# THE POLITICAL ECONOMY OF HUNGER

# WIDER

*Studies in Development Economics* embody the output of the research programmes of the World Institute for Development Economics Research (WIDER), which was established by the United Nations University as its first research and training centre in 1984 and started work in Helsinki in 1985. The principal purpose of the Institute is to help identify and meet the need for policy-oriented socio-economic research on pressing global and development problems, as well as common domestic problems and their interrelationships.

# The Political Economy of Hunger

Edited by

JEAN DRÈZE AND AMARTYA SEN

Volume 2

*Famine Prevention*

CLARENDON PRESS · OXFORD
1990

Oxford University Press, Walton Street, Oxford OX2 6DP

Oxford New York Toronto
Delhi Bombay Calcutta Madras Karachi
Petaling Jaya Singapore Hong Kong Tokyo
Nairobi Dar es Salaam Cape Town
Melbourne Auckland

and associated companies in
Berlin Ibadan

Oxford is a trade mark of Oxford University Press

Published in the United States
by Oxford University Press, New York

British Library Cataloguing in Publication Data
The political economy of hunger. – (WIDER studies in
development economics).
Vol. 2, Famine prevention
1. Food supply
I. Dreze, Jean II. Sen, Amartya III. Series
363.8
ISBN 0–19–828636–8

Library of Congress Cataloging in Publication Data
The Political economy of hunger / edited by Jean Drèze and Amartya Sen.
p. cm.—(WIDER studies in development economics)
Includes bibliographical references and indexes.
Contents: v. 2. Famine prevention.
1. Famines—Africa, Sub-Saharan—Case studies. 2. Food relief—
Africa, Sub-Saharan—Case studies. 3. Famines—South Asia—Case
studies. 4. Food relief—South Africa—Case studies. 5. Hunger—
Case studies. I. Drèze, Jean. II. Sen, Amartya Kumar.
III. Series.
HC800.P653   1990  363.8'83'0967—dc20  90-7663
ISBN 0–19–828636–8

Typeset by Rowland Phototypesetting Ltd
Bury St Edmunds, Suffolk

Printed and bound in
Great Britain by Biddles Ltd,
Guildford and King's Lynn

*In fond memory of*
*Sukhamoy Chakravarty*

# PREFACE

This collection of twenty-six papers, presented in three volumes, represents the result of work undertaken at and for the World Institute for Development Economics Research (WIDER) in Helsinki. This programme of joint research was initiated in the summer of 1985. The first versions of most of the papers were presented at a WIDER conference on 'food strategies' held in Helsinki in July 1986. The papers as well as the research programme as a whole were subjected to close scrutiny at that conference. Those discussions strongly influenced the work that followed—both extensive revisions of the papers presented and the undertaking of new studies, which are also included in these volumes.

The objective of this programme has been the exploration of a wide range of issues related to hunger in the modern world. The papers are concerned with diagnosis and causal analysis as well as policy research. The focus is particularly on Africa and Asia, but there are also two papers on hunger and deprivation in Latin America and a few contributions on more general theoretical issues. The full list of papers in the three volumes can be found at the beginning of each volume. Our 'Introduction' to the three volumes, discussing the papers and their interrelations, is included in full in volume 1, but the parts relevant for the subsequent volumes are also included in the respective volumes, i.e. volumes 2 and 3.

The tasks of revising the papers and carrying out the follow-up studies proved to be quite challenging, and the entire project has taken much longer than we had hoped. We are extremely grateful to the authors for their willingness to undertake substantial—and in some cases several rounds of —revisions, and for putting up with long lists of suggestions and requests. The revisions have been enormously helped by the contributions of the discussants who participated in the 'food strategies' conference in July 1986, including Surjit Bhalla, Susan George, Keith Griffin, S. Guhan, Iftekhar Hussain, Nurul Islam, Nanak Kakwani, Robert Kates, Qaiser Khan, Henock Kifle, Stephen Marglin, Siddiq Osmani, Martin Ravallion, Sunil Sengupta, Mahendra Shah, Nick Stern, Paul Streeten, Megan Vaughan, and Samuel Wangwe. Carl Eicher's comments and suggestions contributed greatly to the improvement of a number of papers. Very helpful comments and suggestions were also received after the conference from Sudhir Anand, Susan George, Judith Heyer, Nurul Islam, Robert Kates, B. G. Kumar, and François-Régis Mahieu.

For their participation in the conference, and their help in planning these studies, we are also grateful to Frédérique Apffel-Marglin, Juha Ahtola, Tuovi Allén, Lars-Erik Birgegaard, Pekka Harttila, Cynthia Hewitt de Alcantara, Eric Hobsbawm, Charles Kindleberger, Michael Lipton, Kaarle Nordenstreng, Kimmo Pulkinnen, Shlomo Reutlinger, Tibor Scitovsky, Darrell Sequiern, Heli Sirve, Marjatta Tolvanen, Matti Tuomala, Tony Vaux, and Hannu Vesa.

For editorial and logistic assistance, we are greatly in debt to Asad Ahmad, Robin Burgess, Nigel Chalk, Jacky Jennings, Shantanu Mitra, Sanjay Reddy, Sangeeta Sethi, Pekka Sulamaa and Anna-Marie Svedrofsky. We would like to thank Judith Barstow for doing the subject index.

Finally, we are grateful to WIDER for its generous support. We owe special thanks to Lal Jayawardena, the Director, for being immensely helpful at every stage of this project.

J.D.
A.S.
*November 1989*

# CONTENTS

# LIST OF PAPERS

## Volume 1: Entitlement and Well-Being

## Volume 2: Famine Prevention

## Volume 3: Endemic Hunger

# LIST OF CONTRIBUTORS

SUDHIR ANAND is University Lecturer in Quantitative Economic Analysis at the University of Oxford, and Fellow and Tutor at St Catherine's College.

KAUSHIK BASU is Professor of Economics at the Delhi School of Economics, and currently Visiting Professor of Economics at Princeton University.

PARTHA DASGUPTA is Professor of Economics at the University of Cambridge, and Professor of Economics and Philosophy at Stanford University.

MEGHNAD DESAI is Professor of Economics at the London School of Economics.

JEAN DRÈZE, formerly Lecturer in Development Economics at the London School of Economics, is now a freelance development economist.

CHRISTOPHER HARRIS is University Lecturer in Public Economics at the University of Oxford, and a Faculty Fellow of Nuffield College.

BARBARA HARRISS is University Lecturer in Agricultural Economics at Queen Elizabeth House, University of Oxford, and Fellow of Wolfson College.

JUDITH HEYER is Lecturer in Economics at the University of Oxford, and Fellow and Tutor at Somerville College.

FRANCIS IDACHABA is Vice-Chancellor of the University of Agriculture, Makurdi, on leave of absence from the Department of Agricultural Economics, University of Ibadan.

S. M. RAVI KANBUR is Editor of the World Bank Economic Review and Senior Adviser on the Social Dimension of Adjustment at the World Bank, on leave from Professorship in Economics at the University of Warwick.

B. G. KUMAR is Associate Fellow at the Centre for Development Studies, Trivandrum, Kerala, India.

S. R. OSMANI is Research Fellow at the World Institute for Development Economics Research, Helsinki, Finland.

KIRIT S. PARIKH is Director of the Indira Gandhi Institute of Development Research, Bombay, and from 1980 to 1986 was Program Leader at the Food and Agriculture Program of the International Institute for Applied Systems Analysis, Austria.

JEAN-PHILIPPE PLATTEAU is Professor of Economics at the Facultés Universitaires, Namur, Belgium.

N. RAM is Associate Editor of *The Hindu*, a leading national daily newspaper in India, based in Madras.

MARTIN RAVALLION is Senior Economist in the Agricultural Policies Division of the World Bank, Washington DC, on leave from the Australian National University, Canberra, Australia.

DEBRAJ RAY is Professor, Planning Unit, Indian Statistical Institute, New Delhi.

CARL RISKIN is Professor of Economics at Queens College, City University of New York, and Senior Research Scholar at the East Asian Institute, Columbia University.

IGNACY SACHS is Professor at the Écoles des Hautes Études en Sciences Sociales, and Director of its Research Centre on Contemporary Brazil in Paris.

AMARTYA SEN is Lamont University Professor at Harvard University.

REHMAN SOBHAN was formerly the Director of the Bangladesh Institute of Development Studies, Dhaka, with which he is still associated.

PETER SVEDBERG is a Senior Research Fellow at the Institute for International Economic Studies, Stockholm.

SAMUEL WANGWE is Professor of Economics at the University of Dar es Salaam.

ANN WHITEHEAD is Lecturer in Social Anthropology at the University of Sussex, England.

# LIST OF TABLES

# Introduction[1]

## Jean Drèze and Amartya Sen

The facts are stark enough. Despite the widespread opulence and the unprecedentedly high real income per head in the world, millions of people die prematurely and abruptly from intermittent famines, and a great many million more die every year from endemic undernourishment and deprivation across the globe. Further, hundreds of millions lead lives of persistent insecurity and want.

While all this is quite obvious, many things are unclear about the characteristics, causation, and possible remedies of hunger in the modern world. A great deal of probing investigation—analytical as well as empirical—is needed as background to public policy and action for eradicating famines and eliminating endemic undernutrition. In this collection of twenty-six papers in three volumes, serious attempts have been made to address many of these momentous issues.

## 0.1. *Organization and structure*

These studies were initiated in 1985 when the World Institute for Development Economics Research (WIDER) was established in Helsinki. First versions of most of the papers were presented at a conference on 'food strategies' held at WIDER in July 1986. In that meeting there were extensive discussions of the analyses presented in the various papers, and some of the debates continued well beyond the conference. The papers have been revised in the light of these exchanges, and further discussions among the authors and the editors. A few new studies were also undertaken during 1986–8 to fill some identified gaps. This book of three volumes represents the fruits of these efforts. It is meant to be a wide-ranging investigation of the causal antecedents, characteristic features, and policy demands of hunger in the modern world. The focus is primarily on sub-Saharan Africa and South Asia, but the experiences of several other countries—from China to Brazil—have also been examined.

Though three of our own essays are included in these volumes, our role has been primarily organizational and editorial. We have, however, also written a monograph of our own, *Hunger and Public Action*,[2] which deals with related issues, and there is a clear connection between the two works. The planning and the design of these three volumes of essays, *The Political Economy of*

---

[1] This Introduction draws on the fuller and more general Introduction to the set of three volumes presented in vol. 1.

[2] Also published by Oxford University Press in the series of WIDER Studies in Development Economics: Drèze and Sen (1989).

*Hunger*, have been closely related to the approach explored and developed in *Hunger and Public Action*, and in turn, in that book, we have drawn on the results of the studies presented in these three volumes.

We should, however, emphasize the obvious. We, as editors, must not be identified with all the views that have been expressed in these essays. These three volumes of essays, which are mainly revised conference papers, present investigations and conclusions that deserve, in our view, serious consideration. But although we have been involved at every stage of these studies, and have also presented our critical comments on the various versions, it was not our aim to soldier on with requests for revision until we all agreed. The analyses and the views are those of the respective authors.

## 0.2.   *Political economy*

The essays in the first volume deal with 'general matters'—including the nature and diversity of the problem of world hunger. They set the background for the analysis of government policy and public action. The second volume includes studies of famines and of anti-famine strategies, and altogether there is an attempt here to identify what is needed for the eradication of famines. The third volume takes up endemic deprivation and undernourishment, discusses successes and failures of different lines of action, and investigates the lessons for public policy aimed at eliminating persistent hunger. The different volumes, thus, deal with distinct but interrelated aspects of what we have called 'the political economy of hunger'.

The meaning of the expression 'political economy' is not altogether unambiguous. To some it simply means economics. It is indeed the old name of the discipline, common in the nineteenth century, and now rather archaic. To others, political economy is economics seen in a perspective that is a great deal broader than is common in the mainstream of the modern tradition. In this view, the influences of political and social institutions and ideas are taken to be particularly important for economic analysis and must not be pushed to the background with some stylized assumptions of heroic simplicity. Political economy thus interpreted cannot but appear to be rather 'interdisciplinary' as the disciplines are now standardly viewed.

Even though the two interpretations are quite distinct, there is a clear connection between them in the sense that the dominant tradition of economics is much narrower now than it was in the classical political economy of Adam Smith, Robert Malthus, David Ricardo, Karl Marx, John Stuart Mill, and others.[3] Thus the old and archaic term for economics as such is also a reminder of the breadth of the earlier tradition of the subject. Many of the analyses of the kind that are now seen as interdisciplinary would have appeared to Smith or

---

[3]  On this issue, see Sen (1984, 1989).

Mill or Marx as belonging solidly to the discipline of political economy as a subject.

It does not, of course, really matter whether political, social, and cultural influences on economic matters are counted inside or outside the discipline of economics, but it can be tremendously important not to lose sight of these influences in analysing many profoundly important economic problems. This is particularly the case with the problem of hunger. The title of the book, *The Political Economy of Hunger*, is meant to be an explicit reminder of the need to adopt a broad perspective to understand better the causation of hunger and the remedial actions that are needed.

## 0.3. *Entitlements and famine prevention*

As was mentioned earlier, the essays included in the first volume of this book deal with rather general matters that serve as background to policy analysis. The topics covered include the characteristics and causal antecedents of famines and endemic deprivation, the interconnections between economic and political factors, the role of social relations and the family, the special problems of women's deprivation, the connection between food consumption and other aspects of living standards, and the medical aspects of undernourishment and its consequences. Several contributions also address the political background of public policy, in particular the connection between the government and the public, including the role of newspapers and the media, and the part played by political commitment and by adversarial politics and pressures.[4]

This second volume is concerned with famine prevention. Since the analysis of famine prevention issues in several of the papers refers to the 'entitlement approach' to famine analysis, it may be helpful to recall briefly the nature of that approach in this introduction. The approach, presented elsewhere (see Sen 1977, 1981), points to the need for focusing on the 'acquirement' of food by the respective households and individuals, and to the fact that the overall production or availability of food may be a bad predictor of what the vulnerable groups in the population can actually acquire. The entitlement approach concentrates instead on the forces that determine the bundles of commodities over which a family or an individual can establish command. A person can be reduced to starvation if some economic change makes it no longer possible for him or her to acquire any commodity bundle with enough food. This can happen either because of a fall in endowment (e.g. alienation of land, or loss of labour power due to ill health), or because of an unfavourable shift in the conditions of exchange (e.g. loss of employment, fall in wages, rise in food prices, drop in the price of goods or services sold by the person, reduction of social security provisions).

In this framework, averting famine can be seen essentially as a question of

---

[4] On these questions see also Drèze and Sen (1989).

'entitlement protection', i.e. of re-creating the lost entitlements of vulnerable groups. The prevention of famines in the long run involves broader areas of action, including the promotion of participative economic growth, the diversification of rural livelihoods, the protection of the environment, the abolition of armed conflicts, and the development of social security systems. The last chapter in this volume, by Jean-Philippe Platteau, addresses some of these long-term issues. The other five chapters are primarily concerned with the more elementary and urgent challenge of developing entitlement protection systems in famine-prone countries.

## 0.4.  *The Indian experience*

Jean Drèze's chapter 'Famine Prevention in India' scrutinizes India's achievement in preventing droughts, floods, and other natural disasters from developing into famines as they used to in the past. A major step was taken in that direction in the 1880s when the 'Famine Codes' were formulated. These codes included instructions for recreating lost incomes through wages to be paid in public works programmes, supplemented by some unconditional relief for those who could not be employed. Food trade was left almost entirely to private traders throughout the pre-independence period.

The Famine Codes, though clear-headed in analysis, were only a partial success in practice. Sometimes the relief offered was too little and too late, and in one notorious occasion—the Bengal Famine of 1943—the Famine Codes were not even invoked (the famine was simply 'not declared'). In post-independence India the relief system has become more systematic and extensive, but no less importantly, the governments—pressured by the news media and opposition parties—do not any longer have the option of ignoring famine threats. The last major famine in India occurred in 1943, preceding independence in 1947.

Drèze presents a discussion of the rationale of the Famine Codes (and other insights of the Famine Commission Reports), and he also investigates the changes that have been brought about since independence. Aside from a major political transformation, the latter include a considerable increase in the real resources devoted to famine relief, a broadening of the range of support measures, direct state involvement in food trade without eliminating private traders, and the maintenance of a substantial volume of food in public stock. Food management in India seems to have produced a large measure of food price stability, but India's success in famine prevention is still thoroughly dependent on the recreation of lost entitlements through wage-based employment, supplemented by unconditional relief.[5]

---

[5]  There are few empirical studies of the role played in practice by unconditional relief measures. The interregional contrasts within India in this respect are important. For further discussion and some empirical material relating to the 1987 drought in Gujarat, see Drèze (1988).

Jean Drèze provides two specific case-studies, namely the food crisis of 1966–7 in Bihar and the non-famine of 1970–3 in Maharashtra despite a disastrous drought. These two case-studies, along with the general analysis presented in the rest of the paper, provide important lessons for famine prevention elsewhere.[6]

## 0.5. *African successes in famine prevention*

India's success in the eradication of famines is fairly widely acknowledged, even though the reasons for this success are often misunderstood.[7] In contrast, the experiences of successful famine prevention in sub-Saharan Africa are often unacknowledged and ignored. The harrowing tales of unprevented famines in that subcontinent seem to dominate the international perception of what has been happening in Africa.

In his second chapter in this volume ('Famine Prevention in Africa: Some Experiences and Lessons'), Jean Drèze concentrates specifically on recent success stories in sub-Saharan Africa, and examines the lessons that can be drawn from them. The case-studies include experiences of averted famines in Botswana, Cape Verde, Kenya, and Zimbabwe. At a very general level, these experiences confirm that public policy for recreating lost entitlements provides a major clue to success in famine prevention. Neither rapid economic growth (as in Botswana), nor rapid growth of agriculture (as in Kenya), nor even rapid growth in food production (as in post-independence Zimbabwe), are by themselves an adequate safeguard against famines. The distinguishing achievements of these countries (as well as of Cape Verde) really lie in their having provided direct public support to their populations in times of crisis.

Aside from this general observation, there are many other lessons to learn from the experiences examined by Drèze. The lessons are partly concerned with the strategy of entitlement protection, and partly with the politics of early action.[8] Regarding the former, Drèze discusses a range of policy issues including the role of food supply management in famine prevention, the question of early warning, the case for greater use of cash support and

---

[6] Drèze also points to the limitations of the Indian anti-hunger policy, which eliminates famines but tolerates massive endemic undernutrition. On this see also Drèze (1988).

[7] It is often presumed that famines have been eliminated in independent India through a revolutionary increase in food production. There certainly has been some rise in food production per capita since independence (and the 'green revolution' has been effective in the production of wheat in particular), but the increase in food production per head has not been very large. Indeed, the average per capita food availability in India today is not substantially greater than in the late 19th century (a decline over the first half of this century having been balanced by an increase after independence). The causes of success of Indian famine prevention policy have to be sought elsewhere—in the process of entitlement protection through various measures of income generation and price stability, and in the compulsion generated by adversarial politics that ensures early public intervention. On this last see ch. 6 in vol. 1 of this book.

[8] See also Drèze and Sen (1989: chs. 5–8).

employment provision, the interconnections between private trade and public distribution, and the long-run importance of economic diversification. As far as early action is concerned, the case-studies presented in the chapter confirm that, in Africa no less than in India, the response of governments has been more a question of political incentives to intervene against a famine than one of relying on formal 'early warning techniques' to anticipate a crisis. There is some diversity in the precise nature of political incentives that have prompted the governments of these African countries to counter resolutely the threat of famine. But one of the features that does emerge again in this context is the importance of public accountability in making it hard for a government to allow a famine to develop.

## 0.6.  Famines in Ethiopia

The success stories from Botswana, Cape Verde, etc. have to be contrasted with failures in famine prevention elsewhere. The case of Ethiopia is often cited in this context. In Chapter 3, B. G. Kumar examines the famines in Ethiopia during 1973–5 and 1982–5. The former set of famines began during Haile Selassie's rule and, in fact, he was deposed during those famines. But the government that followed has not been able to eliminate famines from Ethiopia.

Kumar explains the occurrence of famines and the composition of the destitute population by examining the collapse of entitlements to food of different occupation groups. He also argues, however, that there were substantial declines in food availability in each of the famines, and these declines were among the factors that had a major influence on the entitlements of different groups.[9] Kumar also investigates the demographic and social impacts of the Ethiopian famines.

On matters of policy, Kumar's analysis underlines the usefulness of employ-

---

[9] As far as the 1973 famine is concerned, discussed earlier in Sen (1981), Kumar disputes Sen's view that the famine was not caused by any significant decline in food availability. Sen's diagnosis referred to food availability in Ethiopia as a whole, whereas Kumar's point is about a decline in food availability specifically in the famine province of Wollo (this decline was, in fact, noted and discussed by Sen, pp. 88–96). Since there was no ban on food movement between the different provinces during the famine of 1973, the question as to whether Wollo's low food supply should be treated as an endogenous variable governed by local food production in Wollo (as Kumar suggests), or as being governed by the low purchasing power of the Wollo population connected with the local agricultural decline (as Sen suggests) turns on the physical possibility of transporting food across the boundaries of Wollo from the rest of Ethiopia. In this context, the undisputed existence of a major highway linking Dessie (the capital of Wollo) to Addis Ababa and Asmera (the highway was in fact used for moving some food out of Wollo to elsewhere, on which see Sen 1981: 94), is crucial to the point at issue. Further, the fact that food prices in Dessie did not rise and remained roughly similar to those in Addis Ababa and Asmera (Sen 1981: 95–6), despite the famine conditions in and around Dessie, would seem to support the view that the food available in the rest of Ethiopia could not be pulled into Wollo because of the lack of purchasing power of the Wollo population (not because of a transport bottleneck).

ment creation and the use of cash wages. He also emphasizes the importance of an early response. In this respect Kumar attaches some importance to improving formal 'early warning' systems, but argues that the main delays in responding have been caused by political factors rather than by technical inadequacies. These lessons have clear affinity with those emerging on the 'other' side, from case-studies of success in India and in sub-Saharan Africa.

## 0.7. *Early warning systems*

There is general agreement on the need to act quickly to defeat threatening famines. 'Early warning systems' are aimed at making it possible to act without delay by making policy makers aware of famine threats. Unfortunately, there is also some agreement that the existing formal systems of early warning are seriously defective.

From here we can go in one of two different directions. One is to abandon the search for an adequate 'early warning' model, and to concentrate on getting the necessary warnings in other ways, e.g. through an active news media reporting early cases of hardship and worsening hunger.[10] The other way is to try to improve the models that have been so far devised. Meghnad Desai takes the second route in Chapter 4, and suggests ways in which the exercise of early warning can be much improved.

One of the reasons why formal analysis of early warning is difficult is the fact that a famine can develop from a variety of causes. The initiating factor can be a natural phenomenon (e.g. a drought), or an economic one (e.g. widespread loss of employment and income), or a socio-political event (e.g. a civil war). Desai discusses how these processes can respectively—in different ways—affect the economic system and lead to the collapse of entitlements of vulnerable groups.

Desai's analysis throws much light on the requirements of a good early warning system.[11] There may be some scope for doubt as to whether these requirements can be typically fully met given the complexities of the relations involved and the need for speed in data gathering and analysis. That question remains somewhat open at this stage. But even if a fully adequate system of early warning were not to emerge rapidly, the connections that Desai explores can be of a great deal of use in devising anti-famine policies. An analytical system of early warning, of the kind that Desai has explored, relies on unpacking the different components involved in the collapse of entitlements, and those components have to be clearly understood for the formulation of effective policies of entitlement protection and famine prevention. Thus, the scope of Desai's chapter is considerably broader than the title suggests.

---

[10] On this see chs. 2 and 6 in vol. 1 and chs. 1 and 2 below. See also Drèze and Sen (1989).

[11] See also Desai (1988), and the chapter by D'Souza (1988) in the same volume.

## 0.8.  *Anti-hunger policy and market responses*

In Chapter 5, Martin Ravallion takes up the complex issue of how market responses affect the effectiveness of various public measures to combat hunger of particular groups. This investigation draws on general-equilibrium analysis of the kind that Ravallion has already used very successfully in his previous studies of famines (particularly in his book *Markets and Famines*, Ravallion 1987).

Ravallion considers the major types of measures that have been used in this field, including pure transfer payments, wages for relief work, public grain storage, food price policies, foreign trade, and public information and famine forecasting. In each case, he investigates the ways in which the markets may respond, and their implications for public policy. For example, the overall transfer benefits (inclusive of 'multiplier effects') of public employment programmes will be larger when the wage elasticity of demand for labour is small, and this provides one argument for providing such employment at times when it competes with other employment, rather than just in lean seasons. Of course, these particular considerations have to be integrated with other elements of a full assessment of alternatives, including in this case the 'stabilization benefits' that may be associated with income generation in lean seasons.

Ravallion puts particular emphasis on the less obvious elements of anti-hunger policy. In contrast with the much-discussed cases of relief work and pure transfers, he also investigates the considerable benefits for the poor and the hungry that may result from price stabilization policies, improvement of rural credit, etc. The relative effectiveness of these different lines of action has to be assessed in the light of their respective market responses. Altogether Ravallion has provided an important exploration of alternative anti-hunger policies, the effects they may have (operating *inter alia* through the market), and how their effectiveness may be respectively assessed. The lessons have relevance in combating endemic hunger as well as in devising policies of famine prevention.

## 0.9.  *Policy variables and structural constraints*

One of the issues facing public policy analysis to combat famines and hunger in sub-Saharan Africa concerns the assignment of responsibility for its present predicament. Policy mistakes in the past have often been identified as the major offenders in bringing Africa to its present plight. For example, African governments typically have much control—direct and indirect—over prices of agricultural goods in general and food prices in particular, and it has been frequently argued that it is the tendency to keep these prices artificially low that has been a major cause of low food production in Africa.[12]

In so far as the problems of sub-Saharan Africa are seen as arising primarily or largely from policy mistakes, there may be some reason to hope that a solution of these problems may be readily available in the form of reversing these policy mistakes. For example, 'getting prices right' has appealed to many as an obvious and sure-fire way of liberating Africa from its present predicament.

While there is clearly some truth in the diagnosis of policy errors, and while price incentives can indeed be important, it is not easy to see a ready salvation for Africa through a simple 'policy reversal'. For one thing, each of these policies has many aspects. To illustrate, high food prices may give more production incentives, but they also make it harder for food buyers to acquire food, and a substantial proportion of the African poor have to rely on the market—rather than on home production—for getting the food they eat. For another, the remedy of African poverty calls for a rapid increase in productions and incomes in general, and the demands of this have to be distinguished from the policy imperatives of maximizing food production as such. Even though there have undoubtedly been policy mistakes that have contributed to Africa's present problems, straightforward remedies, such as raising food prices, may not be as promising and unproblematic as they have been made to look.[13]

What is at issue is not merely the effectiveness of changes in prices and of other policy variables that the governments can easily control, but also the need to address the harder and less easily influenceable features of the economy and the society. Jean-Philippe Platteau in Chapter 6 discusses many of the structural features that have had a profound bearing on famines and hunger in Africa, particularly through influencing food production. The domain of Platteau's investigation is wide, and he identifies the important influences exercised by land tenure and other institutions, technological constraints, political limitations, and even cultural obstacles. His analysis of Africa's predicament draws on a long-ranging study of history, and he argues strongly in favour of taking fuller note of structural parameters and constraints in understanding African hunger and in seeking effective and lasting remedies.

Platteau's institutional analysis importantly supplements the concentration on easily influenceable policy variables in many other studies. The recurrence of famines in Africa has many aspects and it relates to different antecedent circumstances. The demands of rapidity and durability in remedying the situation include the need for attention being paid to policy issues of widely different kinds.

[12] This position has been forcefully presented in several contributions by the World Bank and its policy analysts; see e.g. World Bank (1986), Ray (1988).

[13] We have gone into these issues in Drèze and Sen (1989), particularly in chs. 2, 9, and 13. There is an extensive literature on this; see e.g. Lipton (1987), Streeten (1987), Pinstrup-Andersen (1989).

The chapters included in this volume, taken together, provide a fairly comprehensive investigation of the underlying issues and the different considerations that have to be taken into account in eradicating famines from Africa. While there is scope for much optimism, especially in view of the successes already achieved in some parts of sub-Saharan Africa and elsewhere, the need for deep-rooted, constructive changes cannot be overemphasized.[14] The call for rapidity should not be confused with a search for the 'quick fix'.

[14] The positive opportunities that can be effectively used have also been discussed in Drèze and Sen (1989: chs. 5–8).

# References

DESAI, MEGHNAD (1988), 'The Economics of Famine', in Harrison, G. A. (ed.), *Famines* (Oxford: Oxford University Press).

DRÈZE, JEAN (1988), 'Social Insecurity in India', paper presented at a Workshop on Social Security in Developing Countries held at the London School of Economics, July.

——and SEN, AMARTYA (1989), *Hunger and Public Action* (Oxford: Oxford University Press).

—— ——(1990), 'Public Action for Social Security', in Ahmad, S. E., Drèze, J. P., Hills, J., and Sen, A. K. (eds.) (1990), *Social Security in Developing Countries* (Oxford: Oxford University Press).

D'SOUZA, FRANCES (1988), 'Famine: Social Security and an Analysis of Vulnerability', in Harrison, G. A. (ed.), *Famines* (Oxford: Oxford University Press).

LIPTON, MICHAEL (1987), 'Limits of Price Policy for Agriculture: Which Way for the World Bank?', *Development Policy Review*, 5.

PINSTRUP-ANDERSEN, PER (1989), 'Assuring a Household Food Security and Nutrition Bias in African Government Policies', paper presented at the 9th World Congress of the International Economic Association, Athens, Aug.

RAVALLION, MARTIN (1987), *Markets and Famines* (Oxford: Oxford University Press).

RAY, ANANDARUP (1988), 'A Response to Lipton's (June 1987) Review of "World Development Report 1986"', *Development Policy Review*, 6.

SEN, AMARTYA (1977), 'Starvation and Exchange Entitlements: A General Approach and its Application to the Great Bengal Famine', *Cambridge Journal of Economics*, 1.

——(1981), *Poverty and Famines* (Oxford: Oxford University Press).

——(1984), *Resources, Values and Development* (Oxford: Basil Blackwell).

——(1989); 'Economic Methodology: Heterogeneity and Relevance', *Social Research*, 56.

STREETEN, PAUL (1987), *What Price Food?* (London: Macmillan).

World Bank (1986), *World Development Report 1986* (Washington, DC: World Bank).

# 1

# Famine Prevention in India

*Jean Drèze*

## 1.1. *Introduction*

India's record of famine prevention in recent decades has often been presented as a highly impressive one, and several attempts have been made to draw out the possible lessons of this experience for other countries. This alleged success arguably needs to be put in proper perspective, and it has to be remembered that the various influences which combine to ensure the sustenance of the people in times of crisis do little more than keep them barely alive. As this chapter comes to completion, a frightening drought is hitting large parts of India, and while large-scale starvation will no doubt be averted once again, the hardships endured by the rural population offer a sobering picture.

Having said this, if India's recent 'success' in preventing famines is hardly a definitive achievement, it still remains a creditable one against the background of continuing failures elsewhere. While the 'lessons from India' are by no means easy to draw, the rich experience of this country with famine prevention strategies remains well worth scrutinizing.

How, then, has India avoided major famines since independence in 1947? It is tempting to attribute her relative success in this field to a steady improvement in food production. A close look at the facts, however, quickly reveals the

For many helpful comments and suggestions, I am extremely grateful to Harold Alderman, Arjun Appadurai, David Arnold, Kaushik Basu, A. N. Batabyal, Nikilesh Bhattacharya, Crispin Bates, Sulabha Brahme, Robert Chambers, V. K. Chetty, Stephen Coate, Lucia da Corta, Nigel Crook, Parviz Dabir-Alai, Angus Deaton, Guvant Desai, Meghnad Desai, V. D. Deshpande, Steve Devereux, Ajay Dua, Tim Dyson, Hugh Goyder, S. Guhan, Deborah Guz, Barbara Harriss, Judith Heyer, Simon Hunt, N. S. Iyengar, N. S. Jodha, Jane Knight, Arun Kumar, Gopalakrishna Kumar, Jocelyn Kynch, Peter Lanjouw, Michael Lipton, John Levi, Michelle McAlpin, John Mellor, B. S. Minhas, Shantanu Mitra, Mark Mullins, Vijay Nayak, Siddiq Osmani, Elizabeth Oughton, Kirit Parikh, Pravin Patkar, Jean-Philippe Platteau, Amrita Rangasami, N.P. Rao, J. G. Sastry, John Seaman, Kailash Sharma, P. V. Srinivasan, Elizabeth Stamp, Nicholas Stern, K. Subbarao, P. Subramaniam, V. Subramaniam, Peter Svedberg, Jeremy Swift, Martin Ravallion, David Taylor, Suresh Tendulkar, A. M. Vidwans, A. Vaidyanathan, Peter Walker, Tom Walker, Michael Windey, and Sheila Zubrigg. I owe even more to the many labourers, farmers, administrators, and activists who helped me during my field work in Bihar, Gujarat, and Maharashtra in 1986. Amartya Sen, who invited me to undertake this study, provided me with constant inspiration during several years of highly rewarding collaboration, and his own work on famine-related issues has greatly influenced the analysis presented in this paper. My greatest debt is to Bela Bhatia, not least for reminding me that India's relative success in averting large-scale famines in the recent past should not deflect our attention from the persistent and unnecessary sufferings of her people—the need for concern, pressure, and action remains as great as ever.

inadequacy of this explanation. Indeed, the half-century preceding independence witnessed steadily *declining* levels of food production per head, along with a reduction in the frequency of famines compared to the nineteenth-century experience. Since independence in 1947, total food output has admittedly grown at a healthy rate, but per capita food production levels have *not* dramatically increased; they appear, in any case, to remain lower than late nineteenth-century levels, and also lower than per capita food output levels in many countries affected by famines today. Moreover, the increase of production has resulted first and foremost in the reduction of imports and the accumulation of increasingly large stocks, so that the net consumption of food has stayed remarkably stagnant over the last forty years. Last but not least, almost every year large and heavily populated parts of India suffer from devastating droughts which, through the 'entitlement failures' they threaten to precipitate, remain quite capable of causing large-scale starvation.

It is more plausible to attribute the disappearance of large-scale famines in India during recent decades to the overall evolution of the economy. Sources of livelihood for the rural population are increasingly diversified, and in some areas at least the rapid advance of productivity in agriculture has substantially raised general living standards and further reduced the insecurity of rural life. The government's general food policy, though far from flawless, has largely succeeded in stabilizing food prices and in insulating consumption from fluctuations in production. In many States a wide array of more or less successful 'poverty alleviation programmes' provide a measure of protection against destitution to poor households, and by some accounts at least a discernible trend towards decreasing poverty has emerged since the mid-1960s. So goes the argument.

But even this optimistic interpretation of recent changes in economic opportunities and policies does not seem to be quite enough to account for the prevention of famines. In the semi-arid parts of India, the stagnation or near-stagnation of yields, population pressure, and the increasing frequency of droughts keep the rural population at the mercy of the monsoon. The vulnerability of impoverished classes (particularly agricultural labourers) remains extreme, and the need persists for a very extensive and effective *relief system*. When food crises have assumed unusual proportions (as in 1966–7, 1972–3, 1979–80, and 1985–7), this relief system has played an undeniably crucial role in averting large-scale starvation. This chapter examines the role played by famine relief policies in ensuring the prevention of famines in India in the last few decades.

This enquiry will inevitably involve a brief excursion into the historical origins of India's relief policies as they exist today. This is the theme of section 1.2, where attention is drawn particularly to the role and content of the Famine Codes introduced by the British administration towards the end of the nineteenth century.

Section 1.3 takes a closer look at the nature of entitlement crises in India since independence. On the basis of a tentative comparison between India and the Sahel, as well as of a reassessment of crisis management in the State of Bihar in 1966–7, India's continued exposure to famine threats is underlined.

The effectiveness of relief policies in dealing with these threats is illustrated in section 1.4, which is devoted to a case-study of famine prevention in Maharashtra during the devastating drought of 1970–3. This example, it must be stressed at the outset, is not in any sense 'representative' of India's experience with famine prevention. Indeed, the scope and effectiveness of famine relief measures in India vary considerably between different regions and periods. Nevertheless, the drought of 1970–3 in Maharashtra is well worth studying, partly because it has the merit of bringing out the *potential* of India's relief system, and partly because it is extremely well documented and provides rich material for an empirical examination of many important problems connected with famine prevention in general. Close attention will be paid, *inter alia*, to the familiar issues of early warning, food availability, private trade, public distribution, cash relief, targeting mechanisms, employment programmes, cost-effectiveness, and political pressure. A summary of the findings, and some concluding remarks, are contained in the final section.

This chapter is based primarily on research carried out in 1985–6. Since little material was available at that time on droughts and famine prevention in the 1980s, this study essentially concentrates on the pre-1980 period. There is much to say on the developments that have taken place since then (including the alarming problem of ecological devastation), and in particular on famine prevention during the drought of 1985–7, but no attempt has been made here to cover these issues.[1] It would be surprising, however, if recent events called for a major reassessment of the analysis presented in this paper.

## 1.2. *The emergence of India's famine relief system*

The history of famine relief in India is a fascinating area of research, and deserves attention from everyone concerned with the problem of famines in the modern world—scholars and practitioners alike. It is beyond the scope of this paper to review this history in any depth, or to contribute fresh insights to it. The interested reader is referred to the large literature on the subject.[2] My wish here is only to provide a selective account of the emergence of a famine relief system in India, as a background for the study of famine prevention since independence. The following is a selective chronological sketch of the history

[1] For some relevant studies, see Pinstrup-Andersen and Jaramillo (1985), Caldwell *et al.* (1986), Bandyopadhyay (1987), Agarwal (1988), Bhatia (1988), Hubbard (1988), Kumar (1988), Rao *et al.* (1988), Reddy (1988), Chen (1989), Drèze (1989, 1990), the collection of papers in Centre for Social Studies (1988), Government of India (1989), and the further literature cited in Mac (1988).

[2] On the history of famines and famine prevention in India, see Dutt (1900, 1904), Loveday (1914), Ghosh (1944), Bhatia (1967), Srivastava (1968), Ambirajan (1978), Alamgir (1980), Jaiswal (1978), McAlpin (1983), Ghose (1982), Brennan (1984), Klein (1984), among others.

of famines and famine relief in India during the period on which this section
will focus.

1770            Formidable famine in Bengal
1770–1858       Frequent and severe famines
1858            End of East India Company
1861            Report of Baird Smith on the 1860–1 famine
1861–80         Frequent and severe famines
1880            Famine Commission Report, followed by the introduction of
                Famine Codes
1880–96         Very few famines
1896–7          Large-scale famine affecting large parts of India
1898            Famine Commission Report on the 1896–7 famine
1899–1900       Large-scale famine
1901            Famine Commission Report on the 1899–1900 famine
1901–43         Very few famines
1943            Bengal Famine
1945            Famine Commission Report on the Bengal Famine
1947            Independence

## (a)  Famines in nineteenth-century India

Numerous famines occurred in India throughout the nineteenth century, and
their victims were often counted in millions.[3] There is a fair amount of
agreement among nineteenth-century analysts and later economic historians
concerning the proximate causes underlying these catastrophes. In most
(nearly all) cases, famine followed massive crop failures resulting from
drought. The immediate effect of these crop failures was not only to reduce
food availability in the affected region, but also, and more importantly, to
disrupt the rural economy. In particular, landless agricultural labourers found
little employment as field activity was brought to a standstill while general
impoverishment simultaneously enlarged the supply of casual labour. Food
prices increased as the less vulnerable groups strived to maintain reasonable
food consumption levels (possibly by selling assets), while trade was often slow
to move food to the affected area from other regions. Money wages lagged
behind price increases, further aggravating the plight of agricultural
labourers.[4] The operation of the so-called 'moral economy' did little to mitigate
their sufferings, which all too often ended only in death. Thus severe famines

---

[3] For chronologies of Indian famines in the 19th century, and estimates of their impact on
mortality, see Loveday (1914), Bhatia (1967), Dando (1980), Jaiswal and Kolte (1981), Greenough
(1982), Visaria and Visaria (1982), and Government of India (1880).

[4] The reduction of real wages in rural India during periods of rapid price increases (including
famines) has been observed by numerous authors—see e.g. the evidence, discussions, and further
references provided in Breman (1974), Bhatia (1975), Bardhan (1977), Lal (forthcoming),
Ravallion (ch. 5 below), and Government of India (1898).

frequently took place even when crop failures were only localized (as well as short-lived) and food was far from wanting in the country as a whole.

This recurring scenario was aptly summarized by Baird Smith's well-known statement to the effect that famines in India were 'rather famines of work than of food'.[5] The same verdict was arrived at later by successive Famine Enquiry Commissions, as well as by most independent analysts—though there has predictably been much more controversy about the underlying causes of mass poverty in the same period. The Famine Commission Report of 1880 (the first major report of its kind) is worth quoting here, not least as an early example of 'entitlement analysis':

The first effect of drought is to diminish greatly, and at last to stop, all field labour, and to throw out of employment the great mass of people who live on the wages of such labour.[6]

. . . distress is mainly among the agricultural portion of the population thrown out of work by the failure of their ordinary employment, and the few small trades and handicrafts which are chiefly dependent upon them for sale of their manufactures . . . among this class, distress arises, not so much from an actual want of food, as from a loss of wages—in other words, money to buy food . . . as a general rule, there is an abundance of food procurable, even in the worst districts at the worst time; but when men who, at the best, merely live from hand to mouth, are deprived of their means of earning wages, they starve, not from the impossibility of getting food, but for want of the necessary money to buy it.[7]

Two aspects of this description are particularly relevant to an appreciation of later relief policies. The first is the recognition of *agricultural labourers and rural artisans* as the main victims of traditional Indian famines. During very severe famines cultivators became vulnerable to starvation as well, in spite of the then widespread practice of storing large quantities of grain;[8] and when epidemics broke out they caused victims among large sections of the population. But these qualifications apart, the outstanding vulnerability of agricultural labourers and artisans has been widely noted.[9]

Another important aspect of the received analysis of nineteenth-century famines is the view that entitlement failures occurred amidst plenty rather than in the context of a fierce battle for scarce food. A rather striking degree of agreement on this question can be found in the official reports of the British administration at the time, as well as among commentators of very diverse

---

[5] Baird Smith (1861), quoted in Srivastava (1968: 53 n.).

[6] Government of India (1880: 35); this is the preamble of a fuller discussion of 'The Classes that suffer from famine'.

[7] Government of India (1880: Appendix I, p. 205).

[8] 'Everyone knows that all the well-to-do farmers have very large hoards of grain, which they keep in pits, especially in the dry districts, often for many years' (Government of India 1880: Appendix I, p. 204).

[9] See e.g. Bhatia (1967, 1975), Srivastava (1968), Ghose (1982), and the Famine Commission Reports (Government of India, various years).

persuasions (e.g. Baird Smith 1861, Naoroji 1900, Ray 1901, Ray 1909, Loveday 1914, Srivastava 1968, Ghose 1982, McAlpin 1983, and Guz 1987, among many others). The literature on nineteenth-century famines is replete with statements such as the following:

What does a drought mean? It is not a question of food; the scarcity of food in a district affected by drought is the least of the evils with which the Government of India have to deal. There is nearly always a sufficiency of food in India to feed all the people within its limits; and owing to the development of the railway, the British Government was able, no matter what part of the country may be affected, to pour in sufficient food to maintain the people of the district.[10]

The consensus on this question should, admittedly, be approached with caution. The view that aggregate food availability was never a serious problem during Indian famines was, after all, largely propagated by the official Famine Commission Reports.[11] These lean heavily on the initial calculations of the Famine Commission Report of 1880, which might have been misleading. The Famine Commission Report of 1898 formed its own view on the subject partly on the evidence of the non-exhaustion of stocks and continued food exports in famine years (see below). But this piece of evidence is not particularly convincing: it only proves that extra food was available *at the margin*—but not necessarily enough to feed the whole population. Finally, it may be argued that the dismissal of food shortage problems served the interests of the British authorities by obviating the need for intervention in grain trade, which—as we shall see—they were so obsessively anxious to avoid.

Detailed investigations would be required to ascertain whether or not the absence of a food availability problem during nineteenth-century famines in India was a myth propagated by the Famine Commissions. There is, however, little indication that the myth theory should be taken very seriously. The fabrication of a myth would have triggered dissent, of which there is very little trace. Indeed, it is rather striking that commentators of all persuasions, including many radical ones, concurred with the views of the Famine Commissions on the issue of food availability; the distinction of the radical writers was not to challenge the notion of sufficiency of food, but rather to trace the lack of purchasing power of the masses to colonial exploitation.[12] As far as quantitative evidence is concerned, several independent rounds of food availability calculations were carried out (in 1878, 1898, and 1902); they were based on

[10] Statement made by Lord George Hamilton (3 Feb. 1902), quoted in Ray (1909: 10).

[11] The idea, however, did not originate from the Famine Commission Reports. As we have seen, the very first report on an Indian famine under British rule (that of Baird Smith in 1861) already considered Indian famines as 'rather famines of work than of food; when work can be had and paid for, food is always forthcoming' (Smith 1861, quoted in Srivastava 1968: 53 n.).

[12] See e.g. Ray (1901) and Ray (1909). The former argued that 'Close students of Indian economical history know, and none have ever seriously questioned the fact, that India, on the whole, produces enough of crops every year, good or bad, to feed her aggregate population' (Ray 1901: 33).

food consumption allowances which were extremely generous by contemporary standards and yet they all arrived at the firm conclusion that a substantial surplus of food was available in India in normal years.[13] Since multi-year storage was a widespread practice in nineteenth-century India, and most famines were localized, the argument that most nineteenth-century famines had little to do with a problem of physical availability of food seems convincing enough.

An exception may, however, have to be made in this respect for the last two famines of the nineteenth century—those of 1896–7 and 1899–1900. In these two cases, famine occurred against an exceptional background of massive crop failures virtually throughout the country at times when stocks were already diminished, and much greater caution is required in assessing the aggregate food availability situation. I shall argue below that the case against the existence of a food availability problem is much less convincing in this context.[14]

## (b)  Early famine relief efforts

Famine relief has a very long history in India. One of the very first treatises on government, written more than 2,000 years ago and commonly attributed to Kautilya, pronounces that when famine threatens a good king should 'institute the building of forts or water-works with the grant of food, or share [his] provisions [with the people], or entrust the country [to another king]'.[15] According to Srivastava, 'the chief methods of famine relief adopted by Indian rulers included free distribution of raw grains, opening of free kitchens, opening of public grain stores to the people, remission of revenue, payment of advances, remission of other taxes, construction of public works, canals and embankments, sinking of wells, encouragement of migration, and increase in the pay of soldiers. Even sold children in the time of Shahjahan are reported to have been ransomed by the Government and restored to their parents.'[16] However, the evidence is inadequate to judge the real efficacy of relief efforts

[13]  See e.g. Bhatia (1967: Table 33), and Government of India (1898: para. 587).

[14]  Bhatia (1967), for one, has challenged the idea of food sufficiency in 19th-century India, as a background to the thesis that the responsibility for 19th-century famines lay largely with the government's refusal to interfere with private trade. His counterargument, however, is not very persuasive. He criticizes the official food availability estimates of 1878, 1898, and 1902 for their lack of accuracy (pp. 225–8), but fails to show a systematic bias or to suggest more plausible magnitudes. The main piece of evidence he puts forward on the existence of food shortages is the substantial rise in prices *throughout India* during the late 19th-century famines. This observation, however, refers specifically to the famines of 1896–7 and 1899–1900 which, I have argued, should be regarded as exceptions in this regard. Indeed the Famine Commission of 1898 referred to 'the uniform level of prices all over the country' as 'one of the most remarkable features in the recent (1896–97) famine', underlying the novelty of the phenomenon (on this see also Loveday 1914). It is, in any case, argued below that the policy of complete non-interference with private trade in British India had little to do with any particular appraisal of the food availability situation.

[15]  *Arthasastra*, quoted in Chetty and Ratha (1987: 3).

[16]  Srivastava (1968: 28).

before the nineteenth century, and it is not implausible that they were often far from systematic and comprehensive.[17]

Under the rule of the East India Company, famines were frequent and severe—sometimes extremely severe, as with the calamitous famine of 1770 in Bengal. Relief efforts were, moreover, at best half-hearted, and in any case lacking in effectiveness. The laconic remarks of the Famine Commission of 1880 on this subject are revealing enough:

. . . the earlier despatches of the Bengal Government, while breathing a tone of sincere compassion for the sufferings occasioned by famine, are busied rather with its fiscal results, as affecting the responsibility of the Company towards its shareholders, than with schemes, which would have seemed wholly visionary, for counteracting the inevitable loss of life.[18]

How did the 'breath of sincere compassion' gradually turn into a serious preoccupation with the prevention of famines after the British administration took over in 1858? In other words, why were the British rulers so concerned to avert famines in India? Oddly enough, the answers that have been proposed to this question have remained extremely fragmented and speculative.[19] The report of the Famine Commission of 1880 repeatedly invokes the 'duty of the State' in this context.[20] But what this rhetoric actually masked is rather hard to say. The desire to preserve political stability or the revenue base, a feeling of obligation to the people arising from the more obviously deleterious aspects of colonial expansion (such as the ruin of the weaving industry), the so-called 'weight of irresponsible public opinion in England',[21] concern with the administration's image in the eyes of the British public, and genuine human-itarian concern may all have played a more or less important role. It is unlikely that this issue could be satisfactorily resolved without also considering British policy in Ireland and even in Africa, where very similar situations and debates were encountered. This, however, would take us far beyond the scope of this chapter and can only be proposed here as a theme for further research.

[17] See Curley (1977) for an interesting account of traditional Mogul famine policy in 18th-century India.

[18] Government of India (1880: 31).

[19] For some useful discussions, see Bhatia (1967), Ambirajan (1976, 1978), and Brennan (1984).

[20] Under the heading 'Obligation of the State to give relief in time of famine', for instance, the Famine Commission Report of 1880 states that 'there can be no doubt that a calamity such as famine, exceptional in its nature and arising from causes wholly beyond human control, which deprives an entire population of its customary food supply, and arrests the ordinary employments of the wage-earning classes, is one which in a country such as India wholly transcends individual effort and power of resistance. It accordingly becomes a paramount *duty of the State* to give all practicable assistance to the people in time of famine, and to devote all its available resources to this end; and this duty is emphasized by the fact that the Government stands in the place of landlord to the agriculturists, who form the great mass of the population' (Government of India 1880: 31–2; my italics).

[21] Government of India (1880: Appendix I, p. 117).

Referring to caste prejudices against forbidden food, Sir Bartle Frere lamented, in an important prelude to the later Famine Codes, that 'no one whose experience is confined to the poor of other countries can imagine the difficulties of dealing with starving Hindoos, even when you have the most ample means at your disposal'.[22] However, the really important difficulties initially experienced by the British administration in organizing relief went much beyond the cultural idiosyncrasies of 'starving Hindoos'. In fact they were strikingly reminiscent of the familiar stumbling blocks of famine relief elsewhere even today: confused information, faulty forecasts, absence of contingency planning, weak motivation, delays, transport bottlenecks and other logistical nightmares, poor administration, inertia of private trade, etc. The Famine Commission Report of 1880 contains a vivid account of the nature of relief efforts before the Famine Codes:

What often happens now is that they wander from their village, crowd into towns, die about the roads, and otherwise attract the attention of the officials. Then a survey is made, a relief-work is started, and then follows all the train of difficulties attendant on the endeavour to get masses of wretched, demoralized, half-starved creatures to work and be paid after some sort of method. The work is generally started too late to save life; numbers, from one cause or another, do not get within its scope; every department is strained to supply supervision, and the supervision is generally quite inadequate for anything like real control; the wage is a hopeless dilemma; if you give a low rate, the people desert and die; if you give a high one, you drain the labour market and the thing gets beyond control.[23]

To be fair, the prevention of famines during the greater part of the nineteenth century was also handicapped by infrastructural deficiencies which were to diminish substantially in later decades. The Famine Commission Reports often laid great stress on the need to develop *irrigation* and, even more importantly, *communications* (mainly railways). For future reference, and given the considerable importance ascribed to public and private trade issues in discussions of famine relief, the role of communications is worth probing.

Before the large-scale development of the railways from the 1870s onwards, private trade in foodgrains within India notably lacked dynamism, and local scarcities precipitated very severe price hikes.[24] Often, the 'lack of satisfactory communications . . . severely restricted the movement of food grains so that while in one part of the country people died of lack of food, in another, only a few miles away, there was an abundance of cheap food'.[25] Entitlement failures were exacerbated by the sluggishness of trade and the large price disparities prevailing between adjacent regions:

[22] Frere (1874: 15).

[23] Government of India (1880: Appendix I, p. 113). For a more detailed account of mismanagement in famine relief before the Famine Codes, see e.g. Srivastava (1968: chs. 2–5) and Bhatia (1967: ch. 3).

[24] On this question see Bhatia (1967), Srivastava (1968), and particularly McAlpin (1983).

[25] Srivastava (1968: 7).

. . . while in one bazar, famine prices of four rupees per maund might be ruling, in another, not thirty miles off, the price would be but about rupee one and a half for the same quantity, yet no flow from the full to the exhausted market could take place, because roads were not in existence and means of carriage unknown.[26]

In his famous *Report on the Past Famines in the Bombay Presidency*, Etheridge (1868) attributed the inertia of private trade in that period to the lack of 'animal spirits' among Indian merchants, who sometimes 'altogether failed . . . to take advantage of the high prices ruling'; 'the Hindoo merchant', said Etheridge, 'is slow of action even when [his] own interests are deeply concerned'.[27] But later experience belied this peculiar view of the Hindu merchant. Indeed, only a few years later the Famine Commission of 1880 described a completely different state of affairs:

The extension of railways, and the connection of trunk lines, has so increased the rapidity of communication that mercantile relations now subsist between the Native traders of all parts of India, and these traders keep themselves well posted up in the state of the most distant markets, being keenly alive to the advantage of the telegraphic communication . . . The combined effect of Railway and Telegraph extension throughout the length and breadth of India, has permitted Government to rely upon the activity of private trade for the supply of foods to all districts immediately served by railways . . . Moreover, the area from which food supplies can be drawn has been extended from the limit of 100 miles, which, with a cart-carriage, in a famine-striken country, destitute of fodder for cattle, or oxen with pack-bullocks or cooly labour, is a maximum to a range of over 2000 miles . . . as certainly as a strong demand arises for grain or other country produce, either for a famine district or for export, the railway stations of all districts from which export is possible, are crowded with stores of grain, while the railway officials are besieged by applicants for early despatch of their consignments.[28]

The sudden dynamism of private trade may have been somewhat exaggerated by the Famine Commission which, as we shall see, was very anxious to rationalize the policy of non-interference recommended—it thought—by what Etheridge called the 'supposed infallible laws of the great Masters of Economic Science'.[29] However, it was certainly not a myth, and as a matter of fact the 'remarkable tendency to a common level of prices throughout India' during the 1896–7 famine, and again during the 1899–1900 famine, has been reliably documented.[30] Nor can the key role played by the railways in this context be seriously questioned.

While the expansion of the railways was undoubtedly *effective* in promoting private trade, it is much less obvious how *beneficial* this development was to various sections of the Indian people. This question has, not surprisingly, been

---

[26] Baird Smith (1861), quoted in Srivastava (1968: 53).     [27] Etheridge (1868: 3, 11).

[28] Government of India (1880: Appendix I, pp. 198–9).     [29] Etheridge (1868: 3).

[30] See e.g. Holderness (1897), Loveday (1914), McAlpin (1983), and Government of India (1898). The expression quoted in the text is taken from the latter report, p. 359.

a matter of some debate.[31] In the Indian context as elsewhere, radical writers have often blamed the growth of commercialization for the impoverishment of the people, and even held 'capitalist penetration' responsible for the occurrence of famines. But it is arguable that the source of exploitation and persistent poverty should be sought in the domain of *ownership* much more than in the domain of exchange *per se*.[32] This is not the place to pursue this complex question, and our attention here will be confined to a somewhat narrower issue, namely the consequences of railway extension for food movements during famines.

The Famine Commissions regarded the greater 'market integration' permitted by the railways as an unambiguous, if not completely unmixed, blessing. They did feel uncomfortable about the occasional facilitation of *exports* from famine-stricken areas (see below). And they gave a rather muddled response to the criticism of growing disincentives against private storage.[33] But on the long-run advantages of the railways they had no doubt, and the Famine Commission of 1898 pronounced that 'one of the most remarkable features in the recent famine was the uniform level of prices all over the country which is attributable to the ever-extending system of railways and which, *if it increased the area, greatly diminished the intensity of distress*'.[34] Analysts such as Loveday emphatically concurred with this view, arguing that 'the desirability of a system by which the prosperous should help to bear the burden of the distressed is unquestionable'.[35] But there also existed another school of thought, which stressed the evils of the railway in general, and its possible role in facilitating exports from famine-striken areas in particular.

Economic analysis confirms the scope for ambiguity in the effects of railway extension on food entitlements. There can be little doubt that the expansion of the railways resulted in a greater tendency towards uniformity of

[31] For a useful introduction to the controversy, see Michelle McAlpin (1974, 1975, 1980, 1982, 1983). McAlpin herself has strongly argued, on the basis of detailed empirical work, that the expansion of the railways in India led to a considerable reduction in poverty and famine vulnerability, and in particular that 'probably by the end of the nineteenth century and certainly by the beginning of the twentieth century, the movement of grain into regions with harvest shortfalls was a routine process' (McAlpin 1983: 156). For rejoinders, see Appadurai (1984), Bates (1985), Rangasami (1985), and Guha (1986).

[32] As Marx emphasized, 'the relation of capitalist and wage labourer . . . has its foundation in the social character of production, not in the mode of exchange . . . It is, however, quite in keeping with the bourgeois horizon, everyone being engrossed in the transaction of shady business, not to see in the character of the mode of production the basis of the mode of exchange corresponding to it, but vice-versa' (Marx 1970: 120). On railways in India specifically, Marx predicted that 'the railways system will become, in India, truly the forerunner of modern industry' (cited in Bhatia 1967: 307).

[33] 'It is true that to a certain extent cultivators, who formerly stored grain, because it could neither be sold nor removed, have ceased to do so because they can see to advantage; and that, owing to their improvidence, the money slips through their fingers' (Government of India 1901: 74).

[34] Government of India (1898: 351) (italics added).

[35] Loveday (1914: 111).

prices.[36] One may also generally expect a reduction of price disparities to reflect greater food movements towards famine-affected areas, and to result in an improvement of the food entitlements of vulnerable sections of the population in these regions. However, it is easy to think of counterexamples, of which two are particularly important here.

First, in the absence of international trade regulation, the smoother flow of grain towards high price regions took place across, as well as within, national boundaries, and the large-scale export of grain abroad during famine periods was a frequent phenomenon in the nineteenth century.[37] It must be remembered in this context that while regional food price patterns within India could, by and large, be expected to reflect the severity of entitlement crises in different parts of the country, price differences between India and England could certainly not be given the same interpretation—if only because they were heavily influenced by the exchange rate, itself a reflection of numerous factors hardly related to food entitlements. The Famine Commission of 1880 recognized the problem with some embarrassment but viewed it as an 'inevitable' consequence of the broader and essential policy of non-interference with private trade:

Unluckily for the Indian consumer, there have been several bad harvests in England, and this and the exchange have stimulated a great export of grain for the last few years. This gain of the producing class and its adjunct, the bunyah [trader], has been so far the loss of the consuming class. This seems inevitable.[38]

Second, even within a country the reduction of disparities in prices need not always imply a reduction in the severity of famine. In fact, the greater spatial integration of markets can be expected to contribute to alleviating famine if, and only if, two conditions are satisfied:[39] (1) the moderation of price increases improves the entitlements of vulnerable groups, and (2) vulnerable areas are also, as a rule, those subject to strong upward pressures on food prices. The first assumption is safe enough, since few households benefit from higher food prices except those who have some food to *sell*. Regarding the second assumption, a broad correlation has indeed been observed during Indian famines between the level of food prices and the intensity of distress, and the Famine Commission of 1880 even boldly stated that 'it may be said approximately and

[36] See the references cited earlier on this point. It is noteworthy that McAlpin's critics have not seriously challenged the *evidence* she has presented on the progress of market integration towards the end of the 19th century.

[37] For evidence of this, and indeed of the very large *increase* in exports during the famines of the 1870s, see Bhatia (1967). For an interesting econometric study of international trade and food entitlements in British India, see Ravallion (1987b).

[38] Government of India (1880: Appendix I, p. 112).

[39] Strictly speaking, the *violation* of both these conditions would also do, but this possibility is little more than a theoretical curiosum. More importantly perhaps, note that when trade takes place *within* a famine-affected region, one also has to check whether the reduction of disparities in food entitlements within that region does result in lower aggregate mortality. For a detailed examination of this hypothesis, see Ravallion (1987a).

generally that, in time of very great scarcity, prices of food grain rise to three times their ordinary amount'.[40] This statement was admittedly followed by lengthy qualifications, and the use of prices as an indication of distress has met with some notable failures.[41] However, the general observation that famine-affected areas were also areas of high food prices was a robust one.

In sum, and with a major reservation applying to international trade, it is plausible that the improvement of communications towards the end of the nineteenth century did make a major contribution to the alleviation of distress during famines. However, it is also easy to see that this factor alone could hardly account for the very sharp reduction in the incidence of famines in the twentieth century. Indeed, the dynamism of private trade during famines has always been contingent on the existence of adequate *purchasing power* in affected areas. Even today, it is clear that the high level of market integration in India would be of little consolation for agricultural labourers if government intervention did not also protect their market command over food during lean years. The idea of preventing famines by generating purchasing power in affected areas and letting private trade supply the food was the basic inspiration behind the Famine Codes.

### (c) The Famine Codes and their basic principles

The failure of famine prevention during the period 1858–80 (extending from the demise of the East India Company to the birth of the Famine Codes) was not a complete one. A measure of inverse correlation between the extensiveness of relief efforts and the intensity of distress was noticeable even at that time. In particular, during the 'Panic Famine' of 1873–4 in Behar massive relief efforts were quite effective in preventing the worst. However, the shortcomings of *ad hoc* responses were increasingly evident, and while the relative success of relief efforts in 1873–4 was recognized they were also regarded as excessively costly.[42]

[40] Government of India (1880: 27). On the relationship between food prices and famine mortality in 19th-century India, see Lardinois (1982, 1985).

[41] During the famine of 1860–1 in Moradabad, for instance, John Strachey had already observed that 'although the agricultural population has thus suffered comparatively little the prices of food have risen higher in Moradabad than in almost any district of these provinces' (Government of Bengal 1874: 363). The Famine Commission of 1880 itself concluded that 'much caution, however, is requisite in regarding prices as a sound standard by which to estimate the severity of famine or distress' (Government of India 1880: 27), and this point was made even more forcefully by later Famine Commissions.

[42] The Famine Commission of 1880, referring to the Behar famine of 1873–4, did not hesitate to deplore that 'life was preserved, but money was spent profusely' (Government of India 1880: para. 94). It is of some interest to note that the exceptionally large levels of expenditure incurred during this famine were to a great extent due to the costs of food transportation and distribution (both unusual measures), as well as to the poor 'targeting' inherent in a relief strategy largely based on the distribution or subsidization of food (see e.g. ibid. para. 57 and Appendix I, p. 109). For further elaboration of the many interesting issues pertaining to famine relief after 1858 but before the Famine Codes, see particularly the discussion of 'Principles of Famine Relief' in ibid. Appendix I, as well as Loveday (1914).

This period of 'trial and error' (as Srivastava puts it) came to an end after the Famine Commission of 1880, keenly aware of the vital importance of 'prompt and decided action' in matters of famine relief, recommended the promulgation of *Famine Codes* which would contain authoritative guidelines to the local administration for the anticipation, recognition, and relief of famines:

The duties involved in relief measures are complicated and multifarious; their successful performance necessitates the utilisation of large stores of accumulated experience and a carefully considered and prepared plan; they cannot be safely left to individual energy and resource, or be dealt with on a system improvised only when the emergency has arisen. Prompt and decided action in carrying out these measures is of primary importance, and by considering well beforehand the principles that should guide them, much of that hesitation and uncertainty of purpose, which have been found to be so detrimental in the past, will be avoided in the future. We recommend, therefore, that the Government of India should, as soon as possible, issue a set of rules embodying the main principles that should govern the administration of famine relief, and that these rules should be authoritative in all parts of British India.[43]

The introduction of the Famine Codes undoubtedly represented an essential (though not quite decisive) step towards the successful prevention of famines in India.[44] The provisions of these Codes are much too comprehensive to be discussed here in detail.[45] For future reference, however, it is of some interest to recall the basic strategy of famine prevention recommended by the Famine Codes, and its rationale.

The backbone of the famine relief strategy embodied in the Famine Codes was the organization of *massive public works*. More precisely, the first and foremost aim of this strategy was nothing less than to provide employment at subsistence wages and at a reasonable distance from their homes to *all* those who applied for it (wages were to be paid in cash, and public employment

[43] Government of India (1880: 37–8). For a detailed account of the historical events surrounding the birth of the Famine Codes, see Brennan (1984).

[44] The first 'Draft Famine Code' was submitted along with the Famine Commission Report of 1880. Each State was required to frame its own code by adapting the model contained in the Draft Code to its own circumstances. With the passage of time the State Famine Codes underwent occasional revisions, and in independent India they received the name of Scarcity Manuals. In some parts of the country the latter are no longer explicitly used today, but this is partly because the rules they embody have become a matter of routine response to the threat of famine.

[45] The chapter headings of the provincial Famine Codes are as follows: '(I) Duties of revenue and village officers in ordinary times; (II) When serious scarcity is imminent; (III) Duties of superior revenue and engineer officers (during famine); (IV) Circle organization and duties of circle officers; (V) Gratuitous relief; (VI) Famine relief works; (VII) Wages and rations; (VIII) Poor houses; (IX) Kitchens for children; (X) Other measures of relief; (XI) Measures for the protection of cattle; (XII) Utilization of forests; (XIII) Duties of police; (XIV) Duties of medical officers; (XV) Accounts' (Srivastava 1968: 175). These were the recommended chapter headings for the provincial Famine Codes, as per a resolution of the Government of India, 1893 (see Srivastava 1968). The present Bombay Scarcity Manual (Government of Maharashtra 1966) still follows a very similar pattern. For an introduction to the Famine Codes and their provisions, see Srivastava (1968: ch. 6). See also the discussions in Alamgir (1980), McAlpin (1983), Brennan (1984), and Government of India (1945).

was directed to the creation of public assets such as roads and canals). 'Gratuitous relief' for those unable to work, in the form of doles or kitchens, complemented public works to form the core of relief measures.

It is tempting to suspect that the motivation behind this predilection for public works lay with a puritanical prejudice against the provision of unconditional relief. This suspicion is all the more difficult to refute because the Famine Commission Report in fact explicitly referred on occasion to 'the demoralising influences of purely eleemosynary aid'.[46] It is, nevertheless, worth attempting to understand the arguments which the Famine Commissions put forward in defence of the strategy they advocated.

The problem of preventing famine was, naturally, seen by the British administration as one of protecting food entitlements in a situation where the physical availability of food was not itself problematic. One avenue of intervention could, of course, have been to aim primarily at preventing undue increases in food prices. But the success of such measures would have inevitably called for some form of 'interference' with the free market—either in the form of direct price *control*, or at least in the form of government *participation* in trade, storage, and distribution. And this was anathema to the British administration.

Why so? It is hard not to sympathize here with Ambirajan's view that 'when virtually every document relating to the formulation and execution of famine policy over a century refers to Adam Smith and/or John Stuart Mill, it becomes well nigh impossible to dismiss the role of Classical economic ideas in the formation of economic policy'.[47] Indeed these ideas were echoed with striking fidelity in the Famine Commission Reports themselves.[48]

Policies of direct price control had been emphatically criticized by classical economists. John Stuart Mill, for instance, pronounced:

In cases of actual scarcity Governments are often urged . . . to take measures of some sort for moderating the price of food. But the price of a thing cannot be raised by deficiency of supply beyond what is sufficient to make a corresponding reduction of the

---

[46] Government of India (1880: para. 111). Note, however, that what is referred to here is not so much the intrinsically 'immoral' character of gratuitous relief as the adverse effect of gratuitous relief on the 'moral economy': 'Even where the legal right does not exist, the moral obligation of mutual assistance is scarcely less distinctly recognized [in rural India] . . . Any form of relief calculated to bring these rights into obscurity or desuetude, or to break down these habits by showing them to be superfluous, would be an incalculable misfortune' (ibid. para. 108).

[47] Ambirajan (1978: 100); see also Stokes (1959) and Ambirajan (1971, 1976). Bhatia dissents on this point: 'It is difficult to explain this palpably mistaken policy [of free trade] simply in terms of the ideological attachment of the Government of those days to the teachings of Adam Smith and John Stuart Mill . . . It appears that behind the façade of the theoretical argument there was the fear that the Government would have to assume a gigantic financial responsibility in undertaking to feed a vast population during the period of a famine' (Bhatia 1967: 107). But it is hard to take seriously the suggestion that several decades of official writings were consistently manipulated to maintain this 'façade', and the single 'letter' which Bhatia refers to in support of his contention carries little weight in the face of the voluminous evidence gathered by Ambirajan.

[48] See e.g. the lengthy chapter on Food Supply in Government of India (1880).

consumption; and if a Government prevents the reduction from being brought about by a rise of price, there remains no mode of effecting it unless by taking possession of all the food and serving it out in rations as in a besieged town.[49]

This argument implicitly assumes competitive conditions, so that high prices reflect the 'actual scarcity' in the first place rather than collusive practices or speculative hoarding. But the disciples of classical economists did not think that assumption implausible for India, where 'a combination of large dealers with the object of keeping up prices is impossible'.[50]

It is more difficult to understand why the British administration viewed government participation in food trade with abhorrence. It can be argued that in many circumstances, and especially in the presence of important uncertainties and information costs, judicious government involvement in food trade can have many positive effects, including that of stabilizing food prices.[51] But the British administration was deeply sceptical of this view, and strongly feared that government participation in food trade would have harmful *disincentive effects* on private initiative. Here again the influence of classical economists is unmistakable:

Direct measures at the cost of the State, to procure food from a distance, are expedient when, from peculiar reasons, the thing is not likely to be done by private speculation. In any other case they are in great error. Private speculation will not, in such cases, venture to compete with the Government and though the Government can do more than any other merchant it cannot nearly do so much as all the merchants.[52]

It might even become necessary for Government to import grain for sale to the public in such an event as a combination of local dealers to refuse to sell, or only to sell at prices unduly raised above the rates of neighbouring markets . . . But much caution will be required in every case lest interference should aggravate the evil which it is designed to avert, and have the effect of preventing traders from entering the market while it is being operated upon by the Government.[53]

Whether the British administration's obstinate policy of complete non-intervention in the food trade was an effective route to the moderation of price increases in famine situations has been the subject of some controversy.[54] But in any case, the fundamental problem remained that the moderation of price increases could hardly suffice to restore the entitlements of the masses of labourers and artisans whose cash earnings virtually vanished for long periods during droughts. The need for a mechanism of income generation or transfer was therefore inescapable.

[49] J. S. Mill, quoted in Etheridge (1868: 7).

[50] Wallace (1900: 48).

[51] For further discussion, see ch. 5 below. See also Drèze and Sen (1989).

[52] Mill (1848), cited in Bhatia (1967: 107).

[53] Government of India (1880: para. 159).

[54] For different viewpoints, see e.g. Bhatia (1967), Srivastava (1968), Ambirajan (1978), Rashid (1980), McAlpin (1983), and Ravallion (1987b).

It remains to explain why public works (supplemented by 'gratuitous relief' for those unable to work) emerged as the preferred transfer mechanism. At this point it is important to recognize that the British administration, while anxious to prevent starvation deaths during droughts, was also deeply concerned with financial economy. It therefore felt a strong urge to concoct a system by which 'the proper recipients of public charity can be most effectively ascertained',[55] and to ensure that resources were concentrated exclusively on that category. Given the weakness of the administrative structure at the time, and the large numbers of people often affected by famine, it was also felt important that the selection mechanism should rely as far as possible on 'self-acting tests' rather than on discretionary procedures. The latter method, although found necessary for some forms of gratuitous relief (see below), was deemed impracticable as a general approach to the identification of the needy, and a few experiments in that direction were criticized by the Famine Commissions.[56]

Four varieties of 'self-acting tests' were seriously tried at various stages in the early days of famine relief under the colonial administration: (1) the *distance test*: relief is provided (in some form or other) in far-apart places, on the assumption that only those in greatest need will take the trouble of travelling long distances to avail themselves of it; (2) the *residence test*: beneficiaries are required to reside at the place of relief (e.g. a poor-house or worksite), and thereby forgo the presumed pleasure of ordinary social life; (3) the *test of cooked food*: relief is based on the distribution of cooked meals, a source of repulsion to many 'starving Hindoos' at that time (particularly when cooked by, or shared with, people belonging to other castes); and (4) the *labour test*: relief takes the form of subsistence wages in return for hard manual labour.

The distance test and the residence test, both of which required entire families of famine victims to leave their homes before obtaining relief, were quickly rejected because experience repeatedly showed them to be too dangerous. Famine victims were found to be strongly attached to their homes, and only abandoned them in search of food or relief when their physical condition was one of extreme weakness and great vulnerability to disease. The Famine Commission of 1880 had already discouraged recourse to self-acting tests of this kind; later experience repeatedly confirmed their danger, and the Famine Commissions of 1898 and 1901 categorically rejected them:

There is . . . a great accumulation of evidence to the effect that the feeling of people towards relief administered in this form is in most parts of India one of extreme repulsion; and that even in the North-Western Provinces in 1877–78 that repulsion was strong enough to cause many to lose their lives rather than to accept help on those terms;[57]

[55] Government of India (1880: para. 110).
[56] See e.g. Government of India (1880, 1898: 86, and 1901: 25).
[57] Government of India (1880: para. 140).

. . . we do not hold the view . . . that the fact that many will attend works when close to their village, who will not follow them to a distance, necessarily proves that such persons were not in need of relief;[58]

Labour should be the only test; neither a distance test, nor compulsory residence should be imposed.[59]

The choice between the labour test and the test of cooked food was a more subtle one. Three reasons (each prevailing with varying strength over time) seem to have accounted for the precedence taken by the generation of employment over the unconditional provision of cooked food in the Indian system of famine relief. The first reason was the belief (discussed earlier) in the 'demoralizing' influence of gratuitous relief.[60] The second reason was the impracticability of delivering relief on a large scale by means of cooked food:

Acceptance of cooked food is the truest and safest test of the need for gratuitous relief, but the objection to relying exclusively on this form of relief is, that it would be difficult to work on a large scale if there were widespread distress. When a large proportion of a not very dense population has to be relieved, the organization of adequate distribution of cooked food becomes almost impossible.[61]

The third reason appeared only with the Famine Commission of 1901. The Famine Commission of 1898 had pronounced a rather favourable judgement on relief kitchens (as a means of gratuitous relief specifically), and expressed a general preference for kitchens over doles (of cash or grain) as a form of gratuitous relief partly on the grounds that kitchens embodied a self-acting test.[62] Indeed there was evidence from different parts of the country that 'the people showed a very strong reluctance to accept relief in this form'.[63] But the Famine Commission of 1901 radically reversed this judgement, altogether dismissed the idea that kitchens embodied a self-acting test, and therefore strongly favoured (grain) doles as the main vehicle of gratuitous relief:

. . . gratuitous relief can properly be regulated by *personal selection* alone. Every self-acting test that has been tried has broken down;[64]

Non-official opinion is almost unanimous, we gather, in favour of doles. It is now generally admitted by the officers of the Central Provinces that *personal selection* is as necessary for kitchens as it is for village relief. This conclusion deprives the kitchens of the principal advantage expected from them, namely, the enforcement of an automatic test of distress; while the disadvantages attaching to them remain.[65]

---

[58] Government of India (1898: 110).

[59] Government of India (1901: 18).

[60] See e.g. Government of India (1898: 233).

[61] Ibid. 18.          [62] See ibid. 286.

[63] Ibid. 23–4. See also pp. 18–26, 68–74, 80–1, 84–5, 88, 93, 178, 210, 286–7, and 322 of the same report for discussions of the relative merits of kitchens and doles.

[64] Government of India (1901: 44) (my italics).

[65] Ibid. 47 (my italics). 'Village relief' refers to the distribution of doles.

In spite of their perceived superiority over the provision of cooked meals as far as *gratuitous* relief was concerned, doles in cash or grain could obviously not be adopted as a *general* form of relief. This followed from the assumed need for a test of distress, the impracticality of personal selection on a large scale, and the difficulties and confusion to which the granting of doles often led.[66]

The effectiveness of the 'labour test' as a self-acting test, on the other hand, was repeatedly confirmed by practical experience. Public works therefore emerged as the preferred vehicle of income transfers in the Famine Codes.

Having said this, it should be stressed that the provisions of the Famine Codes also included gratuitous relief (usually in the form of doles) for those to whom the labour test could not be applied. Although gratuitous relief has almost invariably assumed much less importance than public works in terms of numbers relieved and expenditure incurred, it has undoubtedly been an irreplaceable component of the 'safety-net' which the relief system sought to provide.[67]

At the risk of repetition, it is worth closing this discussion by quoting at some length the passage where the Famine Commission of 1880 succinctly summarizes the logic of the recommended approach:

. . . we have to consider the manner in which the proper recipients of public charity can be most effectually ascertained. The problem to be solved is how to avoid the risk of indiscriminate and demoralising profusion on the one hand, and of insufficient and niggardly assistance on the other—how to relieve all who really need relief, and to waste as little public money as possible in the process . . . . Again where limited numbers have to be dealt with, and there is a numerous and efficient staff of officials, it may be possible to ascertain by personal inquiry the circumstances of every applicant for relief sufficiently for the purpose of admitting or rejecting his claim. But in an Indian famine the Government has to deal not with limited numbers, but with millions of people, and the official machinery at its command, however strengthened for the occasion, will inevitably be inadequate to the task of accurately testing the individual necessities of so great a multitude. Nor again is it possible to entrust the administration of public charity to a subordinate agency without providing sufficient checks against dishonesty and neglect on the part of its members. Some safeguards then are essential in the interests of the destitute people no less than of the public treasury, and they are best found in laying down certain broad self-acting tests by which necessity may be proved, and which may, irrespective of any other rule of selection, entitle to relief the person who submits to them . . . The chief of these tests, and the only one which in our opinion it is ordinarily desirable to enforce, is the demand of labour commensurate in each case with the labourer's powers, in return for a wage sufficient for the purposes of maintenance but not more. This system is applicable of course only to those from whom labour can reasonably be required . . . but for those who are able to work, we can feel no doubt that

---

[66] 'The drawbacks were that they [relief centres in the Central Provinces, where doles were distributed] tended to become centres of confusion and disorder, where relief was disbursed, without discrimination or enquiry into individual cases' (Goverment of India 1989: 72).

[67] There are, unfortunately, very few empirical studies of how this component of the relief system has worked in practice in different periods. For some recent evidence, see Drèze (1989).

it is the safest and most efficacious form of State help . . . The great bulk of applicants for relief being thus provided for, we believe that it will be possible for an efficient staff of officers to control with success the grant of relief, on the basis of personal inquiry and knowledge of the individual circumstances of each applicant, among the comparatively small numbers of destitute persons to whom the test of labour cannot be applied.[68]

The preceding discussion has attempted to identify the main ingredients of the Famine Codes. It would be naïve to regard the Famine Codes as embodying only enlightened pragmatism, and I have indeed pointed out the role of other influences such as the phobia of 'interference' with private trade and the distrust of gratuitous relief on sheer moral grounds. However, the strategy of open-ended employment for cash wages, supplemented by 'gratuitous relief' for the weak, undeniably had a sound rationale in terms of the objective of preventing all starvation deaths while achieving a measure of financial economy. Since this narrow objective remains, unfortunately, how famine prevention is often conceived, the Famine Codes and their basic principles have not lost their relevance.[69]

### (d)  Modern developments

It would not be easy to 'demonstrate' that the relief system which emerged and evolved from the Famine Codes had a dramatic effect on the incidence of famines before independence in 1947. Such questions are commonly investigated on the basis of famine chronologies,[70] but in the absence of reliable information on the actual excess mortality associated with different events the use of this piece of evidence is fraught with difficulties. In fact, crop failures resulting in a successfully averted threat of famine have sometimes been recorded in the annals of history as a 'famine', even though little or no evidence existed of substantial excess mortality.[71] Reliable data on crop failures and other possible sources of entitlement failures would also be needed in order to assess the severity of the *threats* confronted by the relief system in different periods.

Nevertheless, an examination of the incidence of famines in India before and after the Famine Codes strongly suggests a contrast between the earlier period

[68]  Government of India (1880: paras. 110–11).

[69]  Brennan (1984) has rightly emphasized the importance of 'personalities and politics' in the framing of the first Famine Code. He does not, however, imply that the actual content of that Code significantly reflected the uninformed prejudices or self-interested inclinations of the members of the Famine Commission of 1880. The remarkable continuity of the basic principles of famine relief in India to this day, in spite of substantial changes in 'personalities and politics', strongly discredits any implication of that sort.

[70]  See n. 3 above for some references of famine chronologies for India.

[71]  *Vide* the 'famine' of 1906–7 in Darbhanga, when 'the death rate was *unusually low* during the greater part of the famine period when relief measures were organised and in working order' (Government of India 1908: 30; italics added). The 'famine' of 1907–8 in the United Provinces is another example (see Bhatia 1967: 265–70). On the methodology of historical famine assessment, see Murton (1984).

of frequently recurring catastrophes, and the latter period when long stretches of relative tranquillity were disturbed by a few large-scale famines (see the 'chronological sketch' in section 1.2). This pattern is unmistakable, for instance, in a comparison between the twenty years preceding and the twenty years following the Famine Commission Report of 1880. The period from 1860 to 1880 was a calamitous one. From 1880 to 1896, by contrast, great success was encountered in preventing local crop failures from developing into famines, allowing the Famine Commission of 1898 to assert that 'scarcities occurring over limited areas while the rest of the Indian continent is prosperous, can be successfully dealt with by a very moderate expenditure of money without disturbing the ordinary administration'.[72] Then, in 1896–7 and again in 1899–1900, disaster struck with renewed force. During the twentieth century, the incidence of famines was remarkably small even before independence; the main failure was of course the Bengal Famine of 1943.[73]

Why did the relief system experience these intermittent failures to prevent large-scale starvation?[74] Without attempting to assess their relative importance, I will suggest here four elements of answer to this question.

First, it is important to note that the existence of the Famine Codes does not automatically ensure their *application*, let alone their early and energetic application. The Famine Codes did include very specific (and 'authoritative') guidelines on how to recognize and 'declare' a famine, and it was not their least achievement to reduce the risk of deliberate ignorance or neglect of a crisis —an attitude which has been described as 'one of the most predictable responses by Government officials' in times of famine.[75] Nevertheless this 'early warning system' remained *within* the Famine Codes, and the problem of triggering remained an important one. During the Bengal Famine of 1943, for instance, the Famine Codes were deliberately ignored for political reasons —and this fault may well be responsible for a large part of the extraordinary excess mortality associated with that famine.[76]

Second, even for the narrow purpose of ensuring the mere survival of the population, famine relief under the British administration often had an

[72] Government of India (1989: 5). There are several interesting first-hand accounts of successful famine prevention in pre-independence India, e.g. Carlyle (1900).

[73] Considerable mortality also occurred in 1918–19, but this was mainly the result of a terrible influenza epidemic which affected many other parts of the world as well. On this see Mills (1986). On the prevention of famines during the first half of this century, see Christensen (1984), Kachhawaha (1985), and McAlpin (1985), among others.

[74] Note that even when famine did occur, the relief system may have succeeded in ensuring a considerable moderation of excess mortality. The Famine Commission of 1898, for instance, claimed that 'the success actually attained in the relief of distress was, if not complete, far greater than any that has been recorded in famines that are at all comparable with it in extent, severity, and duration' (Government of India 1898: 196). Demographic statistics also showed a clear inverse correlation between the extent of relief and that of excess mortality (Visaria and Visaria 1982: 130).

[75] Carlson (1982:9).

[76] On the Bengal Famine of 1943, and the question of non-declaration of famine in that event, see Sen (1981), Greenough (1982), Brennan (1988), and the literature cited in these studies.

excessively punitive character. In particular, the level of wages paid on relief works was extraordinarily low—the extreme of stinginess being reached with the so-called 'Temple ration' of 1lb of grain per day (this standard was fortunately abrogated without delay).[77] As a result, during the most severe crises the availability of work did not always prevent a considerable enfeeblement of affected people, and their enhanced vulnerability to epidemics. This factor seems to have played a particularly important role during the famines of 1896–7 and 1899–1900.[78]

Third, in the case of the latter two famines the policy of strict non-interference with private trade was particularly questionable because the existence of abundant food supplies in India as a whole could no longer be so safely assumed. The crop failures which triggered these famines had unique severity for the nineteenth century, and they also had the exceptional feature of affecting very large parts of the country. The collapse of production for the country as a whole was unprecedented, and prices rose throughout India. The fact of continued food exports during the 1896–7 famine, taken by the Famine Commission of 1898 as evidence of the persistence of a surplus, could obviously not be interpreted in that way. It is hard to deny that in this case the refusal to prohibit exports or arrange for imports may have had disastrous consequences.[79]

Finally, it must be recognized that while epidemics are often exacerbated or even triggered by food entitlement failures, they do have an influence of their own as well. This was most obvious in the case of the 1918 influenza epidemic, which affected large parts of the world. The Famine Commissions of 1898 and 1901 also stressed the independent role of cold weather, contaminated water, and epidemics during the famines of 1896–7 and 1899–1900. In his rejoinder to some of the conclusions of the Famine Commission Report of 1898, Holderness even argued that in some places excess mortality had altogether little to do with food deprivation.[80]

[77] The proper level of wages, keeping in view the objective of preventing starvation deaths while simultaneously ensuring the greatest possible measure of financial economy, was discussed at nauseating length in most Famine Commission Reports. The issue was all the more important because the supply of labour to public works was repeatedly observed to be extremely sensitive to the level of wages. For some examples of strong expansion or contraction of labour supply in response to small wage revisions, see e.g. Bhatia (1967: 85, 95, 249) and Government of India (1898: 25, 26, 34, 76, 77, 80, 83, 168, 177).

[78] See e.g. Bhatia (1967), Guz (1987), Hebert (1987), and particularly Klein (1984).

[79] This question is pursued at some length in Holderness (1897), with reference to the 1896–7 famine. Holderness argued that 'there is . . . a strong probability that the production of the year was much below the requirements of the population' (p. 11), estimated the decline in foodgrain production to represent as much as 18 or 19 million tons (p. 13), and cited a letter published in early 1897 in the *Gazette of India* invoking the usual reasons for not interfering with private trade in any way: 'The Governor-General in Council believes that the intervention of Government as a purchaser or importer would do infinitely more harm than good, as it would cripple and discourage the agency which is best able to gauge the need, which is impelled by self-interest to anticipate it, and which alone is best able to supply it effectively' (quoted on p. 33).

[80] See the Appendix of Government of India (1898).

While the control of epidemics obviously demands intervention measures beyond the mere restoration of food entitlements, the first three of the above factors point to defects of the entitlement protection system itself. As we shall see, these three defects were largely remedied after independence, an event which must count as marking the second turning-point in the history of famine relief in India over the last two centuries. The government of independent India rapidly did away with the policy of strict non-interference with private trade in food, and its price stabilization measures in particular have often played an important role in averting famine threats. The punitive and avaricious nature of relief provisions has not altogether disappeared (far from it), but the value attached to human life has nevertheless appreciated compared to the colonial days. Last but not least, commitment to respond to the threat of famine has increasingly assumed the character of a political compulsion.

### 1.3. Food crises in India after independence

This section consists of two fairly self-contained parts. The first is devoted to a general overview of food crises in India since independence. The second discusses famine relief in Bihar during the drought of 1966–7, with particular attention to its shortcomings. The intention of these explorations is essentially to strengthen the background against which relief operations in Maharashtra in 1972–3 (the subject of section 1.4) will be evaluated. The reader familiar with the food situation in contemporary India and lacking interest in the Bihar crisis may wish to go straight to section 1.4.

### (a) The reality and nature of recent food crises

According to official statistics, per capita food production in India consistently declined in the first half of this century (see Table 1.1). In fact, official statistics unambiguously show consistently declining *total output* over this period.[81] Even if we take official statistics for the pre-independence period with a pinch of salt, it is clear that by the time of independence per capita foodgrain production levels in India were dangerously low, and they remained so until very recent years when a mild trend upward has slowly emerged. It is,

---

[81] This conclusion is extremely robust with respect to alternative manipulations of these statistics—for further discussion, see Blyn (1966), Mukerji (1965), Sen (1971), and Sivasubramoniam (1960, 1965). The fact that the Famine Commissions (in 1880, 1898, and 1901) asserted the existence of a surplus of foodgrains in India in normal years on the basis of consumption allowances which far exceeded contemporary standards provides further support for the thesis of declining per capita production levels in the first half of this century. In a widely discussed rejoinder, Alan Heston (1973, 1978, 1982) has expressed scepticism about the plausibility of output trends derived from official statistics because they imply (he argues) the doubtful finding of declining yields over the same period. Heston's own estimates of production trends, based on the assumption of stable yields, affect the force, but not the substance, of the argument presented in this section. Indeed, the growth of *acreage* of foodgrains lagged behind population growth during the first half of this century (see McAlpin 1985).

**Table 1.1** Production and availability of foodgrains in India,
1893–1985

| Period | Production per capita (1961 = 100) | Availability per capita (1961 = 100) |
|---|---|---|
| 1893–4 to 1895–6 | 146 | — |
| 1896–7 to 1905–6 | 140 | — |
| 1906–7 to 1915–16 | 136 | — |
| 1916–17 to 1925–6 | 134 | — |
| 1926–7 to 1935–6 | 115 | — |
| 1936–7 to 1945–6 | 99 | — |
| 1956 | 94 | 92 |
| 1961 | 100 | 100 |
| 1962 | 98 | 99 |
| 1963 | 94 | 95 |
| 1964 | 92 | 96 |
| 1965 | 100 | 102 |
| 1966 | 79 | 87 |
| 1967 | 80 | 86 |
| 1968 | 99 | 98 |
| 1969 | 98 | 95 |
| 1970 | 100 | 97 |
| 1971 | 107 | 100 |
| 1972 | 101 | 99 |
| 1973 | 90 | 90 |
| 1974 | 96 | 96 |
| 1975 | 90 | 87 |
| 1976 | 106 | 91 |
| 1977 | 96 | 92 |
| 1978 | 107 | 100 |
| 1979 | 109 | 102 |
| 1980 | 89 | 88 |
| 1981 | 102 | 97 |
| 1982 | 103 | 97 |
| 1983 | 98 | 93 |
| 1984 | 113 | 102 |
| 1985 | 106 | 99 |

*Notes*: Availability is calculated (following the usual conventions in Indian food statistics) as net production + net imports − net additions to government stocks, where net production consists of production less 12.5% for 'feed, seed, and wastage'.

There are a number of other estimates of pre-independence trends in per capita food production (e.g. Blyn 1966, Mukerji 1965, Sen 1971, and Sivasubramoniam 1960, 1965); but all those based on official statistics lead to the same conclusion of a *declining* pre-independence trend (see text).

In the post-independence calculations based on the *Economic Survey*, 'foodgrains' is understood as the sum of 'cereals' and 'pulses' (following the usual practice in Indian statistics). For pulses, 'net availability' is taken to be synonymous with 'gross production'—the resulting bias in the estimates of foodgrain production is negligible.

*Sources*: pre-independence: calculated from Bhatia (1967: 315), itself summarizing the work of Daniel Thorner; post-independence: calculated from *Economic Survey 1985–86* (Government of India 1986: 120).

moreover, very striking that production gains after independence have resulted mainly in reduced imports as well as in the accumulation of large stocks, leaving net 'availability' remarkably stagnant (see Table 1.1, and also Fig. 1.2 below).[82] There are compelling reasons, therefore, to attribute India's success in preventing famines after independence to other factors than the improvement of food availability.

Another important point to note is that the growth of food and agricultural output since independence has been very uneven across different parts of India.[83] While in irrigated regions the so-called 'Green Revolution' has permitted impressive increases in yields and total output, large unirrigated tracts have (until very recently at least) experienced virtual stagnation against a background of rapidly growing population. Accordingly, there is little evidence of increasing rural incomes and employment in unirrigated areas, which still cover around two-thirds of the total cropped area. These regions have also experienced huge ecological problems (such as deforestation, soil erosion, and falling water tables), and in this respect it is far from clear that they have fared better than Sahelian countries. Last but not least, there have been droughts and crop failures almost every year in some part or other of the country since independence, and the 'entitlement failures' which threatened to ensue remained quite capable of causing massive starvation in the absence of a vigorous relief system. The case-studies of drought in the States of Bihar (1966–7) and Maharashtra (1970–3) analysed further in this chapter unambiguously confirm that the growth of food production alone would have fallen far short of ensuring the prevention of famines in India in the last few decades.

The latter point can also, to some extent, be appreciated from a comparison of the recent experiences of India and the Sahel in terms of vulnerability to famine. Needless to say, any comparison of this kind must remain highly tentative, considering the quality of the available data and the wide variations in country-specific circumstances; in fact it is attempted here only with the greatest reluctance. I have nevertheless assembled in Tables 1.2 and 1.3 some evidence on levels of production and 'availability' of cereals for India and the Sahel over the 1960–80 period (see also Figs. 1.1 and 1.2).[84] Here 'availability' simply refers to the sum of production (net of 12.5 per cent allowance for feed, seed, and wastage), net recorded imports, and, in the case of India, net depletion of government stocks. This definition, largely imposed by the nature of the available data, neglects unrecorded imports (e.g. all private imports in the case of Maharashtra and Bihar) and the depletion of private stocks; it will, therefore, usually overestimate the instability of consumption. The neglect of

[82] See Lipton (1984) for further discussion of this point.

[83] For a detailed analysis of District-wise output trends during the 1960s and early 1970s, see Bhalla and Alagh (1979).

[84] I follow the definition of 'Sahel' used in Sen (1981). The comparison with the Sahel is emphasized because for that region in recent decades food availability fluctuations have been particularly sharp and closely associated with famines.

**Table 1.2** 'Production' of cereals per capita, India and Sahel, 1961–1980 (½ kg/cap./day = 100)

| Year | India | Sahel (A) | Sahel (B) | Maharashtra | Bihar | Palamau (A) | Palamau (B) | Chad | Mali | Mauritania | Niger | Burkina Faso | Senegal |
|---|---|---|---|---|---|---|---|---|---|---|---|---|---|
| 1961 | 86 | 124 | — | 93 | — | — | — | 194 | 141 | 52 | 145 | 89 | 90 |
| 1962 | 86 | 130 | — | 75 | — | — | — | 172 | 156 | 52 | 150 | 108 | 90 |
| 1963 | 82 | 124 | — | 77 | — | — | — | 164 | 127 | 52 | 151 | 108 | 101 |
| 1964 | 82 | 127 | — | 74 | 70 | — | — | 146 | 115 | 51 | 144 | 140 | 110 |
| 1965 | 87 | 120 | — | 74 | 68 | — | — | 141 | 118 | 60 | 132 | 117 | 113 |
| 1966 | 69 | 113 | — | 49 | 63 | — | — | 124 | 116 | 49 | 130 | 117 | 91 |
| 1967 | 72 | 124 | — | 62 | 35 | 12 | 20 | 119 | 128 | 59 | 141 | 117 | 133 |
| 1968 | 88 | 126 | — | 68 | 75 | — | — | 120 | 110 | 27 | 133 | 115 | 79 |
| 1969 | 87 | 116 | — | 67 | 79 | — | — | 109 | 129 | 55 | 129 | 108 | 122 |
| 1970 | 90 | 98 | — | 63 | — | — | — | 101 | 89 | 41 | 135 | 105 | 75 |
| 1971 | 96 | 102 | 96 | 51 | — | — | — | 103 | 123 | 37 | 117 | 88 | 100 |
| 1972 | 92 | 75 | 105[a] | 46 | — | — | — | 59 | 89 | 25 | 97 | 85 | 51 |
| 1973 | 83 | 78 | 83 | 27 | — | — | — | 72 | 72 | 15 | 101 | 80 | 81 |
| 1974 | 88 | 115 | 76 | 62 | — | — | — | 84 | 79 | 25 | 140 | 111 | 122 |
| 1975 | 82 | 95 | 104[a] | — | — | — | — | 79 | 98 | 15[b] | 104 | 124 | 87[b] |
| 1976 | 96 | 104 | 102[a] | — | — | — | — | 81 | 116 | 14 | 156 | 115 | 77 |
| 1977 | 87 | 93 | — | — | — | — | — | 81 | 96 | 11 | 171 | 91 | 54 |
| 1978 | 97 | 109 | — | — | — | — | — | 83 | 124 | 9 | 169 | 97 | 102 |
| 1979 | 99 | 99 | — | — | — | — | — | 82 | 101 | 15 | 173 | 99 | 66 |
| 1980 | 82 | 91 | — | — | — | — | — | 84 | 76 | 10 | 184 | 82 | 64 |

[a] Excluding Mauritania.
[b] Discrete jump in population estimates.

*Note:* Bold type indicates a year of famine or averted famine.

*Sources:* The estimates presented in the table were obtained as follows: India: calculated from the *Economic Survey 1985–86* (Government of India 1986: 120). Sahel: the estimates for individual Sahelian countries (Burkina Faso, Chad, Mali, Mauritania, Niger, and Senegal) have all been derived using the same formula, and the estimates for 'Sahel (A)' are calculated by aggregation over individual countries. Production as well as (mid-year) population estimates are taken from the *FAO Production Yearbooks* (the FAO population series, unlike those of the *United Nations Demographic Yearbook*, are adjusted to achieve consistency across years). Whenever different production (population) estimates for a given year appeared in different *FAO Production Yearbooks*, the figure mentioned in the *latest* Yearbook in which a production (population) estimate was available for that year has been used. The alternative estimates 'Sahel (B)' are calculated from Club du Sahel (1977) and the *United Nations Demographic Yearbook 1977*. They are not directly comparable to 'Sahel (A)' on a year-to-year basis because of differences in calendars. Maharashtra: production figures from the *Economic Review 1973–74* (Government of Maharashtra 1974) and the *Bulletin on Food Statistics*, 1975, 1976. Population estimates (mid-year) from the *Bulletin on Food Statistics*, 1975 and 1982–4. To obtain per capita production, population in calendar year $t$ was combined with production in agricultural year ($t − 1, t$). Bihar: production figures from the *Bulletin on Food Statistics*, 1967, 1968, and 1971: Table 4. Population figures from the *Bulletin on Food Statistics*, 1972. Palamau: See Table 1.7 below.

The *Economic Survey* production figures for India have been preferred to the FAO figures, because the latter include rice in the husk, which is about 50% heavier than husked rice (used in the *Economic Survey* figures); the latter is more directly comparable to other cereals (e.g. in terms of calorie content per kg) than rice in the husk. Apart from this discrepancy, however, the FAO figures are broadly comparable to the *Economic Survey* figures, and the latter are generally considered as fairly accurate. The FAO figures for the Sahel, on the other hand, can at best be regarded as rough estimates. I am grateful to the Statistics Division of FAO for helpful personal communications on these issues.

**Table 1.3** 'Net availability' of cereals per capita, India and Sahel, 1961–1980 (½ kg/cap./day = 100)

| Year | India | Sahel (A) | Sahel (B) | Maharashtra | Bihar (A) | Bihar (B) | Palamau | Chad | Mali | Mauritania | Niger | Burkina Faso | Senegal |
|---|---|---|---|---|---|---|---|---|---|---|---|---|---|
| 1961 | 80 | 115 | — | — | — | — | — | 170 | 123 | 66 | 121 | 79 | 109 |
| 1962 | 80 | 120 | — | — | — | — | — | 151 | 137 | 70 | 126 | 97 | 109 |
| 1963 | 77 | 114 | — | — | — | — | — | 145 | 112 | 63 | 125 | 96 | 120 |
| 1964 | 80 | 118 | — | — | — | 71 | — | 129 | 102 | 63 | 120 | 124 | 137 |
| 1965 | 84 | 113 | — | — | 65 | 68 | — | 124 | 106 | 74 | 110 | 104 | 139 |
| 1966 | **72** | 105 | — | — | **62** | **63** | — | 109 | 103 | 66 | 109 | 104 | 115 |
| 1967 | **73** | 115 | — | — | **45** | **53** | **≈55[b]** | 106 | 113 | 67 | 118 | 106 | 150 |
| 1968 | 81 | 118 | — | 75 | 85 | 72 | — | 106 | 97 | 53 | 110 | 103 | 104 |
| 1969 | 80 | 111 | — | 74 | 75 | 74 | — | 97 | 117 | 73 | 107 | 97 | 151 |
| 1970 | 81 | 93 | — | 68 | — | — | — | 90 | 105 | 66 | 111 | 95 | 95 |
| 1971 | 84 | 101 | 95 | **55** | — | — | — | 91 | 114 | 67 | 96 | 79 | 136 |
| 1972 | 84 | **76** | 102[a] | **57** | — | — | — | **53** | **85** | **59** | **80** | **79** | **83** |
| 1973 | 76 | **85** | 90 | **46** | — | — | — | **66** | **79** | **60** | **86** | **74** | **129** |
| 1974 | 82 | 120 | 87 | 73 | — | — | — | 81 | 92 | 77 | 134 | 104 | 148 |
| 1975 | 73 | 92 | 98[a] | — | — | — | — | 70 | 97 | 51 | 90 | 110 | 99 |
| 1976 | 75 | 104 | — | — | — | — | — | 74 | 101 | 65 | 140 | 103 | 112 |
| 1977 | 77 | 94 | — | — | — | — | — | 74 | 84 | 64 | 152 | 84 | 91 |
| 1978 | 85 | 110 | — | — | — | — | — | 75 | 114 | 62 | 154 | 91 | 132 |
| 1979 | 87 | 101 | — | — | — | — | — | 74 | 91 | 43 | 153 | 93 | 108 |
| 1980 | 76 | 94 | — | — | — | — | — | 74 | 73 | 66 | 166 | 78 | 96 |

[a] Excluding Mauritania.

[b] This includes estimates of private imports.

*Note:* Bold type indicates a year of famine or averted famine.

*Sources:* As explained in the text, the definition of 'net availability' used here is the following: net availability = net production + recorded imports + recorded stock depletion, where net production is obtained by deducting 12.5% from gross production for 'feed, seed, and wastage'. The production and population estimates are the same as in Table 1.2 for every region. Other sources are as follows: India: all figures obtained from *Economic Survey 1985–86* (Government of India 1986: 120). Sahel: there are no recorded changes in stocks. Import and export estimates for each year were taken from the latest *FAO Trade Yearbook* for which figures for that year were available. Maharashtra: see Table 1.18 below. Bihar: see Table 1.6 below. Palamau: see Table 1.7 below.

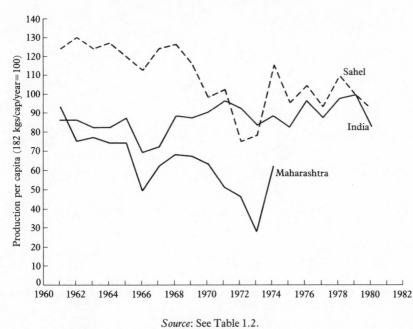

*Source*: See Table 1.2.

**Fig. 1.1** Production of cereals per capita, 1961–1980

unrecorded trade is likely to be particularly serious in the case of individual States within India, and that of private stocks in the case of the Sahel. Note that much of the discussion in this section will concentrate on 'cereals' or 'foodgrains' rather than 'calories'; however, a comparison between India and the Sahel based on available calorie data leads to broadly similar conclusions.[85]

Many complex issues are, of course, involved in deciding what these figures tell us about the potential severity of entitlement crises in different places at different times. It is arguable, for instance, whether the comparison made here should be primarily based on (1) *production* or *availability* figures; and (2) *levels* or *change*. Answers to these questions are highly contingent upon our view of how the food entitlement process works in a particular place. Regarding the first question, production and availability figures obviously give us different and complementary clues. While 'availability' sounds more closely related to consumption than production, it suffers particularly badly from being an aggregative measure. If entitlement failures are seen to arise mainly as a

---

[85] See also Sen (1986). For our purposes, foodgrains are probably not a bad proxy for calories in India, where they form an overwhelming proportion of total calories. Svedberg (1987) has argued that this approximation may not be too inaccurate for Sahelian countries either. Throughout this paper I shall use the usual convention in Indian statistics of defining 'foodgrains' as the sum of 'cereals' and 'pulses'. The share of pulses in total foodgrains in India was less than 10% in the early 1980s (Government of India 1986: 120).

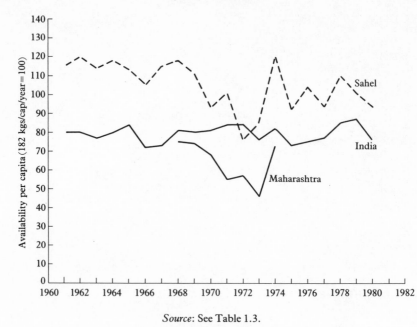

*Source*: See Table 1.3.

**Fig. 1.2** Availability of cereals per capita, 1961–1980

consequence of the loss of employment or income associated with bad harvests, it is arguable that production is a more significant variable. In this case, however, it is total agricultural output rather than food output which is of interest. The recognition of this simple fact was indeed at the centre of the 'annewari' system of early warning in India, based on assessments of harvest quality.

The second question is also important, particularly in the case of availability figures. If food consumption responds little to income and price changes (except perhaps for pure 'income effects' at very low income levels), then even with a fairly high base consumption level small *declines* in net food availability are likely to have serious consequences, because the burden of adjustment will fall on the poorest. On the other hand, if food consumption is highly responsive to short-run price and income changes, then small changes in food availability around a high base level may be fairly unalarming, and the long-term level of food consumption may be the more important variable to focus on. The contrast is of some importance in this context, because the evolution of (aggregate) cereal production and consumption in India during the period 1960–80 seems to have been marked by much lower base levels but also smaller fluctuations than those experienced in the Sahel (see Figs 1.1 and 1.2).

A further issue is that of appropriate standards for comparing availability levels. In principle, one should at least adjust for differences in calorie 'requirements' and in the importance of cereals in the diet. While the latter adjustment would not be likely to change the results, the basis of the former is a matter of fierce controversy (on this see Chapters 7 and 8 in the first volume of this book).

No attempt will be made here to take all these considerations explicitly into account. They are, to some extent, of secondary importance, in so far as our purpose is not primarily to compare actual or potential entitlement crises in India and the Sahel, but rather to show that the prevention of famines in contemporary India cannot be convincingly explained solely in terms of food production or availability. The data in Tables 1.2 and 1.3 allow us to compare both levels and change (for production as well as availability), and in the absence of fairly large differentials in consumption standards between India and the Sahel the following tentative observations would appear to be valid:

1. The interpretation of a comparison of food 'production' and 'availability' between *India as a whole* and *Sahel as a whole* over the 1960–80 period hinges greatly on whether one compares levels or change. India has not suffered from a declining trend in production over that period, but nevertheless poduction and availability levels have remained consistently lower in India than in the Sahel.

2. If one compares *Sahel countries* or groups of countries with *areas* of similar (or greater) population size in India, it always seems possible to find an area in India which has fared no better than the corresponding area in the Sahel (e.g. Maharashtra 1960–75 vs. Sahel 1960–75, or Bihar 1965–70 vs. Chad 1970–5). This holds in terms of both 'production' and 'availability'.

3. If we compare *India as a whole* with *individual Sahel countries*, some among the latter (e.g. Chad and Mauritania) have undoubtedly faced more severe food crises by any criterion.

Before moving on, it is worth reflecting for a moment on the issue of food security and national boundaries. The contrast between India and the Sahel suggests that food security tends to be enhanced by the integration of vulnerable areas within wider national boundaries. This observation is confirmed by an examination of State-wise cereal production and consumption data in India (Table 1.4). Not only do we find that consumption differences across States are much narrower than production differences, but consumption differentials themselves appear to be extraordinarily stable over time and therefore must have very little to do with production differentials as such. Thus, in contemporary India, consumption instability is very effectively insulated from production instability for individual States; though not perfectly, as the consumption 'dips' in Maharashtra (1972–3), Gujarat (1972–4), and West Bengal (1973–4)—all coinciding with local crop failures—illustrate.

The finding that a large country tends to achieve a greater level of food security, *ceteris paribus*, than a collection of small countries is hardly surprising. But the precise mechanism underlying this contrast deserves further

**Table 1.4** Cereal production and consumption in India, State-wise (kg/cap./month)

| State | Cereal consumption per capita | | | | Cereal production per capita |
|---|---|---|---|---|---|
| | 1970–1 | 1972–3 | 1973–4 | 1977–8 | 1977–8 |
| Andhra Pradesh | 16.05 | 15.25 | 15.80 | 15.85 | 14.30 |
| Assam | 15.70 | 14.81 | 15.33 | 14.38 | 11.18 |
| Bihar | 16.39 | 15.58 | 14.99 | 16.16 | 11.42 |
| Gujarat | 15.00 | 13.32 | 13.87 | 13.44 | 9.78 |
| Haryana | 18.13 | 17.57 | 16.56 | 15.22 | 30.16 |
| Jammu and Kashmir | 20.14 | 18.72 | 19.09 | 17.97 | 16.36 |
| Kerala | (7.99) | (7.97) | (7.69) | (9.18) | 4.44 |
| Madhya Pradesh | 16.51 | 17.28 | 17.12 | 16.08 | 17.51 |
| Maharashtra | 12.83 | 12.60 | 13.45 | 13.52 | 13.40 |
| Karnataka | 15.71 | 15.63 | 15.61 | 16.01 | 16.03 |
| Orissa | 16.12 | 15.22 | 15.80 | 15.97 | 16.27 |
| Punjab | 15.46 | 15.38 | 14.89 | 14.35 | 52.85 |
| Rajasthan | 17.91 | 18.17 | 18.76 | 18.18 | 13.56 |
| Tamil Nadu | 13.95 | 14.53 | 14.72 | 13.85 | 13.56 |
| Uttar Pradesh | 16.32 | 16.83 | 16.24 | 16.57 | 15.12 |
| West Bengal | 13.35 | 13.64 | 12.97 | 14.74 | 13.97 |
| India | 15.35 | 15.26 | 15.09 | 15.25 | 14.88 |

*Note*: Figures for Kerala are not strictly comparable with those for other States because of the great importance, in the former case, of food items classified as 'Cereal Substitutes' by the National Sample Survey.

*Sources*: Consumption figures for 1970–1, 1972–3, 1973–4 from National Sample Survey (25th, 27th, and 28th Rounds), as summarized in *Sarvekshana*, Jan. 1979. Consumption figures for 1977–8 from the Draft Report No. 311 of the National Sample Survey, relating to the 32nd Round. Production figures are calculated from the *Bulletin on Food Statistics*, 1980: 13–14, using population projections (for 1 Oct. 1977) from the *Bulletin on Food Statistics*, 1982–4: 8–9 (assuming a constant population growth rate during the 1971–81 decade, within each State).

investigation. Does a poor 'integration' of food markets across national boundaries obstruct some evening out of food surpluses and shortages? Does the restricted movement of factors impinge on the diversification of income sources and exacerbate the consequences of crop failures? Is there an un-utilized potential, within the Sahel for instance, for improving food security through co-operation or trade? All of these questions may well deserve prudently affirmative answers. But in the case of India it is also important to recognize a less frequently mentioned source of security, namely the possibility of implementing large *transfers* of resources towards vulnerable States during bad years. The financial resources allocated by the central government to drought-affected States have indeed reached impressive levels in recent years, and they certainly represent a very important factor of risk pooling at the national level.[86]

[86] These financial transfers have, in fact, become a bone of contention among economists and politicians. See Rangasami (1986) for a discussion of this and related problems.

This section will conclude with a brief overview of food crises in India since independence, as a background to the more detailed case-studies analysed in the remainder of the chapter. Over this period, localized crop failures (mainly due to drought) have occurred in different parts of the country almost every year.[87] In non-irrigated areas they recur at more or less frequent intervals. When crop failures are only local in character, food is usually forthcoming from neighbouring areas at reasonable prices, and hence the 'Famine Codes strategy' of generating purchasing power in the affected areas and stimulating private trade tends to work well. The actual determination with which relief has been provided has varied from State to State and from time to time, and some obvious failures have occurred (such as in Assam in 1974–5).[88] However, on the whole and by international standards the operation of the famine relief system in India in the context of local crises can undeniably be considered as impressive.

Besides dealing with these numerous local crises, India has had to cope with the threat of major disaster on three occasions since 1947: in 1966–7, 1972–3, and 1979–80.[89] The first of these crises occurred in the wake of a very rare instance of virtually country-wide crop failures for two consecutive years. In both 1965–6 and 1966–7, the all-India level of foodgrain production was nearly 20 per cent below the average for the previous five years (see Table 1.2 above). In terms of the magnitude and geographical coverage of crop failures, a disaster of this magnitude had not occurred since the catastrophic famine of 1899–1900. The situation was all the more precarious considering the very low base level of production, the large numbers of people affected, the sharp regional variations in distress, and the virtual disappearance of 'surplus areas'. In Bihar, a State then counting more than 50 million people (more than twice the combined population of all six Sahel countries at that time), foodgrain production in 1966–7 was only about 54 per cent of the average 1961–5 level.[90]

Disaster was narrowly avoided. Public food stocks being negligible at the time, massive imports were undertaken. But the net availability of food per capita remained dangerously low in several States (including Bihar), and a large-scale famine would undoubtedly have occurred in the absence of extensive measures of direct entitlement protection. These took the familiar form of a combination of employment generation and unconditional relief.

[87] It is worth remembering that when a 'localized' drought extends over, say, a single State, it still typically affects tens of millions of people! Note also that in the 19th century the vulnerability of agricultural labourers was so acute that localized crop failures occurring in a single year often caused famine—see e.g. Government of India (1880: paras. 76–7).

[88] See e.g. Prabhakar (1975) and Baishya (1975). It is noteworthy that this particular failure occurred in circumstances where the traditional 'early warning' system was likely to fail (because the famine was not, in this instance, caused by drought).

[89] The years 1985–7 were also a period of acute vulnerability. As stated in the introduction, however, this chapter focuses primarily on the pre-1980 period.

[90] Calculated from *Bulletin on Food Statistics*, various issues. See also Table 1.2 above, or Table 1.5 below.

Officially, no starvation deaths occurred. One is inclined to be suspicious of official figures in this respect when local authorities are accountable for starvation deaths, and indeed there were non-official allegations of starvation deaths. However, the numbers involved were undoubtedly very small. On the other hand, short of starvation deaths every possible kind of damage occurred to an alarming degree: hunger and severe nutritional deterioration, massive loss of livestock, depletion of assets, and possibly even substantial excess mortality. Eye-witness accounts of the situation evoke sadly familiar pictures of destitution and hunger.

In spite of this, the 1966–7 experience has been hailed as a grand 'success story' by many commentators.[91] Considering the gravity of the crisis this verdict may not be entirely exaggerated. I shall nevertheless express considerable reservations about it in the next section, where the 1966–7 crisis is further examined with special reference to Bihar.

India's great 'success story' of famine prevention is more justly dated in 1972–3, when another very severe drought hit large parts of the country. The worst affected State was that of Maharashtra (again, more than 50 million people at the time), which suffered the exceptional calamity of three successive drought years from 1970–1 to 1972–3. The cornerstone of relief operations consisted of open-ended public works of the cash-for-work type. At the peak of distress, as many as 5 million people attended the relief works in Maharashtra alone.

Inter-State private trade in foodgrains was prohibited, and the government undertook to fill the food deficit in affected States with food sales through the public distribution system. However, public food deliveries fell far short of needs, and crucial inter-State food movements also took the form of illegal private transactions. These were stimulated by large price differentials between States, and tolerated by pragmatic (or corrupt) government officials.

Even after allowing for these food movements, it appears that food consumption in Maharashtra during the drought was substantially lower than in normal years, but that famine was averted because the food deficit was rather well *distributed* among different socio-economic groups. There is also some evidence to the effect that nutritional damage during the Maharashtra crisis was not very great. Another important achievement of famine relief operations was to prevent a major and lasting disruption of the rural economy.

In many respects, therefore, famine relief in 1972–3 represented a great improvement over the 1966–7 experience. The former success was all the more impressive considering that it was achieved with little help from abroad, and with little resort to food imports. Section 1.4 is devoted to a case-study of the 1972–3 relief operations.

The drought of 1979–80 was short-lived, but its intensity and widespread geographical coverage were exceptional. Compared with the average of the

[91] See e.g. Nossiter (1967), Verghese (1967), Harvey (1969), Scarfe and Scarfe (1969), Berg (1972), Aykroyd (1974), and Singh (1975).

*Source*: Brass (1986).

**Map 1.1** Bihar Districts, 1967

previous four years, foodgrain output fell by about 30 per cent in north India as a whole, and by much more in individual States. By then, however, India had accumulated large buffer stocks of foodgrains and these were used both to prevent excessive increases in food prices and to finance public works programmes. The crisis was anticipated with impressive foresight and a huge employment programme of the food-for-work type was undertaken. The country seems to have taken the drought in its stride with remarkable ease. This episode, however, will not receive further attention in this chapter.

### (b) Famine averted in 1966–1967: a reassessment

A proper 'case-study' of the 1966–7 drought is beyond the scope of the present enquiry. There is, nevertheless, some merit in attempting a brief re-examination of this important event, partly in order to question some of the interpretations it has lent itself to, and partly to bring out an instructive contrast with the Maharashtra drought of 1970–3 examined in section 1.4.[92]

Bihar is widely regarded as one of the most 'backward' regions of India. In the early 1980s this State had, among all the States of India, the lowest net domestic product per capita, the lowest proportion of non-agricultural employment to total employment, the second lowest literacy rate for both sexes, the third highest crude death rate, and the fourth highest incidence of rural poverty.[93] Bihar is also prone to droughts and floods, and in 1966 only a very small proportion of the cultivated area was irrigated. Yields were dangerously stagnating, and the State-level foodgrain deficit in an ordinary year around 1966 was officially estimated at 1.3 million tonnes.[94] By any account Bihar in the mid-1960s was a highly vulnerable spot.

In fact it can be said without exaggeration that India itself looked like a big 'vulnerable spot' at that time. In the early 1960s, output levels were pitifully low, yields were stagnating, the Green Revolution was hardly in sight, and output gains through expansion in cultivated areas were increasingly difficult

[92] An in-depth analysis of the 1966–7 drought would undoubtedly provide most valuable insights into many issues related to famine relief. Unfortunately, no comprehensive study of this event seems to be available. The most widely used source on the subject is Singh's (1975) very valuable book *The Indian Famine, 1967*. The author was District Collector in Palamau (one of the worst affected Districts) in 1967, and for this reason the book is well documented but not entirely detached; nor is it always a masterpiece of academic rigour. The Government of Bihar (1973) issued its own Report on the drought, and similar comments apply to this document. There exist a number of other interesting accounts and analyses of the 1966–7 events, including Indian Institute of Public Administration (1967), Sen (1967), Verghese (1967), Scarfe and Scarfe (1969), Swaminathan *et al.* (1969), Central Institute of Research and Training in Public Cooperation (1969), Ramlingaswami *et al.* (1971), Berg (1972, 1973), Gangrade and Dhadda (1973), and Brass (1986). None of them, however, provides a comprehensive and carefully documented analysis of the events. A further report by Professor Michael Windey, to whom a great deal of credit for orchestrating famine relief in Palamau should probably have gone, was handed to Indira Gandhi who later pronounced that it was 'too important to be disclosed' (Michael Windey, personal communication).

[93] These observations are based on Vaidyanathan (1987). All figures refer to 1982–3, except poverty incidence (1977–8) and crude death rate (average of 1979–81).

[94] Government of Bihar (1973: 75).

to achieve. India's future was not regarded with greater optimism in the early 1960s than Africa's future is today, and when widespread drought hit the country twice consecutively in 1965–6 and 1966–7, a terrible famine was widely predicted.

Massive imports were undertaken to augment available supplies of food. Most of the imported food consisted of food aid under the American PL-480 programme and there were, at times, complicated politics involved in securing the required supplies.[95] A policy of internal 'zoning' was in force, under which private trade in foodgrains across broad zones within the country was prohibited. The official purpose of this policy was to facilitate procurement from surplus zones—and presumably transfer this surplus to deficit zones.[96]

Complementary to these attempts at improving food supplies in deficit areas was the more traditional battery of relief measures, including relief works and unconditional relief. The efforts of the government were supplemented by those of voluntary agencies (local as well as international), which mainly organized free-feeding programmes.

The food situation in Bihar was very serious. Cereal production per capita was already on a dangerous downward trend, and collapsed dramatically in 1966–7 (see Tables 1.2, 1.3, and 1.5).[97] The final official estimates of cereal production in Bihar for the year 1966–7 (after a substantial *upward* revision of initial estimates) were put at 3.4 million tonnes.[98] If we use the average level of cereal consumption in Bihar over four rounds of the National Sample Survey in the 1970s as the 'normal consumption' standard, this represents barely *one-third* of cereal consumption requirements.

In order to arrive at an estimate of net availability of food in Bihar in 1966–7, the production figure needs to be adjusted in order to take into account (1) private stocks, (2) private trade, and (3) public distribution.[99]

No data exist, as far as I know, on private foodgrain stocks for that period; but there is every reason to believe that in this case the adjustment required to allow for private stocks would be minimal. As noted earlier, the practice of multi-year foodgrain storage by farmers was widespread in nineteenth-century India, but declined markedly towards the end of that century.[100] There are strong presumptions that nowadays the extent of on-farm storage across years

---

[95] On this see e.g. the contemporaneous issues of *Economic and Political Weekly*.

[96] See Bhagwati and Chakravaraty (1969), and Krishna and Chhibber (1983), for evaluations of zoning policies.

[97] In Bihar, the most damaging crop failure affected the *kharif* crop in the second part of 1966. The year 1966–7 covers both the 1966 *kharif* crop and the *rabi* crop (early 1967). Note that there is some discrepancy in India between the 'agricultural year' (July–June) and the 'financial year' (Apr.–Mar.).

[98] *Bulletin on Food Statistics*, 1968.

[99] Strictly speaking, one should also make an allowance for food aid not merged with central stocks, e.g. moved and distributed directly by international voluntary agencies such as CARE. But quantitatively this item was negligible (see Singh 1975: 201).

[100] See e.g. the discussions in Srivastava (1968: 331) and McAlpin (1974, 1983).

**Table 1.5** 'Outturn of crops' in Bihar, 1966–1967

| District | 'Outturn of crops' (in 000 tonnes) | | | 1966–7 as % of 'normal' |
|---|---|---|---|---|
| | 'Normal' | 1965–6 | 1966–7 | |
| Patna | 540 | 542 | 119 | 22.0 |
| Gaya | 698 | 606 | 138 | 19.7 |
| Shahabad | 918 | 888 | 435 | 47.4 |
| Saran | 434 | 422 | 325 | 74.9 |
| Champaran | 437 | 488 | 280 | 64.1 |
| Muzaffarpur | 374 | 432 | 220 | 58.8 |
| Darbhanga | 515 | 473 | 246 | 47.8 |
| Monghyr | 484 | 487 | 283 | 58.5 |
| Bhagalpur | 251 | 291 | 129 | 51.4 |
| Saharsa | 178 | 161 | 122 | 68.5 |
| Purnea | 471 | 397 | 249 | 52.3 |
| S. Pargana | 523 | 522 | 323 | 61.8 |
| Hazaribagh | 297 | 252 | 79 | 26.6 |
| Ranchi | 362 | 335 | 179 | 49.4 |
| Palamau | 176 | 148 | 48 | 27.2 |
| Dhanbad | 85 | 85 | 21 | 24.2 |
| Singhbum | 383 | 280 | 156 | 40.7 |
| STATE | 7,403 | 7,122 | 3,564 | 48.1 |

*Notes*: It appears that 'outturn of crops' refers specifically to the output of *foodgrains*, and that 'normal outturn' is simply the outturn in 1963–4 (see Government of Bihar 1973: 87).

The District-wise figures do not precisely add up to the State figure because of the addition in the latter of 'Other crops for which district break-up not available'.

*Source*: Government of Bihar (1973: 108–9).

is extremely small, at least in north India.[101] Nor are the reasons for this difficult to understand. The confidence with which grain prices in India can be predicted to fall after a harvest is now so great (partly due to public storage and distribution policies) that storing grain across a major harvest is a very unattractive way of holding wealth, particularly with high interest rates. The same argument makes it unlikely that merchants store much grain across years. In any case, whatever the level of private storage might have been in Bihar in a normal year, foodgrain stocks in 1966–7 must have been particularly small since the preceding year itself was one of poor harvest. Singh (1975) confirms this hypothesis for Palamau District.[102]

[101] In the village of Palanpur (Uttar Pradesh), where I conducted intensive field work in 1983–4, the practice of grain storage across years (more precisely, storage across the main rabi harvest in Apr.–May) has virtually disappeared. Already in 1958, the reported total grain stocks held before the arrival of the rabi crop amounted to less than 5% of the current rabi harvest. During recent field work in other parts of north India as well as Maharashtra I have also been repeatedly told that only a small percentage of large farmers, at best, store across years.

[102] Singh (1975: 36, 227).

Private trade is also unrecorded, but again it is very likely that the adjust-ment required on this count would be minimal. Zonal restrictions of the 'single-State' type were in force at the time and they seem to have been effective.[103] Here again, a priori reasoning is directly confirmed for Palamau District.[104]

The report of the Government of Bihar (1973) on the drought (*Bihar Famine Report*) arrived at very similar conclusions on the importance of private stocks and unauthorized grain trade, and considered a margin of 10 per cent of food availability figures as a 'liberal allowance' on these counts.[105]

There remains the question of public distribution. The *Bulletin on Food Statistics* publishes State-wise annual series on 'Net Imports', 'Issues' (through the public distribution system), 'Procurement', and 'Closing Stocks' of cereals and foodgrains. 'Net Imports' refer to imports by 'Rail and River', which should closely coincide with total net imports on government account. When this is the case the identity

$$(\text{Net imports}) - (\text{Addition to stocks})$$
$$= \qquad\qquad (1.1)$$
$$(\text{Issues}) - (\text{Procurement})$$

theoretically holds.[106] Unfortunately it is not possible to verify this identity on a year-to-year basis because net imports are reported for the 'financial year' (March to April), whereas other items refer to the 'calendar year' (January to December). However, this problem hardly arises if we attempt to verify the identity over a period of several years, and indeed over the period (say) 1964–5 to 1968–9 the figures tally well. Moreover, the *Bulletin on Food Statistics* figures are also consistent with the month-by-month figures on 'off-take' from the public distribution system appearing in Government of Bihar (1973: 162), and using these month-by-month figures we can check the above identity for the year 1966–7.[107] Again, the numbers tally fairly nicely. It seems, therefore,

[103] See e.g. ibid. 39, 98–9, 157, 227. On p. 156 of his book, Singh alludes casually to private trade 'not covered by zonal restrictions' of 1.3 million tonnes. But this is almost certainly a confusion with the same figure of 1.3 million tonnes for 'total net imports' mentioned in Government of Bihar (1973: 160). In fact, 1.3 million tonnes exceeds the likely magnitude of private trade even in a normal year (an idea of this can be obtained by comparing 'net availability' figures with 'consumption' figures from the National Sample Survey), and Singh himself emphasizes that private trade had slowed down considerably in 1966–7.

[104] See Singh (1975: 36, 46, 99).

[105] Government of Bihar (1973: 93–4).

[106] This is not strictly true because of minor details such as the fact that stocks are partly held by the central government and partly by the State government. But since stocks were anyway very small in this case we can safely ignore these qualifications.

[107] In doing this I have assumed that monthly issues over the period Apr.–Sept. 1966 (for which month-by-month data are not available in the Bihar Famine Report) were constant. This assumption is plausible and in any case rather unimportant. Monthly issues from July 1966 onwards for Palamau District are given in Singh (1975: 96), and they were fairly stagnant until Oct. 1966.

**Table 1.6** Cereal availability in Bihar, 1966–1967

| Year | Population[a] (000s) | Production[b] | Issues[c] | Procurement[c] | Closing stocks[c] | Net imports[d] | Net availability per capita (kg/year) (A) | (B) |
|---|---|---|---|---|---|---|---|---|
| 1964 (1963–4) | 49,580 | 6,282 | 765 | — | 74 | — | — | 129 |
| 1965 (1964–5) | 50,552 | 6,293 | 758 | 36 | 214 | 436 | 118 | 120 |
| 1966 (1965–6) | 51,537 | 5,902 | 806 | 67 | 169 | 662 | 113 | 115 |
| 1967 (1966–7) | 52,532 | 3,377 | 2,092 | 10 | 195 | 1,288 | 81 | 95 |
| 1968 (1967–8) | 53,536 | 7,343 | 658 | 44 | 186 | 1,891 | 155 | 132 |
| 1969 (1968–9) | 54,547 | 7,864 | 485 | 76 | 184 | 532 | 134 | 134 |

[a] Mid-year estimates.
[b] Agricultural year (July–June).
[c] Calendar year.
[d] Financial year (Apr.–Mar.).

*Note:* Unless otherwise specified, all figures are in thousand tonnes.

*Sources:* All figures except 'net availability' are taken from the *Bulletin on Food Statistics*, 1967, 1968, 1971, and 1972, Tables 1, 2, and 4. 'Net availability (A)' is calculated as 'net production' + 'net imports' + 'depletion of stocks'. 'Net availability (B)' is calculated as 'net production' + 'issues' – 'procurement'. 'Net production' is calculated by deducting 12.5% from 'production' for 'feed, seed, and wastage'. Series (A) and (B) are not quite comparable for a *single* year because they refer to different 12-month periods. But they should be compatible over a number of years. See text for details.

that one can alternatively use the 'Net Imports' figures or the 'Issues, Procurement and Closing Stocks' figures to arrive at net availability estimates. Table 1.6 presents two sets of estimates, based on these alternative series of figures. It is reassuring to note that these calculations are fairly consistent with those reported by Singh.[108]

The estimates of Table 1.6 ignore private trade and stocks altogether, but there is every reason to believe that both of these played a *greater* role in the years preceding 1966–7 than in 1966–7 itself: trade, because zonal restrictions were particularly stringent in 1966–7; and stocks, because in that year they must have been largely exhausted (see above). Thus, the figures in Table 1.6 probably *underestimate* the *change* in net availability in 1966–7 (as discussed earlier, they may also underestimate the *level* by up to 10 per cent).

Even then, an inescapable conclusion emerges: in spite of massive imports, a dramatic decline of net foodgrain availability accompanied the drought of 1966–7 in Bihar—a decline of the order of 30 per cent compared to ordinary levels.

There is, moreover, strong independent evidence of a sharp decline in aggregate consumption of foodgrains. By collating various bits and pieces of information contained in Singh (1975), we can perform similar calculations to the previous ones for Palamau District. This district, slightly more populated than Mauritania (1.19 million inhabitants according to the 1961 Census), was one of the worst-affected ones in 1966–7. But it was also one where relief measures were notoriously far-reaching,[109] and on balance there is no reason to believe that net food availability was better or worse in Palamau than elsewhere. Table 1.7 summarizes the possible calculations; the results for Palamau are quite similar to those for Bihar as a whole in the same year.

Further evidence can be gathered from direct consumption studies. In the 1960s the National Sample Survey was unfortunately not collecting data on quantities of foodgrains consumed, and inferring quantities from expenditure data is a hopeless exercise when prices change rapidly, as they did in 1966–7. However, three useful nutrition surveys were carried out during the drought by (1) the Public Health Institute, Patna (hereafter PHI); (2) the Nutrition Research Laboratories, Hyderabad (hereafter NRL); and (3) the All-India Institute of Medical Sciences, New Delhi (hereafter AIIMS). The quality of these surveys is difficult to ascertain, and the evidence they individually provide is very patchy; however, the tone of their common findings is clear enough.

Regarding the first of these surveys, Singh (1975) mentions that it found foodgrain intake to be 33 per cent lower in July–August 1966 compared to a similar baseline survey carried out in March 1964 (17.9 ounces per consumer

---

[108] Singh (1975: 146, 156).

[109] For instance, over the period Jan.–Sept. 1967, the 'daily number of persons receiving cooked food' in Palamau was about one-third of the total for the whole State—while its population was only around 2.5% of the State population (Government of Bihar 1973: 276–8).

**Table 1.7** Net availability of foodgrains, Palamau District, 1966–1967

| Period | Gross production (tonnes) | | Public distribution (tonnes) | Private imports (tonnes) | Net availability (kgs/cap./year) | |
|---|---|---|---|---|---|---|
| | (A) | (B) | | | (A) | (B) |
| July 1966–Aug. 1967 | 29,400 | 48,000 | 73,972 | 26,390 | 97 | 107 |
| Aug. 1966–Sept. 1967 | 29,400 | 48,000 | 80,665 | 26,126 | 101 | 112 |
| Sept. 1966–Oct. 1967 | 29,400 | 48,000 | 85,812 | 22,235 | 102 | 113 |
| Oct. 1966–Nov. 1967 | 29,400 | 48,000 | 87,836 | 17,976 | 101 | 111 |

*Sources*: For 'gross production (B)', see Table 1.5 above. All other figures except 'net availability' are calculated from Singh (1975: 8, 36, 96–9, 104) (the agricultural year 1966–7 being considered, following the usual practice, as the sum of *kharif* 1966 and *rabi* 1966–7). 'Net availability' is calculated as 'net production' + 'public distribution' + 'private imports', where 'net production' is obtained from 'gross production' by deducting 12.5% for 'feed, seed, and wastage'.

unit per day in 1966 as opposed to 26.6 ounces in 1964).[110] A resurvey in March 1967 found that foodgrain consumption had crashed to 8.1 ounces per consumer unit per day before rising again to 17 ounces per consumption unit per day as 'the nutrition and feeding programmes intensified and distribution of foodgrains extended'.[111]

The relevant results of the NRL survey conducted in May 1967 in four drought-affected districts are summarized in Tables 1.8–1.10. In this study, cereal intake in 'severely affected areas' was found to be 34 per cent below that in 'least affected areas' (44 per cent below for 'labourers' and 22 per cent below for 'cultivators'). Moreover, the NRL report states that 'there had been a substantial reduction in the dietary intake in the villages affected by drought, when compared to the diets of four selected districts surveyed prior to the onset of drought'.[112]

Both studies also reveal the sharp drop in *calorie* consumption which accompanied the drought (see Table 1.9, and Singh 1975: 241).

The third study, by the All-India Institute of Medical Sciences, presents no data on consumption but mentions that 'diet surveys conducted by the State Department of Nutrition at intervals of time in various parts of South Bihar between 1966 and 1967 showed that in several regions the calorie intake dropped from 2,200 per capita per day to nearly 1,200 calories'.[113]

Yet another confirmation of the large decline in food intake comes from socio-economic surveys. In a survey carried out by the Central Institute of Research and Training in Public Cooperation (hereafter CIRTPC) in the districts of Palamau and Gaya in 1967 and covering 555 households, 37 per cent of the respondent households reported 'missing meals' as a 'step to overcome their hardships'; and 95 per cent mentioned that food was one of the sources of 'hardship'.[114] A hint may also be taken from a report on a survey carried out in Dolchi (Uttar Pradesh, adjacent to Bihar and also severely affected by drought) in 1967, which states: 'During the preceding year 17 out of 24 households were taking three meals a day, 6 two meals a day and one household only one meal a day. But during 1966–67 the number of households taking 3 meals a day came down to 15 from 17 last year. On enquiry it was found that as many as 9 out of 24 households (37.5%) were either half-fed or on the brink of total starvation.'[115]

Finally, numerous eye-witness accounts of people eating wild leaves and roots, picking pieces of grain from the dust around railway sidings, undergoing appalling 'skeletonization', and even starving to death corroborate the finding of severe food deprivation.

[110] Singh (1975: 241). The area where the survey was conducted is not mentioned.
[111] Ibid. 246.   [112] Swaminathan *et al.* (1969: 214).
[113] Ramlingaswami *et al.* (1971: 95).   [114] CIRTPC (1969: 227, 231).
[115] Agricultural Economics Research Centre, Allahabad (1972: 18).

**Table 1.8** Consumption of cereals and calories in drought-affected areas of Bihar, May 1967

| | Cereal intake (gm/day) | | | Calorie intake (cal./day) | | | No. of households |
|---|---|---|---|---|---|---|---|
| | Cultivators | Labourers | All classes | Cultivators | Labourers | All classes | |
| SAFA | 445 | 306 | 371 | 1,840 | 1,210 | 1,450 | 50 |
| MAFA | 453 | 312 | 388 | 1,740 | 1,280 | 1,510 | 42 |
| LAFA | 573 | 545 | 566 | 2,660 | 2,280 | 2,470 | 40 |

SAFA = 'Severely affected area'.
MAFA = 'Moderately affected area'.
LAFA = 'Least affected area'.

*Notes*: This table shows the results of a survey conducted by the Nutrition Research Laboratories (Indian Council of Medical Research, Hyderabad) in 7 villages of Gaya, Hazaribagh, Palamau, and Patna Districts in May 1967.

The data on cereal consumption do not take into account food intake in relief kitchens. But the authors describe the consumption at free kitchens as follows: 'It was observed that about 25–30% of the vulnerable segments of the population (preschool children, expectant and nursing mothers) surveyed, were deriving the benefits of the supplements provided through free kitchens functioning in the villages. This amounted to 300–500 calories per person per day.' Clearly, if calorie intake from relief kitchens was so low even among these narrowly-defined 'vulnerable segments' of the population, the figures of average cereal intake in Table 1.8 can be taken as reasonably accurate.

*Source*: Swaminathan *et al.* (1969: Tables III, IV, and V).

**Table 1.9** Percentage distribution of calorie intake in
drought-affected areas of Bihar, May 1967

| Level of per capita calorie intake per day | SAFA[a] | MAFA[a] | LAFA |
|---|---|---|---|
| <500 | 8.2 | — | — |
| 500–899 | 6.1 | 5.7 | — |
| 900–1,299 | 18.4 | 14.3 | — |
| 1,300–1,799 | 26.5 | 31.4 | 15.0 |
| 1,800–2,299 | 30.6 | 40.0 | 25.0 |
| >2,300 | 10.2 | 8.6 | 60.0 |
| TOTAL | 100.0 | 100.0 | 100.0 |

[a] Including contribution of calories from feeding centres.
*Note*: See Notes and Source to Table 1.8.

Not surprisingly, food deprivation led to acute and widespread malnutrition.
The findings of the NRL and AIIMS studies in this respect are reported in
Swaminathan *et al.* (1969) and Ramlingaswami *et al.* (1971), respectively. The
first study found a close relationship between malnutrition (assessed by
anthropometric measures) and the severity of crop failures; a close positive
relationship between nutritional status and the extent of relief measures; and a
greater incidence of malnutrition among children than adults as well as among
labourers than non-labourers.[116] The AIIMS study confirmed all these

**Table 1.10** Income and assets in drought-affected areas of Bihar, 1967

| Village | Per capita income (Rs./year) | | | % change in possession of livestock (1965–6 to 1966–7) | No. of households surveyed |
|---|---|---|---|---|---|
| | Agricultural sources | Other sources | Total | | |
| SAFA | | | | | |
| Kundah | 57 | 53 | 110 | −49 | 21 |
| Nawagarh | 62 | 41 | 103 | −36 | 22 |
| Adarshagram | 41 | 32 | 74 | −38 | 7 |
| MAFA | | | | | |
| Massaurah | 35 | 77 | 112 | −27 | 25 |
| Tarwadi | 56 | 46 | 101 | −28 | 17 |
| LAFA | | | | | |
| Ranipur | 162 | 161 | 323 | +33 | 17 |
| Kothwan | 177 | 180 | 357 | +30 | 23 |

*Note*: See Notes and Source to Table 1.8.

[116] Swaminathan *et al.* (1969: 214–15).

findings; added 'the elderly' to the list of vulnerable groups; and noted the widespread prevalence of 'famine oedema'.[117] Significantly, out of 49 patients suffering from oedema and selected for intensive clinical study only four owned any land; five died in the hospital and the autopsies revealed that 'massive oedema was the characteristic feature and the body cavities were filled with fluid'.[118] The only consolation against this nutritional disaster was the absence of epidemics.

The occurrence of a sharp decline in food intake during the drought, accompanied by widespread nutritional damage, is thus clear enough. It is much more difficult to ascertain the consequences of deprivation in terms of excess mortality. The reasons are that (1) mortality estimates from various sources (such as the National Sample Survey, the ordinary system of Registration, and the new Sample Registration Scheme initiated in 1965) are not even remotely comparable, and (2) the use of a time-series for a given source is also fraught with difficulties, because the methods used to estimate vital statistics changed rapidly in the late 1960s. In principle, these problems could be circumvented by looking at month-wise data from a particular source over a short period covering the drought; but this method would itself have to deal with the sharp element of seasonality present in such statistics.

A rigorous analysis of the demographic impact of the drought is beyond the scope of this chapter. Some of the available evidence is summarized in Appendix 1.1, and with due reservations the following conclusions can tentatively be drawn:

1. the mortality figures reported in Singh (1975) for Bihar as a whole are internally inconsistent as well as in conflict with the published results from the Sample Registration Scheme, from which they are supposed to originate (Table 1.26);
2. the Sample Registration Scheme provides no evidence of a noticeable increase in mortality in Bihar as a whole during the crisis (Table 1.26);
3. National Sample Survey data suggest (quite implausibly) that while the death rate in Bihar was lower than in India as a whole during the years preceding the crisis, it was higher by about 20 per cent in the year 1966–7 (Table 1.27);
4. mortality estimates based on 'registered' deaths show a noticeable increase in Bihar as a whole during the crisis, the death rate being 34 per cent higher in 1967 than in 1968 (Table 1.28);
5. if the data reported in Singh (1975) for the severely affected Districts of Palamau, Hazaribagh, and Gaya are accepted (in spite of the discrepancies pertaining to Bihar as a whole), mortality appears to have shot up in these Districts during the crisis (Table 1.29); this is confirmed by published data on registered deaths, which show even larger increases in

---

[117] Ramlingaswami *et al.* (1971: 98–9).          [118] Ibid. 104.

mortality (of the order of 100 per cent for the infant mortality rate—see Table 1.28).

Of all these indications, those provided by published data on 'registered deaths' are probably the least unreliable. While registered deaths do not provide accurate estimates of *levels* of mortality, they are generally thought to be quite useful for the assessment of *change*. The fact that, according to this source, the death rate in Bihar in 1967 was 34 per cent above its 1968 value (with much higher increases for the more severely drought-affected Districts) is certainly alarming. Even if we reject these findings as based on unreliable data, one thing is clear: there is precious little evidence to support the self-congratulatory statements that have commonly been made about the Bihar famine, e.g. 'no exceptional mortality was recorded' or 'no one died of starvation'.[119]

While the severity of a famine is usefully measured by the extent of overall excess mortality, it may be worth commenting briefly on the question of 'starvation deaths' specifically. To the extent that the popular notion of 'starvation deaths' can be made precise, it seems to refer to deaths directly attributable to the inability to acquire any food, rather than to the indirect consequences of enfeeblement. The question of how many 'starvation deaths' occurred in 1966–7 was, as always, a highly sensitive one. Ever since the Famine Codes made it the clear duty of the authorities to protect the people against starvation, food crises have prompted public allegations of 'starvation deaths', and official refutations (or sometimes outright 'camouflage').[120] In fact, controversies around the existence and extent of starvation deaths have often provided a focus for public pressure, and played an important instrumental role in prompting the government to act. The 1966–7 drought was no exception.

Bihar alone accounted for almost half of the all-India total of 2,353 officially acknowledged 'alleged starvation deaths'.[121] At one point the government admitted 217 actual starvation deaths (all-India); but, as Singh puts it, 'later it was clarified that these were cases of suicide by "voluntary starvation" and had nothing to do with . . . the non-availability of food . . . the allegations about deaths from starvation were thus not substantiated'.[122] These statements need no comment, and eye-witness accounts leave no doubts as to the grim reality of numerous 'starvation deaths'.[123] I have already referred to the five patients

[119] Aykroyd (1974: 140). Authors such as Singh (1975) and Verghese (1967) went even further and asserted that health conditions *improved* during the crisis. What is, however, plausible is that mortality and morbidity did come down sharply after large-scale relief operations were undertaken. As we shall see, one of the main defects of remedial action in this event was its tardiness.

[120] The report of the Puri Famine Enquiry Committee of 1919, for instance, contains a convincing account of how starvation deaths were disguised by directly instructing the *chowkidars*—here village enumerators—to record starvation deaths as deaths due to sickness.

[121] Singh (1975: 182–3).     [122] Ibid. 182–3.

[123] Such accounts can be found, *inter alia*, in the journalistic literature on the drought of 1966–7 in Bihar.

who died from famine oedema while under clinical observation, and there is no reason to believe that they were isolated cases.

Let me conclude this overview of the effects of the Bihar drought by considering briefly the *distribution* of hardship. It may seem obvious that during a crisis of this magnitude the poor are the hardest hit. But the Maharashtra drought of 1970–3 will provide an interesting example of a remarkably egalitarian famine (or rather, 'non-famine'), and one may ask whether the Bihar crisis of 1966–7 was of the same type. Indeed it *has* been boldly asserted that the success of relief operations converted this potential tragedy into 'a bonus year . . . a year of great blessing' for the destitute masses.[124]

The evidence, however, strongly suggests a very different picture. First, we have already noted the high incidence of deprivation among landless labourers reported in the NRL and AIIMS studies (see also Tables 1.8–1.10). Informal accounts of the drought confirm this observation, which conforms to the traditional pattern of Indian famines (see section 1.2). Second, there appears to have been a pronounced maldistribution of hardship across areas more or less severely affected by crop failures (see Tables 1.8–1.10, and also Appendix 1.1 on mortality estimates). Finally, informal reports strongly suggest that the peak of hardship occurred towards the end of 1966 (before the beginning of large-scale relief operations) and subsided considerably in the following months. This is plausible in itself considering the inverse correlation between relief and distress mentioned earlier. It is also confirmed by some interesting survey results reported by Singh (see Table 1.11). While the observation is a testimony to the effectiveness of relief operations, it also indicates the maldistribution of hardship across time caused by their notorious tardiness. Thus, the occupational, geographical, and temporal distribution of hardship during the drought of 1966–7 in Bihar appears to have been characterized by great unevenness.

A crucial question remains: were all these disastrous outcomes the inevitable consequence of an extremely precarious situation, or did they partly betray a failure of the relief system?

The received assessment, as was mentioned earlier, points in the former direction, and crisis management during the 1966–7 drought has indeed been hailed by many commentators as a grand success. However, there are good reasons to be suspicious of this received assessment, which has been based partly on the self-congratulatory writings of government administrators and partly on the writings of foreign observers who were inclined to contrast Bihar in 1967 with Bengal in 1943. The effectiveness of relief operations in 1966–7 needs to be re-examined.

A comprehensive reassessment will not be attempted here. I shall confine myself to pointing out three aspects of famine relief in 1966–7 which would

---

[124] Verghese (1967), quoted in Aykroyd (1974: 140).

**Table 1.11** Subjective assessment of the severity
of hardship in different months, Bihar 1966–1967

| Months considered hard | Responses |
| --- | --- |
| June 1966 | — |
| July 1966 | 3 |
| August 1966 | 39 |
| September 1966 | 171 |
| October 1966 | 252 |
| November 1966 | 361 |
| December 1966 | 363 |
| January 1967 | 368 |
| February 1967 | 82 |
| March 1967 | 14 |
| April 1967 | 12 |
| May 1967 | 90 |
| June 1967 | 151 |
| July 1967 | 166 |
| Total response | 2,072 |

*Source*: Singh (1975: 228).

call for serious scrutiny as part of the needed reassessment: the delayed 'declaration' of famine; the limited provision of employment; and the policy of zoning.

The Famine Commissions had all recognized the critical importance of diligence in starting relief operations. The Famine Commission of 1880 itself insisted that 'the great thing is to begin on time'.[125] Experience repeatedly showed that early relief measures promised a great economy of efforts and much better chances of success. This in fact was one of the very reasons for drawing up detailed contingency plans in the form of Famine Codes. The importance of a speedy response also explained the prominence given in the Famine Codes to an elaborate system of 'early warning', according to which the authorities had the obligation to 'declare' famine, and hence set in motion the provisions of the Famine Codes, once a number of well-defined signs of imminent distress manifested themselves (e.g. crop failures, rise in prices, unusual migration or sales of assets, etc.).

Famine was 'declared' in Bihar on 20 April 1967.[126] This was very late indeed. It is well known that once the monsoon breaks (normally in late June for Bihar), relief operations become extremely difficult to carry out, and declaring famine only two months ahead of the rains hardly seems worth the trouble. Relief operations did take place before the official declaration of

[125] Government of India (1880: Appendix I, pp. 119–20).
[126] Government of Bihar (1973: 77).

famine, but relief policy in that period was rather *ad hoc*, and in fact even later measures were explicitly confined to a mere 'intensification' of that policy.[127]

The reasons for delaying the declaration of famine were mainly of a political nature, and closely connected in particular with the general election of February 1967 as well as with centre–State intrigues. The reader is referred to Brass (1986) for further discussion of this issue.[128] The belated and politicized nature of relief efforts during the Bihar crisis in 1967 is undoubtedly an area of failure.

A second query, closely related to the first, concerns the failure to guarantee employment. According to the Bihar Famine Code, public works are supposed to form the backbone of relief operations, and moreover employment is to be provided through small-scale 'village works' near the homes of the affected people.[129] The actual pattern of relief operations in 1967 is summarized in Table 1.12. Clearly the contribution of public works to the overall relief strategy was rather small. The main plank of relief, in fact, was a huge free-feeding programme organized by CARE and UNICEF with the co-operation of the government. The beneficiaries of this scheme, mainly children and expectant or nursing mothers, received one meal a day at the local school. Also of great importance were free kitchens, organized mainly by the Bihar Relief Committee under the leadership of Jayaprakash Narayan. This pattern is quite interesting because it provides a rather impressive example of success-ful co-operation between government and voluntary agencies (both local and international). However, one suspects some abdication of responsibility on the part of the government.

In particular, it is very hard to believe that the 'employment guarantee' of the Famine Code was actually honoured, unless the free-feeding programmes induced a massive withdrawal of labour supply from public works.[130] Indeed, the figures of labour attendance on relief works are rather poor for a crisis of this intensity. Over the period January to June 1967 (the period of peak labour attendance), the average number of labourers employed on relief works was nearly 450,000 (Table 1.12). During the same months of 1973 in drought-affected Maharashtra, average attendance as a proportion of the population was nearly eight times as high! The difference may partly be due to the fact that the Maharashtra drought was a prolonged one, adding many farmers to the ranks of the drought victims along with agricultural labourers (see section 1.4). It is also hard to disprove the existence of a large 'withdrawal effect' due to free-feeding in the case of Bihar. However, *ex post* 'distress' in Bihar in 1967

---

[127] Singh (1975: 148); Government of Bihar (1973: 77).

[128] See also Singh (1975: 144–9), and CIRTPC (1969: 20).

[129] CIRTPC (1969: 42).

[130] There is some evidence that, to a certain extent at least, a withdrawal effect did operate. The CIRTPC study, for instance, noted that 'in many instances, it was true that people did not work on labour-schemes and hung around the free-kitchens' (CIRTPC 1969: 178).

**Table 1.12** Relief operations in Bihar, 1967

| Month | Average no. of people (000s) benefiting from | | | | |
|---|---|---|---|---|---|
| | Cooked food | Mid-day meal (CARE/UNICEF) | Red Cross scheme (free meals) | Relief works | 'Red cards' (gratuitous relief) |
| | (A) | (B) | (C) | (D) | (E) |
| Jan. 1967 | 33 | 373 | n/a | 228 | n/a |
| Feb. 1967 | 163 | 1,118 | n/a | 318 | n/a |
| Mar. 1967 | 436 | 3,269 | 244 | 374 | n/a |
| Apr. 1967 | 487 | 3,916 | 509 | 432 | n/a |
| May 1967 | 636 | 4,282 | 500 | 607 | n/a |
| June 1967 | 795 | 4,054 | 500 | 692 | n/a |
| July 1967 | 700 | 4,549 | n/a | 324 | 783 |
| Aug. 1967 | 537 | 4,767 | n/a | 68 | n/a |
| Sept. 1967 | 527 | 4,553 | n/a | 22 | n/a |
| Jan–June average | 425 | 2,835 | n/a | 442 | n/a |

*Notes*: In addition to relief works, 'plan schemes' employed 223,400 persons on average over the period Jan.–June 1967 (Government of Bihar 1973: 100).

Relief works started in Oct. 1966, and gratuitous relief started in Dec. 1966 (CIRTPC 1969).

*Sources*: (A) and (D) are from Government of Bihar (1973: Annexures 3.7 and 10.15). Other figures are from CIRTPC (1969).

was, as we shall see, much more severe by any criterion (food deprivation, nutritional damage, excess mortality, distress sales of assets, etc.) than in Maharashtra in 1973. Hence, unless Biharis have a much higher 'reservation wage' than Maharashtrians at a comparable level of income (an unlikely proposition), there must have been a large pool of unsatisfied labour supply in Bihar in 1967.[131] To take another point of comparison, peak labour attendance in Maharashtra in *1966* was itself of the order of 500,000, even though the drought affecting Maharashtra at that time was less severe, and the population less vulnerable, than was the case in Bihar in 1967.[132] The Bihar government appears to have not only delayed the application of the Famine Code, but also violated one of its most crucial provisions throughout the crisis.

Third, one may question how the national 'zoning' policy, prohibiting private trade in food across different States, affected food entitlements in different States of India. This is not the place to go into the controversy about

---

[131] Note that the observed contrast cannot be explained with reference to wage levels on public works: wage levels in Maharashtra in 1973 were extremely low (see section 1.4), and they could hardly have been lower in Bihar in 1967.

[132] The figure is from Singh (1975: 177). Note that the total population of Maharashtra is *smaller* than that of Bihar.

the general merits or demerits of 'zoning' in India.[133] But a few remarks on the specific relationship between zoning and famine prevention are in order, if only because bureaucratic restrictions on private trade are often seen as essential in famine situations.

If private trade in grain is competitive, it is easy to show that a zoning system is essentially equivalent to a set of taxes on food movements.[134] As we have already seen in section 1.2, a policy of this kind may well have some merit when vulnerable areas are *exporting* food; but this was definitely not the case in 1966–7 (see below). Otherwise, a case for zoning can still conceivably exist if the government desperately needs extra resources for financing relief measures and no socially preferable means exist of raising funds—but this is a rather remote possibility.

This argument, admittedly, runs in terms of a competitive food market. There is little evidence that food markets in India easily lend themselves to collusion and manipulation. But in any case, where collusive practices do exist it is rather hard to see how a policy of zoning helps to counter their deleterious effects. If anything, zoning is likely to facilitate such practices.

None of this implies, of course, that food trade, storage, and distribution offer no scope for a positive involvement of the government. On the contrary, public distribution schemes can definitely have a major impact on food entitlements, and the influence of public storage and food pricing policies on private expectations and hoarding decisions can be a decisive one in famine situations. But the point is that zoning does not, as a rule, strengthen the scope for this type of intervention.

To summarize, it is hard to see how a zoning policy could help to reduce the threat of famine under the conditions prevailing in India, and if anything one would expect its effects to operate in the opposite direction. Careful empirical studies strongly confirm that zoning policies, when in force, have considerably increased the dispersion of food prices across Indian States (and thus increased hardship for deficit households in deficit States). In fact, the dispersion of wheat prices reached an all-time high for the post-independence period precisely during the 1965–7 droughts.[135] In Bihar in 1967, the price of coarse rice (the staple cereal) increased by leaps and bounds and in August 1967 was more than four times as high as in Haryana (Table 1.13)! Price differentials of this magnitude between States are quite abnormal, and there undoubtedly existed a big untapped potential for advantageous food reallocation within the country in 1966–7. Without going as far as to claim that India could have taken

[133] For an introduction to the debate, see Bhagwati and Chakravarty (1969) and Krishna and Chhibber (1983).

[134] If procurement and/or public distribution take place at preferential prices rather than at open-market prices, the system will also involve the implicit lump-sum taxes and transfers associated with 'dual pricing' policies. These taxes and transfers may or may not be socially desirable, but in any case their operation is independent from that of zoning.

[135] See the work of Krishna and Chhibber (1983) on the effects of zoning in India.

**Table 1.13** Cereal prices in North India, August 1967 (Rs/quintal)

|       | Bihar | Uttar Pradesh | Haryana | Punjab |
|-------|-------|---------------|---------|--------|
| Rice  | 288   | 150           | 63–7    | 83–9   |
| Wheat | 163   | 117–20        | 100–2   | 99–100 |
| Maize | 125   | 95–6          | —       | 55–63  |

*Source*: Government of Bihar (1973: 98).

the drought in its stride in the absence of zoning, one does wonder how much this policy exacerbated the very problem it sought to relieve.

### 1.4. A case-study: the Maharashtra drought of 1970–1973

The drought of 1970–3 in Maharashtra offers ideal material for a case-study of successful famine relief operations: the crisis was of extreme severity, famine was uncontroversially averted, and the events are well documented. In this section we shall see how the sudden emergence of an alarming gap between food production and food requirements failed to develop into a famine. This gap was, in the first instance, considerably narrowed by the combined operation of the public distribution system and private trade movements—the latter stimulated by the generation of purchasing power in affected areas through public works programmes. Equally importantly, the remaining short-fall was very evenly shared between different socio-economic groups, as employment programmes protected the purchasing power of the more vulnerable groups. The role of markets, politics, public works, food distribution, informal security systems, and other contributing influences will be investigated.[136]

### (a) Background and impact of the drought

In terms of several conventional indicators of 'development' (including literacy, urbanization, life expectancy, and average incomes), Maharashtra appears as one of the more 'developed' States of India. However, aggregate statistics hide enormous regional disparities, and this vast State strikes the

---

[136] The following case-study draws *inter alia* on the scattered but already voluminous literature (in English) on the Maharashtra drought. Important sources include Subramaniam (1975), who gives an extremely detailed and useful (though far from detached) account of the events from the point of view of a high-level government servant; Ladejinsky (1973), a vivid first-hand report; Oughton (1982), whose analysis, however, differs from mine in some important respects; the enquiry carried out by the Government of Maharashtra (1973b) itself; the studies of administrative, nutritional, and other specific issues in Jodha (1975), Krishnamachari *et al.* (1974), Mathur and Bhattacharya (1975), Mundle (1974a, 1974b), and Somwanski (1979); the detailed micro-studies of Borkar and Nadkarni (1975), Brahme (1983), and particularly Kulkarni (1974); the field reports of voluntary agencies such as Oxfam (1972, 1973); various contributions to the *Economic and Political Weekly* from 1972 to 1974; and a large number of newspaper reports.

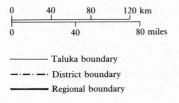

Taluka boundary
District boundary
Regional boundary

*Note*: The area within the thick line indicates the 10 Districts most affected by drought in 1972–3 (see text).

*Source*: Brahme (1983).

**Map 1.2** Political map of Maharashtra

traveller by its great diversity. The urban–rural contrast is particularly sharp, and the relative prosperity of the State as a whole hides a great deal of rural poverty. Thus, while Maharashtra had the third highest State Domestic Product per capita among all Indian States in 1977–8, it also had the third highest proportion of rural population below the poverty line, next only to Orissa and Madhya Pradesh.[137] Within the rural sector, there are enormous regional differences in productivity, particularly between the 'high' or 'assured' rainfall areas of coastal and eastern Maharashtra, and the semi-arid drought-prone areas of inland western Maharashtra.[138] Finally, even within fairly homogeneous rural regions, one cannot fail to be struck nowadays by the sharp contrast between irrigated and non-irrigated agriculture—not only in terms of yields but far more importantly in terms of incomes and employment. On the lush and busy patches of irrigated land (which constituted only 8.5 per cent of total gross cropped area in 1970–1),[139] 'progressive' farmers devote a large proportion of sown area to highly rewarding cash crops such as sugarcane, bananas, papayas, and even grapes, while in the non-irrigated expanses the meagre harvest of coarse grains remains a gamble on the monsoon and the land offers a spectacle of desolation and dust during the slack season.

At the time of the onset of the terrible drought of 1970–3, Maharashtra was facing problems of agricultural decline similar to those described earlier for Bihar: stagnant area under cultivation; stagnant yields; and rapidly increasing population pressure (Table 1.14). As a result, per capita food production was on a sustained downward trend.[140] This downward trend turned into a disastrous crash in the early 1970s, when the exceptional calamity of three successive drought years shattered the rural economy of Maharashtra. While the aggregate picture is bad enough, the District-wise figures of food production bring out even more clearly how in several Districts agricultural production and incomes, already so low to start with, were sharply depressed for several years (see Table 1.15). By any criterion, the severity of agricultural decline in Maharashtra before the early 1970s, and the extent of crop failures during the drought, dwarf the food crises which led to dramatic famines in the Sahel over the same period (see Tables 1.2–1.3 and Figs. 1.1 and 1.2 above). The sharply contrasting outcomes of these respective economic disasters in terms of human deprivation and mortality enhance the importance of understanding how famine was averted in the former case.

The sufferings occasioned by the Maharashtra drought were, indeed, very much smaller than one might have expected given the almost complete collapse

---

[137] Vaidyanathan (1987: Table 1).

[138] The agroclimatology of Maharashtra, and its relation to drought and famine, is discussed in detail in Vincent (1981). See also Brahme (1983).

[139] Statistical Abstract of Maharashtra State for the year 1970–1, quoted in Brahme (1983: 14).

[140] In fact, this trend probably started several decades earlier—see the discussion of trends in food production in India during the first half of this century, in section 1.3.

**Table 1.14** Cultivated area, cereal yields, and cereal production in Maharashtra, 1956–1974

| Year | Population (000) | Gross cropped area (000 ha) | Cereal yields (kg/ha) | Cereal production per capita kg/year) | Three-year averages | |
|------|------|------|------|------|------|------|
| | | | | | Yields (kg/ha) | Production per capita (kg/year) |
| | (A) | (B) | (C) | (D) | (E) | (F) |
| 1956–7 | 36,337 | 18,770 | 522 | 146 | | |
| 1957–8 | 37,115 | 18,596 | 522 | 142 | 534 | 146 |
| 1958–9 | 37,909 | 18,764 | 559 | 151 | 530 | 143 |
| 1959–60 | 38,720 | 18,978 | 510 | 136 | 569 | 152 |
| 1960–1 | 39,880 | 18,823 | 637 | 169 | 560 | 147 |
| 1961–2 | 40,487 | 19,094 | 532 | 137 | 576 | 149 |
| 1962–3 | 41,806 | 18,963 | 560 | 141 | 547 | 138 |
| 1963–4 | 42,798 | 19,174 | 548 | 135 | 556 | 137 |
| 1964–5 | 43,825 | 19,216 | 559 | 134 | 497 | 120 |
| 1965–6 | 44,886 | 18,972 | 384 | 90 | 475 | 112 |
| 1966–7 | 45,982 | 19,191 | 482 | 113 | 471 | 109 |
| 1967–8 | 47,115 | 19,253 | 548 | 124 | 530 | 120 |
| 1968–9 | 48,284 | 19,367 | 561 | 122 | 553 | 120 |
| 1969–70 | 49,490 | 19,435 | 550 | 114 | 523 | 110 |
| 1970–1 | 50,709 | 19,398 | 458 | 93 | 478 | 97 |
| 1971–2 | 51,927 | — | 427 | 83 | 395 | 75 |
| 1972–3 | 53,159 | — | 301 | 49 | — | 82 |
| 1973–4 | 54,404 | — | — | 113 | — | — |

*Sources*: (A) *Bulletin on Food Statistics*, 1975 and 1982–4, for 1961 onwards (population figures correspond to the middle of the second of the two calendar years). Pre-1961 population figures were obtained by assuming a constant population growth rate (of 2.14%) between the 1951 and 1961 Censuses.

(B) Government of Maharashtra (1974: 72).

(C) Calculated from ibid. 72 and 74.

(D) See Table 1.2.

(E), (F) Calculated from (C) and (D). The three-year average for each year is calculated as an unweighted average for the preceding year, the current year, and the following year.

of agricultural incomes, employment, and wages in many areas for a prolonged period. Mortality rose only marginally, if at all, and disparities in mortality rates do not seem to have widened either between males and females or between infants and adults (Table 1.16).[141] There were no confirmed instances of 'starvation deaths'. Though no longitudinal studies of nutrition are available for that period, a survey conducted by the National Institute of Nutrition (Hyderabad) in February 1973 in the 'worst affected taluka' of each of four

[141] I am extremely grateful to Nigel Crook (SOAS) and Tim Dyson (LSE) for helping me to probe the evidence on this question. According to work in progress by Arup Maharatna (LSE), mortality during the last year of the drought *fell* in the most severely drought-affected Districts, and rose a little in the *other* Districts (where relief operations were less extensive).

Districts among the worst-affected observed that 'the incidence of the various deficiency signs is somewhat similar to that frequently seen among the poorest sections of rural population in many other parts of the country'.[142] Eye-witness accounts mention very little of the appalling emaciation that struck countless observers of the Bihar drought, and indeed a comparison of two nutrition

**Table 1.15** District-wise cereal production in Maharashtra, 1969–1973

| District | Index of cereal production (1967–8 = 100) | | | | Cereal production per capita, 1972–3 (kg/year) |
| --- | --- | --- | --- | --- | --- |
| | 1969–70 | 1970–1 | 1971–2 | 1972–3 | |
| Ratnagiri | 99 | 117 | 103 | 86 | 85 |
| Yeotmal | 131 | 65 | 104 | 85 | 86 |
| Amravati | 103 | 61 | 68 | 79 | 62 |
| Chandrapur | 129 | 109 | 105 | 71 | 118 |
| Jalgaon | 89 | 74 | 59 | 70 | 72 |
| Wardha | 97 | 59 | 73 | 68 | 80 |
| Nagpur | 96 | 71 | 76 | 67 | 49 |
| Kolaba | 78 | 101 | 81 | 67 | 131 |
| Kolhapur | 93 | 110 | 115 | 65 | 53 |
| Buldhana | 122 | 68 | 82 | 63 | 86 |
| Akola | 132 | 55 | 89 | 61 | 64 |
| Bhandara | 121 | 139 | 114 | 58 | 92 |
| Dhulia | 106 | 119 | 74 | 49 | 54 |
| Osmanabad | 108 | 54 | 58 | 45 | 61 |
| Poona | 90 | 70 | 73 | 43 | 38 |
| Thana | 88 | 110 | 97 | 42 | 46 |
| Satara | 98 | 103 | 91 | 41 | 45 |
| Parbhani | 76 | 54 | 42 | 41 | 66 |
| Ahmednagar | 109 | 80 | 59 | 33 | 47 |
| Greater Bombay | 77 | 81 | 54 | 31 | n/a |
| Nanded | 77 | 36 | 48 | 29 | 51 |
| Nasik | 81 | 107 | 55 | 26 | 32 |
| Aurangabad | 89 | 74 | 48 | 20 | 31 |
| Sangli | 90 | 86 | 90 | 18 | 20 |
| Sholapur | 92 | 51 | 63 | 18 | 27 |
| Bhir | 120 | 97 | 54 | 17 | 27 |
| MAHARASHTRA | 99 | 83 | 74 | 47 | 49 |

*Source*: Calculated from the *Annual Season and Crop Reports* (Government of Maharashtra) of the corresponding years. Per capita production figures for 1972–3 (last column) are based on District-wise population estimates (for 1973) obtained by assuming identical 1973–1971 population ratios for each District. District-wise population estimates for 1971 are from the Census (as given in Brahme 1983: 13–14).

[142] Krishnamachari *et al.* (1974: 22).

**Table 1.16** Mortality in rural Maharashtra, 1968–1978

| Year | Registered deaths | | Sample Registration Scheme | |
|------|-------------------|---|---------------------------|---|
| | Crude death rate | Infant death rate as ratio of crude death rate | Crude death rate | Male death rate as % of female |
| | (1) | (2) | (3) | (4) |
| 1968 | 12.3 | n/a | 13.9 | n/a |
| 1969 | 12.9 | n/a | 15.5 | n/a |
| 1970 | 12.1 | n/a | 13.0 | 96 |
| 1971 | 11.3 | 6.19 | 13.5 | 96 |
| 1972 | 10.5 | 6.76 | 14.5 (13.2)[a] | 95 |
| 1973 | 11.2 | 6.96 | n/a (13.1)[a] | 96 |
| 1974 | 9.1 | 6.59 | 12.6 | 95 |
| 1975 | 9.1 | 6.70 | 12.2 | 97 |
| 1976 | 8.6 | 6.28 | 12.5 | 94 |
| 1977 | 9.3 | 6.67 | 14.5 | n/a |
| 1978 | 7.3 | 6.44 | 11.3 | n/a |

[a] Figures in brackets relate to the first half of the calendar year.

*Notes*: The Sample Registration Scheme (SRS) in Maharashtra was disrupted during the second half of 1973. An explicitly 'unreliable' figure of 15.6 for the crude death rate in 1973 was later published by the *Sample Registration Bulletin* (July 1975 issue), apparently based on a rough extrapolation from 1970–2 figures.

While crude death rates based on 'registered deaths' are not very accurate estimates of mortality *levels*, they are generally thought to be useful for the assessment of *change*.

*Sources*: (1) *Vital Statistics of India*, various issues.

(2) Unpublished data kindly supplied by Nigel Crook (School of Oriental and African Studies, London).

(3) *Sample Registration Bulletin*, Apr. 1974 and June 1979.

(4) Unpublished data kindly supplied by Tim Dyson (London School of Economics).

surveys conducted respectively in Bihar (1967) and Maharashtra (1973) confirms the reality of the suggested contrast (Table 1.17). The loss of livestock was considerable, but the disposal of other assets was not large, and land sales (an indication of acute distress) were minute.[143] The extent of migration was also moderate (see below).

In contrast to Sahelian countries, of course, Maharashtra had the ability to draw fairly easily on the 'surplus' available in neighbouring areas. It also had the general advantage, discussed in the preceding section, of being integrated within a larger economic and political entity. I shall argue, however, that these factors fall far short of providing a satisfactory explanation for the successful

[143] Interesting observations on the disposal of assets and the loss of livestock during the Maharashtra drought can be found in a number of microstudies, including those reported in Kulkarni (1974), Borkar and Nadkarni (1975), Subramaniam (1975), and Jodha *et al.* (1977). Land sales are also discussed in Cain (1981), where a sharp contrast is drawn with the incidence of land sales during food crises in Bangladesh.

**Table 1.17** Prevalence of nutritional deficiency signs among children (aged 0–5) in severely affected areas of Bihar (1967) and Maharashtra (1973)

| Deficiency sign | Prevalence (%) | |
|---|---|---|
| | Bihar (1967) | Maharashtra (1973) |
| Without any clinical sign | 37.9 | 69.1 |
| Marasmus | 16.1 | 2.4 |
| Kwashiorkor | 2.3 | 1.6 |
| Number of cases observed | 87 | 151 |

*Sources*: Swaminathan *et al*. (1969: Table VI), and Krishnamachari *et al*. (1974: Table III).

*Notes*: The Bihar survey was carried out in May 1967 among randomly selected households in areas classified by the State government as 'severely affected'. But the authors note that 'the pattern of malnutrition in the community could have been considerably influenced beneficially by the energetic ameliorative programmes which were already in operation' (Swaminathan *et al*. 1969: 215).

The Maharashtra survey was carried out in Feb. 1973 in 'the worst affected taluk of each of the Districts of Poona, Ahmednagar, Bihar and Aurangabad' (themselves among the very worst affected Districts—see text). The subjects were drawn from households of labourers (male and female) employed on relief works; but the authors argue that the people 'could be considered as representing the population of the surrounding drought stricken villages' (Krishnamachari *et al*. 1974: 20).

prevention of famine in Maharashtra—once again, the relief system played an essential role.

### (b)   *Production, availability and consumption*[144]

As in the discussion of nineteenth-century famines in section 1.2, we have to consider here two closely related but nevertheless distinct effects of crop failures: the sharp reduction of food availability in affected areas, and the threat to food entitlements arising from the collapse of rural incomes. In the case of Maharashtra, it is quite clear that the improvement of food availability was an inescapable pre-condition to the protection of food entitlements. It is natural, therefore, to begin our investigation with a brief assessment of the food situation in Maharashtra in the year 1972–3, which marked the peak of the crisis.

Calculations of 'net availability' of foodgrains very similar to those performed in the previous section for Bihar can be carried out for Maharashtra using the same sources (mainly the *Bulletin on Food Statistics*). This has in fact already been done by Oughton (1982). Oughton takes the route of the left-hand side of equation (1.1) on p. 51 above, and I have attempted my own (rough) calculations via the right-hand side. Private stocks and private trade (the latter

[144] In arriving at the conclusions reached in this subsection, I have benefited from extensive discussions with several leading experts on Indian statistics, including N. Bhattacharya, B. S. Minhas, S. Tendulkar, A. Vaidyanathan, and A. M. Vidwans. I am also indebted to Michael Lipton for several useful suggestions.

again prohibited across States in 1972–3) are ignored throughout; I shall comment on this below. The results are summarized in Table 1.18.[145]

The two series of net availability estimates for foodgrains give a consistent picture of *change*, although in terms of *levels* my series appears to be somewhat lower than Oughton's. The discrepancy widens substantially in 1971 and 1972, and this may be due to the removal of zoning in 1970–1 and 1971–2 (if private trade takes place by rail or river, equation (1.1) ceases to hold). For the year we are concerned with, however, the discrepancy narrows down considerably. According to official statistics, then, net foodgrain availability per capita in Maharashtra for the year 1972–3 was somewhere between 90 and 100 kg, and roughly 60 per cent of the average 1968–70 level—a picture not very different from that obtained for Bihar in 1966–7.

This finding, however, is completely unbelievable. Field reports, nutrition surveys, socio-economic microstudies, and, finally, the National Sample Survey all converge to indicate that the decline in foodgrain *consumption* in 1972–3 must have been far smaller.

For the time being, let us neglect all other sources of evidence and only consider the most important one: the National Sample Survey (hereafter NSS). According to the 27th Round of the NSS (October 1972–August 1973), average monthly cereal consumption per person in Maharashtra in 1972–3

**Table 1.18** Net availability of foodgrains in Maharashtra, 1968–1974

| Year | Net production (000 tonnes) | Issues (000 tonnes) | Procurement (000 tonnes) | Net availability per capita (kg/year) | | |
|------|------|------|------|------|------|------|
| | | | | Oughton | Drèze | Drèze (cereals) |
| 1968 | 5,972 | 1,942 | 567 | 167 | 156 | 137 |
| 1969 | 6,262 | 1,728 | 439 | 160 | 156 | 134 |
| 1970 | 6,050 | 1,609 | 400 | 167 | 147 | 124 |
| 1971 | 4,891 | 1,244 | 254 | 138 | 116 | 101 |
| 1972 | 4,334 | 1,677 | 122 | 132 | 113 | 103 |
| 1973 | 2,670 | 2,404 | 236 | 96 | 91 | 84 |
| 1974 | 6,230 | 1,979 | 231 | 157 | 147 | 133 |

*Sources*: Production, issues, and procurement are from the *Bulletin on Food Statistics*, 1971 to 1976. 'Net production' is obtained by deducting 12.5% from gross production for 'feed, seed, and wastage'. Production figures relate to the agricultural year (starting in July of the preceding calendar year). Issues and procurement figures relate to the financial year (Apr.–Mar.). Oughton's estimates of 'net availability' (see Oughton 1982: 180) are obtained as net production + net imports + net depletion of government stocks. My estimates are obtained as net production + issues − procurement (see text for details). Population estimates are as in Table 1.2.

[145] Brahme (1983: 79) presents similar calculations (for cereals), based on the various issues of *Maharashtra, An Economic Review* (1983). The broad picture is the same, though there are year-to-year discrepancies. Brahme, however, appears to have neglected changes in public stocks, and her results have, therefore, not been reported here.

**Table 1.19** Cereal consumption in Maharashtra,
1972–1973

| | Cereal consumption per capita | | No. of households sampled |
|---|---|---|---|
| | kg/month | kg/year | |
| Rural | 12.60 | 153 | 5,249 |
| Urban | 8.95 | 109 | 6,181 |

*Source*: *Sarvekshana*, Jan. 1979: 133, reporting the results of the 27th Round of the National Sample Survey (Oct. 1972–Aug. 1973). The figures on yearly consumption are derived from those on monthly consumption, and are provided here to facilitate comparison with Table 1.18.

amounted to 12.6 kg in rural areas and 8.95 kg in urban areas (Table 1.19). With the rural–urban population proportions of the 1971 Census, this represents an average per capita consumption per year of 140 kg, and implies an embarrassing discrepancy of around 50 kg per head (a little more than 2.5 million tonnes) with our previous estimate.

Let us examine the possible sources of this discrepancy. First, could the NSS figures be wild overestimates? It is well known that NSS estimates of cereal consumption systematically exceed, at the all-India level, the 'net availability' estimates arrived at by the sort of method used in Table 1.18.[146] The reasons for this are an old and unsolved riddle in Indian statistics, and many experts believe that the NSS series are on the high side. However, even if we (unreasonably) put the whole blame for this chronic inaccuracy on the NSS series, we are only led to revise it downwards by about 15–16 per cent in the 1970–3 period and at most 20 per cent in 1972–3,[147] whereas our concern here is with an adjustment of about 35 per cent. We are still far off the mark.

Are there reasons why overestimation in the NSS figures should increase in a drought year? A complete answer to this question would lead us into the intricate (and rather boring) issue of the *source* of alleged overestimation in the NSS data, and only a few general conjectures can be made here. It is fairly well agreed that sampling errors in NSS data are small if one is concerned with aggregate magnitudes such as average cereal consumption. Among possible non-sampling errors leading to overestimation, the most frequently cited ones are the double counting or faulty recording of wages in kind, gifts (including meals at marriage feasts), animal feeding, and the like. But these sources of overestimation are not likely to increase in a drought year. A more relevant possibility is that respondents often report 'normal' or 'ideal' rather than

---

[146] For an excellent discussion of this problem, see Vaidyanathan (1986). On the quality of NSS data, see also Bhattacharya *et al.* (1985), Mukherjee (1986), Srinivasan and Bardhan (1974), and Suryanarayana and Iyengar (1986).

[147] See Vaidyanathan (1986: 133, Table 3) and Bhattacharya *et al.* (1985: 275–83).

'actual' diets. Overestimation on this count *is* likely to increase in a drought year when people frequently miss meals but may fail to report the associated reduction in intake compared to usual levels. A similar conjecture is that NSS estimates partly reflect the perceptions of the investigator, and as a result underestimate change. Indeed Table 1.4 indicates astonishingly small year-to-year changes in cereal consumption, though this may also reflect robust consumption habits. What all this adds up to precisely is far from clear, but it hardly explains the gross discrepancy we are concerned with here.

Nor can migration solve the riddle. There is no trace of large-scale migration outside Maharashtra in the many first-hand accounts and newspaper reports on the drought. In his very careful survey of drought conditions in Sinnar taluka (Nasik District), Kulkarni (1974) found that a significant proportion of individuals and households had migrated in 1972–3, but 86 per cent of the migrating households had moved less than 50 miles away, and the author incidentally notes that 'most of the immigrants moved within taluka at the scarcity work centres'.[148] Subramaniam (1975) also forcefully denies the occurrence of large-scale population movements.[149]

What about the reliability of the 'net availability' calculations? Maharashtra is reputed to have one of the best statistical systems in India, and the transactions on government account (procurement, issues, changes in stocks, and imports) in all probability involve reasonable margins of error. Crop-cutting techniques are now well developed in India and production estimates are believed to be very accurate. It is sometimes suggested that individual States purposely and grossly 'falsify' production reports to the centre in order to achieve various political aims, but it is difficult to take these allegations very seriously. There remains the question of private stocks and trade. Private stocks can safely be ignored (for the same reasons as in the case of Bihar) since we are looking at the third successive drought year. We must, however, re-examine the issue of private trade.

During the year 1972–3, inter-State movements of foodgrains on private account were banned. The shortfall in food availability in Maharashtra was supposed to be met by the public distribution system. The Food Corporation of India organized the transport of foodgrains (mainly wheat) from other parts of the country, and their distribution at subsidized prices through a network of nearly 30,000 'Fair Price Shops' scattered all over the State. However, the achievements of the public distribution system fell far short of targets. Numerous formal and informal reports testify to the fact that all over Maharashtra the actual per capita allocation of grain in Fair Price Shops fell

---

[148] Kulkarni (1974: 207, and Table 8.3). A 'taluka' is a small administrative unit within a District. One civil servant who had been Collector of one of the peripheral Districts at that time told me that large-scale employment programmes had attracted migrant labourers *into* Maharashtra during the drought.

[149] Subramaniam (1975: 463–5, 528–9).

pitifully short of the initial official allocation of 12 kg per month.[150] The quantum of actual allocations naturally varied from place to place, but the reported figures vary from 'hardly 2 kg per month' (Kulkarni 1974; Anon 1972b) and '5 to 10 per cent of needs'; (Patil 1973) to 4 kg per month (Brahme 1983). Subramaniam (1975), who is not inclined to admit government failures, concedes that 'the public distribution system was able to supply hardly 3 to 4 kg per month per adult'.[151] And indeed, according to official statistics themselves per capita issues of foodgrains through the public distribution system were only 2.7 kg per month in 1972 and 3.8 kg in 1973 (Table 1.18). By all accounts, public food distribution in 1972–3 represented only a very small proportion of consumption requirements.

Meanwhile, however, the purchasing power generated by huge public works programmes put an upward pressure on prices all over the State, and widening price differentials between Maharashtra and the neighbouring States promised huge profits to illegal private trade. Interestingly enough, private trade was also actively (though unofficially) encouraged by government authorities. During interviews with former District Collectors of the worst affected Districts, I have repeatedly heard the same story: 'smuggling' of grain across State borders was tacitly approved by government officials in Bombay, and openly promoted at the District level.[152] This policy was not just the result of common sense and concern for the people; in many cases its motivation arose directly from a strong anxiety about possible law and order problems ensuing from food shortages and price increases.[153] Illegal private trade was therefore brisk throughout the drought period in spite of the official ban. The microsurveys cited above all confirm that the bulk of food purchases drew on the 'open' (or black) market rather than on the public distribution system.

Attributing the whole of the discrepancy between the 'net availability' and the 'consumption' estimates to illegal private trade amounts to putting around 2.5 million tonnes of foodgrains on that account in 1972–3 (see above). This is a staggering figure: it exceeds the amount of foodgrains moved on government account over the same period, and suggests a picture of hundreds of trucks crossing the State borders every day 'illegally'. Thus while the most reasonable hypothesis seems to be to assign the bulk of the discrepancy to private trade, the other sources of inaccuracy discussed earlier may have played a significant role as well.

Let us now revert to the issue of the magnitude of food deprivation in

[150] See e.g. Kulkarni (1974: Table 6.7), Borkar and Nadkarni (1975: 58), Brahme (1983: 69), Mody (1972: 2482), Oxfam (1972, 1973), Oughton (1982: 182), Patil (1973: 1617), Anon. (1972b), and Subramaniam (1975).          [151] Subramaniam (1975: 128).

[152] The State government also made representations to the central government in favour of the removal of 'zoning' (Subramaniam 1975: 254).

[153] One former District Collector even claimed that, fearing imminent food riots, he had literally 'hijacked' a large quantity of government-owned grain consigned by rail to Karnataka and emptied it in the nearest go-down! Law and order is one of the main responsibilities of the District Collector.

**Table 1.20** Cereal consumption in rural India and Maharashtra, 1967–1978

| Year | Cereal consumption (kg/cap./month) | | |
|---|---|---|---|
| | India | Maharashtra | Maharashtra (10 drought-affected Districts) |
| 1967–8 | n/a | n/a | 14.01 |
| 1970–1 | 15.35 | 12.83 | n/a |
| 1972–3 | 15.26 | 12.60 | 11.74 |
| 1973–4 | 15.09 | 13.45 | 13.90 |
| 1977–8 | 15.25 | 13.52 | n/a |

*Sources*: Figures for all-India and Maharashtra are from the Central Sample of the National Sample Survey, as reported in *Sarvekshana*, Jan. 1979: 133, and Bhattacharya *et al.* (1985). The 1967–8 and 1972–3 figures for the 10 worst-affected Districts are from Subramaniam (1975: 443), and are based on tabulations of the State Sample of the National Sample Survey. Figures for 1973–4 for these Districts have been calculated by Vijay Nayak and myself (using the Central Sample of the National Sample Survey, 28th Round) at the Development Economics Research Centre, University of Warwick, in Aug. 1986.

Maharashtra during the peak drought year. The figure of 12.6 kgs per capita per month for cereal consumption in rural Maharashtra in 1972–3 is the lowest ever for any State and for any round of the National Sample Survey for which such data are available (see Table 1.4).[154] It is also 17 per cent lower than the all-India figure for the same year; but this is not necessarily a good indication of the effect of the drought because, as was mentioned earlier, there seem to exist fairly substantial State-to-State variations in cereal intake which bear no obvious relation to price and income differentials and are more likely to be related (at least partly) to 'dietary habits'.

Table 1.20 presents cereal consumption figures for rural India and Maharashtra during the drought period as well as for the nearest years for which comparable data are available for the relevant regions. The table also shows similar figures for the ten Districts most affected by drought within Maharashtra, representing a combined population of more than 20 million in 1971 (nearly 80 per cent rural).[155] As before, it is worth noting the striking stability of cereal consumption estimates over time, and the fact that if

[154] This statement ignores Kerala, where there is a high propensity to consume food items classified in the National Sample Survey as 'cereal substitutes' (e.g. tapioca).

[155] Population figures are from Government of India (1979: 3–12). The definition of '10 worst-affected Districts' follows Subramaniam (1975) and includes Poona, Ahmednagar, Shola-pur, Satara, Sangli, Aurangabad, Bhir, Osmanabad, Nasik, and Dhulia. Subramaniam does not motivate this definition explicitly, but implies that this was an official classification, and Table 1.15 above strongly suggests that the severity of drought was assessed on the basis of food or agricultural production estimates. An independent attempt at classification in Anon. (1972*b*) identifies the 8 worst-affected Districts, all of which belong to the above list.

**Table 1.21** Cereal consumption and total consumer expenditure in the rural areas of 10 drought-affected Districts in Maharashtra

| Household class | Monthly cereal consumption per capita (kg) | Per capita expenditure (nominal) (Rs/month) | Real per capita expenditure (1967–8 Rs/month) | | No. of households |
|---|---|---|---|---|---|
| | | | (1) | (2) | |
| *Large cultivators* | | | | | |
| 1967–8 | 15.55 | 33.50 | 33.50 | 33.50 | 147 |
| 1972–3 | 12.77 | 41.35 | 29.68 | 28.98 | 89 |
| 1973–4 | 15.26 | 57.71 | 38.07 | 37.67 | 130 |
| *Small cultivators* | | | | | |
| 1967–8 | 13.37 | 31.36 | 31.36 | 31.36 | 73 |
| 1972–3 | 11.08 | 33.87 | 24.31 | 23.74 | 50 |
| 1973–4 | 12.90 | 61.38 | 40.49 | 40.07 | 77 |
| *Farm labourers* | | | | | |
| 1967–8 | 14.47 | 24.01 | 24.01 | 24.01 | 111 |
| 1972–3 | 11.45 | 32.85 | 23.58 | 23.02 | 218 |
| 1973–4 | 13.68 | 44.69 | 29.48 | 29.17 | 166 |
| *Industrial workers* | | | | | |
| 1967–8 | 13.15 | 34.17 | 34.17 | 34.17 | 29 |
| 1972–3 | 12.02 | 37.23 | 26.72 | 26.09 | 28 |
| 1973–4 | 13.34 | 48.29 | 31.85 | 31.52 | 51 |
| *Others* | | | | | |
| 1967–8 | 12.38 | 33.14 | 33.14 | 33.14 | 40 |
| 1972–3 | 10.79 | 42.37 | 30.41 | 29.69 | 54 |
| 1973–4 | 12.07 | 79.83 | 52.66 | 52.11 | 59 |
| *All households* | | | | | |
| 1967–8 | 14.01 | 30.70 | 30.70 | 30.70 | 400 |
| 1972–3 | 11.74 | 36.34 | 26.08 | 25.47 | 439 |
| 1973–4 | 13.90 | 55.53 | 36.63 | 36.25 | 483 |

(1) = Calculated by using the Consumer Price Index (CPI) for Agricultural Labourers (General Index).
(2) = Calculated by using the Consumer Price Index (CPI) for Agricultural Labourers (Food Index).

*Notes*: The estimates of 'real' per capita expenditure are almost certainly overestimates, because the price indices used apply to Maharashtra as a whole, whereas the increase of prices (especially food prices) was more pronounced in the 10 worst-affected Districts. However, it is noteworthy that the difference in prices between these Districts and Maharashtra as a whole was in fact quite moderate (see text), so that the overestimation involved is not considerable.
   'Small cultivators' are those with operational holdings of less than 7.5 acres.

*Sources*: Nominal consumption and expenditure for 1967–8 and 1972–3 are from Subramaniam (1975: 442–3, 435); they are based on the State Sample of the National Sample Survey (22nd and 27th Rounds). The corresponding figures for 1973–4 have been calculated by Vijay Nayak and myself, using the Central Sample of the 28th Round of the National Sample Survey at the Development Economics Research Centre (University of Warwick). Real expenditure figures are calculated by deflating the nominal expenditure figures. The deflator used to calculate real expenditure in 1972–3 is the ratio of the CPI for 1967–8 to the CPI for Oct. 1972–Sept. 1973 (unweighted average of monthly index), the period covered by the State Sample; and similarly for 1973–4 (using the sample period Oct. 1973–June 1974).

anything the NSS figures are likely to underestimate consumption fluctuations from year to year. In spite of this, a drop of 16 per cent in average cereal consumption is noticeable in 1972–3 for the 10 worst-affected Districts compared to either of the nearest two normal years for which comparable data are available. Given the possibility of a small underestimation of the consumption decline in the NSS figures, we can tentatively but reasonably conclude that average cereal consumption in rural areas of the 10 worst-affected Districts in 1972–3 was somewhere between 15 and 20 per cent below 'normal' levels.[156]

Consumption changes of this order of magnitude are nowhere as frightening as those which took place in Bihar in 1966–7. But when they affect such a large population they remain quite capable of entailing disastrous consequences. It is easy to see, for instance, that if the deficit had been concentrated on (say) the poorest 30 per cent of an already greatly impoverished population, the results in terms of excess mortality could have been catastrophic. This raises the question of the *distribution* of the food deficit, and brings us to a crucial aspect of the mechanism of famine prevention in Maharashtra.

Table 1.21 presents cereal consumption figures by socio-economic groups for the rural areas of the ten worst-affected Districts during the peak drought year (1972–3), as well as for the nearest two 'normal' years for which comparable data are available (see also Fig. 1.3). The emerging picture of consumption adjustments is interesting. Its most striking feature is the broad spread across socio-economic groups of the aggregate reduction in cereal intake, and the surprising *evenness* of the distribution of cereal intake in 1972–3. The consumption level of farm labourers in 1972–3, for instance, was very near the overall mean.

Taken on its own, this piece of evidence indicating a fairly 'egalitarian' reduction of food consumption during the Maharashtra drought is admittedly rather thin. However, further evidence from microstudies abundantly confirms the scope for relief measures to shift the burden of consumption adjustment away from the most deprived sections of the population. Indeed, reducing food intake (including cereal consumption) seems to be a common response to adverse changes in real income during droughts in rural India, not only on the part of landless labourers and poor artisans but also on the part of cultivators over a very wide range of landholding size groups. Some supporting evidence appears in Appendix 1.2, where I have assembled the results of several microstudies on food consumption during recent droughts in Maharashtra and other States.[157] The following findings are particularly noteworthy.

[156] More detailed and painstaking estimations, based on alternative inferences from NSS figures for all available years (Central Sample as well as State Sample), were carried out in an earlier draft of this paper (Drèze 1986). They led to very similar results.

[157] The findings reported in Appendix 1.2, and discussed here, are further supported by a recent study of drought in Gujarat in 1987 (see Chen 1989, especially Table 39). In fact, there are many striking similarities between the episodes of drought and averted famine in Maharashtra in 1970–3 and in Gujarat in 1985–7 (see Drèze 1990).

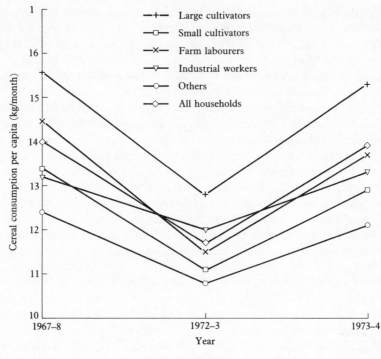

*Source*: Table 1.21.

**Fig. 1.3** Cereal consumption decline in Maharashtra by household class, 1972–1973

A pioneering study of 144 'farming households' carried out by Jodha during the 1963–4 drought in Rajasthan (Table 1.30) clearly shows that (1) a very large proportion of households reduced their consumption of foodgrains during the drought, and (2) frugality in consumption set in largely before the process of asset depletion, mortgaging, and migration.

A study of 108 households during the drought of 1974–5 in Gujarat by Desai *et al.* (Table 1.31) arrived at strikingly similar results: the great majority of cultivators in all landholding size classes were found to reduce their cereal consumption, even though the depletion of assets only reached very moderate proportions.[158] Incidentally, much as in the case of Maharashtra in 1972–3 this study found that the proportion of households experiencing a reduction in cereal intake during the drought was significantly *lower* for labourers and artisans than for cultivators in any landholding size class (see Table 1.31). The authors themselves persuasively relate this phenomenon to the disproportionate involvement of labourers and artisans in relief works.

A somewhat similar, though less striking, pattern of cereal consumption

[158] The 'depletion' of assets in this case consisted mainly of livestock deaths (see Desai *et al.* 1979: 79–80).

changes is noted by Choudhary and Bapat during the 1969–70 droughts in Gujarat and Rajasthan (Table 1.32).

In a study of food consumption during drought and non-drought years in sample villages of Tamil Nadu, Pinstrup-Andersen and Jaramillo (1985) found, once again, that a large reduction of food intake was a feature of consumption patterns in drought years even for 'large farmers' (see Table 1.33). In this case, the relative deprivation of landless labourers in terms of food consumption during drought years remained important, possibly due to the apparent absence of extensive relief measures in these villages.

In their study of survival strategies during the 1983 drought in Karnataka, based on a survey of nearly 400 households, Caldwell et al. note: 'Eating less . . . was universal . . . The important point is that most families still regard their ability to weather droughts as being based on savage cutbacks in their living standards, dominated by reducing food to the minimum. The rich families moved from three to two meals a day, and many ordinary families from two to one.'[159] Once again, moreover, the protection of the productive base took precedence over the protection of consumption standards (see Table 1.34).

To the best of my knowledge, no comparable studies exist for Maharashtra in 1972–3. However, the survey of two villages in Aurangabad District by Borkar and Nadkarni in May–June 1973 contains some useful hints. This study does not cover cereal consumption as such, but presents data on purchases of cereals for different socio-economic groups (Table 1.35). No indication is given about the size of stocks, but these were most probably negligible by that time for most households. On the other hand the authors state that 'in May and June when they reported peak employment and earnings through scarcity works, the households purchased slightly in excess of their current requirements because of the expected rise in the prices of food articles and the decline in their incomes in the immediate future (due to discontinuance of scarcity relief works)'.[160] Thus purchases are not a very good approximation for consumption in this case. Nevertheless the rather egalitarian pattern of current purchases is itself revealing. The market command of agricultural labourers was, for instance, *greater* than average in both villages.

Two closely related objections can be raised against using these studies and surveys as evidence of 'equal sharing' of the food deficit during the Maharashtra drought. The first is that landholding size is not a good proxy for 'normal-year income', so that a fairly uniform pattern of food intake reduction across landholding size groups is quite compatible with a concentration of the burden of adjustment on the poor. The second objection is that, regardless of whether or not landholding size is a good proxy for average income, *within* each landholding class only the very poor may have suffered.

The first objection may seem surprising, but it has been seriously argued

---

[159] Caldwell et al. (1986: 687–8).     [160] Borkar and Nadkarni (1975: 58).

that, in the semi-arid areas of India, average 'normal-year' incomes do not increase with landholding size over a very wide range of landholding sizes at the lower end of the scale—there is a 'threshold effect'.[161] This is not the place to enter into a general assessment of this interesting theory—though it is worth noting in passing that the NSS data in Table 1.21 clearly show a large gap between the expenditure levels of farm labourers and 'small cultivators' in non-drought years. In section 1.4c I shall comment on the available evidence on incomes and expenditure for Maharashtra around 1972–3, and suggest that if a 'threshold effect' existed at all in this context, it must have occurred at very low levels of landholding size. It would therefore be hard to invoke the threshold hypothesis to explain the observed adjustments in food consumption since, as Table 1.21 indicates, considerable reductions of food intake appear to have taken place even in the largest landholding size groups.

In any case, neither this first objection nor the second one square with further evidence on the pattern of reduction in food intake from the National Sample Survey. As Table 1.22 unambiguously shows, a significant proportion of the reduction in cereal intake in the ten worst-affected Districts took place among high-consumption groups: the percentage of all rural households consuming more than 15 kg of cereals per capita per month fell from 39.0 in 1967–8 to 15.9 in 1972–3, and rose again to 36.1 in 1973–4. Moreover, since 'cereals' invariably appear to have a positive and large expenditure elasticity in rural areas according to NSS data, high cereal consumption groups also correspond to high expenditure groups in this case.

A consistent and fairly solid picture emerges, then, indicating a significant reduction in aggregate cereal consumption during the peak drought year, spread rather evenly across different socio-economic groups—poor and less poor, landless and landed, blue-collar and white-collar and no-collar. If we trust consumer price indices, we may also conclude that every socio-economic group experienced a severe cut in 'real per capita expenditure' during the drought year, *except* farm labourers (see Table 1.21). The latter conclusion must be treated with some caution, especially because it is based on all-Maharashtra price indices whereas the increase of prices was somewhat more pronounced in the severely affected Districts than elsewhere.[162] Nevertheless, using a different price index would not invalidate the finding that the propertied classes suffered a much larger *percentage* reduction in real expenditure

---

[161] See Visaria (1978) and particularly Lipton (1985). It should be mentioned that the evidence presented by Visaria does not really provide much support for the 'threshold effect' hypothesis. Indeed, this evidence is precisely based on data relating to Maharashtra and Gujarat in 1972–3, when, as we shall see, the distribution of income and expenditure was very significantly less unequal than in normal years. In fact Visaria's evidence can be interpreted as *confirming* that, in normal years, per-capita income must be positively related to landholding size.

[162] On this, see e.g. the (fairly consistent) data on retail prices in Subramaniam (1975) and Brahme (1983). In June 1973, the price of cereals in 'Scarcity Areas' was higher than in 'Non-scarcity Areas' by a margin ranging from 6% for bajra to 34% for jowar (Brahme 1983: Table 4.15).

**Table 1.22** Percentage distribution of population by levels of per capita monthly cereal consumption in the rural areas of 10 drought-affected Districts in Maharashtra

| Household class | Per capita intake of cereals (kg/month) | | | Total |
|---|---|---|---|---|
| | up to 12 | 12–15 | 15+ | |
| *Large cultivators* | | | | |
| 1967–8 | 25.5 | 28.7 | 45.8 | 100.0 |
| 1972–3 | 44.7 | 30.0 | 25.3 | 100.0 |
| *Small cultivators* | | | | |
| 1967–8 | 53.0 | 19.0 | 28.0 | 100.0 |
| 1972–3 | 61.2 | 25.2 | 13.6 | 100.0 |
| *Farm labourers* | | | | |
| 1967–8 | 41.4 | 19.9 | 38.6 | 100.0 |
| 1972–3 | 60.9 | 25.3 | 13.8 | 100.0 |
| *Industrial workers* | | | | |
| 1967–8 | 42.8 | 21.7 | 35.5 | 100.0 |
| 1972–3 | 65.3 | 27.1 | 7.6 | 100.0 |
| *All households* | | | | |
| 1967–8 | 38.5 | 22.5 | 39.0 | 100.0 |
| 1972–3 | 58.9 | 25.2 | 15.9 | 100.0 |
| 1973–4 | 37.2 | 26.7 | 36.1 | 100.0 |

*Note*: For sample sizes and other details, see Table 1.21.

*Source*: All figures relating to the years 1967–8 and 1972–3 are from Subramaniam (1975: 446), and were derived from the State Sample of the National Sample Survey (22nd and 27th Rounds). The figures for 1973–4 were calculated as in Table 1.21.

than agricultural labourers. And this is itself quite striking, considering that famines are generally believed to exacerbate existing inequalities.[163]

The significance of these findings should not be exaggerated. Comparable percentage reductions of consumption at different income levels are not, of course, the same as comparable declines in well-being, and it is likely enough that the hardship endured by agricultural labourers remained much greater than the sufferings of the propertied classes. While many first-hand accounts of the Maharashtra drought go so far as to suggest that, thanks to bright employment prospects on relief works, agricultural labourers were actually *better-off* in the peak drought year than in normal years, there is little evidence supporting the view that agricultural labourers 'enjoyed the drought'.[164] The

---

[163] Even in the case of the Maharashtra drought, there remained some clear examples of widening inequalities. Oughton (1982), for instance, emphasizes the contrast between general impoverishment and the enrichment of large farmers growing cash crops on irrigated land.

[164] This view has been expressed in Anon. (1972b: 2480), Garcia (1981: 124), Subramaniam (1975: 491), Aykroyd (1974), and Oxfam (1972, 1973), among others. Liz Oughton, who conducted extensive field work in a village of Sangli District in 1982, met a poor labourer who told her that he 'liked droughts' because they improved his employment prospects (personal communication).

bulk of the evidence (reviewed in the next section) and of the better-informed first-hand accounts suggests a more plausible assessment closely agreeing with our previous observations: the plight of agricultural labourers during the drought varied from place to place and in some cases they may have found themselves better off than in ordinary years; as a rule, however, their real earnings declined.[165] The reason is simply that while labourers were getting more work than usual, and higher money incomes, their *real* wages were very meagre indeed.[166]

This said, the fact that the traditional victims of Indian famines not only remained safely protected from starvation but also experienced a surprisingly moderate deterioration in their living standards is remarkable enough. The precise mechanism underlying the observed 'redistribution of hardship' to-wards the more privileged classes is investigated in the next section.

### (c)   The entitlement process

Famines, it is now well understood, can and sometimes do occur without a substantial decline in aggregate food availability (Sen 1981). The symmetric question of whether, and to what extent, famines can be contained in spite of an irreducible decline in food availability has received comparatively little atten-tion. This question is of great importance for the design of famine relief policies, and in particular for the issue of whether the implementation of famine relief schemes in situations of food scarcity should be conditional upon the timely arrival of additional food supplies. The Maharashtra experience does seem to provide an example where famine was averted in spite of a partial failure of the food delivery system, mainly through *redistribution*. The factors which account for this success are worth exploring.

Why did cultivators in all landholding size classes reduce their food con-sumption during the Maharashtra drought? Why did people who owned many acres of land as well as other valuable assets such as animals and jewellery decide to go hungry rather than (or as well as) to deplete their wealth or to borrow? Before attempting to answer these questions, it is useful to take a closer look at the nature of income, expenditure, and price changes that accompany a drought of the kind that hit Maharashtra in 1970–3.

For this purpose, I have assembled in Appendix 1.3 such evidence as I could

[165] On this, see particularly the careful studies of Borkar and Nadkarni (1975), Kulkarni (1974), and Brahme (1983), as well as the National Sample Survey evidence presented above, and Ladejinsky (1973). On careful questioning (the distinction between money and real incomes always poses a problem), most of the eye-witnesses I interviewed myself concurred with the assessment proposed here. Labourers gave different answers in different places, according to the intensity of the drought and the effectiveness of relief measures in that area. In the worst affected places the events of 1972–3 often evoked very painful memories.

[166] Brahme estimated the average daily wage rate on relief works for Maharashtra as a whole at Rs. 1.90 for the period Apr.–July 1973 (Brahme 1983: 102). Using the figures which the same author presents on food prices in drought-affected areas in June 1973, this represented a little less than 1 kg of staple cereals!

gather from microstudies and household surveys on income and expenditure patterns in Maharashtra and adjacent States around 1972–3. Many of the studies reported there, it must be said, use rather rough survey methods—particularly when they attempt to estimate 'normal year income' retrospectively. Put together, however, they form a remarkably consistent picture, and their results can be summarized as follows. First, there is a clear correlation (in this region and for this period) between landholding size and 'normal year' per-capita income, at least across broad landholding size classes.[167] This correlation may or may not survive in a drought year, depending *inter alia* on the nature and effectiveness of relief measures. Second, during the Maharashtra drought the distribution of *current incomes* was considerably more equal than in normal years. Third, a tendency towards much greater equality in *current expenditure* was also noticeable. Finally, greater equality was accompanied by a considerable reduction in *average* real incomes and expenditure; the latter resulted from the combination of a dramatic loss of output (pushing most households into the 'food deficit' category) and sharply rising prices.[168]

The observed changes in income patterns are not difficult to understand. In an ordinary year, large cultivators reap the profits of better endowments. In a drought year, however, cultivators may get only small returns on cultivation expenses, and 'net profits' per acre can drop to very low—possibly even negative—values. What happens to the distribution of income then depends largely on whether or not cultivators in different landholding size groups decide to join the relief works (when they exist). During an isolated drought following one or more 'good years', most cultivators commonly abstain from doing so, and this together with negative profits per acre accounts for the impressive 'reversal' of the ordinary income scale observed by Desai *et al.* (1979) during the 1974–5 drought in Gujarat (see Table 1.41). However, when droughts recur for several years in succession, cultivators gradually lose their resilience and start flocking to the relief works in increasing numbers. This is precisely what happened in Maharashtra in 1972–3 (see below), which explains why in this event the distribution of current incomes, while far less unequal than in other years, retained the ordinary pattern.

It is, of course, not easy to predict how pronounced declines in current income for different socio-economic groups will affect their current expenditures. In principle, credit transactions and informal insurance arrangements (including patronage and reciprocity practices) could allow individual households to protect their current expenditures from income fluctuations. To the

---

[167] The correlation does not always appear in small samples, partly because the variance of incomes is high. The relationship can also get blurred in places where small farms happen to have better access to irrigation facilities than large farms (presumably an exceptional situation).

[168] See Pandey and Upadhyay (1979) for similar results on the effects of the 1972–4 drought in Haryana. An important exception to the operation of equalizing forces must be made for the accentuation of inequality between irrigated and non-irrigated farming. See Brahme (1983) for a detailed discussion.

extent that the arrangements involved are imperfect and costly, a measure of correlation over time between income and expenditure would remain for individual households even if household incomes were largely uncorrelated and therefore potentially amenable to mutual insurance. In the event of a drought, however, we are concerned with income fluctuations which are not only large but also have a strongly collective nature. A reduction of living standards is especially inescapable in this context.[169]

There is plenty of evidence to support the validity of these speculations for rural India. Several careful empirical studies have indeed shown that informal insurance arrangements are active—though far from perfect—in rural India, and allow a substantial degree of insulation of expenditure levels from income fluctuations. During droughts, however, the effectiveness of insurance mechanisms is considerably eroded. In particular, the strategy of temporarily depleting assets to preserve ordinary consumption standards becomes extremely costly as widespread sales drive asset prices down. The insurance opportunities provided by alternative strategies such as borrowing, income transfers (including remittances), patronage, sharing, or storage are also severely limited in times of drought.[170]

Understandably enough, then, droughts in India do entail large cuts in household expenditures, not only for agricultural labourers but also for cultivators (large and small). Moreover, the available empirical evidence strongly suggests that the inclination of the propertied classes to protect their asset base during droughts by reducing consumption expenditure is much stronger than one might have thought (see the discussion in the preceding section, and the evidence presented in Table 1.21 and Appendices 1.2 and 1.3). This explains, *inter alia*, why household consumption expenditure during the peak year of the Maharashtra drought was found to be remarkably constant over a wide range of landholding sizes at the lower end of the scale (see particularly the NSS-based data in Table 1.40 of Appendix 1.3). As was discussed earlier, empirical studies also bring out clearly that reduction in consumption expenditure during droughts typically involves substantial reductions in food intake, even among the relatively privileged classes.

The widespread responsiveness of food consumption to sharp changes in real income has far-reaching implications for relief policies. Thus, even when some reduction of aggregate consumption appears inevitable, there is no reason why the burden of readjustment should necessarily fall on the most

[169] For further discussion of the theoretical issues involved, see Platteau (1988), Newbery (1989), and Martin Ravallion in ch. 5 below. The imperfection of insurance opportunities does not, of course, apply uniformly to all classes. The special disadvantages of agricultural labourers in this respect account for their traditional vulnerability to starvation, and the function of the relief system can be precisely seen as one of providing them with a form of insurance and shifting the burden of uncertainty towards the propertied classes.

[170] For reviews and discussions of the relevant empirical studies, see Torry (1986a), Agarwal (1988), Platteau (1988), Drèze and Sen (1989: ch. 5), and Martin Ravallion in ch. 5 below.

vulnerable groups. In principle, suitable income support measures (e.g. in the form of employment generation) can succeed in protecting their entitlements.

Before concluding this section, a word must be said about the role of prices in this scenario. At the risk of simplification, the changes in real incomes which took place in Maharashtra in 1972–3 can be seen as having resulted from the combination of three influences: (1) the loss of crops and agricultural employment; (2) direct income transfers through relief measures; and (3) the increase of prices (especially food prices).[171] The latter was due, in part, to the generation of purchasing power resulting from large-scale income support measures (mainly in the form of cash-for-work schemes). Exactly how much extra upward pressure relief measures were actually putting on food prices is, however, difficult to ascertain, and would have depended *inter alia* on the elasticity of supply. As was discussed earlier, the supply of food to Maharashtra in 1972–3 was far from completely inelastic, and it was not the least success of relief measures to attract large quantities of food from other parts of the country. Nevertheless, substantial increases in food prices did occur in Maharashtra in 1972–3.

If we ignore 'substitution effects', an increase in food prices operates very much like a lump-sum tax applying to all households *proportionately to their food purchases*.[172] The soundness of a relief strategy relying on an implicit tax of this kind to release the resources needed to support the entitlements of vulnerable groups depends largely on two conditions being satisfied. First, there must be a substantial pool of households whose food purchases are responsive to declines in real income but who are not immediately at risk. Second, the number of households who buy food but *are* at risk and have no access to the relief system must be small. In Maharashtra, the existence of many cultivators struggling to preserve their asset base in the face of massive crop losses ensured that the first condition was met. As we shall see, moreover, the policy of open-ended public works supplemented by unconditional relief for households without fit adult members ensured that the second condition was, by and large, also met. In these circumstances, it was hardly a mistake to provide massive cash relief to the poor without waiting for a definitive improvement in food availability.

If food consumption is also responsive to food price changes through substitution effects, the scope for using the incomes–prices mechanism to protect the entitlements of vulnerable groups can be expected to be correspondingly greater. Whether substitution effects are in fact important is hard to ascertain. Econometric studies would have us believe that the consumption of food (whether interpreted as 'total food', 'calories', or even

---

[171] For further details on incomes, wages, and prices in Maharashtra in 1972–3, see Oughton (1982). See also Appendix 1.3 of this chapter.

[172] This follows from the 'Slutsky equation'. A substitution effect is a change in consumption in response to a change in price occurring over and above the effect that one would expect merely on account of the induced change in real income (with unchanged relative prices).

**Table 1.23** Per capita cereal
consumption in urban Maharashtra,
1970–1978

| Year | Per capita cereal consumption (kg/month) |
|------|------------------------------------------|
| 1970–1 | 9.75 |
| 1972–3 | 8.95 |
| 1973–4 | 9.24 |
| 1977–8 | 9.92 |

*Source*: National Sample Survey (25th, 27th,
28th, and 32nd Rounds), as reported in *Sarvek-shana*, Jan. 1979: 133, and Draft Report No.
311 of the National Sample Survey.

'cereals') is subject to strong income *and* substitution effects at *all* income levels.[173] There are, however, good reasons to be cautious in interpreting these results,[174] and even if they are valid 'at the sample mean', they become quite suspect in the kind of price and income ranges relevant to a drought situation. This said, it is interesting to note that at least one clear case of a significant substitution effect can be detected for the Maharashtra drought: urban consumption of cereals fell in 1972–3 in response to sharp price increases, even though cereals appear to be an 'inferior' commodity group in urban Maharashtra (Table 1.23).[175]

One should not, of course, exaggerate the extent to which limited food supplies can be fairly 'shared' through the prices–incomes mechanism. In the event of a severe food shortage, the scope for redistribution will inevitably be limited. Further, it cannot be disputed that food entitlements are generally easier to protect the more comfortable the state of food supplies. Cash relief schemes should not (and need not) *substitute* for public involvement in food supply management.

The argument of this section can be summarized as follows. It is tempting to believe that, in a situation of severe food availability decline, the restraint of consumption will inevitably be concentrated on the poorest groups. Careful

[173] On this, see particularly the review of evidence in Alderman (1986).

[174] In the case of India, the need for caution arises particularly from (1) the virtually universal use of a single source of data (the National Sample Survey) in econometric studies of consumption; (2) the common practice of estimating functional forms (such as the Linear Expenditure System and its variants) which impose very strong a priori restrictions on substitution effects (or their relation to income effects); (3) the striking robustness, noted above, of cereal consumption for individual States in non-drought years.

[175] For evidence that cereals are an inferior commodity in urban Maharashtra, see e.g. the results of the 27th Round of the National Sample Survey reported in the Jan. 1979 issue of *Sarvekshana*.

reasoning as well as empirical evidence do not lend support to this presumption, at least for India. In the event of a severe crop failure, a broad section of the rural population experiences a dramatic decline in current income, to which food consumption appears to be responsive. In such a situation we can also expect food consumption to be widely responsive to price changes, if only through income effects. Hence, as long as the food deficit is not too large, income support policies for the most vulnerable groups should be successful (as they have been in Maharashtra) in spreading the burden of consumption reduction over a broad section of the population. This is not an argument for dealing with food shortages by engineering a redistribution of food from the poor to the poorest and neglecting the problem of food supply management. Rather, it is a plea to support the poorest by priority *irrespective* of the success achieved in improving food supplies. While this recommendation may sound trivial, it runs contrary to much current practice and thinking in famine relief.[176]

### (d)  Public works, public pressure and public distribution

By any criterion the drought of 1970–3 in Maharashtra must have marked an all-time record for the scale and reach of public works programmes in a famine relief operation. At the peak of employment in May 1973, nearly five million labourers attended relief works every day, and over the twelve-month period from August 1972 to July 1973 almost exactly one billion person-days of relief employment were provided. The average attendance in April–June 1973 exceeded 20 per cent of the total rural population in 7 out of 26 districts, and it was as high as 35 per cent in Bihar District.[177] Many informal as well as formal reports testify to the fact that in many villages, most of the labour force was employed on relief works. Even though real wages were very meagre, the contribution of relief works to total village income in 1972–3 was often enormous (see Table 1.24, and Table 1.36 in Appendix 1.3).

Wages were paid in cash. The idea was to enable labourers to purchase food themselves, mainly from 'Fair Price Shops' where grain rations of 12 kg per head per month were meant to be available. As was discussed earlier, the public distribution system actually met only a very small fraction of the population's food needs, and the bulk of purchases were made on the open market. The payment of cash wages ensured that delays and failures in public food delivery did not paralyse the provision of relief.

[176] It is noteworthy that even during the Maharashtra drought, when plenty of cheap food was available within India, the mode of intervention of international relief agencies still consisted mainly of importing wheat, biscuits, milk powder, and high-protein soya from countries as varied as Canada, Israel, and Australia, for direct feeding programmes.

[177] Figures calculated from Subramaniam (1975: Table II.3). Strictly speaking, these figures are based on attendance on the last day of each month. One cannot rule out a margin of exaggeration in the official employment figures, and indeed there is some discrepancy between the employment and expenditure figures reported by Subramaniam (I am grateful to Siddiq Osmani for drawing my attention to this point).

**Table 1.24** Earnings from relief works and total income in 70 drought-affected villages of Maharashtra, 1972–1973

| Contribution of earnings on relief works to total income (%) | No. of villages |
|---|---|
| 0.0–20.0 | 7 |
| 20.1–40.0 | 8 |
| 40.1–50.0 | 9 |
| 50.1–60.0 | 10 |
| 60.1–70.0 | 14 |
| 70.1–80.0 | 15 |
| 80.1–90.0 | 6 |
| 90.1–100.0 | 1 |
| TOTAL | 70 |

*Source*: Brahme (1983: 59). The villages were located in the Districts of Poona, Ahmednagar, Sholapur, Aurangabad, Bhir, and Osmanabad (all severely drought affected).

The works undertaken had, initially at least, the intended 'productive' nature (as with road building, soil conservation, and irrigation works). There came a point, however, where the capacity to plan and implement productive works on an increasingly large scale came under severe strain. Among the less productive assets created under the relief programme was a mountain of nearly 30 million cubic metres of broken stones, which took years to utilize.[178] Some authors have chosen to emphasize the productive value of relief works (Ladejinsky 1973; Godbole 1973), others their wastefulness (Jaiswal and Kolte 1981; Morris 1975). There is little doubt that the total quantity of assets created was impressive, but equally clearly the average productivity of labour must have been extremely low. Serious cost–benefit studies of these questions are not available, and would in any case face extremely complex methodological problems.[179]

Productive achievements, however, are certainly not the most important aspect of public works in the context of famine relief. While this is not the place to go into a discussion of the general merits and shortcomings of employment provision as a relief strategy, the Maharashtra experience does underline particularly clearly a number of positive features of the approach. Special mention should be made of the effectiveness of public works as a 'selection mechanism'.

The importance of the 'selection problem' for famine prevention strategies

---

[178] Subramaniam (1975: 185). In some parts of Maharashtra the drought is remembered as 'the drought of stone-breaking'.

[179] For a brave attempt at solving some of these problems, see Mundle (1974a, 1974b).

has been discussed elsewhere.[180] Any relief system must come to grips with the challenge of defining and reaching the population entitled to public support. In this context, a dilemma often arises between the 'security objective' and the 'targeting objective'. The security objective refers to the need to ensure that all those at risk of starvation are protected. The targeting objective is concerned with the possible importance of withdrawing public support from relatively privileged groups, in order to impart an adequately redistributive bias to the relief system.[181] The 'self-selection' feature of employment-based relief programmes is attractive from the point of view of both objectives. The experience of famine prevention in Maharashtra amply illustrates this point.

As far as the security objective is concerned, the open-ended provision of employment to all those who wished to join the relief works certainly went a very long way towards providing universal protection against starvation.[182] It may seem incredible that an actual guarantee of employment was successfully provided to a rural population of 35 million. Surely there were loopholes and people were deprived of work in many places? Because the question is so important, I have asked a large number of witnesses of the drought (in the administration, in voluntary agencies, in villages) whether they thought that the guarantee of employment had been effective in 1972–3. In the vast majority of cases the answer was basically in the affirmative, though occasional qualifications were expressed on account of short-run delays and bottlenecks.[183] And the employment figures, too, are eloquent enough.

Even more eloquent, to say the least, is Subramaniam's rather inflated but nevertheless revealing version of the story:

In every visit which was undertaken by the Chief Minister, he propounded a new slogan which in Marathi runs as 'maagel tyala kaam' or 'Work for all who want it'. The reverberations of this slogan from village to village, from worksite to worksite, coupled with the phenomenal industry displayed in the organisation of relief measures and the allotment of the necessary funds for implementing these measures, spread as it were a new gospel of faith and cheer and courage throughout the entire countryside, as a result

---

[180] See Drèze and Sen (1989), particularly ch. 7.

[181] The basic distinction between these two objectives is a familiar one in the income support literature, both for developed countries (see e.g. Atkinson 1987) as well as for developing ones (Cornia *et al.* 1987; Kumar and Stewart 1987).

[182] The guarantee of employment was supplemented with unconditional relief for those unable to work or to rely on able-bodied relatives. Unfortunately, the actual functioning of this component of the relief system has been little studied.

[183] An anonymous and impressionistic contribution to *Janata* in 1972 (Anon. 1972*a*), later quoted in Jaiswal and Kolte (1981: 19), themselves cited in Torry (1986*a*: 17), asserts that at one point in 1972 the amount of employment provided barely reached one-quarter of the amount demanded. Subramaniam himself admits that 'the number of works sanctioned in the initial stages fell far short of the number required to absorb the needy people' (Subramaniam 1975: 402), and Kulkarni also notes that 'in almost all the sample villages, scarcity works were available to the persons willing to work only since October 1972' (Kulkarni 1974: 169). There is clear evidence, however, that the lull of the first half of 1972 proved short-lived (see Fig. 1.5 below).

of which there was an electric charge in the rural atmosphere. The slogan of 'maagel tyala kaam' was not merely a myth; it was a reality.[184]

What accounted for this 'phenomenal industry' of the government machinery? Why did the Chief Minister suddenly prove so zealous and resourceful? One would like to think that humanitarian concern played a role, but other factors must obviously have been at work as well. Two different but highly complementary types of incentives can be identified here, arising respectively from the *meritocratic* nature of the Maharashtrian administration, and the *democratic* nature of Indian politics.

Meritocratic pressures were most evident in the behaviour of the District Collectors, who were often found to be incessantly working during the crisis. It must be remembered that District Collectors in India are very powerful, carefully trained, and often highly motivated individuals. In the event of a drought, they assume full responsibility for the management of relief operations typically covering several million people. This is a rare and often much awaited opportunity to achieve distinction, or, as one District Collector put it frankly, to 'boost one's ego'.[185]

Having said this, the reasons why the successful conduct of relief operations should be a cause for distinction in the first place cannot be understood without reference to the political influences and pressures which made the prevention of famine a chief preoccupation of the government. The role of opposition parties and the press in this context is obvious enough, if only from the 696 drought-related questions asked in the Maharashtra Legislative Assembly and Council in 1973 alone, as well as from the numerous journalistic reports which appeared in newspapers and periodicals such as *Economic and Political Weekly*, *Janata*, *Statesman*, *Times of India*, *Hindu*, and *Economic Times*, to mention only a few.[186] Popular demands for relief were also strongly backed by voluntary agencies (a very dynamic force in rural Maharashtra) and by local leaders (for whom the drought was an opportunity to build political capital).

Direct public pressure on the part of drought-affected populations also deserves emphatic mention. Employment for all was not only a clear instruction of the Bombay Scarcity Manual, it was also a *perceived right* which millions of poor men and (especially) women were determined to claim—if necessary

---

[184] Subramaniam (1975: 189–90). Many first-hand accounts of the public response to the drought provide a similar, if less flowery, picture of administrative dynamism.

[185] Personal communication from a former District Collector. It is hard to avoid a parallel with Mrs Thatcher's attitude during the Falklands Campaign: 'When you've spent half your political life with humdrum issues like the environment . . . it's exciting to have a real crisis on your hands' (quoted in *Pacifist*, 25/6, Nov. 1987, p. 16).

[186] A useful guide to many English-medium newspaper articles on the drought can be found in Luthra and Srinivas (1976). See also Subramaniam (1975: ch. IV.4), where many interesting details (including the figures cited above) can be found on the influence of newspapers and opposition parties during the drought. On the general role of adversarial journalism and politics in reducing the threat of famine in India, see Sen (1982), and ch. 6 in the first volume of this book.

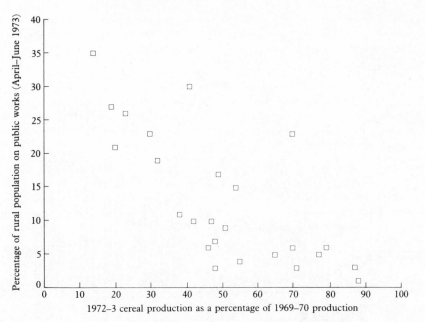

*Source*: Calculated from Subramaniam (1975: Appendix). Each point in the figure represents one District of Maharashtra.

**Fig. 1.4** Drought intensity and public relief in rural Maharashtra by District, 1972–1973

by marching, picketing, and rioting. As one labourer aptly put it, 'they would let us die if they thought we would not make a noise about it'.[187]

It is, in fact, quite interesting that relief operations, particularly employment programmes, were the focus of a great deal of radical political activity, especially on the part of rural women.[188] This observation calls into serious question the common view that public works are merely short-term relief measures, which create 'dependency' and reduce the militancy of the masses.

[187] Cited in Mody (1972: 2483). Many vivid accounts of popular protest during the drought can be found in the columns of *Economic and Political Weekly* (see e.g. Mody 1972, Anon. 1973, and Patil, 1973). Women were commonly found to be 'more vociferous and articulate in voicing their needs and complaints than men' (Padgaonkar 1973). On this see also Bhatia (1986).

[188] On the long-term influence of drought-related political activity on the women's movement in Maharashtra, see Omvedt (1980). The success of a State-wide strike by relief labourers for higher wages in 1973 is another example. It could be argued, of course, that political activism had more to do with the impoverishment of the masses during the drought than with the relief operations. However, solidarity and organization are not typical features of famine situations, which lead more commonly to unorganized revolt and increasing individualism. See Kynch (1988), and Drèze and Sen (1989: chs. 4 and 5).

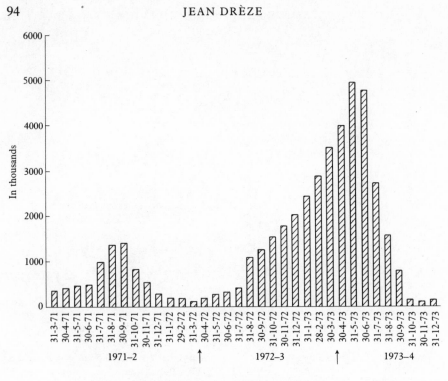

*Source*: Subramaniam (1975: Appendix).

**Fig.** 1.5 Month-by-month labour attendance on relief works in Maharashtra, 1971–1973

Turning to the 'targeting' objective, we can examine the redistributive effects of employment programmes along four distinct dimensions: (1) between areas more or less vulnerable to famine, (2) over time, (3) between different socio-economic groups at a given time and place, and (4) between different household members.

As far as the distribution of relief between different areas is concerned, Fig. 1.4 indicates a striking correlation, across Districts, between 'vulnerability' (as measured by the extent of crop failures) and 'relief' (as measured by the percentage of the rural population employed in relief works).

Regarding distribution over time, Fig. 1.5 suggests that relief operations in 1972–3 were highly concentrated on the period when the threat of famine was most serious: the summer months from April to June when, in the absence of relief, employment comes to a standstill and household resources run out. In both these respects (targeting over space and time), the Maharashtra experience sharply contrasts with the all too familiar nightmare of relief arriving at the wrong time and/or in the wrong place.

The distribution of relief between different socio-economic groups at a given time and place is less easy to assess. Usually the bulk of participation on public works schemes in India is accounted for by agricultural labourers, sometimes joined (particularly in non-irrigated areas) by marginal or small farmers. Income support through public works therefore typically assumes a strongly redistributive character.[189] During very severe droughts, however, the participation of cultivators is observed to increase sharply.[190] For this reason, the distribution of work in Maharashtra in 1972–3 was less progressive than usual if one takes landholding size as an indication of ordinary prosperity. In fact, the available evidence suggests that, during the peak months of the crisis and in the worst-affected districts, only a small measure of inverse correlation between household income from relief works and landholding size survived.[191]

However, a more sharply redistributive pattern would almost certainly emerge if one considered the entire drought period. Note also that the inverse correlation between relief employment and current (non-relief) *income* must have been much stronger than that between relief employment and landholding size. Indeed, large farmers were notoriously reluctant to join the crowd of lesser mortals on relief works, and those who eventually did so must have been driven by acute hardship.

Special mention should be made in this context of the employment of women on public works, because the redistributive effects of employment programmes arise partly from higher rates of female participation among the poorer groups. Maharashtra has a strong tradition of female wage labour, and women always form a very large proportion of the labour force on public works, often outnumbering men altogether. Relief works in 1972–3 were no exception to this rule.[192] Moreover, female wage labour tends to confer a low social status, and thus to be restricted to households of poor economic condition or (so-called) low caste. While in 1972–3 hardship was so widespread that no few stories of 'respectable' women joining the relief works could be heard, female participation must have remained significantly higher among

[189] This is evident, for instance, from the findings of Desai *et al.* (1979) for Gujarat in 1974–5, where participation on relief works was very strongly and inversely correlated with landholding size. Similarly, in her study of the Employment Guarantee Scheme of Maharashtra, Dandekar (1983) found that 90% of the labourers belonged to households owning less than 3 acres of land, almost always non-irrigated. See also Chen (1989: Table 43) on participation in relief works during the 1987 drought in Gujarat.

[190] This phenomenon was already commonly observed during pre-independence famines (see Bhatia 1967), and was noticed by many observers of the Maharashtra drought including the authors of most of the microstudies cited earlier. For a more recent example, relating to the drought of 1985–7 in Gujarat, see Chen (1989).

[191] On this, see Borkar and Nadkarni (1975: Table XI), Subramaniam (1975: Table IV.3(iv)), Kulkarni (1974: Table 7.21), and Brahme (1983: Table 4.13).

[192] See Dandekar (1983) for an in-depth study of female employment on public works schemes in Maharashtra (her survey of 3,080 EGS workers in 1978–9 found females to outnumber males, though official statistics put the percentage of female labour to total EGS labour at about 40% only in 1979 and 1980). In his survey of Sinnar taluka (Maharashtra) during the 1972–3 drought, Kulkarni (1974) found female labourers to be almost as numerous as male labourers on relief works, even though women were heavily underrepresented in the total working population.

Table 1.25 Female participation in relief works, Maharashtra 1972–1973

| Household class | % of female household members attending relief works | |
| --- | --- | --- |
| | Ahmednagar District | Osmanabad District |
| Large cultivators | 39.6 | 22.3 |
| Small cultivators | 47.8 | 38.8 |
| Agricultural labourers | 56.6 | 40.9 |
| Village artisans | 39.0 | 29.3 |

*Source*: Subramaniam (1975: Table IV-3(iv)).

disadvantaged groups. The only piece of evidence I could find on this question is shown in Table 1.25, and confirms the hypothesis.[193]

The issue of female participation relates closely to that of intrafamily distribution—the fourth dimension of 'targeting' mentioned earlier. It may be argued that employment-based relief strategies fail to exert a positive influence on the distribution of resources (particularly food) within households. Indeed, the popularity of feeding programmes among relief agencies arises partly from the conviction that direct feeding can strongly tilt intrahousehold distribution towards more vulnerable individuals (e.g. women or children). It has been argued elsewhere that the benefits of individual targeting have often been exaggerated, partly because in practice it is extremely hard to exert a strong influence on intrafamily distribution, and partly because intrafamily inequalities typically supplement in a relatively minor way the debilitating forces operating in a famine situation.[194] Moreover, given the high involvement of women in public employment programmes in India, and the generally positive effects of this involvement on the position of women within the family, employment-based relief strategies can be seen as having some important advantages from the point of view of intrahousehold distribution. As was discussed earlier, mortality differentials between age and sex groups do not appear to have widened during the Maharashtra drought (see Table 1.16).

The performance of public works as a selection mechanism, in terms of both

[193] Hopefully there are better reasons for women outnumbering men on public works than that 'women themselves did not like their husbands to be employed as they are not in a mood to complete the given task and ultimately women have to assist in their work' (Lodha and Khunteta 1973). A distinct possibility is that the comparatively narrow wage differentials between men and women on public works make this employment opportunity relatively more attractive to women, who experience strong wage discrimination on the private labour market. Surveys carried out in Poona, Ahmednagar, and Osmanabad Districts of Maharashtra in 1972–3 indicate wage differentials of the order of 20% on relief works, arising mainly from the remuneration of men as 'diggers' and of women as 'carriers' (see Subramaniam 1975: 613, and Brahme 1983: 102–3).

[194] See Drèze and Sen (1989: chs. 4, 5, 7). On the general question of intrafamily distribution of food in India, see ch. 10 in the first volume of this book. Gender issues in relation to Indian famines are examined in Kynch (1987) and Guz (1987).

the 'security' and 'targeting' objectives, contrasts especially favourably with that of the public distribution system. Clearly, if the resources which the Indian government was prepared to devote to famine relief in 1972–3 had been allocated through the indiscriminate (in fact, urban-biased) channel of the Fair Price Shops network, many of the impoverished labourers for whom relief was the main source of sustenance during the drought would have received too little support to survive. Once again, this is not to say that government intervention in foodgrain trade and distribution has no positive role to play. But the role of India's public distribution system needs to be put into proper perspective, because it is often given exaggerated credit for the elimination of famines in that country.[195]

The contrast between the strategy of relief works and the public distribution system also draws our attention to the merits of cash relief in this particular event. In spite of India's very considerable expertise with the logistics of food, the difficulties encountered in storing, transporting, and distributing large quantities of food made themselves very strongly felt.[196] It is quite plain that if the scale of relief had been limited by the capacity of the public distribution system to handle food, enormous hardship would have ensued. Under the cash-for-work strategy, however, the logistical resources of the public distribution system were effectively augmented by those of the private sector, and the relief system was largely protected from failures of public food delivery.

None of this, of course, amounts to a general and unqualified case in favour of the cash-for-work approach to famine relief. The choice of a relief strategy involves a broad range of issues, going well beyond the observations made in this section. Some of these issues are examined in other contributions to this book.[197]

### 1.5. Summary and conclusions

India's success in preventing droughts and other natural disasters from developing into large-scale famines since independence is not a spurious one. The entitlement system defined by the operation of the economy and the ordinary level of State provisioning leaves a large part of the population highly vulnerable to starvation in times of crisis. On several occasions, famine would undoubtedly have occurred in the absence of early and effective intervention to protect the entitlements of vulnerable groups. If the government of India can and should be criticized for having gone little further than espousing the earlier

---

[195] The public distribution system deserves credit for price stabilization, not direct income generation. The former goal depends on aggregate food supply management much more than on decentralized distribution through Fair Price Shops.

[196] See Subramaniam (1975: ch. 7) for further details.

[197] For a general discussion of alternative famine prevention strategies, see Drèze and Sen (1989).

colonial view that 'while the duty of the Government is to save life, it is not bound to maintain the labouring community at its normal level of comfort',[198] the measure of success it has achieved in the pursuit of this narrow objective is, by international standards, impressive.

At a general level, a reliable system of famine prevention can be seen to consist essentially of two distinct elements. The first is an intelligent and well-planned intervention procedure, based on a sound understanding of how the entitlements of vulnerable sections of the population may be threatened and can be protected. The second is a mechanism to ensure that an early decision to act is taken by the responsible authorities in the event of a crisis. This part of the system has, inevitably, an important political dimension. At the risk of some oversimplification, the emergence of these two components of India's famine prevention system can be traced to two historical milestones: the birth of the Famine Codes at the end of the nineteenth century, and the achievement of independence in 1947.

The Famine Commission of 1880 saw the loss of employment and wages for agricultural labourers and artisans during droughts as the primary cause of famines, while it pronounced that food was rarely in short supply for the country as a whole. Accordingly, the famine relief strategy embodied in the Famine Codes consisted of generating purchasing power in affected areas, and letting private trade ensure the physical supply of food. Moreover, the preferred income transfer mechanism consisted of open-ended public works supplemented by 'gratuitous relief' for the weak. The self-selection feature of relief works was relied upon to ensure financial economy while providing a universal guarantee against starvation. These principles remain at the core of the Scarcity Manuals of independent India.

It would be simplistic, however, to regard India's present relief system as a mere legacy of the British administration. In fact, important changes have occurred since independence. Some of these changes relate to the practicalities of a strategy of entitlement protection. In particular, the government of independent India has resolutely entered the previously sacrosanct domain of food supply management, and ensured a large measure of price stability through the public distribution system. However, the more fundamental changes have occurred in the political sphere, as the undependable commitment of the British administration to preventing starvation deaths evolved into a political compulsion to respond to famine threats.

A case-study of the drought of 1970–3 in Maharashtra, while admittedly concentrating on one of the most striking successes of public action for famine prevention in India, clearly underlines the high standards of effectiveness which the relief system is capable of achieving. Against the background of a dramatic and prolonged collapse of agricultural production and food availabil-

---

[198] Circular of the Government of India No. 44F, 9 June 1883, quoted in Government of India (1901: 35).

ity, massive programmes of income generation through public employment succeeded in attracting considerable amounts of food into Maharashtra, in a situation where the public distribution system had proved unequal to the task of filling the initial gap between availability and requirements. Large-scale provision of employment to the deprived sections of the population was also successful in ensuring that the remaining deficit was distributed with astonishing evenness between different socio-economic groups. The effectiveness of relief measures largely explains why this devastating drought caused relatively little damage in terms of excess mortality, nutritional stress, and asset depletion.

This case-study also highlighted the crucial role played (*inter alia*) by public pressure, cash relief, and public works in averting a tragedy. Public pressure from political parties, the media, voluntary agencies, and—last but not least—affected populations themselves galvanized the government into action at an early stage and kept it on its toes throughout the crisis. Cash relief enabled the logistical resources of the public sector to be supplemented with those of the private sector, and insulated income support strategies from food delivery failures. The reliance on public works as the main income transfer mechanism ensured both a sharp concentration of resources on the needy (the 'targeting objective') and, perhaps even more importantly, the provision of a nearly universal protection against starvation (the 'security objective').

It is fit to conclude this chapter by tempering its congratulatory tone. In fact, it can be argued that the diagnosis of success in crisis management is contingent upon the existence of acute and lasting famine vulnerability in the first place. The disappearance of large-scale famines in India has indeed coexisted with the resilient persistence of mass poverty and hunger. As with the prevention of famines, public action will be a crucial ingredient of success in confronting this colossal and inadmissible failure.

# Appendix 1.1: Mortality in Bihar, 1966–1967

This Appendix presents some evidence on the impact of the food crisis of 1966–7 in Bihar on mortality rates. The findings are discussed in the text (section 1.3*b*).

**Table 1.26** Death rate in rural Bihar (Sample Registration Scheme)

| Period | Source | |
|--------|--------|---|
| | Singh | *Sample Registration Bulletin* |
| July 1966–July 1967 | 16.8 | |
| Aug. 1966–July 1967 | | 15.4 |
| July 1966–Dec. 1966 | 16.9 | 16.9 |
| Jan. 1967–June 1967 | 14.2 | |
| July 1966–June 1967 | | 15.7 |
| July 1967–June 1968 | 13.2 | 15.0 |
| July 1967–Dec. 1967 | 10.3 | |
| Nov. 1966–Oct. 1967 | | 14.6 |
| Jan. 1968–June 1968 | 11.6 | 11.8 |
| 1968 | | 14.9 |
| 1970 | | 14.5 |
| 1971 | | 14.6 |
| Jan.–June 1971 | | 12.7 |
| July–Dec. 1971 | | 16.9 |
| 1972 | | 19.0 |
| Jan.–June 1972 | | 15.1 |
| July–Dec. 1972 | | 22.6 |

*Note*: It can be seen that the figures reported by Singh are internally inconsistent (since 16.8 could hardly be an average of 16.9 and 14.2 with roughly equal weights), and also in conflict with the official figures of the *Sample Registration Bulletin*.

*Source*: Singh (1975: 243) and *Sample Registration Bulletin*, 1968, 1973, and 1974, various issues.

**Table 1.27** Rural death rate in Bihar and India,
1963–1964 and 1966–1967 (National Sample Survey)

| Period | Bihar | India |
|---|---|---|
| Feb. 1963–Jan. 1964 | 10.1 | 12.4 |
| July 1966–June 1967 | 12.4 | 10.4 |

*Notes*: The individual observations consist of a death rate for
365 days before the date of interview. Hence, the reference
period '1963–4' (say) strictly speaking spans the period
Feb. 1962–Jan. 1964, but with a very small weight on the
beginning of the latter period.

*Source*: National Sample Survey, Report Nos. 175 (18th
Round) and 210 (21st Round).

**Table 1.28** Registered deaths in Gaya, Palamau, and Hazaribagh Districts of Bihar
and in Bihar as a whole, 1966–1968

| | Death rate (per 000) | | | Infant mortality rate (per 000 live births) | | |
|---|---|---|---|---|---|---|
| | 1966 | 1967 | 1968 | 1966 | 1967 | 1968 |
| Gaya | 14.7 | 24.6 | 8.1 | 107 | 132 | 63 |
| Palamau | 13.5 | 17.1 | 13.6 | 93 | 112 | 60 |
| Hazaribagh | 11.3 | 22.7 | 10.7 | 62 | 63 | 42 |
| Bihar | 11.4 | 13.9 | 10.4 | 74 | 72 | 51 |

*Source*: *Annual Report on Vital Statistics of Bihar, 1968* (Patna: Government of Bihar), and
*Condensed Annual Vital Statistics Report for the Years 1966 and 1967* (Patna: Government of Bihar).

**Table 1.29** Singh's mortality estimates for Gaya, Palamau, Hazaribagh, and Bihar,
1966–1967

| Period | Death rate | | | |
|---|---|---|---|---|
| | Gaya | Palamau | Hazaribagh | Bihar |
| July 1966–Dec. 1966 | 17.2 | 19.2 | 19.8 | 16.9 |
| July 1967–Dec. 1967 | 16.6 | 12.6 | 12.3 | 10.3 |

*Source*: Singh (1975: 243), who presents this as data collected by the Sample Registration Scheme
(but see Table 1.26 above).

# Appendix 1.2: Food Consumption Adjustments during Drought Years in Rural India

This Appendix presents some evidence on food consumption adjustments by different socio-economic groups during drought years in Maharashtra, Gujarat, Karnataka, Rajasthan, and Tamil Nadu. It clearly emerges that even the relatively privileged classes often substantially reduce their food consumption in drought years, rather than maintaining ordinary food consumption levels by depleting their assets (see section 1.4b for further discussion).

**Table 1.30** Food consumption and asset depletion for a sample of 52 farming households from a village in Jodhpur District, Rajasthan, 1963–1964 (drought year)

(a)

| Foodgrain consumption class (gm/day) | % of households in each consumption class | | | | | | |
|---|---|---|---|---|---|---|---|
| | Oct. 1963 | Nov. 1963 | Dec. 1963 | Jan. 1964 | Feb. 1964 | Mar. 1964 | Apr. 1964 |
| 300–450 | 7.7 | 21.3 | 34.6 | 48.1 | 57.7 | 60.5 | 69.2 |
| | (—) | (—) | (1.9) | (5.7) | (3.8) | (5.7) | (7.6) |
| 451–600 | 21.2 | 25.0 | 38.5 | 34.6 | 35.5 | 32.7 | 25.0 |
| | (67.3) | (73.0) | (69.2) | (74.9) | (76.8) | (78.7) | (78.7) |
| 601–750 | 71.1 | 53.8 | 26.9 | 17.3 | 5.8 | 5.8 | 5.8 |
| | (32.7) | (27.0) | (28.9) | (19.4) | (20.4) | (15.4) | (13.9) |

(b)

| Asset depletion step | % of households which took the indicated step | | | | | | |
|---|---|---|---|---|---|---|---|
| | Oct. 1963 | Nov. 1963 | Dec. 1963 | Jan. 1964 | Feb. 1964 | Mar. 1964 | Apr. 1964 |
| Sold inventories | 22.9 | 40.9 | 55.0 | 50.1 | 52.2 | 35.3 | 36.7 |
| Sold assets | — | 1.4 | — | — | 2.1 | 0.7 | 4.2 |
| Mortgaged assets | 0.7 | — | 2.8 | 5.6 | 14.5 | 26.4 | 22.2 |

*Notes*: Figures in parentheses indicate the corresponding details for the year *following* the drought year.

'Inventories' here refer to items such as fuel wood, dung cakes, timbers, ropes and mats, spun wool, ghee, pickles, stocks of provisions, clothing, etc. (see Jodha 1975: 1620).

*Source*: Jodha (1975: 1613, 1615).

**Table 1.31** Changes in cereal consumption for 108 households in Dandhuka taluka, Gujarat, 1974–1975

| Household class and nature of change | All cereals | Wheat | Rice | Jowar | Bajra | No. of households |
|---|---|---|---|---|---|---|
| *Large cultivators* | | | | | | 24 |
| Increased | — | 5 | — | 22 | 14 | |
| Decreased | 75 | 22 | 59 | 5 | 7 | |
| Stopped | — | — | 23 | — | 36 | |
| No change | 25 | 73 | 18 | 73 | 43 | |
| *Medium cultivators* | | | | | | 24 |
| Increased | — | — | — | 7 | 7 | |
| Decreased | 75 | 23 | 65 | — | 29 | |
| Stopped | — | — | 15 | — | 50 | |
| No change | 25 | 77 | 20 | 93 | 14 | |
| *Small cultivators* | | | | | | 24 |
| Increased | — | 5 | — | 10 | 6 | |
| Decreased | 85 | 32 | 35 | 20 | 50 | |
| Stopped | — | — | 47 | — | 19 | |
| No change | 15 | 63 | 18 | 70 | 25 | |
| *Labourers* | | | | | | 30 |
| Increased | — | 7 | — | 9 | 14 | |
| Decreased | 47 | 33 | 36 | 22 | 29 | |
| Stopped | — | — | 29 | — | — | |
| No change | 53 | 60 | 35 | 69 | 57 | |
| *Artisans* | | | | | | 6 |
| Increased | — | — | — | — | — | |
| Decreased | 50 | — | 50 | — | 33 | |
| Stopped | — | — | 50 | — | — | |
| No change | 50 | 100 | — | 100 | 67 | |

*Note*: Each entry in the table indicates the percentage of households which were consuming the specified item in 1973–4 (a good year) and adopted the specified 'change' in 1974–5 (a severe drought year). Maize was not consumed by any household in 1973–4 and for this reason does not appear in the table.

*Source*: Desai *et al.* (1979: 4–5, 72).

**Table 1.32** Consumption of foodgrains in Gujarat and Rajasthan villages, 1970–1971 (normal year) and 1969–1970 (drought year) (gm/adult unit/day)

| Size of operational holding | Gujarat | | | Rajasthan | | |
|---|---|---|---|---|---|---|
| | Normal year (1970–1) | Drought year (1969–70) | No. of households | Normal year (1970–1) | Drought year (1969–70) | No. of households |
| 'Big' | 956 | 895 (94%) | 1 | 668 | 593 (89%) | 7 |
| 'Large' | 996 | 780 (78%) | 10 | 715 | 605 (85%) | 17 |
| 'Medium' | 812 | 732 (90%) | 29 | 595 | 507 (85%) | 40 |
| 'Small' | 648 | 577 (89%) | 36 | 612 | 512 (84%) | 31 |
| Non-operators | 557 | 523 (94%) | 24 | 578 | 603 (104%) | 5 |
| All households | 740 | 657 (89%) | 100 | 626 | 535 (85%) | 100 |

*Notes*: For Rajasthan, 'foodgrains' here includes foodgrain substitutes (*kair ki chhal, bhurat, chandalia*, etc.). During the drought year, the consumption of foodgrain substitutes virtually disappeared in each landholding size group, while that of foodgrains marginally increased.
Numbers in brackets indicate 'drought year' consumption as a percentage of 'normal year' consumption.

*Source*: Choudhary and Bapat (1975: 394).

**Table 1.33** Calorie and protein consumption in sample villages of Tamil Nadu during drought and non-drought years

| | Calorie consumption per adult equivalent | | | Protein consumption (gm) per adult equivalent | | |
|---|---|---|---|---|---|---|
| | Drought years | | Non-drought year | Drought years | | Non-drought year |
| | 1973–4 | 1982–3 | 1983–4 | 1973–4 | 1982–3 | 1983–4 |
| Large farmers | 2,038 | 2,232 | 3,456 | 44 | 48 | 82 |
| Small farmers | 1,666 | 1,714 | 2,953 | 35 | 37 | 73 |
| Landless labourers | 1,662 | 1,783 | 2,572 | 33 | 40 | 67 |

*Source*: Pinstrup-Andersen and Jaramillo (1985: Table 6.6).

**Table 1.34** 'Disaster-avoidance strategies' reported by 365 households during the 1983 drought in Karnataka

| Type of strategy | Specific action | % of households concerned |
|---|---|---|
| Reducing consumption | Eating less food: all levels | 'Nearly all' |
| | Eating less food: to point of hunger | 35 |
| | Changing type of food eaten | 9 |
| | Spending less on festivals | 18 |
| | Spending less on clothing | 15 |
| | Postponing marriages | 7 |
| | Spending less on entertaining and visiting | 3 |
| | Removing children from school | 1 |
| Selling possessions | Animals | 6 |
| | Valuables | 2 |
| | Land | 1 |
| Employment | Changing rural employment | 3 |
| | Changing to non-rural employment | 3 |
| | Working on natural resources | 1 |
| | Some family members migrating | 2 |
| Exchange transactions | Securing loans | 13 |
| | Food from members of their community | 1 |

*Note*: This drought was far less severe than that of Maharashtra in 1970–3. On the other hand, relief operations were only undertaken on a modest scale (at least in the sample villages).

*Source*: Caldwell *et al.* (1986: Table 1).

**Table 1.35** Purchases of cereals in May–June 1973 in two villages of Aurangabad District, Maharashtra

| Household class | Quantity purchased (kg/head/month) | | No. of households | |
| --- | --- | --- | --- | --- |
| | Adul | Bhadji | Adul | Bhadji |
| Cultivating 50 acres and above | 14.2 (25.0) | 15.4 (25.0) | 1 | 1 |
| Cultivating 25–50 acres | 14.8 (25.0) | 12.6 (25.7) | 3 | 5 |
| Cultivating 15–25 acres | 14.1 (25.0) | 17.3 (26.6) | 10 | 5 |
| Cultivating 10–15 acres | 14.9 (22.8) | 14.5 (23.0) | 5 | 6 |
| Cultivating 5–10 acres | 14.5 (24.3) | 18.5 (31.2) | 22 | 7 |
| Cultivating less than 5 acres | 14.7 (23.7) | 18.7 (31.45) | 17 | 4 |
| Agricultural labour | 14.7 (25.5) | 16.4 (24.4) | 17 | 4 |
| Artisans | 13.7 (26.6) | 15.2 (29.6) | 7 | 4 |
| Others | 13.3 (28.4) | — | 10 | 0 |
| All households | 14.4 (24.9) | 15.4 (26.9) | 105 | 36 |

*Notes*: Figures in brackets indicate the percentage of purchases made at Fair Price Shops.

The authors note that 'in May and June, when they reported peak employment and earnings through scarcity works, the households purchased slightly in excess of their current requirements because of the expected rise in the prices of food articles and the decline in their incomes in the immediate future (due to discontinuance of scarcity relief works)' (Borkar and Nadkarni 1975: 58).

No indication is given about the size of initial stocks, but these were most probably negligible for most households.

*Source*: Calculated from Borkar and Nadkarni (1975: 14–15, 48–9).

# Appendix 1.3: Income and Expenditure Patterns in Drought Years in Rural Western India

This Appendix presents some evidence on the relationship between landholding size and income or expenditure in drought and non-drought years for Maharashtra and nearby States around the time of the 1970–3 drought. The findings are discussed in the text (section 1.4*c*).

**Table 1.36** Incomes in two villages of Aurangabad District, Maharashtra, 1972–1973

| Landholding size class (acres) | Village Adul | | | | | Village Bhadji | | | | |
| --- | --- | --- | --- | --- | --- | --- | --- | --- | --- | --- |
| | Household income per capita (Rs./year) | | | | No. of households surveyed | Household income per capita (Rs./year) | | | | No. of households surveyed |
| | Relief works | Farming | Other income | Total income | | Relief works | Farming | Other income | Total income | |
| >50 | 91 | — | — | 91 | 1 | 188 | 61 | 1 | 250 | 1 |
| 25–50 | 165 | −36 | 23 | 152 | 3 | 94 | 104 | 88 | 286 | 5 |
| 15–25 | 359 | −22 | 25 | 362 | 10 | 167 | −21 | 43 | 189 | 5 |
| 10–15 | 210 | −7 | 21 | 224 | 5 | 138 | −24 | 181 | 295 | 6 |
| 5–10 | 239 | −22 | 7 | 224 | 22 | 193 | −1 | 21 | 213 | 7 |
| <5 | 240 | −5 | 40 | 275 | 17 | 259 | −11 | 1 | 249 | 4 |
| Agricultural labour | 287 | 16 | 30 | 333 | 17 | 193 | 13 | 168 | 374 | 4 |
| Artisans | 169 | 56 | 79 | 304 | 7 | 183 | 63 | 65 | 311 | 4 |
| Others | 83 | −16 | 346 | 413 | 10 | | | | | |
| All households | 230 | −6 | 59 | 283 | 92 | 153 | 28 | 76 | 257 | 36 |

*Note:* Adul was much more affected by the drought than Bhadji.

*Source:* Calculated from Borkar and Nadkarni (1975: Tables I, II, and XI).

**Table 1.37** Incomes in Nasik District, Maharashtra, 'normal year' and 1972–1973

| Landholding size class (acres) | Household income per capita (Rs./year) | | Population |
|---|---|---|---|
| | 'Normal year' | 1972–3 | |
| >10 | 481 | 206 | 820 |
| 5–10 | 274 | 168 | 741 |
| 0.01–5 | 202 | 146 | 763 |
| Landless agricultural labourers | 138 | 152 | 288 |
| Other landless | 212 | 205 | 314 |
| All households | 293 | 175 | 2,926 |

*Note*: From the text in Kulkarni (1974), it seems that 'normal year' refers to 1971–2.
*Source*: Calculated from Kulkarni (1974: Tables 7.21, 7.23).

**Table 1.38** Incomes in six villages of Satara District, Maharashtra, 1972–1973

| Landholding size class (ha) | Household income per capita (Rs./year) | | No. of households surveyed |
|---|---|---|---|
| | 'Normal year' | 1972–3 | |
| >4.0 | 446 | 283 | 139 |
| 2.1–4.0 | 251 | 218 | 204 |
| 0.1–2.0 | 260 | 213 | 526 |
| Landless | 215 | 208 | 121 |
| All households | 286 | 222 | 990 |

*Note*: A very similar pattern of income changes was observed in a village of Sholapur District (Brahme 1983: 73–5). In another sample of households in Poona District, incomes were found to be unrelated to landholding size both in the drought period and in the previous year, but (1) the sample was drawn exclusively from among relief workers, and (2) the author notes that large-scale relief works were in operation during both periods (Brahme 1983: 66–8).
*Source*: Brahme (1983: 76).

**Table 1.39** Incomes in two Districts of Maharashtra, 1972–1973

| Household class | Household income per capita (Rs./month) | | | |
| --- | --- | --- | --- | --- |
| | Ahmednagar District | | Osmanabad District | |
| | Latest normal year | 1972–3 | Latest normal year | 1972–3 |
| Large cultivators | 36 | 24 | 32 | 23 |
| Small cultivators | 23 | 24 | 16 | 20 |
| Agricultural labourers | 21 | 24 | 16 | 22 |
| Village artisans | 18 | 17 | 28 | 24 |

*Note*: Small cultivators are those 'possessing' less than 7.5 standard acres of land.

*Source*: Subramaniam (1975: 436, 598). Based on a survey of 27 households for each household class in each District, carried out by the Directorate of Economics and Statistics, government of Maharashtra.

**Table 1.40** Poverty and landholding size,
Maharashtra and Gujarat, 1972–1973

| Operational holding size | % of households below the 'poverty line' | |
| --- | --- | --- |
| (acres) | Gujarat | Maharashtra |
| 0 | 36.8 | 60.0 |
| <1.0 | 44.0 | 63.6 |
| 1–2.5 | 39.8 | 66.6 |
| 2.5–5.0 | 41.2 | 59.4 |
| 5.0–7.5 | 37.3 | 58.8 |
| 7.5–10.0 | 29.9 | 57.5 |
| 10.0–20.0 | 24.4 | 47.7 |
| >20 | 13.5 | 36.1 |
| All households | 34.7 | 57.3 |

*Note*: The 'poverty line' is defined here as an expenditure level of Rs. 15/month/capita at 1960–1 prices.

*Source*: Visaria (1978), itself based on a tabulation of the 27th Round of the National Sample Survey.

**Table 1.41** Household incomes in Dandhuka taluka, Gujarat, 1972–1974

| Household class | Income per household (Rs./year) | | | | No. of households surveyed |
| --- | --- | --- | --- | --- | --- |
| | Relief works | Other wage income | Non-wage income | Total | |
| *Large farms* | | | | | |
| 1973–4 | 0 | 33 | 4,213 | 4,246 | 24 |
| 1974–5 | 240 | 121 | −764 | −403 | |
| *Medium farms* | | | | | |
| 1973–4 | 0 | 65 | 3,326 | 3,391 | 24 |
| 1974–5 | 189 | 163 | −763 | −411 | |
| *Small farms* | | | | | |
| 1973–4 | 0 | 530 | 1,242 | 1,772 | 24 |
| 1974–5 | 254 | 2,260 | −87 | 427 | |
| *Landless labourers* | | | | | |
| 1973–4 | 0 | 826 | 17 | 843 | 30 |
| 1974–5 | 447 | 413 | 7 | 867 | |
| *Landless artisans* | | | | | |
| 1973–4 | 0 | 1,533 | 0 | 1,533 | 6 |
| 1974–5 | 442 | 799 | 0 | 1,241 | |

*Note*: 1974–5 was a drought year in Gujarat, but *not* 1973–4.
*Source*: Desai *et al.* (1979: 4–5, 65).

**Table 1.42** Household incomes in Panchmahal District, Gujarat, 1972–1973

| Landholding size (ha) | Income per household (Rs./year) | | | No. of households surveyed |
| --- | --- | --- | --- | --- |
| | Farm | Non-farm | Total | |
| Above 5.0 | 7,585 | 41 | 7,627 | 8 |
| 4.1–5.0 | 7,055 | 1,428 | 8,482 | 5 |
| 3.1–4.0 | 4,084 | 1,298 | 5,382 | 8 |
| 2.1–3.0 | 2,951 | 437 | 3,388 | 19 |
| 1.1–2.0 | 1,827 | 950 | 2,777 | 97 |
| 0.1–1.0 | 1,180 | 633 | 1,813 | 57 |
| Landless | 0 | 1,325 | 1,325 | 5 |
| All classes | 2,156 | 809 | 2,964 | 199 |

*Source*: Sambrani and Pichholiya (1975: 95–6).

**Table 1.43** Household expenditure in rural Gujarat and Rajasthan, 1969–1970 and 1970–1971

| Size of operational holding | Total household expenditure (Rs./year) | | | |
|---|---|---|---|---|
| | Gujarat | | Rajasthan | |
| | Normal year (1970–1) | Drought year (1969–70) | Normal year (1970–1) | Drought year (1969–70) |
| Big | 3,985 | 5,087 | 1,489 | 1,378 |
| Large | 3,693 | 3,812 | 1,950 | 1,743 |
| Medium | 2,124 | 1,595 | 1,766 | 1,581 |
| Small | 1,305 | 1,203 | 1,135 | 1,019 |
| Non-operators | 1,010 | 855 | 916 | 1,137 |
| All households | 1,737 | 1,532 | 1,540 | 1,398 |

*Note*: Data collected from two samples of 100 households each from villages of Gujarat and Rajasthan.

*Source*: Choudhary and Bapat (1975: Table V.6).

**Table 1.44** Incomes in 15 villages of drought-prone Districts of Andhra Pradesh, Karnataka, and Tamil Nadu, 1978–1979

| Household class | Total income per household (Rs./year) | | | |
|---|---|---|---|---|
| | Anantapur (Andhra Pradesh) | Bijapur (Karnataka) | Coimbatore (Tamil Nadu) | All villages |
| Large farmers (above 10 ha) | 37,906 | 24,753 | 91,732 | 51,464 |
| All cultivators | 4,669 | 3,408 | 9,921 | 5,999 |
| Marginal farmers (below 1 ha) | 2,201 | 2,067 | 5,082 | 3,117 |
| Agricultural labourers | 1,942 | 1,812 | 2,954 | 2,236 |
| Artisans | 3,231 | 11,051 | 5,269 | 6,517 |
| Others | 4,442 | 3,137 | 8,609 | 5,396 |
| All households | 3,676 | 3,094 | 6,308 | 4,359 |

*Source*: Nadkarni (1985: Table 9.1). The year 1978–9 was *not* a drought year.

# References

AGARWAL, BINA (1988), 'Social Security and the Family: Coping with Seasonality and Calamity in Rural India', paper presented at a workshop on Social Security in Developing Countries held at the London School of Economics, July 1988; to be published in Ahmad, S. E., Drèze, J. P., Hills, J., and Sen, A. K. (eds.), *Social Security in Developing Countries* (Oxford: Oxford University Press).

Agricultural Economics Research Centre, Allahabad (1972), *Study of Drought Conditions in Dolchi*, Ad Hoc Study No. A.2(a) (Allahabad: AERC).

ALAMGIR, M. (1980), *Famine in South Asia* (Cambridge, Mass.: Oelgeschlager, Gunn & Hain).

ALDERMAN, HAROLD (1986), *The Effect of Food Price and Income Changes on the Acquisition of Food by Low-Income Households* (Washington, DC: IFPRI).

AMBIRAJAN, S. (1971), 'Political Economy and Indian Famines', *South Asia*, 1.

——(1976), 'Malthusian Population Theory and Indian Famine Policy in the Nineteenth Century', *Population Studies*, 30.

——(1978), *Classical Political Economy and British Policy in India* (Cambridge: Cambridge University Press).

Anon. (1972*a*), 'Scarcity: Government Accepts Reality but Fails to Do its Duty', *Janata*, 27/42–3.

Anon. (1972*b*), 'For Most, Metal-Breaking', *Economic and Political Weekly*, 7.

Anon. (1973), 'Food Riots: Hungry Stomachs Must Hunger On', *Economic and Political Weekly*, 28 Apr.

Anon. (1987), 'A Historical View of Famines and Famine Policy', mimeo (Ahmedabad: Centre for Social Knowledge and Action).

APPADURAI, A. (1984), 'How Moral is South Asia's Economy? A Review Article', *Journal of Asian Studies*, 43.

ATKINSON, A. B. (1987), 'Income Maintenance and Social Insurance: A Survey', in Auerbach, A., and Feldstein, M. S. (eds.), *Handbook of Public Economics* (Amsterdam and New York: North-Holland).

AYKROYD, W. R. (1974), *The Conquest of Famine* (London: Chatto & Windus).

BAISHYA, P. (1975), 'Man-Made Famine', *Economic and Political Weekly*, 10.

BANDYOPADHYAY, J. (1987), *Ecology of Drought and Water Scarcity* (Dehradun: Research Foundation for Science and Ecology).

BARDHAN, KALPANA (1977), 'Rural Employment, Wages and Labour Markets in India: A Survey of Research', *Economic and Political Weekly*, 12.

BATES, CRISPIN (1985), review of *Subject to Famine* (McAlpin 1983), *Modern Asian Studies*, 19/4.

BERG, ALAN (1972), 'Famine Contained: Notes and Lessons from the Bihar Experience', *Tropical Science*, 2; also in Blix *et al.* (1971).

——(1973), 'Nutrition in Disasters: A Case Study', Appendix A in Berg, A., *The Nutrition Factor* (Washington, DC: Brookings Institution).

BHAGWATI, J., and CHAKRAVARTY, S. (1969), 'Contributions to Indian Economic Analysis: A Survey', Supplement to *American Economic Review*, Sept.

BHALLA, G. S., and ALAGH, Y. K. (1979), *Performance of Indian Agriculture: A District-Wise Study* (New Delhi: Sterling Publishers).

BHATIA, BELA (1986), 'Drought Relief Work in North Sabarkantha: A Reality', mimeo (Ahmedabad: Centre for Social Knowledge and Action).

——(1988), 'Official Drought Relief Measures: A Case Study of Gujarat', *Social Action*, 38.

BHATIA, B. M. (1967), *Famines in India 1860–1965* (London: Asia Publishing House).

——(1975), 'Famine and Agricultural Labour in India: A Historical Perspective', *Indian Journal of Industrial Relations*, 10.

BHATTACHARYA, N., COONDOO, D., MAITI, P., and MUKHERJEE, R. (1985), *Relative Price of Food and the Rural Poor: The Case of India* (Calcutta: Indian Statistical Institute).

BLAIR, C. (1874), *Indian Famines: Their Historical, Financial and Other Aspects* (Edinburgh and London: W. Blackwood & Sons).

BLIX, G., HOFVANDER, Y., and VAHLQUIST, B. (eds.) (1971), *Famine: Nutrition and Relief Operations* (Uppsala: Swedish Nutrition Foundation).

BLYN, G. (1966), *Agricultural Trends in India, 1891–1947* (Philadelphia, Penn.: University of Pennsylvania Press).

BORKAR, V. V., and NADKARNI, M. V. (1975), *Impact of Drought on Rural Life* (Bombay: Popular Prakashan).

BRAHME, S. (1973), 'Drought in Maharashtra', *Social Scientist*, 12 July.

——(1983), *Drought in Maharashtra 1972*, Gokhale Institute Series No. 68 (Pune).

BRASS, PAUL (1986), 'Political Uses of Famine', *Journal of Asian Studies*, 45.

BREMAN, JAN (1974), *Patronage and Exploitation* (Oxford: Oxford University Press).

BRENNAN, LANCE (1984), 'The Development of the Indian Famine Codes: Personalities, Politics and Policies', in Currey and Hugo (1984).

——(1988), 'Government Famine Relief in Bengal, 1943', *Journal of Asian Studies*, 47.

CAHILL, KEVIN (ed.) (1982), *Famine* (New York: Orbis Books).

CAIN, M. (1981), 'Risk and Insurance: Perspectives on Fertility and Agrarian Change in India and Bangladesh', *Population and Development Review*, 7.

CALDWELL, J. C., REDDY, P. H., and CALDWELL, P. (1986), 'Periodic High Risk as a Cause of Fertility Decline in a Changing Rural Environment: Survival Strategies in the 1980–1983 South Indian Drought', *Economic Development and Cultural Change*, 34.

CARLSON, D. G. (1982), 'Famine in History: With a Comparison of Two Modern Ethiopian Disasters', in Cahill (1982).

CARLYLE, R. W. (1900), 'Famine in a Bengal District in 1896–1897', *Economic Journal*, 10.

Central Institute of Research and Training in Public Cooperation (1969), *Famine Relief in Bihar: A Study* (New Delhi: CIRTPC).

——(1970), *People can Avert Famine* (New Delhi: CIRTPC).

——(1971), *Famine Relief and Reconstruction (Report of a Workshop)* (New Delhi: CIRTPC).

Centre for Social Studies (1988), *Drought and Famine 1980s: Crises and Response* (Surat: Centre for Social Studies).

CHANDRA, N. K. (1982), 'Long-Term Stagnation in the Indian Economy, 1900–75', *Economic and Political Weekly*, 17.

CHARLESWORTH, N. (1982), *British Rule and the Indian Economy 1800–1914* (London: Macmillan).

CHATTERJEE, B. B., and SRIVASTAVA, H. P. (1968), *Challenge of Famine: A Study of the Working of Free Relief Kitchens in Naugarh, Varanasi* (Varanasi: Amitabh Prakashan).

CHEN, MARTHA (1989), 'A Gamble on the Monsoon: Coping with Seasonality and Drought in Western India', Ph.D. thesis, Harvard Institute for International Development; to be published as a monograph.

CHETTY, V. K., and RATHA, D. K. (1987), 'The Unprecedented Drought and Government Policies', mimeo (New Delhi: Indian Statistical Institute).

CHOUDHARY, K. M., and BAPAT, M. T. (1975), 'A Study of Impact of Famine and Relief Measures in Gujarat and Rajasthan', Research Study No. 44 (Ahmedabad: Agricultural Economics Research Centre, Sardar Patel University).

CHRISTENSEN, R. O. (1984), 'Famine and Agricultural Economy: A Case Study of Haryana during the British Period', *South Asian Studies*, 1.

Club du Sahel (1977), *Marketing, Price Policy and Storage of Food Grain in the Sahel: A Survey* (University of Michigan: Center for Research on Economic Development).

CORNIA, G., JOLLY, R., and STEWART, F. (1987), *Adjustment with a Human Face* (Oxford: Oxford University Press).

CURLEY, D. L. (1977), 'Fair Grain Markets and Mughal Famine Policy in Late Eighteenth-Century Bengal', *Calcutta Historical Journal*, 2.

CURREY, B., ALI, M., and KOHMAN, N. (1981), *Famine: A First Bibliography* (Washington, DC: Agency for International Development).

——and HUGO, G. (eds.) (1984), *Famine as a Geographical Phenomenon* (Dordrecht: Reidel).

DANDEKAR, KUMUDINI (1983), *Employment Guarantee Scheme: An Employment Opportunity for Women* (Pune: Orient Longman).

DANDEKAR, V. M., and PETHE, V. P. (1962), *A Survey of Famine Conditions in the Affected Regions of Maharashtra and Mysore (1952–53)* (Pune: Gokhale Institute of Politics and Economics).

DANDO, WILLIAM (1980), *The Geography of Famine* (New York: John Wiley).

DESAI, G. M., SINGH, G., and SAH, D. C. (1979), *Impact of Scarcity on Farm Economy and Significance of Relief Operations*, CMA Monograph No. 84 (Ahmedabad: Indian Institute of Management).

DIGBY, WILLIAM (1878), *Famine Campaign in Southern India*, 2 vols. (London: Longmans, Green & Co.).

DRÈZE, JEAN (1986), 'Famine Prevention in India', draft paper presented at a Conference on Food Strategies held at the World Institute for Development Economics Research, Helsinki, July 1986.

——(1989), 'Social Insecurity in India', mimeo (Development Economics Research Programme, London School of Economics).

——(1990), 'Famine Prevention', transcript of a presentation made at a conference on Hunger and Public Action held at WIDER (Helsinki), July 1990.

——and SEN, AMARTYA (1989), *Hunger and Public Action* (Oxford: Oxford University Press).

DUTT, R. C. (1900), *Open Letters to Lord Curzon on Famines and Land Assessment in India* (London: Kegan Paul, Trench Trubner & Co.).

——(1904), *The Economic History of India* (London: Kegan Paul, Trench Trubner; repr. 1969, New York: A. M. Kelley).

DYSON, TIM (1987), 'The Historical Demography of Berar, 1881–1980', mimeo (London School of Economics).

ETHERIDGE, A. T. (1868), *Report on the Past Famines in the Bombay Presidency* (Bombay: Education Society's Press).

FRERE, Sir BARTLE (1874), *The Bengal Famine: How it Will Be Met and How to Prevent Future Famines in India* (London: John Murray).

GANGRADE, K. D., and DHADDA, S. (1973), *Challenge and Response: A Study of Famines in India* (Delhi: Rachana Publications).

GARCIA, R. V. (1981), *Drought and Man: The 1972 Case History* (Oxford: Pergamon).

GHOSE, A. K. (1979), 'Short-Term Changes in Income Distribution in Poor Agrarian Economies: A Study of Famines with Reference to the Indian Sub-Continent', World Employment Programme Research Working Paper (Geneva: ILO).

——(1982), 'Food Supply and Starvation: A Study of Famines with Reference to the Indian Subcontinent', *Oxford Economic Papers*, 34.

GHOSH, K. C. (1944), *Famines in Bengal, 1770–1943* (Calcutta: Indian Associated Publishing Co.).

GODBOLE, A. (1973), 'Productive Works for the Rich', *Economic and Political Weekly*, 8.

GOPALAN, C. (1973), 'Nutrition Survey in Drought Areas of Maharashtra', *Hindu*, 21 Mar.

Government of Bengal (1874), *Administrative Experience Recorded in Former Famines* (Calcutta: Bengal Secretariat Press).

Government of Bihar (1957), *The Bihar Famine and Flood Relief Code* (Patna: Revenue Department).

——(1973), *Bihar Famine Report, 1966–67* (Patna: Secretariat Press).

——(undated), *Bihar Fights the Drought* (Patna: Secretariat Press).

Government of India (1880), *Report of the Indian Famine Commission 1880* (London: HMSO).

——(1898), *Report of the Indian Famine Commission 1898* (Simla: Government Central Printing Office).

——(1901), *Report of the Indian Famine Commission 1901* (Calcutta: Government Printing Office).

——(1908), *Final Report on the Famine Relief Operations in the District of Darbhanga during 1906–1907* (Calcutta: Bengal Secretariat Press).

——(1945), *Famine Inquiry Commission: Report on Bengal* (New Delhi: Manager of Publications).

——(1966), *Review of Scarcity Situation and Measures Taken to Meet It* (New Delhi: Ministry of Food, Agriculture, Community Development and Cooperation).

——(1967), 'Review of the Food and Scarcity Situation in India (January 1967, March 1967, July 1967, November 1967)' (New Delhi: Ministry of Food, Agriculture, Community Development and Cooperation).

——(1973): 'Review of Drought Situation in India', mimeo (New Delhi: Department of Food, Ministry of Agriculture).

——(1979), *Statistical Abstract, India 1978* (New Delhi: Central Statistical Organisation).

——(1986), *Economic Survey 1985–86* (New Delhi: Ministry of Finance).

Government of Maharashtra (1966), *The Bombay Scarcity Manual (draft)* (Bombay: Revenue Department).

——(1973a), *Scarcity: A Compendium of Government Orders*, 2 vols. (Bombay: Mantralaya).

——(1973*b*), *Report of the Fact Finding Committee for Survey of Scarcity Areas of Maharashtra State*, 2 vols. (Bombay: Mantralaya).

——(1974), *An Economic Review, 1973–74* (Bombay: Bureau of Economics and Statistics).

——(various years), *Maharashtra Season and Crop Report* (Bombay: Directorate of Agriculture).

GREENOUGH, PAUL (1982), *Prosperity and Misery in Modern Bengal: The Famine of 1943–1944* (Oxford: Oxford University Press).

GUHA, S. (1986), review of *Subject to Famine* (McAlpin 1983), in *Indian Economic and Social History Review*, 23.

GUZ, DEBORAH (1987), 'Population Dynamics of Famine in 19th Century Punjab, 1896–7 and 1899–1900', mimeo (London School of Economics).

HARRISS, BARBARA (1988), 'Limitations of the "Lessons from India"', in Curtis, D., Hubbard, M., and Shepherd, A. (eds.), *Preventing Famine* (London and New York: Routledge).

HARVEY, P. (1969), 'Development Potential in Famine Relief: The Bihar Model', *International Development Review*, Dec.

HEBERT, J. R. (1987), 'The Social Ecology of Famine in British India: Lessons for Africa in the 1980s?', *Ecology of Food and Nutrition*, 20.

HESTON, ALAN (1973), 'Official Yields per Acre in India, 1886–1947: Some Questions of Interpretation', *Indian Economic and Social History Review*, 10.

——(1978), 'A Further Critique of Historical Yields Per Acre in India', *Indian Economic and Social History Review*, 15.

——(1982), 'National Income', in Kumar (1982).

HOLDERNESS, T. W. (1987), *Narrative of the Famine in India in 1896–97* (Simla: Government Central Printing Office).

HUBBARD, MICHAEL (1988), 'Drought Relief and Drought Proofing in the State of Gujarat, India', in Curtis, D., Hubbard, M., and Shepherd, A. (eds.), *Preventing Famine* (London and New York: Routledge).

Indian Institute of Public Administration (1967), *Administrative Survey of the Food and Relief Organisation of the Bihar Government* (New Delhi: IIPA).

——(n.d.), *Crisis Administration* (New Delhi: IIPA).

JAISWAL, N. K. (1978), *Droughts and Famines in India* (Hyderabad: National Institute of Rural Development).

——and KOLTE, N. V. (1981), *Development of Drought-Prone Areas* (Hyderabad: National Institute of Rural Development).

JODHA, N. S. (1975), 'Famine and Famine Policies: Some Empirical Evidence', *Economic and Political Weekly*, 10.

——(1978), 'Effectiveness of Farmers' Adjustment to Risk', *Economic and Political Weekly*, 13.

——(1980), 'The Process of Desertification and the Choice of Interventions', *Economic and Political Weekly*, 15.

——(1981), 'Role of Credit in Farmers' Adjustment against Risk in Arid and Semi-arid Tropical Areas of India', *Economic and Political Weekly*, 16.

——ASOKAN, M., and RYAN, J. G. (1977), 'Village Study Methodology and Resource Endowment of the Selected Villages', Economics Program Occasional Paper No. 16 (Hyderabad: ICRISAT).

——and MASCARENHAS, A. C. (1985), 'Adjustment in Self-Provisioning Societies', in

Kates, R. W., Ausubel, J. H., and Berberian, M. (eds.), *Climate Impact Assessment* (New York: John Wiley).

JODHA, N. S. and WALKER, T. (1986), 'How Small Farmers Adjust to Risk', in Hazell, P., *et al.* (eds.), *Crop Insurance for Agricultural Development* (Washington, DC: IFPRI).

KACHHAWAHA, O. P. (1985), *Famines in Rajasthan* (Delhi: Hindi Sahitya Mandir).

KLEIN, IRA (1973), 'Death in India, 1871–1921', *Journal of Asian Studies*, 32.

——(1984), 'When the Rains Failed: Famine, Relief and Mortality in British India', *Indian Economic and Social History Review*, 21.

KRISHNA, R., and CHHIBBER, A. (1983), 'Policy-Modelling in a Dual Grain Market', Research Report No. 38 (Washington, DC: IFPRI).

KRISHNAMACHARI, K. A. V., *et al.* (1974), 'Food and Nutritional Situation in the Drought-Affected Areas of Maharashtra: A Survey and Recommendations', *Indian Journal of Nutrition and Dietetics*, 11.

KULKARNI, S. N. (1974), *Survey of Famine Affected Sinnar Taluka* (Pune: Gokhale Institute of Politics and Economics).

KUMAR, B. G. (1988), 'Consumption Disparities, Food Surpluses and Effective Demand Failures: Reflections on the Macroeconomics of Drought Vulnerability', Working Paper No. 229 (Trivandrum: Centre for Development Studies).

——and STEWART, FRANCES (1987), 'Tackling Malnutrition: What Can Targeted Nutritional Intervention Achieve?', paper presented at a Conference on Poverty in India, Queen Elizabeth House, Oxford, Oct.

KUMAR, DHARMA (ed.) (1982), *The Cambridge Economic History of India* vol. ii (Cambridge: Cambridge University Press).

KYNCH, JOCELYN (1987), 'Some State Responses to Male and Female Need in British India', in Afshar, H. (ed.), *Women, State and Ideology: Studies from Africa and Asia* (London: Macmillan).

——(1988), 'Scarcities, Distress and Crime in British India', paper presented at the 7th World Congress of Rural Sociology, Bologna, July.

LADEJINSKY, W. (1973), 'Drought in Maharashtra: Not in a Hundred Years', *Economic and Political Weekly*, 8.

LAL, DEEPAK (forthcoming), *The Hindu Equilibrium*, vol. ii: *Aspects of Indian Labour* (Oxford: Oxford University Press).

LARDINOIS, ROLAND (1982), 'Une conjoncture de crise démographique en Inde du Sud au XIXe siècle', *Population*, 37.

——(1985), 'Famine, Epidemics and Mortality in South India', *Economic and Political Weekly*, 20.

LIPTON, MICHAEL (1984), 'Conditions of Poverty Groups and Impact on Indian Economic Development and Cultural Change: The Role of Labour', *Development and Change*, 15.

——(1985), 'Land Assets and Rural Poverty', World Bank Staff Working Paper No. 744 (Washington, DC: World Bank).

LODHA, S. L., and KHUNTETA, B. K. (1973), *An Economic Survey of Famine in Beawar Sub-division* (Beawar: SD Government College).

LOVEDAY, A. (1914), *The History and Economics of Indian Famines* (London: A. G. Bell & Sons; repr. New Delhi: Usha Publications, 1985).

LUTHRA, S., and SRINIVAS, S. (1976), 'Famine in India: A Select Bibliography', mimeo (New Delhi: Social Science Documentation Centre).

MAC, M. R. (1988), *Drought, Famine and Water Management: A Select Bibliography* (Surat: Centre for Social Studies).

McALPIN, MICHELLE (1974), 'Railroads, Prices, and Peasant Rationality, India 1860–1900', *Journal of Economic History*, 34.

——(1975), 'Railroads, Cultivation Patterns, and Foodgrains Availability: India 1860–1900', *Indian Economic and Social History Review*, 12.

——(1980), 'Impact of Trade on Agricultural Development, Bombay Presidency', *Explorations in Economic History*, 17.

——(1982), 'Price Movements and Fluctuations in Economic Activity (1860–1947)', in Kumar (1982).

——(1983), *Subject to Famine: Food Crises and Economic Change in Western India, 1860–1920* (Princeton, NJ: Princeton University Press).

——(1985), 'Famines, Epidemics and Population Growth: The Case of India', in Rotberg, R. I., and Rabb, T. K. (eds.), *Hunger and History* (Cambridge: Cambridge University Press).

——(1987), 'Famine Relief Policy in India: Six Lessons for Africa', in Glantz, M. (ed.), *Drought and Hunger in Africa* (Cambridge: Cambridge University Press).

McMINN (1902), *Famine: Truth, Half-Truths, and Untruths* (Calcutta: Baptist Mission Press).

Maharashtra Economic Development Council (1974), *Droughts in Maharashtra* (Bombay: MEDC).

MARX, K. (1970), *Capital*, vol. ii (London: Lawrence & Wishart).

MATHUR, K., and BHATTACHARYA, M. (1975), *Administrative Response to Emergency: A Study of Scarcity Administration in Maharashtra* (New Delhi: Concept).

MAYER, JEAN (1975), 'Management of Famine Relief', in Abelson, P. H. (ed.) (1975), *Food: Politics, Economics, Nutrition and Research* (American Association for the Advancement of Science).

MENARIA, R. K. (1975), 'Famine Relief Operations in the Princely States during the British Period', *Economic Studies*, 15.

MEREWETHER, F. H. S. (1898), *A Tour Through the Famine Districts of India* (London: A. D. Innes & Co.).

MILL, J. S. (1848), *Principles of Political Economy*, ed. W. Ashley (New York: Reprints of Economic Classics, Augustus M. Kelley).

MILLS, I. D. (1986), 'The 1918–1919 Influenza Pandemic: The Indian Experience', *Indian Economic and Social History Review*, 23.

MODY, N. (1972), 'To Some, a God-Send', *Economic and Political Weekly*, 7.

MOOLEY, D. A., and PANT, G. B. (1981), 'Droughts in India over the Last 200 Years: Their Socio-economic Impact and Remedial Measures for them', in Wigley, T. M. L., Ingram, M. J., and Farmer, G. (eds.), *Climate and History* (Cambridge: Cambridge University Press).

MORRIS, M. D. (1974), 'What is a Famine?', *Economic and Political Weekly*, 9.

——(1975), 'Needed: A New Famine Policy', *Economic and Political Weekly*, 10.

MUKERJI, K. M. (1965), *Levels of Economic Activity and Public Expenditure in India: A Historical and Quantitative Study* (Bombay: Asia Publishing House).

MUKHERJEE, M. (1986), 'Statistical Information on Final Consumption in India and the National Sample Survey', *Economic and Political Weekly*, 21.

MUNDLE, S. (1974a), 'Relief Planning in Maharashtra', *Indian Journal of Public Administration*, 20.

——(1974*b*), 'Planning and Resource Deployment in Drought Relief Operations: A Study in Aurangabad District, Maharashtra, 1972–73', mimeo (New Delhi: Indian Institute of Public Administration).

MURTON, B. (1984), 'Spatial and Temporal Patterns of Famine in Southern India before the Famine Codes', in Currey and Hugo (1984).

NADKARNI, M. V. (1985), *Socio-economic Conditions in Drought-Prone Areas* (New Delhi: Concept).

NAOROJI, D. B. (1900), *Poverty and Un-British Rule in India* (London: Swan Sonnenschein & Co.).

NEWBERY, DAVID (1989), 'Agrarian Institutions for Insurance and Stabilization', in Bardhan, P. K. (ed.), *The Theory of Agrarian Institutions* (Oxford: Oxford University Press).

NOSSITER, B. D. (1967), 'Bihar's Famine Relief Viewed as a Model', *Washington Post*, 6 Nov.

OMVEDT, GAIL (1980), *We Will Smash This Prison! Indian Women in Struggle* (London: Zed).

OUGHTON, ELISABETH (1982), 'The Maharashtra Droughts of 1970–73: An Analysis of Scarcity', *Oxford Bulletin of Economics and Statistics*, 44.

OXFAM (1972, 1973), Unpublished field reports.

PADGAONKAR, D. (1973), 'Maharashtra after Rain', *Times of India*, 26–7 July.

PANDEY, S. M., and UPADHYAY, J. N. (1979), 'Effects of Drought on Rural Population: Findings of an Area Study', *Indian Journal of Industrial Relations*, 15.

PASSMORE, R. (1951), 'Famine in India: An Historical Survey', *Lancet*, 18 Aug.

PATIL, S. (1973), 'Famine Conditions in Maharashtra: A Survey of Sakri Taluka', *Economic and Political Weekly*, 8.

PINSTRUP-ANDERSEN, P., and JARAMILLO, M. (1985), 'The Impact of Technological Change in Rice Production on Food Consumption and Nutrition in North Arcot, India', mimeo (Washington, DC: IFPRI).

PLATTEAU, JEAN-PHILIPPE (1988), 'Traditional Systems of Social Security and Hunger Insurance: Past Achievements and Modern Challenges', paper presented at a Workshop on Social Security in Developing Countries held at the London School of Economics, July; to be published in Ahmad, S. E., Drèze, J. P., Hills, J., and Sen, A. K. (eds.), *Social Security in Developing Countries* (Oxford: Oxford University Press).

PRABHAKAR, M. S. (1975), 'Death in Barpeta', *Economic and Political Weekly*, 10.

RAMLINGASWAMI, V., DEO, M. G., GULERIA, J. S., MALHOTRA, K. K., SOOD, S. K., OM PRAKASH, and SINHA, R. V. N. (1971) 'Studies of the Bihar Famine of 1966–67', in Blix *et al.* (1971).

RANGASAMI, AMRITA (1978), 'A Study of Some Aspects of Famine-Affected Areas in India', unpublished Ph.D. thesis, University of Delhi.

——(1985), 'McAlpin's Capers', *Economic and Political Weekly*, 20.

——(1986), 'Mismanagement of Financing Drought Relief', paper presented at a Seminar on Control of Drought, Desertification and Famine, held at the India International Centre, New Delhi, May.

RAO, H. C. H. *et al.* (1988), *Unstable Agriculture and Droughts* (New Delhi: Vikas).

RAO, N. V. K. (1974), 'Impact of Drought on the Social System of a Telangana Village', *Eastern Anthropologist*, 27.

RASHID, S. (1980), 'The Policy of Laissez-faire during Scarcities', *Economic Journal*, 90.

RAVALLION, MARTIN (1987a), *Markets and Famines* (Oxford: Oxford University Press).

——(1987b), 'Trade and Stabilization: Another Look at British India's Controversial Foodgrain Exports', mimeo; forthcoming in *Explorations in Economic History*.

RAY, P. C. (1901), *Indian Famines: Their Causes and Remedies* (Calcutta: Cherry Press).

RAY, S. C. (1909), *Economic Causes of Famines in India* (Calcutta: Baptist Mission Press).

REDDY, G. P. (1988), 'Drought and Famine: The Story of a Village in a Semi-arid Region of Andhra Pradesh', mimeo.

RYAN, J. G., *et al.* (1984), 'The Determinants of Individual Diets and Nutritional Status in Six Villages of Southern India', Research Bulletin No. 7 (Hyderabad: ICRISAT).

SAMBRANI, S., and PICHHOLIYA, K. (1975), 'An Enquiry into Rural Poverty and Unemployment', mimeo (Ahmedabad: Indian Institute of Management).

SCARFE, W., and SCARFE, A. (1969), *Tiger On a Rein: Report on the Bihar Famine* (Melbourne: Geoffrey Chapman).

SEN, AMARTYA (1981), *Poverty and Famines* (Oxford: Oxford University Press).

——(1982), 'How is India Doing?', *New York Review of Books*, 29.

——(1986), 'India and Africa: What Do We Have to Learn from Each Other?', C. N. Vakil Memorial Lecture delivered at the Eighth World Congress of the International Economic Association, New Delhi, Dec.; pub. in Arrow, K. I. (ed.) (1988), *The Balance between Industry and Agriculture in Economic Development*, i: *Basic Issues* (London: Macmillan).

SEN, M. (1967), 'Famine in Purulia and Bankura', *Modern Review*, 121.

SEN, S. R. (1971), *Growth and Instability in Indian Agriculture* (Calcutta: Firma K. L. Mukhopadhyay).

SHUKLA, R. (1979), *Public Works during Drought and Famines and Its Lessons for an Employment Policy* (Ahmedabad: Sardar Patel Institute of Economic and Social Research).

——(1981), 'Employment Implications of Drought Situations: Issues and Experience', in *Employment, Poverty and Public Policy*, Monograph Series, No. 9 (Ahmedabad: Sardar Patel Institute of Economic and Social Research).

SINGH, S. K. (1975), *The Indian Famine, 1967* (New Delhi: People's Publishing House).

SIVASUBRAMONIAM, S. (1960), 'Estimates of Gross Value of Output of Agriculture for Undivided India, 1900–01 to 1946–47', in Rao, V. K. R. V., *et al.* (eds.), *Papers on National Income and Allied Topics*, vol. i (Bombay).

——(1965), 'National Income of India, 1900–01 to 1946–47', unpublished Ph.D. thesis, Delhi University.

SMITH, B. (1861), *Report on the North Western Provinces Famine of 1860–61* (London: HMSO).

SOMWANSKI, S. A. (1979), 'Impact of Drought on Cooperative Agricultural Credit in Aurangabad District', unpublished Ph.D. thesis, Marathwada University.

SPITZ, P. (1983), 'Food Systems and Society in India: A Draft Interim Report', mimeo (Geneva: UNRISD).

SRINIVASAN, T. N., and BARDHAN, P. K. (eds.) (1974), *Poverty and Income Distribution in India* (Calcutta: Statistical Publishing Society).

SRIVASTAVA, H. S. (1966), 'The Indian Famine 1876–79', *Journal of Indian History*, 44.
——(1968), *History of Indian Famines and Development of Famine Policy 1858–1918* (Agra: Sri Ram Mehra and Co.).
STOKES, E. (1959), *English Utilitarians and India* (Oxford: Oxford University Press).
SUBRAMANIAM, V. (1975), *Parched Earth: The Maharashtra Drought 1970–73* (Bombay: Orient Longman).
SURYANARAYANA, M. H., and IYENGAR, N. S. (1986), 'On the Reliability of NSS Data', *Economic and Political Weekly*, 21.
SVEDBERG, PETER (1987), 'Undernutrition in Sub-Saharan Africa', mimeo (Helsinki: WIDER).
SWAMINATHAN, M. C., *et al.* (1967), 'Food and Nutrition Situation in Drought-Affected Areas of Andhra Pradesh', *Indian Journal of Medical Research*, 55.
——*et al.* (1969), 'Food and Nutrition Situation in the Drought-Affected Areas of Bihar', *Journal of Nutrition and Dietetics*, 6.
TORRY, WILLIAM (1984), 'Social Science Research on Famine: A Critical Evaluation', *Human Ecology*, 12.
——(1986a), 'Drought and the Government–Village Emergency Food Distribution System in India', *Human Organization*, 45.
——(1986b), 'Morality and Harm: Hindu Peasant Adjustments to Famines', *Social Science Information*, 25.
VAIDYANATHAN, A. (1986), 'On the Validity of NSS Consumption Data', *Economic and Political Weekly*, 21.
——(1987), 'Poverty and Economy: The Regional Dimension', paper presented at a Workshop on Poverty in India held at Queen Elizabeth House, Oxford, Oct.
VERGHESE, G. (1967), *Beyond the Famine* (New Delhi: Bihar Relief Committee).
VINCENT, L. (1981), *Dry Spells, Drought Risk and Agricultural Production in Maharashtra State*, Monographs in Development Studies No. 9 (University of East Anglia).
VISARIA, L., and VISARIA, P. (1982), 'Population (1757–1947)', in Kumar (1982).
VISARIA, P. (1978), 'Size of Land Holding, Living Standards and Employment in Rural Western India, 1972–73', Working Paper No. 3 (Joint ESCAP-IBRD Project on the Evaluation of Asian Data on Income Distribution).
WALKER, T. S., SINGH, R. P., and ASOKAN, M. (1986), 'Risk Benefits, Crop Insurance, and Dryland Agriculture', *Economic and Political Weekly*, 21.
WALLACE, R. (1900), *Lecture on Famine in India* (Edinburgh: Oliver & Boyd).
World Bank (1984), 'Situation and Prospects of the Indian Economy: A Medium Term Perspective, vol. iii: Statistical Appendix', Report No. 4962-IN (India Division, World Bank).
——(1986), *Poverty and Hunger: Issues and Options For Food Security in Developing Countries* (Washington, DC: World Bank).
WRIGHT, A. (1968), 'Note on the Bihar Drought', *Journal of the Bombay Natural History Society*, 65.

# 2

# Famine Prevention in Africa:
# Some Experiences and Lessons

*Jean Drèze*

## 2.1. *Introduction*

Faith in the ability of public intervention to avert famines is a relatively new phenomenon. Not so long ago, even James Mill felt compelled to use the most fatalistic language to inform his friend David Ricardo of his apprehensions as to the consequences of a spell of adverse weather in England:

Does not this weather frighten you? . . . There must now be of necessity a very deficient crop, and very high prices—and these with an unexampled scarcity of work will produce a degree of misery, the thought of which makes the flesh creep on ones bones—one third of the people must die—it would be a blessing to take them into the streets and high ways, and cut their throats as we do with pigs.[1]

Ricardo had full sympathy for Mill's feelings, and assured him that he was 'sorry to see a disposition to inflame the minds of the lower orders by persuading them that legislation can afford them any relief'.

Fatalism to such a degree would be extremely hard to defend today. An enormous amount of evidence now bears testimony to the potential effectiveness of concerted action for famine prevention.[2] More than ever, the occurrence of a famine in the modern world is an incontrovertible sign of some massive failure of public intervention—often originating in war situations.

This observation applies as much to sub-Saharan Africa as to the rest of the world. At the risk of some oversimplification, it could be argued that even in this region the phenomenon of large-scale famine is now mainly confined to war situations. Contrary to popular belief, there is considerable evidence that famine vulnerability in sub-Saharan Africa has significantly decreased this

This chapter is an outgrowth of collaborative work with Amartya Sen, published in our book *Hunger and Public Action* (Drèze and Sen, 1989). I am most grateful to John Borton, Diana Callear, Jane Corbett, Rob Davies, Thomas Downing, Carl Eicher, Jim Gordon, Roger Hay, Judith Heyer, Renée Loewenson, Siddhartha Mitter, S. T. W. Mhiribidi, Richard Morgan, David Sanders, Lucy Spyckerelle, and Daniel Weiner for many helpful comments, suggestions, and personal communications relating to the case-studies appearing in section 2.4. I have also greatly benefited from extensive comments by Robin Burgess on an earlier draft of this chapter.

[1] Letter of Mill to Ricardo, 14 Aug. 1816. Quoted in Jacqemin (1985: Annexe historique, p. 18), where Ricardo's reply is also quoted.

[2] For a few examples of the ability of public intervention to prevent or contain famine mortality in the most diverse historical and socio-economic contexts, see Valaoras (1946), Binns (1976), Smout (1978), Will (1980), Kiljunen (1984), Otten (1986), and Drèze (1988), among many other studies.

century, and also that this reduced vulnerability is partly attributable to the improved quality of public intervention.[3] African countries, however, receive little credit for this achievement. The disasters that periodically visit (usually war-torn) countries such as Ethiopia, Sudan, or Mozambique tend to over-shadow the more positive experiences that have taken place elsewhere.

This chapter investigates some of these experiences. It will be argued that a number of impressive examples of successful famine prevention can be found in contemporary Africa, from which there is a great deal to learn. To start with, section 2.2 provides some elementary observations on the strategy of famine prevention. Section 2.3 brings out some of the perception biases which divert attention away from positive experiences of famine prevention in contemporary Africa. Section 2.4 is devoted to selected case-studies of such experiences. The last section offers some concluding remarks.

## 2.2. Famine prevention and entitlement protection

It is now well understood that famines can be fruitfully analysed as 'entitlement failures' suffered by a large section of the population.[4] Those who cannot establish command over an adequate amount of food have to perish from starvation. Famine prevention is essentially concerned, therefore, with the *protection of entitlements*. That much might be obvious enough, but a few interpretational issues should be addressed straightaway to avoid misunder-standing the content of that superficially simple message.

First, while famines involve—and are typically initiated by—starvation, many of the people who die from a famine die in fact not from starvation as such, but from various epidemic diseases unleashed by the famine. This happens primarily through the spread of infectious diseases helped by debilita-tion, attempts to eat whatever looks eatable, breakdown of sanitary arrange-ments, and massive population movements in search of food.[5] Famine preven-tion is, in fact, intimately connected with the avoidance of epidemics, even though the first and basic culprit may be the failure of food entitlements.

[3] On this see e.g. Wrigley (1976), Caldwell (1977, 1984), Bryceson (1981a, 1981b), Kates (1981), Herlehy (1984), Hugo (1984), Bernus (1986), Borton and Clay (1986), Downing (1986), Wood et al. (1986), World Food Programme (1986a), Caldwell and Caldwell (1987), de Waal (1987), Hill (1987), Iliffe (1987), Vaughan (1987), and Kates et al. (1988). Of course, it is arguable that this record of reduction in famine vulnerability remains shamefully poor when viewed against a background of rapidly increasing opulence at the world level over the same period.

[4] On the 'entitlement approach' to famine analysis, see Sen (1981). For various critiques of this approach, see Rangasami (1985), Bowbrick (1986), Devereux (1988), de Waal (1988b), Eicher (1988), and Kula (1989).

[5] This emerges clearly from a large number of empirical studies of famine mortality, including those of Foege (1971), Stein et al. (1975), Sen (1981), de Waal (1987), Dyson (1988), and O'Grada (1988), among others. Interestingly, it is also possible to find cases of famines where excess mortality has been attributed mainly to direct 'starvation deaths' (see Valaoras 1946, on the Greek famine of 1941–2, and Biellik and Henderson 1981, on the Karamoja famine of 1980). On related matters, see also Sorokin (1942), Rotberg and Rabb (1983), and Hugo (1984).

Thus, when acute deprivation has been allowed to develop, the task of containing famine mortality may require substantial attention to health care and epidemiological control. This consideration links with the general importance of seeing hunger and deprivation in terms of entitlement failures in a broader perspective than that of *food* entitlements only (see Drèze and Sen 1989). At the same time, it is important to bear in mind that in the case of famines the collapse of food entitlements is the initiating failure in which epidemics themselves originate, and that the protection of food entitlements at an early stage is often a more effective form of action than medical intervention at a later stage.[6]

Second, while the entitlement approach asserts the *inadequacy* of aggregate food availability as a focus for the analysis of famines, it does not assert its *irrelevance*. Aggregate food availability remains important, but its influence has to be seen only as an element of a more complex entitlement process. This general point is of obvious relevance in the context of analysing the causation of famines, but it also has to be borne in mind when the attention is turned to the *prevention* of famines. In particular it is important to see that (1) the improvement of food availability can play a helpful or even crucial role in preventing the development of a famine, whether or not the threat of famine is accompanied by a decline in food availability, and (2) at the same time, many other influences are at work, and a broad view should be taken of possible options for action—including that of protecting the food entitlements of vulnerable groups even when it is not possible to bring aggregate food availability to a particular level.

Third, the protection of entitlements in the short run has to be contrasted with the general promotion of entitlements in the long run. In the short run, famine prevention is essentially a question of countering an immediate threat of entitlement failure for vulnerable groups. In the long term, of course, a durable elimination of vulnerability involves more diverse areas of action, including the expansion of general prosperity, the reduction of insecurity through economic diversification, the prevention of armed conflicts, and the protection of the environment. However, even within a long-term perspective, the task of building up reliable entitlement protection systems remains quite crucial. Indeed, in most cases it would be rather naïve to expect that efforts at eliminating vulnerability could be so successful as to allow a country to dispense with distinct and specialized entitlement protection mechanisms. While famine prevention is not exclusively concerned with the protection of entitlements, much of the discussion in this chapter will concentrate on this elementary and urgent aspect of the problem.

---

[6] Empirical studies sharply bring out the effectiveness of famine prevention measures which concentrate on protecting entitlements to staple foods, supplemented with basic health care services such as vaccination, oral rehydration, and the provision of simple vitamins. See e.g. Swaminathan et al. (1969), Ramalingaswami et al. (1971), Berg (1973), Krishnamachari et al. (1974), Otten (1986), de Waal (1987) and Drèze (1988).

Fourth, the task of entitlement protection also has to be distinguished from a notion of 'famine relief' which conjures up the picture of a battle already half lost and focuses the attention on emergency operations narrowly aimed at containing large-scale mortality. Devising planned, coherent, effective, and durable entitlement protection mechanisms is a much broader enterprise. Entitlement crises have many repercussions on the rural economy and on the well-being of affected populations, and a comprehensive strategy for dealing with the scourge of famine must seek to ensure that human beings have both secure *lives* and secure *livelihoods*.

This is not just a question of immediate well-being, but also one of development prospects. Consider, for instance, the so-called 'food crisis in Africa', discussed in a number of contributions to this book (see especially Chapter 6 below). The current débâcle of agricultural production in much of sub-Saharan Africa has, not without reason, been held partly responsible for this region's continued vulnerability to famine. But one is also entitled to wonder how farmers who are condemned every so often to eat up their productive capital in a desperate struggle for survival can possibly be expected to save, innovate, and prosper. There is indeed considerable evidence of the lasting adverse effects of famine on productive potential as well as on the distribution of assets.[7] It is reasonable to think that improved entitlement protection systems in Africa would not only save lives, but also contribute to preserving and rejuvenating the rural economy. The alleged dilemma between 'relief' and 'development' is a much exaggerated one, and greater attention needs to be paid to the *positive* links between famine prevention and development prospects.

Finally, seeing famine prevention as an entitlement protection problem draws our attention to the plurality of strategies available for dealing with it. Just as entitlements can be threatened in a number of different ways, there are also typically a number of feasible routes for restoring them. Importing food and handing it over to the destitutes is one of the more obvious options. The overwhelming preoccupation of the journalistic and institutional literature on African famine relief has been with the logistics of food aid and distribution, reflecting the continued popularity of this approach. But there is a good case for taking a broader view of the possible forms of intervention, and indeed the rich history of famine prevention over the world reveals a great variety of possible strategies for the protection of entitlements.

In this respect, the sort of relief methods commonly employed in many parts of Africa today are bound to look somewhat unimaginative and unambitious. Particularly problematic are intervention strategies that are contingent on the

---

[7] See e.g. Swanberg and Hogan (1981), Chastanet (1983), de Waal (1987), Glantz (1987*b*), McCann (1987), and Hay (1988). Numerous reports on the 1983–5 famines in sub-Saharan Africa also emphasize the acute problems caused (*inter alia*) by shortages of seeds, oxen, or human labour during the recovery period, often resulting in a shrinkage of sown area and other forms of production losses.

rapid arrival of food aid from the other side of the globe.[8] While effective action is undoubtedly first and foremost a question of political motivation and pressure, it also requires a sound choice of intervention strategy. Both problems plague famine-prone countries in Africa and both need to be urgently addressed.

## 2.3. *African challenge and international perception*

It is widely believed that most African countries lack the political structure (perhaps even the commitment) for successful pursuit of comprehensive strategies of entitlement protection. There may be truth in this in some cases. The inaction and confusion of some governments in the face of crises have been striking. The role of war in exacerbating food crises in Africa also needs persistent emphasis. Nevertheless, an excessive concentration on failure stories has probably given an exaggerated impression of the apathy, incompetence, and corruption of African governments in the context of famine prevention. As was mentioned earlier, there is some evidence that the willingness and ability of many African countries to respond to crises have been improving over time, in some cases to a very considerable degree.

Furthermore, state action is not immune to the influence of political ideology, public pressure, and popular protest, and there is nothing immutable in the nature of contemporary African politics. It is, of course, true that the development of a workable system of famine prevention calls for political as well as economic restructuring, but political changes—no less than economic transformations—are responsive to determined action and popular movements.

While examining experiences of success and failure in famine prevention, it has to be recognized that international perceptions of these past experiences are often seriously distorted. In particular, for reasons of journalistic motivation (which has its positive side as well, on which more presently), the media tend to overconcentrate on stories of failure and disaster. To the extent that successes do get reported, the balance of credit is heavily tilted in favour of international relief agencies, which enjoy—and need—the sympathy of a large section of the public.

This phenomenon is well illustrated by an episode of successful famine prevention in the State of Maharashtra in India in 1972–3. The impressive success achieved at the time by the government of Maharashtra in preventing a severe drought from developing into a famine by organizing massive public works programmes (at one point employing as many as five million men and women) has been described in some detail elsewhere.[9] This event, however,

---

[8] The mode of operation of international agencies bears some responsibility for the perpetuation of these intervention strategies. See McLean (1988) for a perceptive discussion of this issue.

[9] See ch. 1 in this volume.

caused very few ripples in the Western press, and received extraordinarily little attention from social scientists outside India until recently.[10]

While the government of Maharashtra was employing millions of people on relief works, various international agencies were involved in feeding programmes on a relatively tiny scale—often importing modest amounts of wheat, biscuits, and milk powder from the other side of the globe. However, the role of the latter appeared to be oddly exaggerated. One of the relief organizations —indeed one that has altogether distinguished itself for many years by its far-sighted initiatives and actions—had no hesitation in reporting in its *Bulletin* how a poor peasant sighed that the drought 'may be too big a problem for God; but perhaps OXFAM can do something'. There are other self-congratulatory snippets in the same vein about OXFAM's heroic deeds in Maharasthra and other drought-affected parts of India at that time:

I suddenly realised that, driving 20 miles out of Ajmer on the road to Udaipur, all the scattered green patches I saw in the brown desert were in some way or another due to OXFAM.

In spite of the feeding programme the children have not gained weight. Stina at first thought her scale was wrong, but she discovered that the children now get almost nothing to eat at home. One shudders to think what would have happened to them without the feeding scheme. What's happening in other villages, where we aren't feeding?[11]

The donor's exaggerated perception of its achievements is coupled with a somewhat astonishing lack of information about what the government was doing on an enormously larger scale. As late as December 1972, by which time the government-led relief programme was in full swing, the same *Bulletin* reports: 'we have no information as yet of the extent of the Indian government's programme'. The fact that an organization with as remarkable a record of helpful action and leadership as OXFAM could fall into this trap of making mountains out of molehills and molehills out of mountains shows the difficulties of objective perception and reporting on the part of an institution directly involved in the act of relief and dependent on the preservation of a particular public image.

The highly selective focus of public discussions on famine is also evident in the case of Africa. For instance, until recently Botswana's remarkable record of famine prevention had received very little recognition, to the point that a

[10] The first in-depth analysis of the Maharashtra drought published in an international professional journal outside India is that of Oughton (1982), who focuses, however, more on the crisis of entitlements than on the success of public response. On the latter, see ch. 1, and the further contributions cited there.

[11] These citations are from OXFAM (1972, 1973) and Hall (1973). It must be emphasized that it is not the intention here to blame OXFAM in particular for sharing in a form of disaster reporting that seems to be, in fact, common to the publications of many relief agencies when these are addressed to the wider public. The point is simply to illustrate certain biases which an institution of this kind seems to find it hard to resist, for understandable reasons.

leading expert on Africa described it as 'Africa's best kept secret'.[12] Examples of underreported successes in famine prevention in Africa, most of them involving large-scale government intervention, can also be found in countries as varied as Burkina Faso, Cape Verde, Kenya, Lesotho, Mali, Mauritania, Niger, Tanzania, Uganda, Zimbabwe, and even to some extent Chad and Ethiopia.[13]

It is arguable that popular interpretations of the recent 'African famine' of 1983–5 have themselves involved important misperceptions. Though drought threatened a large number of African countries at that time, only some of them—notably war-torn ones—actually experienced large-scale famine. There was no uniform disaster of the kind that has often been suggested. In fact, a probing interpretation of the mounting evidence on this tragedy could well uncover many more reasons for hope than for despair.[14]

It is, moreover, far from clear that those countries where large-scale famine did occur were the ones most affected by drought. Such an impression is certainly *not* borne out by available food and agricultural production indices (see Table 2.1).[15] I shall argue, in fact, that the sharp contrasts which can be observed in the relationship between drought and famine in different countries have a lot to do with the contrasting quality of public action in various parts of Africa. In particular, a number of countries where drought was extremely severe in 1983–4 (indeed often more severe than in the much-discussed cases of Ethiopia or Sudan, in terms of declines in food and agricultural production indices) met with notable success in averting large-scale famine. Vivid illustrations of this fact are found in the experiences of Botswana, Cape Verde, Kenya, and Zimbabwe (see Table 2.2).[16] There is as much to learn from these 'quiet successes' as from the attention-catching failures that can also be observed elsewhere in Africa. Some of these success stories are further examined in the next section.

[12] Eicher (1986: 5). The experience of this country will be further discussed in section 2.4.

[13] See e.g. Kelly (1987) on Burkina Faso; Freeman *et al.* (1978) and van Binsbergen (1986) on Cape Verde; Borton and Clay (1986), Cohen and Lewis (1987), and Downing *et al.* (forthcoming) on Kenya; Bryson (1986) on Lesotho; Steele (1985) on Mali; UNDRO (1986) on Mauritania; de Ville de Goyet (1978), CILSS (1986), and World Food Programme (1986c) on Niger; Mwaluko (1962) on Tanzania; Brennan *et al.* (1984) and Dodge and Alnwick (1986) on Uganda; Bratton (1986) on Zimbabwe; Holt (1983), Nelson (1983), Firebrace and Holland (1984), Peberdy (1985), Grannell (1986), and World Food Programme (1986b) on Ethiopia (including Tigrai and Eritrea); and Autier and d'Altilia (1985), Brown *et al.* (1986), and World Food Programme (1986a) on Chad.

[14] A large number of the references cited in the previous footnote deal with the 1983–5 crisis.

[15] Nor is this impression confirmed by meteorological information—see J. Downing *et al.* (1987).

[16] Table 2.2 includes four of the five countries appearing at the top of Table 2.1. The fifth (Niger) is not included for lack of detailed and reliable information on the experience of that country. It is, however, interesting to note that, according to at least one authoritative study, 'Niger is probably one of the few African countries where the government has, for more than a decade, proclaimed and shown a strong commitment to guarantee the subsistence of the population' (CILSS 1986; my translation).

**Table 2.1** Food and agricultural production in sub-Saharan Africa, 1983–1984

| Country | Per capita food production 1983–4 | | Per capita agricultural production 1983–4 | Growth rate of agricultural production per capita 1970–84 |
|---|---|---|---|---|
| | (1979–81 = 100) (1) | (1976–8 = 100) (2) | (1979–81 = 100) (3) | (% per year) (4) |
| Cape Verde | 62 | n/a | n/a | n/a |
| Zimbabwe | 73 | 68 | 82 | −1.4 |
| Niger | 83 | 78 | 83 | 0.7 |
| Botswana | 83 | n/a | 84 | −3.8 |
| Kenya | 87 | 82 | 93 | −1.3 |
| Senegal | 88 | 70 | 89 | −2.1 |
| Mozambique | 88 | 75 | 87 | −4.3 |
| Ethiopia | 88 | 94 | 88 | −0.6 |
| Sudan | 89 | 72 | 93 | −0.5 |
| Togo | 90 | 93 | 90 | −1.1 |
| Zambia | 92 | 89 | 93 | −1.1 |
| Angola | 93 | 81 | 91 | −5.6 |
| Guinea | 93 | 92 | 94 | −1.0 |
| Malawi | 93 | 100 | 96 | 0.1 |
| Tanzania | 95 | 91 | 93 | −0.6 |
| Burundi | 95 | 87 | 95 | 0.5 |
| Ivory Coast | 95 | 111 | 90 | 0.5 |
| Cameroon | 96 | 83 | 95 | −0.8 |
| Burkina Faso | 98 | 90 | 99 | −0.2 |
| Uganda | 98 | 96 | 100 | −1.7 |
| Ghana | 98 | 80 | 98 | −3.9 |
| Nigeria | 98 | 88 | 98 | −1.0 |
| Zaire | 101 | 97 | 102 | −0.6 |
| Liberia | 102 | 100 | 99 | −1.4 |
| Benin | 103 | 85 | 104 | −0.3 |
| Sierra Leone | 104 | 84 | 101 | −0.5 |
| Mali | 106 | 90 | 105 | 0.8 |
| Guinea-Bissau | 114 | 92 | 114 | −0.9 |

*Note*: The countries included in this table are all those for which data are available from each of the three sources; Cape Verde has been added using van Binsbergen (1986: Table 3). Figures for 1983–4 have been calculated as an unweighted average of 1983 and 1984.

*Sources*: (1) and (3): Calculated from FAO, *Monthly Bulletin of Statistics*, Nov. 1987. (2): Figures given by the United States Department of Agriculture, reproduced in J. Downing *et al.* (1987: Table 1.1). (4): Food and Agriculture Organization (1986: Annex I, Table 1.2).

## 2.4. *Famine prevention in Africa: selected case-studies*

Declines in food or agricultural production are not, by themselves, reliable indicators of threats of large-scale entitlement failures. The fact that countries such as Botswana or Cape Verde have suffered very sharp production declines in recent years (without experiencing famine) hardly establishes the existence of a serious threat of famine in these countries. Nor does it tell us a great deal about how this threat—if real—was averted. These issues are taken up here for further scrutiny, for each of the four 'successful' countries appearing in Table 2.2. On closer examination it will clearly emerge that, in each case, a serious threat of famine *was* averted through determined public intervention.

### Cape Verde

In his distinguished history of the Cape Verde Islands, Antonio Carreira wrote that 'everything in these islands combines to impose on man a hard, difficult and wretched way of life'.[17] A prominent aspect of the harshness of life in Cape Verde is the recurrence of devastating droughts, which have regularly affected the islands ever since their 'discovery' in the middle of the fifteenth century by the Portuguese. Many of these droughts have been associated with large-scale famine.[18]

In fact, it is hard to think of many famines in history that have taken a toll in human life proportionately as high as those which have periodically decimated Cape Verde in the last few centuries. Some of these famines are believed to have killed nearly half of the population (see Table 2.3). Even allowing for some exaggeration in these estimates, there are very few parallels of such wholesale mortality even in the long and terrible history of famines in the world.

These historical famines went almost entirely unrelieved. When one of the very few exceptions to this pattern occurred in 1825, the Governor of the islands was sacked for using Crown taxes to feed the people.[19] Left to its own devices, the population had little other refuge than the attempt to emigrate —often encouraged by the colonial authorities. Cape Verde's history of persistent migration is indeed intimately connected with the succession of famines on the islands. However, for most people this option remained a severely limited one, and as recently as the 1940s large-scale mortality was a predictable feature of prolonged drought.

---

[17] Carreira (1982: 15). According to several analysts, the climate of Cape Verde is even harsher, and the droughts visiting it more frequent and severe, than those of other Sahelian countries. See e.g. Meintel (1984: 56).

[18] For a chronology of droughts and famines in Cape Verde, see Freeman *et al.* (1978). For further discussion of famines in the history of Cape Verde, see Cabral (1980), Carreira (1982), Moran (1982), Meintel (1983, 1984), and Legal (1984).

[19] Freeman *et al.* (1978: 18). A strikingly similar incident occurred during the famine of the early 1940s (Cabral 1980: 150–1). A significant attempt at providing relief was however made during the famine of 1862–5, when employment was provided (with cash wage payments) on road-building works (see Meintel 1984).

Table 2.2 Drought and famine in Africa, 1983–1984: contrasting experiences

| Country | Decline of production since 1979–81 (%) | | Growth rate of per capita total gross agricultural production (1970–84) | Outcome |
|---|---|---|---|---|
| | Food | Agriculture | | |
| Cape Verde | 38.5 | n/a | n/a | Mortality *decline*; nutritional *improvement* |
| Zimbabwe | 37.5 | 18.5 | −1.4 | Mortality *decline*; no sustained nutritional deterioration |
| Botswana | 17.0 | 16.5 | −3.8 | Normal nutritional situation; no starvation deaths |
| Kenya | 13.5 | 7.5 | −1.3 | No starvation deaths reported; possibility of nutritional deterioration |
| Ethiopia | 12.5 | 12.5 | −0.6 | Large-scale famine |
| Sudan | 11.0 | 7.0 | −0.5 | Large-scale famine |

*Sources*: The figures on food and agricultural production performance are from the same sources as Table 2.1. The assessment of 'outcome' in Botswana, Cape Verde, Kenya, and Zimbabwe is discussed further in this chapter. For estimates of excess mortality in Sudan and Ethiopia during the 1983–5 famines, see e.g. Otten (1986), de Waal (1987), Jansson *et al.* (1987), and Seaman (1987).

In recent years, Cape Verde may well have been the worst drought-affected of all African countries. Indeed, uninterrupted drought crippled the country's economy for almost twenty years between 1968 and 1986—leading to a virtual extinction of domestic food supplies and a near standstill of rural activity.[20] Half-way through this prolonged drought in the middle 1970s, the event was already described as 'the longest and most severe [drought] on record' for the country.[21] In this case, however, not only was famine averted but, even more

[20] In 1970, 70% of agricultural products consumed in Cape Verde were produced in the country (CILSS 1976: 8). This ratio had fallen to 1.5% by 1973 (CILSS 1976: 8), and only rose marginally thereafter (van Binsbergen 1986). According to one study, 'during the drought over 70% of the agricultural labour force has been unemployed' (Economist Intelligence Unit 1984: 38). It is not clear, however, how this calculation treats labour employed on public works programmes (on which more below).                   [21] Freeman *et al.* (1978: 98).

**Table 2.3** History of famine mortality in Cape
Verde, 1750–1950

|  | Mortality attributed to famine (% of total population) |
| --- | --- |
| 1773–6 | 44 |
| 1830–3 | 42 |
| 1863–6 | 40 |
| 1900–3 | 15 |
| 1920–2 | 16 |
| 1940–3 | 15 |
| 1946–8 | 18 |

*Source*: Moran (1982: Table 1). The famines indicated
here are only those for which an estimate of famine
mortality is provided in that table. For the same period,
the author mentions 22 further large-scale famines for
which no mortality estimates are available.

strikingly, significant *improvements* in living conditions took place during the
drought period.

It is convenient to divide the drought period into two parts, separated by the
independence of Cape Verde from Portugal in 1975. The first part of the
drought period is marked by an untypical attempt on the part of the Portuguese
rulers at providing large-scale relief.[22] Relief was provided almost exclusively
in the form of employment for cash wages in makeshift work (the adequacy of
food supplies being ensured separately by food imports). According to one
study, 55.5 per cent of the labour force was unemployed in 1970, but as much
as 84 per cent of total employment was provided by drought relief
programmes.[23]

These preventive measures succeeded to a great extent in averting a severe
famine. There were no reports of large-scale starvation deaths, and the overall
increase in mortality seems to have been moderate. The estimated infant
mortality rate, for instance, which had shot up to more than 500 per thousand
during the famine of 1947–8, was only a little above the 1962–7 average of 93.5
per thousand in the period 1968–75 (Table 2.4). On the other hand, a
significant intensification of undernutrition during the same period has been
reported in several studies.[24]

[22] Several commentators have argued that, in this case, action was motivated by the concern of
the Portuguese government for its international image. See e.g. Meintel (1984: 68), CILSS (1976:
4), Davidson (1977: 394), and Cabral (1980: 134).

[23] Calculated from CILSS (1976: 3–4). This was the policy of *apoio* or 'support', which was
later criticized by the government of independent Cape Verde for the unproductive nature of the
works undertaken (see CILSS 1976, Legal 1984, and Meintel 1983, 1984).

[24] See e.g. Meintel (1984: 68–9), CILSS (1976: 14), and Freeman *et al.* (1978: 149, 203).

**Table 2.4** Infant mortality in Cape Verde, 1912–1986

| Year | Estimated infant mortality rate (deaths per 1,000) | |
|---|---|---|
| | (1) | (2) |
| 1912 | 220.6 | |
| 1913 | 174.2 | |
| 1915 | 117.9 | |
| 1920 | 155.0 | |
| 1927 | 217.6 | |
| 1931 | 206.7 | |
| 1937 | 223.4 | |
| 1943 | 317.9 | |
| 1946 | 268.7 | |
| 1947[a] | 542.9 | |
| 1948[a] | 428.6 | |
| 1949 | 203.9 | |
| 1950 | 130.7 | |
| 1962 | 106.1 | |
| 1963 | 109.7 | |
| 1964 | 85.3 | |
| 1965 | 76.7 | |
| 1966 | 83.6 | |
| 1967 | 99.9 | |
| 1968 | 91.7 | |
| 1969 | 123.1 | |
| 1970 | 95.0 | |
| 1971 | 130.9 | |
| 1972 | 90.9 | |
| 1973 | 110.6 | |
| 1974 | 78.9 | |
| 1975 | 103.9 | 104.9 |
| 1980–5 | | 77.0 |
| 1985 | | 70.0 |
| 1986 | | 65.0 |

[a] Famine years.

*Sources*: For the period 1912–75 (col. 1), Freeman *et al.* (1978: Table V.26) (very close estimates are also reported for the 1969–74 period in CILSS 1976: Table VI). For 1975–86 (col. 2), *World Health Statistics Annual 1985* and UNICEF (1987, 1988).

Since independence in 1975, Cape Verde has been ruled by a single party with a socialist orientation, namely the Partido Africano da Independencia da Cabo Verde (PAICV).[25] This party, described by the current Prime Minister as 'reformist, progressist and nationalist',[26] is flanked by the Popular National Assembly, which is elected every five years by popular ballot (on the basis of a single-party system). The government of independent Cape Verde has been consistently credited with progressive social reforms and development programmes. Notable areas of improvement have been those of education and health. Drought relief has been among the top political priorities.

Cape Verde's entitlement protection system since independence has consisted of three integrated components.[27] First, a competent and planned use of food aid has ensured an adequate and predictable food supply in spite of the nearly total collapse of domestic production. Food aid is legally bound to be *sold* wholesale in the open market, and the proceeds accrue to the National Development Fund.[28]

Second, the resources of the National Development Fund are used for labour intensive public works programmes with a 'development' orientation. In 1983, 29.2 per cent of the labour force was employed in such programmes.[29] The works undertaken include afforestation, soil conservation, irrigation, and road building, and according to a recent evaluation 'the results of these projects are positive, even on the basis of high standards'.[30]

Third, unconditional relief is provided to selected vulnerable groups such as pregnant women, undernourished children, the elderly, and the invalid. This part of the entitlement protection system includes both nutritional intervention (such as school feeding) and cash transfers, and is integrated with related aspects of social security measures. In 1983, direct food assistance covered 14 per cent of the population.[31]

The effectiveness of this fairly comprehensive and well-integrated entitlement protection system is visible from the impact of the drought after 1975.[32]

---

[25] In fact, until 1981, Guinea-Bissau and Cape Verde were jointly ruled by the binational Partido Africano da Independencia da Guine e Cabo Verde, which led the independence struggle against the Portuguese rulers.  [26] *Courier* (1988: 27).

[27] For further details, see CILSS (1976), Freeman *et al.* (1978), USAID (1982), Meintel (1983), Legal (1984), and particularly van Binsbergen (1986).

[28] This rule does not apply when the sale of food aid violates the conditions of delivery, e.g., in the case of the comparatively small quantities of food donated to Cape Verde under the World Food Programme. These are used for supplementary feeding.

[29] Economist Intelligence Unit (1984: 38).

[30] van Binsbergen (1986: 9). See also *Courier* (1988).   [31] van Binsbergen (1986: 10).

[32] In both the pre-independence and the post-independence periods, remittances from abroad also played an important role in mitigating the effects of the drought. Note, on the other hand, that remittances would not seem to explain the better record of famine prevention in the post-independence period, during which the world economic conditions were less favourable and emigration from Cape Verde considerably less common than during the first period (see e.g. Freeman *et al.* 1978: 139–40).

**Table 2.5**  Child undernutrition in Cape Verde, 1977 and 1984

| District | School children suffering from undernutrition (moderate to serious) (%) | |
| --- | --- | --- |
| | 1977[a] | 1984[b] |
| Boa Vista | 41.8 | 7.8 |
| Porto Novo | 49.2 | 9.2 |
| Ribeira Grande | 54.3 | 5.8 |
| São Vicente | 38.1 | 10.7 |
| Tarrafal | n/a | 7.8 |
| TOTAL | 46.4 | 8.8 |

[a] Children aged 7–15 years.
[b] Children aged 6–18 years.

*Source*: van Binsbergen (1986: Table 2). According to the author, the two studies on which this table is based are 'reasonably comparable', and 'although the methodologies used by the different studies were not identical, it is safe to conclude that the nutritional status of school age children has significantly improved since 1977' (van Binsbergen 1986: 3–4). An independent study carried out in 1973 estimated that 38% of children aged 7–14 suffered from 'moderate protein-calorie malnutrition' (Freeman *et al*. 1978: Table V.24).

Indeed, the adverse effects of the drought on the living conditions of human beings seem to have been remarkably small.[33] In addition to the successful prevention of famine, there are indications that the post-1975 part of the drought period has witnessed: (1) a *decline* in the infant mortality rate (see Table 2.4); (2) a significant *increase* in food intake;[34] and (3) a significant *improvement* in the nutritional status of children (see Table 2.5).[35] By any criterion, the success achieved by the government of independent Cape Verde in protecting the population from the adverse effects of a drought of unprecedented magnitude must be seen as an exemplary one.

### Kenya

The history of Kenya, like that of Cape Verde, has been repeatedly marked by grim episodes of drought and famine.[36] As recently as 1980–1, famine struck

[33] There is a revealing contrast between this observation and the fact of huge livestock losses, which provide another measure of the intensity of the drought and of the threat of famine. The decline in livestock between 1968 and 1980 has been estimated at 12% for goats, 30% for pigs, 50% for sheep, and 72% for cows (calculated from Economist Intelligence Unit 1983: 43).

[34] On this, see Legal (1984: 12–16), who notes large increases in the consumption of maize, wheat, and rice in the post-independence period compared to the pre-drought period. The average consumption of calories, which 'for the vast majority of the population did not exceed 1500 calories per day' at the time of independence (CILSS 1976: 8; my translation), is now believed to have 'moved closer to the required level of 2800 calories per day' (van Binsbergen 1986: 3).

[35] A USAID study dated 1982 also mentions, without explicitly providing supporting figures, that 'by providing employment, the Government of Cape Verde's rural work program has had an acknowledged major effect on improving nutritional status' (USAID 1982: 15).

[36] See e.g. Wisner (1977), O'Leary (1980), Herlehy (1984), and Ambler (1988).

substantial parts of the population in the wake of a drought of moderate intensity. The government of Kenya has been widely praised, however, for preventing a much more widespread and intense drought from developing into a famine in 1984. This event has been extensively studied elsewhere.[37] I shall only recall here the main features of this successful response, and comment briefly on some of its neglected aspects.

Like Cape Verde, Kenya has a single-party system and an elected parliament. Since independence in 1963, the country has enjoyed a degree of political stability which compares favourably with many other parts of Africa. The freedom of the national media is somewhat limited but nevertheless far more extensive than in most African countries. The country also has a high degree of visibility in the international press.

More than 80 per cent of Kenya's population (around 19 million in 1984) is rural, and derives its livelihood largely from agriculture and livestock. The rural economy is more diversified, and has experienced more rapid growth since the early 1960s, than in most other parts of Africa. However, large parts of the country remain vulnerable to climatic and economic instability, particularly in the largely semi-arid areas of the Eastern and North-eastern Provinces (and parts of the Rift Valley).

The strategies adopted by rural households in Kenya to cope with drought or the threat of famine appear to be increasingly geared to the acquisition of food on the market and the diversification of economic activities (partly through wage employment).[38] The importance of off-farm activities in the rural household economy can be seen from the fact that, according to a survey carried out in six districts of the Central and Eastern Provinces in 1985, more than half of smallholder households had at least one member in long-term wage employment (see Table 2.6 below).

The 1984 crisis followed a massive failure of the 'long rains' in March and April 1984. According to Cohen and Lewis:

it was the worst shortage of rains in the last 100 years. Production of maize, the nation's principal food crop, was approximately 50% below that normally expected for the main rains of March–May. Wheat, the second most important grain, was nearly 70% below normal. Potato production was down by more than 70%. Pastoralists reported losing up to 70% of their stock. The situation had the potential for a famine of major proportions.[39]

[37] For in-depth analyses of the 1984 drought and the government's response, see Ray (1984), Deloitte et al. (1986), Cohen and Lewis (1987), Corbett (1987), J. Downing et al. (1987), and Downing et al. (forthcoming). A particularly thoughtful and well-documented account of this event can be found in Borton (1988, forthcoming).

[38] For insightful studies of coping strategies in Kenya, see Wisner (1977), Bertlin (1980), Campbell (1984), Swift (1985), Downing (1986), Akong'a and Downing (1987), Sperling (1987a, 1987b), Anyango et al. (forthcoming), and Kamau et al. (forthcoming).

[39] Cohen and Lewis (1987: 274). The existence of a serious threat of large-scale famine in this event is also argued in detail in Corbett (1987). For statistical information on rainfall patterns and crop production during the drought, see Downing et al. (forthcoming).

Regional disparities accentuate the alarming nature of these aggregate statistics. In the Central and Eastern Provinces, food production for the agricultural year 1984–5 was estimated by the FAO at 14 per cent and 26 per cent (respectively) of the average for the previous six years. In districts such as Kitui and Machakos, maize production was virtually nil both in 1983 and in 1984.[40]

While in specific areas the drought of 1984 meant the second or even third consecutive crop failure, for most areas the crisis was one of limited duration. The 'short rains' of October to December 1984 were above average. However, in terms of intensity and geographical coverage the drought of 1984 was certainly an exceptional one, and distress continued until the harvest of mid-1985.

The use of formal 'early warning' techniques apparently played little role in precipitating action. The need for action seems to have been detected partly from the visible failure of rains in early 1984 (followed by evident crop failures), and partly from the unusual increase in food purchases from the National Cereals and Produce Board later in the year.[41] While Cohen and Lewis stress the role of 'political commitment' in ensuring an early and adequate response, others comment that 'the government felt the need to forestall political instability that would result in the event of a widespread famine'.[42] The threat of political unrest seems to have been exacerbated by the fact that, somewhat unusually, the drought of 1984 strongly affected a number of politically important and influential areas of the Central Provinces as well as Nairobi.

Active public response to the crisis began in April 1984.[43] The first step taken by the government to deal with the threat of famine was to import large amounts of food on a commercial basis. The initial availability of substantial food stocks ensured that the lags involved in the importation of food did not have disastrous consequences. Additional food aid pledges were also obtained, but with a few minor exceptions their fulfilment occurred only in 1985, several months after the arrival of commercial food imports. The ability of the government to buy large amounts of food on the international market was

[40] See Borton (1988: Table 3), and Maganda (forthcoming: Table 9.4).

[41] Cohen and Lewis describe the symptoms of an impending crisis as follows: 'By April 1984, the situation was obvious. The sun was shining beautifully, when it should have been raining; no early warning system was required' (Cohen and Lewis 1987: 276). Other authors, however, have stressed the role of rapidly increasing purchases from the National Cereals and Produce Board in arousing concern for the possibility of a crisis (see e.g. Corbett 1987, and Downing 1988).

[42] J. Downing et al. (1987: 266). It appears that the drought enjoyed only limited coverage in the local media, but attracted considerable international attention and concern (Downing 1988).

[43] For detailed accounts of the famine prevention measures, the reader is referred to Cohen and Lewis (1987), J. Downing et al. (1987), Borton (1988, forthcoming), and Downing et al. (forthcoming). This case-study concentrates mainly on the government response, which represents the greater part of these measures, though the involvement of non-government agencies was not insignificant.

greatly helped by the availability of foreign exchange reserves and the peak in export earnings resulting largely from high world prices for tea and coffee.

Entitlement protection measures took two different forms. First, the government used food imports to ensure the continued availability of food at reasonable prices through normal commercial channels. In ordinary times, interdistrict food movements are exclusively organized by the National Cereals and Produce Board, which subcontracts the transport and distribution of food to licensed private traders. This arrangement was preserved and intensified during the drought, and most of the food imported was sold through the intermediation of private traders at 'gazetted' prices fixed by the government.

Second, direct support was provided to vulnerable households in affected areas. Initially, the government intended to provide such support mainly in the form of employment for cash wages.[44] In practice, however, the generation of employment fell far short of target, due to a lack of preparedness and supervisory capacity. On the other hand, the provision of unconditional relief in the form of free food rations (mainly from food aid) assumed considerable importance. In August 1984, nearly 1.4 million people, or 7 per cent of the total population, were estimated to be in receipt of free food distribution, and in January 1985 a very similar estimate was reported.[45] In drought-affected areas, the proportion of the population receiving food rations was much larger, and the survey of smallholders in Central and Eastern Kenya mentioned earlier found that over the same period the proportion of households receiving food assistance in the surveyed districts was as high as 45 per cent (see Table 2.6). The size of the rations distributed, however, appears to have been very small before the large-scale arrival of food aid in 1985.[46]

The allocation of relief to the needy was the responsibility of the provincial administration, which itself relied on famine relief committees and local 'chiefs' to identify those in need of support. The precise way in which this system actually worked is far from clear. According to Cohen and Lewis, the local chiefs 'knew the needs of their people, and by most reports did an effective, equitable job of distributing the government-supplied grain'.[47]

---

[44] The two slogans propounded by the government early on during the crisis were 'planning, not panic' and 'food imports and employment generation' (J. Downing et al. 1987: 265).

[45] Deloitte et al. (1986: 12). In 1985, the numbers in receipt of unconditional relief gradually decreased, though the amount of food distributed increased with the enlarged flow of food aid.

[46] The same survey reveals that, between July and Dec. 1984, the median food ration per recipient household varied between 197 and 633 calories per day in different regions (Downing 1988: Table 4.19). For the same period, Anyango et al. (forthcoming) estimate that 'the food relief averaged 5–10 percent of individual requirements' for the recipients (see also Kamau et al. forthcoming). In 1985, the size of food rations was much larger, and did not in fact differ very much on average from the 'target' of 10 kgs of maize per person per month (Borton 1988, forthcoming).

[47] Cohen and Lewis (1987: 281). The authors had an active personal involvement in the government relief programmes, and provide a somewhat uncritical account of their implementation.

Another account, however, states that 'moving in the path of least resistance, the GOK [government of Kenya] would seem to rather divide the available food equally among recipients at the distributions thus defusing potentially uncomfortable situations'.[48]

It is not implausible that the allocation of food within specific communities was largely indiscriminate, and that 'targeting' operated mainly between different villages or regions (the impact of the drought was highly uneven geographically). On the other hand, an important factor facilitating the fair allocation of free food was the fact that most of it consisted of *yellow* maize, which is generally considered an inferior commodity in Kenya. The element of 'self-selection' involved in distributing a commodity that is somewhat disliked has been said by a number of commentators to have contributed to an allocation more geared to the most desperate.

Some indicators of the impact of the drought on the rural population in different ecological zones of Central and Eastern Kenya appear in Table 2.6. They reveal, *inter alia*, the importance of wage employment and remittances in sustaining affected households, and the broad coverage of food distribution in these districts at that time. The large cattle losses also confirm the exceptional severity of the drought.[49]

The precise impact of the drought on the well-being of the affected populations is hard to ascertain. Most commentators consider that 'famine was averted'. The apparent absence of confirmed reports of 'starvation deaths', as well as of distress migration on the part of entire families, lend some support to this view. On the other hand, there is clear evidence of widespread hunger as well as rising malnutrition in 1984.[50] Available data do not, unfortunately, seem to allow a detailed and reliable analysis of the demographic and nutritional impact of the drought.

While the credit which the Kenyan government has been given for averting a severe famine in 1984 appears to be largely deserved, an important query can nevertheless be raised as to whether the strategy it adopted made good use of available opportunities. A particularly compelling query, which seems to have escaped the attention of most commentators, concerns the balance between income support and price stabilization measures. Considering the small size of food distribution to vulnerable households in per capita terms (at least until

[48] Ray (1984: 2). Independent personal communications from two persons who were involved in the 1984 relief efforts confirm that food distribution centres typically did not discriminate between different groups of people, and provided identical rations to all recipients.

[49] For further details of livestock losses, see Borton (1988), Downing *et al.* (forthcoming: ch. 1), Kamau *et al.* (forthcoming), Anyango *et al.* (forthcoming), and Mwendwa (forthcoming). The picture presented in other surveys is, if anything, grimmer than that offered by Table 2.6. According to Borton (1988), the 1984 drought may have depleted the *national* cattle herd by as much as 50% (p. vii).

[50] See the surveys of Anyango *et al.* (forthcoming), Neumann *et al.* (forthcoming), and Kamau *et al.* (forthcoming). The relative absence of distress migration is discussed in Anyango *et al.* (forthcoming).

**Table 2.6** The 1984 drought and smallholder households in Central and Eastern Kenya

| Characteristic | Households with the specified characteristic, by ecological zone (%) | | | | | |
|---|---|---|---|---|---|---|
| | 1 | 2 | 3 | 4 | 5 | All zones |
| Household member moved during 1984 | 23 | 7 | 21 | 26 | 38 | 25 |
| Has a member in permanent employment | 58 | 47 | 61 | 54 | 54 | 56 |
| Received cash remittances from relatives or friends during drought | 34 | 28 | 40 | 57 | 46 | 43 |
| Major food changed during 1984 | 84 | 78 | 76 | 67 | 67 | 73 |
| Received famine relief (from govt. or NGOs) | 14 | 35 | 25 | 67 | 77 | 45 |
| Slaughtered, sold, lost, or consumed cattle[a] | 41(26) | 45(35) | 33(29) | 44(46) | 32(51) | 38(58) |

[a] In brackets, the percentage decrease in cattle holding, averaged over all households surveyed in the respective zone.

*Source*: Anyango *et al.* (forthcoming: Tables 13.6, 13.9). Based on survey data collected in Jan. 1985 by the Central Bureau of Statistics on behalf of the National Environment Secretariat. In Kenya, a smallholder is 'typically defined as a rural landowner with less than 22 hectares' (Akong'a and Downing 1987: 92). Ecological zones appear in increasing order of drought-proneness, based on rainfall data.

1985), it appears that famine prevention measures attempted to operate mainly through the level of food prices rather than through the generation of compensating incomes.[51] In turn, the stability of prices was pursued through a policy of commercial imports from abroad into the worst-affected districts. At the same time, however, government regulations prevented private traders from moving food from surplus to deficit areas within Kenya.

As was mentioned earlier, interdistrict food movements in Kenya are tightly regulated by the National Cereals and Produce Board, which subcontracts food transport to licensed private traders. Several studies have shown that restrictions on interregional movements have the effect of exacerbating the intensity of local shortages and the disparity of retail prices between regions.[52]

[51] According to Borton (1988), free distribution of food accounted for only 15% of the cereals imported between Sept. 1984 and June 1985 (p. 19).

[52] On this, see particularly Olsen (1984). See also Akong'a and Downing (1987) and Sperling (1987a). Note that the volatility of retail prices is compatible with the control of 'gazetted prices' mentioned earlier.

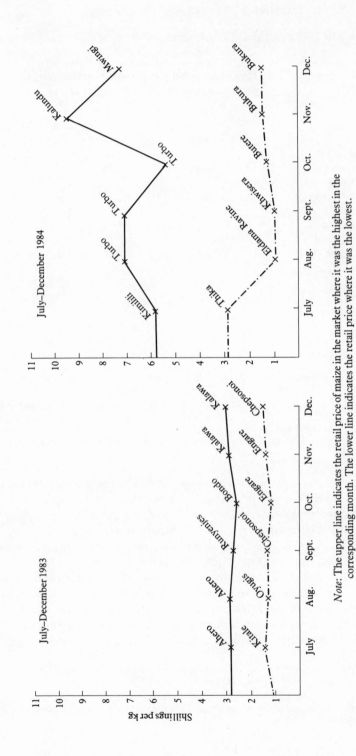

*Note:* The upper line indicates the retail price of maize in the market where it was the highest in the corresponding month. The lower line indicates the retail price where it was the lowest.

*Source:* As in Table 2.7.

**Fig. 2.1** Minimum and maximum retail price of maize in Kenya, 1983 and 1984

**Table 2.7** Retail prices of maize in Kenya, 1984

| Market | Jan. 1984 (Kshs/kg) | Nov. 1984 (Kshs/kg) | Increase (%) | Province |
|---|---|---|---|---|
| Kalundu | 2.50 | 9.31 | 272 | Eastern |
| Mwingi | 2.50 | 9.00 | 260 | Eastern |
| Kiambu | 2.14 | 5.30 | 148 | Central |
| Machakos | 2.40 | 5.76 | 140 | Eastern |
| Iciara | 2.53 | 5.94 | 135 | Eastern |
| Limuru | 2.02 | 4.19 | 107 | Central |
| Runyenjes | 2.57 | 4.70 | 83 | Eastern |
| Thika | 2.86 | 4.91 | 72 | Central |
| Kandara | 2.84 | 4.76 | 68 | Central |
| Embu Town | 2.92 | 4.89 | 67 | Eastern |
| Eldoret | 2.00 | 2.92 | 46 | Rift Valley |
| Kitale | 1.51 | 2.11 | 40 | Rift Valley |
| Bondo | 2.50 | 3.33 | 33 | Nyanza |
| Ahero | 2.51 | 3.19 | 27 | Nyanza |
| Sondu | 2.31 | 2.73 | 18 | Nyanza |
| Mumias | 2.35 | 2.69 | 14 | Western |
| Luanda | 2.71 | 2.57 | −5 | Western |

*Source*: Republic of Kenya, Central Bureau of Statistics, Ministry of Finance and Planning, *Market Information Bulletin* (Jan.–June 1984 and July–Dec. 1984 issues). The markets in the table are all those for which data are provided in the *Bulletin* for both months.

This phenomenon was clearly visible during the drought year itself: while food prices were sharply rising in drought-affected districts, they were only sluggishly rising or even *falling* in many others (see Fig. 2.1 and Table 2.7). Maize prices in different markets varied, at one point, by a factor of nearly *ten*.[53] Even between adjacent districts, price disparities seem to have been exceptionally large (Table 2.8).

The detrimental effects of this policy of trade restrictions on the entitlements of vulnerable groups in drought-affected areas are not difficult to guess. For instance, after stressing the role of food shortages and high prices in undermining the entitlements of poor households in the Samburu district of northern Kenya, Louise Sperling comments:

[The] problem of local distribution was sufficiently severe to result in the convening of a district-level meeting as early as 14th June 1984. The District Commissioner called together the eleven or twelve wholesalers to discuss 'the erratic supply of commodities'. Maize prices are strictly controlled by the state, and the local traders claimed they were losing money on maize sales. The allowed mark-up could not cover the costs of

[53] For details of food price patterns during the drought, see the government of Kenya's *Market Information Bulletin*, and also Maganda (forthcoming). Careful econometric analysis of time-series data on food prices in Kenya confirms that the interregional disparity of prices sharply increased in 1984 (Jane Corbett, Food Studies Group, Oxford, personal communication).

**Table 2.8** Maize prices in Central and Eastern Kenya, 1984

| Zone | Price of white maize (Kshs/kg) | | Increase (Jan.–Dec.) (%) |
|------|-----------|-----------|------|
|      | Jan.–Mar. | Oct.–Dec. |      |
| 1    | 3.98      | 5.94      | 49   |
| 2    | 3.25      | 5.50      | 69   |
| 3    | 2.80      | 6.20      | 121  |
| 4    | 2.94      | 7.22      | 146  |
| 5    | 3.49      | 10.24     | 193  |

*Note*: The ecological zones are the same as in Table 2.6.

*Source*: Anyango *et al.* (forthcoming: Table 13.10).

transport and loading to these more remote areas. Even considerable government pressure to encourage traders to keep their shelves full did not result in an increase in the local availability of maize . . . Again, the poor disproportionately suffered from these shortages. They could not afford to buy grain in bulk when it did arrive. Equally, they did not have the means to purchase alternative, more costly foodstuffs.[54]

It is not completely surprising, then, if the 1984 drought is remembered by some of the affected populations as *Ni Kwa Ngweta*, or 'I could die with cash'.[55] The strangulated flow of food through different parts of the country must have accounted for much of this paradoxical perception.

To conclude, while the efforts made by the government of Kenya in 1984 to import food and distribute it in drought-affected areas well ahead of large-scale famine were no doubt remarkable, it may be that certain aspects of the relief programme have not received adequately critical scrutiny. To some extent, the acute need to rush food from abroad into the worst-affected regions was a result of the parallel efforts that were made, partly for political reasons, to prevent food exports from surplus areas (or to direct such exports towards Nairobi). It appears that, in some respects, government intervention during the drought was undoing with one hand the harm it had done with the other.

### Zimbabwe

The so-called 'Zimbabwean miracle' in food production has received wide attention recently. By contrast, the impressive programmes of direct entitlement protection adopted by the Zimbabwean government to prevent the prolonged drought of 1982–4 from precipitating a major famine seem to have been relatively neglected.[56] The assumption, presumably, is that a country

[54] Sperling (1987a: 269).                [55] Downing (1986: 7).

[56] To the best of my knowledge an in-depth analysis of these events has not been published to this day. However, see Government of Zimbabwe (1986a, 1986b), Gaidzanwa (1986), Leys (1986), Bratton (1987), Davies and Sanders (1987a, 1987b), Loewenson (1986), Loewenson and Sanders (1988), Mitter (1988), Tagwireyi (1988), and Weiner (1988), for many valuable insights.

with growing food supplies cannot possibly know the threat of famine. The experience of famines all over the world, however, shows how misleading and dangerous this assumption can be. In the case of Zimbabwe too, a closer examination of the facts reveals that the prevention of a famine in 1982–4 must be attributed as much to far-reaching measures of public support in favour of affected populations as to the abundance of food supplies.

Since independence in 1980, Zimbabwe has been ruled by the elected and re-elected ZANU (Zimbabwe African National Union) party led by Robert Mugabe, though the political system involves a multi-party structure. A notable feature of ZANU is its very wide and largely rural support base, inherited from the independence struggle. Political debate is intense in Zimbabwe, and the press is one of the most active and unconstrained in Africa. The press played, in fact, a conspicuous role in keeping the government on its toes throughout the drought period.[57]

In spite of the socialist aims of the government, the economy has retained private ownership and market incentives. On the other hand, the government of independent Zimbabwe has carried out a major revolution in the area of social services. The great strides made since 1980 in the areas of health and nutrition have, in particular, received wide recognition.[58]

In comparison with most other African countries, Zimbabwe's economy (including the agricultural sector) is relatively prosperous and diversified. However, the heritage of the colonial period also includes massive economic and social inequalities. The agricultural sector is highly dualistic, the larger part of the more fertile land being cultivated by a small number of commercial farms while peasant production remains the dominant feature of 'communal areas'. Even within the communal areas, sharp regional contrasts exist both in productive potential and in access to infrastructural support.[59] Further divisions exist between racial and class groups as well as between rural and urban areas. As a result, large sections of the population live in acute poverty in spite

[57] On the extensive coverage of the drought in the Zimbabwean press, see the accounts of Leys (1986), Bratton (1987), and Mitter (1988). Some of the more widely circulated newspapers, such as the *Herald*, did not always take a sharply adversarial stance given their generally supportive attitude *vis-à-vis* the ZANU government. However, even they played a role in maintaining a strong sense of urgency by constantly reporting on the prevalence of undernutrition and hardship in the countryside, echoing parliamentary debates on the subject of drought, calling for action against profiteering, and exposing the 'scandal' of rural women driven to prostitution by hunger (on the latter see the *Herald* 1983).

[58] See e.g. Donelan (1983), Government of Zimbabwe (1984), Waterson and Sanders (1984), Mandaza (1986), Davies and Sanders (1987a, 1987b), Loewenson and Sanders (1988), and Tagwireyi (1988). To mention only two important areas of rapid advance, the percentage of children fully immunized in Zimbabwe increased from 27% in 1982 to 85% in 1988 (Tagwireyi 1988: 8), and school enrolment increased at an annual rate of 20% between 1979 and 1985 (Davies and Sanders 1987b: 297).

[59] This point is stressed in Weiner (1987) and Weiner and Moyo (1988). For further discussion of production relations in Zimbabwe's rural economy and their implications for living standards and famine vulnerability, see also Bratton (1987), Rukuni and Eicher (1987), Rukuni (1988), and Weiner (1988).

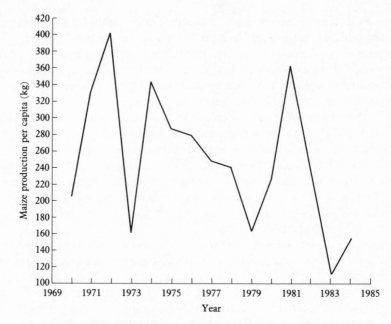

Source: Calculated from production figures provided in Rohrbach (1988: Fig. 1), and from
population data given in UNICEF (1988: Tables 1 and 5).

**Fig. 2.2** Maize production per capita in Zimbabwe, 1970–84

of the relative prosperity of the economy as a whole. At the time of independence, health and nutrition problems in Zimbabwe were extremely serious,
even in comparison with other African countries.[60]

The 'production miracle' in Zimbabwe is of relatively recent origin. In fact,
from the early 1970s until after the drought period, there was—to say the
least—little evidence of any upward trend in food production per capita (see
Fig. 2.2). On the other hand, it must be remembered that, over the same
period, Zimbabwe remained a net *exporter* of food in most years. The plentiful
harvest which immediately preceded the drought ensured that large stocks of
maize were available when the country faced the threat of famine.[61]

---

[60] See e.g. Sanders (1982), World Bank (1983), Loewenson (1984), and Government of
Zimbabwe (1984). These studies give a clear picture of the connections between this poor record
and the massive inequalities in economic opportunities and access to public services of the colonial
period. In the early 1970s, for instance, the life expectancy of a European female was more than
twenty years longer than that of an African female (Agere 1986: 359).

[61] It is worth noting that while the Zimbabwean 'miracle' has often been attributed to the
astonishing power of price incentives (see e.g. *The Economist* 1985 and Park and Jackson 1985), the
expansion of the rural economy since independence has in fact involved a great deal more than a
simple 'price fix'. On the extensive and fruitful involvement of the government of independent
Zimbabwe in infrastructural support, agricultural extension, credit provision, support of co-
operatives, etc., see Bratton (1986, 1987), Eicher and Staatz (1986), Eicher (1988), Rohrbach
(1988), and Weiner (1988).

The drought lasted three years, and was of highest intensity in agroclimatic terms during the second year (i.e. 1983). In the drier parts of the country, the maize crop (Zimbabwe's principal staple crop) was 'a total failure throughout the drought years'.[62] Maize sales to the Grain Marketing Board fell by more than two-thirds between 1980–1 and 1982–3. Livestock losses between 1978 and 1983 have been estimated at 36 per cent of the communal herd.[63]

For many rural dwellers, remittances from relatives involved in regular employment or migrant labour were a crucial source of support during the drought. As in the case of Kenya (discussed earlier), it was found in Zimbabwe that 'the households most engaged in selling labour to the wider economy . . . are the least susceptible to drought'.[64] Many households, however, did not have access to this source of sustenance, and for them government relief was often the main or even the only source of food.

The drought relief programme of the government was an ambitious and far-reaching one. Famine prevention measures were taken early in 1982, and given a high political and financial priority throughout the drought. The main entitlement protection measures were large-scale distribution of take-home food rations to the adult population, and supplementary feeding for children under 5. Commenting on the importance of free food distribution for the survival of the poor, one study of drought relief in southern Zimbabwe comments that 'for those without access to cash and other entitlements it was their only food intake'.[65]

It is not easy to assess how large a part of the population benefited from free food distribution. Estimates of 2 to 3 million people being fed in rural areas at the peak of the programme, as against a total rural population of 5.7 million in 1982, have been cited in various studies.[66] A survey of 464 households carried

[62] Bratton (1987: 224). This statement, more precisely, refers to the two least fertile among Zimbabwe's five agroecological regions. These two regions account for 64% of Zimbabwe's land, 74% of the 'communal lands', and about two-thirds of the communal area population.

[63] Bratton (1987: 223–5). Weiner (1988) reports declines in draught stock during the drought period of 47% and 21% respectively in the two agroecological regions mentioned in the previous footnote.

[64] Leys (1986: 262). On the importance of wage labour and remittances for the rural economy of Zimbabwe in general, and for mitigating the impact of the drought on the rural population in particular, see also Bratton (1987) and Weiner (1987).

[65] Leys (1986: 270). Similarly, Weiner (1988) states that 'during the 1982–4 period the government drought relief programme became the primary means of survival for about 2.5 million people' (p. 71). While the present discussion focuses largely on the food distribution component of the drought relief programme, it is worth noting that (1) policy developments during the drought included an increasingly marked preference for public works programmes (supplemented by unconditional relief for the destitute) as opposed to large-scale distribution of free food, and (2) the drought relief programme had a number of other important components, such as water supply schemes, cattle protection measures, and inputs provision. On both points, see Government of Zimbabwe (1986a).

[66] See e.g. Government of Zimbabwe (1983: 21), Bratton (1987: 237), and Mitter (1988: 4). The official version seems to be that 'at the height of the drought about 2.1 million people had to be fed every month' (Government of Zimbabwe 1986a).

**Table 2.9** Drought and drought relief in Chibi district, Zimbabwe, 1983–1984

| Village | No. of households | % of cattle which died in previous twelve months | % of population receiving food rations[a] |
|---------|-------------------|--------------------------------------------------|-------------------------------------------|
| A | 52 | 28 | 62 |
| B | 36 | 34 | 64 |
| C | 44 | 32 | 68 |
| D | 39 | 47 | 54 |

[a] Per capita rations of 20 kg per month.

*Source*: Constructed from Leys (1986). According to the author, Chibi was one of the worst affected districts.

out in four communal areas selected for their environmental diversity found that more than 50 per cent of the surveyed households were receiving free maize in 1982–3 and 1983–4.[67] Another study, focusing on four villages in one of the most affected districts, reveals a proportion of population in receipt of free food rations ranging from 54 to 68 per cent (see Table 2.9). Very similar findings are reported in a number of further household surveys.[68] While the precise extent of food distribution is difficult to ascertain, its scale was undoubtedly impressive. The size of individual food rations—officially 20 kg of maize per head per month—was also astonishingly large.

Of course, the task of organizing food distribution on such a gigantic scale was by no means an easy one. The implementation of relief measures, much helped by the popular mobilization, the administrative dynamism, and the political stability associated with the post-independence reconstruction efforts, has attracted favourable comments from many observers. But frequent complaints on the part of recipients about the delays, uncertainties, and frauds involved in food distribution have also been reported.[69] In relieving logistic constraints, the subcontracting of food delivery to the private sector played a major role. However, the aberrations involved in organizing complex procurement operations from rural areas to central government depots before hauling food back to the countryside for free distribution have been pointed out.[70] And disruptions in food deliveries seem to have intensified after the attempt was made (in September 1983) to substitute government transport for private transport.[71]

[67] Bratton (1987: Table 10.8(b)).

[68] See especially Weiner (1988: Table 6.4), and Matiza *et al.* (1988).

[69] On both of these viewpoints, see e.g. USAID (1983), Leys (1986), Bratton (1987), Davies and Sanders (1987*b*), and Mitter (1988).

[70] Bratton (1987: 238).       [71] Leys (1986: 270).

The free distribution of food raised its own problems. The population eligible for food rations seems to have been considered, in practice, as that of households without a member in regular employment.[72] How fairly this criterion was actually applied is not easy to ascertain, and conflicting views have been expressed on this question. For instance, one author reports on the basis of extensive field work in southern Zimbabwe that 'as far as I could assess, these criteria were applied fairly and, at the sub-district level, were felt to be fair', and the evidence presented from four village studies in one of the worst-affected districts broadly supports this assessment.[73] But another author suggests the possibility that 'in practice, the distribution pattern was indiscriminate; those who were ineligible received relief food, while those who were truly needy may have gone short'.[74]

The politicization of food distribution during the drought was also apparent in a number of ways (with both negative and positive implications). First, party cadres have played a major role in many places in implementing the distribution of food, and this seems to have led to some favouritism along party lines.[75] Second, the coverage of the drought relief programme in Matabeleland, the stronghold of political dissidents, has been described as 'exceedingly patchy'.[76] Third, food distribution was restricted to rural areas—a highly interesting feature of the relief programme given the frequent bias of public distribution systems in favour of urban classes. It is tempting to interpret this 'rural bias' as a reflection of the politics of ZANU and the predominantly rural character of its support base.

In spite of these reservations, the overall effectiveness of entitlement protection measures during the drought is beyond question. It is not only that 'starvation deaths' have been largely and perhaps even entirely prevented.[77] A

[72] Bratton (1987) describes the eligible population as 'the "needy" . . . defined as those with insufficient grain in the home granary and without a close family member working for a wage' (p. 238). Leys (1986), on the other hand, states that free food distribution was intended for 'the members of households in which the head of the household earned an income under the statutory minimum wage' (p. 269), but later adds that this involved 'distinguishing between those households where the head of household held a formal sector job' and others (p. 270). In practice it is likely that the two sets of criteria described by these authors did not diverge substantially.

[73] Leys (1986: 270). Mitter (1988) also gives credit to the ZANU government for 'the smooth running of the relief committees' (p. 5).

[74] Bratton (1987: 238). The viewpoint expressed by Bratton is based on a personal communication from a colleague at the University of Zimbabwe and would seem to be less robustly founded than that of Leys.

[75] Daniel Weiner (University of Toledo), personal communication. See also Leys (1986).

[76] Leys (1986: 271). The government put the blame on dissidents for disrupting relief efforts, and even at one stage held them 'responsible for the drought' (see Mitter 1988 for further discussion).

[77] According to Bratton, 'it is safe to say that no person in Zimbabwe died as a direct result of starvation' (Bratton 1987: 225). According to Leys, 'one consequence of the drought for some of the rural African population was hunger, and on occasion and specific places, deaths from starvation' (Leys 1986: 258).

**Table 2.10** Nutritional status of children in Zimbabwe, 1981–2 and 1983

| Area | % of children (aged 0 to 5) suffering from second or third degree malnutrition | | | |
| --- | --- | --- | --- | --- |
| | Weight for age | | Weight for height | |
| | 1981–2 | 1983 | 1981–2 | 1983 |
| Commercial farming area | 42 | 14, 20[a] | 16 | 8, 7[a] |
| Communal area[b] | 20 | 11 | 13 | 3 |
| Mine area | 22 | 9 | 6 | 4 |
| Urban area | 6 | 4 | 6 | 2 |

[a] These figures refer respectively to (1) farms benefiting from a health project initiated in 1981–2, and (2) farms excluded from the health project.

[b] Resurvey (1983) area adjacent to that of baseline survey (1981–2) area.

Source: Loewenson (1986: Table 3). Based on a sample survey of nearly 2,000 children in Mashonaland Central. For further details and discussion, see also Loewenson (1984).

further achievement of the government's ambitious relief programme, in combination with the general expansion of health and education facilities since independence, has been a noticeable improvement in the health status of the population of rural Zimbabwe in spite of the severe drought. An important indication of this improvement is the substantial reduction of infant mortality during the drought period.[78] A significant decline in child morbidity, at least in relation to immunizable diseases, has also been reported, and related to the government's vigorous immunization campaigns.[79]

The evidence on the nutritional status of the population during the drought is mixed. There was concern, with good reason, about sharply rising levels of undernutrition in the early phase of the drought, and these were expressed in many informal reports.[80] There is, however, some evidence of declining undernutrition after the relief programme expanded on a large scale in 1983 (see Table 2.10).[81] Taking the drought period as a whole, the available evidence suggests the absence of marked change in the nutritional status of the Zimbabwean population.[82] This is remarkable enough, given the severity of the initial threat.

[78] For detailed discussions of mortality decline in Zimbabwe since independence, see Davies and Sanders (1987a, 1987b), Loewenson and Sanders (1988), and Sanders and Davies (1988). It has been claimed that the extent of mortality reduction in Zimbabwe between 1980 and 1985 was as large as 50% (The Times 1985; Bratton 1987: 238).

[79] See Loewenson and Sanders (1988).

[80] See e.g. Bratton (1987: 224), Mitter (1988: 3–4), and Moto (1983).

[81] See Loewenson (1984, 1986) for further discussion of these findings.

[82] See Davies and Sanders (1987a, 1987b), Loewenson and Sanders (1988), and Sanders and Davies (1988) for detailed reviews of the evidence. See also the results of regular surveys (carried out by the government of Zimbabwe) presented in Tagwireyi (1988).

## Botswana

As a land-locked, sparsely populated, and drought-prone country experiencing rapid population growth, massive ecological deterioration, and shrinking food production, Botswana possesses many of the features that are thought to make the Sahelian countries highly vulnerable to famine. There are, of course, also important contrasts between the two regions. One of them arises from the highly democratic nature of Botswana's political regime, and—relatedly perhaps—the comparative efficiency of its administration. Also, while many Sahelian countries have suffered from declining or stagnating per capita incomes in recent decades, Botswana has enjoyed a growth rate which is estimated as one of the highest in the world.

Economic growth in Botswana has, however, followed a highly uneven pattern. In fact, much of this rapid growth has to do with the recent expansion of diamond mining, a productive sector of little direct relevance to the rural poor. Against a background of booming earnings in industry, there is some evidence of increasing rural unemployment and falling rural incomes since the early 1970s. One study goes so far as suggesting that rural incomes in Botswana (inclusive of transfers and remittances) have been *declining* in real terms at the rate of 5 per cent per year during the period 1974–81.[83] The year 1981–2 marked the beginning of a prolonged and severe drought which lasted until 1986–7, and which would certainly have been accompanied by an even sharper deterioration of income and employment opportunities in the absence of vigorous public support measures. Fast overall economic growth is no guarantee of protection against famine.

The rural economy, mostly based on livestock, crop production, and derived activities, suffered a predictable recession during the drought. The output of food crops fell to negligible levels (Table 2.11). Cattle mortality increased substantially, and the decline of employment opportunities further aggravated the deterioration of rural livelihoods.[84] In a socio-economic survey of 284 rural households carried out in 1984, more than half of the respondents reported 'having no cash income' (other than relief income).[85]

By 1981–2, however, Botswana had set up an entitlement protection system

---

[83] See Hay et al. (1986), especially Table 2. A published summary of the main results of this major study of drought relief in Botswana can be found in Hay (1988). On the rural economy of Botswana, see Chernichovsky et al. (1985).

[84] For details, see Hay et al. (1986) and Quinn et al. (1987). It should be mentioned that while livestock losses during the drought were perhaps not dramatic in *aggregate* terms (according to Morgan 1986, the size of the national cattle herd declined by 22% between 1982 and 1986), it has been frequently noted that these losses disproportionately hit small herds. Cattle deaths in small herds have been estimated at 'more than 40% for several years' (Diana Callear, National Food Strategy Coordinator, personal communication). Also, poor households in rural Botswana derive a greater than average part of their total incomes from crops (even harder hit by the drought than livestock). The threat which the drought represented to the entitlements of vulnerable groups was therefore much more serious than aggregate figures about livestock mortality and the importance of livestock in the rural economy would tend to suggest. [85] Hay et al. (1986: 85).

**Table 2.11** Food crop performance in Botswana,
1968–1984

| Year | Area planted (000 ha) | Yield (kg/ha) | Output (000 tonnes) |
|------|------------------------|---------------|----------------------|
| 1968 | 200 | 180 | 36 |
| 1969 | 240 | 258 | 62 |
| 1970 | 202 | 69  | 14 |
| 1971 | 246 | 293 | 72 |
| 1972 | 251 | 343 | 86 |
| 1973 | 139 | 101 | 14 |
| 1974 | 255 | 290 | 74 |
| 1975 | 250 | 284 | 71 |
| 1976 | 261 | 295 | 77 |
| 1977 | 255 | 290 | 74 |
| 1978 | 260 | 192 | 50 |
| 1979 | 160 | 62  | 10 |
| 1980 | 268 | 172 | 46 |
| 1981 | 274 | 201 | 55 |
| 1982 | 193 | 89  | 17 |
| 1983 | 226 | 63  | 14 |
| 1984 | 197 | 36  | 7  |

*Source*: Hay *et al.* (1986: Tables 5, 6).

exemplary in its scope and integration. This system was, in fact, the outcome of a long process of experimentation, evaluation, and learning. Moderately successful but instructive experiments with famine relief in the 1960s and early 1970s were later followed by a series of evaluations and debates which provided the crucial foundation of Botswana's outstanding relief system.[86] The drought of 1979–80 played a particularly important role in this respect.

Famine relief during the 1979–80 drought was essentially an experiment in what may be called the 'strategy of direct delivery', based on the transportation of food into famine affected areas and its distribution to the destitute.[87] The operation was considerably hampered by logistic difficulties connected with the transportation and distribution of food, though a noticeable improvement occurred after the adoption of extensive subcontracting to private truckers.

[86] The Sandford Report (Sandford 1977) provided a useful background investigation of drought in Botswana. The Symposium on Drought in Botswana (Botswana Society 1979) which was convened, quite remarkably, in spite of the then prosperity of agriculture and the economy, was an invaluable forum of discussion on numerous aspects of the problem. Gooch and MacDonald (1981a, 1981b) provided an illuminating evaluation of relief efforts during the 1979–80 drought and far-reaching recommendations for improvement. For an excellent analysis of the development of Botswana's entitlement protection system, see Borton (1984, 1986).

[87] See Drèze and Sen (1989) for further discussion of this approach to famine prevention. The following details are based on Relief and Development Institute (1985), Morgan (1985), and especially Gooch and MacDonald (1981a, 1981b).

Food deliveries in different parts of the country matched poorly with the extent of distress. The allocation of food within the rural population was largely indiscriminate, partly because the selective distribution of food was found to be 'socially divisive'.[88] While a large-scale famine was averted, the relief operations did not succeed in preventing increased malnutrition, excess mortality, or even starvation deaths.[89]

The lessons of this experiment were not lost, however. In fact, the detailed evaluation carried out by Gooch and MacDonald made a crucial contribution to the design of Botswana's entitlement protection system as it exists today. Their recommendations included: (1) the issue of a Relief Manual providing clear and coherent advance guidelines to the administration about the provision of drought relief; (2) the adoption of a famine prevention strategy based on the unlimited provision of employment to the able-bodied (for a subsistence wage paid in cash), supplemented by unconditional relief for vulnerable groups. These recommendations, while not literally implemented to this day, have provided the basis for a sustained improvement in famine prevention measures.[90]

Careful planning (and buoyant government revenue) would not have gone far enough in the absence of a strong motivation on the part of the government to respond to the threat of famine. Drought relief, however, has consistently been a high political priority in Botswana, and an object of rival promises and actions on the part of competing political parties. It is also revealing that, when drought struck the country again in 1981–2, early action was forthcoming in spite of the absence of a formal early warning system.[91] As in India, the politics of famine prevention in Botswana are intimately linked with the accountability of the ruling party to the electorate, the activism of opposition parties, the vigilance of the press, and—last but not least—the rising demands for public support on the part of the affected populations.[92]

The drought of 1982–7 provided a severe test of the country's growing

---

[88] Gooch and MacDonald (1981b: 11). In other cases, the distribution of food was vulnerable to frank abuses.

[89] On this, see Gooch and MacDonald (1981b: 12–13).

[90] In the absence of an explicit Relief Manual, the Gooch–MacDonald Report itself has served as a surrogate contingency plan during the recent drought (Holm and Morgan 1985), and the associated measures have gradually 'sunk into' the administrative routine (Richard Morgan, personal communication).

[91] Botswana does have a well-developed 'nutrition surveillance' system, but this is used mainly for the purposes of monitoring and targeting rather than as a warning device, and the decision to launch a major relief operation in 1982 was taken long before the system detected a significant increase in undernutrition. Nor do other components of Botswana's evolving early warning system seem to have played a major role in triggering the government's response in 1982 (see e.g. Relief and Development Institute 1985).

[92] For a detailed discussion of this issue, and of 'the political value of drought relief' in Botswana, see Holm and Morgan (1985) and Holm and Cohen (1988). On the politics of famine prevention in India, see Sen (1982), Ram (1986), and ch. 1 in this volume.

ability to prevent famines. The entitlement protection measures invoked to avert the threat of famine in Botswana in this event involved three areas of action: (1) the restoration of adequate food availability, (2) the large-scale provision of employment for cash wages, and (3) direct food distribution to selected groups.[93]

Unlike in 1979–80, the restoration of food adequacy in 1982–7 relied on a more varied and discerning strategy than that of 'direct delivery'. While Botswana did receive large amounts of food aid during the drought, the support of incomes through employment generation (financed out of general government revenue) was not *tied* to the receipt of food aid. Moreover, food aid was substantially complemented by private imports of food from abroad, and it is plausible that had food aid been interrupted or delayed this alternative source of food supply would have enabled the relief system to operate with no major loss of effectiveness.[94]

Trade and distribution within the country has been largely ensured by Botswana's 'widespread and highly competitive retail network operating in all but the remoter areas'.[95] The effectiveness of this system, and of the process of spatial arbitrage, is visible from the remarkable degree of uniformity in the level of food prices in different parts of the country during the drought (Table 2.12). The contrast with our earlier findings on Kenya is striking.

Another important contrast between drought relief in 1982–7 and in 1979–80 has been the much greater reliance, in the former case, on cash-based employment generation as a vehicle of income generation. The provision of employment has, in fact, fallen short of the vision of 'employment guarantee' contemplated by Gooch and MacDonald, and it has been repeatedly observed that the demand for employment has exceeded the number of jobs available.[96] Nevertheless, the extent of income support provided to vulnerable households by 'Labour-Based Relief Programmes' has been considerable. In 1985–6 they provided around 3 million person-days of employment to 74,000 labourers. It

---

[93] It should be mentioned that the drought relief programme as a whole went far beyond these measures of short-term entitlement protection. Public intervention was also very significant in areas such as the provision of water and the promotion of agricultural recovery. For comprehensive analyses of the drought relief programme, see Tabor (1983), Borton (1984, 1986), Holm and Morgan (1985), Relief and Development Institute (1985), Morgan (1985, 1986, 1988), Hay *et al.* (1986), Quinn *et al.* (1987), Hay (1988), and Holm and Cohen (1988). See also Government of Botswana (1980, 1985*a*, 1985*b*, 1987, 1988).

[94] Botswana belongs to the South African Customs Union (SACU), which *inter alia* allows the free movement of food between South Africa, Botswana, Lesotho, and Swaziland. According to Tabor (1983: 71), 'in 1981, 89% of Botswana's imports came from South Africa or through South African borders'. See Cathie and Herrmann (1988) for an econometric analysis of the effect of SACU membership on food prices and food security in Botswana.

[95] Morgan (1985: 49).

[96] See e.g. Hay *et al.* (1986) and Quinn *et al.* (1987). This finding must be interpreted bearing in mind that the level of wages paid was 'roughly equivalent to the salary earned by maids and security guards in urban areas and considerably more than cattle herders earned on cattle-posts' (Quinn *et al.* 1987: 18).

**Table 2.12** Price of maize meal in different regions, Botswana 1980–1983

| Region | Price in August 1980 (Pula/bag) | Price in April 1983 (Pula/bag) | Increase (%) |
|---|---|---|---|
| Ramotswa | 3.84 | 4.73 | 23 |
| Francistown | 3.56 | 4.41 | 24 |
| Mmadinare | 3.73 | 4.70 | 26 |
| Maun | 4.22 | 5.38 | 27 |
| Tonota | 3.59 | 4.68 | 30 |
| Molepolole | 3.70 | 4.81 | 30 |
| Mochudi | 3.41 | 4.55 | 33 |
| Gaborone | 3.39 | 4.51 | 33 |
| Lobatse | 3.34 | 4.48 | 34 |
| Kanye | 3.41 | 4.58 | 34 |
| Serowe | 3.56 | 4.80 | 35 |
| Palapye | 3.36 | 4.54 | 35 |
| Mahalapye | 3.48 | 4.86 | 40 |
| Selibe-Pikwe | 3.33 | 4.71 | 41 |
| Shoshong | 3.38 | 4.82 | 43 |
| Thamaga | 3.35 | 4.97 | 48 |
| Moshupa | 3.38 | 5.02 | 49 |
| All regions, unweighted average | 3.53 | 4.74 | 34 |

*Source*: Tabor (1983: Table 4.5).

has also been estimated that Labour-Based Relief Programmes 'replaced' almost one-third of rural incomes lost from crop failures between 1983 and 1985.[97] Informal evaluations of the productive value of the works undertaken suggest that the contribution of these programmes to national investment has been far from negligible.[98]

Along with this strategy of employment generation, free food has been distributed on a large scale, mainly in the form of 'take-home' rations. The eligibility conditions for food distribution in rural areas are very broad, and include not only the destitute but also other categories such as all preschool children, all children in primary school, all children aged 6–10 not attending school, and all pregnant or lactating women. As a result, the proportion of Botswana's population in receipt of free food rations was as high as two-thirds in 1985.[99] It has been argued, moreover, that 'this food is taken home, mixed in

[97] Quinn *et al.* (1987: 18, 21). The population of Botswana was a little over one million at the time.

[98] See Hay *et al.* (1986) for a detailed discussion.

[99] Calculated from Hay *et al.* (1986: Tables 10, 11). According to the same source, yearly rations amounted to nearly 60 kg of food (mainly cereals) per recipient. For a succinct account of the various components of Botswana's food distribution programme, see Hay (1988).

the family pot and distributed as usual among the family members'.[100] Thus, in practice the distribution of food rations is largely indiscriminate.

A number of commentators have suggested that Botswana's entitlement protection system could be considerably improved by a better 'targeting' of resources towards vulnerable individuals or households.[101] Indeed, the rural society in Botswana is a highly inegalitarian one, with more than half of rural incomes accruing to the wealthiest decile of the rural population.[102] The indiscriminate distribution of food can be a rewarding form of political patronage, but it does not necessarily work to the greatest advantage of vulnerable groups.

How better targeting could be achieved, however, is not altogether clear. An adjustment in the balance between food distribution and employment generation in favour of the latter is an obvious option, which has indeed been advocated. Its attractiveness depends on how need-orientated the distribution of employment really is. In this case the answer to the latter question is far from clear, given that the conditions of employment seem to attract large numbers and that the available work is often divided equally among applicants.[103]

Be that as it may, the experience of drought relief in Botswana in 1982–7 amply demonstrates the effectiveness of a famine prevention system based on the combination of adequate political incentives and insightful administrative guidelines. While the drought of 1982–7 was far more prolonged and severe than that of 1979–80, and led to a much greater disruption of the rural economy, the extent of human suffering was comparatively small. There is no evidence of starvation deaths or of distress migration on any significant scale.[104] The nutritional status of children only deteriorated marginally and temporarily (Fig. 2.3). One study also reports that 'those who have experienced previous droughts say that the decline in suffering among the disadvantaged is dramatic'.[105] Further, drought relief measures in Botswana seem to

[100] Tabor (1983: 37). On this see also Hay et al. (1986).

[101] See e.g. Gooch and MacDonald (1981a, 1981b), Tabor (1983), Borton (1984), Relief and Development Institute (1985), Hay et al. (1986), and Holm and Cohen (1988).

[102] Chernichovsky et al. (1985: Table 1.2), based on the 1974–5 Rural Income Distribution Survey. The same survey reveals that 5% of the rural population owns 50% of the national herd (Quinn et al. 1987: 5).

[103] See Hay et al. (1986). Note that, according to first-hand observations, about 80% of labourers are women (Tabor 1983; Morgan 1988).

[104] According to Morgan (1988), 'starvation, even among extremely isolated communities, was entirely averted during the droughts' (p. 37).

[105] Holm and Morgan (1985: 469). None of the studies cited in this section provide estimates of excess mortality during the drought. According to Borton, 'mortality estimates are poor in Botswana so it is not possible to estimate whether there has been a significant increase in the death rate' (Borton 1984: 92). Against the initial increase in undernutrition among children, it must be noted that (1) the incidence of severe undernutrition has been very small (Hay et al. 1986; Holm and Morgan 1985), and (2) seasonal fluctuations in nutritional status have virtually disappeared during the drought (Government of Botswana 1985a: Table 5).

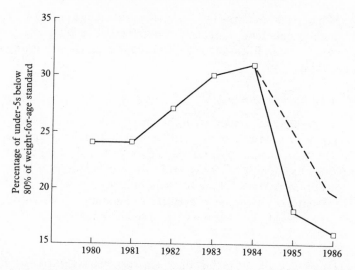

*Note*: The broken line shows the estimated incidence of undernutrition, taking into account changes in the recording system in 1985. The figures are derived from Botswana's Nutrition Surveillance System, which covered about 60% of all under-5s in Botswana in 1984 (Morgan 1985: 45). The increase in observed undernutrition in the early years of the drought may partly reflect the large increase in the coverage of the surveillance system that took place during those years (Hay 1988: 1125).

*Source*: Morgan (1988: Fig. 5).

**Fig. 2.3** Incidence of child undernutrition in Botswana, 1980–1986

have met with an impressive measure of success not only in preventing human suffering but also in preserving the productive potential of the rural economy.[106]

There is another aspect of Botswana's experience which deserves special mention here. A number of components of the drought relief programme, such as the distribution of food to certain vulnerable groups, the rehabilitation of malnourished children, and the provision of financial assistance to the destitute, have acquired a permanent status and are now an integral part of Botswana's social security system.[107] In the future, therefore, it can be expected that famine prevention measures will perhaps take the form of an *intensification* of social security measures applying in ordinary times. Such a policy development would be a natural extension of the current reliance on existing infrastructural and institutional arrangements for drought relief

[106] On this, see Morgan (1986). The preservation of the productive potential of the rural economy is related partly to the entitlement protection measures discussed here, but also partly to a wide array of explicit rehabilitation and recovery programmes. Though they are not the focus of our attention in this chapter, the importance of these programmes should not be underestimated.

[107] See Morgan (1986, 1988) and Holm and Cohen (1988) for further discussion of the interplay between drought relief and social security in Botswana in the last few decades.

purposes. This approach to the protection of entitlements during crises has, in general, much to commend it, in terms of administrative flexibility, likelihood of early response, simplification of logistic requirements, and ability to elicit broad political support.

### 2.5.  *Concluding observations*

The African experiences reviewed in the previous section illustrate the challenging variety of political, social, and economic problems involved in the protection of entitlements in a crisis situation. It would be pointless, indeed inappropriate, to attempt to derive from these case-studies a blueprint for famine prevention in Africa. However, a number of commonalities involved in the recent experiences of famine prevention in Botswana, Cape Verde, Kenya, and Zimbabwe seem to provide the basis of some useful lessons.[108]

*The importance of entitlement protection systems*

There is a tendency, once the dust of an emergency has settled down, to seek the reduction of famine vulnerability primarily in enhanced economic growth, or the revival of the rural economy, or the diversification of economic activities. The potential contribution of greater prosperity, if it involves vulnerable groups, cannot be denied. At the same time, it is important to recognize that, no matter how fast they grow, countries where a large part of the population derive their livelihood from uncertain sources cannot hope to avert famines without specialized entitlement protection mechanisms involving direct public intervention. Rapid growth of the economy in Botswana, or of the agricultural sector in Kenya, or of food production in Zimbabwe, explain at best only a small part of their success in averting recurrent threats of famine. The distinguishing achievements of these countries (as well as of Cape Verde) really lie in their having provided direct public support to their populations in times of crisis.

This is an elementary point, and it is worth stressing only because it tends to be quickly forgotten after threats of famine have subsided. While entitlement protection is, intrinsically, a short-term task, building up flexible and effective response mechanisms is a long-term one. For most countries it involves a lengthy process of experimentation, evaluation, and learning. In countries such as Botswana and Cape Verde (or India for that matter), where a system of disaster response can be said to exist in a state of permanent preparedness, this process has taken several decades. It is encouraging that, after a long period of high exposure to contingencies and of reliance on international assistance, a number of countries in sub-Saharan Africa now attach increasing importance to the development of planned entitlement protection systems. These efforts need sustained attention and promotion.

---

[108]  For a more general discussion of the issues considered in this concluding section, see Drèze and Sen (1989).

*Initiative and agency*

An important feature of recent famine prevention efforts in the four countries studied in this chapter is that, in each case, the initiative and conduct of emergency operations rested squarely with local or national institutions. This is not to say that international agencies played no positive part in such efforts. In fact, their contribution or partnership has, in each case, been helpful. But the essential tasks of co-ordination and leadership belonged primarily to the government and administration of the affected countries.

International perceptions of African governments are steeped in suspicion and sometimes even cynicism. It might be asked how this view squares with the positive involvement of national governments observed in the case-studies of the previous section. Part of the answer lies, undoubtedly, in the special features of the countries concerned. In particular, it is worth noting that the political systems of these countries involve greater pluralism and accountability than would apply in most other African countries.

It may be that, elsewhere in Africa, less confidence can be placed in the ability of national and local institutions to act as the prime agent in famine prevention. This pessimistic view needs, I believe, to be qualified in at least two ways.

First, it must be realized that, in spite of their frequently limited competence and motivation, local and national administrations often have, in many ways, an enormous 'comparative advantage' over international agencies when it comes to the implementation of entitlement protection measures. In particular, international relief agencies frequently find their operations encumbered by heavy and hasty investments in transport, storage, information, communications, administration, and the like when resources of this kind are, to some extent, readily available to the governments of affected countries.

Second, a notable pattern pervading many historical experiences of famine situations is that, when adequate incentives and pressure exist to elicit a response, the behaviour of the local administration is often characterized by an unusual degree of dynamism, initiative, and effectiveness.[109] The functioning of African administrations in ordinary times may therefore be a poor indication of their potential for response in crisis situations.

*Early warning and early response*

Formal 'early warning' techniques appear to have played only a minor role in the famine prevention experiences studied in this chapter.[110] Early response

---

[109] For further discussion of the possible motivations underlying the unexpected behaviour of administrations in crises situations, see Brennan *et al.* (1984) and Drèze (1988). See also the remarkable work of Pierre-Étienne Will (1980) on famine relief under the Qing dynasty in 18th-century China.

[110] This has been explicitly pointed out in the previous section in the cases of Botswana and Kenya. Cape Verde has no early warning system worth the name (CILSS 1986). There is no indication of Zimbabwe having a formal early warning system in any of the references cited earlier in relation to that country.

has been much more a matter of political incentives and motivation than one of informational or predictive wizardry.

As was mentioned earlier, the political systems of these countries are, by African standards, relatively open and pluralist (e.g. they all have an elected parliament). All except Cape Verde also have an active and largely uncensored press. The role of political opposition, parliamentary debate, public criticism, and adversarial journalism in galvanizing the national government into action has been central in Botswana as well as in Zimbabwe, and, to a lesser extent, in Kenya.

The general picture of public pressure that emerges in other African countries is admittedly not a very encouraging one. The opposition is often muzzled. Newspapers are rarely independent or free. The armed forces frequently suppress popular protest. To claim that there are clear signs of change in the direction of participatory politics and open journalism in Africa as a whole would undoubtedly be premature. But there is now much greater awareness of the problem and of the need for change. The long-term value of that creative dissatisfaction should not be underestimated.[111]

Moreover, it would be a mistake to regard sophisticated democratic institutions as indispensable to the existence of strong incentives for a government to respond to the threat of famine. It is true that the ability of a government to get away with letting a famine develop is much greater when there is no direct accountability to the public. But even fairly repressive governments should be—and have often been—wary of the prospects of popular discontent in such an event. Even where such prospects are remote, political ideology—if it takes the form of a commitment to the more deprived sections of the population —can be another creative force in motivating response. In the case of Cape Verde (and probably also Zimbabwe), this influence seems to have been important. As was pointed out in section 2.2, the general attitude of African governments to the threat of famine is certainly not one of apathy and callousness (the main exception being, once again, related to war situations). There are good grounds for hoping that their commitment to famine prevention will receive further stimulation in the near future.

*Food supply management*

In each of the four countries studied in this chapter, the government took necessary steps to ensure an adequate availability of food. But the exact nature of these steps varied a great deal, and appealed to different strategic elements such as government purchases on international markets, private trade, food aid, and the depletion of public stocks.

This strategic diversity contrasts with the common belief that food aid is the only appropriate channel to enhance food availability in a famine-affected

---

[111] On the current role of the press in the context of African famines, and the emerging signs of positive change in some countries, see Yao and Kone (1986), Mitter (1987) and Reddy (1988).

country. It is true that three of these four countries (namely Botswana, Cape Verde, and Kenya) have *made use* of substantial quantities of food aid in their efforts to avert famine, but in no case have their entitlement protection measures been *contingent* on the timely arrival of such aid. In fact, entitlement protection policies have typically preceded the arrival of drought-related food aid commitments.

In this respect, entitlement protection measures in these countries have markedly departed from the strategy of 'direct delivery' commonly recommended or practised by international agencies such as the World Food Programme, which consists of dispatching food to affected countries, transporting it to vulnerable areas, and delivering it (in cooked form or otherwise) to famine victims. The case for exclusive reliance on the latter strategy rests implicitly on the combination of two assumptions: (1) that no effective entitlement protection is possible without a commensurate and simultaneous increase in food availability, and (2) that no reliable channel for increasing food availability exists other than the famine relief system itself. These assumptions appear to be highly questionable on both analytical and empirical grounds.

A particularly significant departure from the strategy of direct delivery is the use of cash support to protect the entitlements of vulnerable groups. This is not the place to assess the general merits and limitations of this approach.[112] But it is worth noting that reliance on cash support, which is sometimes thought to be highly unsuitable in the context of African famines, has been used with excellent effect in two of the four countries concerned (namely Botswana and Cape Verde).

*Private trade and public distribution*

Each of the four countries which have retained our attention has induced private trade to supplement the efforts of the public sector in moving food towards vulnerable areas. In Botswana and Cape Verde, this has taken the form of providing cash support on a large scale and leaving a substantial part of the task of food delivery to the market mechanism. In Kenya and Zimbabwe, it has taken the form of subcontracting to private traders the transport of food to specific destinations. In all cases, private trade could be confidently expected to move food in the right direction, i.e. towards (rather than out of) affected areas.

At the same time, the direct involvement of the public sector in food supply management has also been substantial in each country. The benefits of this involvement were visible not only in terms of its direct effects on the flow of food, but also in the noticeable absence of collusive practices or panic hoarding in the private sector itself. Further, the sharp contrast between the behaviour of food prices in Kenya and Botswana during recent droughts strongly suggests

---

[112] See Drèze and Sen (1989: ch. 6), for further discussion. It must be stressed that the success of a strategy of cash support can depend crucially on its integration with other policy decisions, e.g. those related to food supply management and the role of private trade.

that the positive involvement of the public sector in food supply management is often a far more creative form of intervention than the imposition of negative restrictions on the operation of private trade.

Aside from influencing market prices, public distribution can also perform the role of generating income for the recipients (when food is distributed at subsidized prices). The effectiveness of this particular mechanism of income redistribution depends, *inter alia*, on the extent to which it is possible to ensure that vulnerable groups have preferential access to the public distribution system. The experiences reviewed in this chapter indicate that the scope for redistribution can vary a great deal, depending *inter alia* on the nature of local institutions and politics. The advantages of food distribution *vis-à-vis* other forms of income generation, such as employment provision, depend quite crucially (though not exclusively) on these considerations.

### Diversification and employment

As a final observation, we should note the prominent role played by the diversification of economic activities (especially through wage employment), and by the acquisition of food on the market, in the survival strategies of vulnerable groups during crises. This observation is, in fact, one of the most common findings of the now voluminous literature on survival strategies in different parts of Africa.[113] Two of its implications are worth stressing here.

First, while current food security problems in Africa clearly originate in part from the stagnation or decline of food production in that continent (leading to major losses of income for the rural population), it does not follow that the reduction of famine vulnerability must necessarily take the form of reversing that historical trend. Diversification and exchange have been an important part of the economic opportunities of rural populations in Africa for a long time, and open up alternative avenues of action that also need to be considered.[114]

Second, the potential of employment provision (e.g. in the form of public works programmes) as a tool of entitlement protection in some parts of Africa may be far from negligible. The strategy of employment provision has a number of distinct advantages (notably making possible the use of 'self-selection' and also the provision of cash relief) which cannot be neglected. The fact that affected populations positively look for work in crisis situations suggests this as a natural form of intervention. The scope for employment-based famine prevention strategies in different parts of Africa deserves further investigation.

---

[113] For a review of this literature, see Drèze and Sen (1989: ch. 5).

[114] For an illuminating discussion of the historical role of economic diversification and market exchange in East Africa and the Sahel, see Pankhurst (1985, 1986). For similar observations in West Africa, see Hill (1986).

# References

AGERE, S. T. (1986), 'Progress and Problems in the Health Care Delivery System', in Mandaza (1986).

AHMAD, S. E., DRÈZE, J. P., HILLS, J., and SEN, A. K. (eds.) (forthcoming), *Social Security in Developing Countries* (Oxford: Oxford University Press).

AKONG'A, J., and DOWNING, T. (1987), 'Smallholder Vulnerability and Response to Drought', in Akong'a *et al.* (1987).

———— KONIJN, N. T., MUNGAI, D. N., MUTURI, H. R., and POTTER, H. L. (1987), 'The Effects of Climatic Variations on Agriculture in Central and Eastern Kenya', mimeo (IIASA, Laxenburg); reprinted from Parry, M. L., *et al.* (eds.), *The Impact of Climatic Variations on Agriculture* (Dordrecht: Reidel).

AMBLER, C. H. (1988), *Kenyan Communities in the Age of Imperialism: The Central Region in the Late Nineteenth Century* (New Haven, Conn.: Yale University Press).

ANYANGO, G. J., *et al.* (forthcoming), 'Drought Vulnerability in Central and Eastern Kenya', in Downing *et al.* (forthcoming).

AUTIER, P., and D'ALTILIA, J. P. (1985), 'Bilan de 6 mois d'activité des équipes mobiles médico-nutritionnelles de médecins sans frontières', mimeo (Médecins Sans Frontières, Brussels).

BERG, A. (1973), *The Nutrition Factor* (Washington, DC: Brookings Institution).

BERNUS, E. (1986), 'Mobilité et flexibilité pastorales face à la sécheresse', Bulletin de liaison No. 8 (Paris: ORSTOM).

BERTLIN, J. (1980), 'Adaptation and Response to Drought: Traditional Systems and the Impact of Change', a special study submitted in part fulfilment of the requirements for the M.Sc. in Agricultural Economics, Wye College, University of London.

BIELLIK, R. J., and HENDERSON, P. L. (1981), 'Mortality, Nutritional Status, and Diet during the Famine in Karamoja, Uganda, 1980', *Lancet*, 12 Dec.

BINNS, C. W. (1976), 'Famine and the Diet of the Enga', *Papua New Guinea Medical Journal*, 19/4.

BORTON, J. (1984), 'Disaster Preparedness and Response in Botswana', report prepared for the Ford Foundation by the Relief and Development Institute, London.

——(1986), 'Botswana Food Aid Management', paper presented at the WFP/ADB Conference on Food Aid for Development, Abijan, Sept.

——(1988), 'The 1984/85 Drought Relief Programme in Kenya: A Provisional Review', Discussion Paper No. 2 (London: Relief and Development Institute).

——(forthcoming), 'Overview of the 1984/85 National Drought Relief Program', in Downing *et al.* (forthcoming).

——and CLAY, E. (1986), 'The African Food Crisis of 1982–1986', *Disasters*, 10.

Botswana Society (1979), *Symposium on Drought in Botswana* (Gaborone: Botswana Society).

BOWBRICK, P. (1986), 'The Causes of Famine: A Refutation of Professor Sen's Theory', *Food Policy*, 11.

BRATTON, M. (1986), 'Farmer Oganizations and Food Production in Zimbabwe', *World Development*, 14.

——(1987), 'Drought, Food and the Social Organization of Small Farmers in Zimbabwe', in Glantz (1987*a*).

BRENNAN, L., HEATHCOTE, R. L., and LUCAS, A. E. (1984), 'The Role of the Individual Administrator in Famine Relief: Three Case Studies', *Disasters*, 8.

BROWN, V. W., BROWN, E. P., ECKERSON, D., GILMORE, J., and SWARTZENDURBER, H. D. (1986), 'Evaluation of the African Emergency Food Assistance Program 1984–1985: Chad', report submitted to USAID, Washington, DC.

BRYCESON, D. (1981*a*), 'Colonial Famine Responses: The Bagamoyo District of Tanganyika, 1920–61', *Food Policy*, 6.

——(1981*b*), 'Changes in Peasant Food Production and Food Supply in Relation to the Historical Development of Commodity Production in Pre-colonial and Colonial Tanganyika', *Journal of Peasant Studies*, 7.

BRYSON, J. C. (1986), 'Case Study: The Lesotho Food for Work Programme of Catholic Relief Services', paper presented at the WFP/ADB Conference on Food Aid for Development, Abijan, Sept.

CABRAL, N. E. (1980), *Le Moulin et le pilon: Les Îles du Cap Vert* (Paris: L'Harmattan).

CALDWELL, J. C. (1977), 'Demographic Aspects of Drought: An Examination of the African Drought of 1970–74', in Dalby, D., *et al.* (eds.), *Drought in Africa*, ii (London: International Africa Institute).

——(1984), 'Desertification: Demographic Evidence, 1973–1983', Occasional Paper No. 37 (Development Studies Centre, Australian National University).

——and CALDWELL, P. (1987), 'Famine in Africa', paper presented at a IUSSP Seminar on Mortality and Society in Sub-Saharan Africa, Iford, Yaoundé, Cameroon, Oct.

CAMPBELL, D. J. (1984), 'Response to Drought among Farmers and Herders in Southern Kajiado District, Kenya', *Human Ecology*, 12.

CARREIRA, A. (1982), *The People of the Cape Verde Islands: Exploitation and Emigration* (London: Hurst & Co).

CATHIE, J., and HERRMANN, R. (1988), 'The Southern African Customs Union, Cereal Price Policy in South Africa, and Food Security in Botswana', *Journal of Development Studies*, 24.

CHASTANET, M. (1983), 'Les Crises de subsistances dans les villages Soninke du Cercle de Bakel de 1858 à 1945', *Cahiers d'études africaines*, 89–90, 23/1–2.

CHERNICHOVSKY, D., LUCAS, R. E. B., and MUELLER, E. (1985), 'The Household Economy of Rural Botswana: An African Case', World Bank Staff Working Paper No. 715 (World Bank, Washington, DC).

CILSS (1976), 'Aperçu sur la situation aux Îles du Cap Vert du fait de la continuation de la sécheresse', DPP/5-10-1976 (Comité permanent interétats de lutte contre la sécheresse dans le Sahel).

——(1986), *La Prévision de situations alimentaires critiques dans les pays du Sahel: Systèmes et moyens d'alerte précoce* (Paris: OECD).

COHEN, J., and LEWIS, D. (1987), 'Role of Government in Combatting Food Shortages: Lessons from Kenya 1984–85', in Glantz (1987*a*).

CORBETT, J. (1987), 'Drought and the Threat of Famine in Kenya in 1984', mimeo (Oxford: Food Studies Group).

CORNIA, G., JOLLY, R., and STEWART, F. (eds.) (1987), *Adjustment with a Human Face* (Oxford: Oxford University Press).

*Courier* (1988), 'Country Report: Cape Verde', *Courier*, 107.

DAVIDSON, B. (1977), 'Mass Mobilization for National Reconstruction in the Cape Verde Islands', *Economic Geography*, 53/4.

DAVIES, R., and SANDERS, D. (1987a), 'Stabilisation Policies and the Effects on Child Health in Zimbabwe', *Review of African Political Economy*, 38.

————(1987b), 'Adjustment Policies and the Welfare of Children: Zimbabwe, 1980–1985', in Cornia *et al.* (1987), vol. ii.

DELOITTE, HASKINS, and SELLS (1986), 'Final Monitoring Report on the Drought Emergency Relief Porgram for USAID Mission to Kenya', report prepared for USAID.

DEVEREUX, S. (1988), 'Entitlements, Availability and Famine: A Revisionist View of Wollo, 1972–1974', *Food Policy*, 13.

DE VILLE DE GOYET, C. (1978), 'Disaster Relief in the Sahel: Letter to the Editor', *Disasters*, 2.

DE WAAL, A. (1987), 'Famine That Kills', mimeo (London: Save the Children Fund UK); to be published as a monograph by Oxford University Press.

————(1988a), 'Famine Early Warning Systems and the Use of Socio-economic Data', *Disasters*, 12.

————(1988b), 'A Re-assessment of Entitlement Theory in the Light of Recent Famines in Africa', Ld'A-QEH Development Studies Working Paper No. 4 (Oxford: Queen Elizabeth House).

DODGE, C. P., and ALNWICK, D. (1986), 'Karamoja: A Catastrophe Contained', *Disasters*, 10.

DONELAN, A. (1983), 'Zimbabwe: A Study of the New Nation's Attempts to Progress since Independence, with Particular Reference to Health and Nutrition', report submitted to the University of London in partial fulfilment of the requirements for the Diploma in Food Resources related to Community Development.

DOWNING, J., BERRY, L., DOWNING, L., DOWNING, T., and FORD, R. (1987), 'Drought and Famine in Africa, 1981–1986: The U.S. Response', report prepared for USAID, Settlement and Resources Systems Analysis, Clark University/Institute for Development Anthropology.

DOWNING, T. (1986), 'Smallholder Drought Coping Strategies in Central and Eastern Kenya', paper presented to the Annual Meeting of the Association of American Geographers, Minneapolis, 3–7 May.

————(1988), 'Climatic Variability and Food Security among Smallholder Agriculturalists in Six Districts of Central and Eastern Kenya', unpublished Ph.D. dissertation, Clark University, Worcester, Mass.

————AKONG'A, J., MUNGAI, D. N., MUTURI, H. R., and POTTER, H. L. (1987), 'Introduction to the Kenya Case Study', in Akong'a *et al.* (1987).

————GITU, K., and KAMAU, C. (forthcoming), *Coping with Drought in Kenya: National and Local Strategies* (Boulder, Colo.: Lynne Rienner).

DRÈZE, J. P. (1988), 'Famine Prevention in India', Discussion Paper No. 3 (Development Economics Research Programme, London School of Economics); published as ch. 1 above.

————and SEN, A. K. (1988), 'Public Action for Social Security', paper presented at a Workshop on Social Security in Developing Countries held at the London School of Economics, July 1988; to be published in Ahmad *et al.* (forthcoming).

————————(1989), *Hunger and Public Action* (Oxford: Oxford University Press).

DYSON, T. (1988), 'The Population History of Berar since 1881 and its Potential Wider Significance', mimeo (Department of Population Studies, London School of Economics).

*The Economist* (1985), 'Where Africans Feed Themselves', *The Economist*, 12 Jan.

Economist Intelligence Unit (1983), 'Quarterly Economic Review of Angola, Guinea Bissau, Cape Verde, Sao Tome, Principe: Annual Supplement 1983', The Economist Intelligence Unit.

——(1984), 'Quarterly Economic Review of Angola, Guinea Bissau, Cape Verde, Sao Tome, Principe: Annual Supplement 1984', The Economist Intelligence Unit.

EICHER, C. K. (1986), 'Food Security Research Priorities in Sub-Saharan Africa', keynote address presented at the OAU/STRC/SAFGRAD International Drought Symposium held at the Kenyatta International Center, Nairobi, May.

——(1988), 'Food Security Battles in Sub-Saharan Africa', paper presented at the VIIth World Congress for Rural Sociology, Bologna, 25 June–2 July.

——and STAATZ, J. M. (1986), 'Food Security Policy in Sub-Saharan Africa', in Maunder, A., and Renborg, U. (eds.), *Agriculture in a Turbulent World Economy* (London: Gower).

FIREBRACE, J., and HOLLAND, S. (1984), *Never Kneel Down: Drought, Development and Liberation in Eritrea* (London: Spokesman).

Food and Agriculture Organization (1984), *Assessment of the Agriculture, Food Supply and Livestock Situation: Kenya* (Rome: Office for Special Relief Operations, FAO).

——(1986), *African Agriculture: The Next 25 Years* (Rome: FAO).

FOEGE, W. H. (1971), 'Famine, Infections and Epidemics', in Blix, G., et al. (eds.), *Famine: Nutrition and Relief Operations* (Uppsala: Swedish Nutrition Foundation).

FREEMAN, P. H., GREEN, V. E., HICKOK, R. B., MORAN, E. F., and WHITAKER, M. D. (1978), 'Cape Verde: Assessment of the Agricultural Sector', report CR-A-219A submitted to the US Agency for International Development, General Research Corporation, McLean, Va.

GAIDZANWA, R. (1986), 'Drought and the Food Crisis in Zimbabwe', in Lawrence, P. (ed.), *World Recession and the Food Crisis in Africa* (London: James Currey).

GLANTZ, M. (1987a), *Drought and Hunger in Africa: Denying Famine a Future* (Cambridge: Cambridge University Press).

——(1987b), 'Drought and Economic Development in Sub-Saharan Africa', in Glantz (1987a).

GOOCH, T., and MACDONALD, J. (1981a), *Evaluation of 1979/80 Drought Relief Programme* (Republic of Botswana: Ministry of Finance and Development Planning).

————(1981b), *Evaluation of 1979/80 Drought Relief Programme: Synopsis* (Republic of Botswana: Ministry of Finance and Development Planning).

Government of Botswana (1980), *A Human Drought Relief Programme for Botswana* (Gaborone: Ministry of Local Government and Lands).

——(1985a), *The Drought Situation in Botswana* (Gaborone: Ministry of Finance and Development Planning).

——(1985b), *Report on the National Food Strategy* (Gaborone: Ministry of Finance and Development Planning).

——(1987), 'The Drought Situation in Botswana, March 1987, and Estimated Requirements for Relief and Recovery Measures', *aide-mémoire*, Ministry of Finance and Development Planning, Gaborone.

——(1988), 'The Drought Recovery Situation in Botswana, March 1988, and Estimated Requirements for Relief and Recovery Measures', *aide-mémoire*, Ministry of Finance and Development Planning, Gaborone.

Government of Kenya (1985), 'CBS/NES Survey of Drought Responses, Preliminary Findings', mimeo (National Environment Secretariat, Nairobi).

Government of Zimbabwe (1983), 'Development Policies and Programmes for Food and Nutrition in Zimbabwe', mimeo (Ministry of Finance, Economic Planning and Development, Harare).

——(1984), 'Planning for Equity in Health: A Sectoral Review and Policy Statement', mimeo (Ministry of Health, Harare).

——(1986a), 'Zimbabwe's Experience in Dealing with Drought 1982 to 1984', mimeo (Ministry of Labour, Manpower Planning and Social Welfare, Harare).

——(1986b), 'Memorandum on Drought Relief 1986', mimeo (Ministry of Labour, Manpower Planning and Social Welfare, Harare).

GRANNELL, T. F. (1986), 'Ethiopia: Food-for-Work for the Rehabilitation of Forest, Grazing and Agricultural Lands in Ethiopia', paper presented at the WFP/ADB Conference on Food Aid for Development, Abijan, Sept.

HALL, E. (1973), 'Diary of the Drought', Oxfam News, July.

HAY, R. (1988), 'Famine Incomes and Employment: Has Botswana Anything to Teach Africa?', World Development, 16.

——BURKE, S., and DAKO, D. Y. (1986), 'A Socio-economic Assessment of Drought Relief in Botswana', report prepared by UNICEF/UNDP/WHO for the Inter-ministerial Drought Committee, Government of Botswana, Gaborone.

Herald (1983), 'Hungry Buhera Women Search for Husbands', Herald, 16 Mar.

HERLEHY, T. J. (1984), 'Historical Dimensions of the Food Crisis in Africa: Surviving Famines along the Kenya Coast 1880–1980', Working Paper No. 87 (African Studies Center, Boston University).

HILL, A. (1987), 'Demographic Responses to Food Shortages in the Sahel', paper presented at the Expert Consultation on Population and Agricultural and Rural Development, FAO, Rome, June–July.

HILL, P. (1986), Development Economics on Trial: The Anthropological Case for a Prosecution (Cambridge: Cambridge University Press).

HOLLAND, P. (1987), 'Famine Responses in Colonial Zimbabwe: 1912–1947', mimeo (London School of Economics).

HOLM, J. D., and COHEN, M. S. (1988), 'Enhancing Equity in the Midst of Drought: The Botswana Approach', Ceres, 114.

——and MORGAN, R. (1985), 'Coping with Drought in Botswana: An African Success', Journal of Modern African Studies, 23.

HOLT, J. (1983), 'Ethiopia: Food for Work or Food for Relief', Food Policy, 8.

HUGO, G. J. (1984), 'The Demographic Impact of Famine: A Review', in Currey, B., and Hugo, G. (eds.), Famine as a Geographical Phenomenon (Dordrecht: Reidel).

ILIFFE, J. (1987), The African Poor: A History (Cambridge: Cambridge University Press).

JANSSON, K., HARRIS, M., and PENROSE, A. (1987), The Ethiopian Famine (London: Zed).

JACQUEMIN, J. C. (1985), 'Politiques de stabilisation par les investissements publics', unpublished Ph.D. thesis, Facultés des sciences économiques et sociales, University of Namur, Belgium.

KAMAU, C. M., GITAU, M., WAINAINA, M., ANYANGO, G. J., and DOWNING, T. (forthcoming), 'Case Studies of Drought Impacts and Responses in Central and Eastern Kenya', to be published in Downing et al. (forthcoming).

KATES, R. W. (1981), 'Drought Impact in the Sahelian–Sudanic Zone of West Africa: A Comparative Analysis of 1910–1915 and 1968–1974', Environment and Development Background Paper No. 2 (Center for Technology IDS, Clark University).

——CHEN, R. S., DOWNING, T. E., KASPERSON, J. X., MESSER, E., and MILLMAN, S. R. (1988), 'The Hunger Report 1988' (Providence, RI: The Alan Shawn Feinstein World Hunger Program, Brown University).

KELLY, C. (1987), 'The Situation in Burkina Faso', Disasters, 11.

KILJUNEN, K. (ed.) (1984), Kampuchea: Decade of the Genocide (London: Zed).

KRISHNAMACHARI, K. A. V. R., RAO, N. P., and RAO, K. V. (1974), 'Food and Nutritional Situation in the Drought-Affected Areas of Maharashtra: A Survey and Recommendations', Indian Journal of Nutrition and Dietetics, 11.

KULA, E. (1989), 'Politics, Economics, Agriculture and Famines', Food Policy, 14.

LEGAL, P. Y. (1984), 'Alimentation et énergie dans le développement rural au Cabo Verde', Série énergie, alimentation et développement, No. 2 (Paris: Centre international de recherche sur l'environnement et le développement, école des hautes études en sciences sociales).

LEYS, R. (1986), 'Drought and Drought Relief in Southern Zimbabwe', in Lawrence, P. (ed.), World Recession and the Food Crisis in Africa (London: James Currey).

LOEWENSON, R. (1984), 'The Health Status of Labour Communities in Zimbabwe: An Argument for Equity', dissertation presented for the M.Sc. Degree in Community Health in Developing Countries, University of London.

——(1986), 'Farm Labour in Zimbabwe: A Comparative Study in Health Status', Health Policy and Planning, 1/1.

——and SANDERS, D. (1988), 'The Political Economy of Health and Nutrition', in Stoneman, C. (ed.), Zimbabwe's Prospects: Issues of Race, Class, State and Capital in Southern Africa (London: Macmillan).

McCANN, J. (1987), 'The Social Impact of Drought in Ethiopia: Oxen, Households, and Some Implications for Rehabilitation', in Glantz (1987a).

McLEAN, W. (1988), 'Intervention Systems in Food Crises: The Role of International Agencies', paper presented at the Seventh International Congress for Rural Sociology, Bologna, Italy, June.

MAGANDA, B. F. (forthcoming), 'Surveys and Activities of the Central Bureau of Statistics Related to Food Monitoring', to be published in Downing et al. (forthcoming).

MANDAZA, I. (ed.) (1986), Zimbabwe: The Political Economy of Transition 1980–1986 (Dakar: CODESRIA).

MASON, J. B., HAAGA, J. G., MARKS, G., QUINN, V., TEST, K., and MARIBE, T. (1985), 'Using Agricultural Data for Timely Warning to Prevent the Effects of Drought on Child Nutrition: An Analysis of Historical Data from Botswana', mimeo (Cornell University Agricultural Experiment Station).

MATIZA, T., ZINYAMA, L. M., and CAMPBELL, D. J. (1988), 'Household Strategies for Coping with Food Insecurity in Low Rainfall Areas of Zimbabwe', paper presented at the Fourth Annual Conference on Food Security Research in Southern Africa, Oct.–Nov., Harare, Zimbabwe.

MBITHI, P., and WISNER, B. (1972), Drought and Famine in Kenya: Magnitude and Attempted Solutions (Nairobi: Institute for Development Studies).

MEINTEL, D. (1983), 'Cape Verde: Survival without Self-Sufficiency', in Cohen, R. (ed.), African Islands and Enclaves (Beverley Hills: Sage).

——(1984), *Race, Culture and Portuguese Colonialism in Cabo Verde*, Foreign and Comparative Studies, African Series 41 (Maxwell School of Citizenship and Public Affairs, Syracuse University).

MITTER, S. (1988), 'Managing the Drought Crisis: The Zimbabwe Experience, 1982–83', undergraduate essay, Harvard University.

MORAN, E. (1982), 'The Evolution of Cape Verde's Agriculture', *African Economic History*, 11.

MORGAN, R. (1985), 'The Development and Applications of a Drought Early Warning System in Botswana', *Disasters*, 9.

——(1986), 'From Drought Relief to Post-Disaster Recovery: The Case of Botswana', *Disasters*, 10.

——(1988), 'Social Welfare Policies and Programmes and the Reduction of Household Vulnerability in the Post-Independence SADCC States of Southern Africa', paper presented at a Workshop on Social Security in Developing Countries held at the London School of Economics, 4–5 July; to be published in Ahmad *et al.* (forthcoming).

*Moto* (1983), 'Facing the Drought', *Moto* Magazine, Harare.

MWALUKO, E. P. (1962), 'Famine Relief in the Central Province of Tanganyika, 1961', *Tropical Agriculture*, 39/3.

MWENDWA, H. (forthcoming), 'Agricultural and Livestock Monitoring Using Aerial Photography', in Downing *et al.* (forthcoming).

NELSON, H. (1983), 'Report on the Situation in Tigray', mimeo (Manchester University).

NEUMANN, C. G., *et al.* (forthcoming), 'Impact of the 1984 Drought on Food Intake, Nutritional Status and Household Response in Embu District', in Downing, T. E., *et al.* (forthcoming), *Coping with Drought in Kenya: National and Local Strategies*.

O'GRADA, C. (1988), 'For Irishmen to Forget? Recent Research on the Great Irish Famine', Working Paper No. WP88/7 (Dublin: Centre for Economic Research, University College).

O'LEARY, M. (1980), 'Response to Drought in Kitui District, Kenya', *Disasters*, 4.

OLSEN, W. (1984), 'Kenya's Dual Grain Market: The Effects of State Intervention', mimeo (Oxford: Food Studies Group).

OTTEN, M. W. (1986), 'Nutritional and Mortality Aspects of the 1985 Famine in North Central Ethiopia', mimeo (Atlanta, Ga. Centre for Disease Control).

OUGHTON, E. (1982), 'The Maharashtra Droughts of 1970–73: An Analysis of Scarcity', *Oxford Bulletin of Economics and Statistics*, 44.

OXFAM (1972, 1973), Unpublished field reports.

PANKHURST, A. (1985), 'Social Consequences of Drought and Famine: An Anthropological Approach to Selected African Case Studies', unpublished MA dissertation, Department of Social Anthropology, University of Manchester.

——(1986), 'Social Dimensions of Famine in Ethiopia: Exchange, Migration and Integration', paper presented to the 9th International Conference of Ethiopian Studies, Moscow.

PARK, P., and JACKSON, T. (1985), *Lands of Plenty, Lands of Scarcity: Agricultural Policy and Peasant Farmers in Zimbabwe and Tanzania* (Oxford: OXFAM).

PEBERDY, M. (1985), *Tigray: Ethiopia's Untold Story* (London: Relief Society of Tigray UK Support Committee).

QUINN, V., COHEN, M., MASON, J., and KGOSIDINTSI, B. N. (1987), 'Crisis Proofing the Economy: The Response of Botswana to Economic Recession and Drought', in Cornia *et al.* (1987).

RAM, N. (1986), 'An Independent Press and Anti-hunger Strategies', paper presented at a Conference on Food Strategies held at the World Institute for Development Economics Research, Helsinki, 21–5 July; published in the first volume of this book.

RAMALINGASWAMI, V., DEO, M. G., GULERIA, J. S., MALHOTRA, K. K., SOOD, S. K., OM PRAKASH, and SINHA, R. V. N. (1971), 'Studies of the Bihar Famine of 1966–67', paper presented at a Symposium of the Swedish Nutrition Foundation.

RANGASAMI, A. (1985), '"Failure of Exchange Entitlements" Theory of Famine: A Response', *Economic and Political Weekly*, 20.

RAY, R. T. (1984), 'Drought Assessment: Kenya', mimeo (USAID/Kenya, Nairobi).

REDDY, S. (1988), 'An Independent Press Working Against Famine: The Nigerian Experience', *Journal of Modern African Studies*, 26.

Relief and Development Institute (1985), 'Strengthening Disaster Preparedness in Six African Countries', report prepared for the Ford Foundation, Relief and Development Institute, London.

ROHRBACH, D. D. (1988), 'The Growth of Smallholder Maize Production in Zimbabwe (1979–1985): Implications for Food Security', in Rukuni, M., and Bernsten, R. H. (eds.), *Southern Africa: Food Security Policy Options* (Harare: University of Zimbabwe).

ROTBERG, R. I., and RABB, T. K. (eds.) (1983), *Hunger and History: The Impact of Changing Food Production and Consumption Patterns on Society* (Cambridge: Cambridge University Press).

RUKUNI, M. (1988), 'The Evolution of Smallholder Irrigation Policy in Zimbabwe: 1982–1986', *Irrigation and Drainage Systems*, 2.

——and EICHER, C. K. (eds.) (1987), *Food Security for. Southern Africa* (Harare: UZ/MSU Food Security Project, University of Zimbabwe).

SANDERS, D. (1982), 'Nutrition and the Use of Food as a Weapon in Zimbabwe and Southern Africa', *International Journal of Health Services*, 12/2.

——and DAVIES, R. (1988), 'Economic Adjustment and Current Trends in Child Survival: The Case of Zimbabwe', *Health Policy and Planning*, 3.

SANDFORD, S. (1977), 'Dealing with Drought and Livestock in Botswana', report to the Government of Botswana, Gaborone.

SEAMAN, J. (1987), 'Famine Mortality in Ethiopia and Sudan', paper presented at a IUSSP seminar on Mortality and Society in Sub-Saharan Africa, Yaoundé, Cameroon, Oct.

SEN, A. K. (1981), *Poverty and Famines* (Oxford: Oxford University Press).

——(1982), 'How is India Doing', *New York Review of Books*, 29.

SMOUT, T. C. (1978), 'Famine and Famine-Relief in Scotland', in Cullen, L. M., and Smout, T. C. (eds.), *Comparative Aspects of Scottish and Irish Economic History 1600–1900* (Edinburgh: Donald).

SOROKIN, P. A. (1942), *Man and Society in Calamity: The Effects of War, Revolution, Famine and Pestilence upon Human Mind, Behaviour, Social Organization and Cultural Life* (New York: E. P. Dutton & Co.).

SPERLING, L. (1987a), 'Food Acquisition during the African Drought of 1983–1984: A Study of Kenyan Herders', *Disasters*, 11.

——(1987b), 'Wage Employment among Samburu Pastoralists of Northcentral Kenya', *Research in Economic Anthropology*, 9.

SRAFFA, P. (ed.) (1952), *The Works and Correspondence of David Ricardo* (Cambridge: Cambridge University Press).

STEELE, I. (1985), 'Mali Battles Drought', *Africa Emergency Report*, Apr.–May.

STEIN, Z., SUSSER, M., SAERGER, G., and MAROLLA, F. (1975), *Famine and Human Development: The Dutch Hunger Winter of 1944/45* (New York: Oxford University Press).

SWAMINATHAN, M. C., RAO, K. V., and RAO, D. H. (1969), 'Food and Nutrition Situation in the Drought-Affected Areas of Bihar', *Journal of Nutrition and Dietetics*, 6.

SWANBERG, K. G., and HOGAN, E. (1981), 'Implications of the Drought Syndrome for Agricultural Planning in East Africa: The Case of Tanzania', Discussion Paper 120: 1–49 (Cambridge, Mass.: Harvard Institute for International Development).

SWIFT, J. (1985), 'Planning against Drought and Famine in Turkana, Northern Kenya', mimeo (Institute of Development Studies, University of Sussex).

TABOR, S. (1983), 'Drought Relief and Information Management: Coping Intelligently with Disaster', mimeo (Family Health Division, Ministry of Health, Government of Botswana).

TAGWIREYI, J. (1988), 'Experiences in Increasing Food Access and Nutrition in Zimbabwe', paper presented at the Fourth Annual Conference on Food Security Research in Southern Africa, Oct.–Nov., Harare, Zimbabwe.

*The Times* (1985), 'Harare Health Drive Cuts Infant Mortality', *The Times*, 4 Nov.

TORDOFF, W. (1988), 'Local Administration in Botswana', *Public Administration and Development*, 8.

UNDRO (1986), *UNDRO in Africa 1984–85* (Geneva: Office of the United Nations Disaster Relief Co-ordinator).

UNICEF (1987), *The State of the World's Children 1987* (Oxford: Oxford University Press).

——(1988), *The State of the World's Children 1988* (Oxford: Oxford University Press).

USAID (1982), 'Cape Verde: Food for Development Program', mimeo (Washington, DC: US Agency for International Development).

——(1983), 'U.S. Aid to Zimbabwe: An Evaluation', AID Program Evaluation Report No. 9 (Washington, DC: US Agency for International Development).

VALAORAS, V. G. (1946), 'Some Effects of Famine on the Population of Greece', *Milbank Memorial Fund Quarterly Bulletin*, 24.

VAN APPELDOORN, G. J. (1981), *Perspectives on Drought and Famine in Nigeria* (London: Allen & Unwin).

VAN BINSBERGEN, A. (1986), 'Cape Verde: Food Aid Resource Planning in Support of the National Food Strategy', paper presented at a WFP/ADB Seminar on Food Aid in Sub-Saharan Africa, Abijan, Sept.

VAUGHAN, M. (1987), *The Story of an African Famine: Hunger, Gender and Politics in Malawi* (Cambridge: Cambridge University Press).

WATERSON, T., and SANDERS, D. (1984), 'Zimbabwe: Health Care since Independence', *Lancet*, 18 Feb.

WEINER, D. (1987), 'Agricultural Transformation in Zimbabwe: Lessons for a Liberated South Africa', paper presented at the Annual Meeting of the Association of American Geographers, Portland, Oregon, 23–6 Apr.

——(1988), 'Land and Agricultural Development', in Stoneman, C. (ed.), *Zimbabwe's*

*Prospects: Issues of Race, Class, State and Capital in Southern Africa* (London: Macmillan).

——and Moyo, S. (1988), 'Wage Labor, Environment and Peasant Agriculture', mimeo (Harare: Zimbabwe Institute of Development Studies); forthcoming in *Journal of African Studies*.

WILL, P. E. (1980), *Bureaucratie et famine en Chine au 18ᵉ siècle* (Paris: Mouton).

WISNER, B. G. (1977), 'The Human Ecology of Drought in Eastern Kenya', Ph.D. dissertation, Clark University, Worcester, Mass.

WOOD, D. H., BARON, A., and BROWN, V. W. (1986), *An Evaluation of the Emergency Food Assistance Program: Synthesis Report* (Washington, DC: USAID).

World Bank (1983), *Zimbabwe: Population, Health and Nutrition Sector Review* (Washington, DC: World Bank).

World Food Programme (1986a), 'Lessons Learned from the African Food Crisis: Evaluation of the WFP Emergency Response (Note by the Executive Director)', WFP/CFA: 22/7 (Rome: World Food Programme).

——(1986b), 'Interim Evaluation Summary Report on Project Ethiopia 2488', WFP/CFA: 21/14-A (WPME) Add. 1 (Rome: World Food Programme).

——(1986c), 'Aide alimentaire d'urgence fournie à la suite de la sécheresse 1984–85 au Niger', mimeo (Niamey: World Food Programme).

WRIGLEY, C. (1976), 'Changes in East African Society', in Low, D. A. and Smith, A. (eds.) (1976), *History of East Africa* (Oxford: Oxford University Press).

YAO, F. K., and KONE, H. (1986), 'The African Drought Reported by Six West African Newspapers', Discussion Paper No. 14 (African Studies Center, Boston University).

ZINYAMA, L. M., CAMPBELL, D., and MATIZA, T. (1987), 'Traditional Household Strategies to Cope with Food Insecurity in the SADCC Region', paper presented at the Third Annual Conference on Food Security Research in Southern Africa, 2–5 Nov., Harare.

# 3

# Ethiopian Famines 1973–1985:
# A Case-Study

### B. G. Kumar

## 3.1. Introduction

With the notable exception of sub-Saharan Africa, global food production has
in recent years been keeping abreast of population increase; malnutrition is yet
endemic amongst the poor in the developing world today.[1] Starvation deaths,
resulting from protracted malnutrition, and accentuated by infection,[2] are also
not unusual in many poor contexts. But famines—defined as virulent manifestations of intense starvation causing substantial loss of life[3]—are on the
other hand, comparatively rarer, even though this century has witnessed some
terrible examples.[4] In discussing these issues, it is important to note that while
endemic malnutrition and the associated starvation are in general characterized by the *lowness* of the *typical level* of food consumption and accentuated by a
*declining trend* of food consumption, it is a *sudden collapse* of the level of food
consumption that typically characterizes a famine. The contrast is a crucial one
to appreciate, inasmuch as a dramatic fall in the ability of a group to command
food can occur at a time when the overall trend in food consumption is on the
increase.

An intuitive first approach to the analysis of famines is to focus on the total
availability of food, and to analyse the connections, if any, between a decline in
this statistic and the onset of a famine. This can in fact be quite a revealing

For invaluable comments on previous drafts and other help, I would like to thank, without in any
way implicating, Peter Cutler, Jean Drèze, Judith Heyer, and, especially, John Seaman. Robert
Baulch, Carl Eicher, and John Gray also gave me comments and assistance, for which I am
grateful. The discussions following my seminar presentation in Helsinki proved to be a source of
great stimulation and I should particularly like to acknowledge the penetrating comments made by
my discussant, Henock Kifle. My greatest debt, however, is to Amartya Sen, not only because his
writings served to initiate my interest in this research, but, more proximately, because his
encouragement and support have helped me so much in carrying it out.

[1] A recent estimate by the World Bank (1986) put the figure of malnourished world-wide at a
staggering 730 million. A more conservative estimate, with a review of the methodology used in
measurement, is provided in Lipton (1983).

[2] Cf. Scrimshaw, Gordon, and Taylor (1968).

[3] Cf. Jean Mayer's definition: '. . . a severe shortage of food, accompanied by a significant
increase in the local or regional death rate' (1975: 572).

[4] The recent Ethiopian famine, to be discussed presently, of course comes to mind; but the
most devastating such catastrophe this century was without doubt the Chinese famines of 1958–61
following the failure of the Great Leap Forward, during which close to 30 million people may have
perished. On this, see Ashton, Hill, Piazza, and Zeitz (1984).

exercise. The Irish famine of 1845–7 was the result of a disastrous fall in total food availability brought about by a recurring failure of the pest-ridden potato crop;[5] food availability did decline considerably during the Sahel famine of the 1970s;[6] and, as we shall see, the recent Ethiopian famine was preceded by a dramatic collapse of food availability.

But it should be clear from what has been said above that the connection between the total availability of food and the amount of it going to a particular group or groups is a contingent—and not an inevitable—one. It should therefore come as no surprise that some major famines have occurred with no overall decline in food availability; instead people starved to death either because a sudden increase in food prices cut their ability to buy enough food (as in the Great Bengal Famine of 1943)[7] or because their employment—and hence ability to buy food in a market economy—collapsed as a result of massive flooding (as in the case of the Bangladesh famine of 1974).[8] To understand the causes of starvation and famines, then, one has to go far beyond analysing total food availability, important though the latter may be.

A more general approach to famines, put forward by Amartya Sen,[9] views famines as economic disasters rather than as just food crises. A focus simply on downward trends in the amount of food availability per head—or FAD ('food availability decline') for short—is misleading, according to Sen, because it gives us little clue to the causal mechanism at work, concentrating on aggregates rather than on the *relationship* between people and the food they need. Indeed:

A food-centred view tells us rather little about starvation. It does not tell us how starvation can develop even without a decline in food availability. Nor does it tell us—even when starvation is accompanied by a fall in food supply—why some groups had to starve while others could feed themselves. (1981: 154)

Instead, Sen focuses on what he calls 'entitlements' as an explanatory variable. Entitlements are defined as 'the set of alternative commodity bundles that a person can command in society using the totality of rights and opportunities that he or she faces' (1983: 497). Entitlement relations can be diverse and depend on different facets of the production and distribution system of societies—they can be trade-based, production-based, own labour-based —and so on. Much depends on the type of economy and social structure one is dealing with. In the context of starvation and food supply, each of these entitlement relations represents a different way of ensuring that individuals can command enough food for subsistence, through securing, in one way or another, an entitlement to it. The entitlement may remain safe even though the

---

[5]  See Woodham-Smith (1962) and Mokyr (1983).

[6]  Sen (1981: 113–29).      [7]  Ibid. 52–85.      [8]  Ibid. 131–53.

[9]  See in particular ibid. 1–8, 47–50, and 162–6. Also Sen (1977, 1986a). See Tilly (1985) for an application of this approach to the analysis of European famines occurring between the 17th and 19th centuries.

average availability of food per head has declined. Equally, any entitlement to food can collapse as a result of economic and social changes in the region or country at large even in the absence of any decline in the overall availability of food.

The approach thus presents a framework for analysing famines, and indeed their antecedents—poverty and destitution. It is worth emphasizing, in view of the subsequent discussion, that this framework is a general one and can be usefully applied even to famines where it is evident that the main causal element *has* been a decline in food availability. The wider scope of the entitlement approach can still be used to shed light on the various processes at work which precipitated the famine, and assist us in identifying the broad groups whom it affected.[10]

The purpose of this chapter is to apply this framework to the experience of Ethiopia, a country which in the last decade and a half has been notable for witnessing periodic outbreaks of mass starvation. It has, of course, to be borne in mind that a full account of the reasons for these frequent devastations would require detailed analysis of a host of social and political factors, some with deep historical roots. Such an enterprise is clearly beyond the scope of this chapter, though its importance is obvious. While reference is made below to the political background against which the famines developed, and to the way in which political and military factors operated to intensify the starvation by posing a serious threat to relief operations, the focus throughout is on the development of the famines themselves, the proximate factors which caused them, their social and demographic impact, and the relief policies followed to contain their effects. There is therefore little attempt at social or historical analysis, or consideration of the kinds of political structures the famines were associated with, paradoxical similarities between which have often been noted despite their radically different character. These are no doubt important to the understanding of the political economy of hunger and starvation in Ethiopia, but they are best tackled in a separate paper.

We start, then, with a discussion of the country's agricultural economy, and its continuing vulnerability to the ravages of drought and famine (section 3.2). The experiences of 1972–5 and 1982–5 are then analysed (sections 3.3–3.4), followed by a discussion of the relief policies in operation at the time, and any implications that these might carry for general policy issues (section 3.5). There is, finally, by way of conclusion, an attempt to draw out the main lessons of the Ethiopian experience (section 3.6).

---

[10] This point deserves to be underlined if only because it has been so often misunderstood —witness the persistence of Bowbrick (1986, 1987). The entitlement approach carries no implication that food availability per head is an unimportant variable; it only emphasizes that, even where a food availability decline is a crucial part of the story, an economic—and perhaps social, legal, and political—analysis of the reasons why the availability decline caused a widespread failure of entitlements on the part of a large section of the population needs to be carried out.

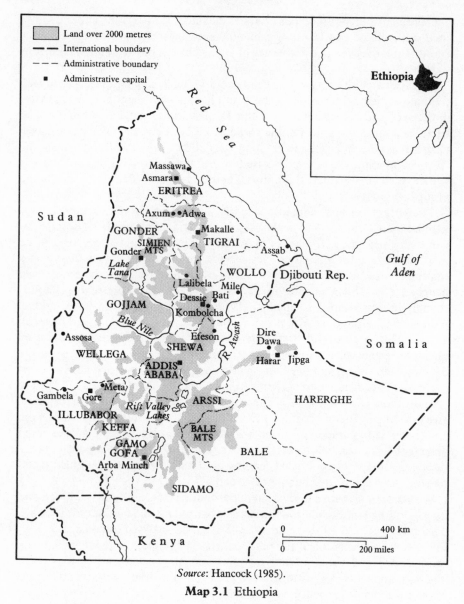

Land over 2000 metres
— — International boundary
— - — Administrative boundary
■ Administrative capital

*Source*: Hancock (1985).

**Map 3.1** Ethiopia

## 3.2. *Famine vulnerability in Ethiopia*

Whereas the long recorded history of Ethiopia provides fascinating insights into the evolution of a distinctive ethos and culture,[11] it is the tragic images of death and destitution caused by famines, recurring time and again, that stay in

[11] For historical accounts, see Ullendorff (1963) and Pankhurst (1961).

the mind. The first recorded famine goes back to the ninth century and no century since then has been free from a major devastation: the thirteenth century witnessed four major famines, and no less than twenty-three are recorded from 1540 to 1800. The worst famine of all, however, occurred towards the end of the nineteenth century: the so-called 'Great Famine' ravaged the country in the years 1888–92, leaving only two-thirds of the population alive. These devastations occurred for a variety of reasons and one cannot really generalize about the historical causes of famine in the country. There is, on the other hand, little doubt that the famine-prone character of the society does not seem to have diminished much in more recent times. A recent study of the vulnerability of the country to the onset of famine makes the astonishing estimate that, 'between two and five million' people died between 1958 and 1977 as a cumulative result of the destitution induced by drought, bad harvests, and famine.[12]

One of the main reasons for this continuing vulnerability lies in the particular characteristics of the largest and most critical sector of the economy: agricultural performance is vital not only for food production, but also for the livelihood of 80 per cent of the working population.[13] Most agriculturists are subsistence farmers who maintain themselves by growing crops or rearing livestock. For most of the year, the vast majority are market-dependent, even for the fulfilment of basic consumption needs. Before the dramatic change of regime of 1974, the agrarian economy was largely feudal in character; a surplus was extracted from a low productivity agriculture by a small group of overlords and cultivating practices were primitive. The new regime introduced radical changes in the social organization of agriculture, such as the nationalization of land, the massive redistribution of usufructuary rights, and the banning of hired labour. These changes, which on the whole proved beneficial to the peasantry, have none the less left unresolved the problem of generating surpluses in the agrarian sector without depressing already low consumption standards. The structural weaknesses of the agrarian economy remain thus another contributory factor to continuing famine vulnerability.[14]

The consequence is that for a large proportion of agriculturists, the famines have only succeeded in making an unfortunate day-to-day situation a tragic one. Evidence in this regard for the 1970s emerges in nutritional surveys carried out in several regions before the 1972–4 famine (Miller and Holt 1975) which revealed very low levels of calorie intake, exacerbated by vitamin

[12] Wolde Mariam (1984: 58).

[13] According to a recent study released by the Ethiopian Relief and Rehabilitation Commission (RRC) 86% of the total population of 42 million live in rural areas. Of the total, 49.4% (17.1 million) are in the 15–59 year working age group and 75.4% (12.9 million) of them are defined as economically active. As regards land use, 65% of the total land area is considered to be suitable for cultivation though at present less than 20% (16.7 million ha) of the total arable land is cultivated. For more details, see Relief and Rehabilitation Commission (1985a).

[14] For a discussion of the problems of agrarian transformation in Ethiopia, see Abate and Kiros (1983), Ghose (1985), and Griffin and Hay (1985).

**Table 3.1** 'Normal' year expected production in Ethiopia

| Region | Population | Av. area under crop (ha/ household) | 'Normal' (i.e. non- famine year) household production (quintals/month) | Share per person per day in a 'normal' year (gm) |
|--------|-----------|------|------|------|
| (1) | (2) | (3) | (4) | (5) |
| Shewa | 8,090,565 | 0.84 | 10.7 | 666 |
| Harerghe | 4,151,706 | 0.45 | 6.9 | 438 |
| Sidamo | 3,790,579 | 0.21 | 2.8 | 174 |
| Wollo | 3,609,918 | 0.79 | 8.3 | 555 |
| Gojjam | 3,244,882 | 1.16 | 11.8 | 740 |
| Gonder | 2,905,362 | 1.05 | 8.9 | 602 |
| Eritrea | 2,614,700 | 0.52 | 4.2 | 247 |
| Keffa | 2,450,369 | 0.45 | 6.4 | 428 |
| Tigrai | 2,409,700 | 0.52 | 4.5 | 287 |
| Wellega | 2,369,677 | 1.05 | 12.3 | 718 |
| Arssi | 1,662,233 | 1.33 | 16.7 | 933 |
| Gamo Gofa | 1,248,034 | 0.54 | 5.8 | 356 |
| Bale | 1,006,491 | 0.95 | 10.1 | 575 |
| Illubabor | 963,327 | 0.59 | 8.9 | 595 |

*Source*: Cols. (1), (3), (4), (5): RRC (1986*a*: 4); col. (2): RRC (1985*a*: 260).

deficiencies and by the presence of goitre: the body fat reserves of the population, as indicated by skinfold thicknesses, were also found to be very low (p. 198). Estimates for more recent years of per person production of food in normal (i.e. non-famine) times (Table 3.1) show six regions, namely Tigrai, Eritrea, Harerghe, Gamo Gofa, Sidamo, and Keffa, falling below the RRC's relief ration of 500 gm per person per day (and of these Tigrai, Eritrea, Gamo Gofa, and Sidamo fall below the critical minimum figure of 400 gm). In some regions, particularly in the southern and south-western parts of the country, the meagre diets of which these statistics are evidence may be supplemented by wild foods or root crops such as 'enset' (false banana). There is little doubt, however, as to the generally poor nutritional situation in the country and the ravages caused by sudden collapses in food entitlement, when the base from which this happens is already so low, can now be seen in some perspective.

Agricultural life in Ethiopia revolves around the country's two principal rainy seasons: *belg* (February to May) and *meher* (June to September). The *belg* season traditionally sees lowlanders planting long-maturing crops such as maize and sorghum. Highlanders, on the other hand, take advantage of the different climate of the mountains to plant short-maturing crops during the *belg* rains, such as barley and wheat, which they harvest in June and July.

The main *meher* (or *kremt*) rains see the planting of long-maturing grains in the highland areas and the main crop is normally harvested in November–December. Although the *belg* season represents only 5–10 per cent of total crop output, it is important to note that it is the more productive season—and occasionally the sole season—in lowland areas like Bale, Sidamo, Gamo Gofa, and particularly Wollo (where 50 per cent of crop production takes place during the *belg* season). A failure of the *belg* rains by itself can thus have a significant impact on the vulnerable crop-dependent population, as will be evident from the discussion that follows.

### 3.3. The famine of 1972–1975

#### (a) Background

The critical events in Ethiopia in the early 1970s can be periodized as follows: in the first phase, namely 1972–3, the north and especially the province of Wollo suffered recurrent crop failure and fell in the grip of famine; the second phase ran from 1973 to 1975 in the course of which the famine moved south and mainly affected the province of Harerghe. Much of the destitution and mortality took place in the first phase and the subsequent discussion will therefore centre on this period, although the fate of the southern pastoralists —hit by drought and animal deaths—will be considered in some detail when we turn to analysing the impact of the famine on different occupational groups.

The erratic behaviour of the weather in 1971–2 did not augur well for future harvests. Although the indications were that weather conditions would deteriorate further, little concern was expressed by the government, and still less any contingency planning carried out. Nature then fulfilled its share of the bargain. The country witnessed a failure of the *meher* rains for 1972, followed by the disastrous loss of the 1973 *belg* harvest. (The former was to have its impact mainly on the lowlands and the latter mainly on the highlands.) By this time, the famine was in full swing in Wollo, and the situation was much as had been described in a Report put out by the Ministry of Agriculture:[15]

The most serious problem is centred in the lowland areas east of the escarpment road in Tigrai and Wello and the lowlands of northern Shewa, with a less serious problem appearing in Eritrea, Harerghe and Begemdir and Simien.[16]

By early 1973, there were signs of the distress in Wollo spilling over to the other regions in the form of migration and roadside destitution: sick and hungry people lined parts of the north–south highway through Wollo, stopping vehicles to beg for food; a march by 1,500 peasants to Addis Ababa to

---

[15] This Report, which related to the 1972 season, was known to the authorities but was deliberately not publicized, for obvious political reasons. It was finally released only in mid-1973.

[16] Quoted in Hussein (1976: 23).

plead for food was turned back by the police[17] and attempts by intellectuals at Addis Ababa University to rouse the authorities into acting against the spreading famine were brusquely brushed aside by the imperial government, which denounced the reports of distress as 'fabrication'.[18] Later in the year, the emperor voiced his views about the famine in an interview: 'Rich and poor have always existed and always will. Why? Because there are those that work . . . and those that prefer to do nothing . . . Each individual is responsible for his misfortunes, his fate.'[19]

The attempts systematically to minimize the seriousness of the situation in the early—and critical—period of the famine, together with the apathy and callousness shown towards the suffering, contributed in no small way to delaying relief efforts. They also ultimately helped to bring about the fall of the imperial regime.

The relief camps that were set up initially were woefully inadequate to deal with the thousands of destitutes who flooded in. Indeed, as Rivers *et al*. (1976) note, 'the crisis of starvation and death occurred from June to August 1973 when the relief camps, exceedingly ill-equipped with food, sanitation or medical services were overwhelmed by some three times the numbers they could shelter, and by August at least 284,000 people had asked for help at administrative centres' (p. 351).

By late 1973 foreign aid had started arriving in considerable strength. Attempts to mobilize it had been greatly helped by the excellent work of the TV journalist Jonathan Dimbleby, who, in his film *The Unknown Famine*, had exposed both the true seriousness of the situation and the shabby attempts at covering it up, and thereby alerted the attention of potential aid givers. By this time, however, the peak of the starvation was already over and the camp population in Wollo had shrunk to 15,000. Indeed by the time the international relief operation went into top gear in early 1974, the famine had moved from Wollo and Tigrai to the south, where fresh destitutes were being created every day. Despite this, owing to a mismatch of aid with real distress, the bulk of the food aid went to the north, with Harerghe, now reeling under the impact of famine, receiving only 8 per cent of relief aid (Rivers *et al*. 1976).

### (b) Food availability decline?

Since the famine was clearly initiated by a drought, it might be plausible to think that the main causal element in the destitution was a drastic decline in food availability brought about by crop failure. There are, however, problems with this explanation.

Consider to begin with the Report referred to a moment ago which the Ethiopian Ministry of Agriculture released after the failure of the main rains in 1972 (Table 3.2). Rather than provide quantitative estimates of output,

---

[17] Wiseberg (1976: 108).    [18] Wolde Mariam (1984: 40).

[19] Quoted in Wiseberg (1976: 108).

**Table 3.2** Aggregate crop production in Ethiopia, 1972–1973

| Region | No. of districts reporting (1) | Normal (2) | Above normal (3) | Below normal (4) | Net below normal (5) = (4) − (3) | Substantially below normal (6) (included in (4)) |
|---|---|---|---|---|---|---|
| Wollo | 21 | 10 | 0 | 90 | 90 | 52 |
| Arssi | 20 | 70 | 5 | 25 | 20 | 10 |
| Harerghe | 22 | 39 | 23 | 39 | 16 | 9 |
| Eritrea | 23 | 78 | 4 | 18 | 14 | 8 |
| Shewa | 72 | 54 | 17 | 25 | 12 | 8 |
| Tigrai | 42 | 84 | 6 | 10 | 4 | 0 |
| Wellega | 35 | 86 | 0 | 14 | 14 | 0 |
| Gamo Gofa | 17 | 82 | 6 | 12 | 6 | 0 |
| Illubabor | 14 | 64 | 22 | 14 | −8 | 0 |
| Gojjam | 22 | 82 | 14 | 4 | −10 | 0 |
| Keffa | 9 | 45 | 33 | 22 | −11 | 0 |
| Begemder and Simien | 29 | 72 | 21 | 7 | −14 | 0 |
| Sidamo | 23 | 78 | 22 | 0 | −22 | 0 |
| Bale | 11 | 9 | 82 | 9 | −73 | 0 |
| TOTAL | 360 | 65 | 14 | 21 | 7 | 7 |

*Source*: Cols. (1)–(4): Ethiopian Ministry of Agriculture (1973) and Hussein (1976: Table 10); cols. (5) and (6): Sen (1981: Table 7.1).

the Report classified districts according to whether production was 'above normal', 'normal', 'below normal', or 'substantially below normal'. This was done for each of the main crops, and for 'aggregate production' for 1972–3. It appears that while 65 per cent of the districts had normal output, 21 per cent had below normal production, and 14 per cent above normal. The below normal category is further split up into those districts that produced 'substantially below normal' and those below normal but not substantially so.

As Sen (1981) argues, attaching the same importance to all the districts, the 14 per cent above normal districts can be 'cancelled out' against the 14 per cent non-substantially below districts. This leaves 65 per cent normal output districts and 7 per cent substantially below normal output. Assuming that nothing was produced in the substantially below normal output districts—a clear understatement—this gives us a figure of displacement from normal output of 7 per cent. As Sen puts it, 'A 7 per cent decline in the output of food crops is hardly a food availability decline (especially in an economy with primarily rain dependent agriculture)' (p. 90). There is thus little indication of a decline in food production coinciding with the famine. The evidence there is rather points to a fall in food production in 1974 after the main impact of the famine had been felt.[20]

### (c) Logistics, food supply and starvation in Wollo

The fact that the evidence points to no dramatic decline in food availability, country-wide, in the famine year 1973 might tempt one to dismiss an explanation premissed on food availability straightaway as unsustainable. This, however, would be rather peremptory. Since the famine was not a generalized phenomenon but had its main impact in the north, and particularly in the province of Wollo, a more disaggregated analysis is necessary before the issue of causation can be settled.

A look at Table 3.2 shows clear evidence of food availability decline in Wollo. Starvation could still in principle have been avoided if food had been moved quickly into the affected areas from other provinces where output had not declined. This tells us that the appropriate unit of analysis in looking at the Wollo famine has to be Ethiopia rather than Wollo itself. And in deciding between competing explanations of the famine, much then depends on whether there were serious logistical problems in bringing food into the province. A view centred on food availability would attribute the failure to avert starvation to the inability to move food sufficiently quickly into the affected areas, and ascribe the responsibility for this failure to the inadequate roads and bad transport with which the country had to live. An alternative view would deny that logistical problems were of paramount importance, since these could in principle have been overcome if the required demand existed, and ascribe the starvation instead to a failure of purchasing power.

Sen's analysis of the Wollo famine is notable for its unequivocal rejection of the former hypothesis. Sen argues that:

the fall in food output in Wollo resulted in *a direct entitlement failure* on the part of the Wollo farmers and a *trade entitlement failure* for other classes in Wollo e.g. labourers and providers of services. There was not merely a decline in the food output to which the Wollo population was directly entitled out of its own production but also a collapse of income and purchasing power and of the ability of the Wollo population to attract food from elsewhere in Ethiopia. (1981: 93–4)

This view is favoured over the transport limitation explanation for three reasons: (1) Roads may be few and bad in Wollo but two highways run through it, including the main north–south road linking Addis Ababa and Asmara. (2) There were some reports of food moving *out* of Wollo through the famine period. (3) Food prices did not go up very much or for long in Wollo, despite the disastrous failure of food output; in fact wholesale price data from Dessie—the main grain market in Wollo—showed very little movement.

---

[20] Direct evidence for this is lacking since the FAO discontinued its food consumption series between 1972 and 1975. However, the data on calorie availability per head in the FAO Production Yearbook (1976) (see also Sen 1981: 93) points to a decline for 1974 compared to any previous year.

In sum, since roads existed and were in fact used to carry food out of the province, transport could not have been a binding constraint on food moving into Wollo: the failure of prices to rise is further indicative of this, since a transport limitation view would have suggested a jump in prices owing to the excess demand arising from supply constraints. A collapse of direct food entitlement, on the other hand, can operate without a rise in market prices.[21] There are, however, reasons to think that this explanation may not be entirely convincing.

First, it is likely that Sen underestimates the extent to which the unsatisfactory road network and the difficult topography of the country could militate against an effective transfer of grain and supplies. In the issue in question, it is not clear that his point that *some* food moved out of Wollo shows anything about food availability and transport not being important limitations, since any attempt to avert starvation in Wollo by moving in supplies would have required an ability to move substantial amounts of food in a sustained manner over a period of time. Further, the inaccessibility of the interior regions of the province—referred to in Sen's analysis (p. 74)—may be more of a problem than he is prepared to acknowledge. It is true, as he says, that some relief camps were set up near the highway where they were accessible to convoys coming in from the capital and also that some destitution was near the main road, posing few logistical problems in terms of administering relief. The overall difficulties created by topography and limited transport have, however, been emphasized by many commentators[22] and clearly did operate as a constraint on the ability to help the starving at a crucial point in the development of the famine: they cannot summarily be ruled out of court.

Second, Sen's use of the apparent stability of prices in Dessie in Wollo to cast doubt on the transport limitation view is questionable. Seaman and Holt (1980), using data from Korem and Alamata in Wollo, have argued that prices did increase as the famine set in. Further, Cutler (1984) has shown that because of distress migration, prices tend not only to rise with a lag, but to rise further and further from the epicentre of the famine zone as the impact of the migration begins to be felt. For these reasons, the data that Sen used, collected as it was from one provincial central market, may not be of the right type to enable a judgement on the price effects of a famine,[23] and his characterization

---

[21] Contrast the case of the Great Bengal Famine of 1943 (Sen 1977) which was a classic inflationary 'boom' famine.

[22] Cf. Gebre-Medhin and Vahlquist's (1977) comment that, '. . . the general inaccesibility of the interior areas, especially of regions like Wollo, due to the mountainous terrain and lack of roads made difficult or impossible the distribution of foods, seeds and animals at the village level' (p. 197).

[23] Cf. Cutler's comment that, 'It may be that Sen misread the situation in Wollo during the last crisis by relying on data from Dessie Market which was a provincial central market getting grain from a large highland non-famine area at that time' (1984: 53).

of Wollo in 1973 as a 'slump' situation is further rendered suspect by the more extensive data collected by Cutler and Seaman and Holt.[24]

Third, the view that transport problems were a principal factor militating against effective relief of the Wollo population—which, in contrast to Sen's presentation, has been highlighted above—might be questioned if it were the case that private trading in foodgrains, by bringing in supplies from other regions of the country, typically provided an important contribution to overall availability in Wollo. Notwithstanding the problems of organizing official relief, it could then be argued that food could potentially have been moved in by traders and surplus farmers (and, by extension, the fact that this did not happen could be taken as evidence that the failure of effective demand was the main causative agent behind the famine). The available evidence, contained in the occasional Reports issued by the Ministry of Agriculture, is patchy, but what there is does not point to interregional trade in foodgrains in Ethiopia occurring on the scale required to even out regional imbalances in production. While private trade was probably not negligible in Wollo in 1973 (since the zoning policies severely restricting it, associated with the post-1974 regime, did not then exist) it is highly improbable that this could have been significant enough to avert starvation during the famine (even assuming for the moment that the requisite purchasing power did exist). In any case, if the earlier argument holds, any substantial private transfer of food would have faced the same sort of logistical problems that, as discussed above, made official relief so difficult.

In so far as a binding transport limitation accentuated the chronic food shortages caused by drought in the province, then, food availability decline has to figure as the major explanatory factor in the famine. Whereas the drought did cause a collapse in purchasing power and limited the ability of the poor in Wollo to command food from outside through the exercise of market pressure, it is clear that supply limitations caused a critical excess demand for foodgrains and that this was reflected in an increase in prices. Despite the centrality of the food availability decline, however, a simple FAD framework cannot be resuscitated to analyse the ramifications of the famine. To understand fully the nature of the starvation and its incidence, we need a more elaborate structure. And a natural way to proceed is to examine the mechanisms through which the decline in food availability caused a collapse in entitlements. It is to this that we now turn.

*(d)   Agriculturists, pastoralists and the collapse of entitlements*

The impact of the famine tended to vary from region to region, depending on the nature of the local economy and the types of entitlement structures in

[24] More fundamentally, perhaps, given the well-nigh universal tendency of prices to rise to reflect scarcity values in a famine situation—either immediately, or with a lag (cf. Cutler 1984: 53)—it is possible to question the analytical value of a formal distinction between 'boom' and 'slump' famines, if it is to be based solely on assumed differences in price movements in the two situations.

operation at the time of the drought. A detailed discussion is difficult in the absence of a systematic survey of the occupational status of the famine victims (as was done, for instance, in the wake of the Bengal Famine of 1943). However, we have substantial field studies to rely on[25] and from these a picture of the destitution can be reconstructed. Broadly speaking, the biggest group of destitutes in the Wollo famine came from an agricultural background, although the relative incidence of starvation was probably greatest for the pastoral people, particularly for the tribe of Afar pastoralists. As for the Harerghe famine, the pastoralists from the Ogaden Somali and Issa Somali groups suffered most, despite the fact that a substantial majority of the population in the province were agriculturists.

A study of the destitutes from the Wollo famine seeking refuge in relief shelters (Belete *et al.* 1977) brings out the fact that the largest occupational category was that of the agriculturist. Unemployed labourers and their dependants, rural water carriers, household servants, and village artisans dominated the shelter population, although the Afar group of nomads were also represented.

What seems to have happened is that, as the crisis operated to reduce crops and the arable grazing land, servants and dependants of farmers were evicted, and were amongst the first to move to look for work elsewhere. Tenants also suffered eviction, and these as well as the small-scale family land (*rist*) holders, were gradually forced to sell livestock, compounding the effects of losing them as part of the impact of the drought. Migration in search of work—never uncommon in Ethiopia—now became a generalized phenomenon. As regards the 'southern' famine, the mortality data from Harerghe[26] show higher rates of mortality amongst the Somali nomads from the Ogaden and Issa groups. Whereas animal mortality and falling livestock prices had a severe impact on rural households in most affected areas of the country, the effect on the southern pastoralists seems to have been nothing short of disastrous, and it is hardly suprprising that they should figure most prominently amongst the destitutes. How exactly did the famine operate to pauperize these various groups?

As far as the agriculturists are concerned, Sen argues that '[t]he entitlement decline here took the form of *direct* entitlement failure . . . without involving the market in the immediate context. The output—typically of foodgrains —was severely reduced and this led to starvation in a direct way' (1981: 101). Thus, the hunger of the Wollo peasant did not depend on the contraction of food output in the region as a whole: rather, it had, as Sen puts it, 'a more direct origin', namely the decline of the food owned and grown by the family. Since the failure of his crop also amounted to a collapse of his source of market

[25] See Gebre-Medhin *et al.* (1977), Gebre-Medhin and Vahlquist (1977), Belete *et al.* (1977), Belete *et al.* (1974), Holt *et al.* (1975), Seaman *et al.* (1974), and Maffi (1975). See also the analysis in Sen (1981: 96–112).

[26] See Seaman *et al.* (1978) and Gebre-Medhin *et al.* (1977).

command (i.e. his income) he could not really supplement his reduced income by market purchase. There was insufficient effective demand for food in the market, and despite widespread starvation, food prices recorded very little increase.

There are, however, reasons to think that in the Ethiopian context, crop failure may work to increase market dependence rather than to decrease it[27] and this would, *inter alia*, accord with our earlier finding that *pace* Sen food prices did on the whole increase during the Wollo famine. When own production possibilities fail agriculturists are forced to find other means of obtaining food by exchanging their endowments—such as their labour or their livestock—in the market, and even by 'economizing' on the quality of foodgrains which they purchase. (Baulch 1985) A failure of direct entitlements thus transforms itself into a desperate search, on the part of the agriculturists, for some kind of market-based entitlement. And as in most such ultimate situations, those closest to the margin of subsistence fall rapidly by the wayside.

Turning now to the fate of the pastoralists during the famine in both regions, their distress was accentuated, as we have seen, by the loss of animals, whether due to drought or to displacement from traditional grazing grounds.[28] But as Sen (1981) points out, perhaps a more immediate reason for their travails was that the exchange entitlement associated with any given stock of animals *vis-à-vis* grain also fell dramatically. Since a pastoralist lives not only by eating animals or consuming animal products like milk, but also by exchanging animals for other means of sustenance like grains—and given that animal calories cost about twice as much as grain calories (Seaman *et al.* 1978)—a pastoral family can survive on a much lower holding of animals if it sells animals to buy grains. Indeed, it has been estimated[29] that in normal times the typical pastoralist tends to meet about half his calorie requirements through agricultural rather than pastoral production. This relative price effect is therefore crucial to understanding the starvation of the pastoralist. Exchange rates between animals and grain did fall generally, but the southern famine in Harerghe was notable for witnessing a precipitous fall in these indices.

The effect of exchange rate declines and losses due to mortality on the pastoral population have been illuminatingly analysed by Sen in his study of the Harerghe famine, and some of the results can be seen in Table 3.3 reproduced from his work. Notice, among other things: (1) the percentage

[27] Thus Cutler and Stephenson (1984) comment, in relation to the current famine: 'When farmers suffer crop failure, they actually become more dependent upon marketing their labour and other assets in order to survive. Even when outright famine rages, starving peasants desperately engage in petty trading in an attempt to make small profits for consumption.'

[28] Large tracts of good land in the Awash Valley were taken over during 1970–1 by foreign-owned companies for growing commercial crops, particularly cotton and sugar, and this obviously led to a serious reduction in grazing land. On this see Bondestam (1974) and Hussein (1976).

[29] Rivers *et al.* (1976: 354).

**Table 3.3** Grain entitlement loss due to animal loss and exchange rate change

| | Average stock of cattle | | |
|---|---|---|---|
| | Southern Ogaden stratum | Northern stratum | Issa stratum |
| Value in pre-drought holdings | 1.0 | 1.0 | 1.0 |
| Animal loss owing to exchange rate $(q)$ (%) | 48 | 57 | 79 |
| Total grain entitlement loss $(p)$ (%) | 70 | 68 | 62 |
| Total grain entitlement loss $(p + q - pq)$ (%) | 84 | 86 | 92 |
| Ratio of exchange rate loss to animal ownership loss $(p/q)$ | 1.46 | 1.18 | 0.78 |

*Source*: Reproduced with some omissions from Sen (1981: Table 7.7, p. 108).

losses of grain entitlement from animal holdings as a combined result of animal loss and exchange rate deterioration are very large for all the pastoral areas, namely 84 per cent for southern Ogaden, 86 per cent for northern Ogaden, and as much as 92 per cent for the Issa desert; (2) in both southern Ogaden and northern Ogaden, the contribution of the exchange rate seems substantially larger than that of animal loss as such.

Given the lower cost of acquiring calories through exchanging animals for grain rather than consuming the animals themselves, hard times push the pastoralist to be more and more dependent on grains acquired through animal sales. Animal mortality combined with a deteriorating exchange rate for grains has therefore a doubly damaging effect on the pastoralist. Faced with such an alliance between nature and the market mechanism, there is really little that he can do to resist incipient starvation.

### (e)  Mortality patterns in the famines

The real crisis of starvation and death in the Wollo famine occurred from June to August 1973, during which time the relief camps were simply overwhelmed by destitute people. Mortality estimates for this period vary considerably. Whereas the official estimate of the Relief and Rehabilitation Commission suggests that only 10,000 people died, a UNICEF study puts the figure at between 50,000 and 100,000.[30] (At this time, the population of Wollo was estimated at 2.4 million of which less than one million lived in the main drought area.) As far as the second phase goes, it appears that mortality had reached its peak by March 1975 when 30,000 people—mainly women and children—had settled around a few large centres in the Ogaden where camps

---

[30] Quoted in Gebre-Medhin and Vahlquist (1977: 197).

were being organized. This number was far in excess of anything the authorities could handle, and the severe overcrowding and the insanitary conditions it
created made the situation potentially disastrous. Oxfam reports speak of a
peak death rate of 150 children a day, which had not fallen below 50 a day by
early April 1975. In the last months of 1975, some 88,000 people were still
believed to be living in 19 relief centres. In total, then, between 1972 and 1975
there were, according to Rivers *et al.* (1976), 'an excess of at least 100,000
deaths due to starvation and associated diseases' (p. 355).

The study of the shelter population in Wollo—referred to earlier—(cf.
Belete *et al.* 1977) documents the appalling conditions that obtained in many of
the impromptu relief camps set up at the time. The lack of basic amenities
made inevitable the spread of infectious diseases—and these particularly
affected children. Diarrhoea, measles, whooping cough, and respiratory
infections claimed a large toll of young lives, though precise estimates are
lacking.

Further insights into the pattern of mortality in Wollo can be gained by
considering the results of a study carried out by Maffi (1975), between
February 1974 and February 1975, i.e. after the worst of the crisis was over.
This allows insights into the famine's demographic impact in the immediate
aftermath of the critical events. Notice from Table 3.4, which reproduces some
of Maffi's estimates, that the eastern lowlands—where a majority of the Afar
pastoralists live—show the highest incidence of excess mortality (both over all
age groups, and amongst children). It was suggested earlier that the eastern
herdsmen were, in relative terms, the group worst affected by the crisis; here
we find further support for this proposition in the mortality pattern that
emerges. Another important point to notice is that the table provides evidence
of the very high proportion of excess mortality amongst infants, indicating
once again the devastating impact of infectious diseases which particularly
affected the young.

**Table 3.4** Excess mortality in Wollo, February
1974–February 1975 (%)

|                  | All ages | Infants |
| ---------------- | -------- | ------- |
| *Wollo Province* | 61       | 119     |
| East             | 61       | 124     |
| West             | 61       | 103     |
| *Lowlands*       | 63       | 128     |
| Eastern          | 65       | 137     |
| Western          | 62       | 106     |
| *Highlands*      | 56       | 100     |
| Eastern          | 54       | 98      |
| Western          | 58       | 103     |

*Source*: Maffi (1975: 17).

**Table 3.5** Mortality amongst under-5s reported by different groups in Harerghe, year ending 1974

| Area | Pastoralists | | | Farmers | |
|---|---|---|---|---|---|
| | Issa desert | North Ogaden | South Ogaden | High land | Main areas |
| Deaths/1000 population 0–4.99 years | 306 | 290 | 290 | 92 | 142 |

*Source*: Rivers *et al*. (1976: 354).

Turning now to the Harerghe famine, the results of surveys carried out in 1974, in the midst of the crisis, provide firm indications into the main trends in the destitution.[31] Nutritional measurements of sample populations showed that the worst effects of the drought had occurred in the Ogaden. Continuing rain failure there had forced pastoralists to migrate, and it is no coincidence that the worst-nourished pastoral groups were found at seasonally unusual locations.[32] Table 3.5 gives evidence of a different sort on the pattern of under-5 mortality in the province. In the year previous to the survey, i.e. 1973, this indicator of impending famine was virtually unchanged for agricultural peoples but increased about threefold amongst pastoralists. The high mortality amongst pastoral groups is associated by the authors with food shortage, especially since this went together with 'a lower herdsize and a tendency to cluster along roads' (Rivers *et al*. 1976: 354)—presumably in search of relief shelters. The acute difficulties caused to the pastoralists as a result of falling animal prices, combined with the increase in grain prices, have already been discussed above; the mortality evidence just reviewed, then, serves as a grim reminder of what this process ultimately led to.

### 3.4.   *The famine of 1982–1985*

#### (*a*)   *Background*

The recent Ethiopian famine, the final impact of which it is still too early to gauge, has been a much bigger catastrophe than the one just discussed. Some commentators have in fact likened it to the 'Great Famine' which ravaged the

---

[31]   See Rivers *et al*. (1976) and Seaman *et al*. (1978).

[32]   Herdsmen tend to treat cattle as a better insurance against drought than carried-over stocks of grain. For this reason, they were tied to the land around water points for their cattle, and were reluctant to move in search of better weather conditions until it was clear that their own land would provide them with nothing. When they finally decided to do so, however, the available water points proved to be too far away, and they ended up suffering not only a harvest loss, but the loss of their cattle. For an elaboration, see Seaman *et al*. (1978).

country in the last decade of the nineteenth century, and suggested that the same heavy toll in human lives would have been paid had not a last minute emergency programme begun to get underway in October 1984.[33] In the event, excess mortality was estimated to have reached 175,000 by mid-1984[34] and it is all but certain that the total mortality figure will be in excess of one million.[35]

The origins of the current famine actually go back to the intermittent food crises of the 1970s, accentuated, among other things, by the effects of the Ogaden conflict of 1977–8. The social convulsions that shook the country during this period, consequent on the coming to power of the military regime, and the debilitating effects of the civil war which the regime was waging against separatist forces in the north of the country, also played no small part in increasing the country's vulnerability to the depredations caused by endemic food shortages. By 1982, the famine had come into its own in the northern provinces, though it took the international community another two years to recognize the true magnitude of the crisis. The regime's own belated recognition of the scale of the impending catastrophe and its increasing preoccupation with the tenth anniversary celebrations of the fall of the imperial order also did much to delay relief efforts. Before the famine itself is analysed, therefore, it is best to begin with a brief review of the interplay between developments in Ethiopia and their perception abroad in the period when the famine was transformed from a localized crisis to a major international media event. This background is important in assessing both the delayed reaction of the international community and the callousness of the country's own regime as elements in the intensification of starvation.

### (b)  Discovering the famine

The existence of a major famine in Ethiopia only became apparent to the outside world in the autumn of 1984, when television crews managed to reach some of the worst-affected relief camps and filmed excruciating scenes of starvation and death. In particular, the evocative reporting from Korem in Wollo by the BBC journalist Michael Buerk and the unforgettable camera work of Mohammed Amin[36] managed to capture world-wide public attention to such an extent as to render further complacency on the part of governments well-nigh impossible and made the organization of relief assistance an urgent

---

[33]  Hancock (1985: 66).

[34]  Cutler and Stephenson (1984).

[35]  To get an idea of the scale of the disaster, consider that an authority on famines like Aykroyd, writing in the mid-1970s, could express the view that, 'a death toll of perhaps over 100,000 [is] . . . inexcusable at this stage in the history of famine' (1974: 203).

[36]  The closing words of Buerk's commentary on the situation in the camp he visited have been much quoted in this context and well illustrate the dimensions of the human tragedy in what was taking place: 'Dawn, and as the sun breaks through the piercing chill of night on the plain outside Korem, it lights up a biblical famine, now, in the twentieth century. This place, say workers here, is the closest thing to hell on earth.'

political priority. The role of the media, firstly in providing a forum through which public concern could be channelled into effective public action— witness the stunning success of the Live Aid Concert organized by the singer and media personality Bob Geldof the following summer—and secondly, in making it impossible for governments to ignore the demands of a concerned electorate for narrow political ends deserves, then, in this context to be both highlighted and praised.[37]

But whereas the media exposure set in motion a sustained relief operation, and must have thereby saved countless lives, the fact that it came only in the closing months of 1984 meant that it had in an important sense come too late: by 1984 Ethiopia was a famine-devastated country and thousands of lives had already been lost. The apparatus of famine forecasting and alert had failed miserably.

Yet it was not as though no warning had been given of the impending crisis. As early as May 1981 a presentation to the United Nations Conference on Least Developed Countries from the Relief and Rehabilitation Commission (RRC) of Ethiopia provided evidence of an alarming deterioration in weather conditions in the country. It was argued that persistent rain failures and drought would certainly lead to famine in the near future unless a co-ordinated international relief programme was set in motion. This appeal, however, aroused as little international interest as the subsequent ones that the RRC advanced—with increasing stridency in 1982 and 1983—as the continuing failure of the rains in the northern provinces confirmed its own worst fears about the gravity of the situation. That these were no false alarms should by then have been clear in view of the accumulating evidence in favour of an incipient crisis.[38]

At the same time as the RRC pursued its international appeals, however, domestic political priorities in Ethiopia dictated that news about the famine should be played down. During the early part of 1984, official attention was directed to the twin tasks of establishing a new party and celebrating the tenth anniversary of the coming to power of the country's military rulers, and news of the famine came as an unwelcome reminder that the celebrations might just be masking a reality that was growing uglier by the day. Groups of starving peasants, who had marched from the provinces of Wollo and Tigrai seeking —as their countrymen a decade ago had done—an escape from desperate hunger, were intercepted at roadblocks seven or eight miles north of Addis Ababa. At the same time, foreigners, and particularly foreign journalists in the capital to cover the anniversary functions, were refused permission to visit the

---

[37] For an account of the background to the famine, and in particular the role of the media in arousing public concern, see Gill (1986).

[38] Major Dawit Wolde Giorgis, the head of the RRC, apparently did his best to get the Politbureau to respond appropriately to the emergency, but 'they just didn't want to know' (quoted in Gill 1986: 100).

north of the country. Nothing, it appeared, was to be allowed to detract from the government's chosen aim of demonstrating its achievements of the previous decade in the most spectacular fashion.

In early 1984, in response to the growing sense of crisis, the UN's Food and Agricultural Organization (FAO) prepared a list of 'calamity affected countries', largely based on expected crop failures, identifying no less than twenty-four countries in Africa in 1984 as in need of aid. There was, however, no attempt to discriminate amongst countries facing varying degrees of emergency and, in particular, no effort was made to highlight the case of Ethiopia. This militated against any concentrated attempt to mobilize support for the famine, which by this time was affecting, on the RRC's calculation, more than five million people, and the relief of which needed some 900,000 tonnes of grain.[39]

In subsequent estimates produced after a series of missions to the country, what seems to have dominated the FAO's thinking was a concern with how much food Ethiopia could distribute, so that as a general rule, any estimates put forward by the RRC were slashed on the grounds that the country did not have the logistical support system to distribute what was being requested. This confusion—if such it was—between *need* and *logistical capacity to meet need* in the event unwittingly provided ammunition to those who wished to challenge the more alarming reports of deterioration in Ethiopia and justified the view that there was really enough grain in the country, the main question being one of adequately mobilizing the available surplus.[40] It was actually only towards the end of 1984 that some sort of parity of views was achieved between the FAO and the RRC: both seemed to agree that the extent of the shortfall was between 1.7 million and 2 million tonnes (representing the consumption of between 6.5 and 8 million people). By then, of course, the famine was in full swing.

The picture, in sum, is one of unconscionable delay on the part of the international donor community in realizing the magnitude of the crisis and co-ordinating the appropriate response to it; the delay seems also to have been compounded by a faulty analysis of the situation. In addition, the misdirected political priorities of the regime and its inability or unwillingness to mobilize wholeheartedly against the famine further added to the problem. What impact did this tardy response have on the ability of the country to fight the famine? Could a well-thought-out initial response have prevented the spread of the devastation? These are questions to be taken up once the famine itself is analysed.

---

[39] This figure for the RRC's estimate at this period is taken from Gill (1986).

[40] That port and transport facilities were at least initially hopelessly inadequate to cope with the volume of relief to be distributed and limited the effectiveness of the emergency operations is of course true and will be further discussed presently. Note, however, that this is, if anything, an argument for trying to improve the distributional capacity, not one for tailoring needs to an estimate of the extent to which they can be fulfilled: doing the latter only confuses the issue.

(c)   *Phases in the disaster*

The recent events in Ethiopia that finally brought forth the international reaction discussed above can, broadly speaking, be partitioned into four phases:[41]

Phase I: from April–May of 1981 to March of 1983;
Phase II: from April–May of 1983 to March of 1984;
Phase III: from April–May of 1984 to September of 1985;
Phase IV: October 1985 and thereafter.

The current crisis first manifested itself in deteriorating conditions in the northern provinces of Wollo, Tigrai, and Eritrea in 1980–1. But what we have called Phase I really revealed itself as the 1982 *belg* season failed in Tigrai and Eritrea (the culmination of five bad harvests in these two regions). An Oxfam study for the period notes that while 'Eritrean dura (sorghum) prices more than doubled in 1982', sections of the population 'managed to survive eating wild fruits such as cactus and wild grass seeds'.[42] The *belg*-producing regions of Wollo, Bale, Gonder, Shewa, and Sidamo—the last two of which had never previously experienced severe droughts—were now being affected. The *meher* rains were also below normal in several regions and there were alarming indications that the drought had transformed itself into something more than a regional manifestation. Some 2,270,000 were by then estimated to have been affected[43] although few indications existed at this stage of general famine mortality. At this stage migration in search of food had started and starving

**Table 3.6** Total number of people affected by famine, Ethiopia 1981–1985

|            | 1981    | 1982    | 1983      | 1984      | 1985      |
|------------|---------|---------|-----------|-----------|-----------|
| Wollo      | 450,000 | 592,000 | 1,100,230 | 1,820,970 | 2,587,420 |
| Shewa      | 239,000 | 533,000 | 195,000   | 204,310   | 851,830   |
| Tigrai     | 500,000 | 600,000 | 1,000,000 | 1,300,000 | 1,400,000 |
| Gonder     | 67,000  | 202,000 | 424,600   | 324,500   | 363,000   |
| Harerghe   | 420,000 | 384,000 | 285,000   | 278,830   | 875,080   |
| Sidamo     | n/a     | 303,000 | 145,000   | 355,040   | 532,500   |
| Gamo Gofa  | 232,000 | n/a     | n/a       | 79,880    | 106,330   |
| Bale       | 275,000 | 109,000 | 35,000    | 52,950    | 192,870   |
| Arssi      | 185,000 | 220,000 | 60,000    | 20,530    | 81,610    |
| Wellega    | n/a     | n/a     | n/a       | n/a       | 23,420    |
| Illubabor  | n/a     | 20,000  | n/a       | n/a       | 20,400    |
| Keffa      | n/a     | n/a     | n/a       | n/a       | 58,000    |
| Gojjam     | n/a     | 83,600  | 20,000    | 35,250    | 76,120    |

*Source*: RRC (1986*b*).

[41] There is, of course, an element of continuity underlying this division.
[42] Quoted in Hancock (1985: 76).        [43] FAO (1983).

**Table 3.7** Trend in per capita per day grain production available for food, 1981–1985 (1981 = 100)

| Region | Relative weight in production | 1982 | 1983 | 1984 | 1985 | Average shortfall 1982–5 | Weighted average shortfall 1982–5 | Weighted average shortfall 1984–5 |
|---|---|---|---|---|---|---|---|---|
| (1) | (2) | (3) | (4) | (5) | (6) | (7) | (8) | (9) |
| Wollo | 0.076 | 83 | 49 | 46 | 14 | −52 | −3.95 | −5.32 |
| Tigrai | 0.039 | 97 | [49] | [46] | [14] | −52 | −2.03 | −2.73 |
| Eritrea | 0.034 | 104 | [49] | [46] | [14] | −52 | −1.77 | −2.38 |
| Gamo Gofa | 0.049 | 75 | 114 | 75 | 75 | +15 | −0.74 | −1.23 |
| Harerghe | 0.060 | 109 | 135 | 100 | 52 | +1 | −0.06 | −1.44 |
| Bale | 0.079 | 183 | 225 | 146 | 62 | +54 | +4.27 | +0.16 |
| Keffa | 0.059 | 68 | 105 | 105 | 65 | +14 | −0.83 | −0.89 |
| Sidamo | 0.024 | 73 | 101 | 93 | 60 | +15 | −0.36 | −0.58 |
| Illubabor | 0.081 | 122 | 194 | 213 | 100 | +14 | +1.13 | +0.57 |
| Gonder | 0.082 | 106 | 149 | 96 | 80 | +8 | +0.66 | −0.98 |
| Shewa | 0.091 | 80 | 108 | 84 | 59 | +18 | −1.64 | −2.63 |
| Wellega | 0.098 | 117 | 129 | 112 | 63 | +5 | +0.49 | −1.27 |
| Gojjam | 0.101 | 100 | 115 | 103 | 117 | +9 | +0.91 | +1.01 |
| Arssi | 0.130 | 108 | 112 | 85 | 64 | +8 | −1.04 | +0.91 |
| TOTAL | 1.000 | | | | | | −4.96 | −9.75 |
|  |  |  |  |  |  |  |  | −27.45 |

*Notes:* Per capita per day calculation is made based on the assumption that post harvest losses are at an average of 10%.

Population is estimated from the 1984 population census results which indicated a 2.9% rate of annual population growth.

The figures in cols. (4)–(6) for Tigrai and Eritrea are not available. However, since it is known that these two regions—along with Wollo—suffered the most in the period 1983–5 we assume in the calculation that their average shortfalls were the same as that of Wollo. This explains why these figures are reproduced in brackets in cols. (4)–(6).

*Source:* Cols. (1), (3)–(9): computed from RRC (1985b); col. (2): Computed from data on production/person/day in a 'normal' year from Table 3.1.

peasants from Korem in Wollo had trekked to the main road near their dwellings in search of relief.[44]

Phase II was marked by the renewed failure of the *belg* season in 1983, and conditions consequently worsened in the northern provinces. Reports speak of hunger and deteriorating health conditions, particularly in Gonder where the influx of people from western Wollo in search of food caused intolerable strains on the resources available. The deepening drought also increased the rate of cattle mortality in these regions, cutting at a stroke the principal source of livelihood for many pastoralists. At this stage, it was still possible to hope that further devastation could be averted. The RRC, as detailed above, was desperately trying to mobilize international assistance during this period. Indeed, the *meher* rains for 1983 actually brought some hope of improvement: the crop harvested was higher than in 1982 and food output in 1983 rose in provinces like Arssi, Gojjam, and Illubabor (Table 3.7).

However conditions had deteriorated in Wollo, Tigrai, and Eritrea, where even the *meher* season had brought no relief and where shortfalls continued to cause severe problems. An important indicator of the imminent spreading of famine conditions was the acceleration of population movement which took place around this period. There was large-scale distress migration out of Tigrai to Gonder and Gojjam from early to mid-1983, involving 500,000 people according to one estimate.[45] In the latter half of 1983 a very heavy migratory spell to Sudan began; the migrants belonged to central Tigrai and north-western Wollo and were middle peasants in origin (rather than the usual desperately poor migrant class) all of whom had been living on the sale of assets for two or three years before this move. Yet, in spite of all this, it remained possible to hope that the famine could still be contained in the few worst-affected areas.

Such hopes were however cruelly exposed as hollow by the failure of the 1984 *belg* season. And as Phase III began, it was clear that the disaster was fated to reach epic proportions. Famine was now raging all over the north—the number of people affected in Wollo and Tigrai was now estimated at over two million (see Table 3.6)—and reports from the many hastily arranged relief camps suggested that the daily death rate had crossed the 100 mark and was climbing upwards. As the *meher* rains came late and very erratically, the country prepared for nature's *coup de grâce*, which duly came with the failure of the 1984 main season. Eleven out of fourteen administrative provinces were now affected, in the grip of a famine the like of which Ethiopia had not witnessed since the 'kifu qan' (evil days) of 1888–92. Overall output between 1984 and 1985 was down by between 25 and 20 per cent—i.e. representing the consumption of between 6.5 and 8 million persons. Besides the devastated provinces of Wollo, Eritrea, and Tigrai, the famine had now spread to Bale, Gonder, and Sidamo. Accounts of the situation in the worst-affected areas

[44] John Seaman: personal communication dated 13 Aug. 1986.    [45] Ibid.

from observers present during this period bear out in full the grim implications of these statistics.[46]

The dramatic loss of cattle, the sharply reduced availability of seeds, and the continuing erratic behaviour of the weather spelt trouble again for the next *belg* season. As expected, output was again drastically curtailed in Wollo, Tigrai, and Eritrea (estimated to be down from normal levels by 70, 60, and 45 per cent respectively)[47] and the drought had by now spread to the prime producing areas of Arssi, Gojjam, and Shewa, wiping out any potential surpluses that might have been available for distribution elsewhere. By March, only 45 per cent of the pledged aid had arrived and the number of people needing relief assistance was now, according to the RRC, reaching 8 million.[48] Despite the international relief efforts now in progress, the limited internal distribution capacity of the country imposed a formidable constraint on the ability to deliver relief quickly. Mortality thus continued to be severe through the first half of 1985. The *meher* rains in 1985 brought cautious room for optimism, signalling a possible change in overall weather conditions; the damage to the land had been such, however, that crop output for the year remained very low. Indeed (Table 3.7), in some previously unaffected regions like Harerghe, the harvest was disastrously bad, reflecting the combined impact of the rain failure and the shortage of seeds in the previous season.

This latter development was indicative of a possible fresh crisis looming in the country. Looking at the trend, one could cautiously hope that the worst of the famine would be over at the end of Phase III. As our Phase IV began, however, there were reports of the prime cereal lands of the south and the south-east being hit by the drought and suffering an output collapse and indications that up to two million people might be in urgent need of food aid.[49] But if we *are* witnessing the start of a fresh wave of devastation—with the famine moving now to the south and the south-east[50]—this would in fact only replicate the pattern of 1972–5, when—as discussed above—the southern pastoralists in the main fell victim to the second attack of drought, the first having primarily claimed the agriculturalists of the north.

[46] Cf. Peter Gill's account of a visit to Korem in Wollo in early Oct. 1984: 'It is surprisingly easy to remain the dispassionate outsider when presented with barely recognizable distortions of the human condition—the scores of bodies laid out each morning for burial, the unnatural quiet of tin huts full of the dying, the misshapen form of the grossly malnourished. Even the numbers involved—tens of thousands in Korem—tended to numb the senses. I found that I could just about cope with the dead and the dying. It was the despair of the living that finally put paid to my sense of detachment.'

[47] FAO (1983).

[48] Since the agricultural sector is a provider of food as well as a source of employment and income for agriculturists, many of those seeking relief would have suffered a loss of employment and hence income as a result of harvest failures. This is an important point to bring out and we shall have more to say on this, although lack of data on employment and trade prevents us from giving any detailed account of the secondary effects of output reductions.

[49] Paul Vallely, 'Ethiopia Food-Producing Sectors Hit by Drought', *The Times*, 2 Dec. 1985.

[50] John Madeley, 'Ethiopia Faces a New Famine', *The Observer*, 26 Jan. 1986.

Taking an overall view of the nature and development of the famine, then, the following points stand out:

1. The famine struck particularly hard in the northern regions of Wollo, Eritrea, Tigrai, and Gonder, though in time it also engulfed the southern regions of Bale, Sidamo, and Gamo Gofa and even threatened Shewa. Merely in terms of geographical coverage, then—not to mention mortality or social impact—it was clearly a much more impressive affair than its predecessor.

2. As a result of successive droughts, the country suffered a catastrophic collapse in food output. For the majority of regions, this decline is most in evidence in 1984 and 1985—the years in which acute famine conditions had gripped most of the country. The trend witnessed, then, is one of sharp regional output collapses, followed by a nation-wide decline in food output and availability.

3. Since excess mortality in mid-1984 was estimated at 175,000 and total excess mortality for the famine by 1985 at more than one million, it appears that the bulk of the mortality occurred in the period mid-1984 to mid-1985, i.e. in what we have called Phase III (although the data available is not sufficient fully to confirm this). Preliminary evidence of the scale of mortality associated with the famine is further discussed in section 3.4e below.

4. While international apathy in the initial periods of the crisis crucially delayed an early response to the spreading famine, the logistical difficulties in distributing large quantities of grain—briefly, the inadequate port facilities, the shortage of trucks, the absence of spare parts and maintenance, and the hopelessly inadequate road networks to the critically affected areas—proved possibly the most binding constraint on the effectiveness of relief policy in saving lives. An effective early response to the famine was also, of course, rendered impossible by political constraints within the country: there was first the diversion created by the decennial celebrations of the fall of the old order, but more critically the fact that the regions most affected by the devastation —Eritrea, Tigrai, and parts of Gonder and northern Wollo—were also those more troubled by the military conflict between the government and the separatist forces.

(d)   *Food availability and entitlement collapse*

It might appear from what has so far been said about the nature of the famine that a dramatic decline in food availability was its major causative agent—and this view is indeed borne out by a consideration of the available data.

Table 3.7 shows the trend in per capita availability of food between 1981 and 1985. Not only is there an overall decline in food availability per head in the country as a whole over this period, but the rate of decline increases as we move into the latter years (which happen to coincide with our Phase III). One can, in fact, identify two broad periods of decline, namely (1) pre-1983 (the initial period when the famine set in); (2) post-1983 (when the famine intensified and

**Table 3.8** FAO tables on food production in
Ethiopia (1974–1976 = 100)

|      | Food | Food per capita |
|------|------|-----------------|
| 1974 | 96   | 99              |
| 1975 | 102  | 102             |
| 1976 | 101  | 99              |
| 1977 | 99   | 95              |
| 1978 | 110  | 104             |
| 1979 | 122  | 113             |
| 1980 | 117  | 106             |
| 1981 | 115  | 102             |
| 1982 | 127  | 110             |
| 1983 | 118  | 99              |
| 1984 | 110  | 90              |
| 1985 | 116  | 92              |

*Source*: FAO Production Yearbooks, 1984; Monthly
Bulletin of Statistics, Jan. 1985.

covered virtually the whole country). If one takes a weighted average of the decline it is, as one would expect, much more marked for the period 1984–5 than for the whole period.[51]

However, different regions shared somewhat unequally in this drought-induced collapse of food output. The impact was clearly greatest in the provinces of Wollo, Tigrai, and Eritrea[52] and—in 1985—in Harerghe. The *belg*-dependent provinces of Sidamo and Gamo Gofa also suffered, as well as, in the later stages, the normally surplus regions of Arssi and Shewa. For some regions, these aggregate figures do not give a true picture of the devastation that occurred; we know for instance that Gonder was critically affected well before 1984 (when output declined according to Table 3.7). Table 3.6 puts the number of people affected in 1983 at 424,600. It thus seems likely that a picture of increasing aggregate availability for the region as a whole masked the extent of starvation before 1983. This is an important point to emphasize, since the

[51] It is interesting to note that using the widely known FAO Production Yearbook data—rather than the RRC data we have used—would provide a different picture of output movements in the last five years. A glance at Table 3.8, which reproduces data from the FAO Yearbooks, shows 1982 to be something of a bumper harvest (with food production per capita in fact higher than in 1977, which was a 'good' year) and 1985 to be a year of output recovery. This, however, does not tally with what we know about the famine's development and impact, and the RRC data are almost certainly more representative of the trend. The discrepancy between the two may be caused *inter alia* by (1) a different definition of agricultural production used by the FAO in its computation; (2) a lower—and in fact obsolete—figure of population growth used for the purpose of deflation.

[52] Since data are not available for the latter two, we have assumed that they shared the same fate as Wollo; this is a defensible assumption in view of what we know about the progress of the famine through the northern regions. Cf. notes to Table 3.7.

presence of more data at a more disaggregated district or 'woreda' level would enable us to highlight more such aspects of the destitution.

The finding that the recent Ethiopian famine was, in all probability, caused by a sustained decline in food availability is important, at one level, in confronting a naïve distributionist view of the incidence of famines that we are sometimes faced with and, at another, in emphasizing the long-term import-ance of investing in agricultural infrastructure, reforestation, soil conserva-tion, etc., so as to ensure a more secure food production situation. This latter point is especially crucial when, as in the Ethiopian case, a substantial proportion of the agricultural population depend on food production, not merely to satisfy their consumption needs, but for employment and incomes. As we have seen, when a decline in food production causes people to starve, such starvation can be understood as the collapse of certain kinds of entitle-ments to food. It is therefore important to enquire, once again, into the mechanisms through which such destitution occurs.

A drought-induced famine reduces food supply but it also cuts the earnings of the agriculturist or the pastoralist and thereby affects his command over food. If we take the case of Wollo, successive droughts will obviously drastically reduce the amount of food available within the province: if there is in addition a transport constraint—and the evidence for this, as we have seen, is not lacking—then, for a given level of demand, the supply of food coming into the province will be reduced.[53]

In addition, when the impact of the famine makes itself felt, there is likely to be a local-level contraction in supplies. This tends to happen when farmers start withholding whatever small surpluses they have from the market, wanting to safeguard their own consumption possibilities, or speculating that prices may rise on account of shortages caused by the famine.

On the other hand, the possibility of exerting effective demand pressures in the market for foodgrains will clearly be reduced on account of the collapse of purchasing power caused by the drought. However, as discussed in the context of the earlier famine, total demand for foodgrains is not always substantially reduced in these conditions. By cutting direct entitlements—or the possibility of meeting basic consumption needs from own production—and by killing off livestock, the crisis operates to force agriculturists to be more rather than less market-dependent and the results may ultimately manifest themselves in *more* local level pressures on foodgrains sold on the market.

Looking at the price data in Table 3.9, the impact of these various effects can now be traced. It is interesting to note that prices did not show much movement in Wollo in the first two years of the famine, namely 1982 and 1983 (and in other less affected areas like Gonder actually recorded a fall). We know

---

[53] There are also disturbing allegations—which at this stage cannot be further substantiated —that Wollo was being 'starved' so that more grain could go to the resettlement areas to the south. (See Paul Vallely 'Starving Wollo: An Empty Excuse', *The Times*, 14 Aug. 1985.)

**Table 3.9** Regional price movements, 1981–1985

| Region and *awraja* | Average monthly wholesale prices in birr/quintal | | | | |
|---|---|---|---|---|---|
| | 1981 | 1982 | 1983 | 1984 | 1985 |
| *Wollo* | | | | | |
| Dessie Zuria | | | | | |
| T | 83 | 93 | 95 | 175 | 255 |
| S | 54 | 70 | 60 | 137 | 219 |
| Rayana Koba | | | | | |
| T | 50 | 75 | 107 | 194 | 252 |
| S | 33 | 50 | 67 | 111 | 184 |
| Ambassel | | | | | |
| T | 72 | 90 | 93 | 198 | 276 |
| S | 63 | 65 | 63 | 138 | 226 |
| Average | | | | | |
| T | 68 | 86 | 98 | 189 | 261 |
| S | 50 | 62 | 63 | 129 | 210 |
| *Gonder* | | | | | |
| Gonder Zuria | | | | | |
| T | 54 | 75 | 58 | 77 | 119 |
| S | 34 | 50 | 35 | 48 | 86 |
| Gayent | | | | | |
| T | 48 | 58 | 52 | 93 | 145 |
| S | 32 | n/a | 30 | 68 | 119 |
| Simien | | | | | |
| T | 55 | 63 | 60 | 72 | 122 |
| S | 23 | 30 | 27 | 39 | 78 |
| Average | | | | | |
| T | 52 | 65 | 57 | 81 | 129 |
| S | 30 | 40 | 31 | 52 | 74 |
| *Harerghe* | | | | | |
| Chercher | | | | | |
| Adelna Gara | | | | | |
| Gurache | | | | | |
| T | 116 | 121 | 92 | 115 | 178 |
| S | 95 | 95 | 94 | 133 | 122 |
| Dire Dawa | | | | | |
| T | 115 | 125 | 120 | 178 | 216 |
| S | 93 | 113 | 73 | 150 | 137 |
| Harer Zuria | | | | | |
| T | n/a | 110 | 114 | 170 | 137 |
| S | 98 | 87 | 69 | 169 | 196 |
| Average | | | | | |
| T | 116 | 119 | 109 | 154 | 177 |
| S | 95 | 98 | 79 | 151 | 152 |

| Region and *awraja* | Average monthly wholesale prices in birr/quintal | | | | |
|---|---|---|---|---|---|
| | 1981 | 1982 | 1983 | 1984 | 1985 |
| Shewa | | | | | |
| T | 79 | 73 | 64 | 121 | 178 |
| M | 45 | n/a | 42 | 78 | 133 |
| Sidamo | | | | | |
| T | 82 | 82 | 74 | 106 | 144 |
| M | 34 | 37 | 30 | 65 | 91 |
| Arssi | | | | | |
| T | 58 | 63 | 61 | 109 | 118 |
| B | 33 | 36 | 30 | 58 | 62 |
| Gamo Gofa | | | | | |
| T | 72 | 76 | 60 | 122 | 97 |
| M | 48 | 31 | 28 | 73 | 75 |
| Bale | | | | | |
| T | 61 | 66 | 67 | 115 | 151 |
| B | 39 | 34 | 30 | 70 | 84 |
| Wellega | | | | | |
| T | 70 | 70 | 60 | 75 | 102 |
| M | 42 | 41 | 44 | 64 | 78 |
| Illubabor | | | | | |
| T | 82 | 66 | 61 | 105 | 104 |
| M | 47 | 33 | 35 | 58 | 78 |

*Notes*: T = teff; S = sorghum; M = maize; B = barley.
  Where one price figure is given for a cereal in a region, the average of prices in three *awrajas* has been taken.
  Prices in Eritrea and Tigrai are not given, because data was not available.
*Source*: RRC (1986*b*).

that output had been severely affected by 1983 (Table 3.7) and the failure of prices to react much is probably due to the fact that a reduced demand went hand in hand with a reduced supply. Prices did however rise considerably in 1984—presumably after the failure of the *belg* crop in that season—and showed a big jump in 1985. Output recorded its biggest fall in this period (Table 3.7) and there must have been substantial withholding of small surpluses for the reasons discussed earlier, so that the reductions in overall supplies caused a shortage which could manifest itself in price rises.[54] But probably crucial also was the increasing level of market dependence leading to local level pressures on prices, now that direct entitlements had been totally

---

[54] Prices of basic cereals like teff, sorghum, and maize have been controlled by the government in the period since the mid-1970s and it is arguable that they are therefore less responsive to demand and supply pressures than if markets were free. It is clear, however, that even these controlled prices are responsive to changes in market conditions, especially when the latter are as pronounced as during a famine. See Saith (1985) for a discussion of price variability in Ethiopia.

**Table 3.10**  Livestock–grain barter terms of trade (quintals)

|              | Sept. 1982 (1) | Oct. 1982 (2) | Nov. 1982 (3) | Jan. 1983 (4) | July 1983 (5) | Oct. 1983 (6) | May 1985 (7) |
|--------------|-----|-----|-----|-----|-----|-----|-----|
| *Korem*      |     |     |     |     |     |     |     |
| Oxen–teff    |     | 2.6 |     | 3.3 | 1.0 | 2.5 | 0.6 |
| Oxen–sorghum |     | 4.3 |     | 5.0 | 1.3 | 3.2 | 0.9 |
| Goat–teff    |     | 0.5 |     | 0.5 | 0.3 | 0.3 | 0.1 |
| Goat–sorghum |     | 0.8 |     | 0.8 | 0.4 | 0.4 | 0.2 |
| *Kombolcha*  |     |     |     |     |     |     |     |
| Oxen–teff    | 3.1 |     | 3.5 | 2.7 |     |     | 0.9 |
| Oxen–sorghum | 4.1 |     | 4.0 | 2.6 |     |     | 1.0 |
| Cow–teff     | 2.4 |     | 2.2 | 1.8 |     |     | —   |
| Cow–sorghum  | 3.1 |     | 2.5 | 1.8 |     |     | —   |

*Source*: Cols (1)–(6): Cutler (1984); col. (7): Baulch (1985).

cut. The increase in migration in search of food at this period could also have had an impact on prices in Wollo. A combination of severely reduced supply and moderately increasing demand would then explain the price trend in the years 1984 and 1985.

So far our analysis has centred mainly on the agriculturists. But the other main group to be affected by the famine was the community of nomadic pastoralists. A drought wreaks havoc by killing off animals. Yet—as we saw in the case of the Harerghe famine of 1974—this may not be the most immediate cause of starvation: what needs to be studied is the variation in exchange rates between livestock and grains.

Data on such exchange rate movements have been collected—again for Wollo—by Cutler (1984) and Baulch (1985). Table 3.10 presents these for Korem and Kombolcha—two major markets in Wollo. Notice that, in both places, the barter terms of trade suffered a decline between 1982 and 1985. Thus whereas one ox could buy 2.6 quintals of teff in Korem in October 1982 and 3.1 quintals of teff in Kombolcha, its exchange value had fallen to 0.6 and 0.9 respectively in these two markets by May 1985. The substantial decline post-1984 probably reflects the combination of the large food price increases in 1984 and the growing number of livestock deaths during this period.[55] More data on livestock and foodgrain prices would have enabled us to make more precise estimates of the grain entitlement loss due to animal loss and exchange rate depreciation. There is little doubt, however, that, as with 1972–5, the

[55] Thus Holt and Cutler (1984) report from south-western Gamo Gofa—a region traditionally inhabited by pastoralists—that drought had forced up the price of grain to around three times its usual level, while the prices of sheep and goats fell to between one-third and one-tenth of normal.

Afar community of herdsmen[56] have suffered in recent times. Once again, the market reinforced the depredations of nature, and both acted to decimate the pastoralist.

### (e)  Mortality during the famine

Estimates of the level of mortality during the famine vary widely; data collection of this kind was obviously not a priority amongst relief and medical personnel in the critical months when the starvation was taking its heaviest toll. In addition, access to the rural areas, where a vast majority of the deaths occurred, was often restricted on account of political and military considerations. As has already been suggested, what evidence there is leads us to suppose that:

1. the estimate of one million deaths would constitute an absolute minimum for the entire famine period and the actual figure could turn out to be more than 1½ million;
2. the bulk of the mortality took place in what we have characterized as Phase III, namely April–May of 1984 to September of 1985.

There is, however, some additional information well worth considering. This is mainly drawn from the records and surveys of medical personnel who worked in roadside camps or in feeding centres set up in the affected regions. While some of the data is of a fragmentary nature, and often uneven in quality, making it difficult to draw any general inferences, the picture that it reveals does give us an invaluable insight into the nature and pattern of the mortality caused by the crisis. The discussion below draws on two studies of this nature, both of which are marked by the immediacy of personal experience.

An analysis of the operation of a child feeding centre at a roadside camp in Korem in Wollo by Tony Nash (1986)—a nutritionist working for Save the Children Fund (SCF)—provides an indication of the conditions prevailing in one of the worst famine-hit areas in 1984 and 1985. The camp registered people who had come from adjoining districts for the grain distribution organized by the RRC, and kept records relating to their medical and nutritional condition. In addition, SCF separately registered children for the purpose of medical surveillance and feeding. The SCF Feeding Centre categorized children into three groups, suitable for (1) general feeding, (2) intensive feeding, and (3) supervised intensive feeding, depending on the severity of their condition as measured by weight loss. The mortality data is based largely on what happened to the children at this feeding centre.

Nash concentrated on the data relating to the period May to July 1984. The number of deaths as a proportion of the numbers fed each day were: May 121/2,800, June 83/2,700, and July 56/2,400. This gives a monthly death rate

---

[56] Baulch (1985) quotes the Save the Children Fund Nutrition Field Workers Reports as saying the Afar were amongst the largest group of beneficiaries registered recently in Kombolcha for food distribution by the RRC.

per thousand of 43/1,000, 31/1,000, and 23/1,000 for the months of May, June, and July respectively. This should be compared to the *annual* figure for the age group of 1–4 for the country as a whole of 31/1,000 deaths and an infant mortality rate of 155/1,000 deaths.

The problems of comparing a monthly rate with an annual rate are clearly recognized in the analysis—especially as some of the mortality data collected are known to be biased for a number of reasons. But Nash argues that the July figure of 23/1,000 is in all likelihood a *minimum* for the entire period between April 1984 and December 1985 during which time the feeding centre was active. If we take into account also the fact that child mortality formed the major proportion of total mortality in Korem (the bulk of fatalities, incidentally, affecting children 14 months old) and that Korem was amongst the worst-affected areas, the data gives us some indication of the minimum mortality rate that must have ruled in Wollo during the height of the famine.[57]

Also instructive is a study of M. W. Otten (1986), this time based on a survey of Yifata na Timuga *awraja* (or subdistrict) in rural northern Shewa in the central region of Ethiopia. One of the objectives of the study was to estimate the contribution of food distribution and emergency health assistance to reducing the extent of famine mortality in 1985, which, as we know, was perhaps the most critical famine year; and for this purpose, a house-to-house survey of 51,274 households using both 7-day and 30-day recall methods was conducted. The mortality figure estimated for Yifata na Timuga before the nutrition and emergency health care operation had its impact in the *awraja* is of considerable interest, for it is one of the very few attempts made to obtain a figure of population mortality for an Ethiopian region for the year 1985. Otten estimates the crude death rate (CDR) for the *awraja* at 98.5 deaths per thousand population per year.[58] Of the deaths that occurred in this period (i.e. before any relief began) three causes, namely diarrhoea, lack of food, and measles, are reported to have caused all but 17 per cent. It was apparently difficult to further break down the mortality pattern though it is obvious that—as in many other famines—the lack of food would by itself have heightened susceptibility to both diarrhoea and measles, and that this would have had its impact mainly on the young.

---

[57] Perhaps more significantly, if one attempted, on the basis of Nash's figures, to make a rough calculation of the total mortality for the entire population in the Ethiopian highlands for the period in question, the resulting figure would turn out to be around 1.5 million deaths (John Seaman: personal communication dated 4 Feb. 1987).

[58] It is worth pointing out, though, that following inputs of food and health care assistance, the CDR decreased from 98.5 to 27.5 in the first months of the relief operation and had dropped to 8.8 in its fourth month. It is remarkable, as Otten points out, that the CDR should drop to non-famine levels by the second month of a relief operation. However, since the region surveyed, northern Shewa, was a relatively peripheral famine area, it is probably more realistic to take the pre-relief CDR in Yifuta as representative of mortality trends elsewhere, rather than the post-relief ones, and this is what the remainder of the section does. (This discussion owes much to two personal communications by John Seaman, both referred to earlier.)

The mortality figure obtained of 98.5 can be contrasted, bearing in mind the usual problems of comparability amongst different surveys relating to different population groups, with a non-famine CDR for Ethiopia as a whole (based on the 1980–1 double round National Household Sample Survey) of 18.4 deaths per thousand per year. It is obviously difficult to extrapolate for the country as a whole from the survey just discussed, but since conditions in other regions, especially in the north, were worse than in Shewa, the sort of magnitude that the figures convey in terms of demographic impact, namely a mortality level four or five times the average, is probably no exaggeration in the current Ethiopian case.

### 3.5. Famine relief and the rehabilitation of victims

#### (a) Kinds of relief

In discussing relief policies in the context of famines, it is useful to make a distinction between (1) short-term relief and (2) long-term rehabilitation. The first is proximately the more important one, being literally a life and death issue in the context of famines such as the ones we have been discussing, and has understandably engaged much attention. However, in terms of rebuilding the famine-ravaged economy and reducing future vulnerability to famine, the second should perhaps receive more careful consideration than it has done so far. Recent attempts in Ethiopia, in the wake of the 1982–5 famine, to orientate short-period relief policy to the demands of longer-term relief (e.g. the organization of food for work or cash for work on soil conservation sites) are clearly a move in the right direction. In what follows, then, different approaches to the provision of relief and rehabilitation are considered, largely on the basis of the recent Ethiopian experiences. Since policies usually operate under huge constraints—only some of which can be foreseen—it is difficult to engage in any kind of prescriptive analysis. Rather, the attempt will be to highlight certain key issues.

#### (b) Food, nutrition and cash

Whether or not food availability decline has an important role to play in the causation of a famine, methods of breaking it clearly call for a large increase in the amount of food available for public consumption. Issues of causation have in this sense to be distinguished from those of policy. This would, in fact, hardly need stating were it not for recent attempts to propound an odd new thesis suggesting that imports of food into the system can only be justified if a food shortage is diagnosed as the *cause* of the famine.[59] Distributing free food and supplementary nutrients in camps and relief centres is one obvious step to take: this can be viewed as providing people with a 'direct entitlement' to food. Indeed, the thrust of relief policy in both famines was to achieve this sort of

[59] See Bowbrick (1986, 1987) and Sen (1986b, 1987)—in that order!

'nutritional maintenance', although in 1983–5 the continuing military conflict made any consistent relief policy in the worst-affected areas of Tigrai and Eritrea difficult.

The management of food supplies[60] thus takes on a crucial role and a critical problem is the matching of donor shipments with the available domestic carrying capacity. This has proved to be a major headache in recent times in Ethiopia, largely because of (1) totally inadequate port facilities and (2) severe shortage of trucks and spare parts for maintenance. In fact, when the first large relief supplies arrived in 1984, the main Ethiopian ports of Assab and Massawa could handle only 8,000 to 11,000 tonnes of material a month; the road transport system could, for its part, handle just 5,000 tonnes a month. It was clear that this capability fell far short of what was needed for the massive relief programme to get underway. Strenuous efforts on all sides finally succeeded in increasing the capacity of the network substantially to around 100,000 tonnes a month by early 1985 and this considerably eased the initial constraints on administering relief. This does not alter the fact that, as a general rule, food distribution remains a difficult operation to manage, and the exploration of alternative options therefore becomes an urgent priority.

Whereas creating direct food entitlement might be an obvious choice in terms of relief, it is not the only way of ensuring that different sections of the population have the ability to command food. Depending on the situation in question, other policies (e.g. employment maintenance for attached servants thrown out of work) would also act as entitlement-creating mechanisms. But by far the easiest to administer is simple cash disbursement. The idea here is to *stimulate* the working of the market mechanism rather than *supplant* it. In many instances, on account of a collapse of purchasing power following drought, the peasant or agriculturist may not have sufficient market clout to attract what little food there is. Cash relief will work by giving the deprived additional income and leaving the market and the traders to respond to the new 'pull'[61] through moving food to the cash recipients. There are, of course, deep questions as to the performance of markets in a famine situation[62] and in an extreme situation, where any remaining small surpluses of food have been exhausted, there is no alternative to instituting emergency food relief. But cash relief is not without its merits. One can, in fact, think of advantages in terms of: (1) economizing on the use of scarce transport facilities (released for use elsewhere) if cash relief is instituted; (2) being able to reach areas where the inhospitable terrain would make food distribution (done by means of heavy transport vehicles) impractical; (3) preventing speculative or other food movements *out* of famine affected areas by generating a certain amount of

[60] The term 'food' is here used to include not only foodgrains, but also supplementary feeding materials for children, like the protein mix 'faffa'.

[61] For an elaboration in terms of entitlements approach see Sen (1986a).

[62] Besides the classic discussion of Adam Smith (1776: Book IV, ch. V) see Rashid (1980) and Ravallion (1985).

'pull'; (4) regenerating the local famine-struck economy via the 'lubricating' effects of more cash in circulation; and (5) providing the basis for longer-term development activities, for instance through instituting cash-for-work programmes.[63] The balance between the two types of relief systems is an issue that repays careful consideration; in fact, except in the critically affected areas—where emergency feeding is an overriding need—the two can probably be used in a complementary fashion.

*(c)  Famine shelters*

One of the recurring problems of coping with an emergency like a famine is that it leads to unpredictable movements of population: for the agriculturist, hunger makes migration in search of food the only survival strategy left, whereas for a pastoralist, the destruction of grazing land brought about by drought again necessitates movement in search of fresh pasture. As we saw, it was the sight of migrating destitutes from Wollo, stopping cars on the north–south highway, that provided the first indication of crisis in the famine of 1973; similar sorts of movements have been noticed in more recent years as the destitution reached the northern parts of Ethiopia.

In the Wollo famine of 1973, such movements were for a time accommodated by housing the destitutes in shelters. Studies of the shelter population in Wollo[64] bring out the strengths and weaknesses of this kind of relief. Among the first plus points that deserve to be noted is that these relief shelters provide quite an efficient and cost-effective way of administering food and medical assistance. This is especially important to note in a context where, as we have seen, it is otherwise difficult to reach many of the starving in the more remote rural areas. Gebre-Medhin and Vahlquist (1977) underline this point when they note that the shelters 'saved thousands of lives with their food distribution and delivery of at least simple health services' (p. 198). They then go on to emphasize the dangers of such large populations of destitutes being housed in makeshift camps lacking proper sanitation and hygiene. First, not surprisingly, the conditions in the shelters made the outbreak of disease inevitable: in fact mortality was accentuated by the fact that many people—having walked long distances to reach the camps—were already in a state of exhaustion when they arrived. Second, shelter life often broke up families and created intolerable social and psychological strains on many of the inmates; there is, for instance, evidence of psychosomatic illnesses developing amongst some of them.[65] The latter problem may initially be considered less acute than the former; but if shelter life is to continue over a period of time, in the absence of

[63] Some of these putative benefits are admittedly of greater relevance to a region like Shewa than to a critically affected area like Wollo. In the former, cash distribution schemes sponsored by UNICEF appear, on the whole, to have been successful. For a discussion see Kumar (1985).

[64] Gebre-Medhin and Vahlquist (1977) and Belete *et al.* (1977), both referred to earlier, in the course of discussing the situation in Wollo.

[65] Gebre-Medhin and Vahlquist (1977: 197).

any other succour, it may at length become more serious. This serves to highlight the fact that, while this form of relief has its merits—especially in the context of large and unforeseen migrations of destitutes—it should essentially be looked upon as a temporary relief measure. The return of normal social and familial living should be arranged at the earliest opportunity.

### (d) Rehabilitation and resettlement

So far, we have mainly been concerned with various approaches to short-term relief policy. Turning now to longer-term questions, the overriding concern must be to prevent the recurrence of disasters like the ones earlier analysed. While a full discussion of this complex issue would take us beyond the scope of this paper, there are some important points to make.

One of the main contributing factors to the weakness of the agricultural system and its proneness to drought and famine has been the deterioration of the natural environment in which agricultural production takes place. There has over the years been an extreme degradation of the soil and a massive loss of forest cover. It has been estimated that Ethiopia loses 80,000 hectares of land per year through soil erosion—enough in fact to feed 66,000 families.[66] Further, recent studies[67] have emphasized the extent to which the processes of soil denudation and desertification are exacerbated by short-sighted development programmes which upset age-old migration patterns amongst pastoralists and make rampant overgrazing inevitable. A main priority must therefore be to restore the health of the agricultural system and increase its productive capacity. One promising way to start this process is explicitly to link relief and development work, e.g. by investing substantially in, say, afforestation programmes, and by instituting cash- or food-for-work programmes as a means of carrying them out.[68] This would have the effect of simultaneously attacking destitution, opening up employment opportunities, creating productive assets, and, perhaps most important of all, enhancing the productive capacity of the agricultural system and making it less susceptible in future to the effects of drought.

Many of these programmes will yield benefits in areas where agriculture *can* be regenerated from the ravages of drought. In some of the worst affected northern areas, however, it appears that soil regeneration is doomed to fail, owing to the scale of the devastation. Rather than try and restart cultivation when faced with such obstacles, the government's approach has for some time been to encourage a controversial resettlement programme, involving the movement of the affected population away from these wasted agricultural

---

[66] Estimate quoted in D'Souza and Shohan (1985: 527).

[67] Cf. Sinclair and Fryxell (1985).

[68] Note that even a simple increase in agricultural and food production, without an explicit employment target, will probably engineer an increase in employment and income—and hence create more secure entitlements to food—to the extent to which the agricultural sector is an employer as well as a producer.

regions to areas in the south and south-west, where the impact of the drought has been much less severe.

In October 1984, an acceleration of the resettlement programme was announced, involving 1½ million people from Tigrai, Wollo, and Shewa being relocated in Wellega, Illubabor, and Keffa (see Map 3.2). There is, at one level, a socio-ecological justification for this policy, as will be evident from what has been said before: its proponents argue also that it will reduce vulnerability to famine in the highlands by reducing population pressure and improving the environment. But it is the political dimension of the move that has attracted the most attention,[69] and it has even been alleged that the main motive was to empty rebel niches of potential recruits by forcibly removing the population in the guise of resettlement.[70]

Given the charged political atmosphere, national and international—and the backdrop of the civil war against which these policies are being carried out—the economic or ecological justifications for resettlement in the end get lost in the mêlée of charges and denials that pass for analysis on this question. Without delving any further into the rights and wrongs of the issue, we close this discussion with two general remarks. First, even if one grants that resettlement is a valid option for any government confronted with environmental degradation on a vast scale, it is difficult to escape the conclusion that it was attempted far too hastily and that little serious advance planning had been done as to how best to carry out the move.[71] Second, the policy requires a long-term investment commitment which Ethiopia would very likely be unable to manage on its own;[72] this highlights the need to mobilize other sources of funding and to present the rationale of the policy in a much clearer manner than has been done so far.

### 3.6.  Concluding observations

Famine seems to be the last, the most dreadful resource of nature . . . premature death must in some shape or other visit the human race.

Thus wrote the Reverend Thomas Malthus in 1798, at the time of announcing his famous prognosis of doom (Malthus 1798). Two hundred years later, we

[69] While recognizing the hardship and deaths caused by the population movements, there is no need to take seriously some of the more extravagant claims of the policy's antagonists, which imply that more people died during the resettlement process than as a result of the famine.

[70] This view is advanced in, for instance, a leader in The Times ('Feeding the Tyrants', 11 Oct. 1985). For a more sympathetic account of the government's motivation, see Hancock (1985).

[71] A pamphlet produced by the group Survival International (1986) argues that the proposed new sites in the south are completely unsuitable for cultivation, since no money has been spent on them, nor any machinery acquired for the purpose of the proposed cultivation.

[72] Cf. Survival International (1986) which calculates (p. 42) that the government's target of resettling 1.5 million people would cost 2.1 billion birr—at the rate of 1,400 birr each—whereas the entire national budget of the country is 2.9 billion birr.

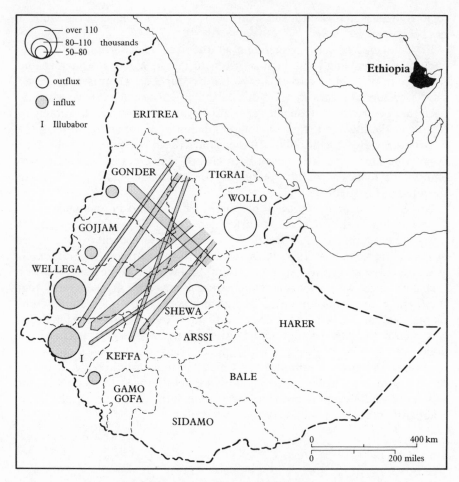

*Source*: Survival International (1986).

**Map 3.2** Ethiopia's resettlement programme

live in a world in which that counsel of despair has not, on the whole, been
borne out. The power of population has not been 'so superior to the power of
the earth to provide sustenance' as Malthus visualized. Yet it would not be easy
to convince a Malthusian visitor to Ethiopia—or indeed large parts of Africa
—that his predictions were not grounded in fact. In these regions, there is
evidence that food production is falling behind rates of population increase.
The situation in Sudan, for instance, has recently sharply deteriorated and
there are fears of an imminent emergency on the Ethiopian scale; to the south
in Mozambique, conditions have been getting steadily worse and the lethal
combination of war and famine could once again precipitate a crisis. And
Ethiopia itself has witnessed mass outbreaks of starvation twice in the last

decade and a half: there is in addition reasonable expectation of more to come. Is famine then the most dreadful resource of nature?

To say 'yes' would be to give an incomplete and possibly misleading answer. A falling level of food consumption per head on account of population increase may of course make a country more susceptible to the onset of a famine, but there is, as we have seen, no *necessary* connection between the overall availability of food in a society, and the propensity of some groups in it to starve. The analysis of famine causation has then to go beyond merely considering the broad parameters laid down by demography and nature to investigating the specific mechanisms at work that cause certain groups to starve for want of food. It is in this sense, illustrated by the Ethiopian examples of recent years, that famines are social and economic crises rather than demographic manifestations. And quite a number of issues relating to these crises have been specifically investigated in the course of the preceding analysis. Rather than attempting an overall summary, then, some points may be worth underlining here while concluding in order to provide a perspective to the discussion as a whole.

First, we have seen that both the Wollo famine of 1973 and the current larger devastation were in important, though different, ways the result of a decline in food availability caused by drought. In the former case, the problem seems to have been that a collapse in food output in the province of Wollo itself created a fall in availability which was then compounded by an inability, largely on account of logistical constraints, to bring food from outside the province to relieve starvation. In the latter event, the country witnessed sharp regional shortfalls in food output, followed in this case by a country-wide collapse in output. This emphasizes, then, the critical role of food availability at a time of famines. Equally, in a policy sense, it highlights both short-term and long-term imperatives of ensuring a minimum level of availability for a population vulnerable to such devastations. The short-term issues are concerned largely with overcoming transport and other problems in moving food during critical periods: they devolve naturally into considerations of the optimum form of relief during famines and are therefore more fully discussed under that head. The longer-term issues, on the other hand, have to do with rebuilding the country's food-growing capability and ensuring more secure long-term access to food for the majority of the population; these in turn, relate to the question of long-term rehabilitation of the famine-stricken economy and are further taken up then.

Second, emphasizing food availability does not mean that an analysis should concern itself only with this variable (as in a simplistic FAD framework). Though food availability decline played a major role in both the major famines discussed above, understanding the precise causal mechanisms at work that ultimately led to starvation requires an investigation of how the drought affected various occupational groups differently and this can be done to telling effect by using the analytical structure of an entitlements approach. Thus, we saw how, amongst the various groups affected by the two famines, own producers suffered a cut in direct entitlement and were forced to become market-dependent, and thereby more vulnerable, whereas pastoralists were hit by a combination of livestock deaths and exchange rate variations and consequently saw a collapse in their exchange entitlements. Wage labourers paid in cash, on the other hand, saw a cut in the amount of food they could buy with a given wage and consequently lost their market-based entitlements. The point is that the distributional effects are crucial even when the causative agent is a collapse in food output.

Third, turning to the question of relief, the infrastructural and other constraints that the country was faced with did, as discussed above, severely limit the effectiveness of relief efforts even after international aid was forthcoming on the scale required. This highlights the necessity of adequate investment in transport infrastructure in order to augment future domestic distribution capacity at a time of regional shortfalls. Also, policy should concentrate in the short term on evolving a more decentralized food stocking system, so that a mechanism is created to even out regional surpluses and deficits; it could also be used to establish stocks of food for emergency public distribution in case of sudden regional shortfalls. Given the existing limitations on the ability to distribute food aid quickly and efficiently, there may in certain cases be good grounds for trying out other forms of relief aid—most obviously cash disbursement—which help to economize on overstretched transport resources.

Fourth, despite the importance of devising more effective approaches to short-term relief, the major challenge probably lies in the area of longer-term relief and, specifically, in the extent to which the country's critical vulnerability to recurring famine can be reduced. This actually relates quite crucially to the issue of causation and food availability raised earlier. Long-term policy would have to see a massive investment in agriculture, aiming to consolidate and extend domestic food growing capability, while at the same time promoting a more diversified crop-growing pattern. Sustained efforts through soil enrichment programmes, etc., would also be needed to rehabilitate the country's drought-ravaged environment.[73] Resettlement of population is in this context an option fraught with difficulties and could only have a limited role to play in any overall restructuring policy.

Fifth, it is apparent that relief would have been greatly helped in both famines—but particularly in the more recent one—had there been in each case an early response to the incipient crisis, from the national governments involved and from international donors. While hard evidence on mortality is hard to obtain, it is clear that the toll of deaths in both cases was sharply increased because of delays in co-ordinating a proper response to the famine.

[73] For a recent discussion of the critical issues involved in transforming African agriculture see Eicher (1986).

There is on the other hand little doubt that both the famines were anticipated, in the sense that responsible groups had issued warnings about the scale of the crisis that was imminent, and that these warnings were in both cases initially played down for largely political reasons. One might therefore be tempted to argue that early warning systems have little impact, and that attempts to improve them would have very limited pay-offs. But this may be too negative a view. The better the quality of the warning system and the track record of the agency managing it, the more difficult it will be to avoid an early response.[74] An effective famine monitoring and anticipating system with guarantees of adequate support in case of impending disaster could well form part of an international agreement amongst the potential donors to deal with future crises.

Whereas the potential for improvements in warning systems may exist, however, the reasons for the lack of response—despite the warnings—in the cases we have studied deserve to be emphasized. And this, finally, brings us to the issue which perhaps underlies many others discussed here, namely, the essentially political nature of famines. And this political dimension shows up striking similarities in two otherwise very different situations. In both cases, the delay in co-ordinating a response to the crisis was on account of political expediency: the imperial regime tried to minimize the severity of the developing famine because it felt its own crumbling power base might be completely exposed by a crisis of this magnitude; the Dergue on the other hand were engaged in a process of consolidating power and did not want to let the untimely news of famine disturb the progress of populist celebrations. Both regimes initially used state resources for the purpose of self-aggrandizement, both were fighting a costly and debilitating war on the borders, and both ultimately were forced to rely on massive foreign aid to relieve a starving population. The importance of the institutional, policy, and other dimensions of the Ethiopian famines, discussed at length in this chapter, should not of course be minimized. But what stands out in the end is the responsibility claimed by sheer human folly for the hapless plight of the famines' victims.

[74] On the role of proper forecasting in reducing famine mortality, see the illuminating work of Ravallion (1987).

# References

ABATE, A., and KIROS, F. G. (1983), 'Agrarian Reform, Structural Changes and Rural Development in Ethiopia', in Ghose, A. K. (ed.), *Agrarian Reform in Contemporary Developing Countries* (London: Croom Helm).

ASHTON, B., HILL, K., PIAZZA, A., and ZEITZ, R. (1984), 'Famine in China 1958–61', *Population and Development Review*, 10.

AYKROYD, W. R. (1974), *The Conquest of Famine* (London: Chatto & Windus).

BAULCH, R. J. (1985), 'Entitlements and the Wollo Famine of 1982–85', mimeo.

BELETE, S., *et al.* (1977), 'Study of Shelter Population in the Wollo Region', *Journal of Tropical Pediatrics and Environmental Child Health*, 23.

——MARIAM, B. H., and GEBRIEL, Z. W. (1974), *Profile of Wollo under Famine* (Addis Ababa: Ethiopian Nutrition Institute).

BONDESTAM, L. (1974), 'People and Capitalism in the North East Lowlands of Ethiopia', *Journal of Modern African Studies*, 12.

BOWBRICK, P. (1986), 'The Causes of Famine: A Refutation of Professor Sen's Theory', *Food Policy*, 11.

——(1987), 'An Untenable Hypothesis on the Causes of Famine', *Food Policy*, 12.

CUTLER, P. (1984), 'Famine Forecasting: Prices and Peasant Behaviour in Northern Ethiopia', *Disasters*, 8.

——and STEPHENSON, R. (1984), *The State of Food Disaster Preparedness in Ethiopia* (Addis Ababa: Relief and Rehabilitation Commission).

D'SOUZA, F., and SHOHAN, J. (1985), 'The Spectre of Famine in Africa: Avoiding the Worst', *Third World Quarterly*, July.

EICHER, C. K. (1986), *Transforming African Agriculture* (San Francisco: The Hunger Project).

Ethiopian Ministry of Agriculture (1973), *Final Report of the Crop Condition Survey for 1972–73 Harvest* (Addis Ababa: Imperial Ethiopian Government).

FAO (1983), *Special Report on Foodcrops and Shortages* (FAO: Rome).

GEBRE-MEDHIN, M., HAY, R., LICKE, Y., and MAFFI, M. (1977), 'Initial Experience of a Consolidated Food and Information System Analysis of Data from the Ogaden Area', *Journal of Tropical Pediatrics and Environmental Child Health*, 23.

——and VAHLQUIST, B. (1977), 'Famine in Ethiopia: The Period 1973–75', *Nutrition Reviews*, 35.

GHOSE, A. K. (1985), 'Transforming Feudal Agriculture: The Case of Ethiopia', *Journal of Development Studies*, Oct.

GILL, P. (1986), *A Year in the Death of Africa: Politics, Bureaucracy and the Famine* (London: Picador).

GRIFFIN, K., and HAY, R. (1985), 'Problems of Agricultural Development in Socialist Ethiopia: An Overview and a Suggested Strategy', *Journal of Peasant Studies*, 13.

HANCOCK, G. (1985), *Ethiopia: The Challenge of Hunger* (London: Gollancz).

HOLT, J., and CUTLER, P. (1984), *Review of the Early Warning System of the Relief and Rehabilitation Commission* (Addis Ababa: UNICEF/Relief and Rehabilitation Commission).

——SEAMAN, J., and RIVERS, J. (1975), 'Famine Revisited', *Nature*, 225.

HUSSEIN, A. M. (ed.) (1976), *Rehab: Drought and Famine in Ethiopia* (London: International Africa Institute).

KUMAR, B. G. (1985), *The Ethiopian Famine and Relief Measures: An Analysis and Evaluation* (Addis Ababa: UNICEF).

LIPTON, M. (1983), 'Poverty, Undernutrition and Hunger', World Bank Staff Working Paper No. 597 (Washington DC: World Bank).

MAFFI, M. (1975), *Wollo: Two Years after the Crisis* (Addis Ababa: Consolidated Food and Nutrition System).

MALTHUS, T. R. (1798), *Essay on the Principle of Population as it Affects the Future Improvement of Society* (London).

MAYER, J. (1975), 'Management of Famine Relief', *Science*, 5.

MILLER, D. S., and HOLT, J. F. J. (1975), 'The Ethiopian Famine', *Proceedings of the Nutritional Society*, 34.

MOKYR, J. (1983), *Why Ireland Starved: A Quantitative and Analytical History of the Irish Economy 1800–1859* (London: Allen & Unwin).

NASH, T. (1986), Untitled report on the operation of the SCF Child Feeding Centre, Koren, mimeo.

OTTEN, M. W. (1986), 'Nutritional and Mortality Aspects of the 1985 Famine in North Central Ethiopia', mimeo (Atlanta, Ga.: Centre for Disease Control).

PANKHURST, R. (1961), *An Introduction to the Economic History of Ethiopia from Early Times to 1800* (London: Lalibela House).

——(1966), 'The Great Ethiopian Famine of 1888–1892: A New Assessment', *Journal of the History of Medicine and Allied Sciences*, 21.

RASHID, S. (1980), 'The Policy of Laissez-faire during Scarcities', *Economic Journal*, 90.

RAVALLION, M. (1985), 'The Performance of Rice Markets in Bangladesh during the 1974 Famine', *Economic Journal*, 95.

——(1987), *Markets and Famines* (Oxford: Oxford University Press).

Relief and Rehabilitation Commission (RRC) (1985*a*), *The Challenges of Drought* (Addis Ababa: RRC).

——(1985*b*), *Food Situation in Ethiopia 1981–85: A Trend Analysis Report* (Addis Ababa: RRC).

——(1986*a*), *Food Supply Prospect: Crop and Livestock Dependent Food Supply System: 1st Report* (Addis Ababa: RRC).

——(1986*b*), *Early Warning System Reports* (Addis Ababa: RRC).

RIVERS, J., et al. (1976), 'Lessons for Epidemiology from the Ethiopian Famines', *Annales Société belge de médecine tropicale*, 56.

SAITH, A. (1985), 'The Distributional Dimensions of Revolutionary Transition: Ethiopia', *Journal of Development Studies*, Oct.

SCRIMSHAW, N. S., GORDON, J., and TAYLOR, C. E. (1968), *Interactions of Nutrition with Infection* (Geneva: WHO).

SEAMAN, J., and HOLT, J. (1980), 'Markets and Famines in the Third World', *Disasters*, 4/3.

—— ——and RIVERS, J. (1974), *Hererghe under Drought* (Addis Ababa: Relief and Rehabilitation Commission).

—— —— ——(1978), 'The Effects of Drought on Human Nutrition in an Ethiopian Province', *International Journal of Epidemiology*, 7.

SEN, A. K. (1977), 'Starvation and Exchange Entitlements: A General Approach and Its Application to the Great Bengal Famine', *Cambridge Journal of Economics*, 1.

——(1981), *Poverty and Famines: An Essay on Entitlement and Deprivation* (Oxford: Oxford University Press).

——(1983), 'Development: Which Way Now?', *Economic Journal*, 93.

——(1986a), 'Food, Economics and Entitlements', *Lloyds Bank Review*, Apr.; repr. in the first volume of this book.

——(1986b), 'The Causes of Famine: A Reply', *Food Policy*, 11.

——(1987), 'Famine and Mr. Bowbrick', *Food Policy*, 12.

SHEPHERD, J. (1975), *The Politics of Starvation* (New York: Carnegie Endowment for International Peace).

SINCLAIR, T., and FRYXELL, J. M. (1985), 'The Sahel of Africa: Ecology of a Disaster', *Canadian Journal of Zoology*, 63.

SMITH, A. (1776), *An Inquiry into the Nature and Causes of the Wealth of Nations*.

Survival International (1986), *Ethiopia's Bitter Medicine: Settling for Disaster* (London).

TILLY, L. A. (1985), 'Food Entitlement, Famine and Conflict', in Rotberg, R. I., and Rabb, T. K. (eds.), *Hunger and History* (Cambridge: Cambridge University Press).

ULLENDORFF, E. (1963), *The Ethiopians: An Introduction to Country and People* (Oxford: Oxford University Press).

WISEBERG, L. (1976), 'An International Perspective on the African Famines', in Glantz, M. H. (ed.), *The Politics of Natural Disaster: The Case of the Sahel Drought* (New York: Praeger).

WOLDE MARIAM, M. (1984), *Rural Vulnerability to Famines in Ethiopia: 1958–1977* (New Delhi: Vikas).

WOODHAM-SMITH, C. (1962), *The Great Hunger: Ireland 1845–9* (London: Hamish Hamilton).

World Bank (1986), *Poverty and Hunger: Issues and Options for Food Security in Developing Countries* (Washington, DC: World Bank).

# 4

# Modelling an Early Warning System
# for Famines

## *Meghnad Desai*

### 4.1. *Introduction*

*Droughts are a natural phenomenon; famines are not.* Rains fail periodically but
cannot be caused or hindered (except in the very long-run economic-ecological
context) by social forces. Famines however are social phenomena. Droughts
may lead to failure of harvests if certain supporting conditions are present: lack
of foresight, lack of irrigation water, etc. Failure of harvests may in their turn
lead to acute starvation if certain other supporting conditions are present: lack
of stocks of foodgrains, lack of availability of foodgrains at prices people could
afford, lack of activity outside food growing to generate adequate purchasing
power widely distributed. If starvation occurs then the starving may undertake
various actions: migration to other areas for instance. These may exacerbate
the severity of famine if the result is to heighten the unevenness of the
distribution of goods as well as of purchasing power.

But famines can also occur without a prior 'natural' disaster. A central
proposition of *Poverty and Famines* (Sen 1981) is that droughts or harvest
failures are neither necessary nor sufficient for famines to occur. Famines can
occur due to political shocks—wars, civil wars, drastic changes in legal rights
that define entitlements (e.g. the collectivization campaign in Russia), etc.
Once the external shock occurs the variables defining the endogenous response
of the food production system are the same as in the case of a natural
shock—lack of stocks of foodgrains, etc. The intensity of the response may be
different in response to a natural as against a political shock, but the linkages
are the same as we shall see below.

Our knowledge of the complex and dynamic interrelationship between
various economic and non-economic variables that go into turning an initial
shock (natural or socio-political) into a full-scale famine has improved
tremendously in recent years, mainly thanks to the framework provided by Sen
(1981), which has been used in many cases, criticized and expanded upon in
others. Thus one way in which the entitlement approach has helped is in
interpreting the methods used in the past by various societies to cope with
impending or actual famines. Famine relief systems as in the Indian Famine
Code (see Chapter 1 above) embody an implicit model of the causal nexus

I am grateful to Martin Ravallion, Jean Drèze, and Amartya Sen for their comments and in case of
the latter two for their forbearance in face of my procrastination. I am grateful to the Map Division
of the London School of Economics for the Figures. All the blemishes are mine, of course.

which leads to famine and the ways of coping with it. As has been argued (Rangasami 1985), relief operations did take a broad entitlements view of the causes of famine. There have also been strategies to warn of impending famines, both historically and much more so in recent years. These 'early warning systems' are the concern of this paper.

I shall try to study the logic of early warning systems, not so much as a description of their present existence but as a logical exercise in the way they could be devised, in two steps. First, I shall articulate a model of how famines develop from initial shocks. If we are successful in articulating the full dynamic process that turns an initial shock, natural or socio-political, into a famine, then this dynamic should immediately suggest the appropriate ways of devising an early warning system. Indeed, to argue that there is no dynamic process that transmutes a shock through an economic system into a famine is to say that famines are pure chance occurrences, unpredictable and hence impossible to insure against, literally acts of God. But while some famines do occur from very sudden shocks (shocks of Type 3, as they are called below), there is much in the dynamics of interaction of natural and economic processes in food production and distribution that is exploitable in devising an early warning system.

In discussing ways of devising an early warning system, we are to some extent analysing the familiar. It is not so much that we need to reinvent the wheel but we do need to understand the physics of motion which may help us to understand how wheels work and devise better wheels. Thus societies have used early warning systems before. As Rangasami (1985) has pointed out, the Indian *annawari* system of estimating the harvest from the standing crop (and then expressing the harvest as a percentage of the norm or as so many annas (of sixteen) in the rupee) was an early warning device. It was used to mitigate the severity of revenue demand but it also served as warning. At another stage in the food cycle, unseasonal price rises and hoarding activity on the part of food traders forewarn of trouble to come, although often the trouble may be exaggerated (see the discussion of merchants' hoarding behaviour and price expectations in Chapter 5 below).

A cogent argument made concerning the devising of an early warning system is that it is not so much that warnings are not given early enough or clearly enough. It is the failure of the public agencies (local and international) to respond to such a warning that is more the nub of the problem. Ideally alongside a design of the early warning system, one should have a design of a policy response system. This can however raise many issues about the institutional structures, national and international politics, and the recent history of an area. It is beyond the scope of this chapter to get into such issues though I return to them in the conclusion.

In the next section I set out a general system theoretic model of the process that leads to a famine. The idea here is to articulate the main blocks and their interconnections. Special attention is paid here to the lags in the linkages between the blocks and the interplay of simultaneity and/or recursiveness

among the blocks. Once this has been done, in the third section there is a
discussion of forecasting the major variables so that the dynamic system yields
devices for early warning. I distinguish between the different types of shocks,
their distinction being based on when they occur and how foreseeable they are.
Together these two sections should give us a framework for designing an early
warning system. I conclude in the last section by briefly examining the
implementability of such a system and the benefits that may flow from it. There
is no attempt at this stage to implement such a system econometrically. That
remains a task, a formidable task without doubt, for the future.

## 4.2.  *Modelling famines*

Before we can understand famines, we must understand how the food production and food supply systems work in 'normal times'. These 'normal times'
may witness some portion of the population going hungry or suffering from
malnutrition and its attendant diseases. But we still regard them as 'normal'
since we wish to study the pathology of the system which leads to famines. If we
were interested in eradication of hunger and poverty, we might regard the
normal system itself as pathological but our present interest is in famines. We
need therefore a general model in which even after a shock has occurred, there
is no certainty that a famine will occur. The probability of famine occurrence
should be an endogenous and hence variable magnitude. But the system should
also be such that we can distinguish sharply between its normal functioning
and its pathological state. In constructing this system, we benefit from the
descriptive studies of famine recently made available, many of them inspired
by the entitlement approach. (For details, see the bibliography of Drèze and
Sen 1989.)

The economies which are vulnerable to famines are predominantly agrarian,
poor ones. Thus a model must give prominence to this aspect whether in the
normal or the pathological state. Food production is thus a pivotal part of the
system. To model its nature and its effect on the other sectors is virtually to
model the entire economy. Bearing this in mind, the economic activities of the
system can be thought to be food production and food delivery, the rest being
non-food production. The latter can be rural or urban. Influencing these
economic sectors are the non-economic forces. These can be natural or
socio-political. The initial shocks to the economic system emanate from these
non-economic forces. Thus these non-economic system have to be regarded as
exogenous (weakly exogenous in the sense of Hendry *et al.* 1983) while the
economic system is endogenous. A distinction which will later emerge is that in
normal times the economic sectors are mutually and simultaneously dependent
on each other but in famine times, the food production system becomes pivotal
and recursive with respect to the non-food production system. Thus famine
represents a disjuncture in the normal functioning of the system.

(*a*)  *The general structure of the system*

In Fig. 4.1, the systems structure of the economy is depicted. (I rely here on Desai 1987.) There are three basic blocks, one of which has four subblocks:

1. the nature system;
2. the socio-political system;
3. the economic system;
    (*a*)  the food production system;
    (*b*)  the non-food production rural system;
    (*c*)  the non-food production urban system;
    (*d*)  the food delivery system.

Each system is in itself composed of subsystems which interact but for our present purposes we treat each block as a single homogenous one. Within each system, there are stock variables and flow variables. Stocks of course change slowly and by accretion from flows. There is not much that a policy response

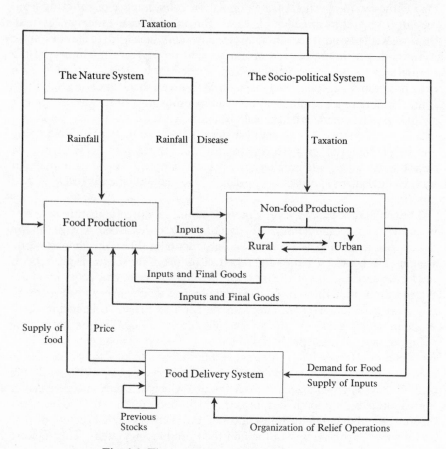

**Fig. 4.1** The system structure of the economy

can do about stocks in the short run but stocks have to be modelled because they condition flows. They are to that extent *predetermined* variables though not exogenous.

In Fig. 4.1, we see the major interconnections between the systems treated as homogeneous blocks. Thus the nature system is primary in time. It affects food production via the amount, the timing, and the spatial incidence of rainfall. Although droughts are not the only reasons for famines, they often are major triggering factors. But the nature system will also affect the non-food production system. It can do this either via drought affecting outputs or via disease which may for example affect the livestock. The stock variables of the nature system will be the ecological conditions—land fertility and erosion, the distribution of forests as against clear land, etc. The mapping of the ecological state is an important step in any anti-famine strategy (see Shah and Fischer 1984).

Parallel to the nature system as an exogenous block is the socio-political system. Of course, continued economic failure will affect the socio-political system. In this sense it is only weakly exogenous but we take it as given for the time being. Civil wars and rebellions, war conditions and external invasions, sudden changes in the taxation regimes—all these are external shocks to the economic system. They can often cause drastic changes in entitlements either by disputing the legality of existing claims (as when a region is under disputed sovereignty by one side or other in a civil war) or by changing the legal framework itself (as when a political revolution changes rights of ownership as happened after the October Revolution in rural areas of Russia). A third example is change in the taxation regime, say from money payments to compulsory requisition. All these would be shocks to the system which could trigger further changes. On the other hand the socio-political system will also provide a public relief system. This is the part that is at the heart of the response to any early warning system.

In Fig. 4.1, the nature system is shown to influence the food production system via rainfall and the non-food production system via rainfall and disease. The only influence of the socio-political system is written as taxation but the broader context of likely changes in entitlements should be kept in mind. The other influence of the socio-political system is on the food delivery system via the organization of relief operations.

The food production system supplies food to the food delivery system and inputs to the non-food production system. Such inputs may be used to produce other edible products e.g. bread from flour. The food delivery system pays the food production system a sum of money determined by the price. The non-food production system demands food from the food delivery system and provides it with inputs e.g. transport equipment, warehousing facilities. Within the non-food production system there is likely to be mutual exchange between the rural and urban for the food production system as well as final goods for consumption.

## (b) The economic system interactions

These are the bare bones of the system structure. But a very important aspect of any economy is the group of agents who form part of any block. It is necessary to open up the black box that each system is since different groups have different entitlements and are differentially vulnerable to the random shocks. In Fig. 4.2, a simple elaboration is attempted. Thus the food production system (FPS) consists of landlords and tenants, owner farmers on the one hand and share-croppers and labourers on the other. The former can be seen as a single group whose primary access to the harvest is guaranteed by their position in the production structure as against labourers and share-croppers who have to contract to get their food supplies. Of all these groups, labourers are again in a peculiar position since if they get paid in money wages they are linked to the food delivery system even in normal times. Apart from that

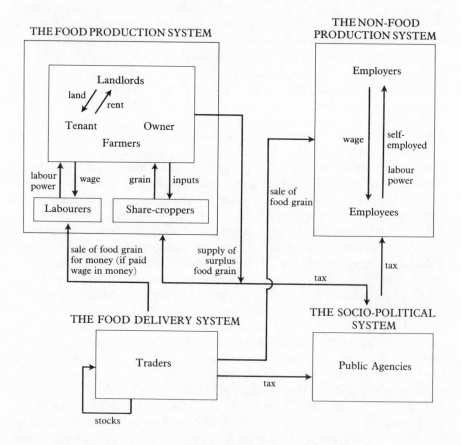

**Fig. 4.2** The system under normal conditions

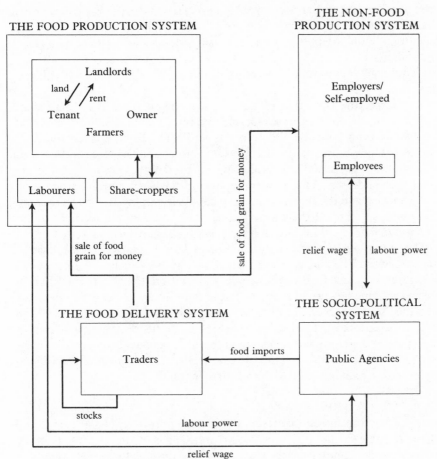

**Fig. 4.3** The system under famine conditions

linkage, the FPS is self-contained as far as its own food supply is concerned. In normal times it contributes a surplus of foodgrain to the food delivery system.

The food delivery system (FDS) consists of traders. They have their previous stocks plus what the FPS supplies. They pay a tax to public agencies as does the FPS. The FDS sells foodgrains to the non-food production system (NFPS). Within the NFPS, there are employers, self-employed, and employees. There is an exchange of labour power for wages between the employers and employees. The NFPS pays tax to the public agencies.

This set of interactions occurs in normal times. If for whatever reason the system is in famine conditions, the interactions are different (Fig. 4.3). Thus the FPS no longer contributes surplus food to the FDS. It also fails to provide jobs for the labourers in the FPS. These labourers thus need the public agencies to provide relief work so they can buy food from the FDS. Similarly in the NFPS, there are difficulties in providing jobs. Employees there also may have to rely on the public agencies to provide a relief wage. These public agencies have to supplement the traders by food imports as stocks may be inadequate by themselves. Then alone can the FDS sell food to the NFPS and the labourers.

Of course, the condition of distress may be so acute that some share-croppers, owner farmers, or tenants are also forced on to relief but we separate out labourers in both the FPS and the NFPS to highlight their vulnerable position. Their entitlements are the most volatile. Similarly for employers and self-employed in the NFPS, it is always possible that they suffer a loss of status in famine conditions. Thus in Sen's account of the Great Bengal Famine it was the fishermen and the rural barbers, typically self-employed, who were among those who suffered. (I deliberately classify fishing as a non-food production activity; in extreme times, it is food grains which count as food.)

The important contrast between Fig. 4.2 and Fig. 4.3 is the changed position of the FPS and the way in which the public agencies become the crux of the matter. Once food surplus ceases to flow from the FPS to the FDS, the normal system has broken down. Those with access to land and as a con-sequence to the harvest, however meagre, will insulate themselves from the rest of the economy. They will no longer buy inputs or final goods from the NFPS since they have no surplus food to sell. This puts everyone who has to buy food on the defensive. They are marginalized *vis-à-vis* the FPS. It is this asymmetry which is crucial to the entitlement failure story.

### (c)   The temporal sequence

So far we have discussed the system structure in normal and famine times. But there are some further questions to explore. One is the temporal sequence in which a shock in one part of the system can feed through the rest of the system. An important corollary of this temporal sequence is the information it provides for devising systems to stem the further adverse effects of the shock by forewarning. The articulation of the blocks and the specification of their linkages are not designed to convey determinacy of the outcome.

In the sequence from the natural system to the food delivery system, no link may be *necessary* but any one can be *sufficient* to cause distress. Thus a failure of the rains is not necessary for a famine to occur nor is a diminution of food supply. An exogenous shock to the non-food system (say spread of a cattle disease) may itself trigger a decline in non-food incomes and cause starvation. Wars, even small, local ones, are notorious for causing food shortages. Mistiming of release of stockpiles of food, the regional/national political machinations that may misdirect food supplies in relation to where they are needed, are other examples of variables sufficient for causing famines (Brass 1986 on the political causes of the Bihar famine of 1974–5).

This lack of a strong necessity of the 'natural' sequence of events or, what is the same, *the variety of possible causal linkages which lead to famine makes the devising of an early warning system for famines tricky.* Since any of the links could fail they all have to be modelled with equal care to yield ways which will make them forecastable. But if a failure occurs at an early stage then an early warning system will help in triggering mechanisms for offsetting its effect at later stages but also in warning to make doubly sure that later blocks in the chain do not malfunction. Time in this sense imposes an asymmetry. If rains fail and we are forewarned then steps can be taken to offset likely effects. There may also be a willingness on the part of various agencies to take such action since they cannot be held responsible for the failure of nature. There need not be recriminations. But if failure occurs in one of the later blocks, despite good rains, then action is much more urgent since anticipation is difficult. But at the same time, there may be a political or bureaucratic resistance to recognizing that action is needed. Droughts are relatively easier to forecast than civil wars, or misman-agement of food stocks. An early warning system can thus rule out failures at earlier stages of the cycle but should never lead to complacency. This is why it is necessary to link the early warning systems for each block in the model with each other. Otherwise, disaster having been successfully ruled out at the natural stage, the need to continue to monitor the progress of food from seed to the mouths of recipients at all stages may be overlooked. Thus good rainfall may trigger premature drawing down (even exports) of food stocks, only to be followed by the discovery that harvests have failed because of locusts, or that breakdown of transport facilities lets harvested grain rot. The linkages of the blocks in the model should force a similar structured linkage in the early warning systems and systems reacting to early warnings.

In order therefore to minimize the adverse effects of a natural or a political shock, i.e. to prevent it from becoming a failure, it is necessary to be able to model the multivariate dynamic character of the complex of events that constitute a famine. It is necessary to set out the sequence of events, i.e. model its temporal structure, as well as specify the other conditioning variables at each stage which are necessary and/or sufficient to trigger the next phase in the chain of events. As one stage leads to the next, a recursive chain of blocks of variables has to be constructed clarifying the nature of the exogenous influences, those variables that are susceptible to policy manipulation and those that can be merely forewarned against.

Let us assume a very simple input–output process in food production. Output or harvest relative to input or planting is a function of rainfall. There is a lag of $2r$ periods between planting and harvest and rainfall should ideally occur midway between them, i.e. $r$ periods before harvest. After harvest, land lies fallow for $r$ periods. Thus the total length of period between successive harvests is $3r$. To clarify the essential ingredients of an early warning system, assume that the production process is (logarithmically) additive and stochastic. Thus

$$Y_{ht} = \alpha Y_{pt-2r} + \beta R_{t-r} + \varepsilon_{1t} \qquad (4.1)$$

where $Y_{ht}$ is the (logarithm of) harvest, $Y_{pt}$ is the (logarithm of) plantings, $R_t$ is rainfall, and $\varepsilon_{1t}$ is a random error. It is also assumed that rainfall follows a simple AR1 process:

$$R_t = \gamma R_{t-1} + \xi_{1t} \qquad (4.2)$$

Nothing hinges on the process being AR1 but it is convenient for the exposition. This simple model enables us to distinguish between three different types of shocks than can emanate from the nature system on to the food production system. Each type of shock requires a different response from the public agencies. This is because of the peculiarities of the temporal sequence.

In addition to the harvest, the most important variable is the price level of foodgrains. Following the simple set up of (4.1) and (4.2) let us say that the (logarithm of the) price level today deviates from its level at the same time in the previous harvest cycle by the deviation of the harvest from expected harvest. Let us say:

$$p_t = p_{t-1} + \delta(Y_{ht} - E_{t-1}Y_{ht}) + e_{pt} \qquad (4.3)$$

In (4.3), the previous level $p_{t-1}$ stands for the equilibrium level reflecting the demand and supply pressures of normal years. In what follows, I first analyse the ways in which the structure of (4.1) and (4.2) yields interesting insights for the device of an early warning system. The analysis of price behaviour is left to the next section.

Thus, the sequence is as follows:

*Panel 1*; as of $t$:

    (*a*) $Y_{ht}$ is known; $R_t$ is unknown;
    (*b*) forecast rainfall in $t + 1$ i.e. $E_t(R_{t+1}/R_t)$;
    (*c*) forecast harvest in $t + 1$ i.e. $E_t(Y_{ht+1}/Y_{ht}, E_t R_{t+2r})$.

This panel says that as of the end of this harvest, the first task is to forecast next period's rainfall knowing this period's rainfall (as well as all past history of rainfall). This gives the expectation $(E)$ of rainfall in $t + 2r$, given the information as of $t$. This information then also helps us forecast next period's harvest. The operational consequence then is to check if next period's rainfall is likely to fail and if as a consequence next period's harvest is likely to fail.

    (*d*) compute $R_t - E_t(R_{t+1}/R_t) = \hat{\xi}_{1t}$;
    (*e*) compute $Y_{ht} - E_t(Y_{ht+1}/Y_{ht}, E_t(R_{t+1}/R_t)) = \hat{\varepsilon}_{1t}$.

At this stage if $\hat{\xi}_{1t}$ is large and positive we know that trouble is brewing ahead: rains are likely to fail. Since harvests depend crucially on rainfall, $\hat{\varepsilon}_{1t}$ will be positive if $\hat{\xi}_{1t}$ is. This is a shock emanating in the nature system but it is an early shock. The lag between input and output allows us an interval of time to act upon this shock. I label this shock of Type 1.

Since this shock is forecast early, various actions are open to the public agencies. They may release alternative water supplies if any are available. They may advise farmers to switch to other crops which may need less water. They may build up public stocks now by buying in the domestic market. This may give private traders a signal to buy as well and the price may rise unseasonally i.e. be higher than the price of the previous post-harvest period. They may alternatively place orders abroad for imports of foodgrains. Thus, we have

if $\hat{\xi}_{1t}$ is high:

(f) prepare to release alternative water supply if available;
(g) if not, advise alternative 'drier' cropping pattern;
(h) if neither (f) nor (g), buy food in local markets for stockpiling and future release;
(i) monitor price movements to detect private hoarding;
(j) prepare relief activities;
(k) buy food in international markets.

The first two actions (f) and (g) refer forward to the FPS. The other four foresee that the system would be in famine condition (Fig. 4.3) rather than normal (Fig. 4.2). Forecasting of rainfall is thus a primary task. In the next section, this is discussed further.

As of $t + r$

Let us now assume that rainfall is forecast to be normal as of $t$. Thus farmers plant normally. We have however further information during this interval since the last harvest and the forecast then made. Thus winter temperature is often a leading indicator of unseasonal rainfall in $t + r$ rather than in $t + 2r$. All this additional information is in the information set $\Omega_{t+r}$ so:

*Panel 2:*

(a) forecast rainfall again $E_{t+r}(R_{t+1}/\Omega_{t+r})$;
(b) compute $R_t - E_{t+r}(R_{t+1}/\Omega_{t+r}) = \hat{\xi}_{1,t+r}$;
(c) compute $Y_{ht} - E_{t+r}(Y_{ht+1}/Y_{ht}, E_{t+r}R_{t+1}/\Omega_{t+r}) = \hat{\varepsilon}_{1,t+r}$.

If planting has already taken place then the forecast of low rainfall in the next period i.e. $\hat{\xi}_{1,t+r}$ being high can only confirm that harvest will be low i.e. $\hat{\varepsilon}_{1,t+r}$ will be high. This is still a Type 1 shock since there is a window of time within which public agencies can act. Of the responses discussed in Panel 1, (f) may still be possible but (g) is not likely to be if plantings have occurred. It may be difficult to pursue 1(h) except by buying from private traders or farmers' private hoards. It would be futile to pursue 1(i). So realistically only (j) and (k) are left. Thus:

if $\hat{\xi}_{1,t+r}$ is high

(d) release alternative water supply if available; if not:
(e) prepare relief activities;
(f) buy food from international markets.

Although $2(e)$ is the same as $1(j)$, it is now later in the production cycle. The same applies to $2(f)$ $(=1(k))$ and of course given the acute sensitivity of international grain markets to weather forecasts, prices may be higher now. But even so, there is time for public agencies to act.

As of $t + 2r$

Now we are in $t + 2r$. Rainfall has happened and we now know, i.e. do not need to forecast, whether it is high or low. Thus we can compare the actual rainfall with our forecast. If our forecast was for a high rainfall i.e. $\hat{\xi}_{1t}$ and $\hat{\xi}_{1,t+r}$ were low, but the rainfall is low, this is a severe shock. I label this shock of Type 2. There is now little time left before the harvest fails. But even so there is a period to go before the crisis and the public agencies can do something.

*Panel 3:*

(a) compute $R_{t+2} - E_{t+2r}(R_{t+1}/\Omega_{t+r}) = \hat{\xi}_{2,t+2r}$;

(b) compute $Y_{ht} - E_{t+2r}(Y_{h,t+1}/R_{t+2r'}Y_{p,t+r}) = \hat{\varepsilon}_{2,t+2r}$.

If $\hat{\xi}_{2,t+2r}$ is *negative*, then the public agencies have to act fast. By now only two options are available.

(c) prepare relief activities;

(d) buy food from international markets.

Of course, as said above in discussion of $2(f)$, buying abroad will cost even more money. As far as $2(e)$ or $3(c)$ are concerned, unless there is previous experience of organizing relief activities (as for example in the case of Maharashtra examined in this volume by Jean Drèze), it is not likely to be very effective.

As of $t + 3r$

The worst possible case of a natural shock is the last one. Let us now suppose that rainfall was normal as expected and with normal planting, we expect a normal harvest. At this stage, there is a shock. This could take the form of unseasonal rain (or frost), or of an attack of locusts, etc. This is a shock of Type 3. This is unforecastable and hence there can be no advance warning about its occurrence. It causes the maximum chaos, since relief has to be organized rapidly and grain imports need to be arranged suddenly. In this case computing the shortfall is only useful as a guide to what might need to be done.

*Panel 4:*

(a) compute $Y_{ht+1} - E_{t+2r}(Y_{ht+1}/R_{t+2r}) = \varepsilon_{3t+1}$;

(b) import as rapidly as possible some portion of $\varepsilon_{3t+1}$;

(c) release stocks of foodgrain.

Since early warning is not possible in this case, the lesson here is that if the public agency has its own stocks of foodgrains, it should not release them prematurely. Thus if rainfall is good, it is no excuse for premature drawing down of stocks. There will be other responses required as well to prevent distress selling of assets, panic migration to other areas, etc., but we concentrate on food-related activities here.

*Shocks from the socio-political system*

At this stage something should be said here about the shocks emanating from the socio-political system. If the change in the system is revolutionary, it may entail redistribution of land and a changed status for landlords, tenants, share-croppers, and labourers. It is hard to predict the effects of this. It is said however that land seizure by the Russian peasantry following the October Revolution led to a decline in the surplus available for the urban area i.e. for the NFPS. The response of the public agencies was to try compulsory requisition to augment their supplies.

What this implies is that while it would be possible to model the shocks from the socio-political system, this is hardly likely to help devise an early warning system. After all an early warning system is designed to give public agencies time to respond, always given the implicit assumption that they will act benevolently. Shocks emanating from the socio-political system that are of interest in famine relief arise from the fact that public agencies are part of the problem and cannot be automatically assumed to be interested in solving the problem. Thus while it would be possible to elaborate a model of the food delivery system, with taxation, etc., this is not relevant to our present concerns.

Having outlined the basic temporal sequence, I now look at the problems that are caused within each block and the information which is available to tackle the forecasting problem. Much work has been done on individual blocks in the past and this will be helpful in constructing a usable model.

### 4.3.  *Forecasting system behaviour*

#### (a)  *The nature system*

Droughts are 'extreme events' and hence appear to be random shocks, yet our ability to model their occurrence has improved considerably (Heathcote 1985). There are now well-established patterns of long and short cycles in climate (for pioneering work on this Lamb 1982, see also Wigley *et al.* 1981, Kates *et al.* 1985). Long cycle evidence is not so helpful in early warning although it can explain a fundamental ecological shift in a region. Thus for the Sahel there have been studies of the longer-run changes in rainfall pattern as well as of the recurring long cycle. Data are of course sparse but not entirely lacking and the field of climate history has made substantial advances here. Thus Nicholson's work on the Sahel climate spans both the last 200 years and the early geological records. Data on river and lake levels stretching back over two or three centuries can be obtained and these point to interesting cycles. Thus, there were numerous droughts in the 1820s and 1830s in Southern Africa as well as further north towards the Sahel. But if 1820–40 was a rainfall deficient period, 1870–95 was surplus, and 1895–1920 was again deficient (Nicholson 1981, and references therein). There are parallels in the rainfall pattern in the two successive drought years 1912–13 and again 1972–3 in the Sahel region (Bowden et al. 1981).

A difficulty with long cycle data is that we cannot rely on them for forecasting purposes. By their very nature, long cycle phenomena yield very few complete cycles and the mean cycle length calculated from such data is subject to large standard errors. Thus, even if we suspect the recurrence of, say, a fifty-year cycle in climate it could have a deviation of ten years either way. They are useful for qualitative study of changing ecology, etc., but dubious for forecasting.

Long series on droughts can however yield other useful information. Thus a study of 200 years of droughts in India shows that droughts are a random occurrence but their occurrence can be modelled as a Poisson distributed variable. Mooley and Pant found that the probabilities of getting 0, 1, 2, 3 droughts in a five-year period were 0.449, 0.359, 0.144, 0.038. Over a ten-year period these probabilities are 0.212, 0.329, 0.255, 0.132, 0.046 (Mooley and Pant 1981).

In modelling climatic variations with a view to early forecasting, if the data are there, techniques exist to exploit the information contained in them. Our ability to extract cyclical phenomena from random ones has improved tremendously with ARIMA modelling of Box Jenkins type, dynamic econometric modelling, and the more recent structural methods of Kalman filter type. Thus, in a recent study with Brazilian data, Harvey and Souza were able to detect short-run cycles in rainfall using structural modelling which Box Jenkins type techniques could not reveal. Since structural models incorporate varying parameters and hence allow for variation in cycle length, they are more useful than methods which posit constant parameters (Harvey and Souza 1986).

Harvey and Souza have applied structural modelling to annual rainfall data for 1849–1979 from Fortaleza in north-east Brazil. While earlier investigations had found cyclical frequencies of 13 and 26 years, they found a single stochastic cycle of 13.75 years. Using this model for forecasting, they claim a 4.3 per cent improvement in the RMSE of the one year ahead forecast.

There are two caveats to be added here. If a rainfall data series exists, modelling it will signal any forthcoming change. There are however other early warning signs within the climate year which could also be exploited. Thus it is possible to use data on climate in between the two rainfall seasons to improve our forecast. Thus, winter temperature is often a good leading indicator of subsequent rainfall. This would imply that by modelling the two seasonal variables—winter temperature and rainfall—*jointly* we could improve the forecasting ability. Again the techniques are available and are easy to implement.

The other caveat to enter is of a very different sort. This has to do with lack of a continuous series on climatic variables in some countries. This is not as serious as it may be thought since weather monitoring spread quite early on in modern times. Yet it is possible that the series available for many Third World countries may be relatively short while for some developed countries they may be long. One can however exploit here the persistence of stable patterns of spatial cross correlation (called 'teleconnections' in climatology). Thus, say, if the weather in the Sahel region is correlated with that in part of the Soviet Union (not a fanciful idea), and if the stability of this cross correlation can be established, modelling the Soviet climate for forecasting purposes may yield some early warning for the Sahel. Evidence of teleconnections in early modern Europe has been found by Flohn (1981). There is also a fascinating study of such spatial cross correlation in China which exploits 500 years of qualitative and quantitative data on droughts and floods using spatial analysis (Wang Shao-Wu and Zhao Zong-Ci 1981). These correlations are not causal: they are jointly caused by atmospheric variables and hence could prove useful.

Droughts acquire a greater force on the socio-economic system if they recur in two successive years. The example of Sahel in 1912 and 1913 and again in 1972 and 1973 was quoted above. Other examples of clustering of extreme events are the USA 1977–9 (three severe winters); the Sahel 1969–73 (four droughts); three severe winters in Europe during 1939–42. Sometimes a wet year is followed by an excessively dry year as happened in India in 1917–18. Extremes are also connected though occurring spatially wide apart. In such cases teleconnections are also 'autoregressive'. Societies often have the ability to survive one drought. But if the reserves are liable to get exhausted, a second drought could be much more damaging for an already underfed population. Thus special care has to be taken to spot clusters of extreme events. This does not pose problems in statistical modelling but it is important to make the prediction of a subsequent drought a special feature of any early warning system (Heathcote 1985).

### (b)   The food production system

The next block is the food production system. Clearly a lot is known about the input–output system in food production. For our purposes, an early warning system can be devised effectively only if the timing of the various operations between input and output are articulated in detail. Thus what we need is not the static production function but the stage-wise process starting with clearing, hoeing, planting, replanting in the case of rice, guarding the field from creatures which might attack the growing food plant, and finally harvest. The availability of water at the crucial stages in this cycle has to be marked. If water fails to arrive via rainfall, the availability of alternative water sources has to be specified. A failure of rain predicted by the nature system model can give us up to a year's advance warning. The response to this may be by encouraging a change in the cropping pattern and planting crops suitable for drier climates. If this were not possible, alternative rural activities could be prepared for in the meantime. Thus if the drought is successfully forecast, the early warning system can go into action with the longest gap we can expect to have. This is a relatively easy problem to tackle. If our nature system has failed to predict the drought correctly then it is at this stage that various warning systems should go into action. They should first alert to the need for alternative water supply to be made available (from reserves, etc.). If such water is not normally available, then the input–output system tells us that the harvest so many weeks hence will be poor. The water input–harvest output lag is thus a window of warning and gives the various agencies time to act before the failure becomes a panic in the food market.

A much more serious problem arises if the harvest failure is not due to drought or any meteorological extreme event occurring early in the input–output cycle. Thus given the input sequence being up to expectations, a sudden shock may still reduce harvest—locusts, for example. Other events which may spoil harvests could be unseasonal frost or rain as these would be difficult to forecast. In such a case the time gap available for warning is much smaller. A harvest failure is not only adverse for food production but also for employment of landless labour which relies on harvest time employment to earn wages which are sufficiently high to tide it over the lean periods. In as much as there is no advance warning this could be a serious blow.

These three possibilities have thus three dissimilar solutions as far as the relief agencies are concerned, although they all result in lower food production. Two of them are anticipated shocks (shocks Type 1 and Type 2) while the third is unanticipatable. It is the unanticipatable shock just before the harvest (shock Type 3) that is the most serious problem since it is sudden. The contingency planning for these three outcomes has to be different.

The contingency planning will have to take into account factors such as possibility of alternative cropping, alternative water supply, alternative demand for landless labour. The burden on the system here is obviously related to the correlation between the food system and the non-food system. Thus if the natural extreme event affects the non-food system equally adversely then there will be little alternative demand for labour from within the economic system. Thus the food and the non-food system need to be modelled simultaneously especially in relation to their reaction to random shocks. We look again at this issue in considering the non-food system.

At the level of the food production system, the consequences of adverse events are low harvest and low employment. Wages may or may not collapse depending on the hold of customary practices. Since labour demand cannot be increased by merely cutting wages (shift of the labour demand curve rather than movement along being dominant), wages do not play an equilibrating role. Farmers' incomes will also be lower as long as the adverse output effect outweighs the favourable price effect. Thus rural incomes in the food-producing sector will be low. This will adversely affect the demand of this sector for non-food commodities and services.

The movement of food prices will depend upon whether the food supply system has recourse to stocks from previous years or imports from other regions. The early warning in the nature (Type 1 shock) gives an even longer gap for the food supply system to adjust itself. Some reaction may be along familiar lines. Thus a forecast of rain failure might lead to early stockpiling, i.e. buying up within the season when rains were adequate. This stockpiling is partly speculative inasmuch as the forecast may not prove correct. But such stocks will come on the market once the failure is confirmed. The public food stocks will need to react similarly to the private system in this eventuality, i.e. buy food in the good season. This may itself discourage speculative buying or at least modify its adverse effects. Again, timing is crucial. A part of the early warning system package has to be action on the part of those blocks which have a long gap before the crisis hits them (see Chapter 5 below).

In the event of a shock of Type 2, there is a little scope for speculative stockpiling purchases. In this case it will be the rate of release of foodgrains from previous stocks which will slow down. This is perhaps hoarding proper. Such hoarding by not releasing food at the normal rate is possible because the shock is unanticipated but still arrives early in the input–output sequence. There is therefore a time gap for the hoarder to exploit as there is for the relief agency to put into motion counteracting policies.

It is with shocks of Type 3, totally unanticipated shocks with no input–output lag, that there is no room for the private speculator. By this time, the private stocks should have run down in the ordinary course of events. Similarly, the public agency may not be prepared for the sudden collapse in harvest and employment. What is much worse, it may have released its stocks upon arrival of the early rains, i.e. upon absence of a shock of Type 2. It must be one of the lessons of a modelling exercise of this kind to base the rate of release from public stocks on the non-arrival of Type 3 shock, i.e. only after the harvest is in the bag, so to speak.

The point of classifying shocks is firstly to appreciate the window of time with which early warnings can be given. The earlier the warning, the better scope for human agencies to deal with the impending consequences. But the structure is also useful if now we can translate these shocks into their likely effect on other variables—prices, wages, labour demand.

Let me therefore develop the consequences of the structures of the three types of shocks on price modelling. We need to elaborate the simple structure of (4.3). As information filters through about the rainfall forecast, there will be price movement unless the public agencies counter it. Let public stock of foodgrains be $ST_1$ and private stocks $ST_2$. Then price movements can be modelled by expanding (4.3) as follows

$$p_{t+r} = p_t + \delta_1[(E_{t+r}Y_{h,t+2r}|\Omega_{t+r}) - Y_{ht}] + \delta_2(ST_1 + ST_2)_{t+r}$$
$$+e_{p,t+r} \tag{4.3a}$$

In equation (4.3a), we look at the movement in price between $t$ and $t + r$. The variable $p_t$ represents 'normal' demand and supply equilibrium of the previous year. If the harvest forecast of $t + 2r$, given the already observed planting, is substantially below that of last year either due to low rain forecast $E_tR_{t+1}$ or due to severe winter conditions $\hat{\xi}_{1,t+r}$, then prices will rise. This may be further reinforced by the combined effect on stockbuilding of private and public agencies. It may be that the price rise is due to precautionary stockbuilding by public agents to prevent prices from rising sharply in $t + 2r$.

The timing of public stock buying is a crucial variable here. If it is early in the year, say soon after the harvest in $t$ given the low rainfall forecast, then it will cause less problem since the supply is there. Private traders may move later. Thus we may have to split the stockbuilding variables into $\Delta ST_{i,t}/(E_tR_{t+1}/\Omega_t - R_t)$ and $\Delta ST_{i,t+r}/(E_{t+r}R_{t+1}/\Omega_{t+r} - R_t)$. The first should be large and the second small if not of opposite sign for the public stocks i.e. $i = 1$. The private stockbuilding behaviour may be different from the public one in that the second term may exceed the first term for $i = 2$. One way to look at this explicitly would be to write

$$p_{t+r} = p_{t+r-1} + \delta_1[Y_{h,t-1} - (E_{t+r-1}Y_{h,t-1}|\Omega_{t+r-1})]$$
$$+ \delta_2(E_{t+r}Y_{h,t+2r}|\Omega_{t+r}) - Y_{ht}]$$
$$+ \delta_3\Sigma_i(ST_{it} - ST_{it-r}) + \delta_4\Sigma(ST_{it+r} - ST_{it})$$
$$+ e_{p,t+r} \tag{4.3b}$$

In (4.3b), we isolate the change in price over the year for the same month/season. This is then decomposed in terms of Type 2 and Type 3 stock on harvest for the last year plus the Type 1 error for this year. The stockpiling is then split into that after previous harvest and that since the winter. Of course it is always possible that $\delta_1 = \delta_2$, $\delta_3 = \delta_4$. If so, this will simplify (4.3b) considerably.

Typically shocks will not be easily measurable even *ex post*. Thus in modelling price movements, we may only have data on public stocks but not on private stocks. Thus in extracting information about the effect of such shocks in the past, it would be necessary to model the error process carefully. Its pattern will contain very useful information. The observable part of (4.3b) may read

$$\Delta_{p,t+r} = \delta_3(ST_{1t} - ST_{1t-r}) + \delta_4(ST_{1t+r} - ST_{1t}) + e'_{p,t+r} \tag{4.3c}$$

where

$$e'_{p,t+r} = e_{p,t+r} + \delta_1(\varepsilon_2 + \varepsilon_3)_{t+r-1} + \delta_2(\varepsilon_{1t} + \varepsilon_{1t+r})$$
$$+ \delta_3(ST_{2t} - ST_{2t-r}) + \delta_4(ST_{2t+r} - ST_{2t})$$

If our forecasting methods for the natural processes are efficient and if equations (4.1)–(4.3) are not misspecified then the error process $e'_p$ should be random except for the unobserved movements in private stocks. (Even these movements should covariant with $\delta_{1,t+r}$ if the argument above about the size of the two component movements in $ST_1$ and $ST_2$ is plausible.) Any sign of serial correlation in the $p_{t+r}$ variable, i.e. annual changes in monthly price series, is an indication of misspecification in the earlier equations. Once that has been checked, we can use $p_{t+r}$ as a way of extracting information on the various shocks in an indirect way.

A similar extension can be made to the post-harvest prices. I will not elaborate it here but it suffices to write

$$\Delta p_{t+2r} = \delta_5(\varepsilon_{1t} + \varepsilon_{1t+r}) + \delta_6(\varepsilon_{2t+2r}) + \delta_7\varepsilon_{3t+2r}$$
$$+ \delta_8\Sigma(ST_{i,t+2r} - ST_{i,t+r}) + \delta_9\Sigma(ST_{i,t+r} - ST_i) + e_{p,t+2r} \quad (4.3d)$$

For generality $\delta_5$ to $\delta_9$ are allowed to be different from $\delta_1$ to $\delta_4$. We now have all the three types of shocks plus the appropriately dated stock movements.

The message of (4.3c) and (4.3d) then is that price movements must be modelled not as monthly changes but as annual changes. This way we minimize the misspecification in the model being confused with moving average elements in the error terms. For a well-specified model, $\Delta p_t$ series may be a robust instrument, but in any other circumstance it will give false signals.

By modelling the time sequence of the natural (winter, rainfall) and production (planting, harvesting) variables correctly, we have arrived at the ways in which the observable series such as rainfall, winter temperature, and prices can be used to extract advance information. If we can observe planting and harvests, so much the better. Only by modelling these processes as a system can we know which variables to look at in devising an early warning system.

It should be taken as read that such price series should be as regionally specific as possible. The rise in local food prices if detected early is a good signal. In addition, the covariance between regional prices should also be examined. To the extent that they are correlated, anti-famine strategies can be devised. But the monitoring of local prices is clearly the crucial factor (Cutler 1984a, 1985a, 1985b).

Income failure in the food production system relates to decline in demand for hired labour and the collapse in wages. As far as labour demand is concerned, for simplicity let us assume that it is only at harvest time that labour is hired. Thus let $L_{ht}$ be the (logarithm of) labour employed in harvesting.

$$L_{ht} = \lambda_1 Y_{ht} + e_{ht} \quad (4.4)$$

Thus labour demand for harvesting is linearly related to the actual harvest plus an error term. Obviously the labour demand equation in any actually estimated model will be more complicated. Given the structure of the shocks, it should be possible to forecast any shortfall in harvest employment as of $t$ or of $t + r$. There is still the Type 2 shock which arrives just before the harvest and the Type 3 shock to adjust to. The substitution is straightforward. The wage movement can be modelled in a parallel way but its dynamics will differ from that of prices. Thus let me posit a simple process

$$w_{t+2r} = w_{t-1+2r} + \lambda_2 \lambda_1^{-1}[Y_{h,t+2r} - (E_{t+r}Y_{h,t+2r}|\Omega_{t+r})] + e_{w,t+2r} \quad (4.5)$$

Equation (4.5) says that the change in wage level depends upon the actual demand for hired labour relative to that expected as of the end of planting season. The collapse of wages is a result of Type 2 and Type 3 shock. Since $\lambda_2 > 0$, a shortfall of harvest depresses wages and increases food prices. Thus a common structure is imposed on wages and prices with contrasting effects.

Type 1 shocks are not in (4.5) since in some ways if rain failure is forecast, and plantings are low, it will be known that there will be little demand for hired labour and migration to towns or other regions could start early. The serious situation arises when a Type 2 or Type 3 shock causes a collapse in the harvest and hence in wages and employment. Thus in equation (4.5) $\lambda_1^{-1}E_{t+r}Y_{h,t+2r}/\Omega_{t+r}$ serves as an *ex ante* labour supply term to which is confronted actual labour demand $\lambda_1^{-1}Y_{h,t+2r}$.

Wages cannot serve as an early warning system device. They are a consequence of earlier shocks but in their case the seasonality of the labour market precludes observations out of season from being informative. Wages have to be studied to be able to estimate the likely extent of the collapse in incomes.

## 4.4.   *The non-food production system*

Parallel to the food production system will be the non-food system. This will differ according to country and nothing much can be said about it in general. Thus these activities may be pastoral, fisheries, non-agricultural labour, small industry, etc. The key question for the early warning system is to articulate the dependence of the non-food production system on rainfall or any other natural/meteorological variable. In each case where such dependence can be established, the impact of the various shocks would depend on the timing of the input–output sequence and the place of the natural variable in this time sequence. Thus rainfall will matter for a sweetwater fisheries economy but there is no advantage in a Type 1, Type 2 separation as no planting–harvesting lag is relevant. A rainfall failure if forecast (Type 1 shock) provides an early warning that the fish catch will be low if rivers are going to be depleted. Any further useful information will depend on a detailed study of each local economy.

More important may be other shocks of Type 3 variety which may hit the non-food system independently of any rainfall or natural failure. Thus cattle disease can strike in an unanticipated fashion and give a quantity shock to the system though this may be mitigated by a price rise. With a disease, the process by which it spreads over time and spatially may be the most relevant variable to model in order to devise counteracting policies.

With cattle, an important consideration is that the impact effect of a natural failure or a disease spreads out over many years since the life cycle of cattle is longer. Compared to this complex dynamic process, the annual food cycle is easy to model and to counteract. Thus the depletion of cattle due to a disease may make natural restocking very difficult, and special livestock imports will be necessary. Here the birth–death process needs to be modelled fully.

Another consideration is the interaction of the food and non-food systems. Either as suppliers of input or purchasers of output, each system is important for the other. A failure of food harvest may devastate the non-food economy by altering relative entitlements but a failure of the non-food system may also cause problems. This area is not well understood. Detailed general equilibrium models are required here. The important issue here is that a system which is simultaneous in normal times will become recursive in famine times. The non-food system becomes dependent on the food system. The share of food in total expenditure rises as food prices rise and non-food incomes collapse. This is of course parallel to the collapse in income of the groups which are not direct producers of food but dependent as hired labourers on the food production system.

The only role of an early warning system depends on the extent of the direct dependence of non-food incomes on rainfalls or the importance of early detection of an epidemic cattle disease. But a Type 1 shock to the food system even if it did not have quantity effects might still have price effects on the non-food system. Thus a Type 1 shock should signal the need for storing up purchasing power in the non-food system.

### 4.5. *The food delivery system*

The food production system if it functions well and has no adverse shocks will result in an augmentation of the food supply. In case there are anticipated shocks, the behaviour of stocks is crucial. As I have outlined above, a Type 1 shock should give the signal to public authorities to build up stocks. These can either be from the current harvest (in $t$) or from imports ordered ahead in $t$ to be delivered in $t + 2$. Quick reaction to Type 1 shocks is thus absolutely crucial to the usefulness of an early warning system.

If the system faces Type 2 and Type 3 shocks, then the food delivery system becomes strained. The crucial variable here is the availability of public stocks. If this is low, then the lag between order and delivery of imports is the next crucial variable. This lag need not be constant but a famine policy should have a good idea of how long the delay will be.

If stocks are low and imports likely to be delayed, the only policy which works is a rationed distribution of the available food supply. There may be some scope here for studying in detail the lag between availability of stocks in headquarters and delivery on the spot where food is needed. Alternatively some regions may have suffered less than others but here again delivery lags (and the politics of interregional food sharing) are a variable to be studied.

If food is available in sufficient quantity but the price is high, then the income—employment generation scheme can take a different form from when food is rationed. This is because the problem in a rationed system is of quantitative availability, while in the non-rationed system it is one of distribution of purchasing power.

These are not however problems of devising an early warning system. For an early warning system, a Type 1 shock causes action on food stockpiling/food importing fronts and in parallel in creating alternative job opportunities for the seasonal labour which relies on harvesting work for subsistence. A related problem is to devise a policy of releasing supplies from food stocks only after observing any Type 3 shock, i.e. after $t + 2$, not before. Thus a lack of Type 1 shock, or even of Type 2 shock, should not lead to a release of stocks. It is only the unanticipated shock which gives sufficient information on timing of food stock release.

## 4.6. *Conclusion*

The problem of devising an early warning system is one of articulating the various blocks which translate a natural failure into an economic and social disaster. The timing of the events in the blocks and as between the blocks is important. The sequence of natural events and the input–output lag in food production provide a classification of the shocks to the system into three types of shock. Conditional on our ability to model natural data with a view to forecasting, the three types of shocks lead to different consequences for anti-famine policy. Thus shocks of Type 1 are the most important for an early warning system. They provide a warning sufficiently early for action to be possible. But it is Type 3 shocks which are unanticipatable and hence the most difficult to provide against. Type 2 shocks are anticipatable but give a very narrow window of warning. By integrating the three different types of shocks into a dynamic block recursive model of the total system, efficient early warning systems can be devised.

In practical terms this means that past data on famine-prone regions can be used to build appropriate systems for each region. Regions will differ in terms of the type of food being grown, the number of crops per year, the nature of the non-food production system and the food delivery system. Only detailed modelling region by region along the lines suggested here can help.

I would like to argue that such detailed modelling is both feasible and desirable. We now have experience in climate and ecological modelling as references already given above amply demonstrate. Efforts by the UNFAO have already begun in this respect (Mahendra Shah). As far as the economic sectors are concerned, recent experience in computable general equilibrium models, large econometric models linking many countries—Project LINK or the IIASA model reported by Kirit Parikh in volume 1 of this book—and the advances in computing facilities all make such an exercise feasible. It will of course demand resources, human as well as financial. It will also require much international co-operation and co-ordination in information gathering, in bringing together intimate knowledge of local conditions and theoretical expertise of meteorologists, economists, anthropologists, and systems analysts. But the real benefits in terms of the saving of human lives and of improvement of such lives as survive will be immense. If we can devise a system that gives a year's, six months', or even three months' early warning then the task would be worth it. It may be a false warning. If so, so much the better. In matters of life and death, the loss function is asymmetric; we may as well err on the safe side having failed to do so for so long.

# References

BOWDEN, M. J., et al. (1981), 'The Effects of Climate Fluctuations on Human Populations: Two Hypotheses', in Wigley et al. (1981).

BRASS, P. (1986), 'Political Uses of Famine', Journal of Asian Studies, 45.

CUTLER, P. (1984a), 'Famine Forecasting: Prices and Peasant Behaviour in Northern Ethiopia', Disasters, 8.

—— (1984b), 'Food Crisis Detection: Going Beyond the Balance Sheet', Food Policy, 9.

—— (1985a), 'Detecting Food Emergencies: Lessons from the 1979 Bangladesh Crisis', Food Policy, 10.

—— (1985b), 'The Use of Economic and Social Information in Famine Prediction and Response' (report for Overseas Development Administration, London).

DESAI, M. (1984), 'A General Theory of Poverty?', review article of Sen (1981), in Indian Economic Review.

—— (1987), 'Economic Aspects of Famine', in Harrison, G. A. (ed.), Famines (Oxford: Oxford University Press).

DRÈZE, J. P. and SEN, A. K. (1989), Hunger and Public Action (Oxford: Oxford University Press).

FLOHN, H. (1981), 'Climatic Change and the Agricultural Frontier: A Researching Strategy', in Wigley et al. (1981).

HARVEY, A. C., and SOUZA, R. (1986), 'Assessing and Modelling the Cyclical Behaviour of Rainfall in North East Brazil' (Econometrics Programme, London School of Economics).

HEATHCOTE, R. L. (1985), 'Extreme Event Analysis', in Kates et al. (1985).

HENDRY, D. F., ENGLE, R., and RICHARD, J. F. (1983), 'Exogeneity', Econometrica, 18.

KATES, R. W., AUSUBEL, J. H., and BERBERIAN, M. (eds.) (1985), Climate Impact Assessment (New York: John Wiley).

LAMB, H. H. (1982), Climate, History and the Modern World (London: Methuen).

MOOLEY, D. A., and PANT, G. B. (1981), 'Droughts in India over the Last 200 Years: Their Socio-economic Impacts and Remedial Measures for them', in Wigley et al. (1981).

NICHOLSON, S. E. (1981), 'The Historical Climatology of Africa', in Wigley et al. (1981).

RANGASAMI, A. (1985), '"Failure of Exchange Entitlements" Theory of Famine: A Response', Economic and Political Weekly, 20.

SEN, A. K. (1981), Poverty and Famines: An Essay on Entitlement and Deprivation (Oxford: Oxford University Press).

SHAH, M., and FISCHER, G. (1984), 'People, Land and Food Production: Potentials in the Developing World', Options (IIASA Journal), 1984/2.

WANG, S. W., and ZHAO, Z. C. (1981), 'Drought and Floods in China (1470–1979)', in Wigley et al. (1981).

WIGLEY, T. M., INGRAM, M. J., and FARMER, G. (eds.) (1981), Climate and History: Studies in Past Climates and Their Impact on Man (Cambridge: Cambridge University Press).

# 5

# Market Responses to Anti-hunger Policies: Effects on Wages, Prices and Employment

*Martin Ravallion*

## 5.1. *Introduction*

The economy is rarely a passive vehicle for transmitting a policy initiative to its target. People react to policy changes. A policy aimed at one class of people can easily bring with it unexpected gains and losses to others. Nor is it always clear how the target group will be affected, once the economy as a whole has reacted.

In targeting policies towards the needs of the poor in a market economy there will generally be some prices and quantities which appear in their budget constraints but are not controllable by the policy maker. An assessment is called for of how those prices and quantities will respond to the policy intervention before one can determine how welfare of the target group will be affected. Policy design may also be constrained by effects on the welfare of non-target groups. Only policies which keep these effects within certain bounds may be politically feasible in specific settings. For example, in designing policies aimed at raising the welfare of the rural poor one may be constrained to leave the post-tax wage of urban workers unaffected.

This chapter surveys and analyses a broad range of anti-hunger policies in market economies, looking particularly at the way market responses can influence policy design. The method of analysis draws on both theoretical and empirical arguments with the latter applying almost exclusively to South Asia, particularly Bangladesh. The policies examined include direct transfer payments, public employment ('relief work' hereafter), food pricing policies, public buffer stocks, external trade policies, and public information policies. The survey is far from even handed. One policy is given more emphasis than the others, namely relief work, while another potentially important one is not discussed at all, namely land reform. This bias seems in keeping with current emphasis amongst policy makers and this is understandable; in the main, the political pre-conditions for successful land and tenancy reforms have not been present, while there seems more immediate hope for relief work and similar income transfer policies.

A theme of this study is that anti-hunger policies should be concerned with two conceptually distinct aspects of individual consumption: its *level* over a

I have had useful discussions on some of these issues with Jim Boyce, S. Brahme, V. M. Dandekar, Gaurav Datt, N. S. Jodha, Kiran Moghe, Amartya Sen, R. M. Sundrum, Dominique van de Walle, and Tom Walker. I am particularly grateful to Jean Drèze for his detailed comments on the paper. Views expressed here should not be attributed to the World Bank.

period of time and its *variability* within that period. The need to raise the level of food consumed by those who are hungry is obvious enough. The concern with variability is motivated by the following argument. Consider two individuals with the same total food consumption over one week, say. The first consumes the same amount of food each day while the second consumes it all in one day. I would assert that the second will be more hungry. The key assumption here is that 'hunger' is not a simple linear function of the amount of food consumed; rather the amount by which hunger diminishes for a given increment in consumption falls as consumption increases. This seems plausible over a wide range of consumption, although possibly less so at low levels; a small increment in food consumption may make little difference to someone who is on the brink of death by starvation. Fig. 5.1 illustrates the assumed relationship between hunger and food consumption.

'Hunger' is not easily measured. Fortunately, one can say quite a lot about anti-hunger policies without being very specific about the measurement of hunger. It can be used the same way as the concept of 'utility' in economics. But the objectives of anti-hunger policies can sometimes be made more specific if one wishes, and there can be advantages in doing so. To give an example, famine relief is an important part of anti-hunger policy. The most important metric of the success of a famine relief policy is clearly mortality. There are good reasons to believe that the relationship between an individual's chance of death during some interval of time and the individual's food consumption over that interval will look something like Fig. 5.1. The survival prospect may be hopeless at very low levels of food consumption and extra food will do little to alter this. But more generally one would expect that equal increments to food consumption will raise survival chance by progressively smaller amounts until, again, extra food makes little difference (or may even lead to a diminished

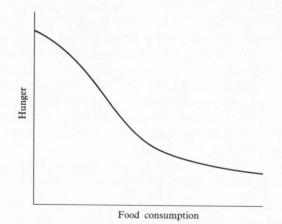

**Fig. 5.1** Assumed relationship between hunger and food consumption

survival chance).[1] There may well be kinks in the relationship at certain biologically critical levels of consumption but this makes little difference to the main argument and its policy implications.

Thus, whether one thinks of the policy objective as the reduction of hunger in general or of mortality as a particular (extreme) consequence of hunger, there is a case for believing that the variability of food consumption over time may be an important concern of anti-hunger policies. And, with possible exceptions at low levels of consumption, there will be an anti-hunger case in favour of reducing consumption variability over time even if this is not accompanied by an increase in the overall level of consumption.

This leads one to distinguish two types of potential benefit to the target group from anti-hunger policies:[2] *transfer benefits* which occur if the policy increases mean food consumption of the target group over some time period and *risk benefits* which arise if the policy also reduces the variability of consumption within that period. Many anti-hunger policies will have both transfer and risk effects (and they need not be in the same direction). None the less, it is convenient that most policies can be broadly classified as either *transfer policies* (where their main effects entail transfer benefits) or *stabilization policies* (which mainly yield risk benefits). The following two sections use this classification.

## 5.2.   Transfer policies

### (a)   The price effects of transfers

Much has been said about the possibly adverse effects of transfer payments made to the poor on the prices they face for the goods they consume intensively, such as food.[3] A well-known result here is that, under regular conditions in a stable and competitive exchange economy for two goods, the interpersonal transfer of an amount of one of those goods will raise (lower) its relative price if it is a good for which the donor has a lower (higher) marginal propensity to consume (mpc) than the recipient. The rural poor tend to have a high mpc for food, and it is likely to exceed that of potential donors. Under these conditions, supplementary food aid to the rural poor will result in them paying higher prices for the rest of their food. Such price effects will mitigate the transfer benefits of the aid to its recipient. If there are only two income groups in the economy—those containing the donor and recipient—then the

---

[1]   See Ravallion (1987a, 1987b). Empirical evidence of convexity can be found in Preston (1975, 1980), Rodgers (1979), Schultz (1979), Williamson (1984), and Khan (1985).

[2]   The following terminology is that of Newbery and Stiglitz (1981).

[3]   Adverse price effects have often been identified as a constraint on redistributive policies in LDCs, see e.g. Griffin and James (1981), Sen (1981: Appendix B). The possibility of a 'transfer paradox' in a stable competitive economy has received considerable attention, see Gale (1974), Chichilnisky (1980), Ravallion (1983a), Dixit (1983), and De Meza (1983).

recipient will still be better off. But there are exceptions to even this claim if there is a third income group trading in the same markets as the donor and recipient.

Suppose, for example, that there are two goods, food and a 'luxury' good, and three income groups, one of which (the third group) is not directly involved in the redistribution. The 'donor' can be thought of as a high-income country, the 'recipient' as the rural poor in a low-income country, and the third group as the rich in the low-income country. The two countries trade freely. It can be shown that the recipient will be worse off when comparing general equilibria of the economy described above if:[4]

1. the donor has a higher mpc for the luxury good than the rich in the low-income country,
2. the rich in the low-income country are net demanders of the luxury good (for example, they are rich farmers who trade their food surplus for the luxury good), and
3. the total compensated substitution effect between food and the luxury good is sufficiently small.

Of course, this is only an example. And a well-informed recipient could never be worse off; the aid will simply be refused. But the example does at least illustrate how important market responses to transfer policies can be to their success.

The extent of *integration* between the markets facing donors and recipients is clearly an important determinant of those responses. In the above example, all agents trade freely in common markets. However, if donor and recipient are located in different markets (in that there is no trade between them) then the food transfer will increase supply to the recipient market. And so (under regular conditions) the transfer will lower the prices for food facing the recipient. Then recipients for whom the transfer is a supplement to their market purchases will gain in two ways: they will have higher incomes (which now include the imputed money value of the aid) and they will face lower food prices. An implication of these arguments is that even generous aid policies which are combined with trade liberalization may well be self-defeating; the aid is likely to be worth more to the recipient if it is combined with restrictions on trade.

All of the above arguments can be applied to other transfer policies. For example, in discussing relief work as a transfer policy, the two goods above can be interpreted as leisure and a composite consumption good. However, the underlying model precludes such an important feature of the economy in which relief work is provided—namely sustained unemployment of labour —that its practical relevance is doubtful. The following sections will examine market responses to transfer policies in models which permit unemployment.

[4] The result is proved in Ravallion (1983a).

## (b)  Relief work and transfers to the unemployed

Public employment has often been used as policy for relieving poverty and famines in South Asia and a number of recent studies have given strong support for this form of assistance.[5] It is appropriate to the present enquiry to concentrate on the potential transfer benefit from relief work. However, it should be noted that, in general, this will only be one aspect of the benefits and costs to be considered by a public decision maker. For example, a comprehensive welfare economic evaluation of the case for an extra job on a specific project should also take account of the social value of its extra output, net of that of any sacrificed outputs from the worker's alternative activities.[6]

The *transfer benefit* to a worker from an extra job on relief work is defined as the worker's income gain from that job, net of any costs incurred, including lost (personal) earnings from alternative employment. Ignoring any effects on wages, other employment, or other sources of income, an extra job on a rural works project will raise the worker's income by the amount of the wage rate for the job. More plausibly, both wages and other employment will change, although probably with opposite effects on rural incomes; an increase in public works employment is likely to put upward pressure on the agricultural wage rate leading to a reduction in demand for agricultural labour. Both effects have been observed in (for example) Bangladesh's food-for-work programme (Osmani and Chowdhury 1983; Ahmad and Hossain 1985). Thus the income gain to an otherwise unemployed worker from an extra job could be above or below the wage rate for that job.

A simple model can help clarify the issue. The model includes a prominent feature of this setting, namely the existence of urban unemployment associated with labour market dualism between the traditional (rural) sector and the modern (urban) sector in which real wages are relatively rigid. Large-scale migration from rural to urban areas is common during lean seasons and famines. Appendix 5.1 outlines a model of dual labour markets incorporating the (Harris–Todaro) assumption of unrestricted mobility between the urban

---

[5] Relief works were an important part of the Indian Famine Codes of the late 19th century, see Bhatia (1967), Akyroyd (1974), Currey (1984), and Rangasami (1985). Similar policies have been followed at various times over recent decades in India, Pakistan, and Bangladesh. There have been a number of recent surveys, see Ahmad and Hossain (1985), Bandyopadhyay (1985), Sundaram and Tendulkar (1985). The most famous programme of this sort is probably the 'Employment Guarantee Scheme' (EGS) of the State of Maharashtra in India, see Abraham (1980), Dandekar (1983), Herring and Edwards (1983), Lieberman (1985), Subbarao (1989). The EGS provided substantial relief during the severe 1970–3 droughts in Maharashtra, see Oughton (1982) and Drèze (1990). Recent advocates of relief work as an anti-hunger policy include Jodha (1978), Rath (1985), Walker *et al.* (1986), and Dandekar (1986).

[6] In terms of cost–benefit analysis, the transfer benefit from an extra relief work job is one component of the *shadow wage rate* for that job, which must be exceeded by the social value of its extra output, before the job can be deemed a welfare improvement. But, of course, the shadow wage also includes the marginal social product of labour in its best alternative use. Transfer benefits and costs to other persons may also be involved. For a thorough treatment of the theory of shadow pricing see Drèze and Stern (1985).

and rural sectors. While rigid in the urban sector, wages are assumed to be flexible in the rural sector. Relief workers are paid at the going wage rate in agriculture; there is no scope for undercutting that wage, although this will be relaxed later.

It is shown in Appendix 5.1 that, under these conditions, the marginal effect on employment in the agricultural sector $(N_a)$ of an aid financed change in rural public works employment $(N_g)$ is given by $-\varepsilon_a/(\varepsilon_a + N_u/N_a) < 0$, where $\varepsilon_a$ is the wage elasticity of demand for agricultural labour (defined to be positive), $N_u$ is the size of the urban workforce (including unemployed workers), and the $N$s are normalized so that $N_a + N_g + N_u = 1$. Thus, even though there is unemployment, an increase in rural public works employment will displace at least some employment in agriculture. When the level of urbanization is low the outcome will resemble a full employment equilibrium in which the displacement will be close to one to one; total rural employment will be invariant to the size of the public works programme. For countries such as Bangladesh and India, the level of urbanization $(N_u/N_a)$ is low, say 20 per cent, while the elasticity of demand for agricultural labour is probably in the region of $-0.7$ to $-0.2$ (Evenson and Binswanger 1985). Thus, the displacement effect will be between 20 and 50 per cent of the increase in rural public works employment. While these numbers are only intended to be a very rough guide to the orders of magnitude involved, they do suggest that the displacement of other employment by relief work need not be negligible.

Appendix 5.1 also shows that the marginal effect of an increase in public works employment on total rural income

$$Y = w_a(N_a + N_g) \tag{5.1}$$

is identical to its effect on the agricultural wage; both are positive and given by

$$\frac{\partial Y}{\partial N_g} = \frac{w_a}{\varepsilon_a N_a + N_u} \tag{5.2}$$

This is the recipient's transfer benefit from an extra job on relief work. If it exceeds the wage for that job then extra public expenditure on relief work will have a multiplier effect on rural incomes. This will be the case if the elasticity of demand for labour is less than unity. The necessary and sufficient condition is that $\varepsilon_a < 1 + N_g/N_a$. It can also be shown that, for a given value of $\varepsilon_a$, the multiplier will increase as the level of public employment increases; this is because, for an iso-elastic (or any convex) demand function, successive increments to the public workforce will bid up the agricultural wage rate by increasing amounts. Further details can be found in Appendix 5.1.

The range of figures considered plausible above for a country such as Bangladesh implies that the transfer benefit will exceed the wage rate, and will do so by quite a wide margin if agricultural labour demand is fairly wage inelastic. To give a numerical example, suppose that $\varepsilon_a = 0.25$, $N_a = 0.8$ and $N_u = 0.2$ (so that, initially, $N_g = 0$). Then the first job on relief work will raise rural income by a factor of 2.5 times the wage rate for that job. Clearly this is quite a substantial multiplier effect. And it will increase slightly as the public works programme expands; for example, under otherwise identical conditions, the multiplier exceeds three when $N_g = 0.3$.

It is worth noting that although the above case for public employment rests partly on the existence of unemployment, effective relief work need not be located within the region or sector in which that unemployment is actually found. Thus, relief work even in fully employed rural areas can yield substantial transfer benefits to the poor, although the unemployment is found elsewhere. For the simple model considered above, the transfer benefit is the same whether the extra job is in the urban area or the rural area. More plausibly, food prices will be higher in the cities, in which case the transfer benefit will favour the rural areas.

An alternative to providing relief work is to make transfer payments to the unemployed. There have been numerous, seemingly successful, attempts at targeting transfer policies to the urban poor, such as through rationed food stamps. Can such policies also have a multiplier effect on the total income of the poor, including the rural poor?

A transfer to unemployed urban workers will attract rural workers and so the agricultural wage will be bid up. This will have a positive effect on rural incomes as long as the wage elasticity of demand for agricultural labour is less than unity. The total income of rural workers and the urban unemployed is

$$Y = w_a N_a + T(N_u - N_m) \qquad (5.3)$$

where $T$ is the transfer made to each unemployed urban worker. It is easily demonstrated that, under the same conditions as above,

$$\frac{\partial Y}{\partial T} = \frac{N_u - N_m}{\varepsilon_a N_a + N_u} \gtreqless N_u - N_m \text{ as } \varepsilon_a \lesseqgtr 1 + N_g/N_a \qquad (5.4)$$

Comparing this with (5.2) it can be seen that the income gain from extra public expenditure on relief work in rural areas equals that from the same expenditure on transfer payments to the urban unemployed. The two policies are perfect substitutes under these conditions. Again this would change in favour of rural relief work if (as is plausible) food prices are higher in urban areas.

*(c)   Rural unemployment and the wage rate for relief work*

There is a widely held view that hiring *unemployed* workers in a public employment scheme will have little or no effect on wages and employment elsewhere in the economy. The validity of this view is questionable. For example, as in the model of the previous section, relief work can attract workers out of both (urban) unemployment and (rural) employment, with a positive effect on wages in the latter. Wage and employment effects also arise if existence of relief work for unemployed workers alters the bargaining power of employed workers. In a Nash bargaining game (for example) between workers and employers, the wages available on relief work are likely to influence the workers' threat point; the higher the wage rate on relief work, the higher (in general) the bargained wage rate for other employment.

Relief work can also have important short-run effects on labour markets which are in the process of adjusting toward a long-run (market clearing) equilibrium. To illustrate, consider a market in which, because of adjustment costs such as due to contracts, the wage rate does not adjust fully to its market clearing level in any one season; instead, it changes by increments which depend on the level of unemployment—the higher the unemployment, the higher the rate at which wages fall. (This is a standard assumption in analysing the stability of a competitive equilibrium.) Then, under regular conditions (including a downward sloping excess demand function for labour), relief work will raise wages above the level which would have otherwise obtained.

These effects have bearing on the policy choice of a wage rate for relief work, when the available budget for the policy is fixed. A worker's expected wage rate is the weighted mean wage rate for all jobs, with weights given by the probabilities of getting each job (including unemployment). If there are no effects on the wages for other jobs or the probabilities of getting those jobs, and both the budget and size of the workforce are fixed, then an increase in the wage rate for relief work will not affect the worker's expected wage; it will be offset exactly by the (consequent) fall in the number of relief jobs available and, hence, the probability of obtaining one of them. However, this ceases to be true if the wage rate for other employment is bid up. It can be shown that the effect on the worker's expected income of an increase in the wage rate on relief work is positive if (and only if) the wage elasticity of demand for labour in other work is less than $1/(1 + \phi)$ where $\phi = w_g N_g/(w_a(1 - N_a)^2)$; see Appendix 5.1.

For example, suppose that the wage rate on relief work is set at the value $w_g^*$ such that all workers who want a relief job at that wage can have it (as recommended by Basu 1990). Then $\phi = w_g/(w_a N_g)$ and so an increase in the relief wage will increase (decrease) a rural worker's expected wage if the elasticity of demand for labour in other work is less (greater) than $N_g/(N_g + w_g^*/w_a)$. For example, if the level of unemployment is high so that $w_g^*$ is small relative to other wages then an increase in $w_g$ will make workers better off on average as long as the elasticity of demand for labour is less than unity. As I have noted, this is plausible. Of course, unemployment will not still be zero, and workers may prefer to sacrifice some of the gain from a higher expected wage (as a result of a higher relief wage) so as to avoid the risk of their unemployment. I shall consider the risk aspect further in section 5.3.

### (d) Financing transfer policies

The above arguments give an optimistic view of the potential rural income gains from an aid-financed expansion of a rural public works programme or transfers to the urban unemployed. And this is so even if (as I have assumed) the output of the public works programme has no value to agricultural workers. However, the advantages of these policies are less obvious if the expansion occurs at the expense of other non-labour sources of income for the poor. In particular, suppose that the extra expenditure on relief work is financed entirely by a reduction in rural workers' non-labour income from another source, such as transfer receipts. It is clear that, without any effect on their other wage income, workers would gain nothing from such a change; their total income would be the same (although they may naturally prefer not to have to work more).

However, this ceases to be true when their employment and wages from other sources are affected by the policy change. For the same model of a dualistic labour market used in section 5.2$b$, it can be shown that the introduction of a rural public works programme financed by a reduction in workers' other (non-labour) income will increase total income as long as $\varepsilon_a < 1$; a revenue neutral policy change away from transfer payments to relief work will have a positive transfer benefit. Furthermore, it is possible that the transfer benefit from an extra job on public works will continue to exceed the wage rate for that job; for example this will hold for $\varepsilon_a < 1/2$ when both the degree of urbanization and initial transfer receipts are small. Appendix 5.1 demonstrates the above results.

This has an implication for the recent debate in India between proponents of public employment policies (such as Maharashtra's Employment Guarantee Scheme) and those who prefer transfer policies (such as payments in cash or kind made under the government of India's Integrated Rural Development Programme). Under the above conditions, workers' expected incomes can be raised by cutting their transfer receipts and using the funds so generated to finance extra employment. The same holds for transfer payments to the urban unemployed.

An alternative way to finance transfers is by taxes levied on the modern sector. For example, a large share of the cost of Maharashtra's EGS is financed this way. Such financing will reduce the transfer benefit to the poor if the tax is passed on in modern sector wage rates, leading to diminished employment opportunities in that sector. However, even if the tax is passed on fully in urban wages, it can be shown that relief work or transfer payments to the unemployed will still produce positive transfer benefits and that, under the same basic conditions as before, that benefit will continue to exceed the government's outlay.[7] The detailed argument is given in Appendix 5.1.

*(e)  The seasonal allocation of relief work*

There is little that can be done about the natural constraints on the seasonal allocation of relief work, such as the monsoon. But there are also some

---

[7] It can also be remarked that, under similar conditions, the value of a transfer payment to rural workers financed by a tax on urban workers will be diminished by its effects on wages and employment. Indeed, it can be shown that rural workers' wage rate will fall by·more than the amount of the transfer payment in a Harris–Todaro economy for which the wage elasticity of labour demand is greater in the modern sector than in agriculture (Ravallion 1984).

man-made constraints. It is often recommended that the timing of relief work should be chosen to avoid competition with the private sector. For example, work on Maharashtra's EGS has often been terminated as soon as harvesting begins. It may well be that the social value of any forgone output from providing relief work in harvest periods is higher than at other times. However, the transfer benefits of relief work are also relevant here. This is obvious when the sole concern is relief from hunger. The transfer benefits also matter when the objective in allocating relief work is to maximize a broader concept of social welfare. The appropriate shadow wage rate for the evaluating relief work is then the marginal social product of labour in alternative employment less the marginal social value of all transfers involved, including that of the worker's income gain (Little and Mirrlees 1974, Dreze and Stern 1987).

Following the arguments of previous sections, it is clear that the practice of avoiding competition with other employment could well reduce the transfer benefits from relief work. It is precisely the existence of competition between public and private employment which makes it possible to achieve high transfer benefits.

The model of dualistic labour markets used in section 5.2b can be used to illustrate this point. Suppose that a given amount of aid is to be allocated as relief work between the peak and off-peak periods. Also suppose that:

1. the wage rate is lower in the off-peak period,
2. the wage elasticity of demand for labour is unity in the off-peak period, but less than unity in the peak period.

It is then easily demonstrated that, at the point of introducing relief work, the transfer benefit from an extra job (averaged over the two seasons) will be greater if that job is provided in the peak period. Condition (2) above can be relaxed a good deal without altering the outcome; it is not even necessary that the elasticity of labour demand is greater in the lean period. Denoting the values of all relevant variables in the two periods by the superscripts: $h$ for the peak ('harvest') period and $l$ for the off-peak ('lean') period, the necessary and sufficient condition for the marginal effect on income of an extra job in the peak period to exceed that for the off-peak period is that (from equation 5.2):

$$\frac{w_a^h}{\varepsilon_a^h N_a^h + N_u^h} > \frac{w_a^l}{\varepsilon_a^l N_a^l + N_u^l}$$

Under this condition, the transfer benefit will be greater if the extra job is provided in the peak period.

There are two important caveats on this argument:

1. The extra relief job in the peak period will cost more to the funding agency. When the latter's budget is fixed, the relief work should only be provided in the peak period when the transfer benefit from doing so exceeds that from an off-peak job by a margin sufficient to cover the extra cost to the budget. And

note that that cost will exceed the initial wage rate since the latter will be bid up. The problem sounds complicated but in fact with a little algebra it can be shown that the decision criterion with a fixed budget is quite simple. The relief work should be provided in the peak period if (and only if):

$$(\varepsilon_a^l - 1)N_a^l > (\varepsilon_a^h - 1)N_a^h$$

Appendix 5.1 proves this result and also discusses the general problem of finding the optimal seasonal allocation of relief work.

2. In addition to the transfer benefit, it is likely that there will also be a stabilization benefit from providing relief work during low-income periods. And this could outweigh the case in favour of letting all relief work compete with peak period activities. I shall return to this point in section 5.3.

Of course, the benefits to the poor have not been the sole reason for providing relief work in the past. For example, one motive for the introduction of Maharashtra's EGS in the early 1970s appears to have been to discourage worker migration to urban areas during the lean seasons and drought-affected years, since some workers were not returning for the next harvest.

Taking the argument a little further, it is not difficult to imagine circumstances in which rural relief work provided in lean periods can have negligible (or even a negative) effect on workers' annual income. By encouraging workers to stay in the village during the off-peak season or during lean years, relief work can be used to keep down the peak period wage rate.

However, there is another argument in favour of restricting competition between relief work and other employment. And this is motivated by a concern for transfer benefits to the poor. The argument is that relief work can be made *self-targeting*, by setting the wage rate low enough to discourage better-off workers. This is an advantage over direct transfer payments for which effective targeting has often proved difficult.

Targeting is effective, however, only if wages for public employment are substantially below market wages. Otherwise, public employment will attract people other than the poor and will displace private employment. (World Bank 1986: 38)

Clearly this assumes unemployment of the strict (Walrasian) kind in which the wage rate is somehow prevented from falling to its market clearing level. Then there will be idle people who would like to work at the going wage rate, and will also take the work at some lower wage rates (as long as their supply schedule is rising).

While work requirements do appear to have been effective in discouraging participation by the non-poor, targeting performance is not the only factor to consider in setting the relief work wage.[8] As was pointed out in section 5.2c,

---

[8] Note that if an employment 'guarantee' is provided then the wage rate depends on the budget allocated to the scheme, and only certain budgets may then be feasible. On the case for and against a guarantee see Ravallion (1990a). For a general discussion of 'targeting' issues in this context see Ravallion (1990b).

when there is unemployment and labour demand is not too wage elastic, the expected income of a rural worker (who has at least the average chance of getting a job) will fall if the relief wage rate is cut, holding total public expenditure on the policy constant.

Nor is the assumption of (Walrasian) unemployment plausible in all the circumstances in which relief work *could* be provided, and so one should be cautious in applying the self-targeting argument generally. It is clearly inappropriate to the peak seasons of high labour demand. As I have already argued, there are likely to be large transfer benefits to workers from stimulating competition in rural labour markets in such periods. And this undoubtedly includes workers who would be attracted at other times into relief work at low wages. Faced with the option, poor workers could easily do better by saving the transfer gains generated by relief work in the peak period than by taking the low wage in off-peak work.

Nor is it obvious that Walrasian unemployment in off-peak seasons is the sole cause of rural poverty. In many places in the subcontinent, real wage rates are highly seasonal, often falling considerably in off-peak seasons as a result of higher food prices and/or lower money wages; see, for example, Chaudhury (1981). Even so, one suspects that this is rarely enough to clear the markets without adjustment on the supply side. But it is not uncommon in the subcontinent for rural labour markets also to adjust to the seasonality of demand by migration. The able people who remain in the villages generally do some sort of remunerative work, but at a low wage rate or a low rate of profit from self-employed activities.

Under these conditions, the primary cause of rural poverty and hunger in off-peak seasons is not unemployment (again in the strict sense of the term), but low real wages due to low demand for labour. There will be little scope for undercutting the wage rate. Relief work will displace other rural employment and some workers who would have otherwise migrated elsewhere will no longer do so. But these changes are an essential part of the adjustment mechanism which, as previous sections have illustrated, can give rise to substantial transfer benefits from relief work.

### (f) Wage and employment effects of food pricing policies

A reduction in the nominal price of food which is not accompanied by an equi-proportional fall in income will raise an individual's food entitlement. More generally, the various prices and quantities which determine income will also respond and so influence the transfer gains from anti-hunger policies such as food price subsidies or export taxes.

In discussing these effects I will concentrate on landless (or near landless) rural workers as the policy's main target group. Then our interest is to determine the effects of changes in food prices on their wages and employment.

An important distinction here is between policies which drive a wedge between consumer and producer prices and those which do not. A potential link between food prices and wage earnings in agriculture is through the demand side of the labour market. This link is broken if the fall in the price paid for food by a consumer can be achieved without altering the price received by the producer.

However, consumer price subsidies on foodgrains can be costly. The government must finance the subsidized component of grain consumption, and not just for the poor. (Although limited price discrimination is usually possible in urban areas and this is one way of making transfers to the urban poor, such as discussed in section 5.2b.) The enforcement cost can also be high in rural areas. For this reason, many governments have preferred intervention aimed at keeping the domestic market price low (for both producers and consumers). A common means of doing so is by taxing food exports. Another is by promoting domestic production of (non-traded) foods, such as by subsidizing inputs to their production.

The anti-hunger case in favour of such a food pricing policy is contentious when other prices and quantities determining food entitlements of the poor are responsive to the policy. In particular, it has been argued that, by stimulating food production and the demand for agricultural labour, high food prices may actually benefit workers, even when they are net demanders of food.[9] This argument rests heavily on the assumption that, through the demand side effects on the agricultural labour market, higher (lower) food prices will lead to (at least) equi-proportionally higher (lower) agricultural wages.

Is this plausible? I would be surprised if anyone who has observed the movements over time in agricultural wages in South Asia would argue that food price increases were generally passed on fully in wages within, say, the current season. Short-run stickiness of wages in both directions is a common feature of agricultural labour markets in South Asia and elsewhere.[10]

The argument may be a good deal more plausible over a longer period of time sufficient for markets to clear. In a simple partial equilibrium model of an agricultural labour market which clears at notional labour demand and supplies, themselves depending solely on the real wage in terms of food, an increase in the nominal price of food will be passed on fully in the nominal wage rate.

But this is not generally true in a dualistic labour market in which, although rural wages are flexible, the modern sector wage rate is fixed (in terms of either one good, or a composite good). Under similar assumptions to those made in previous sections, it can be shown that an increase in the price of food will lead to a deterioration in the food wage rate in agriculture, except in the special case

---

[9]  See e.g. Brown (1979) and Lipton (1984). This is presumably the reasoning behind a recent World Bank Policy Study when it argues that (in reference to countries such as India and Bangladesh): 'Low food prices clearly benefit the urban poor, but they have no effect on subsistence farmers and an ambiguous effect on the landless' (World Bank 1986: 40).

[10]  For evidence, see Rath and Joshi (1966), Lal (1989), and Ravallion (1982). Further evidence for Bangladesh is given below.

in which both labour demand and the food wage rate are fixed in the modern sector. (See Appendix 5.1 for details.)

Bangladesh's experience over the last three decades does not suggest that food price increases are passed on fully in the agricultural wage rate, even in the long-run. Boyce and Ravallion (1988) have examined the dynamics of agricultural wage adjustment to the prices of agricultural and industrial goods over this period. With some simplifications, their econometric model can be written as

$$w_t = \alpha_0 + \alpha_1 w_{t-1} + \beta_0 p_t + \beta_1 p_{t-1} + \gamma_0 q_t + \gamma_1 q_{t-1} + \delta f(t) + \mu_t \qquad (5.5)$$

where $w_t$ is the nominal wage rate at time $t$, $p_t$ is the money price of rice, and $q_t$ is the money price of cloth. All these prices are in log form. If the long-run real wage rate in terms of food is neutral to an equi-proportional change in both goods prices (leaving the relative price of food for clothing constant) then this model must satisfy the following homogeneity restriction on its parameters:

$$\alpha_1 + \beta_0 + \beta_1 + \gamma_0 + \gamma_1 = 1 \qquad (5.6)$$

This assumption is strongly supported by the data; on imposing homogeneity, one obtains the following estimate (in error correction form[11]):

$$\Delta w_t = \begin{matrix} 0.81 & -0.20(w-p)_{t-1} & -0.13(p-q)_{t-1} \\ (4.0) & (3.9) & (2.8) \end{matrix}$$

$$\begin{matrix} +0.23\Delta p_t & +0.15\Delta q_t \\ (4.2) & (2.9) \end{matrix}$$

$$\begin{matrix} +0.23 \times 10^{-2}t & -0.39 \times 10^{-3}t^2 \\ (1.6) & (2.5) \end{matrix} \qquad (5.7)$$

$$R^2 = 0.81 \quad SEE = .054 \quad D-W = 1.69 \quad n = 31$$

The short-run elasticity of the agricultural wage rate to the price of rice is 0.23, implying that the rice wage rate has a short-run elasticity of $-0.77$ to the price of rice. Adjustment is more complete in the long run, but even so the implied long-run elasticity of the rice wage rate to the price of rice is $-0.45$.[12]

It appears then that, for Bangladesh at least, the desirable short-run effects of lower food prices on the incidence of hunger would be reinforced by the more long-term effects on real wage rates. While the final transfer benefit may be mitigated by reduced demand for labour in rice production, it is likely to be

[11] For further discussion of this dynamic specification see Hendry et al. (1984) or Hendry and Richard (1983). For a similar application see Ravallion (1982). Further specification tests on the model are presented in Boyce and Ravallion (1988), including LM tests for serial correlation of the model's residuals. All test results were satisfactory.

[12] This is obtained by setting $\Delta w_t = \Delta p_t = \Delta q_t = 0$ and solving for $(w-p)_t = (w-p)^*$ for all $t$ as a function of $(p-q)_t = (p-q)^*$. Also note that the time trend $t$ in (5.7) is set to zero at the mid-point of the series (so that $t$ and $t^2$ are orthogonal). The result in (5.7) suggests a turning point in real wages at about the midpoint (1965); real wages in Bangladesh's agriculture have been on a downward trend since then.

positive since wage elasticities of demand in this setting are unlikely to exceed unity.

### 5.3.  Stabilization policies

(a)  Are stabilization policies needed?

The anti-hunger case in favour of stabilization is less straightforward than that for transfer policies. This is because, even in the most traditional societies, there already exist practices and institutions which are involved in spreading risks over time and sharing them between people. And it is conceivable that they work quite well.[13]

To illustrate, consider the (hypothetical) situation of an individual who holds rational expectations of his or her future income and has access to a perfect capital market. This person will be able to make food consumption invariant to fluctuations in food entitlements around their lifetime mean. He or she could, of course, still starve; but this will be because of an inadequate lifetime wealth rather than the volatility of food entitlements.

However, if these (admittedly very strong) conditions do not hold in practice then there will also be scope for policy interventions aimed at expanding the individual's opportunities for buffering consumption from fluctuations in entitlements. For example, government loans or subsidies may be used to stimulate the use of private but co-operatively used storage facilities. There are also possibilities for intervention in rural credit markets (such as the widely praised Grameen Bank in Bangladesh; see Ahmad and Hossain 1985). To give another example, the introduction of a government-backed financial asset with guaranteed food-purchasing power could offer an attractive alternative to storage and would avoid the familiar problem of declining real asset prices in terms of food during famines.

So how well do existing risk-sharing institutions work?

The traditional practice for spreading food risk over time is asset storage. The main asset used is foodgrain stock, although other real assets (such as land) and money are also used in market economies. Foodgrain storage can be done in the simplest subsistence economy and is undoubtedly the most long-standing risk-sharing practice. In the more complex rural societies typical of Asia, a number of social institutions are also involved in risk-sharing; these can be classified under two headings: the *moral economy* and *markets*.

A widely accepted historical picture of the evolution of risk-sharing practices and institutions in South and South-east Asia suggests increasing reliance by the poor on markets.[14] It is believed that, as transport and communications

---

[13] For example, though little evidence is presented, Morris's (1974) faith in existing risk-sharing practice and institutions has led him to be critical of famine relief policies. For a critical assessment of Morris's views see Jodha (1975). Also see Torry's (1986a) recent discussion of the debate.          [14] See e.g. Bhatia (1967) and Béteille (1980).

started to improve from about the mid-nineteenth century, trade progressively replaced on-farm asset storage. Also, increasing rural landlessness (particularly over recent decades) has been associated with an increasing reliance by the poor in the subcontinent on markets for labour, credit, and grain. It is also widely believed that the moral economy has declined in importance as a risk-sharing institution in South and South-east Asia.[15] And there is some evidence that institutions such as patronage are vulnerable to severe shocks such as famines.[16]

The reasons for some of these changes are far from clear and their full explanation is beyond the scope of this chapter. But they do suggest that variability of consumption over time may depend a good deal on performance of markets as risk-sharing institutions in agrarian economies. I shall briefly discuss some of the empirical evidence on the performance of rural credit markets and foodgrain markets in South Asia, and its bearing on anti-hunger policies.

*Credit markets*  Popular opinion in the subcontinent is that rural credit markets work rather badly. In fact, the debts arising from access to credit from professional money-lenders have been widely identified as an important cause of the impoverishment and vulnerability to famine of the peasantry. Many observers have thought the levels of indebtedness found in rural India to be excessive; by this view, the problem is not the lack of access to credit but its abundance.

The basis for this judgement has not always been obvious, and appears often to be more a reflection of the observer's values than problems facing the indebted agriculturalist. Take, for example, Malcolm Darling's description of the extravagance he found in Ferozepore in central Punjab after the expansion of irrigation:

The sudden acquisition of wealth, due more to good fortune than to effort, partially demoralized the people, stimulating extravagance, dissipation and drink. The money-lender, who might have been shaken off altogether, secured a firmer hold than ever. (Darling 1947: 71)

It is hard to see why someone should not want to go into debt in order to raise current consumption after an unanticipated increase in future income. And this is exactly what the peasants of Ferozepore appear to have done. The only genuine cause for concern here would seem to be if future income is systematically overestimated or if there are monopolies or other distortions to credit

[15]  This has been argued by Scott (1976), Jodha (1978), Béteille (1980), and Collier (1981). None the less, Ravallion and Dearden (1988) find that the pattern of voluntary transfer payments in rural areas of central Java is inequality reducing. However, this is not so in urban areas, suggesting that redistributive transfers decline with urbanization.

[16]  See e.g. Lewis and Barnouw (1958), Jodha (1978), Greenough (1982). Also see Torry (1986*b*) who argued that the ways in which the 'moral economy' of a Hindu Indian village changes during a famine are consistent with pre-famine moralities and social structures.

markets. Such conditions would prevent the peasant from achieving her or his most desired spread of consumption over time, consistent with lifetime wealth at competitive rates of interest. While there can be no a priori presumption that such conditions did not exist, the evidence in the literature is far from convincing.

Careful observation of the way rural credit institutions work in practice can, however, provide very useful insights. Studies of rural credit institutions in India have often revealed a complex, highly fragmented structure involving a variety of interest rates and contractual agreements often involving interlinkage with other markets. But it is difficult to come to a firm conclusion about market performance from such studies. For example, although the rationing of credit according to collateral (particularly land) is common, it may be unavoidable when lenders are risk averse and they face incomplete information and imperfect insurance markets (Stiglitz and Weiss 1981; Binswanger and Sillers 1983). As a consequence, even a landless worker with very good future income prospects can readily starve. To give another example, the fact that the interest rates charged by professional money-lenders typically exceed those charged by formal (government-sponsored) sources need not reflect a market imperfection. Money-lenders can often provide credit far more quickly than the formal market, and farmers are often willing to pay a higher rate of interest for this service (Bhende 1983; Binswanger et al. 1985).

An alternative approach to assessing market performance in this setting is to examine the way consumption is actually allocated over time, looking particularly for signs of a divergence from the allocation one would expect to be made in a perfect capital market in which agents hold rational expectations of future income prospects. The main result used in this approach is due to Robert Hall (1978), who demonstrated that the joint life-cycle/rational expectations hypotheses imply that the residuals from regressing consumption against its own lagged value in the previous period should be uncorrelated with all information available in that period. Past tests of the Hall hypothesis have largely been based on aggregate time-series data for developed countries.[17] Elsewhere I have tested the Hall proposition on household-level panel data over 1976–80 for three villages in dry regions of peninsular India (Ravallion 1986b). These data give a convincing rejection of the proposition; a number of variables in the lagged information set are found to have individually and jointly significant correlations with the residuals of an AR1 model of consumption. The intertemporal allocation of household consumption in these villages is not consistent with the optimal allocation of lifetime wealth that one would expect in a perfect (including informationally efficient) capital market.

This said, it must also be remarked that households in these villages are

---

[17] These have been motivated by the long-standing concern of economists and policy makers with the effectiveness of temporary changes in national income as a macroeconomic stabilization policy.

generally able (quite substantially) to insulate their consumption from income fluctuations. When averaged over all households, the short-run marginal propensity to consume out of current income is low, ranging from 0.18 to 0.29. It does increase as income or wealth falls, but at a slow rate, so that even households with negligible wealth have, on average, a low marginal propensity to consume from current income; my estimates range from 0.17 to 0.35. Risk-sharing practices and institutions may not work as well as they could, but they are certainly active in these villages.

*Foodgrain markets*    Nor has the popular opinion been that foodgrain markets work well. The interests of buyers and sellers are naturally opposed over price. Relations between merchants and the rural and urban poor in the subcontinent have often deteriorated to the point of violence when food prices rise. 'Hoarding' by merchants is a popular explanation for the high grain prices observed during many famines.[18]

While hostility toward the private grain trade during famines is common, and can be readily understood, it does not necessarily reflect a sound judgement of market performance. Hoarding can be a highly desirable response of current foodgrain markets to future scarcity. And it can be desirable from the point of view of the survival chances of the rural poor as well as the profits of speculative traders; anyone close to death now from starvation is likely to want food stocks to be released, but it is possible for this to result in many more people starving in the future. The crucial question here is how well stock-holders have anticipated future scarcity.

But one should be equally cautious of the faith in markets which some economists hold. Consider, for example, Peter Bowbrick's claim that:

There is an enormous literature on speculation, hoarding and storage dating back at least to Adam Smith. One thing is agreed—that the uninformed layman's criticisms of speculation are unfounded . . . Hoarding, like speculation, is a bogeyman invoked by politicians and administrators. (Bowbrick 1986: 118–21)

As Sen (1986) has noted (in response to Bowbrick), anyone familiar with the theoretical conditions needed to support such a faith in markets should be reluctant to share that faith without some good evidence.[19] And the evidence provided by many past studies of agricultural market performance has been of doubtful value.[20]

---

[18]  See e.g. Das (1949), Greenough (1982), Hartmann and Boyce (1979), Arnold (1984), and Steele (1985).

[19]  Not even the 'ideal' conditions of competitive (price taking) behaviour with perfect foresight are sufficient to guarantee that speculation is price stabilizing, see Hart and Kreps (1986).

[20]  The conventional (and popular) tests for 'efficiency' through spatial and temporal market integration have been criticized by Blyn (1973), Harriss (1979), Rudra (1982), and Ravallion (1986b, 1987b), in which alternative tests for market integration are proposed which avoid the main problems of the received methods. And the new tests suggest very different conclusions

Elsewhere I have examined the 'hoarding' issue at length and have offered some evidence for Bangladesh (Ravallion 1985a, 1985b, 1987b). I shall only summarize my conclusions here.

A convincing case can be made to support the view that rice hoarding before anticipated production losses was excessive during the 1974 famine in Bangladesh, when compared with the likely outcome under competitive conditions with rational expectations. Overreaction to new information on future scarcity appears to have had a destabilizing influence on the markets. Rice prices rose to unnecessarily high levels, particularly in the autumn of 1974 when agricultural employment was also low (and probably even more so than is usual for that season). And prices fell equally dramatically before the arrival of the next winter's (late and heavily depleted) harvest. Thus the worst months of the famine in terms of deaths occurred *before* the decline in food output due to flooding. The high and unstable foodgrain prices in Bangladesh cannot plausibly have been generated by an efficient market and they do appear to have been a major contributing factor to excess mortality.

In summary: from the available (albeit rather sketchy) evidence it appears that there is scope for anti-hunger policies which aim to improve the performance of existing risk-sharing practices and institutions.[21] The remainder of this section will examine likely market responses to some of the policies that have been advocated in the past.[22]

### (b)  Public storage

A policy implication of the above results is that price stabilization may have an important role in anti-hunger policies, particularly famine relief. Public buffer stocks are the traditional instrument for this purpose.

The effects of public storage in stabilizing consumption by the poor depend crucially on the way markets work. Policy makers and governments have often been ignorant of these effects; indeed, they have sometimes acted as if private storage does not exist. But an increase in the government's stocks will invariably displace at least some amount of private storage. Indeed, if markets are competitive and the price expectations on which private storage decisions are based are rational then the displacement effect will be one to one; changes

about the 'performance' of rice markets in Bangladesh during the 1974 famine. Heytens (1986) has applied some of my (1983b) methods to Jones's (1972) data for Nigeria and shown that the results cast considerable doubt on Jones's earlier conclusion that the Nigerian markets for food staples are well integrated.

[21]  It should be emphasized that the aim of stabilization policies in this context is not to raise mean consumption opportunities from income fluctuations. It can be argued that stabilization is an important part of the *social* security function of anti-hunger and other 'basic-needs' orientated social policies such as those pursued by Sri Lanka up to 1977. Failure to consider this aspect of such policies can lead to confusion when interpreting evidence on their basic-needs performance; for an example, see my (1986c) comments on Bhalla and Glewwe (1986).

[22]  I shall largely omit discussion of subsidized rural credit policies; see Braverman and Guasch (1986) for a critical survey. Also see Ahmad and Hossain (1985).

in the government's stock level will have no effect on the total amount of storage in the economy. Of course, this is a very special case and (as I have argued above) an implausible one. More generally, public storage probably matters. But it is also clear that the effects of buffer stocks depend crucially on the nature of the private grain trade.

A brief elaboration of this point will illustrate just how important market responses can be. My work in Bangladesh rice markets has taught me how influential *information* can be on markets. An important part of that information is the level of the government's foodgrain stock, itself determined by the government's past procurement efforts and by food aid and imports. When this is believed to be low, the traders expect future prices to be high. But they do not have rational expectations; I found that their *ex post* forecasting errors are generally and quite strongly correlated with *ex ante* information (Ravallion 1987*b*). Combining these observations, one can paint a rather grim picture of what can happen to such an economy if public stocks get too low and this is known. Indeed, it is entirely possible that, at low levels of public storage, an injection of grain into the economy will be completely ineffective in bringing the price of grain down; all of the drop in public stocks will be absorbed into private storage. The markets will make a successful speculative attack on the government's stock position. I have argued elsewhere that this is quite a plausible interpretation of conditions in Bangladesh during the 1974 famine (Ravallion 1987*b*). Indeed, this may well be the most important lesson from Bangladesh's experience in 1974. And it can be argued that greater public confidence in the government's ability to stabilize food consumption was an important reason why Bangladesh was able (narrowly) to avoid further famines in 1979 and 1984 (Osmani 1990).

### (c)  Trade and stabilization

International trade in food has recently been advocated as an alternative and less costly stabilization policy to buffer stocks.[23] The essence of the partial equilibrium argument is simple: by raising the local food price relative to prices elsewhere, shocks to domestic consumption opportunities should be at least partly offset by an increase in imports or fall in exports. Then trade should help buffer aggregate domestic consumption from random shocks to, for example, price expectations or production possibilities.

Of course the effects of trade on the interpersonal distribution of consumption are also of concern here; for example, while famine mortality can be reduced by stabilizing consumption over time, trade is also likely to affect mortality via its effects on interpersonal distribution. If (as is common) restrictions on trade are used to keep domestic grain prices below world prices

---

[23] See e.g. Weckstein (1977), Bigman and Reutlinger (1979), Reutlinger (1982), and World Bank (1986).

then free trade could well have sufficiently adverse effects on interpersonal distribution to mitigate its stabilizing influence on intertemporal distribution.

The experience of British India around the turn of this century provides a rare opportunity for studying a famine vulnerable economy with easy access to foreign markets. British India had virtually unrestricted external trade for many decades before the First World War and highly variable aggregate foodgrain production. The subcontinent was a net exporter of foodgrains (particularly rice) for most of the period, which included a number of severe famines (Bhatia 1967; Ghose 1982).

Thus free trade in foodgrains is likely to have reduced British India's aggregate grain consumption. To the extent that price elasticities of (net) demand for staple foodgrains tend to decline with the amount consumed, higher grain prices are also likely to have adversely affected interpersonal distribution.[24] But did it help stabilize consumption over time? Sluggishness in trade's response to domestic scarcities can arise from, for example, domestic price stickiness, the existence of long-term contracts, and delays due to transport. Following Sen's (1981) theory of 'slump famines', strong and adverse income effects in the famine region can also undermine the potential for stabilization by trade.

The stabilizing performance of trade can be tested by regressing exports against output; a positive coefficient indicates that trade helped buffer domestic availability from output fluctuations. Allowing for dynamic effects and using Blyn's (1966) estimates of foodgrain output ($Y$) and net trade flows ($X$) for British India (excluding Burma) over the period 1982 to 1914, I obtained the following result (both quantities in million tons; see Ravallion 1987$c$):

$$X_t = -6.9 + 0.51X_{t-1} + 0.075(Y_t + Y_{t-1})$$
$$\quad\;\; (4.7) \quad (4.0) \qquad\quad (5.0)$$

$R^2 = 0.67$ Durbin $h = 0.34$ \hfill (5.8)

A significant positive marginal rate of export is indicated, although the effect is small in the short run: only 7.5 per cent of a fall in output would have been passed on to trade. Export sluggishness is also indicated by the significantly positive effect of lagged exports. And so the long-run marginal rate of export of about 30 per cent is a good deal higher than the short-run figure. None the less, even in the long run, the stabilization of aggregate availability by free trade was far from complete.

While these results are not encouraging, there may be scope for government intervention using trade taxes or quotas aimed at enhancing the responsiveness of external trade to domestic prices. A stabilizing tax on trade is one in which exports are taxed (imports subsidized) when output is below normal while otherwise exports are subsidized (imports taxed). The main drawback of such policies is thought to be the induced instability of tax revenue (Reutlinger

---

[24] Income effects are likely to reinforce this; see Ravallion (1987$b$).

1982). Elsewhere I have calculated a fully stabilizing trade tax, designed to be revenue neutral in the long-run (Ravallion 1987*b*: ch. 7). The revenue variation would have been considerable. For example, as a percentage of the total budget of the government of India in 1900, tax revenue would have ranged from 73 to 66, with a standard deviation of 34. These results confirm the view that revenue instability of a stabilizing trade tax is likely to be large. This suggests that some form of monetary buffer stock, such as the IMF's food financing facility, may be essential for the future success of such policies.[25]

### (d)   Relief work as an income stabilizer

It has been argued that relief work policies can also generate sizeable stabilization benefits when the available work is allocated to low-income periods. One recent study which compared the risk benefits of such a scheme to crop insurance policies for dryland agriculture in India concluded that, despite its shortcomings, '. . . a public works programme like the EGS is the best institutional bet to protect a large number of poor rural households from the ravages of income variability' (Walker *et al.* 1986: A-86).

The stabilization case for relief work can make it desirable to provide work in off-peak seasons even when this reduces the transfer benefit. To illustrate, consider the problem of allocating a fixed budget for relief work between two seasons. Wages and employment behave according to the basic model of section 5.2*b*; to reiterate: workers are mobile between the rural sector in which real wages are flexible and an urban sector in which the wage rate is fixed above its market clearing level. The seasonal allocation of relief work is chosen to minimize hunger over the year, where hunger in each season is a convex function of that season's income. For analytical convenience that function is also assumed to have a constant elasticity, the value of which (following common practice in risk analysis) is interpreted as a measure of (relative) aversion to the risk of hunger. Appendix 5.1 shows that the budget set $B$ of affordable seasonal distributions of relief work is strictly convex; as depicted in Fig. 5.2. However, as Appendix 5.1 also shows, there is the possibility of a non-convexity in the set $H$ of all possible seasonal distributions of relief work which guarantee that annual hunger does not exceed any given amount. This is also illustrated in Fig. 5.2. Furthermore, the lower the aversion to hunger risk, the more likely it is that there will be a non-convexity in $H$. (Noting that seasonal income is a strictly convex function of relief work under the above assumptions; see Appendix 5.1 for details.) For example, if hunger is linear in income (so that the policy objective is simply to maximize annual income) then $H$ will not even be weakly convex. But as aversion to the risk of hunger increases, the lower boundary of $H$ will become more linear, and eventually the set is convex.

[25] For further discussion of the IMF's food financing programme see Huddleston *et al.* (1984) and World Bank (1986).

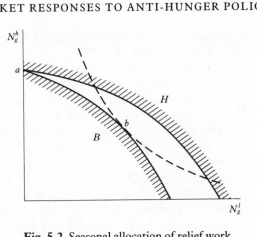

**Fig. 5.2** Seasonal allocation of relief work

Consider now the situation in which annual income is maximized by providing all of the relief work in the peak period (as will be the case under the conditions in section 5.2$e$). Then, following the above argument, there will be some degree of aversion to the risk of hunger which would justify shifting some of the available work to the off-peak season. This is illustrated in Fig. 5.2 where the dotted line indicates the new lower bound for $H$ obtained with (sufficient) aversion to risk. This shifts the optimal seasonal distribution of the relief work from $a$ to an interior point such as $b$.

An important caveat on this argument is that relief work may not be the best way to achieve the benefits to the poor of greater stability of consumption over time. As I have discussed earlier, assets generated in peak periods can be saved. There may also be useful ways of combining public employment and credit schemes, to permit workers in lean times to borrow from their future labour incomes, paying the loan back in the form of relief work. While it is likely that some consumption stabilization will make poor people less hungry, it is also desirable that the policy pursued should minimize the cost (in terms of annual or lifetime wealth of the poor) of achieving a given degree of stability.

*(e)  Public information*

There have been a number of recent attempts to identify key indicators for early warning on food crises in vulnerable economies such as Bangladesh and Thiopia.[26] The idea is not new. For example, the Madras Famine Code of 1883 strongly recommended monitoring grain prices as an indicator of famine (Rangasami 1985), and the Bengal Famine Code of 1918 outlined an elaborate early warning system (Currey 1984). And it seems that quite a few of the severe famines in Asia and Africa over the last 100 years or so were anticipated, and

---

[26]  See e.g. Eusuf and Currey (1979), Crow (1984), Cutler (1985), Desai (1990).

within a reasonable time; this is true of the last major famine in each continent, i.e. the 1974 famine in Bangladesh and the recent famine in Ethiopia.[27]

In the light of these observations, one is naturally left wondering whether further effort at famine forecasting is called for. It seems that the main problem here is lack of response, rather than lack of warning. But this may be too negative a view. Further work on early warnings may be justifiable on two counts: (1) it is clear that *publicity* matters, particularly if it draws international attention to domestic inertia, and (2) existing early warning systems can undoubtedly be improved upon.

The anti-hunger case for public information policies in general (of which famine early warnings are an example) also rests on the nature and performance of existing institutions. For example, there are conditions under which the prices observed in a competitive market with rational expectations will fully reveal all relevant inside information to market participants.[28] Then governmental efforts aimed at information dispersal will be futile.

However, as I have argued above, these conditions are implausible for the foodgrain markets of at least one famine vulnerable economy, Bangladesh. The existence of significant informational inefficiencies in Bangladesh rice markets suggests that there may be a useful role for government in providing better information. Information may be an important consumption stabilizer.

So, what information should be collected? Much attention in the recent famine forecasting literature has focused on the price of the staple foodgrain.[29] This variable is often used as an indicator of aggregate foodgrain supply, although this seems misguided since aggregate supply may be a poor indicator of the food entitlements of famine vulnerable individuals (Sen 1981). But the price of the staple foodgrain is one of the key variables determining the latter. This is obvious enough for the relative price of food. There are also some compelling reasons for suspecting that the *nominal* price of food matters as well. As I have argued in section 5.2f, in economies in which the poor depend heavily on their trade entitlements one often observes short-run stickiness of another important price: the nominal wage in agriculture. Thus an increase in the money price of food results in a deterioration in the food entitlement of the main asset of the poor, their capacity for work. There is now a good deal of empirical evidence suggesting that the money price of food matters to the poor.[30]

---

[27] On the early warnings of the Bangladesh famine see e.g. Alamgir (1980), Ravallion (1987b: ch. 3). On the Ethiopian famine see Kumar (1990), and Jansson *et al.* (1987).

[28] This is demonstrated by Grossman (1976). Also see Grossman and Stiglitz (1980).

[29] See e.g. Cutler (1985), Desai (1990).

[30] For example, past famines in South Asia have often revealed a strong and almost instantaneous association between an increase in the money price of food staples and famine mortality (Ravallion 1987a, 1987b: ch. 2). There is also empirical evidence for India of a positive association between the money price of food staples and the incidence of poverty; see e.g. Saith (1981) and Dharm Narain's work reported and discussed in Mellor and Desai (1985).

Following these observations, the econometric problem of forecasting the money price of the staple foodgrain can be viewed as central to the more general problem of anticipating the short-run collapses in the food entitlements of the rural and urban poor which cause their starvation during famines (Sen 1985). So, what is the best way to go about forecasting food prices?

Grain is storable and stockholders can be presumed to care about profits so their expectations about *future* prices matter for predicting *current* prices. For example, I have argued elsewhere that traders' price expectations were an important driving force in the crucial short-run dynamics of rice price formation during the Bangladesh famine. And, as was noted in section 5.3*a*, there were very significant departures of actual price movements from those implied by a competitive equilibrium with rational expectations.

This raises a problem for the design of early warning systems: it is the old problem Keynes talked about of how to forecast the forecasts of others. It is far from clear how an agency should go about forecasting the diverse forecasting *errors* of others, but at least we know that when expectations are non-rational they do generate errors which are predictable from *ex ante* information. For example, the forecasting errors of rice stockholders during the Bangladesh famine appear to have been particularly sensitive to two items of information widespread around mid-1974: (1) the numerous reports of flood damage to the next winter rice harvest, particularly around the time of its transplanting, and (2) the information accumulated over the previous six months or so suggesting that neither the Bangladesh government nor foreign sources could be relied upon to stabilize future food availability (Ravallion 1987*b*). I have also looked closely at the price expectations of a number of prominent Bangladeshi rice traders in the winter of 1983–4. Then I found that each one of twenty-two sampled traders systematically overestimated changes in rice prices over 70 trading days; forecasting errors (expected–actual) were positively correlated with lagged prices and expectations (Ravallion 1985*b*, 1987*b*). All such correlations can be exploited to achieve improved forecasting precision.

These observations lead me to suggest another source of information for an early warning system. Why not ask the traders what they expect? There are two obvious problems that might arise here: Firstly, the traders might not tell you, or they might mislead you. The way relations sometimes are between private grain traders and governments this is plausible. But it is a common form of madness for governments to adopt a position of hostile ignorance to the private trade. I have found that wholesale rice merchants in Bangladesh can be quite forthcoming about their expectations provided you can get their confidence. The second problem to be anticipated is that, as I have already noted, their expectations could well be informationally biased. However, I have found that even surveyed expectations which are biased can provide very substantial improvements in the post-sample forecasting performance of the sorts of time-series extrapolations commonly employed (such as univariate ARIMA models). For example, my survey information on traders' expectations in

Bangladesh permits an impressive 80 per cent drop in the ten-day ahead forecasting error variance of a model of day-to-day rice prices based solely on past prices and a time trend (Ravallion 1987b: ch. 6). While the traders may be prone to the same psychological 'follies' which lead many of us to hold biased expectations of our future, they do know a lot about the things that determine foodgrain prices, including, of course, their own expectations.

As a final comment, forecasting famines is unlike more familiar econometric forecasting problems in one important respect. In econometric forecasting it is common, indeed (to my knowledge) universal, to use the conditional mean of the forecasted variable for a given model as the forecast. In the language of statistical decision theory, this will be the optimal forecast for a least squares loss function defined on forecasting errors, or, more generally, any convex symmetric loss function.[31] Is this symmetry assumption appropriate to famines? I suspect not. When forecasting the probability of a famine next year, it is likely to be worse in terms of lives lost if one underestimates that probability by a given amount than if one overestimates it by that amount. Then to minimize mortality one should use a biased estimate of the probability of famine. Of course, the econometrician must then be willing to forgo some loss in terms of that favourite goal, forecasting precision.

## 5.4. Conclusions

Market responses can enhance or undermine anti-hunger policies. This chapter has tried to illustrate how an understanding of those responses can provide important clues for policy analysis and design.

Transfer policies such as relief work or payments to the unemployed can have significant multiplier effects on incomes of the poor. In a dualistic economy with mobility between a rural flexi-wage sector and an urban fixed-wage sector with unemployment, the multiplier effect will be large when the wage elasticity of demand for labour in agriculture is low. Such multiplier effects can be exploited in policy design to achieve the most cost-effective aid.

For example, relief work is generally confined to alleviating poverty from rural unemployment in lean periods. While the social opportunity cost from such a restriction on the policy is likely to be low, this is also true of the transfer benefit to the poor, once market responses are considered. Indeed, under this restriction, the policy cannot generally be expected to achieve the most cost-effective aid—in the sense of maximizing the recipient's transfer benefit for a given outlay on the policy. It is likely that a greater benefit to the poor will be possible for the same public expenditure by allocating some of the relief work to times and places at which it competes with other employment. The potential gains from doing so exist for various methods of financing the

[31] For further discussion see Granger (1969) and De Groot (1970).

policy—including revenue neutral financing from the worker's other transfer receipts.

Low prices for staple foods can also have significant transfer benefits to both urban and rural poor. And this is so even when likely market responses are considered. Past experience in South Asia suggests that changes in food prices are unlikely to be passed on fully in the agricultural wage rate, even in the long run. The desirable short-run effects of low food prices on the welfare of the rural poor would probably persist.

The extent of a person's hunger over a period of time is also likely to depend on the variability of food consumption within that period. There is evidence suggesting that the poor face imperfect (or even non-existent) risk-related markets and that there has been an erosion over time of traditional risk-sharing practices and institutions (such as patronage). Thus the stabilization benefits to the poor from alternative anti-hunger policies should also be considered.

Public employment policies illustrate how there can be a trade-off between the transfer and risk benefits to the poor of a policy change. For example, in spite of the potential transfer benefit from not doing so, there may be a stabilization case for providing relief work in lean periods of low and wage elastic labour demand.

However, it is far from clear that relief work and similar transfer policies are the best available instruments for this purpose. There are other policies which can help here, such as rural credit schemes, and which might fruitfully be integrated with transfer policies. There is also a potentially important role for price stabilization policies, using public storage and/or external trade. The choice between these policies depends crucially on market responses, including the way speculative foodgrain markets respond to information on the government's actions. There is also scope for improved public information as part of stabilization policy. Studies of the way markets have worked in the past, particularly during food crises, can throw considerable light on appropriate policy initiatives.

# Appendix 5.1

The following argument proves the claims made in section 5.3*b* concerning the effects of relief work on rural incomes under labour market dualism. The model is:

$$w_i = f_i(N_i) f_i' < 0, i = a,m \tag{A.1}$$

$$N_a + N_u + N_g = 1 \tag{A.2}$$

$$w_a N_u = w_m N_m \tag{A.3}$$

where $w_i$ is the real wage rate in sector $i$, which can be either agriculture ($i = a$) or manufacturing ($i = m$) and $N_i$ is the number of workers in sector $i$. $N_u$ denotes the number of workers in the urban sector comprising those employed ($N_m$) and those unemployed ($N_u - N_m$). $N_g$ workers are employed on public works projects at the going wage rate in rural areas $w_a$ and their wage bill is financed by aid. Unemployment arises because the wage in the manufacturing sector is assumed to be fixed above its market clearing level. The model is closed by the assumption (following Harris and Todaro 1970) of free mobility between urban and rural sectors which, under risk neutrality, implies equality of the agricultural wage rate with the expected urban wage, $w_m N_m / N_u$, as indicated in equation (A.3).[32]

Fixity of $w_m$ implies that $N_m$ and, hence, $w_a N_u$ are also fixed. Then,

$$w_a dN_u + N_u f_a' dN_a = 0 \tag{A.4}$$

Also, from (A.2):

$$dN_u + dN_a + dN_g = 0 \tag{A.5}$$

The solution of the last two equations for

$$dN_a/dN_g = \frac{-w_a}{w_a - N_u f_a'} = -k\varepsilon_a N_a < 0 \tag{A.6}$$

as claimed, where $k = 1/(\varepsilon_a N_a + N_u)$ and $1/\varepsilon_a = -f_a' N_a/w_a$. From (A.1), the corresponding effect on the agricultural wage of an expansion of relief work is

$$dw_a/dN_g = kw_a \tag{A.7}$$

Consider now the effect of public works employment on total rural income $Y: = w_a(N_a + N_g) = w_a(1 - N_u)$ by (A.2). Since $w_a N_u$ is fixed by the manufacturing wage, the effect of a change in $N_g$ on $Y$ is identical to its effect on $w_a$ as given by (A.7). By inspection, it follows that

$$dY/dN_g \gtrless w_a \text{ as } \varepsilon_a N_a + N_u \gtrless 1$$

as claimed in section 5.2*b*. Thus $k$ is the rural income multiplier associated with an expansion of relief work. Also note that $\varepsilon_a N_a + N_u \geq 1$ implies (with A.3) that $\varepsilon_a \geq 1 + N_g/N_a \geq 1$. So $dY/dN_g > w_a$ as long as $\varepsilon_a < 1$. Furthermore, for given $\varepsilon_a$, the

[32] This will overestimate the expected urban wage if incoming workers have a lower probability of obtaining a job than the incumbents (see e.g. Mazumdar 1976). The following analysis can be modified to permit incomplete labour turnover without substantial change to the main argument in section 5.2*b*. For a critical overview of the Harris–Todaro model see Basu (1984).

rural income multiplier is a strictly increasing function of $N_g$; on noting that $k = 1/((\varepsilon_a - 1)N_a - N_g)$ and that (A.6) holds, one finds that

$$\partial k/\partial N_g = k^3(\varepsilon_a^2 N_a + N_u) > 0$$

Section 5.2*b* also discusses the transfer benefits from payments to the urban unemployed. In this case, equations (A.1) and (A.2) are unchanged, but (A.3) is replaced by

$$w_a N_u = w_m N_m + T(N_u - N_m) \tag{A.8}$$

(since the expected urban income of a rural worker now includes the transfer payment $T$ to the urban unemployed). The analysis proceeds as before and equation (5.4) in section 5.2*b* is readily obtained.

The result used in section 5.2*c* is obtained as follows. A proportion $N_a$ of the workforce gets farm employment at the wage $w_a$. A number $N_g$ of the remainder get public employment at the wage $w_g$ while the rest remain unemployed. The (expected) income of a worker is then:

$$Ew = w_a N_a + w_g N_g/(1 - N_a) \tag{A.9}$$

(noting that the probability of getting public employment is $N_g/(1 - N_a)$). The public budget is $R = w_g N_g$ and this is assumed to be fixed. A change in $w_g$ affects $N_a$ through its effect on $w_a$. Then,

$$\frac{\partial Ew}{\partial w_g} = N_a(1 - \varepsilon_a(1 + \phi)) \; \frac{\partial w_a}{\partial w_g} \gtreqless 0 \tag{A.10}$$

as $\varepsilon_a \gtreqless 1/(1 + \phi)$ whenever $\partial w_a/\partial w_g > 0$, as claimed in section 5.2*c*, and where

$$\phi = \frac{R}{w_a(1 - N_a)^2} > 0$$

Note that the inequalities in (A.10) reverse if $\partial w_a/\partial w_g < 0$.

The argument in section 5.2*d* concerning the choice between income transfers and relief work is based on equations (A.1)–(A.3), augmented to include an additional source of income for rural workers in the form of a transfer payment $T$ per worker. (A.1) and (A.2) remain the same, but (A.3) becomes

$$(w_a + T)N_u = w_m N_m \tag{A.11}$$

The expansion of relief work is now at the expense of transfers; the total public budget for redistribution is

$$R = (N_a + N_g)T + w_a N_g \tag{A.12}$$

which is fixed. Using (A.1) and (A.2) to eliminate $w_a$ and $N_u$ from (A.11) and (A.12), one obtains equations in which $N_a$ and $T$ are implicit functions of $N_g$, $w_m N_m$ and $R$, noting again that fixity of $w_m$ implies that $w_m N_m$ is also fixed. It is readily verified that the slopes with respect to $N_g$ of these implicit functions are:

$$\frac{\partial N_a}{\partial N_g} = (w_a + T)/\mathcal{J} < 0 \tag{A.14}$$

$$\frac{\partial T}{\partial N_g} = -(w_a + T)(f'_a N_u - w_a)/\mathcal{J} < 0 \qquad (A.13)$$

when both are evaluated at $N_g = 0$ and where the Jacobian has the value:

$$\mathcal{J} = -N_a(w_a - f'_a N_u) - T \qquad (A.14)$$

The total income of agricultural workers is now:

$$Y = (w_a + T)(N_a + N_g) = w_a N_a + R \qquad (A.15)$$

Differentiating with respect to $N_g$ and using (A.1), (A.12), (A.13), and (A.14) one obtains, after some straightforward algebra:

$$\frac{\partial Y}{\partial N_g} = (w_a + T)(1 - 1/\varepsilon_a)w_a/\mathcal{J} \qquad (A.16)$$

And so

$$\frac{\partial Y}{\partial N_g} \gtreqless w_a + T \text{ as } \varepsilon_a \lesseqgtr \frac{N_a}{1 - N_a + T/w_a}$$

Thus, when $N_u = T = 0$, $\partial Y/\partial N_g > w_a + T$ iff $\varepsilon_a < \frac{1}{2}$, as claimed in section 5.2d.

Consider next the case discussed in section 5.2d in which the relief work is financed by a tax on employed workers in the modern sector. The model again includes equations (A.1) and (A.2). However, the equilibrium condition between the two sectors, (A.3), must be replaced by

$$w_a N_u = \bar{w} N_m \qquad (A.17)$$

where $\bar{w}$ is the (fixed) post-tax wage in the modern sector,

$$\bar{w} = w_m - t \qquad (A.18)$$

The budget constraint on the policy is now:

$$w_a N_g = t N_m \qquad (A.19)$$

Rural income is again given by $Y = w_a(N_a + N_g)$, except that now modern sector employment will be affected by changes in rural public works employment via their effect on the pre-tax wage rate. Then it is readily verified that, for $\varepsilon_a < 1$ and $\varepsilon_m < 1$,

$$\frac{\partial Y}{\partial N_g} = \frac{\partial w_a}{\partial N_g} + \varepsilon_m N_m \frac{\partial w_m}{\partial N_g} > w_a \qquad (A.20)$$

where, on implicitly differentiating the model with respect to $N_g$ at $N_g = 0$.

$$\frac{\partial w_a}{\partial N_g} = k w_a(1 - \varepsilon_m) > 0 \qquad (A.21)$$

$$\frac{\partial w_m}{\partial N_g} = w_a/N_m > 0 \qquad (A.22)$$

(noting that $k = 1/(\varepsilon_a N_a + N_u) > 1$ for $\varepsilon_a < 1$).

To examine the effects of a change in the price of food (as discussed in section 5.2f), wages in the basic model above are now interpreted as nominal wage rates. The labour demand functions now equate the nominal wage rates to marginal revenue products:

$$w_a = pf_a(N_a) \tag{A.23}$$

$$w_m = qf_m(N_m) \tag{A.24}$$

Equations (A.2) and (A.3) are unchanged. The real wage rate in the modern sector is now fixed in terms of a composite good with weights $a$ and $b$ on food and clothing respectively. Thus

$$w_m/(ap + bq) = \overline{w} \tag{A.25}$$

On differentiating the model with respect to $p$ and solving for the implicit derivative of $w_a$ one obtains, in elasticity form:

$$\frac{\partial \log w_a}{\partial \log p} = \frac{cN_u(1 - \varepsilon_m) + N_a\varepsilon_a}{N_u + N_a\varepsilon_a} < 1 \tag{A.26}$$

if $\varepsilon_m < 1$, where $c = ap/(ap + bq)$, as claimed in section 5.2f.

The following variation on the basic model is used in discussing the optimal allocation of relief work between seasons in sections 5.2e and 5.3d. As in section 5.2e, superscripts $l$ and $h$ are used to denote the values of all variables in the off-peak ('lean') and peak ('harvest') periods. The policy problem is to allocate a fixed revenue $R$ between expenditure on rural relief work in the two seasons so as to maximize the workers' welfare over the year. Welfare in each season is an increasing and strictly concave function of income in that season and this is simply summed across seasons to give total annual welfare. Following the discussion in section 5.1, 'welfare' may here be interpreted as the absence of hunger. Wages and employment in each season satisfy the basic model above.

The problem is then to choose $N_g^l$ and $N_g^h$ to maximize

$$u(Y^l) + u(Y^h) \quad u' > 0, u'' < 0 \tag{A.27}$$

subject to the budget constraint

$$w_a^l N_g^l + w_a^h N_g^h \le R \tag{A.28}$$

where wages and employment satisfy equations (A.1) to (A.3) in each season. On noting that (A.27) is strictly quasi-concave in incomes, the problem will have an interior solution if (1) income for each season is at least weakly concave in public employment and (2) the set of $N_g^l$, $N_g^h$ values satisfying the constraints is (at least weakly) convex. However, while the latter condition holds for this model, the former one need not. The key point is that the wage rate for each season can be a strictly *convex* function of the amount of relief work provided in that season; on differentiating equation (5.2) in section 5.3b with respect to $N_g$ at constant demand elasticities:[33]

$$\frac{\partial^2 w_a}{\partial N_g^2} = (1 + kN_u + \varepsilon_a^2 kN_a)w_a k^2 > 0 \tag{A.29}$$

While this implies that the constraint set satisfying (A.28) is strictly convex, it also means that the objective function (A.27) need not be quasi-concave in employment. Indeed, it will be strictly quasi-convex for linear $u$.

---

[33] Noting that $dN_u/dN_g = -kN_u$; this follows from (A.5) and (A.6), recalling that $k = 1/(\varepsilon_a N_a + N_u)$.

Section 5.2*e* discusses the seasonal allocation when only transfer benefits matter, i.e. *u* is linear. For the transfer benefit from an extra peak period job to be positive, when that job is financed by a cut in the budget allocation to the lean period, one requires that

$$\frac{\partial Y^h}{\partial N_g^h} + \frac{\partial Y^l}{\partial N_g^l} \cdot \frac{\partial N_g^l}{\partial N_g^h} > 0 \tag{A.30}$$

where the last derivative on the LHS is evaluated along the upper boundary of the budget constraint (A.24), giving

$$-\frac{\partial N_g^h}{\partial N_g^l} = \frac{w_a^l + N_g^l \partial w_a^l / \partial N_g^l}{w^h + N_g^h \partial w_a^h / \partial N_g^h} \tag{A.31}$$

The decision criterion used in section 5.2*e* is then readily obtained.

The result discussed in section 5.3*d* and illustrated in Fig. 5.2 follows from the fact that starting from the point *a* ($N_g^l = 0$, $N_g^h = R/w_a^h$) an increase in the elasticity of the function *u* will reduce the (absolute) slope of the contours of (A.27). By continuity of the function *u*, there will exist a critical value of that elasticity above which the problem will have an interior solution.

# References

ABRAHAM, A. (1980), 'Maharashtra's Employment Guarantee Scheme', *Economic and Political Weekly*, 15.

——(1985), 'Subsistence Credit: Survival Strategies among Traditional Fishermen', *Economic and Political Weekly*, 20.

AHMAD, Q. K., and HOSSAIN, M. (1985), 'An Evaluation of Selected Policies and Programmes for the Alleviation of Rural Poverty in Bangladesh', in Islam, R. (ed.), *Strategies for Alleviating Poverty in Rural Asia* (Bangkok: ILO).

ALAMGIR, M. (1980), *Famine in South Asia: Political Economy of Mass Starvation* (Cambridge, Mass.: Oelgeschlager, Gunn & Hain).

ARNOLD, D. (1984), 'Famine in Peasant Consciousness and Peasant Action: Madras, 1876–8', in Guha, R. (ed.), *Subaltern Studies*, iii (Delhi: Oxford University Press).

AYKROYD, W. R. (1974), *The Conquest of Famine* (London: Chatto & Windus).

BANDYOPADHYAY, D. (1985), 'An Evaluation of Policies and Programmes for the Alleviation of Rural Poverty in India', in Islam, R. (ed.), *Strategies for Alleviating Poverty in Rural Asia* (Bangkok: ILO).

BASU, K. (1984), *The Less Developed Economy* (Delhi: Oxford University Press).

——(1990), 'The Elimination of Endemic Hunger in South Asia: Some Policy Options', in vol. iii of this book.

BÉTEILLE, A. (1980), 'The Indian Village: Past and Present', in Hobsbawn, E. J., *et al.* (eds.), *Peasants in History: Essays in Honour of Daniel Thorner* (Calcutta, Calcutta University Press).

BHALLA, S., and GLEWWE, P. (1986), 'Growth and Equity in Developing Countries: A Reinterpretation of the Sri Lankan Experience', *World Bank Economic Review*, 1.

BHATIA, B. M. (1967), *Famines in India: A Study of Some Aspects of the Economic History of India, (1860–1965)* (London: Asia Publishing House).

BHENDE, M. J. (1983), 'Credit Markets in the Semi-arid Tropics of Rural South India', ICRISAT Economics Programme, Progress Report 56, Patancheru, Andhra Pradesh, India; See also *Economic and Political Weekly* (1986), Review of Agriculture, 21.

BIGMAN, D., and REUTLINGER, S. (1979), 'National and International Policies toward Food Security and Price Stabilization', *American Economic Review (Proceedings)*, 69.

BINSWANGER, H. P., BALARAMAIAH, V., BAHSKAR RAO, M. J., BHENDE, and KASHIRSAGOR, K. V. (1985), 'Credit Markets in Rural South India: Theoretical Issues and Empirical Analysis', Discussion Paper No. ARU 45 (Agriculture and Rural Development Department, Operational Policy Staff, World Bank).

——and SILLERS, D. A. (1983), 'Risk Aversion and Credit Constraints in Farmers' Decision Making', *Journal of Development Studies*, 20.

BLYN, G. (1966), *Agricultural Trends in India, 1891–1947: Output Availability and Productivity* (Philadelphia, Penn.: University of Pennsylvania Press).

——(1973), 'Price Series Correlation as a Measure of Market Integration', *Indian Journal of Agricultural Economics*, 28.

BOWBRICK, P. (1986), 'The Causes of Famine: A Refutation of Professor Sen's Theory', *Food Policy*, 11.

BOYCE, J., and RAVALLION, M. (1988), 'The Dynamics of Wage Determination in

Rural Bangladesh', mimeo (Washington, DC: Agricultural Policies Division, World Bank).

BRAVERMAN, A., and GUASCH, J. L. (1986), 'Rural Credit Markets and Institutions in Developing Countries: Lessons for Policy Analysis from Practice and Modern Theory', *World Development*, 14.

BROWN, G. (1979), 'Agricultural Pricing Policies in Developing Countries', in Schultz, T. W. (ed.), *Distortions of Agricultural Incentives* (Bloomington, Ind.: Indiana University Press).

CHAUDHURY, R. H. (1981), 'The Seasonality of Prices and Wages in Bangladesh', in Chambers, R., Longhurst, R., and Pacey, A. (eds.), *Seasonal Dimensions to Rural Poverty* (London: Frances Pinter).

CHICHILNISKY, G. (1980), 'Basic Goods, the Effects of Commodity Transfers and the International Economic Order', *Journal of Development Economics*, 7.

CHOWDHURY, O. H. (1983), 'Profile of Workers in the Food-for-Work Programme in Bangladesh', *Bangladesh Development Studies*, 11.

CLAY, E. J. (1981), 'Seasonal Patterns of Agricultural Employment in Bangladesh', in Chambers, R., Longhurst, R., and Pacey, A. (eds.), *Seasonal Dimensions to Rural Poverty* (London: Frances Pinter).

COLLIER, W. L. (1981), 'Agricultural Evolution in Java', in Hansen, G. E. (ed.), *Agricultural and Rural Development in Indonesia* (Boulder, Colo.: Westview Press).

CROW, B. (1984), 'Warnings of Famine in Bangladesh', *Economic and Political Weekly*, 19.

CURREY, B. (1984), 'Coping with Complexity in Food Crisis Management', in Currey, B., and Hugo, G. (eds.), *Famine as a Geographical Phenomenon* (Dordrecht: Reidel).

CUTLER, P. (1985), 'Detecting Food Emergencies: Lessons from the 1979 Bangladesh Crisis', *Food Policy*, 10.

DANDEKAR, K. (1983), *Employment Guarantee Scheme: An Employment Opportunity for Women* (Bombay: Orient Longman).

DANDEKAR, V. M. (1986), 'Agriculture, Employment and Poverty', *Economic and Political Weekly*, Review of Agriculture, 21.

DARLING, M. (1947), *The Punjab Peasant in Prosperity and Debt* (Bombay: Oxford University Press).

DAS, T. (1949), *Bengal Famine (1943) as Revealed in a Survey of the Destitutes in Calcutta* (Calcutta: University of Calcutta).

DE GROOT, M. H. (1970), *Optimal Statistical Decisions* (New York: McGraw-Hill).

DE MEZA, D. (1983), 'The Transfer Problem in a Many-Country World: Is it Better to Give than Receive?', *Manchester School*, Sept.

DESAI, M. (1990), 'Modelling an Early Warning System for Famines' in this volume.

DIXIT, A. (1983), 'The Multi-Country Transfer Problem', *Economics Letters*, 13.

DRÈZE, J. P. (1990), 'Famine Prevention in India', in this volume.

——and STERN, N. (1987), 'The Theory of Cost–Benefit Analysis', in Auerbach, A., and Feldstein, M. (eds.) (1987), *Handbook of Public Economics*, ii (Amsterdam: North-Holland).

EUSUF, A. N. M., and CURREY, B. (1979), 'The Feasibility of a Famine Warning System for Bangladesh' (Ministry of Relief and Rehabilitation, Government of Bangladesh).

EVENSON, R. E., and BINSWANGER, H. P. (1984), 'Estimating Labor Demand Functions for Indian Agriculture', in Binswanger, H. P., and Rosenzweig, M. R. (eds.),

*Contractual Arrangements, Employment and Wages in Rural Labor Markets in Asia* (New Haven, Conn.: Yale University Press).

GALE, D. (1974), 'Exchange Equilibrium and Coalitions: An Example', *Journal of Mathematical Economics*, 1.

GHOSE, A. K. (1982), 'Food Supply and Starvation. A Study of Famines with Reference to the Indian Subcontinent', *Oxford Economic Papers*, 34.

GRANGER, C. W. J. (1969), 'Prediction with a Generalized Cost of Error Function', *Operations Research Quarterly*, 20.

GREENOUGH, P. R. (1982), *Prosperity and Misery in Modern Bengal: The Famine of 1943–1944* (Oxford: Oxford University Press).

GRIFFIN, K., and JAMES, J. (1981), *The Transition to Egalitarian Development* (London: Macmillan).

GROSSMAN, S. J. (1976), 'On the Efficiency of Competitive Stock Markets where Traders have Diverse Information', *Journal of Finance*, 31.

——and STIGLITZ, J. E. (1980), 'On the Impossibility of Informationally Efficient Markets', *American Economic Review*, 70.

HALL, R. (1978), 'Stochastic Implications of the Life Cycle—Permanent Income Hypothesis: Theory and Evidence', *Journal of Political Economy*, 86.

HARRIS, J. R., and TODARO, M. P. (1970). 'Migration Unemployment and Development: A Two-Sector Analysis', *American Economic Review*, 60.

HARRISS, B. (1979), 'There is Method in my Madness: Or is it Vice Versa?', *Food Research Institute Studies*, 17.

HART, O., and KREPS, D. (1986), 'Price Destabilizing Speculation', *Journal of Political Economy*, 94.

HARTMANN, B., and BOYCE, J. K. (1979), *Needless Hunger: Voices from a Bangladesh Village* (San Francisco, Calif.: Institute for Food and Development Policy).

HENDRY, D. F., PAGAN, A. R., and SARGAN, J. D. (1984), 'Dynamic Specification', in Griliches, Z., and Intriligator, M. D. (eds.), *Handbook of Econometrics*, ii (Amsterdam: North-Holland).

——and RICHARD, J.-F. (1983), 'The Econometric Analysis of Time Series', *International Statistical Review*, 51.

HERRING, R. J., and EDWARDS, R. M. (1983), 'Guaranteeing Employment to the Rural Poor: Social Functions and Class Interests in the Employment Guarantee Scheme in Western India', *World Development*, 11.

HEYTENS, P. J. (1986), 'Testing Market Integration', *Food Research Institute Studies*, 20.

HUDDLESTON, B., JOHNSON, D. G., REUTLINGER, S., and VALDÉS, A. (1984), *International Finance for Food Security* (Baltimore, Md.: Johns Hopkins).

ISLAM, R. and LEE, E. (1985), 'Strategies for Alleviating Poverty in Rural Asia', in Islam, R. (ed.), *Strategies for Alleviating Poverty in Rural Asia* (Bangkok: ILO).

JANSSON, K., HARRIS, M., and PENROSE, A. (1987), *The Ethiopian Famine* (London: Zed).

JODHA, N. S. (1975), 'Famine and Famine Policies: Some Empirical Evidence', *Economic and Political Weekly*, 10.

——(1978), 'Effectiveness of Farmers' Adjustments to Risk', *Economic and Political Weekly*, 13.

JONES, W. O. (1972), *Marketing Staple Food Crops in Tropical Africa* (Ithaca, NY: Cornell University Press).

KAHN, Q. (1985), 'Household Wealth, Mother's Education and Child Mortality in South Asia', Discussion Paper (Philadelphia, Penn.: Centre for Analysis of Developing Countries, University of Pennsylvania).

KUMAR, G. (1990), 'Ethiopian Famines 1973–1985: A Case-Study', in this volume.

LAL, D. (1989), *The Hindu Equilibrium, ii: Aspects of Indian Labour* (Oxford: Oxford University Press).

LATHAM, A. J. H., and NEAL, L. (1983), 'The International Market in Rice and Wheat, 1964–1914', *Economic History Review*, 36.

LEWIS, O., and BARNOUW, V. (1958), *Village Life in North India* (Urbana, Ill.: University of Illinois Press).

LIEBERMAN, S. S. (1985), 'Field-Level Perspectives on Maharashtra's Employment Guarantee Scheme', *Public Administration and Development*, 5.

LIPTON, M. (1984), 'Urban Bias Revisited', *Journal of Development Studies*, 20.

LITTLE, I. M. D., and MIRRLEES, J. A. (1974), *Project Appraisal and Planning for Developing Countries* (London: Heinemann).

MAZUMDAR, D. (1976), 'The Rural–Urban Wage Gap, Migration and the Shadow Wage', *Oxford Economic Papers*, 28.

MELLOR, J. W., and DESAI, G. M. (eds.) (1985), *Agricultural Change and Rural Poverty: Variations on a Theme by Dharm Narain* (Baltimore, Md.: Johns Hopkins).

MORRIS, M. D. (1974), 'What is a Famine?', *Economic and Political Weekly*, 9.

NEWBERY, D. M. G., and STIGLITZ, J. E. (1981), *The Theory of Commodity Price Stabilization* (Oxford: Oxford University Press).

OSMANI, S. R. (1990), 'The Food Problems of Bangladesh', in vol. iii of this book.

—— and CHOWDHURY, O. H. (1983), 'Short Run Impacts of Food for Work Programme in Bangladesh', *Bangladesh Development Studies*, 11.

OUGHTON, E. (1982), 'The Maharashtra Droughts of 1970–73: An Analysis of Scarcity', *Oxford Bulletin of Economics and Statistics*, 44.

PANDA, M. K. (1981), 'Productivity Aspect of Wages in Food for Work Programme', *Economic and Political Weekly*, 16.

PRESTON, S. H. (1975), 'The Changing Relation between Mortality and Level of Economic Development', *Population Studies*, 29.

——(1980), 'Causes and Consequences of Mortality Declines in Less Developed Countries during the Twentieth Century', in Easterlin, R. A. (ed.), *Population and Economic Changes in Developing Countries* (Chicago: University of Chicago Press).

RANGASAMI, A. (1985), '"Failure of Exchange Entitlements" Theory of Famine: A Response', *Economic and Political Weekly*, 20.

RATH, N. (1985), '"Garibi Hatao": Can IRDP do it?', *Economic and Political Weekly*, 20.

—— and JOSHI, R. V. (1966), 'Relative Movements of Agricultural Wage Rates and Cereal Prices: Some Indian Evidence', *Artha Vijnana*, 7.

RAVALLION, M. (1982), 'Agricultural Wages in Bangladesh before and after the 1974 Famine', *Bangladesh Development Studies*, 10.

——(1983a), 'Commodity Transfers and the International Economic Order: A Comment', *Journal of Development Economics*, 13.

——(1983b), 'Method with Less Madness: Modelling Market Integration in Agriculture', mimeo (Oxford: Queen Elizabeth House).

——(1984), 'How Much is a Transfer Payment Worth to a Rural Worker?', *Oxford Economic Papers*, 36.

——(1985a), 'The Performance of Rice Markets in Bangladesh during the 1974 Famine', *Economic Journal*, 95.

——(1985b), 'The Informational Efficiency of Traders' Price Expectations in a Bangladesh Rice Market', *Oxford Bulletin of Economics and Statistics*, 47.

——(1986a), 'A Test of the Rational Expectations—Life Cycle Hypothesis for Three Villages in Rural India', mimeo (Department of Economics, Research School of Pacific Studies, The Australian National University).

——(1986b), 'Testing Market Integration', *American Journal of Agricultural Economics*, 68.

——(1986c), 'Growth and Equity in Sri Lanka: A Comment', Trade and Development Working Paper 86/12 (The Australian National University).

——(1987a), 'Towards a Theory of Famine Relief Policy', *Journal of Public Economics*, 33.

——(1987b), *Markets and Famines* (Oxford: Oxford University Press).

——(1987c), 'Trade and Stabilization: Another Look at British India's Controversial Foodgrain Exports', *Explorations in Economic History*, 24.

——(1988), 'The Economics of Famine: An Overview of Recent Research', in Pearce, D. W., and Rau, N. J. (eds.), *Economic Perspectives: An Annual Survey of Economics*, 1988.

——(1990a), 'On the Coverage of Public Employment Schemes for Poverty Alleviation', *Journal of Development Economics*, forthcoming.

——(1990b), 'Reaching the Poor through Rural Public Works: Arguments, Evidence and Lessons from South Asia', mimeo (Washington, DC: Agricultural Policies Division, World Bank).

——and DEARDEN, L. (1988), 'Social Security in a "Moral Economy"', *Review of Economics and Statistics*, 60.

REUTLINGER, S. (1982), 'Policies for Food Security', in Chisholm, A., and Tyers, R. (eds.), *Food Security* (Boston, Mass.: Lexington Books).

RODGERS, G. B. (1979), 'Income and Inequality as Determinants of Mortality: An International Cross-Section Analysis', *Population Studies*, 39.

RUDRA, A. (1982), *Indian Agricultural Economics: Myths and Realities* (New Delhi: Allied Publishers).

SAITH, A. (1981), 'Production, Prices and Poverty in Rural India', *Journal of Development Studies*, 17.

SCHULTZ, T. P. (1979), 'Interpretation of Relations among Mortality, Economics of the Household and the Health Environment', Working Paper No. 78 (Geneva: Population and Labour Policies Programme, ILO).

SCOTT, J. C. (1976), *The Moral Economy of the Peasant* (New Haven, Conn.: Yale University Press).

SEN, A. K. (1981), *Poverty and Famines: An Essay on Entitlement and Deprivation* (Oxford: Oxford University Press).

——(1985), 'Dharm Narain on Poverty: Concepts and Broader Issues', in Mellor and Desai (1985).

——(1986), 'The Causes of Famine: A Reply', *Food Policy*, 11.

STEELE, J. (1985), 'Millionaire "Grain Barons" Hoarding Supplies in Sudan', *Guardian Weekly*, 133, 20 Oct.

STIGLITZ, J. E., and WEISS, A. (1981), 'Credit Rationing in Markets with Imperfect Information', *American Economic Review*, 71.

SUBBARAO, K. (1989), 'Interventions to Combat Household-Level Food Insecurity', mimeo (Delhi: Institute of Economic Growth).

SUNDARAM, K., and TENDULKAR, S. D. (1985), 'Anti-poverty Programmes in India: An Assessment', in Mukhopadhyay, S. (ed.), *The Poor in Asia: Productivity-Raising Programmes and Strategies* (Kuala Lumpur: Asian and Pacific Development Centre).

SUNDRUM, R. M. (1987), *Growth and Income Distribution in India: Policy and Performance since Independence* (New Delhi: Sage Publications).

TOLLEY, G. S., THOMAS, V., and WONG, C. M. (1982), *Agricultural Price Policies and the Developing Countries* (Baltimore, Md.: Johns Hopkins).

TORRY, W. I. (1986a), 'Drought and the Government–Village Emergency Food Distribution System in India', *Human Organization*, 45.

——(1986b), 'Morality and Harm: Hindu Peasant Adjustments to Famines', *Social Science Information*, 25.

WALKER, T. S., SINGH, R. P., and ASOKAN, M. (1986), 'Risk Benefits, Crop Insurance, and Dryland Agriculture', *Economic and Political Weekly*, 21.

WECKSTEIN, R. S. (1977), 'Food Security: Storage vs. Exchange', *World Development*, 5.

WILLIAMSON, J. G. (1984), 'British Mortality and the Value of Life, 1781–1931', *Population Studies*, 38.

World Bank (1986), *Poverty and Hunger: Issues and Options for Food Security in Developing Countries* (Washington, DC: World Bank).

# 6

# The Food Crisis in Africa:
# A Comparative Structural Analysis

*Jean-Philippe Platteau*

A large part of Africa is chronically affected by a severe food crisis which threatens the food security of many of her inhabitants. A peculiarity of this continent is that food production is not only a source of food but also a source of incomes for the numerous smallholder producers who form the most important group exposed to the risk of hunger. Therefore, growing food insecurity is generally associated with a crisis of food production. This chapter is an attempt to analyse various structural factors which underlie this production crisis. It is grounded on the hypothesis that these factors are far more constraining than the inadequate policy mixes which have received so much attention in the economic literature, and that their impact tends to impose serious handicaps on Africa compared to Asia and Latin America.

## 6.1. *Africa's food crisis in perspective*

### (a) *Food security and food self-sufficiency*

There are two striking features or components in the so-called food crisis which faces many developing countries in Asia, Latin America, and Africa: a rapidly increasing number of people who are chronically hungry or malnourished on the one hand, and a quickly rising dependence on food imports on the other hand. While the former problem—that concerned with food security—is especially acute in Asia and (sub-Saharan) Africa, the second problem—that concerned with food self-sufficiency—is typical of all the three continents. It is now a well-known fact that the two problems are not necessarily linked together. In other words, food self-sufficiency does not lead automatically to food security, and vice versa. Indeed, food imports arise whenever domestic supply falls short of demand at the macrolevel, whereas poverty and malnutrition have often to be traced back to a lack of purchasing power among certain vulnerable groups of the population (Sen 1981; Mellor and Desai 1985; Pacey and Payne 1985; World Bank 1986*a*). Thus, it is not difficult to imagine situations in which malnutrition continues unabated although the rate of national food self-sufficiency increases. India and Chile are two cases in point. And it is equally easy to think of situations in which the opposite would

I am greatly indebted to Jean Drèze, Carl Eicher, and Jean-Marie Baland for their helpful comments and criticisms on an earlier version of this paper. Responsibilities for the views expressed remain, however, entirely mine.

occur—decreasing incidence of food hunger and rising dependence on food imports. The example of Taiwan suggests itself as a good illustration of this second possibility.

There is today a growing agreement among economists that the objective of food security should always be given precedence over that of food self-sufficiency. In other words, food security ought to be pursued even at the cost of increased food imports. A good case can however be made for qualifying the above statement. As a matter of fact, if the search for complete food self-sufficiency is a political objective hard to justify in welfare terms except in some peculiar circumstances, there are valid reasons for not letting food dependence develop too far. Uncertainties related to the world food market; shortage of physical facilities to handle large volumes of food imports; foreign exchange constraints; high internal transport costs due to low population densities; low import and capital intensiveness of domestic food production compared with alternative employment opportunities; social, spatial, and environmental considerations; income distribution objectives; all these factors may militate against allowing a decrease in domestic production of staple foods, especially if this decrease is sharp, sudden, or irreversible. The issue of irreversibility deserves to be emphasized since technical progress may cause radical shifts in the structure of comparative advantages and it is practically impossible to recreate a peasantry after having allowed its destruction. Of course, to the extent that the pursuit of food self-reliance threatens food security, the latter ought to be preserved by resorting to compensating measures (like state subsidies).

## (b)   The context of Africa's food crisis

An important feature of many African countries is that the bulk of the food output is produced by small family-operated farms whose members form the largest group facing food insecurity. Indeed, if the number of landless people is no doubt rising in Africa, especially so in areas of high population pressure, it still forms a rather low proportion of the agricultural population. In sub-Saharan Africa, more than three-quarters of the population are engaged in smallholder food production (Delgado et al. 1987: 5). In the case of Africa, therefore, the objectives of food security and food self-sufficiency are potentially more compatible than in the countries of Asia and Latin America where the majority of people at risk are net food buyers. Thus, widespread increases in the productivity of agricultural smallholders are likely to lead to both improved food security and diminished dependence on food imports. Furthermore, in so far as such increases can be obtained without entailing a drop in the production of agricultural exportables, the balance-of-payments constraint will be eased, a consideration of the utmost importance in most African countries ridden with serious problems of national economic management.

Conversely, the close link between food security and food self-sufficiency in Africa tends to make the effects of a slowdown in food production more dramatic. This is precisely what has happened during the long period 1960–84 when disappointing agricultural growth performances were widely observed throughout most of the continent. Thus, the trend rate of growth of food output was not only lower than that of consumption but, in addition, it turned out to be significantly less than the rate of population growth. During the years 1960–84, food output per head in sub-Saharan Africa decreased at an alarming rate of about 1 per cent per annum. The situation was even worse during the years 1970–84, not only in sub-Saharan Africa but also in North Africa: food production in the whole of Africa then grew at only half the population growth rate. If a few countries did not conform to this general picture and could increase their food output per head during the period under consideration (e.g. the Ivory Coast, Malawi, Swaziland, Tunisia), the situation was worse still for the not-so-few countries in which total food output actually declined or stagnated during the period 1970–84 (Mellor and Johnston 1984: 534–9; FAO 1985: 32–51; World Bank 1986a: 14; Eicher 1986b: 4; FAO 1986: Appendix I; IFRI 1986: 123; Paulino 1987: 23–38).

In the specific context of Africa, a production crisis of this size could only result in growing food deprivation among the mass of rural small-scale producers and in increasing reliance on food imports. In 1985, about 100 million people, or roughly one-quarter of the African population, were estimated to be hungry and malnourished (Eicher 1985: 84). Too much importance should not be attached to this figure because the reliability of data on poverty in Africa is open to serious question and there is probably a tendency to overestimate it. However, and this is more relevant to our discussion, there are many hints that hunger and undernutrition have in-creased markedly in quite a number of African countries during the last decades. At the same time, the food import bill of many African states has increased dramatically. In the mid-1980s food import expenditures repres-ented 20 per cent of the total export earnings of Africa, compared to 16 per cent in 1980 and much less in 1970 (FAO 1985: 58 and Marot 1987). In the low-income countries, this proportion was much higher. Food imports there-fore contributed significantly to mounting balance-of-payments deficits and, given the bleak prospects of both agricultural and non-agricultural export markets, the drain on foreign exchange which resulted from decreasing food self-sufficiency was particularly harmful. It is also noteworthy that food output grew so slowly in sub-Saharan Africa during 1960–84 that per capita consump-tion fell despite high growth rates in imports. In other words, had staple food imports not increased dramatically,[1] the per capita consumption of food items would have sunk to intolerable levels (Mellor and Johnston 1984: 538 and FAO 1985: 32–4).

In Asia and Latin America, the 'food crisis' took a different shape. In these two continents, indeed, agricultural growth has usually been quite remarkable

[1] The import content of total calorie consumption for Africa as a whole more than doubled within a decade: from 6% of total calorie supplies in 1969–71 to 13% in 1979–81 (FAO 1985: 34).

during the last two decades (averaging 3 per cent per year), and the production of staple food has increased at a higher rate than population. None the less, with the notable exception of India (and of China during some periods of time), the growth of output has been slower than that of consumption because of regular and significant increases in per capita food consumption. In sharp contrast to the situation observed in Africa, the rapid growth of net food imports has made such increases possible in many Asian and Latin American countries.[2] Provided that the rural masses have an equitable share in the agricultural growth occurring in these countries, there is much reason to expect the rising food imports to be accompanied by a reduction in poverty and malnutrition, at least in the countryside. If this is not the case, attention must obviously be directed to distributive considerations to find the villain of the piece.

Since in Africa food production is not only a source of food but also the main source of incomes for the majority of people facing food insecurity, it is impossible to understand the causes of rising chronic poverty and undernutrition (as well as of increasing food dependence) unless we get a good grasp of the factors responsible for the disappointing growth records of local food production during the last decades. It is the main contention of this chapter that a number of structural factors and constraints act as supply bottlenecks that tend to limit the long-term opportunities for agricultural growth in Africa far more seriously than the inappropriate policy mixes on which economists have focused most of their attention. Furthermore, the hypothesis will be advanced that these structural factors are generally far more constraining in Africa than in Asia and Latin America, so that the former continent suffers from a real handicap in exploiting its agricultural growth potential. It is suggested that the relatively slow growth of African agriculture during the last three decades compared to the performances achieved by the other two continents must be to a large extent ascribed to this structural handicap.

This being said, it would be a mistake to neglect the consumption or demand aspects which have recently been shown to play a crucial role in the food crises of both Asia and Latin America (Mellor and Johnston 1984; Yotopoulos 1985; FAO 1985). As a matter of fact, some demand-related factors have a direct or indirect effect on the smallholders' incentives to produce as well as on the quality of their main productive resource (land). Thus, at least in some areas, rapid population growth creates land pressure with the result that increasingly marginal lands are brought into cultivation and the fertility of existing lands is reduced due to environmental degradation. On the other hand, drastic shifts in consumption patterns towards import-intensive food baskets tend to lower the

---

[2] Bear in mind the exception of India where per capita consumption levels have remained more or less stagnant because increased production has essentially served the purpose of replacing previous food imports (and to build up sizeable stocks of grain). In Chile, during the period 1977–85, the same type of import substitution strategy has created a situation in which average nutrition levels declined while wheat production increased rapidly.

prices of traditional, locally produced, staple foods. Moreover, the rising food import bill following from the above two phenomena—rapid population growth and changes in food consumption patterns—may also constrain agricultural growth in so far as the scarcity of foreign exchange sharply limits the governments' ability to finance imports of modern inputs (fuel, fertilizers, sacks and bags, etc.), capital goods (farm implements, irrigation equipment, etc.), and, perhaps, incentive consumption goods needed to increase agricultural production.

Note that it would be wrong to infer from the above diagnosis that equity issues are non-existent in Africa. In the course of the analysis of some structural growth-inhibiting factors, it will in fact be shown that, in Africa as in Asia and Latin America, there are powerful forces at work that tend to make for discriminatory access to scarce productive resources and for inequitable distribution of growth benefits.

In section 6.2 below, the role of demand factors in Africa's food crisis will be examined. Section 6.3 will be devoted to a discussion of the 'price-focused' doctrine which ascribes this crisis to distortions of the operations of the market by inadequate agricultural policies. Section 6.4 will form the core of the chapter since it will analyse in some detail the main structural constraints that inhibit agricultural development in Africa. In section 6.5, the central results of this study will be summarized.

A final remark is in order. It could be objected that, during the years 1986–7, food production has increased notably in a group of sub-Saharan countries, and that in some of them (e.g. Mali, Sudan, Zimbabwe) increases were such as to lead to sizeable grain surpluses. Given that these were generally good years from a climatic viewpoint, it would be premature to conclude that the downward production trend observed during the last decades has come to an end. Repeated observations and an extension of these positive production performances to many more countries (after all, the three aforementioned countries have a relatively good agricultural growth potential) would be needed before one could safely say that the structural thesis put forward in this chapter is not supported by recent empirical evidence.

## 6.2. *The role of demand factors*

### (a) *Changes in consumption patterns*

To account for the quickly rising per capita demand for cereals in many Asian and Latin American countries during the last decades, one must be able to explain why the elasticity of demand with respect to income has taken on much higher values than could perhaps be expected on the basis of Engel's law. The answer has to be found in the increased use of cereal as livestock feed (FAO 1985: 43). It is 'the voracious appetite of middle-class consumers for animal protein' that has caused a change in total grain demand significantly over and above the effect of population growth (Yotopoulos 1985: 476). Underlying this disproportionate impact of the (mainly urban) demand for animal protein is a well-known mechanism: the low conversion efficiency of primary (plant) calories to secondary (livestock product) calories. It works in such a way that even a relatively small increase in per capita income, or a moderate shift in consumption patterns towards animal protein diets, or a moderate increase in the size of the (urban) middle classes, can lead to a sizeable increase in indirect cereal consumption, that is in indirect demand for feed use. The income elasticities of demand for feed are actually so high that 'the weighted income elasticity of demand for cereals may well rise to a value larger than the initial value of the elasticity for food use alone' (Mellor and Johnston 1984: 541).

The relationship between the above phenomenon and the food crisis is particularly evident in the case of the trade component. Indeed, since economic growth gives rise to a rapid increase in consumption of livestock products—especially so when most of the income gains accrue to middle classes or when they enable more people to graduate into these classes—the ensuing growth of aggregate demand for foodgrain is likely to outpace that of domestic production, unless the latter increases very fast also. Food imports will then be called for to fill this mounting gap. There may also be a causal link between booming indirect cereal consumption and the incidence of poverty and hunger if food use is crowded out when feed use increases. In other words, as people compete with people for the indirect versus direct consumption of cereals, the distribution of purchasing power between the rich and the poor becomes an important determinant of access to available food supplies (Yotopoulos 1985: 476–9). Note that this human struggle for cereals may take place on a national scale if the domestic food market is sheltered from the forces of international competition. If not, it arises at the world level in which case it is the huge demand of developed countries for feed that is the main claimant on world supplies of cereals.

How does Africa fit in with the above pattern? The declining trend of per capital cereal consumption in this continent could create the impression that the food–feed competition is not at work there. This would be a hasty conclusion, however. As a matter of fact, during the period 1966–80, use of major food crops for animal feed expanded at more than 3 per cent a year, implying that per capita feed use in Africa increased with an income elasticity close to one (Paulino 1987: 31; Yotopoulos 1985: 469).[3] Between 1974–5 and

[3] Africa actually achieved the world's highest rate of growth of total feed use during the years 1966–80, that is 6.2% per year as against 2.9% for food use (Yotopoulos 1985: 468). It is true, however, that this continent started from a very low base, with a share of feed use in total consumption of cereals amounting to 8.3% on an average during the years 1966–70 and reaching 10.3% on average during the years 1976–80. Note that in this respect North Africa is far ahead compared to sub-Saharan Africa: while in the former region, the above proportion was 16.6 and 21.0% during the two periods considered, respectively, it was only 5.6 and 6.1% in the latter region. For all the developing countries (including China) taken together, the share of feed use was 14.1 and 15.7% during the same time periods (adapted from IFPRI 1986). In sub-Saharan Africa, the low share of feed use in total domestic utilization actually reflects the fact that 'livestock feeding in the region is still largely dependent on open range and waste products' (Paulino 1987: 31).

1982–3, the share of livestock products in total agricultural output increased by as much as 17.6 per cent in Africa and that of meat in particular by 13.8 per cent, as against average rates of change of 8.8 and 9.4 per cent, respectively, for the whole developing world (FAO 1985: Table 1–19, p. 51). In order to accommodate this increase in consumption of livestock products in conditions of declining per capita supplies of cereals, the direct consumption of cereals, presumably by the lower-income classes, had to be reduced to a much larger extent than would have been necessary if animal protein diets had not expanded among the urban classes. In the words of Yotopoulos, 'a shortfall in per capita supply is not necessarily shared equally by proportional decreases in food and feed' (Yotopoulos 1985: 469–70).

What needs to be stressed is that in the case of Africa the crowding-out effect does not work itself out through an upward pressure on food prices as is apparently suggested by Yotopoulos. On the contrary, a persistent claim made by so many authors and reports about African agriculture is that consumer food prices have been kept at artificially low levels, due to overvaluation of exchange rates, subsidies, international food aid, etc. (see e.g. CILSS 1979: 119–22; World Bank 1981: ch. 5, 1986b: 87–94; IFRI 1986: 143–6; FAO 1986: Annex I, ch. 3; Giri 1983: 243–6, 1986: 66–72; Bates 1981; Rose 1985). In Latin America and Asia, many poor people are net buyers of food (urban low-income classes and landless or near landless rural workers) and, as a result, the food–feed competition may affect them directly to the extent that it leads to rising prices on the local food markets. In large parts of sub-Saharan Africa, however, most poor households are net food sellers who suffer from the 'negative pricing policies' followed by their government (Eicher 1984: 463). By contrast, enriched urban middle classes can all the more easily shift to animal protein diets as the cost of feed is artificially low. In Nigeria, for example, because of a huge overvaluation of the national currency, the prices of US imported maize and wheat—both of which can be fed to animals (particularly to chickens)—were much lower than local costs at the mill gate during the early 1980s. Thus, in 1983, the price of imported maize was about $315 per ton compared with $1,200 for local maize delivered in Lagos (Giri 1986: 76–7; Andrae and Beckman 1986; FAO 1986: Main Report, ch. 1, para. 1.6).

If there is a crowding-out effect arising from food–feed competition in Africa, it is definitely not a market-engineered effect operating through a price increase, but rather a government-engineered effect operating through a price decrease. Indeed, in the face of the mounting craze of urban middle-income classes for livestock products, the government would be impelled to cheapen the foodgrains—for example, by letting the national currency appreciate in real terms—to the detriment of domestic producers who thereby get impoverished.

Now, it is important to realize that so far the bulk of African imports of cereals are intended for direct consumption. The fast-growing food import bills of many African states are less the outcome of increasing adoption of animal protein diets in the cities than of massive displacement of local staples or local food grades by foreign foods or grades. This substitution effect is partly the result of the low prices of imported foods (thanks to foreign food aid or export subsidies granted to foreign food producers, at least for some products during some periods), currency overvaluation, and depressed world prices following overproduction in developed countries and of blatant distortions in the marketing and transport systems, and partly the outcome of radical changes in consumer preferences.

Concerning the price effect, it is interesting to note that in 1982 'while the international price of rice was three times that of sorghum, in West Africa it was rarely more than twice as much and sometimes only the same' (World Bank 1986b: 92). As for the price of wheat flour, it was about the same as that of maize in Nigeria and the Ivory Coast while the ratio of the former to the latter was much higher in the international market (ibid.). But the macroeconomic and price policies of African governments are not always responsible for odd price ratios between 'superior' imported foods and traditional staples. Thus, during the years 1983–4, the retail price of millet grown locally exceeded that of rice (mostly imported) in the free market of Dakar (Berg et al. 1986: Fig. 9, p. 55), as a result of a marked fall in the international price of rice in the world market. Turning to the marketing and transport systems, the main point to emphasize is that these systems have been built up during the colonial period to facilitate the export–import trade rather than to move local produce from the countryside to the urban markets. Finally, changes in consumer tastes have been induced by various forces among which we may note: rapid rates of urbanization; the international demonstration effect of what many urban dwellers in Africa consider as superior goods (US quality maize in Nigeria, short broken rice in Sahelian countries, white bread and skimmed milk all over large parts of the continent, Italian tomato sauce with chemical ingredients in Senegal, etc.); the aggressive advertising campaigns of transnational food corporations; and, last but not least, the existence of various intrinsic advantages of foreign over local foods (low perishability, low time-intensiveness of the required culinary preparations, especially so when foreign foods can be consumed in attractive and convenient processed forms, like wheat in the form of bread).

The importance of trend changes in African food consumption patterns and their dramatic impact on food imports can be illustrated with reference to West Africa. Here, per capita consumption of wheat products and rice grew at an average annual rate of 8.5 and 2.8 per cent, respectively, between 1966–70 and 1976–80. By contrast, consumption of traditional foods locally grown either barely increased (by 0.27 per cent for maize) or declined (by 1.5 per cent for millet and 1.7 per cent for sorghum) (World Bank 1986b: 92). In the Sahelian region only, demand for rice increased by more than 8 per cent a year during the period 1976–82 whereas domestic production hardly expanded. As a consequence, Sahelian countries today produce only half of the quantities of rice they consume. The situation is worse still with regard to wheat and wheat products. Consumption has grown at the high rate of 11 per cent per year, although local wheat production is practically non-existent. No wonder then that these countries produce only 5 per cent of the wheat they consume (Giri 1983: 77–8). Moreover, Giri noted that 'the demand for bread does not spring any more only from the urban classes which have more or less adopted European modes of consumption, but also from low-income urban classes and even from rural populations . . . Thus, in the valley of the Senegal river, the traditional breakfast composed of millet couscous and vegetables has largely given way to a "Europeanized" meal with soluble coffee, concentrated milk or milk powder, and bread' (ibid., 78). This is confirmed by a consumption survey conducted during the late 1970s in Dakar (the capital city of Senegal) and in two small towns of the interior of the country (Louga and Linguère). Indeed, this study has come to the conclusion that (1) rice and bread absorbed almost 90 per cent of the total household budget devoted to cereal consumption, and (2) this proportion did not vary significantly across various income classes (CILSS 1979: 245).[4]

In the Ivory Coast—one of the few sub-Saharan countries which recorded a rise in its per capita food output during the last decades—around 15 per cent of the total import bill is spent on food items. The import content of domestic cereal consumption exceeds one-third while that of consumption on meat, fish, and milk products is higher than one-half. On the whole, food imports have grown at a much higher rate than domestic food production, per capita food imports have increased rapidly, and the import content of aggregate food consumption has risen significantly. Cereals and cereal-based products (almost exclusively wheat and rice) represented 27 per cent of the country's food imports on average for the years 1978–80, which was much less than the share of meat and milk products (38 per cent), but much more than the share of other product categories (12.5 per cent for fish and fish derivates and 10 per cent for beverages and tobacco). Finally, it has been estimated that half the food expenditures by urban dwellers were spent on imported items in the early 1980s (Haubert and Frelin 1985: 21–2).

Table 6.1 compares the respective rates of increase in the imports of various food products during the 1960s and 1970s for the whole of sub-Saharan Africa.

The following trends emerge from an analysis of food imports into Africa during the last decades:

- rising per capita food imports;
- preponderant share of cereals in total food imports (contrary to what was observed in the particular case of the Ivory Coast);

---

[4] However, expenditures on cereal consumption represented only 30% of total food expenditures. Note also that, for the whole of Africa, per capita production (and consumption) of traditional staples has increased at the following negative rates during the period 1970/1–1983/4: millet: −3.9%; sorghum: −3.2%; roots and tubers: −1.3%; cassava: −1.6%; pulses: −2.0% (FAO, *Production Yearbook, 1975, 1985*).

**Table 6.1** Average annual rates of growth of imports of various food products in sub-Saharan Africa, 1961–1984 (in volume)

|  | 1961–3 to 1969–71 (%) | 1970–1 to 1983–4 (%) |
|---|---|---|
| Cereals | 9.0 | 9.7 |
| Wheat | 12.9 | 9.6 |
| Rice | 4.9 | 10.4 |
| Maize | 8.7 | 12.6 |
| Milk products | 7.2 | 7.9 |
| Sugar | 2.5 | 5.0 |
| Meat | 1.3 | 11.1 |
| Animal and vegetable oil | 11.5 | 13.0[a] |

[a] This estimate is for the period 1969–71 to 1977–9.

*Source*: Adapted from World Bank (1981: Table 5.3) and FAO, *Production Yearbook and Trade Yearbook, 1975, 1985*.

- near-complete dominance of grain imports by three cereals (wheat —almost 50 per cent; rice—almost 30 per cent; and maize—almost 20 per cent);
- rising import content of domestic food consumption, particularly so in the case of grain, milk products, meat, and edible oils;[5]
- heavy concentration of consumption of imported foods in urban areas: thus, in 1980, 90 per cent of imported cereals were consumed in the cities (FAO 1986: Main Report, ch. 4, para. 16).

To sum up, many African countries have been subject to profound changes in their food consumption patterns during the last two decades. As could be expected, these changes have been especially rapid and marked in big cities: it is probably not fortuitous that by and large countries which have recorded the highest growth rates of food imports during the 1970s are also those which urbanized at the fastest pace (see FAO 1985: 109). However, the new consumption patterns are gradually spreading to small towns and to rural areas. Therefore, low production performances, and even declining yields per

---

[5] Between 1969–71 and 1979–81, for example, the share of rice and wheat in total grain consumption increased from 18% to 25% (FAO 1986: Main Report, ch. 2, para. 43). In 1982–4, the import content of domestic consumption of milk and milk products exceeded 50% in 15 out of 43 African countries for which data are available (FAO 1986: Annex I, ch. 3, para. 20). Note also that the cereal deficit in Africa amounted to about 25 million tonnes on average during the years 1982–4 (15.7 million for North Africa and 9.1 million for sub-Saharan Africa). This figure compares rather well with the grain deficit of the USSR during the 1980s (more than 30 million tonnes per year). However, what is really alarming in the case of Africa is the prospect for the future: thus, according to FAO projections, Africa's grain deficit would reach 70 million tonnes in the year 2010 (43.5 million for North Africa and 26.6 million for sub-Saharan Africa). See Giri (1986: 48) and FAO (1986: Main Report, ch. 2, Fig. 16).

unit area, in the case of traditional staples (millet, sorghum, yams, cassava, white maize, beans, plantain bananas, etc.) are not necessarily due entirely to supply factors, but may also arise partly from increasingly demand-constrained markets. It is no doubt true that these consumption shifts have been induced, at least in part, by policy-determined factors—like the price policies and the outward-looking strategy of economic development pursued by many African states. But the real question lies in whether they are or have become irreversible, in the sense that they have led African consumers to modify their taste configurations for good.

In other words, can one reasonably expect that drastic measures aimed at reversing the 'faulty' policies—like heavy taxation or strict rationing of 'superior' imported foods—will bring consumer preferences back to their initial position? I think we must realistically assume that changes in consumer tastes such as have occurred in Africa are not easily reversible, especially so for urban dwellers who have been accustomed to the new foods for rather long periods of time. As a consequence, in the numerous African countries where foreign foods cannot be produced locally, or could be produced only at prohibitively high costs, the governments will continue to be under heavy pressure to subsidize their production or their consumption. Evidently, such subsidies are an intolerable drain on these countries' limited resources and their rates of economic growth thereby get reduced. In fact, even if the governments could withstand the pressures from the urban consumers, economic growth performances could still be impaired. This would occur if the demand for 'superior' foods is price inelastic so that it would be maintained at the cost of depressed rates of household savings, were the government to raise food prices drastically.

In these circumstances, reduction of rural poverty and improvement of food security would be best attained through measures of agricultural self-reliance aiming concurrently at protecting traditional local food producers from cheap imports and enhancing the attractiveness of traditional staples. The latter could be achieved through a variety of measures, like the development of more efficient transport and marketing systems; improvements in the quality of traditional foods (better packing, easier storage, new and faster methods of preparation); and the enlargement of their possible uses (e.g. the use of cassava as animal feed; the production of bread from a mixture of wheat and millet or even from millet alone; the invention of new food items using root and tuber crops as ingredients; use of sorghum, maize, or millet together with wheat to make pasta; production of couscous from pre-cooked millet; production of sorghum or millet semolina).[6]

---

[6] Certain attempts have already been embarked upon, like the experimental production of bread from wheat and millet in the Sahelian region (Berg *et al.* 1986: 10). In its recent and comprehensive study of African agriculture, FAO also emphasized the need to improve traditional staples (FAO 1986: Main Report, ch. 4, para. 25).

(b)   Fast population growth

Even assuming a constant pattern of food consumption with no marked shift towards foreign foodstuffs, African agriculture would still be confronted with the dramatic challenge arising from historically unprecedented rates of population growth. Africa is in fact the only region of the world where population growth actually accelerated during the 1970s and the early 1980s. The annual population growth rate in Africa was 2.1 per cent in the mid-1950s, 2.7 per cent in the late 1970s, and as much as 3 per cent during the years 1980–5 (as against 2.2 per cent in Asia and 2.3 per cent in Latin America). Moreover, Africa's population growth rate is projected to continue to increase throughout the late 1980s and the early 1990s until it levels off at about 3.1 per cent by 1995. By that time, population will be growing at 1.9 and 2 per cent per year in Asia and in Latin America, respectively (FAO 1986: Annex I, ch. 2, para. 2.5; Eicher 1984: 457).

What is particularly alarming in the case of Africa's demographic trends is precisely that her population growth will level off at an astronomically high rate (more than 3 per cent), and that this levelling off process will itself last during a rather long period of time. Indeed, for a variety of complex factors which have made for a pro-fertility cultural environment and have created a kind of political indifference to population growth problems (due to a myth of Africa as being a land-surplus continent), there is not much hope that fertility levels will be reduced in the coming years (Eicher 1984: 458, 1986c: 244–5). The situation is especially confounding for more than one-third of African people living in nine countries where population will grow at an average yearly rate equal to or higher than 3.5 per cent during the years 1980–2000 (Kenya, Tanzania, Zimbabwe, Botswana, Rwanda, Libya, Uganda, Nigeria, and Zambia). A number of African countries will reach or have already reached a maximum rate of population growth exceeding the 4 per cent threshold (Kenya—4.3 per cent; Zimbabwe and the Ivory Coast—4.2 per cent; Uganda and Libya—4.1 per cent). Most African countries, however, will have annual population growth rates in the range 2.5–3.5 per cent up to the year 2000. Their maximum rate of growth will typically oscillate around 3.1–3.3 per cent, with the exceptions of the Ivory Coast (see above), Senegal (3.6 per cent), and Malawi (3.5 per cent) (FAO 1986: Annex I, Table 2.1).

Whatever the reasons accounting for these almost incredible trends, the point is that for several decades to come Africa's land, pasture, and forestry resources will be subjected to heavy pressure and the well-known threats to her ecological equilibria will go on increasing. Just to give an example, the aggregate population of Sahelian countries is expected to increase from 31 to 120 million inhabitants between 1985 and 2025 (Pennisi 1986: 55). Only to feed her growing population at the present level of per capita food consumption, Africa would thus need to increase her food production at a rate of, say, 3.2 per cent per year for several decades in succession. This is of course an impossible challenge for her to meet. It is therefore not surprising that in order to reach the conclusion that more than half the African countries could increase or stabilize their rates of food self-sufficiency during the next 25 years, FAO had to make extremely strong assumptions (FAO 1986: Main Report ch. 2). Now, if we leave aside the problem of food self-reliance to focus our attention on the issue of poverty alleviation, the following must be said: even assuming a high rate of job creation in (import-substituting) non-agricultural activities (which will not go without profound reforms in the management of African economies, and in the way they are exposed to international market forces), Africa will need to step up food production, at least in the short and medium term, in order to provide her fast-growing workforce with new incomes and more rewarding employment opportunities. Given that world markets for non-food agricultural products are much depressed, too much hope should not be placed on the expansion of exportable non-food production.

There is yet another demographic trend that must be borne in mind while analysing the agricultural situation in Africa: this is the steady decline in the share of total labour force engaged in agricultural activities. Thus, between 1960 and 1984, the farm labour force has increased at an annual rate much lower than the rate of population growth and the rate of growth of the total labour force (Johnston 1986: 156; Paulino 1987: 25–6). By contrast, the percentage of the population living in urban areas increased from 18.4 to 28.9 per cent between 1960 and 1980 (FAO 1985: 86). In Sudano-Sahelian Africa, urban population has expanded 3.5 times as fast as rural population and, in humid Central Africa, 5.5 times as fast (FAO 1986: Main Report, ch. 1, para. 1.15).

In so far as it helps to mitigate the absolute increase of the farming population and, thereby, to bring down the population pressure on land, the declining share of agriculture in the total labour force might seem to be a welcome trend. However, per capita domestic food supplies will be maintained only if there is a sufficient increase in (per capita) agricultural labour productivity to make up for the relative decline of the farm labour force. In quite a number of African countries, however, this condition is not likely to be satisfied and high rates of urbanization may well result in diminishing per capita food output. The reason for this becomes apparent when it is realized that farm labour is not homogeneous and that rural outmigration modifies the characteristics of the average worker remaining in agriculture. Indeed, it is a common feature of many African countries that internal migration streams are overwhelmingly dominated by single (young) men. Stories of entire villages deserted by their most productive male members are not rare in Africa, particularly so in countries where hard conditions prevail in the countryside (as in arid or semi-arid areas) or where attractive employment opportunities exist outside the agricultural sector (as in the oil-producing countries during the

1970s).[7] That the departure of many young male adult members from the village workforce—where and when it occurs—may seriously hinder agricultural growth is evident from the fact that heavy agricultural tasks are consequently neglected, which is bound to affect the productivity of both the land and labour efforts by the remaining workers. Of course, ordinary effects of labour shortages are also to be feared. Since in Africa demand for agricultural labour is highly seasonal due to single-season rainfall patterns, a labour force mainly composed of women, children, and aged men and sufficient to carry out the ordinary farm works throughout the year will be inadequate for the peak season (Mellor and Delgado 1987: 2; Delgado and Ranade 1987: 124–8). Moreover, 'in the African farming systems seasonal labour shortages are a far more limiting factor in increasing productivity than in Asia, especially in view of the low level of African agricultural technology' (Lele 1984: 445).

It is true that the above effects could be offset or neutralized if, as suggested by some authors (e.g. Collier and Lal 1981; Hyden 1986: 57), migrant workers choose to invest part of their non-agricultural incomes in their home village with a view to introducing new technical configurations (of a labour-saving and/or land-augmenting type) in the family farm. But this poses the problem of the availability of new proven technical packages adapted to the needs of African smallholders. Since these new packages do not generally exist, remittances tend to be spent on consumption purposes, with priority being often given to the purchase of imported foods (Mathieu 1987: i. 33–9).

There are in fact two conditions under which the afore-described situation would probably not be a cause of great concern for many African countries: (1) a sufficient number of sustainable income-earning opportunities exist outside the agricultural sector to absorb the rural migrants productively, and (2) the intersectoral transfer of labour does not result in a tightening of the balance-of-payments constraint (which supposes that increased food imports are offset by new export proceeds). The situation of oil-exporting countries during the 1970s came close to satisfying these conditions but, unfortunately, the world economic crisis put an abrupt end to their growing prosperity. Income-earning opportunities in the oil-producing sector did not turn out to be sustainable and countries like Nigeria, Gabon, and the Ivory Coast were precipitated into a deadlock characterized by a sudden drop of their oil export receipts and by a rapid increase in their food import bill.

---

[7] In African countries which experienced an oil boom during the 1970s (like Nigeria and Gabon), the dearth of young male labour in the countryside created huge problems in the smallholder food-producing sector and was mainly responsible for its bad performance (see Monferrer 1985 for Gabon; Andrae and Beckman 1986; and Aboyade 1987: 246 for Nigeria).

6.3.   *The role of supply factors: price- versus structure-focused analysis*

(a)   *The dominant view*

Since the early 1980s and the publication of the famous Berg report (World Bank 1981), it has become fashionable to locate the most important impediment to agricultural growth in sub-Saharan Africa in 'the nature of incentives offered to producers' and in 'the actions of those who distort the operations of the market' (Bates 1981: 1–2). Crucial determinants of the present food crisis in Africa are seen to be lying in inefficient marketing state monopolies, inadequate distribution of modern agricultural inputs, neglect of agricultural investment in smallholder production, and misguided pricing policies. Yet it is clearly the latter problem—often seen in conjunction with the first one —which has been given most emphasis in many recent publications, particularly those issued by international organizations (CILSS 1979; World Bank 1981, 1986b; IFRI 1986; Berg et al. 1986 (on behalf of CILSS and OECD)). For example, the World Bank has estimated that in a number of African countries effective tax rates—representing the combined effects of currency overvaluation, formal taxation, official pricing policies, and inefficient marketing arrangements—have been such as to reduce the real incomes of agricultural producers below half of the real value of their production as measured by world market prices (World Bank 1981: 55–6; see also World Bank 1986b: ch. 4, pp. 61–84; Giri 1986: 68–9; Lele 1984: 441; Coquery-Vidrovitch 1985: 162–3; Bates 1981; FAO 1986: Annex I, ch. 3, paras 3.4–3.7; Aboyade 1987: 241–52; Oyejide 1987: 257–73).

Heavy effective taxation of agricultural producers is not confined to export crops only, but is also found to be largely prevalent in the case of staple foods. In Mali, for example, an in-depth study of a large irrigated rice production scheme in 1979/80 has revealed that it cost farmers 83 Malian francs to produce a kilo of rice, but that the government paid them only 60 Malian francs (study quoted by Eicher 1984: 463). Another study conducted in the same country reached the conclusion that unit production costs of the two main traditional staples, millet and sorghum, were also higher than official producer prices (Kébé 1982).

Another way of assessing the underpricing of agricultural commodities in many African countries is to compare real official producer prices not with international prices or unit production costs but with current prices ruling in local parallel markets or in neighbouring countries. To refer again to the case of Mali, unofficial market prices for millet, sorghum, maize, and rice were three to five times as high as official prices in the late 1970s (Coquery-Vidrovitch 1985: 162–3; Gueymard 1985: 226 n. 6; Berg et al. 1986: 57).[8] The World Bank

---

[8]   Thus, in Sept. 1981, the average unofficial price for 3 cereals (millet, sorghum, and maize) in 13 market-places of Bamako was 218 Malian francs per kilo while the average official price was only 85 francs (Gueymard 1985: 226 n. 6).

arrived at similar price discrepancies for Tanzania during the same period (World Bank 1986*b*: 75). Even if Mali and Tanzania are extreme cases, there is enough empirical evidence to show that there are often substantial differences —from 100 to 200 per cent according to FAO (1986: Main Report, ch. 4, para. 4.8; see also Anson-Meyer 1985: 277 and Pottier 1986: 51)—between official and unofficial or black market prices.

Two central ideas actually emerge from the dominant price-focused analysis of Africa's food crisis. The first idea follows from a rather straightforward interpretation of the above facts: African small farmers are subject to genuine extortion on the part of the state. This extortion reflects itself in negative pricing and taxation policies devised 'to pump the economic surplus out of agriculture' (Eicher 1984: 463; see also Bienen 1987). The outcome of these exploitative state interferences with market forces is alarming since low food crop prices have discouraged expansion of production for the market and have acted as a disincentive for investment in agriculture. By imposing heavy effective tax rates on export crops, African states have deprived many farmers —who constitute the bulk of Africa's poor—of an important complementary source of monetary income while at the same time denying themselves the possibility of earning scarce foreign exchange. Note incidentally that the tradition of placing relentless fiscal pressure upon the peasant sector was firmly established from the beginning of the colonial state when it was said to produce the same kind of 'demoralization, disaffection and disengagement' as is currently deplored nowadays (Young 1986: 44).

Some authors, rejecting the idea that state agents act irrationally, have tried to explain why African states follow such suicidal or self-defeating strategies of blatant discrimination against farmers (Bates 1981; Hart 1982; Commins *et al.* 1986). Robert Bates has grounded his attempt at understanding African political economy on the assumption that the state essentially tries 'to respond to the political demands it perceives to be important to satisfy in order to retain power' (Colclough 1985: 35). Basically, his socio-political theorization belongs to the 'rural–urban divide' or 'urban-bias' paradigm explored by Michael Lipton with special reference to India (Lipton 1977). The main clientele of most African states are considered to be urban residents (state employees, capitalist employers, merchants, members of the army, organized workers) who operate effectively as an interest group to influence state policies in urban-biased directions. Although Bates's analysis commends itself for its rigour and clarity, and although it offers numerous useful insights into the mechanisms of political patronage in Africa, it can be criticized on several grounds. First, it takes too much for granted that African state policies are systematically and unambiguously biased against agriculturists, a point to which I shall soon return. Second, it often seems to imply that the urban bias is engineered exclusively through state intervention in otherwise unbiased market processes (Toye 1987: 129). Third, the whole demonstration of Bates rests primarily on the assumption that the policy choices made by African governments are relatively unaffected by external factors, like the current world economic crisis, the role of foreign investors, of aid donors, and of international agencies (Bienefeld 1986: 7–9). This assumption is all the more unsatisfactory as growing public deficits in many African countries are to a significant extent the outcome of external forces, a situation which is not likely to change so long as a substantial part of the governments' revenues comes from import and export taxes. Last but not least, Bates' rational choice/public choice framework is questionable and inherently limited in so far as it assumes (a) that individuals implicitly apply a material benefit-cost calculus to their involvement in politics and (b) that policies are the outcome of the competition and interaction of organized social groups. The former assumption rules out any possibility of symbolic and affective actions in politics while the latter implies that 'the state can exist only as a neutral arena or, in the form of the state bureaucracy, as a specially-privileged social group' (Moore 1987: 9–11).

Keith Hart has taken a somewhat different approach to the problem. His pivotal hypothesis is that modern states in Africa cannot be viable and achieve their historical objective of transforming the economy unless they can assure that reliable revenues flow into their treasury. As a result, most of their efforts tend to concentrate on undertaking large-scale projects orientated towards cash crops (state farms, irrigation schemes, settlement, and land reclamation projects), and on controlling agricultural trade through parastatals or publicly sponsored co-operatives which are able to provide the public exchequer with regular and sizeable proceeds for the least administrative cost.[9] And there is a priori no reason to expect that undertakings which are most profitable from the treasury's standpoint (allowing for administrative costs and political feasibility considerations) are also the most socially efficient (Hart 1982, mainly ch. 4). Given that 'the State is not monolithic and does not form a homogeneous bloc directed principally towards exploiting the peasants' (Gentil 1986: 212), perhaps one of the greatest advantages of Keith Hart's hypothesis is that it does not simplistically assume that all state actions are by necessity anti-rural or anti-agriculture. His main point is indeed that treasury considerations can prompt African states to encourage projects or to take steps—including easy acceptance of unscreened foreign aid—that can inhibit agricultural growth. Nowhere does he suggest that governments in Africa consciously neglect or purposefully and systematically exploit the agricultural sector.

This being said, one can rather easily agree with both Robert Bates and Keith Hart that it is not satisfactory to treat all state actions as 'bad' policies, obvious mistakes, or irrational interventions. However, it is no doubt as simplistic an attitude to take the opposite extreme view and to assume that they all form parts of a coherent strategy which would obey the functional exigencies of a rational, single-minded administration or government. In many instances, it is as fruitful a hypothesis to consider that state policies can be

---

[9] For a similar, albeit less articulated, analysis, see Dupriez (1980: 149–58).

unpredictably inconsistent or badly planned[10] for various reasons such as imperfect information, misperception about state interests, or inner conflicts between the government and the state bureaucracy, between different Ministries or departments, etc. As Sara Berry has aptly noted, it is only when Ministries of agriculture, rural development agencies, parastatals, and so forth are assumed to 'act consistently and cooperatively in pursuit of single, well-defined sets of goals' that a theory of the state of the type proposed by Bates (and Hart) can be taken seriously (Berry 1984: 65–6; see also Gephart 1986: 57–9; Bienen 1987: 298).

The second central idea underlying the price-focused analysis of the 1980s is that Africa's agricultural woes are essentially due to misguided, although possibly explainable, government policies. This is taken to imply that Africa's agricultural and other problems could largely be resolved by a domestic realignment of policy measures. Basically, the policy changes advocated are all measures aimed at privatizing the economy, 'getting prices right', and facilitating responsiveness to market signals. It is explicitly assumed that African farmers are highly price-responsive and that a decrease in the effective tax rates they face will pay high dividends in terms of enhanced agricultural production and investment.

To amend the 'faulty' or inadequate pricing policies by eliminating the most glaring price distortions, and to call into question many of the anti-market prejudices which are so common in Africa, are certainly necessary steps to be taken in many countries of the continent. To that extent, the price-focused analysis of the African food crisis has undoubtedly done a good job. In fact, during the last few years, and often under the combined pressures of the International Monetary Fund and the World Bank, many African governments have adopted corrective measures aimed at liberalizing agricultural trade and granting more remunerative prices to agricultural producers, particularly in the case of food crops (see e.g. CILSS 1979: 147; Gueymard 1985: 228–35; Berg et al. 1986; FAO 1986: Main Report, ch. 4, para. 3 and ch. 5, para. 39; Giri 1986: 74–5; Mellor and Delgado 1987: 4; Colclough 1985: 32).[11] Nevertheless, the above interpretation of Africa's predicament is also dangerously misleading in so far as it conveys the idea that food imbalances will be essentially redressed and much rural poverty will be alleviated simply by restoring the market signals and giving the farmers their dues. As one author aptly remarked: '. . . whilst prices are important, they are only *one* element in the process of eliciting a desirable pattern of production and distribution'

[10] This is clearly the path followed by M. Anson-Meyer in her analysis of Benin, Ghana, Nigeria, and Togo (Anson-Meyer 1985: 276–84) and by R. Galli in her case-study of Guinea-Bissau (Galli 1987).

[11] On the whole, it is probably correct to say that real agricultural prices for many food crops have risen since the late 1970s. An outstanding exception is rice in most Sahelian countries where it is mainly produced in governmental irrigation schemes. The situation has been less satisfactory for many export crops, however, and this is in spite of the substantial currency devaluations that occurred in a good number of African countries.

(Colclough 1985: 30). More pointedly, what needs to be emphasized is that 'the lack of technology, not the lack of farmer motivation, is the major brake on expanded food, livestock and export crop production' (Eicher 1986a: 26). Hard realities must be faced squarely: 'Africa's agrarian crisis is complex and it has been building up for several decades. Neither simplistic statements about external forces nor calls for open market, export-led growth, and increased foreign aid are the answers' (Eicher 1985: 98).

### (b)  The deficiencies of a price-focused approach

The dominant, price-focused, thesis on the African food crisis must therefore be seriously qualified and placed in a different and much larger perspective if it is to play a useful role. In the present section, without getting involved in a detailed argument which would take us too far, I would like to make a number of specific points and to give a few warnings which are important in the context of our whole discussion.

*Empirical doubts*  From an empirical viewpoint, the price-focused approach to the African food crisis suffers from several weaknesses which may undermine its credibility. First, it is in fact not quite clear whether the prices of staples have been too low during, say, the last fifteen years. As has been pointed out above, significant price adjustments took place in many African countries during the 1970s which seem to have substantially helped to correct past distortions and to alleviate the tax burden on food producers. Thus, in a report published by CILSS (Comité permanent inter-états de lutte contre la sécheresse dans le Sahel), Elliot Berg himself, the main author of the famous World Bank report on sub-Saharan Africa (1981), confessed that: '. . . up to a certain point, "distortions" prevail that lower the prices [of cereals], and international aid seems to bear heavy responsibility in this situation. But, according to other criteria, it is not clear that official cereal prices ruling [in Sahelian countries] in 1977 were too low' (CILSS 1979: 147; in the same vein, see Colclough 1985: 32). Empirical evidence therefore appears to be much more mixed than is suggested or asserted by many statements or writings on 'peasants' exploitation' in Africa. The truth is that the implicit taxation of African smallholders varies significantly by country, by crop, and by period, so that broad generalizations must always be received with a good dose of scepticism.

Second, it must be realized that there are simply no satisfactory reference prices against which African domestic food prices can be measured to test whether they are 'too low' and to what extent. In particular, there is no way in which we can contend that exchange rates (whether official, or 'black', or 'grey') and world food prices are equilibrium prices. Regarding the latter, what must be emphasized is that international food prices are determined in residual markets, the demand and supply of which may represent only a minor share of world total supply and demand. World prices could only become reliable efficiency signals if agricultural markets in the developed countries were no longer sheltered *vis-à-vis* the international forces of competition, a situation which is not likely to arise, and perhaps rightly so.

Third, even admitting that important price distortions continue to prevail which get reflected in significant differences between official and black market prices, a basic difficulty remains which emerges from the following well-documented fact: in many cases the major part of staple food smallholder production is not actually disposed of through the official channel. Thus, FAO has estimated that only 5–25 per cent of domestic cereal output in most African countries is marketed via state trade organizations, the remainder being sold off in parallel markets (FAO 1986: Main Report, ch. 4, para. 4.8; see also Gueymard 1985: 226). The latter markets are not necessarily illegal since it may be a lack of circulating capital in the hands of the official marketing boards that prevents them from purchasing all the output offered for sale by the farmers. In other words, due to a shortage of liquidity, and to various transport and other logistic problems, many such boards operating in the field of staple food production are unable to exercise effectively the monopsonistic power granted them by the state. As shown by Johan Pottier (1986), government officials are so aware of the difficulties inherent in state marketing boards that they may actively encourage the peasantry to use private channels instead (at least when they are 'off duty'). This being said, it must be admitted that, more generally, 'it is extremely difficult to enforce monopsony for commodities that are primarily consumed in mass domestic markets' (Leonard 1986: 187). But, then, if this is so, one cannot expect that an upward adjustment in official producer prices will enhance total production. The only result it can yield is an increase in the quantities brought for sale in the open, official markets to the detriment of sales in parallel trade networks.[12] As has been actually observed in a number of cases, a rise of official food prices may thus create acute shortages in local or domestic markets (Berry 1984: 72).

Fourth, while insisting on the price-responsiveness of African farmers, too many authors do not carefully distinguish between aggregate supply response on the one hand, and supply response to changes in the prices of particular commodities on the other hand. In fact, they often provide evidence of high price elasticities of output for specific, single crops and then jump to the conclusion that more appropriate pricing policies will automatically boost overall production. This conceptual confusion is all the more serious as

[12] For obvious reasons, farmers are more dependent on state marketing channels in the case of export crops than in that of food crops. Yet, even in the case of export agricultural goods, possibilities of smuggling across borders often exist in Africa as borders are not well guarded and people have a long historical tradition of interregional trade. Thus, to quote an extreme example, the Secretariat for Planning of the Republic of Guinea-Bissau estimated that it lost as much in clandestine trade as it gained in official trade between the year of national independence and 1983 (Galli 1987: 94). In the circumstances a nation state has an obvious interest in raising the official purchase price of the contraband goods in order to avoid regular and important losses of scarce revenue and foreign exchange.

empirical findings concerning supply responses to price changes are not likely to converge whether we consider total production or production of particular commodities. While there is, for Africa as for other developing regions, a good deal of evidence pointing to elastic supply functions for a wide variety of smallholder cash crops, much less is known about aggregate food supply responses to movements in intersectoral terms of trade (Helleiner 1975: 36–41). However, recent evidence available for Asia (Herdt 1970; Krishna 1984), for a large sample of fifty-eight Third World countries (Binswanger et al. 1985), and for a small sample of nine African countries (Bond 1983), all converge to show that under conditions of technologically unchanging traditional agriculture aggregate short-term supply elasticities tend to be positive but low—in the range of 0.0 to 0.2 (see also Askari and Cummings 1977; Scandizzo and Bruce 1980).

According to John Mellor, if aggregate supply responses are low in modern agricultures, they are likely to be even lower in traditional agricultures 'because of the lesser use of purchased inputs and the lesser opportunity for transfer of labour resources to and from productive use in other sectors of the economy' (Mellor 1968: 24). There is thus good reason to believe that the same situation obtains presently in African smallholder agriculture, especially in view of its low level of technical sophistication (many African peasants have still only a hand-hoe as agricultural implement). Moreover, given the absence of specialized capital in African smallholder agriculture as well as the above-noted lack of alternative opportunities for land and labour use, long-term supply elasticities are not likely to be significantly higher than short-term elasticities. It is noticeable that the results obtained by Bond (1983)—although they must admittedly be treated with caution due to the low reliability of the statistical material used—do not show significant differences between these two elasticities for all but one country in the sample. In the case of Africa, therefore, little weight ought to be attached to the World Bank's argument according to which 'estimates of aggregate farm output responses have typically been of a short-term nature and have failed to reflect the fact that changes in prices have a long-term effect on the intersectoral flow of resources' (World Bank 1986b: 69).

Fifth, in many cases it is not clear from the evidence adduced in support of the price-focused thesis to what extent an expansion (depression) of production is due to an increase (decrease) in the price of output. Thus, Eicher has drawn our attention to the fact that the decline in agricultural exports from numerous African countries over the past 15–20 years is not necessarily or entirely to be attributed to misguided pricing policies as is commonly suggested. It increasingly appears that 'some of this decline might be a function of the deteriorating genetic resource base for perennial crops such as coffee, cocoa, coconut palm and oil palm' (Eicher 1986a: 13). Similarly, it would be a mistake to give the entire credit of output growth to rising producer prices when the latter have obviously been only a part of a whole package of reforms including technology, institutions, and agricultural policies. For example, in the case of Zimbabwe—often presented as a perfect illustration of the adequacy of price policy to stimulate agricultural production—we are warned that 'the favourable production response is more complex than higher prices and good weather . . . farmers were able to respond to higher prices because they had access to well-functioning input and output markets, an extension system that has given increasing attention to smallholders in recent years, and one of the strongest agricultural research services in Africa' (Eicher 1985: 92–3, 1986c: 261).

As Helleiner has rightly emphasized, 'what one seeks to understand is the effect of alterations in various packages of influences'. As a consequence, efforts at establishing the price responsiveness of smallholders in African agriculture—that is efforts which consist of selecting only one out of a myriad of influences and of measuring its separate impact on output with the help of the *ceteris paribus* assumption—are bound to be rather sterile and have 'probably already reached a point of rapidly diminishing returns' (Helleiner 1975: 43–4). As for Schäfer, who can certainly not be accused of underrating the role of prices, he admits that 'agricultural production evidently reacts more strongly to certain types of government activity in rural areas (road building, establishment of markets, degree of literacy) than to price increases' (Schäfer 1987: 132).

*Theoretical caveats*  The price-focused doctrine is not exempt from theoretical weaknesses either. In the first place, the presumption that African governments are to be held responsible for a wrong setting of the prices is hardly satisfactory. Indeed, as Sara Berry has pointed out, 'in criticizing African governments for reducing incentives to agricultural producers, economists often implicitly compare the existing situation to one in which state intervention is non-existent' (Berry 1984: 73). To the extent that agricultural markets are not reasonably competitive and can never be so—because a competitive environment is essentially hazardous and therefore tends to breed market controls—such an assumption is unrealistic. In other words, 'the choice facing African governments is often not one of controlled prices versus competitive ones, but of trying to regulate prices themselves or letting someone else take control' (ibid.). In this respect, it is interesting to note that when West African markets work well it is apparently more because they are controlled by well-organized kinship or community-based networks than because they are 'reasonably competitive' (ibid. 72).

Second, the analytical basis from which positive aggregate supply responses to price changes can be derived is far from being as strong as one would wish. In actual fact, it is only in the simple case of complete specialization or pure commercial farming—the entire output of the peasant family is marketed at a given exchange ratio to buy an outside consumer good—that positive price elasticities of agricultural supply can be obtained with unambiguous and rather plausible analytical conditions (Agarwal 1983: 49–50 and Appendix I). In the case of partial specialization or semisubsistence family farming—when only a part of the produce is marketed, the rest being consumed by the peasant family itself—no such clear-cut results can be arrived at, unless we are ready to make very special assumptions (ibid. 50–1; Sen 1966: 436–7; Nakajima 1970). This theoretical indeterminacy obtains whether we consider a model with a single product or with two products (plus leisure), and whether supply refers to output or to marketable surplus. In fact, as soon as we leave the standard and convenient world of pure commercial farms or agricultural *firms*, we are confronted with quite complex income and substitution effects. Take the income effect: an increase in the real income of a peasant family following a rise in the output price may induce it not only to consume more leisure (and, therefore, to work less), but also to consume more of the good produced and, other things being equal, to reduce its marketed surplus. Substitution effects go of course in the opposite direction: at a given real income, the peasant family would respond to a rise in the output price by increasing its work efforts, and by modifying its consumption basket so as to substitute the outside consumer good for the self-produced one (if they are at all substitutable, which is not to be taken for granted). From these considerations, it is apparent that the marketable food surplus will increase as a result of a favourable movement of the intersectoral terms of trade only if the structure of the peasant's preference between leisure, the agricultural self-produced good, and the manufactured outside good is sufficiently skewed in favour of the latter. Note also that because of the role played by leisure the price elasticity of the food market supply might be negative even in the case where food is an inferior good.

Economic theory does not therefore provide the upholders of the price-focused doctrine with the kind of decisive analytical proof they often give the impression of having in the back of their minds. Indeed, there can be no doubt that the situation of most African smallholders is much closer to the model of the semisubsistence farm—that is the model which leads to the most ambiguous analytical results—than to the model of complete specialization. This caveat should not be dismissed lightly on the ground that, since theory does not offer precise guidelines, we can forget about it. As a matter of fact, a good observer of the African scene has recently noted that a rise of income or output may prompt the smallholder in Africa not to increase his marketed surplus and to accelerate his capital accumulation, but to set apart for his own consumption a larger part of his produce and perhaps to shift to the production and consumption of a 'superior' crop (e.g. rice instead of millet) (Coquery-Vidrovitch 1985: 158). Specific evidence confirming the possibility of atypical supply reactions is actually available: for example, Malawian smallholders have responded to a deterioration in their terms of trade by increasing their output (Ghai and Radwan, 1983; Harvey, 1983), while Nigerian food producers have apparently not reacted to a dramatic improvement of their terms of trade in the years 1968–77 (Collier, 1983: 208). For another thing, historical accounts of the experiences of both USSR and China teach us that raising food producer prices may be a counter-productive strategy. This happens because peasants, when they start from a very low level of living, tend to respond to an increase in their real income by retaining a larger proportion of what they produce. Attempts at bettering the standard of living of the mass of individual peasant families may thus result in a decrease in the marketed food surplus, a difficulty which does not arise with estate capitalist or collective farming. Here is a very vexed dilemma of which the Communist leaders of the USSR and China were well aware and which gave rise to heated debates within the Communist Party's structures (Kemp 1983: chs. 3, 5). Conversely, as the experience of the Soviet Union during the 1922–3 'scissors crisis' has revealed, peasants do not necessarily withdraw from the market when the terms of trade are turned against them. This phenomenon, we are told, follows from the attempt of peasant families to maintain their standard of living in the face of a general adverse economic change (Millar 1976: 52–3).

The experiences of the USSR and China apparently also confirm the hypothesis advanced by Thomas Robert Malthus and John Stuart Mill (see Platteau 1978: ii. 431–40, and 1987) according to which the best way to induce the peasants to part with more of their produce lies in increasing the output and the range of consumer goods at prices which they are willing to pay (Kemp 1983: 55). In this case, note that dynamic changes usually occur in the preference functions of the peasants and that a comparative-static framework of analysis is no longer adequate to analyse the effects of changes in output prices. However, by deciding to step up the output of consumer goods or to allocate more foreign exchange to the import of such goods, the government is only replacing one development dilemma by another. In fact, it chooses to slow down the pace of capital accumulation and economic growth in order to increase food market deliveries.

Finally, reverting to a comparative-static framework, it is worth stressing that the impact of agricultural price increases on agricultural production and market sales may be seriously affected by shortages of consumption 'incentive goods'. In the extreme case where the shortage of these goods is so acute that the marginal utility of money is zero, agricultural market supply would be completely price inelastic even if farmers have a strong aversion to leisure. In the context of some poor countries of sub-Saharan Africa, this assumption is not as implausible as it might appear at first sight. In Guinea-Bissau, for example, the dramatic collapse of agricultural exports (mainly oilseeds) and marketed surplus of food crops (mainly rice) in the late 1970s and the early 1980s was to a large extent the result of the reluctance of the peasantry to produce any surplus for the market in a context of severe scarcity of consumption goods.[13] The only regions in which Guinean farmers or fishermen continued to produce marketed surpluses were located along the northern

[13] Consumption and other goods were allocated by priority to the capital city of Bissau.

border and off the Atlantic coast, that is in areas where a contraband trade had developed with the Senegalese which was difficult for the Guinean authorities to check. The same kind of acute scarcity of consumption goods prevails, or at times prevailed, in other African countries as well (Ghana, Mozambique, Sierra Leone, Chad, Benin, Tanzania, Zaïre, etc.). In Mozambique, it resulted in food marketed surpluses being so low at the beginning of the 1980s that many state employees had to take to part-time agricultural occupations to be able to meet their subsistence needs. In countries which have no domestic industrial base and where most consumer goods must therefore be imported, a vicious circle is at work when they are subject to tight balance-of-payments constraints. Indeed, since there is not enough foreign exchange and not enough consumer goods offered for sale in the local markets, peasants are not interested in producing export crops or food crops above their own subsistence needs. As a consequence, the government has to import more food to feed the urban dwellers at a time when its export revenues are at a low level. Its foreign exchange deficit deepens and the macroeconomic situation continues to deteriorate. The above process is a rather accurate description of what actually happened in countries like Guinea-Bissau and Mozambique in the late 1970s and the early 1980s.

*The real African challenge and the role of technical change*   To put the price-focused doctrine in the right critical perspective, one has only to remember the real challenge that Africa will have to face up to during the coming decades. In the words of Carl Eicher: 'Agricultural production must be doubled from the 1970–84 average of 1.8 per cent to the 3.6 to 4.0 range in order to match the annual growth in food demand arising from population growth (3.2 per cent) and increase in per capita incomes' (Eicher 1986b: 36). Even if we make the absurd assumption that a price hike can succeed in doubling the rate of growth of agricultural output in the short term, it is plainly evident that no amount of price policy will ever succeed in sustaining such a high rate of agricultural growth over a period of several decades. On the best assumptions, raising real prices of agricultural goods may enhance their output and, hopefully, their marketed surplus, but this will be essentially a once-for-all effect which is not likely to lead to the continuous increases Africa desperately requires for a long time to come. Mellor and Delgado have actually warned that, in most African countries, such once-for-all effects have already been largely exhausted: 'further increases in food prices where they have been already rising rapidly are less critical than often is supposed' (Mellor and Delgado 1987: 4). And another author has emphasized that 'if there is no modernisation policy making it possible to increase yields, supply can be relatively inelastic in spite of an increase in real prices' (Morrisson 1985: 71).

It can even be argued that, in the absence of technical change, increased real prices could cause a decline of agricultural production in the long run. In the circumstances negative long-term price elasticities of agricultural supplies would result from an overexploitation of fixed land resources. In the short term, the cultivators would assumedly respond to a price rise by putting more land into cultivation. If this extension takes place through a shortening of the fallow period, the fertility of the land would gradually decline and, after a certain time, the initial increase of output on the fallow lands would be erased by a fall in the average land productivity in the surrounding area.

To get out of this trap, either large investments beyond the scope of smallholders will have to be undertaken to reclaim or rehabilitate uncultivated lands, or land-augmenting technical progress will be needed. If labour is scarce, and/or if rural standards of living are to be improved, technical change will also have to enhance labour productivity. Continuous upward shifts of agricultural production functions must therefore be generated in Africa for her agriculture to be able to meet the challenge before her: price policy considerations will be secondary to this crucial requirement. In fact, as the experience of India during the period 1975–6 to 1983–4 shows, agricultural production and investment may well increase rapidly *in spite of* internal terms of trade turning against the agricultural sector (Tyagi 1987: 30–6). For this situation to occur, all that is needed is that 'productivity rises at a rate faster than the rate by which the terms of trade move against the agricultural sector' (ibid. 34). This can happen when rapid technical advances are being made, or when past progress is spreading out to new areas.[14] Neither of these two conditions was satisfied in India between 1952–3 and 1963–64 and, as a consequence, adverse movements of net barter terms of trade during this period resulted in slow growth of agricultural production and investment.

Now, to contend that agricultural production may increase despite adverse movements of intersectoral terms of trade does not imply that agricultural prices should not be raised. A reasonable position would apparently be to argue that, in order to ensure adequate food supplies under conditions of rapid population growth, what is needed is a balanced package of technical change and incentive prices (Krishna 1984; Timmer 1986). There are two serious arguments in favour of policy interventions to raise food prices. First, higher prices may be expected to accelerate agricultural growth by facilitating investment and setting in motion autonomous processes of change. Second, higher prices can be defended on equity grounds since they would have the effect of increasing the real incomes of the smallholder producers from whom most poor people in Africa are drawn. However, there are problems with both arguments which tend to make them much less effective than they appear at first sight. For one thing, because of the relatively egalitarian structure of agricultural holdings in Africa (compared to Asia and Latin America), returns to agriculture are generally low and 'accumulation is difficult in the absence of specific policy

---

[14] The experience of developed countries tells the same story: 'There are many episodes in the record of advanced countries in which the (lagged) terms of trade facing agriculture have stagnated, and yet farm productivity has grown 2–3 percent a year for considerable periods' (Krishna 1984: 170).

interventions to this end' (Delgado *et al*. 1987: 6). For another thing, it must be borne in mind that the effect of agricultural price increases on the producers' real incomes is proportional to their net sales. As a consequence, a price reform is likely to favour comparatively rich farmers while leaving the real situation of poor, quasi-subsistence smallholders almost unaffected. Note that these two objections are to some extent exclusive in so far as an egalitarian agrarian structure tends to entail an egalitarian distribution of rural incomes. There is yet another consideration that may run against raising food prices. This is the classical argument of David Ricardo according to which rising prices for wage goods tend to slow down non-agricultural growth by causing upward pressure on money wages. Because of the (presumed) ensuing erosion of industrial profit margins, both the incentive and the ability to invest would be dampened, the former because the returns on industrial investments are reduced and the latter because the pool of profits is narrowed (Mellor 1968: 27).

*A few queries about the presumed fiscal oppression of agriculture*   It is a proposition currently encountered in both the orthodox and the Marxian literature that African farmers are squeezed by the state. All the blame for the stagnation of agricultural production is then laid upon the price and fiscal policies pursued by most African governments. What deserves to be pointed out, however, is that the evidence adduced in support of this thesis is usually far from satisfactory. In particular, evidence of a heavy tax burden on agriculture is no convincing proof that this sector is discriminated against. Indeed, as Uma Lele has reminded us, 'given agriculture's importance in the GNP, it is natural that the agricultural sector should constitute the major source of government revenues and that governments should control internal agricultural trade to generate revenues' (Lele 1985: 164). A balanced picture of the fiscal treatment of agriculture can be obtained only if we have a rather precise idea of the direction of the intersectoral public capital flows.

   In actual fact, when we look at the overall balance between receipts from direct and indirect taxes and government expenditures in agriculture, we do not find that the agricultural sector has been systematically overtaxed in Africa (Faucher and Schneider 1985: 61; Morrisson 1985: 72). Sara Berry probably comes close to the truth when she writes that 'postcolonial governments have vacillated between extracting surplus from farmers and subsidizing them' (Berry 1984: 80). Nevertheless, it must be admitted that, in the above judgements or calculations, no account has been taken of invisible resource transfers, particularly those which are achieved through movements of the internal terms of trade. Furthermore, estimates of total intersectoral capital flows (whether on public or private account, or both) are not available for Africa. Now, even if reliable estimates existed pointing to systematic net resource transfers from agriculture to the other sectors of the economy, there would still remain the problem of determining the normative criterion on the basis of which such transfers could be regarded as inappropriate or socially inefficient. The question cannot be avoided since 'surplus extraction from agriculture is clearly not always contrary to the interests of the society, nor even to the long-term interests of the peasantry' (Bienefeld 1986: 7).

To discuss this issue is clearly beyond the scope of this chapter. Suffice it to say here that a more or less general feeling is that 'far fewer resources are plowed back into agriculture by most African countries than would seem justified' (Lele 1984: 440). Such a feeling is usually grounded on comparisons of the shares of agriculture in the national budgets as between Africa and Asia. Thus, for example, it appears that independent African states have commonly invested only 5 to 12 per cent of their public development expenditure in agriculture while India's public sector expenditures on agriculture ranged from 23 to 27 per cent over a considerable span of thirty-two years (1951 to 1983). Estimates of roughly the same order obtain for Malaysia over the years 1971–85 (Eicher 1986b: 38–9; see also Eicher and Mangwiro 1986: 17–21; Lele 1984: 440; FAO 1986: Appendix I, ch. 3, para. 10–13; Lipton 1987: Table 16.1, pp. 214–16). In fact, increasing the net flow of resources to agriculture can be justified on the grounds that, for reasons that will be explained later, agricultural technology development in Africa will be a costly process. Moreover, such an increase could help build up the basis from which sizeable net transfers of resources from agriculture to other sectors will be possible in the future (see Mellor 1984). In the short and medium run, however, it will prove very difficult to give effect to this policy reorientation because the international environment is highly detrimental to the interests of Africa (Colclough 1985: 32). A situation of falling agricultural prices, rising public sector deficits, mounting debt repayment obligations, and flagging commitments of foreign aid is hardly one in which substantial reductions of tax rates on agriculture (particularly on export crops) or significant increases in public expenditures on food production are easy to enforce politically and economically.

A final remark is in order. If sufficient attention is not paid to considerations of allocative efficiency in the process of planning public expenditures for agriculture, net intersectoral resource transfers in favour of this sector will not succeed in ensuring its long-term self-sustainability. This issue is especially relevant in sub-Saharan Africa where there are at least three important ways in which public resources for agricultural development have been inefficiently allocated under the joint responsibility of local governments, bilateral donors, and international aid agencies. First, following the colonial pattern of priorities, a disproportionate share of the agricultural national budgets has been devoted to promoting a few export crops. As will be explained later, food crops have been correspondingly neglected in terms of extension, research, marketing arrangements, and public investments.[15] Second, a large part of these

---

[15] A good illustration of this export bias is provided by the striking contrast, in Mali and Burkina Faso, between the neglect of staple food crops and the privileged access of cotton growers to public resources (Morrisson 1985: 70).

budgets in many countries has been spent on subsidies (e.g. subsidies on the price of fertilizers), presumably to compensate for high rates of taxation. As a result, investment expenditures have been kept at a rather low level.[16] Third, government resources have been excessively concentrated 'on a subsector of relatively large-scale farmers' (Johnston 1986: 163), as well as on large-scale, capital-intensive, enclaved, and mostly unprofitable ventures, such as state farms, big land settlement schemes, large-scale and ill-conceived irrigation projects, public co-operatives, agro-business corporations, large-scale ranches equipped with sophisticated infrastructure, etc.[17] Incidentally, this shows that it is not very meaningful to talk about *general* exploitation of agriculturalists in Africa. A small number of large private farms—owned by privileged farmers, wealthy businessmen, or state employees—have often been provided with generous loans, subsidies, infrastructure, and technical assistance (Berry 1984: 80).

### (c)  Conclusion

To sum up, the real challenge confronting African agriculture today is not so much that of finding new political coalitions prepared to reverse 'faulty' pricing policies. It is much more to solve the problem of how to generate technological improvements on an endogenous basis and how to spread them out as quickly as possible to large areas of the continent. This is not to say that a congenial price environment is unnecessary for that purpose: low prices for agricultural goods can indeed hamper agricultural growth by diverting resources to other sectors, by inducing the farmers to consume more leisure, and by discouraging investment in agriculture and the adoption of technical innovations (since real returns are low and the savings pool is restricted). But it must be clearly realized that a technological breakthrough of the kind needed in Africa today will not be price induced. As Raj Krishna has put it, the price regime 'cannot by itself explain the evolution of basic scientific knowledge and the level and growth of public investment in research, extension, infrastructure, and human capital . . .' (Krishna 1984: 170). Therefore, 'the task of accelerating agri-cultural growth is primarily techno-organizational' and the main aim of price policies should be to avoid retarding or frustrating the main techno-organizational effort (Krishna 1970: 190).

Technological change, up to a certain point, can arise from the initiative of the farmers themselves. Yet the cultivators' dynamism alone obviously cannot be expected to produce agricultural innovations at the pace required. If increasing pressure on land resources can lead to adaptive technical changes when the rate of population growth is moderate, population-led agricultural growth of the type analysed by Ester Boserup (1965 and 1981) is not a reliable

---

[16] In Zambia, the percentage of the agricultural budget spent on subsidies exceeds 70% (Lele 1984: 442).

[17] For a case-study of Gabon, see Monferrer (1985).

mechanism when population expands rapidly, say, at more than 2 per cent per year (Eicher 1986*a*: 15; Delor-Vandueren 1988: ch. 4). In the same way, even though we know that peasants are able to respond positively to profit opportunities when the latter are not too risky, there is far less evidence that they can take appropriate decisions when their environment begins to change dramatically and quick responses are called for (Mellor 1970: 217).

In view of the above, the new technology and the institutional innovations that go hand in hand with it will have to be produced by the state as public goods (Lele 1985: 161–2), and as part of a science-based agricultural development strategy. It is in this perspective that the problem of the African state must be looked at and that the urgent need to develop efficient bureaucracies must be assessed. The removal of technological, institutional, and internal market constraints is the primary objective that should serve as a guideline for identifying the reforms required in the organizational structure of the African countries. The main problem with a doctrine concentrating on short-term pricing policy considerations is precisely that organizational and structural issues tend to be neglected (Brett 1986: 22).


6.4. *The role of supply factors: structural constraints and handicaps*

When attention is excessively focused on issues of short-term pricing policy, there is an almost inevitable proclivity to ascribe the present difficulties of African agriculture to 'mistakes' or errors currently made by the local governments. By the same token, the natural constraints Africa is ridden with and the structural problems she has inherited from her historical past tend to be neglected or downplayed. This is particularly evident among orthodox or neo-classical economists who feel more at ease with short-term macroeconomic problems than with long-term issues which often involve many non-economic aspects. Such a neglect is especially regrettable since, as we shall see below, Africa is confronted with structural constraints and handicaps—i.e. growth-inhibiting factors or barriers which cannot be easily removed or will never be eliminated at all—that put her at a clear disadvantage compared to other regions in the Third World. Therefore, whenever comparisons are attempted between Africa and these other regions—e.g. when one contemplates the transfer to Africa of the Green Revolution technology applied in Asia and Latin America—it is absolutely essential that these structural differences be borne in mind. Any strategy of agricultural development which does not take them into account is doomed to failure.

On the other hand, the fact must be reckoned that Africa has little prospect of succeeding in developing non-agricultural production on a large scale, even less in penetrating foreign markets for manufactured products. Structural constraints on agricultural production ought therefore not to be construed as insuperable obstacles to agricultural growth but, rather, as sensitive points on which local governments and foreign actors must concentrate their efforts in the future.

In the remaining part of the chapter, attention will be restricted to such structural constraints and handicaps as appear to have an important bearing on the present food situation in Africa. They involve quite varied aspects which go from soil conditions and water accessibility to land tenure systems and political dysfunctioning, through population densities, technological and infra-structural factors. Wherever possible, explicit comparisons with other Third World regions, particularly with Asia, will be made.

## (a) The effects of a wide dispersal of the population

*Comparative evidence on population sparsity*   A striking demographic feature of Africa is her combination of low population densities and low urbanization rates which make for a very scattered population. This is at variance with the situation observed in Asia where the density of population is very high in most areas; and with that observed in Latin America where comparatively low population densities are counterbalanced by a well-concentrated pattern of population settlement (particularly in the coastal areas).

In the middle of 1984, the density of population was around 110 persons per square kilometre in Asia (excluding the Arab oil-exporting countries except Iran and Iraq); 19 persons in Latin America; and 18 persons in Africa, the latter figure being a weighted average of a density of 24 in sub-Saharan Africa and a density of only 15 in North Africa. In Africa, population densities ranged from 8 persons per square kilometre in Somalia and Sudan to 104 in Nigeria, which is in sharp contrast to densities of 178 in the Philippines, 228 in India, and 681 in Bangladesh.[18] On the other hand, the percentage of total population living in cities was 28 per cent in sub-Saharan Africa in 1984 (as against only 16 per cent in 1965) while it exceeded 40 per cent in all Latin American countries and worked out to as much as 83 per cent in Chile, 72 per cent in Brazil, 85 per cent in Uruguay, and 84 per cent in Argentina (World Bank 1986b: Table 31, pp. 240–1). Finally, it is important to bear in mind that most African countries are small from the standpoint of their population base: more than half of them had actually fewer than 5 million people in the beginning of the 1980s (Eicher 1984: 454).

An immediate and obvious implication of the scattered pattern of population settlement in Africa is the high per capita cost of providing roads, railways, health, schools, agricultural, and other services to the population. Since this issue is quite important and often neglected in the literature on the African food crisis I will look at it a little more closely, trying to highlight several ways in which it affected the history of Africa and determined certain policy choices made by modern African governments.

---

[18] All the figures have been calculated from World Bank (1986b: Table 1, pp. 180–1).

*Looking back into history*    When populations are much scattered, as in Africa, there is little scope for labour specialization and market development: rural families tend to produce themselves all or most of the products which they need, roads or waterways remain undeveloped, and large amounts of natural resources remain out of reach of an existing transport infrastructure. Ester Boserup has reminded us that before the arrival of the Europeans there was practically no labour specialization in the sparsely populated areas of Africa. North Africa and parts of West Africa (most notably, the medieval empires of the Niger bend) seemed to be the only important exception with their long experience of trade (including long-distance trade) in agricultural and non-agricultural goods (Boserup 1981: 146; see also Giri 1983: 15–41 and Bates 1984: 240–1). On the whole, it can therefore be said that, in contrast to the situation observed in Asia and Latin America, large parts of Africa entered the nineteenth century with no transport infrastructure worth the name, with no indigenous merchant classes accustomed to money transactions and urban life, and with no ancient traditions of bazaar trade, 'preindustrial urbanization', and specialized craftsmen. Also, as a result of lack of product specialization and limited exchange of goods, agricultural technologies remained rudimentary, socio-economic differentiation or stratification failed to develop to any significant extent, and the dominant culture tended to reflect peasant values rather than forming a distinct 'élite culture' (Fallers 1961: 110; Hyden 1986: 54–5, 57, 78 n. 10). Moreover, in a number of areas politically structured in empires or kingdoms, Africa's failure to acquire technological advances was reinforced by the fact that the rulers sustained their regimes by appropriating surpluses from long-distance trade and not by promoting agricultural development. In consequence, 'African societies south of the Sahara never developed the institutional mechanisms that tied rulers to a system based on the exploitation of land' as happened in Europe and Asia and, in particular, African pre-colonial cities 'were not productively linked to their rural hinterlands' (Hyden 1986: 54, 69).

The colonial episode has further reinforced the above handicaps of Africa. For one thing, the sparsely populated colonies got very few railways: 'only the Union of South Africa with mass immigration of Europeans had more than six meters of railways per square kilometer in 1970, and six countries had no railways at all' (Boserup 1981: 148). Moreover, 'two-thirds of the African railways built in the colonial period connected mines to a coastal harbour' (ibid.). This was the natural outcome of a colonial policy grounded upon criteria of short- or medium-term economic profitability since railway building was usually uneconomic in the sparsely populated areas of Africa except when it could be justified by the existence of rich mineral deposits. Therefore, 'in most of the African continent, cultivable land, forests, and mineral deposits were not utilized. The sparse population outside the small enclaves of colonial development had the choice of remaining subsistence producers or migrating, assuming that they were not removed by force or prevented from migration by police measures, as often happened' (ibid. 148–9). With the truck revolution a cumulative bias actually developed in large parts of the continent. Areas with small and sparse populations were bypassed by road building because it was not profitable to transform them into areas of cash cropping and there was little incentive to construct roads in regions without railways with which to connect them. To sum up, 'the skewing of the transport system in favour of the enclaves continued to be an important feature in the sparsely populated hot colonies' of Africa (ibid. 150).[19]

For another thing, the policies pursued by most colonial governments and administrations did not encourage the formation of an indigenous merchant class nor that of indigenous skilled craftsmen. In fact, if we except North Africa, coastal West Africa (where mercantile communities were established for a long time), and parts of coastal East Africa (where Zanzibari and Swahili planters were involved in economic intermediation), virtually all the petty trading in urban and rural areas was handled by immigrant communities coming from regions with urban and commercial traditions (Lebanese, Indians, Greeks, Portuguese, Syrians, etc.). And all the other skilled occupations which the indigenous population lacked abilities to fill were equally exercised by foreigners and 'ethnic entrepreneurs' (Boserup 1981: 152; Young 1986: 28). In many instances, however, the colonial governments positively prevented the spontaneous emergence or development of private traders and small entrepreneurs by contracting directly with indigenous village chiefs for the recruitment of labour and the procurement of cash crops, possibly through co-operatives effectively controlled by the colonial governors. These indigenous chiefs were usually made a more or less explicit link in the colonial administrative structure (see below, section 6.4*f*). Therefore, when the trade functions were not performed by foreigners or exercised by intermediaries subjugated to foreign interests, they were often bureaucratized and placed under the strict control of the colonial authorities.

Thus, Catherine Coquery-Vidrovitch has noted that in equatorial Africa 'capitalism intruded at one go, under the then relatively completed form of colonial capitalism, and it did not at all try to strike a bargain; during the years 1885–1910, there was no attempt on the part of the Western countries to raise up, encourage or utilize an indigenous "middle class", quite the contrary' (Coquery-Vidrovitch 1985: 130). In the case of the British colonies in Africa, we are told that 'the eschewing of private enterprise, and the promotion of state agencies to expand colonial production, provoked little or no antagonism from within the British state apparatuses', and one reason advanced by the Colonial Office towards vindicating this policy was that 'colonies ought not to be exploited by private enterprise' (Cowen 1982: 150; see also Bézy *et al.* 1981, 9–47 for the case of the Belgian Congo and Gentil 1986: 35–6 for that of

---

[19] The situation was altogether different in the few African countries endowed with climatic conditions close to those obtaining in the temperate zone (Maghreban countries, Zimbabwe, South Africa), since those regions received massive inflows of European immigrants.

Western Africa). For Crawford Young, it is clear that 'Generally, the new colonial economy required destruction of intra-African trading systems which were not Europe-oriented and the capture of their resources' (Young 1986: 28).

There is also much evidence to show that in commercial and other matters the policies followed by the colonial states were strongly influenced by the interests of the dominant European companies. As a matter of fact, it was usually when those interests became threatened by the active competition arising from the petty trading sector of ethnic immigrants (and, more rarely, of small indigenous merchants) that the colonial administration extended its control over the sphere of circulation (marketing, banking, services). It was at the behest of a foreign merchant class with which it often colluded that the colonial state initiated mercantilist policies designed to control competition and to give monopoly powers to a small class of vested economic interests from the West. Even the creation of state marketing boards was sometimes used to maintain very high profits for the expatriate marketing sector, thus destroying the bargaining power of the independent local small-scale traders (Brett 1973, 1986: 23–4; Bézy *et al.* 1981: 23–6; Berry 1984: 79–80). Sometimes also, marketing board monopolies were conceived by colonial authorities as fiscal devices intended for taxing profits from price booms (notably during the prolonged commodity boom of the 1950s). Thus, in a number of countries, the surpluses earned by those boards were automatically transferred to the state capital account (Giri 1986: 67–8; Young 1986: 33).

It is clear that independent African states have inherited a number of problems which have their roots in the considerable scattering of their populations over huge land areas and which were only exacerbated during the colonial period. First, there is the problem of the racial tensions and latent or open rivalry between the indigenous communities and the immigrant middle classes. By monopolizing the access to all jobs requiring a minimum amount of skill, the latter have prevented the former from entering into contact with modern technology and from experimenting with new ways of thinking and calculating in an environment increasingly dominated by market forces. A considerable gap, both technological and educational, thereby developed between the two groups, undermining the social cohesion of the whole societal fabric (Boserup 1981: 152). Furthermore, it is against this background of sharp ethnic division of labour that the hostility of many African governments towards private trading (easily equated with speculative, exploitative, and antisocial practices) and the free play of market forces can be properly understood (Lele 1976: 297; Johnston 1986: 174). The administrative approach of many colonial governments to trade and commerce is another powerful factor that helps explain the numerous attempts of modern African states at extending their control on domestic purchases and sales of both agricultural and non-agricultural goods. The influence of this historical ante-cedent was, however, greatly reinforced by another circumstance pinpointed by Sara Berry: 'The fact that most postcolonial regimes in Africa took office under pressure—from below, above, and within—to take responsibility for developing their economies meant that they were obliged to adopt an inter-ventionist stance toward economic activities and institutions' (Berry 1984: 67; see also Young 1986: 32).

Second, post-colonial governments have inherited from the previous rulers a highly skewed, export-orientated transport network. Most of the population remained isolated from potential markets and sources of supplies 'by large empty spaces without infrastructure for modern transport'. In this context, many rural families continued 'to keep a low labour input in agriculture' and 'to have a high degree of self-sufficiency of both agricultural and nonagri-cultural products' (Boserup 1981: 150). Consequently, the emergence of specialized craftsmen at the village level was further delayed. In addition, no link was built up between urban and rural areas and 'the imports of European manufactured goods and of products from the lands of origin of the urban middle class acted as a formidable obstacle to development of urban crafts and industries' (ibid. 153). Rural areas devoted to cash cropping exported their surplus production instead of growing food to meet the demand of expanding cities.


*A hard but inescapable dilemma*   In actual fact, the above description fits in rather well with the present situation of many African countries. Rather than counteracting tendencies initiated in their past histories, independent govern-ments have often followed in the footsteps of their colonial predecessors by reinforcing the 'enclave' character of their economies and by developing a host of 'urban biases'. Even today, most African countries have but a small fraction of the roads per square land area that are found in India and in so many other countries of Asia and Latin America (Mellor and Delgado 1987: 4). For another thing, Uma Lele has remarked that investments in the road system have been greater in countries like Kenya and Malawi than in many other African countries with lower population densities and more inadequate trans-port facilities: thus, road mileage per square mile of land area is only 0.02 in Sudan, 0.1 in Zambia, and 0.15 in Zaïre, compared with 0.23 in Kenya and 0.31 in Malawi (Lele 1984: 445). But Lele ought not to be surprised at this: African governments are only following the same logic—the logic of economic profitability—as the previous rulers of Africa. Indeed, sparser populations tend to make the building up of transport systems a more uneconomic proposition since the market potential and the frequency of exchange transac-tions are comparatively lower.

The fact that in Africa human settlements remain small and very much scattered in spite of a tremendous demographic acceleration during the last decades goes therefore a long way towards explaining the major infrastructure deficiencies and the profoundly unbalanced pattern of spatial development commonly observed in this continent. A vicious circle and an unequalizing process of cumulative causation of the type analysed by Myrdal (1963) are evidently at work:

- transport networks are comparatively expensive to build in sparsely populated areas;
- labour emigrates from these areas, sometimes along with their families, sometimes not, to improve their conditions of living and to find better work opportunities in more densely populated areas;
- as a result, the former regions are further depleted of their population and the per capita cost of constructing new lines of communication further rises;
- due to poor transport systems, the per capita cost of providing various services (health, school, agricultural extension, etc.) to the population is correspondingly enhanced.

Because of this process, entire rural regions are increasingly marginalized and vast amounts of potential food production possibly lost.

Many authors have pointed to inadequate rural infrastructures as a crucial factor responsible for the slow growth of food production in Africa, and they have underlined the consequent need to expand the transportation network to and from the isolated rural areas. Thus, Mellor and Delgado have recently expressed the opinion that 'improved rural roads are probably the single most important factor in transforming rural Africa' since 'more and better roads would improve the delivery of farm inputs to and farm products from the widely dispersed smallholder population' (Mellor and Delgado 1987: 4). The dominant literature of today, which emphasizes the commendability of 'small farm' or 'unimodal' strategies of agricultural development (Johnston 1986; Johnston and Kilby 1975; World Bank 1981, 1986b), takes a position very similar to that expressed above. What needs to be stressed here is the simple truism that, however commendable it may be on various theoretical grounds, such a strategy is especially costly and difficult to implement when rural populations are widely dispersed. It is true that village labour could be more intensely mobilized to build up feeder roads in rural areas. Yet, as long as the latter cannot be connected with a national all-weather transport network, their usefulness will remain quite limited (Lele 1984: 450).

There is a serious dilemma here and by bypassing it one runs the risk of indulging in wishful thinking, a luxury which African governments certainly cannot afford. In fact, a number of strategic orientations chosen by them and often regarded as irrational or absurd can be explained on reasonable grounds when the scattered pattern of human settlement in Africa is taken into consideration. The oft-noted preference of the African authorities (and, to a large extent, of the big donor agencies from the West) for large-scale agricultural projects is a case in point. Indeed, such projects allow for a heavy concentration and neat phasing of the government's efforts and avoid the wastes inherent in the sprinkling of these efforts over large, sparsely populated areas. Moreover, the wide dispersion of African smallholders makes for high risks of leakage of revenue and for heavy administrative costs of revenue collection per unit of money gathered by the taxation bureaucracy. In this context, centralized marketing boards are attractive since they enable the state bureaucracy to pass over to the peasants part of the administrative costs of revenue collection: indeed, peasants are forced to bring to some central point the produce upon which implicit or explicit taxes will be levied and to bear the corresponding costs of transportation. Likewise, large-scale agricultural projects and state farms offer the advantage of relatively easy taxability (see above, p. 295).

The above considerations are bound to play a crucial role when the state machineries are new, inexperienced, and short of skilled revenue officers, as is certainly the case in many countries of the African continent. The fact that numerous large-scale agricultural projects and parastatals turn out to be actually ineffective and wasteful of scarce resources only adds to the complexity of the African situation.[20] But it should not lead one to believe that the smallholder-focused strategy of agricultural development is automatically and unambiguously cost-effective as compared to other approaches which give more emphasis to economies of scale and concentration gains. There are clear cases where it would be more economical to reform large-scale projects or state integrating agencies than to wind them up altogether and to rely completely on private decentralized initiative. Thus, for instance, small irrigation schemes along the river Senegal are too dispersed to make private mechanical workshops for the maintenance of tubewells economically profitable. Services have therefore to be provided by the SAED, the parastatal entrusted with the task of organizing and running large-scale irrigation works in the area.

### (b)   Handicaps on the natural resources front

From her low population densities (at least when compared with Asia), can one infer that Africa is a land-abundant continent? After all, contrary to what was observed in Asia and Latin America, most of the output gains in Africa during the last decades resulted from an extension of the agricultural frontier.[21]

Today, however, there is enough evidence to show (1) that this frontier has been extended to its limits in a large number of countries or (2) that in many instances it would be more costly to bring new lands into cultivation than to intensify production on existing agricultural (or pasture) lands. Moreover, Africa is handicapped by difficult climatological and soil conditions, while with respect to water potential and scope for efficient water management she is

[20] Not all large-scale projects and state boards have been failures, however. Famous successes such as Ethiopia's CADU, Rwanda's Coffee Marketing Board, the Kenya Tea Development Authority, the Botswana Meat Commission, the CMDT in Mali, and the SOFITEX in Burkina Faso (both working in the field of cotton production and marketing) are worth bearing in mind (for more details, see Lele 1975 and 1976; Swainson 1986, Morrison 1986).

[21] In sub-Saharan Africa, output per hectare growth rate represented only 8% of the production growth rate during the 1970s, compared with 62% for the whole developing world. During the 1960s, it was −9% (Mellor and Johnston 1984: 536; see also Paulino 1987).

also at a clear disadvantage compared to Asia and Latin America. Let us now examine these various aspects of Africa's land and water resources in greater detail.[22]

*Land reserves*   An FAO study has reached the conclusion that, given the existing technology, Africa's base of cultivable land resources could enable her to feed her whole population in the year 2000 if massive population movements are allowed for (FAO 1986: Annex II, ch. 7). This is of course a completely unrealistic assumption. When attention is drawn to the situation of individual countries, the picture that emerges is quite different because land resources are inequitably distributed across the African continent. Thus, it appears that 21 countries are virtually unable to become food self-sufficient if no technological change is introduced in their agricultural sector. By the end of this century, their number will have risen to 28 even assuming that all their arable lands have been brought under cultivation (FAO 1984 and 1986: Annex II, ch. 7).

As Carl Eicher has remarked, it is time 'to shelve the misleading cliche that Africa is a land abundant continent' and 'to stop thinking of African countries as if they were all the same' (Eicher 1985: 94–5). In fact, only about one-third of the continent can be classified as land abundant (Sudan, Zaïre, Cameroon, Guinea, Sierra Leone, Zambia, Mozambique, and Angola), and in these countries, 'seasonal labor shortages, not land, will be the major constraint on expanding production' (ibid. 95). Of the total land reserve of Africa (estimated at 603 million ha), a large part (75 per cent) is located in two regions: humid Central Africa and sub-humid and semi-arid Southern Africa. It is also noteworthy that 75 per cent of the land reserves in the Sudano-Sahelian region are located in one country, Sudan (FAO 1986: Annex II, ch. 6, para. 6.13).

Another one-third of the African countries are in semi-arid areas where the land frontier is rapidly being exhausted (e.g. Senegal, Niger) and the remaining countries (again one-third of the total) are in a land-scarce environment where the frontier is already exhausted (e.g. Rwanda, Malawi, Burundi) (Eicher 1985: 95). In fact, Africa offers the contrasted picture of large, but very unequally distributed, land reserves coexisting with huge land masses that are and will always remain inhospitable to farming. Around one-third of Africa's soils are too arid to permit any kind of cultivation and 42 per cent of land surfaces are made of either desert or sandy soils (21.8 and 20.3 per cent, respectively). Furthermore, almost half of the African continent is completely unsuited to direct rainfed crop production because the lengths of growing periods are too short (less than 75 days), and only 30 per cent of it is well suited climatically to the rainfed production of millet, sorghum, and maize, the staple food crops (FAO 1986: Annex II, ch. 2, para. 2.7, and ch. 3, Table 3.1).

The situation is made much worse still by the fact that in regions with significant land reserves—that is mainly in tropical humid Africa—there are very serious obstacles to the expansion of the agricultural frontier. These

[22] South Africa is always excluded when reference is made to the African continent.

obstacles may arise from problems of land fertility and soil conservation, from operational difficulties regarding the reclamation and the draining of the lands, and, above all, from health risks affecting both animals and human beings. In many parts of Africa animal trypanosomiasis is the most important constraint to livestock production and to the use of animal draught power in agriculture. The extent of the area affected, estimated at some 38 per cent of the total land area of Africa, covers 37 countries where some 55 million livestock units are at risk. Trypanosomiasis (sleeping sickness) also affects human beings, and since it virtually precludes human settlement on some of the best-watered and most fertile lands, it can really be considered as one of the major scourges of land development in Africa (FAO 1986: Annex II, ch. 6, paras. 29–30; World Bank 1984: 102–3; Eicher 1986*b*: 18). Unfortunately, the control of the vector —tsetse flies—is particularly difficult and, in any case, its success will depend on a high standard of management and follow-up monitoring, on effective public health research, on careful land use planning, and on the willingness of governments and aid donors to incur large expenditures.[23]

To take two other examples, fertile river valleys are closed to human settlement because of the large-scale prevalence of onchocerciasis (river blindness), and schistosomiasis badly affects most of the African continent, particularly the Nile Valley and the countries immediately south of the Sahara, and in East and Central Africa below the equator. As the experience of several water resource development projects has amply illustrated (Aswan Dam in Egypt, Gezira Scheme in Sudan, Volta Lake in Ghana, etc.), any change in the aquatic component of the vector habitat (irrigation, water diversion or impoundment, etc.) is likely to increase the prevalence of schistosomiasis drastically (FAO 1986: Annex II, ch. 6, para. 6.26–7, and Table 6.6).

Given the above constraints, it is not surprising that since the early 1960s, the amount of agricultural land per person in agriculture has gone down regularly in Africa (Cohen 1980: 358), and this despite rising rates of urbanization. The same constraints largely account for the fact that 'despite the abundance of land relative to population, the number of hectares of cropped area per farm worker is small compared with that in other developing areas' (Paulino 1987: 35). In the words of Michael Lipton, much of Africa outside the Nile Valley and Rwanda–Burundi 'contains few persons per acre, yet many persons per efficiency unit of land' (Lipton 1987: 213–17).

*Soil structure*   Perhaps the most serious natural handicap of Africa lies in the highly fragile structure and poor physical characteristics of most of her soils. African tropical soils are often thin and depleted and, if they are easy to cultivate by hand (e.g. with a hand hoe), they are not very productive and they require long periods of time to recover after they have been farmed. These problems have to be traced back to the fact that a large part of the African

---

[23] Trypano-tolerant breeds of livestock exist (e.g. in West Africa) but they can only be used in particular ecological conditions.

continent is made of ancient geological strata which are strongly weathered. Soils are therefore easily degraded and washed away; they present serious deficiencies of mineral salts and they are all the lower in plant nutrients as surface temperatures are very high (FAO 1986: Annex II, ch. 3, para. 3.7, and Annex IV, ch. 2, para. 2.4). Lush vegetation conceals the low inherent fertility of much of the land in the humid tropics. On the other hand, Africa is also badly handicapped by her drought susceptibility: there is a high or very high expectation of drought over 60 per cent of the continent, a problem which was less serious when populations were smaller and unlimited space was available (ibid. Annex II, ch. 2, para. 2.21 and Table 2.4).

In fact, out of the six climatic zones into which Africa can be subdivided (on the basis of temperature and moisture, mainly), only two are relatively well suited to rainfed agriculture: subhumid and mountain East Africa, and subhumid and semi-arid Southern Africa. In the other regions, rainfed agriculture is only possible on a limited percentage of total land area (ibid., Annex II, ch. 2). Moreover, according to FAO, as much as half of Africa's rainfed cultivable land is marginal in quality. Only in regions with a reasonably wide range of moisture conditions, namely Mediterranean and arid North Africa and the afore-mentioned two regions, do marginal lands constitute no more than about one-third the extent of the total potentially cultivable rainfed area (ibid. Annex II, ch. 6, para. 6.12).

As has already been noted, a very large part of the African continent is actually covered by sandy soils of various kinds, which are predominant in the semi-arid and subhumid climates and present the characteristics described above (low content in plant nutrients, fragile structure, high susceptibility to wind blowing). In the humid areas the soils of tropical lowlands predominate 'with their associated problems of acidity, low nutrient retention capacity, aluminium toxicity, low initial phosphate and potassium contents and a tendency to fix phosphate in forms unavailable to plants' (ibid. Annex II, ch. 3, para. 3.7 and 3.8). Even under high-level inputs, sandy soils and acid soils of tropical lowlands have low cultivation factors (corresponding to one or two years of cultivation in every five to seven years) as a result of low inherent fertility. Phosphorous and nitrogen are grossly deficient in many African soils while other nutrient deficiencies are also quite common, in particular potassium, sulphur, calcium, and microelements such as zinc and copper. In the fertile soils of tropical highlands weed growth is often more critical than nutrient constraints. As for dark clay soils, they are difficult to cultivate because they are hard when dry, sticky when wet and prone to waterlogging. Their tendency to compact and harden during the dry season results in high early season runoff and severely restricts pre-season and post-season cultivation (ibid. Annex II, ch. 3, para. 3.11–29; Collinson 1987: 80). Other physical limitations of African soils include: (1) very low structural porosity reducing root penetration and water circulation; and (2) generally poor infiltration (Matlon 1987: 61–2).

To sum up, 'there are practically no extensive areas or soils in Africa without limitations of one sort or another' (FAO 1986: Annex II, ch. 3, para. 3.34). Perhaps paradoxically, conditions for agricultural production tend to deteriorate rather than improve with the transition from dry to wet climate (ter Kuile 1987: 97). Some constraints are irremovable and must therefore be endured: thus, over the third of the continent covered by various soils of arid climates (including shallow soils, shifting dunes, saline, calcareous and gypsiferous soils), intensive development is generally not possible. However, in many cases constraints can be overcome through the farmers' own efforts, community development, or government intervention and, more likely, through a mixed use of these three levels of intervention. From a technical standpoint, success in overcoming or removing these constraints will not be achieved unless appropriate soil management techniques are used which are carefully tuned to the specific characteristics of the agroclimatic environment. Land development or reclamation schemes will have to be grounded on careful analysis of soil structures, moisture conditions, and temperatures (FAO 1986: Annex II, ch. 3, para. 3.9 and 3.34–8).

Land development in Africa is bound to be especially difficult not only because African populations are comparatively scattered (see above), but also because the physical environment for agriculture (and cattle-raising) in this continent is marked by an exceptional diversity of agroclimatic and soil characteristics, of farming systems and socio-economic conditions (Berry 1984: 60 and Johnston 1986: 159). These highly diverse ecological (and socio-economic) conditions are found even within individual countries and within small regions or subregions. Just to take one example, African soils have greatly varying abilities to supply and retain nutrients and to respond to fertilizer applications (be it through organic manures, mineral fertilizers, or biological nitrogen fixation by leguminous plants). Due to such heterogeneity of environmental conditions and wide variations in farming (and livestock) systems by agroecological zones, rigid technical packages have absolutely no chance to succeed. The fact that only highly differentiated strategies of soil management and land development can form a sound basis for agricultural development in Africa makes technological progress a comparatively costly process and, in particular, it compounds to a considerable degree the administrative difficulties created by low population densities. Note that the huge losses resulting from pests, plant diseases, rodents, grasshopper and bird attacks—the latter being an especially serious problem in Africa—can also be remedied only if they are dealt with in a selective way and at a much decentralized level.[24]

---

[24] A well-known parasite in Africa is the striga which attaches itself to the roots of millet and sorghum, two crops often cultivated in association. Quelea (weaver) birds are famous for the havoc they often play in the harvests of these two traditional subsistence crops. On the other hand, rice harvests are also highly susceptible to bird attacks as well as to rats and borers.

There are other sources of great variability which are typical of Africa, particularly of semi-arid areas. Thus, the crop-growing season is short compared to other semi-arid tropics with similar rainfall (Matlon 1987: 60). As a consequence, the seasonality of labour input to agriculture tends to be very high in Africa, 'not only absolutely but also compared to the semi-arid tropics of South Asia' (Delgado and Ranade 1987: 118). Moreover, interyear variability of rainfall is also very high in Africa and this has a considerable impact on agricultural activities in rainfed and traditional irrigation systems. A clear illustration of this is provided by the following example: in the Senegal river valley, the area cultivable under flood recession agriculture varies between 10,000 and 150,000 hectares depending upon the importance of the flood (Mathieu 1987: i. 22).

*Irrigation potential* Lipton has recently expressed the opinion that 'over the next forty years, SSA [sub-Saharan Africa] cannot feed its people without massively expanding the irrigated portion of its cropland' (Lipton 1985: 75). Unfortunately, compared to other regions of the world Africa has a lesser quantity of surface waters per unit of land area while at the same time suffering from greater evaporation. Large rivers like the Nile and the Niger cross vast tracts of interior marshlands (the Sudd in Sudan and the Niger delta) where considerable quantities of water get lost. Several other basins (e.g. Lake Chad) are deprived of any outlet into the sea and lose the totality of their waters through evaporation or percolation (FAO 1986: Annex IV, ch. 2, para. 2.5). There now seems to be a growing consensus that the irrigation potential of Africa is quite limited, in any case much more limited than that of Asia, and that rainfed agriculture will remain the most important and most economical way to increase foodcrop production in most African countries (CILSS 1979: 162–7; Eicher and Baker 1982: 133–9; Lele 1984: 445; FAO 1986: Annex IV; Matlon 1987: 65–9). This is a clear handicap in so far as the potential yield increases that can be obtained from high yield varieties are in general considerably lower under rainfed agriculture than under irrigated agriculture with generous application of fertilizers.

In Africa surface waters are distributed in a very unequal way and most water resources are not located in areas where aridity seriously limits production.[25] Almost half of irrigable land areas are already abundantly watered by rainfall. Out of the remaining potential of 20–5 million hectares, 9.5 million have actually been put under irrigation (between 38–47 per cent), of which 6.1 million hectares represent modern irrigation, mainly under major government schemes (above all in the Maghreb countries, Egypt, and the

---

[25] Thus, the Zaïre basin which covers 16% of the total land area in sub-Saharan Africa carries as much as 55% of the average annual flows running in this region. Unfortunately, the river Zaïre does not flow through areas where low rainfall puts a serious drag on rainfed agriculture. However, some of the large rivers of the continent flow through extensive arid areas (Nile, Niger, and Senegal) (FAO 1986: Annex IV, ch. 2, para. 2.8).

Sudan), and 3.4 million hectares represent small-scale and traditional flood, swamp, surface, and low-lift irrigation developed at the village or household level (above all in Nigeria and Madagascar). Whereas in India and Indonesia about 25 per cent of the total arable land area is under irrigation, the corresponding proportion is less than 5 per cent in Africa and it will take much time and efforts to raise it to its likely maximum of 10–14 per cent. If in North Africa most of the irrigation potential is presently exploited, the same cannot be said of sub-Saharan Africa where as much as 88 per cent of the potentialities are still unused (FAO 1986: Main Report, ch. 2; Annex II, ch. 6, para. 16; Annex IV, i; Paulino 1987: Table 2.8, 36). It is therefore with respect to the latter, yet untapped, potential that one can speak with Lipton about the necessity for Africa to expand massively her irrigated croplands.

Such expansion must actually take place mainly in a group of twelve countries, eight of which have seriously restricted rainfed opportunities (the six Sahelian countries plus Kenya and Botswana), and four of which have a rainfed growing period of less than 120 days on more than a quarter of their territory (Chad, Ethiopia, Sudan, and Tanzania). Other countries with a sizeable portion of their arable lands in the semi-arid zone (e.g. Guinea-Bissau, Nigeria, Cameroon, Angola) also need to develop irrigation in their high-risk tracts (FAO 1986: Annex IV, ch. 6, para. 6.5–6.7). Under all other conditions, according to FAO experts, first priority ought probably to be given to rainfed development because it 'demands fewer scarce government financial or managerial resources; less imported materials, fuel and equipment; does not require profound social change; and has a quicker impact'. However, these experts admit, 'irrigation may *eventually* become essential in these [remaining] countries, but in the short and medium term rainfed development is likely to be a better national strategy for food supply than large-scale modern irrigation' (ibid. ch. 6, para. 6.2; for a similar position, see Spencer 1986: 217).

It is an unmistakable fact that access to water is much costlier and more problematical in Africa than in Asia: thus, for example, the unit cost of water is between two and three times as high in Africa as in India (FAO 1986: Main Report, ch. 2). This is of course the basic reason why most irrigated lands are devoted to export crops (e.g. cotton, sugarcane, and sugar beets) and to 'superior' foodcrops (wheat—essentially in North Africa—and rice—essentially in sub-Saharan Africa). With their low unit values subsistence crops cannot be profitably raised under irrigated agriculture.[26] Note also that,

[26] Between 50 and 60% of the total irrigated land area is devoted to cereal crops. Nevertheless, by far the largest portion of lands under *modern* irrigation schemes is used for raising export crops (FAO 1986: Annex IV, ch. 2, para. 2.60–3). The question could be asked why traditional foodcrops are not displaced by high-value crops under dryland farming systems too. There are two main answers to this question. First, due to technical reasons, most crops with high unit values could not be profitably raised under rainfed agriculture. Second, the food diet in the African countryside still remains heavily biased in favour of traditional staple foods which the farmers are keen to produce themselves and to which they give absolute priority in their time allocation pattern.

institutional and administrative problems apart, traditional irrigation (including flood-recession farming systems, swamp drainage, and irrigation schemes under controlled submersion) is likely to be less cost-effective than modern irrigation with complete control of water. This is due to the fact that crop yields under traditional irrigation systems are generally much lower and much more subject to wild fluctuations arising from natural hazards. At this point, it is interesting to mention a number of technical reasons which tend to make irrigation much more costly and problematic in Africa than, say, in Asia (ibid., Annex IV, ch. 2, para. 2.6–8 and 2.37; ch. 5, para. 5.8–9):

1. High unit costs of imported capital and intermediate goods result from long distances and poor roads, particularly in land-locked countries.

2. Reservoirs and dams are often required to perform the essential function of stabilizing the erratic flows of many African rivers. Because of the central basement complex (shaped like a saucer) of the African continent, suitable dam locations will be found along the rim and these sites 'usually require either considerable lengths of canal to bring the water to the irrigable areas or pumping'.

3. 'Major flood protection dykes are often necessary for irrigation schemes. The lower costs encountered for irrigation in the flood plains in Asia are also due to the fact that such dykes already exist, having been built a long time ago.'

4. The distribution of irrigable soils 'is often patchy, calling for complex water distribution and drainage networks with considerable land levelling where surface irrigation is concerned'.

5. Sources of groundwater are rather few (compared to Asia). Moreover, they are usually scattered and difficult to locate, and they do not replenish themselves easily. They are frequently found at great depths (more than 100 metres), and, as such, they are not suitable for developing cheap small-scale irrigation. None the less, abundant shallow sources of underground water exist along the alluvial beds of some large rivers (like the Nile, Niger, and Senegal).

6. African rivers—except those having their source in the younger geological strata of North Africa or mountain East Africa[27]—carry fewer sedimental matters than rivers in other regions of the world, particularly in Asia. Such a deficiency accounts for the oft-noted fact that the fertility of irrigated fields begins to decline a few years after the completion of irrigation projects, thus making it necessary to apply significant doses of mineral fertilizers to restore economic profitability (see Mathieu 1985a, for irrigation schemes in the Senegal river basin, and 1985b, for schemes along the Niger in Mali). As hinted at above, Asia is in a much more favourable position since her great rivers 'get much of their water and alluvium from head-waters outside the tropics and

---

[27] Sedimental matters can also be locally abundant in the enlarging areas which have lost their plant cover following overgrazing or deforestation. In this instance, however, the nutrients are obtained at the cost of destroying land resources elsewhere in the region: think, for example, of the considerable quantities of sediments flowing away from the Abyssinian plateau as a result of huge deforestation to be eventually dispersed among the fields of Egyptian farmers along the Nile river.

carry a richer load of nutrient-bearing silt'. In addition, 'the permanent snow cover of the Himalayas also represents an enormous resource for recharging underground aquifers, whereas the high rates of evapotranspiration in sub-Saharan Africa reduce significantly available water surpluses' (Eicher and Baker 1982: 134).

7. Other problems arise from heavy clay soils which call for considerable mechanization, and from birds, grasshoppers, and rodents which can cause tremendous destruction by attacking irrigated rice crops in the process of ripening.

8. Finally, possibilities of multiple cropping are far more limited in Africa than in Asia because of the much poorer waterholding capacity of soils in the former than in the latter continent (Matlon 1987; Delgado and Ranade 1987: 126–8).

*Conclusion* The situation of Africa with respect to agricultural natural resources can be summarized in the following way:

1. Africa still possesses considerable land reserves and uncultivated lands are often of high fertility (particularly those located in deltas, swamps, and floodplains). However, these land reserves are very unequally distributed and they are largely inaccessible due to serious animal, plant, and human diseases. This is in contrast to what obtains in other parts of the world where great civilizations of past millennia tamed the infested river valleys and coastal swamps through long-sustained measures of land reclamation and sanitization (Hart 1982: 101 and Bray 1986: ch. 3).

2. A large part of the African continent (around one-third) is covered by various soils of arid climates. In these regions intensive development is usually impossible while prevention of degradation of the sparse vegetation is imperative on the desert margins.

3. African soils are often fragile, shallow, and depleted, and rainfed agriculture is only possible on a limited portion of the total land area which moreover comprises a good deal of marginal lands. In addition, soils in Africa have a very low waterholding capacity.

4. Africa is distinguished by an exceptional diversity of agroclimatic conditions, which further complicates the task of soil management. This is a crucial point since progressive intensification of use of land already cultivated will not be a viable strategy unless highly differentiated and very careful soil management techniques are applied under rainfed agriculture.

5. In semi-arid tropics the crop-growing season is very short and rainfall varies considerably on a year-to-year basis with dramatic effects on rainfed and traditional irrigation agricultural systems.

6. The irrigation potential of Africa is rather limited, especially so if considerations of economic profitability are added to those of technical feasibility. In many countries rainfed development will remain the most cost-effective

way to increase staple food production, at least in the short and medium term. It is mainly in the Sudano-Sahelian belt and in a few other countries—particularly so in deltaic plains and river valleys—that irrigation development will be an essential element of future food strategies.

7. For various technical reasons, the scope for comparatively cheap small- and medium-scale irrigation is much less extensive in Africa than in Asia.

8. Large tracts of Africa's land are drought prone, a problem which has become increasingly serious with the decline of the average annual rainfall observed in sub-Saharan Africa since the mid-1950s.

### (c)  Retarded and biased process of technology generation

*The lack of Green Revolution-type breakthroughs in African agriculture*   In sharp contrast to other developing areas, sub-Saharan Africa has been characterized during recent decades by low and more or less stagnating per acre yields of many subsistence food crops. On average, the yields of cereals in Asia and Latin America are at present twice as high as they are in Africa (Giri 1986: 59). Worse still, in many African countries, yields of traditional foodgrain have declined, sometimes to a marked degree and for a large number of consecutive years. From Table 6.2 a rough idea can be obtained of the comparatively poor performance of sub-Saharan African agriculture with respect to growth of yields per land unit.

Furthermore, recent evidence has shown a picture of small or negative per capita productivity change in the agricultural sector of many parts of the African continent (Paulino 1987: 23–8). On an average (but not at the margin), productivity of agricultural labour seems to be significantly higher in Asia than in Africa in spite of much more acute land scarcity (Delgado and Ranade 1987: 122).

The factors responsible for such a disappointing performance are complex and not always easy to disentangle. There is no doubt, however, that an overwhelming cause lies in the absence of any significant dynamics of technical

**Table 6.2** Average annual percentage change in yields of cereals, 1960–1984

|                                | Wheat | Maize | Rice  | Millet | Sorghum |
|--------------------------------|-------|-------|-------|--------|---------|
| *Developing countries*         |       |       |       |        |         |
| 1960–70                        | 3.54  | 2.47  | 2.20  | 3.19   | 3.53    |
| 1970–84                        | 3.87  | 2.91  | 2.44  | 0.13   | 1.43    |
| *East Africa (south of Sahara)*|       |       |       |        |         |
| 1960–70                        | 2.28  | 0.96  | 1.10  | 1.11   | 0.68    |
| 1970–84                        | 2.73  | −0.58 | −0.42 | −1.00  | −0.90   |
| *West Africa (south of Sahara)*|       |       |       |        |         |
| 1960–70                        | 1.10  | 1.76  | 0.15  | −0.41  | −2.87   |
| 1970–84                        | 1.86  | −0.26 | 1.55  | 0.03   | 2.31    |

*Source*: Adapted from World Bank (1986*a*: Table B-3, p. 60).

change in African agriculture. It is often the lack of new, and adequately tested, technical packages geared towards the needs of small farmers which has prevented them from increasing the productivity of their land and which has led them, in areas subjected to heavy population pressure, to break the fundamental rules of agroecological balance in extensive agriculture, and to cause the land fertility to decrease inexorably. Thus, a group of FAO experts have recently come to the conclusion that there are practically no technical packages ready to be transferred to African farmers with respect to most food crops under rainfed conditions, particularly in the Sudano-Sahelian belt. This is especially disquieting since 'it is also in this belt that possibilities of extension of rainfed area under present practices are extremely limited' (FAO 1986: Annex IV, ch. 6, para. 6.3). Moreover, lack of technical advances in conditions of increasing land scarcity and poor off-farm work opportunities tends to lead to decreasing levels of rural welfare. Indeed, *when technology is held constant*, intensification of land use following a decline in the amount of agricultural land per person in agriculture (e.g. through a move from shifting to permanent cultivation practices) is generally associated with increased labour requirements per unit of land area and, therefore, with diminishing returns to labour.

It would be absurd to envisage the production of new food technology only in terms of the sacrosanct trinity 'seeds–fertilizers–pesticides'. There are apparently many ways in which African farming systems can be made more efficient, e.g. through rotational improvements (including tree crops, leguminous plants, and mixed farming), better integration of crop and livestock production, new crop management practices, improved methods of soil conservation, improvement of intercropping systems, introduction of animal draught power wherever feasible (possibly after controlling severe animal diseases), diffusion of more effective work tools, or of seeds more carefully disinfected and better sorted out. This being said, it cannot be denied that the production of new, high-yield varieties of seeds—and of new, more productive livestock breeds—forms an essential component of the technical revolution which has occurred in agriculture during the present century, and that it can probably not be bypassed by Africa without putting her food-producing capacity in serious jeopardy. It is basically a correct and appropriate attitude to emphasize the deep implicit knowledge which African farmers possess about their natural environment, and to point to the untapped or neglected potentialities which lie in the store of local traditional practices. Nevertheless, this should not mislead us into thinking that, contrary to what has happened in all other areas of the world, Africa does not need to shift gradually from traditional resource-based agriculture to a science-based agriculture in which the discovery of new genetic processes and new plants or breeds occupies a central position. This is all the more so as many African farmers are actually perplexed and even anxious before the new challenges confronting them.

That Africa is far from having completed—or even from having embarked upon—the above shift is plainly evident from the fact that no major breakthrough in high-yield varieties for most food crops has occurred there so far. This is exactly what Eicher means when he writes that 'in fact, the green revolution has barely touched Africa' (Eicher 1984: 464). Apparently, the only exception is maize for which East and Southern Africa have accumulated a backlog of new technology from the colonial period. In fact, Southern Rhodesia was the first country after the United States to release a hybrid variety of maize (the SRI) for commercial farmers and this success was achieved after seventeen years of continuous research efforts (from 1932 to 1949). The dominant variety today—the SR-52—was produced after eleven more years of research, but it is only since the early 1970s that it has been used at the smallholder level (Lipton 1985: 77; Eicher 1986a: 10 n.). In Kenya, research on hybrid maize started only in the mid-1950s and the Kenyan variety known as Kitale was released about ten years later (Lipton 1985: 77; Eicher 1985: 93, 1986a: 10–11). However, even with respect to maize, a lot remains to be done in Africa. For one thing, the new hybrid varieties such as the SR-52 and the Kitale have benefited only a few countries—Zimbabwe, Kenya, Malawi, Tanzania, and Zambia—and, within these pioneer countries, only some regions, while they could be used on an area roughly twice as large as that presently cultivated with them (FAO 1986: Main Report, ch. 2, para. 2.19). For another thing, serious amounts of adaptive research are needed to discover hybrid varieties of maize suited to other agroclimatic regions, particularly to West Africa where research on maize is still in its infancy.

No comparable breakthroughs have taken place for other food crops. As a matter of fact, there is today wide agreement among agricultural experts that, under actual farming conditions (as opposed to ideal conditions prevailing in experimental research stations), traditional local seed varieties remain superior to the new varieties developed through modern genetic research. Either the latter do not give better average yields than the former, or they appear to be much more sensitive to pests, drought, winds, etc., which makes them too risky for most farmers to adopt. Thus, for example, after ten years of research and trials on improved varieties of rice in West Africa, the conclusion has been reached that 'only 2 of over 2,000 imported varieties were yielding as well as the best local varieties' (Eicher 1986a: 9). With regard to sorghum and millet, two important staple foods in low rainfall areas in West Africa, the Sudan, Ethiopia, and Southern Africa, forty-four years of research started by the French during colonial times (1931 to 1975) did not lead to any noticeable improvement in yields. As a result, ICRISAT—an Indian research institute specialized in problems of arid and semi-arid agriculture—was invited to set up a sorghum and millet research programme in the Sahel in the mid-1970s. Today, however, the failure of this attempt at transferring hybrid varieties from India to West Africa is officially admitted (ibid. 9–10 and FAO 1986: Main Report, ch. 2). As a result, 'probably less than 2 per cent of total sorghum, millet, and upland rice area in West Africa is sown with cultivars developed through modern genetic research' (Spencer 1986: 224).

The situation for other African staple foods—like cassava, yams, and root crops—is basically similar to that described above. Again, the same conclusion can be extended to livestock production since the record of recent attempts to introduce new breeds is distressingly poor: local breeds remain superior to the so-called 'improved breeds' developed through scientific approaches, mainly because they turn out to be much more resistant to local diseases (Leonard 1986: 201 and FAO 1986: Annex III, ch. 3, para. 3.54–62).

It would be wrong and dangerous to infer from the afore-mentioned failures that in Africa traditional agricultural technologies and practices have a decisive and permanent advantage over modern technologies and practices derived from a science-based approach. Indeed, it will be argued in the following sections that underlying the bleak picture given above are structural factors, biases, and constraints that can be redressed or released to a significant extent provided drastic corrective measures are taken up. These obstacles and distortions often arise from policy trends that can be traced back to colonial times or to deeply engraved misconceptions about the nature or process of technical change on the part of African governments and international donor agencies. But they may also originate in special difficulties resulting from some structural characteristics of the African continent. The above two categories of technical change-impeding factors will now be analysed in succession with a view to identifying a new set of reasons why Africa is lagging so much behind Asia and Latin America with respect to food technology and production.

*Misguided policy trends: the 'export bias'*   A conspicuous feature of the agricultural strategies followed by most African governments lies in the modest investment in research on food crops compared to similar investments on export crops. Lipton has rightly noted that in Africa 'the lack of "congruence" between research effort and the importance of a crop' takes on extreme proportions and is in fact far more serious than in most of Asia (Lipton 1985: 70). Thus, for example, in 1976, sub-Saharan Africa spent almost twice as much money on national soybean research as on national cassava research, although the area covered by the former crop represented only 3 per cent of that covered by the latter (ibid. 70 n.)! In 1984, only 7 per cent of the agricultural scientists working in this region devoted all their research efforts to millet and sorghum while these two food crops accounted for as much as 41 per cent of total cereal production and almost 60 per cent of the total land area under cereal crops (FAO 1986: Main Report, ch. 1, para. 1.26 and Annex I, ch. 3, para. 3.29). This said, Table 6.3 shows that the discrimination in agricultural research efforts runs essentially against traditional staple foods while 'superior' food crops which are mainly consumed in urban areas (like wheat, rice, beef, pork, and vegetables) fare much better.

The biased allocation of research efforts between (traditional) food crops and export crops is in fact a direct legacy of colonial research systems. As a rule, the agricultural development strategies of colonial powers were 'geared almost

**Table 6.3** Research as percentage of the value of
product, by commodity, average 1972–1979 period

| Crop | Research (%) |
|---|---|
| *Export crops* | |
| Soybeans | 23.59 |
| Coffee | 3.12 |
| Cocoa | 2.75 |
| Sugar | 1.06 |
| Citrus | 0.88 |
| Groundnuts | 0.57 |
| Bananas | 0.27 |
| Cotton | 0.23 |
| *Food crops* | |
| Traditional staple foods | |
|   Cassava | 0.09 |
|   Coconuts | 0.07 |
|   Sweet potatoes | 0.06 |
| Intermediate crops | |
|   Maize | 0.44 |
| 'Superior' food crops | |
|   Pork | 2.56 |
|   Poultry | 1.99 |
|   Beef | 1.82 |
|   Vegetables | 1.56 |
|   Wheat | 1.30 |
|   Rice | 1.05 |

*Source*: Adapted from Judd *et al.* (1986: Table 6, p. 92).

exclusively to the expansion of export crop production for the metropolitan
countries' and, therefore, their research efforts were largely concentrated on
export crops and on the needs of commercial farmers and managers of
plantations (Lele 1984: 447; Eicher 1984: 460; Giri 1983: 237–8; Spencer
1986: 220–1). Quite often, these efforts were highly productive and yielded
impressive results since in many cases new seed or plant varieties were
developed which were well adapted to African agroclimatic conditions. In this
sense, Hart is right in pointing out that 'the colonial period saw the ground-
work laid for the development of a scientific agriculture' (Hart 1982: 98).

Well-known examples of colonial, Green Revolution-type breakthroughs
are: the development of hybrid oil palm in Zaïre, Nigeria, and the Ivory
Coast (thanks to the pioneering research carried out in the INEAC—Institut
national pour l'étude agronomique du Congo—created in 1933 in the Belgian
Congo); of cotton plants adapted to Sahelian conditions in Mali and Burkina
Faso (under the aegis of the CFDT—Compagnie française pour le
développement des fibres textiles); of a new type of coffee—known as

Arabusta—obtained again in the INEAC by crossing Robusta and Arabica types; of varieties of cocoa suited to West African environmental conditions (under the impulse of the West African Cocoa Research Institute in Ghana); and of high-yielding groundnut varieties in Senegal and Gambia (through the efforts made at the research centre of Bambey which was created as early as 1913).

What all these examples converge to show is that a science-based agriculture is possible in Africa as elsewhere: local varieties can be surpassed by modern hybrid varieties, new plants can be adapted to her highly specific conditions, and plant-breeding materials can be successfully transferred from other regions of the world (as demonstrated in the case of imports of oil palm materials from Asia; of cotton and maize materials from the United States; and of coffee materials from South America). There are good reasons to believe that the same positive results could be obtained for food crops if only sufficient resources were devoted to developing an adequate research base and if the research efforts aimed at improving their yields were conducted with the same determination as was encountered in the case of export crops. The success story of hybrid maize in Zimbabwe and Kenya provides further support to this thesis. However, this should not be taken to mean that it is necessarily wise to devote large amounts of research efforts to the development and adaptation of alien plants (like wheat in drought-prone areas or rice in rainfed areas). Such efforts may well be wasteful of scarce research resources which would be better committed to traditional food crops with a long history of adaptation to the African soil. In this respect, the positive research discrimination which 'superior' food crops are presently enjoying in Africa is probably as disquieting as the longer-lived 'export research bias'.

A last remark is in order. Eicher has noted with apparent good sense that the low priority given to investment in research on food crops during the colonial period could be defended because population and demand for food were growing in a relatively slow fashion and surplus land was available which could easily be brought under cultivation by smallholders when the need arose (Eicher 1984: 460). After all, the only real breakthrough which took place in food crop technology was the afore-mentioned development of hybrid maize in Southern Rhodesia (and, later, in Kenya) where an important community of politically influential European farmers were engaged in production of both food and export crops (Johnston 1986: 166). It is also interesting to note that while developing their export-biased agricultural strategies colonial administrators could take advantage of the strong division of work and leisure prevailing in sub-Saharan Africa where most agricultural tasks were performed by women (Boserup 1981: 147). Underemployed men were thus induced or forced to work in the new money economy either as wage labourers on plantations or as peasant producers of export crops. As a result, the new cash crops became 'men's crops', although women often helped to produce them, and the food crops remained 'women's crops' considered as a part of women's traditional obligations to provide for the family consumption (ibid.). Therefore, a kind of collusion was created between colonial administrators and leading male villagers in so far as the latter had no interest in improving the food crops and their whole attention was concentrated on enlarging the scope and increasing the yields of export cash crops.

As is evident from the above discussion, several powerful forces converged during the colonial period to produce an 'export bias' in agricultural development strategies. However, the agricultural research policy followed by the Belgians in Zaïre shows that another approach was possible which gave more weight to long-term considerations and to the well-being of the masses (including women). As a matter of fact, the agricultural research system which was established in 1933 (the INEAC) was not only a strong organization which eventually became the largest of its type in Africa and obtained impressive results (see above), but it also devoted a significant part of its resources to research on food crops. In this respect, it is noteworthy that the INEAC was independent of the colonial administration and that its financing was rather diversified (Eicher 1986a: 13, 1986b: 10).

*Misguided policy trends: the 'technological dependence bias'*   With respect to agricultural technology development and diffusion, the experience of the last decades has taught us a very important lesson: the model of direct 'material' technological transfer does not work because agricultural technology is highly 'location-specific' (Hayami and Ruttan 1985: 271). It is true that the development and rapid diffusion since the Second World War of modern high-yielding varieties of rice, wheat, and maize in Asia and Latin America has followed a dramatic process of agricultural technology transfer. Yet what deserves to be emphasized is the following: if the new seed varieties propagated during the 1960s and the early 1970s were those developed by international agricultural research centres (such as the IRRI for rice and the CIMMYT for wheat and maize), they have been gradually replaced by crosses of the international centre varieties with *local* varieties developed by national research and experiment institutions so as better to suit local environmental conditions (Hayami and Kikuchi 1981: 44–5). This creative process of adaptation of prototype high-yielding varieties (or of other prototypes of genetic material and equipment) developed in temperate zone countries has been made possible 'by a series of institutional innovations in the organization, management, and financing of agricultural research' in the receiving countries themselves. More than the direct transfer of materials and designs, it implied the international migration of scientific manpower and the development of indigenous research capability (Hayami and Ruttan 1985: 264; Johnston 1986: 165). It can therefore be concluded that from a technical standpoint the success of the Green Revolution in Asia and Latin America was due to two main factors: (1) the existence of a large store of scientific and technical knowledge in advanced countries which could be used in tropical countries through the mediation of highly performing international research centres; and (2) a considerable strengthening in the latter countries of capabilities for research, experimentation, and administration of agricultural programmes, through the building up of new institutions (including agricultural universities), a marked increase in the supply of well-trained scientists, engineers, and administrators, and a rapid accumulation of on-the-spot practical knowledge and learning by doing.

In actual fact, the experience of Africa with agricultural technological change during the twentieth century largely bears out the above diagnosis. It does so in both a positive and a negative way. The positive test is provided by the history of technical change during the colonial period. Indeed, it is evident from this history that technical breakthroughs were always the outcome of well-focused and long-sustained adaptive research and experimentation carried out in locally established research-experimentation networks. The story of oil palm technology development, as reported by Eicher, is particularly illustrative in this regard:

INEAC's pioneering research on hybrid oil palms [in the Belgian Congo] laid the foundation for the modern oil palm industry in West Africa. Basic information on oil palm genetics was transferred to Nigeria and after a decade of adaptive research in the 1950s, Nigerian hybrid varieties became the centerpiece of the eastern region's smallholder oil palm scheme in the early 1960s. The Nigerian hybrids yielded 300 per cent more than local (wild) varieties under farm conditions. (Eicher 1986a: 13)

As for the negative test, it is supplied by the numerous cases of failure in international direct transfers of agricultural technology to Africa during the last decades. Such failures even occurred when foodgrain varieties were transferred from other tropical developing areas (like Mexico and India) with apparently similar agroclimatic characteristics. The disappointing results obtained by ICRISAT—a renowned and competent Indian agricultural research centre—when it tried to transfer hybrid sorghum and millet varieties from semi-arid India to Sahelian countries in the late 1970s have already been mentioned. Causes of this failure were located in 'unforeseen problems with disease, variability of rainfall and poor soils' (Eicher 1984: 464), and in 'the difficulty of transferring, crossing or adapting exotic varieties so that they suit local conditions especially regarding striga weeds and quelea (weaver) birds' (Lipton 1985: 78). Other experiences of direct international transfers of agricultural technology in general, and of genetic material in particular, do not tell a different story. After more than two decades of experimentation, optimism about the possibility of transferring the Green Revolution technology to Africa has faded away. FAO experts refer to the 'excessive confidence' which has been put in transfers of imported technologies from other continents (FAO 1986: Main Report, ch. 4, para. 4.75). The US Department of Agriculture considers that high-yielding varieties have distressingly failed to spread to Africa (quoted by Lipton 1985: 77). Bruce Johnston writes that among the factors responsible for inadequate rates of technological progress in

African agriculture are 'overly optimistic expectations about the availability of profitable technical innovations adapted to Africa's diverse environmental conditions and impatience for quick results'. According to him, 'this over-optimism about the potential for direct technological transfer' partly resulted from a misinterpretation of Asia's experience with the Green Revolution (Johnston 1986: 164–5). Finally, Eicher reached the conclusion that 'international technology transfer of plant varieties has been constrained by differences in soil conditions, pest regimes, farming practices' (Eicher 1986b: 24), and, one could add, by differences in rainfall patterns and moisture conditions, in access to water and water quality, and in a host of varied socio-economic conditions. His judgement can be extended to livestock technology and animal genetic material, as is evident from the following excerpt:

Starting with great confidence in the early sixties, western donors imported western models of ranches, capital intensive abattoirs and planeloads of exotic cattle in an attempt to 'bring development' to Africa. But in practice, these livestock improvement programs failed under institutional and environmental conditions that were sharply different from those in North America, Europe and Australia. (ibid. 18; see also Leonard 1986: 201)

In the light of the above analysis, the low pace of technical change in African agriculture must be attributed to an 'absence of effective local scientific capacity to screen, borrow, modify and adapt the most promising technology to local conditions' (Eicher 1986b: 24); to sheer neglect of the potential contribution of local materials (seeds, forest, fish, and livestock species) in development of new varieties or of local systems in development of new technologies (thus, serious research on intercropping started only in the 1970s although in most countries intercropping occupies over 90 per cent of cropped area—Spencer 1986: 224); and to a lack of genuine commitment to, or investment in, improving food crop technology, particularly at the smallholder level. While the latter factor—low priority to investment in food crop research —was at work both during the colonial period and the post-independence era, the other factor—inadequate adaptive agricultural research capacity—is characteristic of post-independence Africa. However, this should not be taken to mean that African governments only are to be held responsible for this dramatic underinvestment in research-building capacity. As a matter of fact, the responsibility of the international aid community is also heavily involved and, moreover, the dearth of trained African scientists and administrators can undoubtedly be traced back to colonial times.[28]

While many Asian countries benefited from sizeable foreign aid programmes with a high priority on long-term objectives of institution-building

[28] Carl Eicher has reminded us that, by the time of independence in the early 1960s, there was only one faculty of agriculture in French-speaking tropical Africa. Furthermore, between 1952 and 1963, only 4 university graduates in agriculture were trained in Francophone Africa, and 150 in English-speaking Africa (Eicher 1984: 459).

and development of graduate training in science and agriculture, Africa had curiously to be content with programmes of more limited size and shorter duration (Johnston 1986: 165). Data compiled by FAO for the period 1974–83 clearly illustrate this distortion: only 3 per cent of donor contributions to agriculture in Africa were used to develop national research systems and training, compared to 5.4 per cent in Asia. Furthermore, during 1974–9, 22 per cent of donor assistance to agriculture went into direct support of crop production in Africa, compared to only 5 per cent in Asia (Mellor and Delgado 1987: 3). Some authors have explained this differential treatment of Asia and Africa in terms of an all-pervasive 'extension bias' in the analysis of the needs of the African continent. Thus, Eicher has noted that after independence, 'donors assumed that inexpensive extension workers (mainly Africans) were a substitute for relatively expensive agricultural research scientists (mainly Europeans)' (Eicher 1986b: 8; see also Evenson 1978 and Johnston 1986: 166). Lagging agricultural development in Africa was seen primarily as the consequence of a failure to make effective use of available technology due to various reasons among which lack of knowledge and motivation among farmers stood foremost. Technical assistance and community development programmes therefore appeared as the best strategy to generate rapid modernization of African agriculture. In varietal research, all that was thought to be needed was 'importing varieties from other parts of the world, testing them for adaptability, and selecting the suitable ones' (Spencer 1986: 225).

To a large extent, however, this 'extension and community development bias' (Eicher) was also at work in Asia, especially during the 1950s (Hayami and Ruttan 1985: 264). It is in fact the availability of *new* technologies tuned to Asia's ecological conditions but requiring on-the-spot adaptation which largely imposed, during the late 1960s, a major revision of past conceptions and strategies. Whatever the reasons may be, there is a clear contrast between Asia and Africa: while in Asia foreign aid has been used to strengthen indigenous scientific capacity to carry out research and field experiments as well as to generate new technologies adapted to local circumstances, in Africa it went mostly into direct assistance projects, thus preventing Africans from developing their expertise and skills. Africa has remained a big builder and receiver of agricultural extension programmes 'which have generally been quite ineffective because they have had so little to extend' (Johnston 1986: 166), and of complex integrated rural development projects which cannot be properly handled due to an evident lack of trained manpower. In this respect, it is probably revealing that in 1980, the ratio of agricultural extension workers to research workers was more than three times as high in Africa (9.9) as in Asia (3.2) and Latin America (2.7) (computed from Judd et al. 1986: Tables 1 and 2, pp. 82–5). Also telling and typical of so many African countries is the case of Senegal where the National School of Agriculture—the first establishment to offer an undergraduate training in agriculture in the country—was not created until nineteen years after national independence (in 1979) (Eicher 1984: 471).

English-speaking countries did not fare much better since in the mid-1960s there were only three African scientists working in research stations in Kenya, Uganda, and Tanzania (Eicher 1986a: 19).

Obviously, Africa will not be in a position to master her long-term process of agricultural development if she does not call radically into question the present human capital model grounded on 'overseas training and the provision of expatriate experts to Africa' (Eicher 1986b: 35). Indeed, the current situation under which the number of African scientists, technicians, and administrators capable of dealing with Africa's agricultural problems is too low and too slowly growing involves many long-term social costs. It cannot be otherwise when national development plans are designed by foreign agencies (often donor agencies), when research priorities are decided by foreign directors or scientists, and, most importantly, when the learning by doing is appropriated by an ever-growing and continuously changing community of expatriate technical experts whose central commitment is elsewhere. Such a deep and chronic dependence on foreign aid and expertise can only alienate and frustrate all the Africans who work—whether formally or not—under the orders of foreigners and, moreover, it is bound to undermine the authority and prestige of national governments (Helleiner 1979; Lele 1984: 450; Lipton 1985: 72; Eicher 1986c: 264; Mellor and Delgado 1987: 3). This is all the more so as foreign technical assistance is very costly, often of mediocre quality, and 'tackled in an *ad hoc* and half-hearted manner' (Eicher 1986b: 41).

Therefore, if Africa is to acquire the capacity to adapt and generate new technologies targeted to her specific conditions—particularly with a view to intensifying agriculture on dryland farming systems—she must increase her education and training programmes for high-level agricultural personnel (biologists, agronomists, irrigation engineers, agricultural economists, rural sociologists, etc.) and change her graduate education priorities by downgrading studies in law, medicine, arts, and social studies. The well-conceived role of the international community would be to encourage this reshuffling of priorities and to support the process of institution-building as it has done with apparent success in Asia.[29]

As a matter of fact, it is not only the level but also the orientation of investment in agricultural research which has been inadequate during the last decades in Africa. Three important sources of misallocation of research resources will be briefly mentioned here. First, instead of pursuing the colonial tradition of strong national or regional research services, donor agencies chose to invest heavily in the establishment of big international research centres (IRC) located in Africa but staffed with expatriates. This decision turned out to be 'a major research policy mistake' since it meant (1) that the building of indigenous scientific capacity got only casual and slight support and (2) that priority was given to international technology transfers over local generation of

---

[29] For more concrete proposals, see Eicher (1984: 472).

new technologies and development of local materials directly relevant to the targeted areas (Eicher 1986*b*: 9–12; Spencer 1986: 225).

Second, too many resources (whether in the IRCs or in national research services) have been committed to applied research at the expense of basic science (soil science, plant physiology and pathology, etc.) (Lipton 1985: 71; Eicher 1986*a*: 11–12; Mellor and Delgado 1987: 4). This bias is obviously the reflection of the 'extension' or 'technological dependence bias' according to which international diffusion of available technologies can be the engine of technical change in African agriculture.

Third, research efforts have been dispersed over too many crops or commodity programmes and over too large a geographical area. Experience in Africa (during the colonial period) and elsewhere has shown that successes have usually been achieved by long-term, highly focused research on one single commodity (Eicher 1984: 470, 1986*b*: 11–13). Lipton has aptly remarked that 'dispersion prevents any one group of scientists from applying, to any agricultural research challenge, the "critical mass" of time and interdisciplinary cooperation needed for progress' (Lipton 1985: 72). This certainly applies to Africa where difficult problems such as low soil fertility, serious livestock diseases, and destructive pest attacks cannot be resolved unless long-sustained research efforts (extending to ten or even twenty years) are devoted to them. In addition, African agricultural research centres have been seriously handicapped by numerous inefficiencies originating in poor personnel management and work discipline, lack of performance incentives and professional advancement, inadequate operating funds, high rates of staff turnover, untimely budgetary allocations, poor financial management and planning of resources (Spencer 1986: 222–3).

*Structural disadvantages: limited size of nation states and traditional consumption patterns*   Two structural disadvantages of Africa deserve to be pointed out in the context of the present discussion. The first one follows from the already noted smallness of many African nation states (see above, p. 309), a feature which was imposed on Africa by the old colonial powers at the time of independence. Indeed, the above argument about the negative effects of dispersion of research efforts on the rate of technical progress in agriculture takes on added significance if the absolute size of the research services or centres is small. Unfortunately, considerations of national prestige and autonomy have led the newly independent African states to dismantle the highly efficient regional research institutes which had been built during the colonial period, and to convert them into national institutes with much more limited resources at their disposal. Thus, for example, the famous EAAFRO (the East African Agriculture, Livestock and Forestry Research Organization) was dismantled after the breakup of the East African Community in 1974 so that 'the scientists in the 94 research stations in the EAAFRO network had to discontinue their cooperative research programs on common problems in Kenya, Tanzania and Uganda' (Eicher 1986*b*: 13–14).

The outcome of this parcelling out of the research set-up inherited from the colonial powers is truly alarming: only one-third of the African countries today have an agricultural research establishment above the critical size—about 100 scientists—required to run and test three adequate commodity programmes. To make matters worse, research workers are usually dispersed into many tiny stations which are supposed to cater to the differentiated needs of various agroclimatic zones and/or farming systems (Lipton 1985: 71–2; Spencer 1986: 233; Mellor and Delgado 1987: 3). Edjem Kodjo is therefore right to call on all African governments to create larger political spaces or entities because only they would allow for more systematic regional co-operation and enable the member-states to meet Africa's present and future challenges in a satisfactory way (Kodjo 1985). Such a move would actually mean a return to a long-established historical tradition in Africa, a tradition which was largely broken down by the colonial powers for political and administrative reasons (Coquery-Vidrovitch 1985: 127–35).

There is a second structural handicap which limits the possibilities of agricultural technical change open to Africa. This handicap arises from traditional consumption patterns that prevent Africa from benefiting from the international pool of scientific and technical knowledge to the same extent as Asia and Latin America. A striking feature about Asia's Green Revolution is that comparatively rapid advances could be made, from a relatively modest research investment, in the development of modern hybrid varieties of wheat and rice (wheat and maize for Latin America) transferable to tropical areas. We know today that such impressive results could not have been obtained if the prototype high-yielding varieties had not already been in existence in advanced, temperate zone countries (Japan, the United States, and Europe). In other words, modern biogenetic research targeted to the needs of Asian (and Latin American) tropical countries was 'able to draw on a large backlog of past research accomplishments on wheat and rice [and maize] in the temperate regions' (Hayami and Ruttan 1985: 270, 279). This is an important feature as it is increasingly recognized today that breakthroughs in agricultural research 'are often a result of past research in which a great deal of work has already been done' (Spencer 1986: 231).

In Africa, however, wheat and rice are not part of the traditional food diet and, even though we have noted that their consumption has risen quickly during the last decades, especially in urban areas, the main African staple foods still remain, with the exception of maize, traditional cereals (sorghum and millet), a variety of root and tuber crops (notably cassava, yams, and sweet potatoes), and pulses. In Central Africa, roots and tubers account for as much as 50 to 65 per cent of calorie intake and the proportion is still higher—from 65 to 80 per cent—in humid West, East, and Southern Africa (Spencer 1986: 232). Since such commodities are not consumed in the temperate regions, there was no backlog of readily available knowledge which African countries could draw upon. As a result, wrote Hayami and Ruttan in a cautious style, 'the flow of new technology from the newer [international research] institutes, and its impact on agricultural production, has proceeded more slowly. Accomplishments have taken the form of incremental gains rather than revolutionary breakthroughs' (1985: 270).

### (d)   The problematic shift to intensive agriculture: the issue of labour availability

*The urgent need for intensification*   Our analysis of Africa's natural resources and constraints has made it clear that the exhaustion of the land frontier in some countries and the high marginal cost of opening new land for cultivation in other countries have led to declining land–labour ratios in response to rising population pressure. It is in fact because land farming systems have remained basically extensive that Africa is characterized simultaneously by relatively low population densities and relatively high land pressure. A shift from extensive to intensive farming and livestock systems has therefore become inevitable if African agriculture is to avoid falling into a deepening crisis of sustainability. This is especially so as 'African soils tend to deteriorate quickly under conditions of increasingly regular or intense exploitation' (Berry 1984: 68; see also Delgado *et al.* 1987: 11). Note, however, that intensification is not an altogether new phenomenon in Africa since high population densities and intensive systems of cultivation were well established in areas of urban growth (e.g. Hausaland) or in areas subject to chronic insecurity (as in northern Cameroon, central Nigeria, and northern Tanzania where slave raiding prevented mountain-dwellers from moving freely into the plains), long before European incursions of the late nineteenth and early twentieth centuries (Berry 1984: 69, 87–8; see also Pingali *et al.* 1987: 49–50).

Intensification of agriculture will not always take the form of irrigation development—particularly that of modern irrigation systems with complete control of water—because, as we saw, Africa's irrigation potential is rather limited and many African irrigation projects are costly in economic terms (see above, pp. 320–2). In many cases, at least for a long time to come, it will have to take place under rainfed conditions within the framework of dryland farming systems. In consequence, most land productivity increases will arise from higher crop yields and better crop mixes rather than from enhanced cropping intensity. This will hold especially true in arid and semi-arid areas where the rainy season is short and access to water difficult or costly.

Now, whatever the circumstances in which it occurs and whatever the exact forms it takes, intensification of land use generally requires the application of increasing amounts of labour (and other inputs) to a given cultivated area. This is so not only because current productive operations (such as land preparation, fertilizing, weeding, harvesting, and animal husbandry) require comparatively large doses of labour when the productivity of the land is increased, but also because many labour investment activities associated with land (such as levelling, destumping, terracing, draining, bunding, and irrigating) are an indispensable component of agricultural intensification. Strictly speaking, the agricultural soil must be gradually 'constructed' (Giri 1983: 222, 1986: 64), as is clearly evident from the history of agricultural development in Europe, Asia, and pre-Columbian Latin America. In these continents, vast amounts of family and village labour have been used to build fences, pick stones, remove stumps, construct flood embankments, level and terrace land, drain water, and so forth, all labour-intensive and hard works which have mobilized many generations of farmers (Boserup 1965; Ishikawa 1981; Bray 1983, 1986; Eicher 1985: 88). Equally important is the fact that investment labour is also required on a recurrent basis in order to maintain the land infrastructures once they have been built. Indeed, if the soil can be 'constructed', it can also be destroyed, and the process of soil destruction is especially rapid in countries—like those of Africa—where problems such as leaching, wind or water erosion, and flooding are permanent threats.

*The problem of labour shortage*   It is, therefore, an inescapable reality that, in Africa as elsewhere, increasing and stabilizing agricultural yields will take time and require enormous inputs of labour. For technical and economic reasons, the use of mechanical devices—assuming that African countries can afford them and have the capacity to service them properly—and of other labour-saving technologies will substitute only partially for labour. As pointed out above, there are historical antecedents of intensive agriculture in Africa. Some areas have overtly stridden along the road to intensification, like the Dogon area in Mali and the Kirdi area in Cameroon (Giri 1986: 64). None the less, the general picture gives much less support for optimism regarding the pace at which Africa will be able to make her transition from extensive to intensive agriculture. Evidence of this is provided by the disappointing performance of irrigated farming, various schemes for intensive culture (including fish culture), and many soil conservation or land improvement programs during the last twenty or thirty years. Moreover, many observers of the African scene would agree with Goran Hyden that 'more labor-intensive husbandry is a necessary corollary to the adoption of yield-increasing technologies. Yet, this is not happening on the average peasant farm in Africa' (Hyden 1986: 60). Since it would be simplistic to assume that this failure can be attributed solely to state mismanagement or corruption, we must look for other factors or constraints operating in the African countryside. In this respect, the increasingly oft-cited evidence of labour shortage (Berry 1984: 86; Lele 1984: 445; Mathieu 1985a; FAO 1986: Main Report, ch. 4; Delgado and Ranade 1987: 124–30) appears to be a central and perhaps paradoxical cause of retarded—or blocked—intensification of agriculture in Africa. What is not clear, however, is the exact nature of this labour scarcity and the factors which account for its emergence.

A first possibility, or a partial explanation of the afore-mentioned phenomenon, is that labour shortages are largely seasonal. In the circumstances, acute dearths of labour during the short peak season—the rainy season in rainfed agriculture—can be reconciled with the fact that 'unemployment and underemployment of rural labor are also increasing, particularly where population pressure on land is rising rapidly' (Lele 1984: 445). The question then is: why do African farmers not make better use of the time available during the off season, as their Asian counterparts did, to build up, consolidate, restore, maintain, and repair rural infrastructures which can improve the land and ensure a better spread of agricultural activities across the year? Another possibility is that labour shortages result largely from rural outmigration (of a transitory, circulatory or permanent kind), or from the development of off-farm work opportunities. This fact is as well documented as that of marked seasonal variations in agricultural demand for labour in dryland farming systems. Thus, it has been found that rural poverty often forces people to seek off-farm employment to supplement meagre income from agricultural activities, and that smallholding households (in countries like Kenya, Lesotho, Tanzania, Burundi, Senegal, Burkina Faso, Zambia, Niger) may derive a substantial part of their annual income from such off-farm sources (Berry 1984: 81–3; Hyden 1986: 55–7; Mathieu 1987: i, ch. 2; FACAGRO and ISA 1989).

A straightforward interpretation of the increasing commitment of African smallholders to non-agricultural activities is that the expected income from these activities is higher than the implicit returns to their on-farm labour (Delgado and Ranade 1987: 129), and/or that vulnerability to risk of falling into distress is thereby reduced thanks to diversification of their activity portfolio. From there, it would be tempting to conclude that intensification of agricultural production is not justifiable on the grounds of allocative efficiency considerations and that African countries would do better to develop by diversifying their production into non-food activities. Even though the necessity of economic diversification in Africa is indisputable, it does not follow from this that agricultural intensification should be eschewed. Indeed, the above conclusion can be criticized from several angles. First, since intensification of agriculture involves the production of capital goods (including land improvements) and since there are obviously no futures' markets where anticipations about future returns could be taken into account, maximizing behaviour on the part of private agents is not conducive to intertemporal social optimality. Of course, uncertainty regarding future returns is not restricted to the agricultural sector and, as such, it cannot be considered as a conclusive argument in favour of encouraging agricultural production. Rather, the point it serves to emphasize is that the existence of comparatively low returns in agriculture is not a sufficient reason for giving up agricultural production if technical changes can be introduced in this sector and if a long-term perspective is adopted (as it should always be when development strategies are discussed). The fact that investments associated with these technical changes require comparatively low amounts of foreign exchange is an important consideration. It should prompt African states to incite their farmers—through education, material incentives, or more direct support—to undertake works and to make technological shifts that are or could be socially profitable in the longer run. Note incidentally that there is a comparatively great role for public sector investments in technological change in Africa since in many parts of the continent the resource base for rural capital accumulation is rather narrow due to low average labour productivity (Delgado and Ranade 1987: 124, 134).

Second, alternative incomes obtained outside the agricultural sector may have a non-productive origin in the sense that they do not result from the creation of new value added but from simple income transfers. Not infrequently, these transfers have a more or less forced character as witnessed by the spawning of thiefs and crooks of all hues in many African big cities.

Third, important externalities are involved in the individual decisions taken by African farmers so that, on this ground also, the market cannot be expected to perform efficiently. For instance, by neglecting to take soil conservation measures on his own plot of land for the sake of increasing his short-term private income, a farmer may cause a decrease in the productive capacity of his neighbours' lands. Therefore, low agricultural incomes obtained in an environment dominated by unhampered competitive market forces (or by inefficient institutional arrangements) do not give a correct idea of the potential incomes which could be earned under a more congenial system of economic regulation.

Finally, it is too simple to assume that migration decisions are exclusively influenced by economic considerations. Thus, the desire to escape from the hierarchical social structure of many African village societies may be an important determinant of migratory moves by young male villagers. Indeed, it is a well-known feature of traditional lineage societies in Africa that social relations are strongly differentiated on the basis of age (and sex).

There is yet another possible cause of labour shortage in intensive farming activities. It deserves to be dealt with at some length not only because, for reasons that will soon become apparent, it is largely ignored or underplayed in the specialized literature, but also because it is capable of resolving questions that are left unanswered by the above two lines of argument. Two such questions arise from facts commonly observed in areas where modern irrigation facilities are available:

- Why is it that, during the peak agricultural season, African cultivators often appear to give preference to traditional rainfed farming over irrigated farming, even though the latter could afford them higher and more reliable incomes than the former?
- How can we account for the fact that, even during the off season, farmers working in modern irrigation schemes tend to treat maintenance and repair works in a rather casual way? And, more generally, how can we

explain that African farmers are 'often more concerned with saving labor than conserving cultivated area' (Berry 1984: 86), even where there is an acute shortage of land?

Related to the latter observation is the well-documented and sobering experience that in the Sahelian states of West Africa, 'the amount of new land being brought under irrigation each year (around 5,000 hectares) is roughly equal to the amount being abandoned each year *because of neglect and lack of maintenance*' (Eicher 1986a: 4; see also Johnston 1986: 170). The situation was somewhat better in Senegal between 1982 and 1983, since the SAED came very close to achieving the ambitious objective set out for it by the government: to bring 2,575 hectares of new land under irrigation in the Senegal river valley. However, half of the tremendous effort made by the SAED (construction of new facilities over 2,400 ha) was lost because 1,200 hectares of irrigated land were in the meantime abandoned following degradation of the infrastructure (Mathieu 1985a: 655).

As for the former observation, a recent FAO in-depth study of African agriculture has reported that:

Modern irrigation schemes have commonly suffered from the farmers' insistence on maintaining the traditional diversity of their rural activities. On projects in Sierra Leone, the Gambia and Madagascar, planting of wet season irrigated rice was delayed until labour was released from work on rainfed crops elsewhere, thus reducing potential yields and overall irrigation intensity. Destitute pastoral nomads settled on small-scale government irrigation schemes in Northern Kenya remained only until they had accumulated enough money to re-establish their herds and resume a nomadic life; plots were then left with women or sharecroppers. (FAO 1986: Annex IV, ch. 5, para. 5.24)

It is worth noticing that the observation that 'priority is given to the rainfed area as soon as the rains arrive' (ibid. para. 5.23) applies not only where the irrigated crop is a cash (export) crop such as cotton or sugarcane, but also where it is an (admittedly unfamiliar) foodcrop such as rice grown in modern irrigation schemes or even a traditional staple food grown in traditional flood irrigation systems (see, for example, Engelhard and Ben Abdallah 1986; Diemer and Van der Laan 1987).

*Aversion to intensive work*   A partial clue to the afore-mentioned relative neglect of intensive farming in Africa lies in the existence of a cultural bias against the type of work implied in intensive farming practices. This bias follows from the fact that Africa has a millenary tradition of extensive agricultural and pastoral activities which get inevitably reflected in her cultural patterns and values. One could therefore argue that Africa is not only characterized by an extensive *agriculture* but also by an extensive *culture*, that is by a culture whose world-view is rooted in the idea of an infinite or boundless space. On the level of labour requirements, extensive agriculture and stock-farming present two noteworthy features. First, the productive tasks involved can be performed with a relatively light work burden because the favourable man–land ratio makes long-fallow agriculture (or pastoral nomadism) possible. Boserup has gathered data showing that labour input is relatively low in different parts of Africa where both subsistence food crops and export crops are being produced: average weekly work hours in agriculture turned out to be fourteen hours for men and boys and fifteen hours for women and girls. The work burden carried by women is of course much larger since they have to perform domestic chores in addition to their agricultural duties. However, for the family as a whole, and for men in particular, the total work burden is no doubt lighter than that of smallholding families in more densely populated areas with more intensive agricultural systems (Boserup 1981: 147–8). Just to take one example, under intensive farming practices, natural processes can no more be relied upon to restore the fertility of the land. Fertilizer must be applied by man and this operation takes time in so far as long walks are needed to collect the required manure, or manure crops have to be grown in some of the fields. Since these operations have to be repeated, off-season periods of leisure or non-agricultural work are bound to be reduced (ibid. 46). This is in stark contrast to the situation obtaining in African dryland systems. Indeed, if African farmers perform long and intense work hours during the relatively short agricultural season (since good soils are rock hard at the end of the dry season farmers cannot prepare the land before the onset of the rains), there is typically little work to be done during the following long dry season (Pacey and Payne 1985: 27–8; Delgado and Ranade 1987: 128). In fact, labour inputs per hectare in most of Africa are reported to be 'very low' (Delgado and Ranade 1987: 122).

A second essential feature of labour performances under extensive farming systems is that productive tasks involve much less drudgery than those required by intensive farming systems. Thus, it is certainly easier to sow broadcast in an open field than to transplant rice seedlings in an irrigation scheme: while the cultivator can almost stand up while accomplishing the former agricultural operation, he (or she) must break his (or her) back and sink into mud to perform the latter. Also, it is apparently a more comfortable task to open a new field through the slash-and-burn technique when the existing land has become exhausted, than to take constant care of the same piece of land (or animals) in order to ensure that its long-term productivity is not impaired. Indeed, the latter strategy involves considerable 'husbandry skill', continuous and painstaking efforts to build up and maintain protective dikes, flood embankments, draining canals, conservation ditches, and so forth.

Intensive farming systems thus involve far more complicated, labour-consuming, and toilsome processes than extensive systems. Therefore, it should not come as a surprise that people who have been accustomed for millenia to extensive (agricultural and stock) farming practices look at the prospect of intensifying production with some strong reluctance and distrust. This attitude is especially noticeable among the old-age classes whose values and beliefs crystallize the history of the society's past practices. As always, young farmers display more enterprise and resilience in the face of new challenges. Consequently, the relative position of the young-age classes in village relations of power is bound to play a determining role in the rate of adoption of intensive farming practices. Opposition of the elders to their aspirations for change—on the basis of traditional authority patterns—can only prompt them to escape from rural poverty through migration, a decision which has long-run adverse effects on the economic future of the villages as well as on the future ability of the domestic food supply systems to feed growing populations.

Several writers have noticed the strong aversion which African village elders may display for the type of work required by agricultural intensification, and many field-observers of African rural realities could join them on this point. Intensive practices are often considered as debasing and status-lowering, just good to be performed by slaves, subordinates, or women. Thus, Catherine Coquery-Vidrovitch has reported that the Zarma peasants in Niger have strong cultural prejudices against the growing of rice in modern irrigation schemes:

Walking backwards for the transplantation of rice is traditionally considered by old people as 'slave's labour' which 'brings misfortunes'. It is for this reason that such people have refused to adopt the work cadences which the Chinese have introduced in the Kolo irrigation scheme at the door of Niamey. The Chinese have since turned to the young . . . and, in spite of the difficulties encountered, the results appear promising. (Coquery-Vidrovitch 1985: 187; my translation)

Another author has pointed out that among the Mandingues rice-growing activities have been entrusted to women (Singleton 1983: 7), which reveals the low status of this occupation since in Africa women are often treated as beasts of burden (Coquery-Vidrovitch 1985: 151). In Zambia, weeding is considered too degrading for men and has remained a typically female activity (Pausewang 1987: 8). In the same vein, it is not uncommon to see old farmers who have taken to irrigated farming entrusting the actual work to share-croppers of inferior socio-economic status (Mathieu 1985b, 1987: i. 148; Engelhard and Abdallah 1986: 141). More generally, Keith Hart has remarked that 'the social and material conditions that would compel a laborer to work like an Asian peasant, up to his knees in paddy water . . . do not yet exist in West Africa' (Hart 1982: 88–9). An FAO study came to a similar conclusion when it emphasized recently that under the present circumstances 'labour availability for intensive production under irrigation is likely to remain a serious concern for some time to come in parts of sub-Saharan Africa with little tradition of intensive irrigation' (FAO 1986: Annex IV, ch. 5, para. 5.23). One of the main barriers to the spread of intensive systems of production would lie in the fact that they demand 'more time and cash' than the African farmers have been accustomed to commit to traditional agriculture (ibid. ch. 3, para. 3.8).

A clear indication of the unwillingness of many African farmers to adopt intensive farming practices—as illustrated again by the case of irrigated farming—is provided by the well-documented fact that acceptable commitment of the irrigators has usually been obtained only where few other options existed for them. For example, small- and medium-scale village irrigation schemes in Senegal (along the river Senegal), Mali (along the river Niger), and Burkina Faso (using small dams) have been successful whenever smallholders could no more satisfy their food consumption needs from rainfed or flood-recession farming due to severe drought conditions (ibid. ch. 2, para. 2.40, and ch. 5, para. 5.30; Boutillier 1980: Hart 1982: 89; Mathieu 1983a, 1983b, 1987). In the Soninké villages of Senegal, it has been observed that the cultivators who have shifted most resolutely to irrigated farming are people from lower socio-economic strata (descendants of slaves, sons of artisans, or outsiders) who do not possess any land of their own and can have access to flood-recession lands only on costly terms (Weigel 1982a: 321–3). Revealingly, however, when some alternative opportunities exist to work outside the village, outmigration is often preferred to intensive farming. Thus, the Sarakollé from the Senegal river valley have migrated almost everywhere in West Africa and, not infrequently, they have travelled much longer distances (up to France) to find work. In the same way, many young Mossi (from Burkina Faso) have settled in Ghana and the Ivory Coast. By contrast, the Mafas of northern Cameroon, blocked in their mountains, first by the persecutions of the empires of the Chadian Basin and thereafter by those of the Foulbé sultans, had no other alternative than to intensify their system of production at the cost of tremendous efforts (Giri 1983: 222).

To sum up, in the many parts of Africa where there is practically no tradition of intensive farming (notable exceptions are Northern Africa, Madagascar, Nigeria, and Guinea-Bissau), villagers usually have a strong aversion to the kind of work required by the intensification of agriculture (and stock farming). Cultural prejudices against intensive work—particularly among the elder male members of the village communities—reveal the profound dislike of African farmers for long work hours and toilsome productive tasks carried out on a continuous basis. Therefore, intensive farming tends to be taken up as a last resort when all other income-earning possibilities have been exhausted or have vanished. And, even then, there is a tendency to entrust the 'dirty' work to low-status people, including women. If intensive farming is not perceived as a survival necessity, villagers are likely to prefer more leisure to more income, so high is the disutility associated with intensive work. Young farmers, none the less, do not necessarily react in this way, especially so if the elder members of the village community allow them a sufficient margin of freedom and if the income prospects afforded by intensive farming are reasonably good.

*Perverse effects, self-defeating strategies or self-fulfilling prophecies*  The above-described situation is typical of a transition period and, as such, it is basically unstable. It is unstable because it is fraught with inner contradictions which

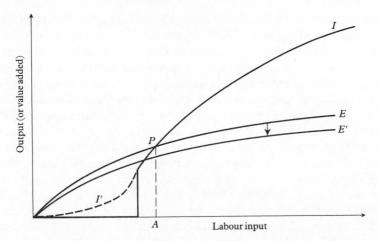

**Fig. 6.1** Hypothetical relations between 'extensive' and 'intensive' production curves with certain outcomes

render the results of many intensive enterprises or projects rather unpredictable. As a matter of fact, intensive agriculture is characterized by 'threshold-effects', meaning that if minimum amounts of labour input are not applied (e.g. for gathering and application of fertilizers, for maintenance of land infrastructure), its productive performance is likely to be inferior to that of current extensive farming practices.[30]

This situation is depicted in Fig. 6.1, where labour input is measured along the horizontal axis and agricultural output along the vertical axis. Curve $E$ is a production curve which shows the maximum amount of produce that, say, a village can get for each amount of labour input through an expansion in cultivated land area (whether this is achieved via additional deforestation, shortening of the fallow period, or otherwise): following Hayami and Ruttan (1985: 310), we may call this strategy 'external land augmentation'. This curve has a conventional Ricardian shape since its slope is continuously decreasing to reflect diminishing returns to labour as lands of lower fertility are brought under cultivation. As for curve $I$, it is supposed to describe an 'internal land augmentation' strategy in which labour efforts are applied to improved land

---

[30] Thus, in a modern irrigation scheme (with complete control of water) in Timbuktu (Mali), it was found that in the plots where the technique of broadcast sowing (without recourse to fertilizer) was used, the average yield per hectare was not much higher than that obtained under more traditional farming systems (including flood irrigation systems). But it was much lower than the average yield obtained by those irrigators who applied fertilizers and used the technique of transplantation. Moreover, the variability of yields was much lower in the latter than in the former case in spite of the fact that the control of water was good in both cases. Calculations of net monetary returns per labour input unit confirmed the above differentials (Islands of Peace 1984, 1985, 1986). The lesson to be drawn from this example is straightforward: there is no sense in applying extensive farming practices (broadcast sowing and no application of fertilizer) to land improvement infrastructures designed for intensive farming.

infrastructure and farmers use land-augmenting technologies. Curve $I$ exhibits a discontinuity to reflect the indivisibility referred to above. Or, alternatively, a curve $I'$ may be constructed which is comprised of two phases: a first phase during which output is low but increases quickly as additional labour inputs are applied, and a second, more conventional phase, during which returns to labour are declining. Because of the pressure of population on land, curves $I$ and $I'$ rise above curve $E$ beyond the crossover point $P$, but if farmers put in less than $OA$ units of labour efforts, the 'internal land augmentation' strategy will be less productive than that of 'external land augmentation'. However, in so far as the latter strategy causes a gradual decline in the fertility of all the existing village lands (e.g. because of increased soil erosion following new encroachments upon the forest lands), the production curve $E$ will shift downward from $E$ to $E'$, thus increasing in due time the relative advantage of intensification for a given amount of labour input and lowering the crossover point beyond which curve $I$ rises above curve $E$.

From the above conceptualization or 'stylization' of the relations between 'internal' and 'external' land augmentation strategies, it is easy to understand how the transition from extensive to intensive agriculture can be arrested due to the operation of 'perverse' effects. Indeed, if African smallholders are reluctant to devote enough time and efforts to intensive agriculture—because of their perception of the risks and costs of adoption of intensive farming practices (including the disutility associated with toilsome intensive work)[31] —a vicious circle 'low returns—insufficient application of inputs—low returns' may easily develop (Platteau 1985: 96–7). This will result in a kind of 'self-fulfilling prophecy', since the farmers will be able to mention the disappointing results obtained from intensification to vindicate and strengthen their belief that it is not worth the trouble and the drudgery it requires.

The problem is in fact more complicated than is suggested by Fig. 6.1, because outcomes are not certain. It could be argued, therefore, that the reluctance of African smallholders to adopt intensive farming practices arises from the fact that these practices are not only perceived as costly in terms of utility, but also considered to increase vulnerability to risk irrespective of their being new and unfamiliar. In this context, the oft-noted observation that African farmers are unwilling 'to abandon the traditional risk-spreading strategy of a mix of agricultural activities in favour of full-time work on the irrigated plot provided by the government' (FAO 1986: Annex IV, ch. 3, para. 3.8) would appear revealing. Yet, this is not an entirely convincing argument since some intensive agricultural technologies are ostensibly designed to reduce risk (Ghatak and Ingersent 1984: 15). Improved water management in drought- and flood-prone areas is a case in point. In the circumstances, risk aversion on the part of smallholders may not be a valid—or complete

---

[31] Bear in mind that labour input units measured along the horizontal axis in Fig. 6.1 are not 'utility-wise' homogeneous since the disutility associated with 'intensive' labour efforts is much higher than that associated with 'extensive' efforts.

—explanation for their reluctance to shift to intensive farming practices on a full-time basis. Once again, it would appear difficult to account satisfactorily for such behaviour without bringing cultural or non-economic factors into the picture.

It has already been noted (1) that African smallholders often have recourse to full-time irrigated farming only when no other alternative is available, and (2) that they tend to return (or give renewed priority) to rainfed farming as soon as the rain comes back in sufficient quantities, be it within the season itself or during a forthcoming agricultural year. The latter phenomenon has been widely observed in West Africa in the years 1985–6, when Sahelian farmers responded to the return of abundant rains by abandoning the modern irrigation schemes in which they had taken refuge during the drought years. What deserves to be stressed in the context of the present discussion is that this kind of unstable attitude on the part of the producers is likely to reinforce the afore-mentioned 'perverse' effect. Indeed, continuous and unpredictable shifts between rainfed extensive farming and intensive agriculture tend inevitably to thwart labour and other investments in land improvements. Unless public agencies are ready to maintain the new land infrastructures when the peasants are not forthcoming to do the job themselves, or to impose upon the latter a minimum of discipline, the capital which these infrastructures represent will be degraded and its future productive capacity will be inexorably impaired. As a consequence of their self-defeating strategies, farmers will thus be caught in a basically precarious situation since their livelihood will no more be guaranteed in times of unfavourable weather.

In Fig. 6.2, a situation has been described in which intensive farming eventually becomes almost technically inferior to extensive agriculture due to

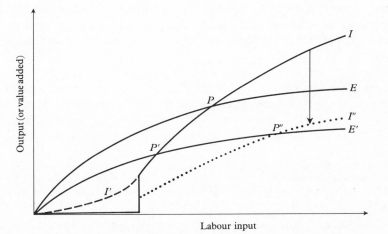

**Fig. 6.2** Hypothetical relations between 'extensive' and 'intensive' production curves with uncertain outcomes

severe neglect and lack of maintenance of land improvement infrastructures. Curve $E$ is the production function which obtains under rainfed farming when rainfall is reasonably adequate in terms of both quantity and timing pattern. Curve $E'$ is also a rainfed farming production curve but it is observed when drought conditions prevail. A single intensive farming production function is assumed to obtain under both 'states of the world', reflecting the fact that intensive agriculture is supposed to be potentially both yield-increasing and yield-stabilizing or risk-reducing. The relative advantage of technology $I$ over technology $E$ is therefore greater when drought conditions occur, not only because the distance between the two curves is then larger, but also because the crossover point shifts leftwards (from $P$ to $P'$). Provided that the disutility associated with intensive work is not too high and that individual preferences are not too skewed in favour of leisure (the marginal rate of substitution of leisure for income is not too high), the farmers would maximize their inter-temporal utility by making a complete shift to intensive agriculture. If this is not the case, however, the risk is high that land improvement infrastructures will not be properly maintained. In Fig. 6.2, such a neglect would be reflected in a downward shift of the intensive production curve from $I$ to $I''$ and there would be a real possibility that intensive farming practices become less profitable than extensive practices, even under conditions of poor weather (curve $I''$ is below curve $E'$ over most of the relevant range). Eventually, the interest of the farmers would lie in sticking to their traditional agricultural system!

It is worth noticing, incidentally, that in conditions such as those analysed above, it is very difficult to assess the comparative profitability of intensive and extensive farming practices. In particular, conclusions that irrigation schemes are unprofitable in many parts of Africa ought to be qualified or stated in a less peremptory way than they often are.[32] It is a lesson to be learned that such comparative exercises or cost–benefit analyses are extremely delicate and difficult to interpret in conditions of agricultural transition or rapid technical change.

*The myth of the good peasant*    The kind of analysis that has been offered here is not much in vogue among development specialists nowadays. Many social scientists consider that one cannot really talk about 'a general cultural bias against labor intensive practices' without implying the 'pejorative view' that

---

[32] It is often suggested that village irrigated agriculture is not (very) rewarding because net monetary income is negative, after having deducted rice for family consumption from the gross produce (Coquery-Vidrovitch 1985: 177; Haubert and Frelin 1985: 27; Mathieu 1985*b*: 55). But this is no convincing evidence since there is no economic sense in effecting this subtraction to arrive at conclusions about the profitability of this technique. However, what the above evidence shows unambiguously is that the irrigated plots are too narrow to provide for the irrigator's family livelihood and that they are just a supplementary source of income and consumption. In fact, such plots are also a narrow basis for employment as it appears that average weekly work hours on them do not usually exceed a few hours.

African farmers are lazy (see e.g. Berry 1984: 69, 97 n. 4). This is of course a *non sequitur* as all economists acquainted with the subjective theories of peasant equilibrium know very well. However, by insisting that farmers in Third World countries behave so as to maximize their (expected) incomes or profits (after allowing for risk considerations and, possibly, for transaction costs), economists have actually lent credence to the view that values play no role in the choices made by agricultural producers. Moreover, this restricted type of peasant rationality is supposed to hold not only with respect to static allocative decisions but also with respect to innovation and change: farmers are receptive to innovation provided that the changes contemplated are 'appropriate', that is low cost, low risk, and fitting well into the traditional agricultural cycle. This myth of the 'good peasant' which emerged as a (rather healthy) reaction against the long-lived prejudiced view of the irrational peasant is also a reflection, in the field of agrarian economics, of the proclivity of the economic profession to produce complete explanations of individual behaviours on the basis of economic variables alone.

In fact, recognition that peasants may have a strong aversion to labour-intensive practices does not imply that they behave irrationally in the economic sense. This is evident from the fact that such an assumption can be easily accommodated into the neo-classical framework by entering two distinct types of labour (extensive and intensive), in addition to income and leisure, into the peasant's utility function, and by assuming that each type of labour is associated with a different production technique. The disutility of intensive labour may then be so high as to exceed the utility increments associated with the extra incomes resulting from application of intensive technologies (assuming constant leisure).

This said, the central problem is not whether agricultural producers behave rationally when considered individually (according to economic theory, they are rational by assumption), but whether the social outcomes they produce together are desirable when assessed in a long-term perspective. The foregoing analysis purported to show that, if sufficient attention is paid to cultural factors such as the norms, values, and beliefs which shape the individuals' preference orderings or limit the range of feasible strategies, there is a real possibility of rational farmers producing socially disastrous long-term results. To understand this, it must be borne in mind that individual behaviours are influenced by collectively produced cultural patterns that reflect past experiences of people's adaptation to their environment as well as the customary ways in which they have been interpreted and evaluated by the society concerned. In most parts of Africa, these experiences are clearly tied to a long tradition of land-extensive agricultural practices. It is therefore no wonder that local cultures have tended to emphasize the merits of the way of life implied by land-extensive farming systems and to underplay or even deride alternative systems of production and social life.

The problem arises because cultural systems do not adjust instantaneously to marked changes in environmental parameters, in particular to rising pressure of population on land resources. To say this is not to contend that African meaning and agrarian systems are fundamentally conservative or rigid. They are bound to change and they have already started to evolve, particularly under the pressure of new dramatic challenges and under the aegis of young age-classes (for evidence of this, see Pingali and Binswanger 1986). But a transitory period cannot be escaped during which Africa will be relatively handicapped because she is equipped with an *extensive culture* at a time when she must shift to *intensive agriculture*. Such a contradiction underlies the observation made by FAO experts that 'only in a relatively few cases has the fundamental conflict between traditional sub-Saharan attitudes to agriculture and the intensive demands of modern irrigation been satisfactorily resolved' (FAO 1986: Annex IV, ch. 5, para. 5.30). Policy makers as well as intellectuals would do well to reflect on this a little more than they usually do. Indeed, the length of the transition period is not a priori determined and, depending upon the approach to rural education and agricultural extension, this period may be rather short or become dangerously long.

It may also be noted that the so-called common property resource problem, to which economists usually refer to explain why individually rational actions sometimes produce socially harmful effects, cannot be analysed without mentioning cultural factors at some point. Thus, a crucial question which suggests itself is why the traditional modes of resource management and of control of access have ceased to play their customary regulatory role.

*Towards a more balanced assessment*   Now, much in the same way as it is simplistic to attribute all the woes of Africa to policy mistakes committed by local governments, it would be absurd to ascribe the rigidity of agrarian systems, to the extent that it exists, solely to inappropriate—even though understandable—attitudes on the part of smallholder producers. Cultural factors in general must also be considered to shed only partial light on the problematic shift of Africa from extensive to intensive agriculture. If they were largely brought into focus in the above discussion, it is only because they are systematically downplayed in most analyses of Africa's current food crisis. In such complex matters, single-factor explanations cannot be trustworthy. It is nevertheless evident that a number of causes which are commonly pointed at in the specialized literature can be roughly summarized under one heading: *organizational problems*. These problems usually originate in both the state and the rural communities:

Group action by farmers or public investment by the government is required and in turn demands both leadership and discipline. These qualities cannot be developed immediately as the need arises; such organizational capacity and habit grow in a rural society only over time, perhaps several generations. (Hayami and Ruttan 1985: 312).

With particular reference to irrigation, one can agree with Uma Lele that 'in most of Africa there is not the complex institutional and managerial capacity to operate irrigation systems indigenously' (Lele 1984: 441). Perhaps the most commonly cited problems of organization are those linked with the rationing or the delayed distribution of crucial inputs, such as fertilizers, new seed varieties, credit, or spare parts for transport, irrigation, and production equipment. Difficulties at the level of national economic management and balance-of-payments deficits, absence or imperfection of essential markets (most notably, capital and insurance markets), and inopportune interferences of the state with the development of local markets are all factors to which such deficiencies may be traced back.

The technical challenge posed by the required technological shift must not be underestimated either. For farmers accustomed to extensive farming practices, intensification of agricultural production represents a complete departure from the past:

It is not only a question of mastering the complexities of the numerous cultural operations involved in the new technology: think of the need for a right spacing of the seedlings in the nursery when the transplanting technique is used for rice cultivation; or of the split application of fertilizers at various stages of the vegetative cycle of the plant; or of the need for an adequate drainage in order to prevent salinity. It is also a question of performing efficiently the mechanical tasks (lest the motor pumps would break down or wear out quickly) as well as the management tasks (if the gasoil is not available in the right quantities in the right time, the whole system is disrupted) which are an essential component of the new technologies. (Platteau 1985: 97)

In the case of irrigated farming again, major problems often arise from structural defects in irrigation systems which are clearly the responsibility of state agencies or foreign contractors and consulting bureaux. When systems of water control are not adequate, farmers lose confidence in timely and adequate water arrivals, and they justifiably tend to run away from irrigation schemes.

It is not difficult to understand how the above mishaps, deficiencies, and dysfunctionings can significantly increase the riskiness of—and reduce the motivation for—adoption of intensive farming practices, thus postponing further the time at which Africa will be able to meet adequately her food challenge. But the fundamental fact must be accepted that it will take time to resolve all these problems. An essential lesson from the Asian experience is precisely that considerable periods of social adjustment and institutional development are needed before intensive agriculture (as well as intensive stock-raising and fish farming) can be made to work satisfactorily. The experience of North Africa points to the same conclusion (FAO 1986: Annex IV, ch. 3). It is no doubt true that sub-Saharan Africa can learn and take inspiration from solutions evolved in Asia (see Lipton 1985) and North Africa. Yet, as in the case of new seed varieties, Africa cannot escape the need to go through the lengthy and painful process of learning by doing which solutions suit best her own environmental and social conditions. In the words of Goran Hyden:

governments and donors alike have ignored the narrow margins of survival that characterize African countries at all levels. Above all, they have failed to adequately look for African solutions to African problems . . . It is high time, therefore, that the present crisis in Africa is recognized to a very large extent as the product of human arrogance and impatience in years past. Africa's problems are not primarily its backwardness and poverty, but rather the unwillingness of those concerned to accept that the continent is caught in its own historical process of development . . . They [African governments] have almost totally ignored the fact that development is a do-it-yourself process. (Hyden 1986: 53, 65)

### (e)    The problematic shift to intensive agriculture: the issue of property rights

*The presumed inadequacy of existing land tenure systems*    Traditional land tenure systems are often regarded as a major impediment to the growth of agricultural output and productivity in Africa. Only a few authors would probably go as far as Jacques Giri when he says that Africa is in need of a genuine land reform (Giri 1983: 271).[33] But it may be taken for granted that most of them would agree with Eicher that 'land tenure and land use policy issues will be of strategic importance in the 1980s and 1990s as the frontier phase is exhausted, land markets emerge, irrigation is expanded, and herders shift from nomadic to seminomadic herding and sedentary farming systems that integrate crops and livestock' (Eicher 1984: 455–6).

The main thrust of the argument could be formulated as follows: there is a fundamental disequilibrium or misfit between existing land arrangements that reflect a long tradition of extensive farming practices and the requirements of growth in the context of intensive agriculture. More precisely, communal control over access to land and the absence of active rural land markets are supposed to discourage investment in land improvements, careful soil husbandry practices, and intense and continuous labour efforts. As a matter of fact, there appear to be two rather distinct theses in this argument which are not always clearly distinguished by their proponents. Both are nevertheless well-known views commonly expounded in the literature about contractual choice, property rights, and transaction costs (see e.g. Demsetz 1967; Williamson 1985; Binswanger and Rosenzweig 1986).

The first thesis assumes the existence of communal tenure (or arrangements allowing multiple interests in a given piece of land) and considers it to be a major disincentive to labour and investment efforts and to conservation practices because decision-making is diffused among many persons (management problem); because the risk of labour-shirking or asset mismanagement is comparatively high while the cost of controlling it is also substantial (transaction cost problem); and because the effectiveness of sharing incentives is low, especially if the produce has to be distributed in accordance with social rules or norms (incentive problem). Of course, all these difficulties are assumed to be

---

[33] Thus, for example, Keith Hart wrote that 'land reform is not a significant issue in West Africa, but reform of the land law is' (Hart 1982: 92).

greater as the size of the social unit in which land rights are vested increases.

Thus, attention has often been drawn to serious deficiencies in land husbandry and conservation measures that result from the open access nature of
many African lands:

Communal and allocated lands are frequently abused because neither farmers nor
graziers feel any responsibility for their conservation. To the farmer there is little to be
gained from constructing conservation ditches if they are to be trampled by another's
cattle when farms are open to communal grazing after harvest. In some rangeland areas
it often pays the herder to over-use the forage; if he does not, someone else will and he
will be the loser. (FAO 1986: Annex II, ch. 9, para. 9.22; see also Platteau 1985: 98;
FAO 1986: Main Report, ch. 4, para. 4.89)

It is interesting to note that the above problem—usually referred to as the
'common-property resource problem' or 'the tragedy of the commons'—
would not arise if land was available in plenty and/or if the internal solidarity or
the authority structure in the group controlling the land was strong enough to
enforce adequate management rules. As we know, the first condition ceased to
characterize most parts of Africa only recently due to increasing pressure of
population on land resources. Violation of the second condition—i.e. the
existence of effective social structures that discourage opportunistic behaviour
on the part of their members—is the result of several complex factors such as
commercialization of agriculture, large incidence of migration, interventions
from state systems of bureaucratic control, redefinition of social rules of access
to productive resources under the impact of colonialism and post-
independence national policies, and so forth. It is also true, however, that the
two conditions are narrowly interrelated since opportunities of conflicts over
land-use rights increase considerably when land becomes scarce, and they may
thereby undermine or thwart the conflict-management capacity of traditional
social systems.

The second and main criticism of communal tenure clearly assumes a system
of individualized occupancy: land is held and controlled by a social group
which allocates it to individual households for their personal use. Here, the
crux of the argument is that traditional systems of communal tenure in Africa
do not provide security of tenure. As a result of this insecurity, farmers are
reluctant to invest in physical capital and to adopt innovations that would
increase the value of their land for fear that the benefits would be appropriated
by other persons and would not accrue to their own children (see e.g.
Christodoulu 1966; Dorner 1972; Cohen 1980: 353–5; Giri 1983: 270–1;
Bachelet 1986: 154). Without ensuring the security of smallholders' rights of
access to land, the 'accretionary type of capital formation whereby family labor
improves land productivity and the productivity of livestock herds over
generations' will not occur in Africa as it did in other parts of the world (Eicher
1985: 88). Moreover, under communal tenure systems, land cannot be used as
a collateral to raise credit and the occupier's ability to invest is correspondingly

restricted (Cohen 1980: 354–5; Noronha 1985: 189–90; FAO 1986: Main Report, ch. 4, para. 4.90). Communal control over access to land is therefore seen as a factor that limits both the willingness and the ability of smallholders to undertake long-term investments in physical equipment and land improvements. Finally, corporate tenure is held to block the flexibility in land use that is considered essential for a dynamic farming sector. In a nutshell, the idea is that land cannot be efficiently used unless it is 'commoditized', that is unless it is transformed into a fully marketable asset (Cohen 1980: 354–5).

The view that existing arrangements with respect to control of, and access to, land resources in Africa are a major factor inhibiting the growth of agricultural output and land productivity is very appealing because it appears to be grounded on commonsense arguments. In fact, as we shall see below, the criticism of communal tenure systems can offer fruitful insights into Africa's disappointing performance of food production only if it is qualified and amended in several important senses. In substance, the main idea that will be developed below is that in many African countries today, the debate over whether to grant formal or customary land titles has become much more critical than the assessment of the relative merits of communal and individual tenure systems.[34]

*Inadequacy of African agrarian systems: a critique of the conventional view*    To start with, there are three important facts that are clearly neglected by the critics of traditional communal tenure in Africa. First, these critics have partly misunderstood the systems of land-use rights they were evaluating. In effect, security of tenure under such systems is often greater than they seem to believe (Cohen 1980: 360; Noronha 1985: 181–95; FAO 1986: Main Report, ch. 4, para. 4.87). It is no doubt true that possession of land under communal tenure is neither exclusive nor definite. Possession of land is personal and statutory, since only someone considered to be a member of the relevant social group is entitled to a portion of the communal resources. However, except in extreme circumstances (as in the case of open conflict with customary chiefs or headmen), the allottee's right of access is safeguarded as long as he keeps cultivating the land.[35] Moreover, the heirs would normally be given the lands that were cultivated at the time of the death of the allottee, even though their rights do not generally extend to lands which had been cultivated by the same but were under fallow when he died. Finally, land can be exchanged, loaned, or gifted (or even pledged) among members of the same landholding group, whereas transfers of land outside the group are subject to strict approval of the

---

[34] While writing this section, I drew much inspiration from a long review paper by Raymond Noronha (1985). Since then, however, I have elaborated the ideas presented here in a more original fashion (see Platteau forthcoming).

[35] This has two obvious implications: (1) the allottee does not have the freedom or the right to decide whether or not to use the land allocated to him; and (2) land in surplus of his requirements can be taken away from him by the customary land authorities.

village chief or the earth priest. In the light of the above, the right of a cultivator under traditional African communal systems cannot be termed a usufructuary right: the scope of the former is obviously larger than that of the latter (Noronha 1985: 195).

It is also evident that when the critics of communal tenure consider that the practice of shifting cultivation leads to insecurity of possession, they are guilty of confusing a system of land usage with title. Indeed, what is then being criticized 'is not so much land law as a form of land usage' since shifting cultivation 'reflects a relative abundance of land and a relative poverty of soils as well as minimal use of other inputs' (ibid. 192). Of course, the point remains essentially correct that land laws corresponding to extensive land usage are not appropriate for the kind of intensive farming practices that are so urgently required in Africa today. It must however be admitted that, contrary to what is suggested by the critics of communal tenure, individual tenures can exist under a system of communal tenure. Garden lands offer a good illustration of this possibility since they 'were always deemed to belong to the family that cultivated them' and did not fall under the scope of the general rules of land allotment and control (ibid. 186–7, 193). Interestingly, especially in areas of high population densities, these lands were usually well settled (possibly terraced or even irrigated) and subject to continuous cultivation thanks to regular application of vegetal manure and careful soil husbandry practices (see e.g. Raynaut 1976: 287–8 and Dupriez 1980: ch. 9).

This takes me to the second, and more important, weakness of the conventional view that communal tenure is a barrier to agricultural growth and investment in Africa. This weakness originates in a clear underestimation of the flexibility and adaptation capacity of traditional African land arrangements. As a matter of fact, there is much evidence to show that the mounting pressure of population and the increasing commercialization of agriculture, particularly since colonial times, have given rise to gradual but meaningful changes in land tenure arrangements in the direction of increased individualization of tenure and growing incidence of land transactions. As noted by John Cohen, 'corporate-tenure land is much less static and inalienable than the ideal model and Western logic lead one to believe' (Cohen 1980: 361).

Apparently, even before the advent of colonialism, exclusive appropriation of land and land sales did occur in some places even though they were strongly prohibited by customary law. What is worth noting, in this respect, is the fact that those 'illegal' practices seem to have mainly taken place in areas where land was becoming increasingly scarce (Boutillier 1963: 116–18; Raynaut 1976). Thus, we are told that, among the Hausas of Niger,

There is no doubt that, even before the arrival of the Europeans, private appropriation and sales of land parcels could occur in areas where population was heavily concentrated, and where land was scarce and subject to intensive farming practices. However, during the expansion period, when large areas of cultivable lands became available again, less clear-cut and more unstable land relations re-emerged. Those fluctuations were more the effect of pragmatic adjustments to evolving environmental conditions than manifestations of profound changes in the people's cultural patterns. (Raynaut 1976: 288—my translation)

The process of individualization of tenure titles has received a decisive impetus—or, in most cases, has been initiated—under the combined effect of population growth, the development of communications, the rise of markets, the adoption of new plants, and the increasing incidence of taxes[36] which characterized the colonial period. From his detailed survey of the existing literature on the subject, Raymond Noronha has concluded that 'the history of tenure during the colonial regime shows a gradual emphasis on individual (or family) appropriation of land for its own use', as well as a growing potential for land sales to non-members of the group following marked increases in land values (Noronha 1985: 105; see also Berry 1980; Pingali and Binswanger 1986). The traditional image of Africa as a 'seemingly changeless society ruled by legislation that only countenanced "communal" tenure' now appears to be a stereotype that cannot even stand the facts pertaining to colonial times (Noronha 1985: 78). The results of the pioneering study of Ghanaian cocoa-farmers by Poly Hill have thus been amply confirmed (Hill 1963). In particular, it is interesting to note that many cash crop growers opted for migration with the main purpose of escaping from the social control of their native village and from their social duty to share the newly earned income. In the new area, on the other hand, the rules of communal tenure could not be applied since there was no group to enforce them (ibid. and Noronha 1985: 79). When the growing of new tree crops was undertaken in the native area itself, customary principles of access to land were adjusted to allow for the new circumstances. As explained by Noronha: 'Now the customary rules of tenure provide that the field is "occupied" when crops are grown', and since trees are crops, as long as they are standing on the field, the field is considered to be 'occupied' (Noronha 1985: 78).

Land sales increased during the colonial period. However, as they were in open violation of customary land laws, they were often disguised under the form of traditional land exchanges or gifts. Moreover, the practice of land pledging began to spread and, apparently, not a few lands changed hands through land foreclosure (Raynaut 1976: 284–5; Coquery-Vidrovitch 1982: 66–71). Finally, it is worth remarking that adaptations of land tenure arrangements were not the only changes generated by the newly emerging socio-economic conditions. Indeed, changes in the patterns of inheritance also

---

[36] Thus, in the already quoted study of a Hausa community in Niger, Claude Raynaut has shown how the increasing burden of taxes led household heads to abdicate their fiscal responsibility for the entire group of their dependants. As a result, junior members of the extended family system began to neglect work on the collective fields and to devote more time to their own, individually controlled, fields (or to wage employment). The collective fields were then subdivided among them and they became personally entitled to the whole produce obtained from these 'individualized' plots of land (Raynaut 1976: 282–3).

occurred (as in Ghana between the two world wars) which usually consisted of a shift from matrilineal to patrilineal inheritance. This shift can be easily understood once it is realized that matrilineal succession loosens the nuclear family solidarity (since property is inherited by persons outside the nuclear family) while, on the contrary, patrilineal succession ensures that the fruits of family labour, investment, and risk-taking will accrue to the children of the deceased father (Noronha 1985: 98–9 and Coquery-Vidrovitch 1985: 155).

It seems ironic that in some cases resistance to change in the traditional system of land rights was offered by the government of the colonial power (that is the 'putative agency of capitalist expansion') against the pressures from members of the indigenous agrarian societies (Coquery-Vidrovitch 1982: 71–80; Bates 1984: 242–8). Thus, in parts of West Africa, in Zambia, and in Kenya, the policy of the colonial government actually promoted tribalism by forbidding any registering of individual titles of land ownership and sale transactions of land. According to Bates, the form of property law encouraged by the colonial powers 'was shaped by the desire of the colonial state for political domination of an agrarian population and by the nature of the political accommodations it had to make in order to secure its hegemony' (Bates 1984: 248). In Kenya and Zambia, two territories where the institution of chieftaincy was non-existent, the British colonial authorities promoted the establishment or the preservation of communal property rights as part of their effort 'to elaborate systems of rural political control over an agrarian population'. This was done by (creating and) empowering local chiefs loyal to the colonial power to allocate the key resource in an agrarian economy according to their own will. In Kenya, interestingly, the demand for enforcement of private rights to land was pressed all the more urgently by the Kikuyu as they felt increasingly insecure 'in the face of the uncompensated seizure of lands by the colonialists'. None the less, in other areas where the colonial authority was not reliant upon the creation of rural élites, the situation was different and the agrarian policies it followed often tilted towards commercialization of land rights or extreme forms of 'Junkerization' of landed relations (ibid. 244–7).

Post-independence Africa has been characterized by the many attempts of national states to pass land laws that would be in accordance with the socio-political philosophy of the ruling regimes. In this respect, Africa has shown considerable diversity and the only common denominator behind all these attempts is the apparent difficulty 'to categorize any nation as falling entirely into the "individual tenure" or "communal tenure" camp' (Noronha 1985: 107). Revealingly, however, the trends initiated during the colonial period—individualization of tenure and increased land transactions—continued unabated in most countries 'despite legislative intervention generally, though at times taking advantage of legislative enactments' (ibid. 108). In the words of John Harbeson: 'patterns of land tenure, insofar as they have changed markedly, appear to have evolved less in response to specific governmental policy initiatives than as a result of, and in conjunction with broader patterns of socio-economic change' (quoted from Noronha 1985: 135; see also Cohen 1980: 356; Mathieu 1985a; Hesseling and Mathieu 1986: 317).

In fact, the movement towards increasing individualization of land tenure, increasing freedom from interference by customary land authorities (as attested by the growing number of sales without permission), and increasing incidence of patrilineal modes of land transmission has accelerated during the last decades as land availability became a more and more acute problem and as opportunities of market involvement multiplied in many African countries. A gradual process of 'wresting of lands from lineage, to sub-lineage, then to extended family, and, finally, to the nuclear family' (Noronha 1985: 184; see also Raynaut 1983: 92) is under way almost everywhere, even though the methods through which it works itself out may vary significantly from country to country depending upon the state laws, the posture of the administration, and other exogenous factors. What Raynaut has said about Niger could be easily extended to most other areas where land has become a scarce factor:

Land possession takes on an increasingly private character, the sharing of family property between the sons becomes the rule, the land is increasingly parcelled out, and land use rights as well as the control of the land are increasingly transferred through other methods than inheritance. (Raynaut 1976: 284—my translation)

A third source of dissatisfaction with current criticism of communal tenure in Africa lies in the fact that group titles to land or communal resource exploitation are deemed to be a priori, and sometimes dogmatically, less efficient—that is, apparently, less conducive to growth of land productivity —than private property rights and family management. To enter into a detailed discussion of this problem is clearly beyond the scope of this chapter. But two points are worth making with a view to calling into question drastic statements of the above kind.[37] First, as has already been pointed out with respect to the 'tragedy of the commons' (see above, p. 353), inefficient collective management of productive resources may arise not only from maladjustment to changing environmental conditions (declining land–population ratios), but also from dissolution of solidarity structure or erosion of authority patterns in traditional landholding groups. Clearly, there are activities subject to externalities, indivisibilities, and scale economies, such as livestock management and irrigated farming in modern irrigation schemes. And the experience of Africa so far does not show unambiguously that private or state management is systematically superior to traditional forms of group management. Thus, for instance, management of watering points has probably never been as efficient—in a long-run perspective—than when these points were the property and the responsibility of well-defined social groups (Leonard 1986: 202). In some cases, it may therefore be wiser to revive or to support such groups than to interfere with their normal functioning by superimposing new structures upon them (Putterman 1985).

[37] For a more theoretical discussion, see in particular Bonin and Putterman (1987).

Second, success stories of communal property and collective management are not rare in Africa, but the informal character of the social group and its relative freedom from inopportune state interventions seem to be important conditions of success. An illustration is provided by the case of Serahuli kinsmen who 'pool their savings to purchase heavy agricultural equipment from the state and have recently begun to grow rice on large, mechanized, irrigated farms worked by labor mobilized within corporate kin groups of up to one hundred or more persons' (Berry 1984: 84; for other examples, see Robertson 1987: 62–63; Diemer and van der Laan 1987; von Braun and Webb 1989). Note in passing that such forms of traditional partnership are not necessarily democratic, since they are bound to reflect the internal inequalities of African village societies.[38] In the light of such experiences, it is difficult to accept uncritically the view that the emergence of innovators and progressive rural entrepreneurs is hampered by corporate patterns of land use.

*Land tenure systems as impediment to agricultural growth: the real issue*   From the above discussion, the impression could be gathered that existing land tenure systems do not pose major problems in Africa since, thanks to their inner flexibility, they gradually adapt to the changing circumstances. To rising land pressure and increasing commercialization of agriculture, African land tenure systems respond by shifting from communal to individual tenure arrangements in which farmers have more incentive to intensify their labour efforts and to undertake investments in land improvement. This is however a grossly simplified view of the process of agrarian evolution at present under way in Africa. An analysis which is so obviously grounded on a mechanicist evolutionist interpretation of human and societal processes can hardly be convincing. Land systems cannot be expected to adjust automatically and harmoniously to satisfy the evolving functional needs of agricultural development and population growth. Historical processes of transition are always characterized by tensions arising from the clashing of contradictory forces. The outcome is necessarily influenced by the way in which the political power—crystallizing the existing class structure of the society—has decided to deal (or to refrain from dealing) with the newly emerging situation, and by the relative bargaining power of the social groups/classes that have an interest in maintaining or breaking the status quo. That agrarian systems can resist pressure for change is evident from the afore-mentioned and currently observed fact that farmers may have to leave their native village and escape from the indigenous system of socio-political control to be able to respond to new challenges and opportunities as they like (see e.g. Geschiere 1984: 18). How far the established power structure will go to meet the new demands will depend upon numerous factors—among which its own interest in the change always comes foremost —and cannot be predicted a priori and mechanically. The following example

---

[38] These inequalities are inherited from the long pre-colonial history of African village settlements and/or they have developed or have been accentuated during the colonial period.

shows clearly that, as in the case of attitudes *vis-à-vis* new agricultural technologies and farming practices, adjustments in land tenure arrangements can never be considered to proceed smoothly and instantaneously:

In sub-Saharan Africa much land for traditional uncontrolled flood irrigation is still allocated on a seasonal basis by community leaders according to ancient custom. Land access for fixed, more intensive forms of irrigation, especially vegetables production, has however been subject to the same trends which have affected land access for the rainfed cultivator. Due to population pressure and commercialization of agriculture, individuals have increasingly *attempted* to claim long-term rights of occupation or personal ownership. (FAO 1986: Annex IV, ch. 4, para. 4.55)

The transition process will be all the more unstable if the new *de facto* emerging rights of access to land are not properly guaranteed, say, because there is a clash or a discrepancy between formal legislation and customary land rights. We have seen how a system of individual property tends to develop over a factor when this factor becomes scarce. But this is not the whole story since, concomitantly, there are likely to be numerous conflicts—actual or potential —with respect to the control and the use of the scarce factor. If such conflicts are not settled in a clear-cut and definite fashion, insecurity over land rights develops which is highly detrimental to investment efforts and, as will be explained below, wasteful of non-land resources as well. In extreme cases, a situation in which communal tenure rights are well established could be more conducive to agricultural growth and investment than another in which individual tenure expands in a quick and anarchic way.

In Africa, unfortunately, many insecurities presently exist because the land laws passed by many governments are ambivalent, confusing, inconsistent, inapplicable, or badly applied. As a result, access to and control of the lands take place 'within a framework of conflicting legal and political principles and practices' (Berry 1984: 92). As Hart noted with respect to West Africa, 'a confusing and conflict-ridden situation has been loosely organized through the erection of a dual system of "traditional" chiefs and law courts' (Hart 1982: 91; see also Mathieu 1983a, 1985a). After a detailed survey of national land policies in a large number of African countries since independence, Noronha has reached a similar conclusion: the insecurity of possession and use of the land 'arises when the "law" is in a state of transition and the individual can then take advantage of two systems: the customary rule that recognizes the right to possession so long as land is being cultivated, and the formal law which will grant individual tenure' (Noronha 1985: 207; see also Marty 1985: ii. 794).

Of course, as the same study shows (Noronha 1985: 107–50), the situation varies a lot from one country to another. There are countries—such as Rwanda, Swaziland, and Tanzania—where confusion about use and possession of land is almost total due to the 'provisional' character of land laws ted by the state, to frequent legislative changes, to non-implementation of d policies or legislation, to inconsistent official statements, etc. In numerous countries—such as Nigeria, Uganda, Zaïre, Kenya, Zambia, and Liberia —long delays are needed until land titles are established, a result which must be attributed to complex procedures of bureaucratic control that tend to breed fraudulent practices. In Liberia, Zambia, and Zaïre, access to land and land transactions are subject to the approval of numerous layers of the administration and the government before the decision is confirmed or denied by the President himself (Hart 1982: 91; Masaki 1987: 93–7). In still other countries —such as Senegal, the Ivory Coast, Lesotho, Cameroon, and Zaïre again—the main insecurity lies in the power of the state to requisition lands for public purposes, to acquire lands with a view to leasing them to agribusiness firms, or to seize them 'in order to fight speculation'. For another thing, there are numerous countries—such as Malawi, Botswana, Kenya, Zaïre, Sudan, Lesotho, Burkina Faso—in which powers of land allocation have been formally transferred from customary authorities to the administration, but where earth priests, headmen, and other traditional land allocators remain in fact powerful. Conversely, some countries have opted for vesting customary village authorities (Ghana, Mauritania, Mali, Guinea-Bissau, Sierra Leone), or Rural Councils representative of both the traditional and the modern worlds (Senegal, Mali), with considerable prerogatives in land matters. There, the main risk is that continuous interferences by state officials or managers of parastatals (like those of the SAED in Senegal) deprive the local bodies or authorities from any genuine autonomy (Mathieu 1985a, 1987).

*The costs of uncertainties of land rights*   In spite of all the above variations, the general picture remains that of countries in which 'formal law has penetrated the rural areas only partially' (Noronha 1985: 143), and the superimposition of a new system of land rights has created serious uncertainties about the application of indigenous rules. The indigenous system of land tenure, despite all its flexibility, loses its effectiveness, particularly in those areas where competition for land is stiff and land has gained commercial value. As a consequence, land disputes have become more and more frequent. The pattern they follow appears 'fairly consistent': first, they arise about 'tribal' boundaries and, somewhat later, about intervillage boundaries; thereafter, they are increasingly concerned with family land boundaries and, finally, they tend to multiply within the (extended) families themselves (ibid. 212). Now, a situation characterized by continuing uncertainty about the effectiveness of land titles and the validity of land claims is bound to inhibit agricultural growth (and even general economic growth). The first way in which this can happen has already been pointed out: since their ability to forecast is greatly impaired by current insecurities regarding the exact nature of their rights, landholders are deterred from making decisions about long-term investments in land improvements. Accumulation of productive capital for development of intensive agriculture is therefore held in check.

Transaction costs are a second kind of social cost arising from ambivalent situations with respect to land titles. They are *ex post costs* when claimants have to waste time and money in long litigation procedures.[39] And they are *ex ante costs* when, through a variety of strategies, people try to insure themselves against the risks generated by the existence of a dual system of land laws.[40] Such strategies may be very costly indeed, from an individual as well as from a social standpoint. Moreover, the greater the insecurities, the higher the premiums people are willing to pay in order to control the above risks. Thus, for example,

It is the fear of expropriation by Government that makes the cultivator in Ivory Coast plant more coffee and cocoa, with very wide spacing, so that the returns are 'inefficient' and the ten hectares planted produce what could have been obtained from three hectares of close-spaced trees. The cultivator is afraid of the lands being acquired and future generations suffering from land shortages (Noronha 1985: 208).

Likewise, it is only for the sake of protecting their customary rights of access to the river Senegal that Peul herders have taken to irrigated farming in the valley near St Louis. In a revealing way, the work on small-scale irrigation schemes has been entrusted to old members of the community who do not take this occupation very seriously. By contrast, the young Peuls continue to devote all their time and efforts to traditional pastoral activities to which they attach overriding importance in spite of low returns (Mathieu 1987: i. 200; see also Le Bris *et al.* 1982: 193).

There are also countless cases where absentee owners living in cities cling to their rural lands in the expectation that they will turn into a useful productive asset, or that land transactions will become (or remain) difficult or costly in the future (or that land value will increase). Such a strategy entails *private* costs: the owners see to it that their lands appear to yield something—even if it is at a loss—lest the rightfulness of their claims to them should be questioned by the land authorities. But *social* costs are also clearly involved in so far as a scarce resource is used in a wasteful way.

Substantial costs—for both the individual and the society—may arise from more 'political' strategies too. Although costly, these strategies may be effective when property rights are 'politicized rather than privatized' (Berry 1984: 92) and when, through the newly established land control system, politicians and bureaucrats are given considerable power of patronage. The latter possibility is all the more easily encountered as, in Africa, there is no respect of 'universalistic civil service norms' within the bureaucracy. According to Brett, the African civil servant cannot be expected to act as a disinterested servant of the state since, being confronted with numerous and urgent demands for assistance, it is inevitable that his decisions come to be powerfully influenced

[39] Note that, almost everywhere in Africa, customary land tribunals have lost the right to settle land disputes (at least in theory).

[40] The distinction between *ex ante* and *ex post* transaction costs was first introduced by Oliver Williamson (1985).

by personal and other sectional interests, as well as by particular considerations and material advantages (Brett 1986: 26–7). In Africa, moreover, there are narrow links between the state bureaucracy and the rural élites—whether old or new—if only because African civil servants were typically recruited from a society of rural small-scale producers and retained their control over productive resources in their native village. 'Being placed in direct control of the resources to be provided by the state to direct producers,' writes Brett, 'it was inevitable that these should be used to extend their own private economic power and that of their kinship network' (ibid. 26; see also Hyden 1986: 57; Bienen 1987: 300–2).

It is in the above context that the strategies of 'politicized but unproductive accumulation' highlighted by Berry, and called 'politics of affection' by Hyden, must be understood (Berry 1984: 89–96; Hyden 1986: 57–63). In substance, the idea is that people have to invest heavily in loyalty and patronage relations in order to gain access to—and retain control of—productive resources, land in particular. The acquisition of resources and the defence of property rights are therefore largely pre-conditioned on 'membership in various social groups or institutions, ranging from the family to the state' (Berry 1984: 91; see also Putterman 1985: 185; Hyden 1986: 62; Mathieu 1987; Bayart 1989). In many countries (e.g. Senegal and the Ivory Coast), the ruling party is actually tied to rural areas 'through a client system that operates via ethnic and factional channels' (Bienen 1987: 302). Group-based modes of access to land and other productive resources thus prevent the farmers from becoming too independent from rural networks of social relations and political power. This is all the more so as loyalty and patronage are 'often associated with ascriptive forms of status or social identity', even though they 'do not flow automatically from them' (Berry 1984: 91). Bear in mind, however, that 'groups of access' are not, strictly speaking, traditional structures or institutions. Most of them, like the Rural Councils in Senegal or the village 'tons' in Mali, are mixed institutions in which elements of the old élites (headmen, councils of 'notables', earth priests, etc.) sit side by side with members of the new élite (members of the trading, business, professional, or military classes) and representatives of the administration and the government.

It is true, as has already been mentioned, that villagers always have the possibility of cutting off their costly socio-political ties with their native area through permanent outmigration. Nevertheless, for the reasons explained above, this is a very risky strategy which may work only under special sets of circumstances (e.g. when freely accessible land does still exist in other, land-abundant, areas). In this respect, it is revealing (1) that most migratory movements in Africa are apparently 'tied migrations' which have been decided or approved by the (extended) family or the kin-group; and (2) that most individual migrants are young people, that is persons belonging to a dependent and low-status social group in the traditional village communities of Africa.

*The need for formal registration of land rights*   From the foregoing analysis, it is evident that large amounts of resources are spent in gaining and protecting access to land. The mechanisms of access which have been outlined are socially wasteful since these resources are no more available for investment in increasing land productivity. Berry is therefore right when she says that 'more stable or less contentious conditions of access and adjudication of rights to productive resources' must be established to ensure future growth of agricultural production capacity in Africa (1984: 96). National and formal registration of land titles—which need not necessarily be private titles—is clearly a step in that direction. The case for introduction of such a system has been cogently argued by Noronha:

The need for land titling (and registration) arises when there are growing uncertainties about the application and effectiveness of indigenous systems to control land transactions. This takes place most often when there are dual systems of control both of which cover land transactions, areas of uncertainty between the two systems, growing land values and pressures on land, and the potential use of land for commercial gain. (Noronha 1985: 220)

This said, an important problem arises from the fact that adjudication and registration of land rights are complex and expensive operations for which many African states are ill prepared or ill equipped. As a matter of principle, they should not be undertaken when the expected social benefits (or reduction in social costs) are smaller than the likely administrative costs. Thus, it may be taken for granted that nation-wide registration and formalization of land titles are not justified in areas where land is abundant and/or has no commercial value, where land transactions and land disputes are few or non-existent, and where other markets are absent or poorly developed (ibid. 215–17, 220).

In a context of stiff competition for land, the security afforded by the traditional system of land control can no longer be relied upon to allocate land and to settle land disputes. A modern system of nation-wide registration and land-titling ought therefore to be substituted for the customary laws and practices. Such a conclusion might be strongly opposed by some authors on the ground that the latter system is more conducive to equality than the former, and that considerations of equity should have precedence over those of efficiency. Unfortunately, even if we agree with the second part of the statement, there is no sufficient reason to change the above-reached conclusion because the first part is seriously open to doubt. We know today that pre-colonial village communities of Africa were not exempt from various sources of socio-economic differentiation (see e.g. Boutillier 1963; Minvielle 1977; Coquery-Vidrovitch 1982; Weigel 1982b; Raynaut 1983; Robertson 1987; Bayart 1989: 159–73). What needs to be especially emphasized here is that, under the combined effect of increasing land pressure and commercialization of agriculture, traditional inequalities have been exacerbated, even in areas where customary rules of communal tenure still apply. Landlessness has increased because ancient village communities have tried to protect their rights of access to available land by imposing more and more stringent conditions of membership upon 'outsiders' (in order to deny them such access, or to drive them into marginal land areas). And processes of socio-economic differentiation have started off or accelerated precisely because customary authorities, like village chiefs and earth priests, have often exploited their privileged position of land-controller to promote their own interests whenever opportunities existed to do so. There is in fact considerable evidence to show that, thanks to their association with members of the new élite, the modern bureaucratic state, the international business community, and foreign aid projects, they have been able to confirm their élite status and to increase their material wealth (Cohen 1980: 357; Mathieu 1985a, 1987; Noronha 1985: 143–4, 203–6; Pingali and Binswanger 1986: 26; Hesseling and Mathieu 1986: 315).

Analysis of income distribution effects of politicized accumulation strategies has led Berry to a similar conclusion: group-based modes of access to productive resources 'have not necessarily served to redistribute income in an egalitarian manner, nor to provide security to the venturesome or to the poor and dependent' (Berry 1984: 94). In view of the above facts, one can strongly doubt that the interests of the poor and the weak would be better protected by divesting the state of all land allocation and adjudication prerogatives and by entrusting them to customary institutions dominated by members of both the old and the new élites.

A final remark is in order if we are to avoid a confusion of issues. To say that property or possession rights in land must be made secure and registered through formal/legal procedures is not at all equivalent to saying that a land market in which private titles to land are freely exchanged ought to be established. In fact, a good case can be made that, given the crucial importance of land assets in countries where most people depend on land for their livelihood, any private land market should be strongly regulated by the state. In the circumstances, indeed, free market transactions can easily lead to processes of land concentration in the hands of the élite and to the concomitant rise of a class of landless people. The important point is, however, that the same undesirable effects are likely to result from the free operation of customary systems of land tenure. As has been contended above, observation of current land situations in many parts of Africa suggests that this perversion of traditional land practices is a possibility that has to be considered very seriously. Therefore, in a context of increasing land scarcity, it is essential that the state takes upon itself the task of regulating the access to available lands and guaranteeing land titles with a view to avoiding all the efficiency and equity costs of non-intervention. Experiences of countries like Taiwan and South Korea show that regulation of the land market so as to protect the rights of smallholders can be effective in holding disequalizing tendencies in check (see e.g. Lee 1979). Moreover, in the case of these two countries, this result does not appear to have entailed substantial efficiency costs compared with a free land market situation.

As I have dealt at great length with this issue elsewhere (Platteau forthcoming), I will not probe further into it here. Suffice it to add that a strategy of control of land market forces does not necessarily imply that customary authorities ought to be divested of all their traditional prerogatives. As has been rightly emphasized by Coquery-Vidrovitch (1982: 83), any African state will be well advised to use the flexibility and adaptive power of indigenous land laws or practices in the design of its 'modern' land policy.

### (f)  Political instability and authoritarianism in the approach to rural development

*The fragility of African states*   In section 6.4*d* above, attention was drawn to some institutional or organizational barriers to agricultural growth in Africa. Probably one of the main lessons which can be learned from the Asian and the Western experiences is that intensive agriculture and rural infrastructures (technical, economic, social, and cultural) cannot be developed very far unless local farmer organizations and decentralized forms of peoples' associations emerge to mobilize communal labour and to take on-the-spot initiatives. Asian experience also teaches us that when the structure of the government is too centralized and too despotic (as in Korea during the Yi dynasty), or when the political situation is too unstable (as in north China when village communities were invaded by the northern tribes), the afore-mentioned developments are dangerously slowed down or blocked altogether. These two kinds of adverse circumstances are frequently encountered in Africa, and this helps explain why rural development and agricultural growth do not proceed at the pace desired.

Political instability, to begin with, is a recurrent feature of the African scene. In most countries, indeed, the state is a relatively new and fragile institution which is continuously threatened with military coups, social turmoils, and ethnic secessions (Hart 1982: 102–5; Leonard 1986: 205). Theodore Mars goes as far as saying that in Africa 'power when examined turns out to be a description of the lack of the existence of an institutional framework for political relationships' (Mars 1986: 17). This is not, however, a correct appreciation of the nature of the state in Africa. Jean-François Bayart (1989) has recently offered us a much more subtle analysis of the African state. According to him, African political systems are in the process of being made: it is even a striking feature of the societies in the south of Sahara that they are able to produce important institutional or administrative innovations which are described as processes of 'creolization' or 'political interbreeding'. The fact that the political construct resulting from these innovations looks very different from the classic Weberian state explains why so many Western observers are misled into thinking that African societies are undergoing a process of political decay or that Africa is a political vacuum (Bayart 1989: 296–300).

This said, it is hard to deny that most sub-Saharan African countries still have a long way to go before achieving a reasonable degree of national integration (see, e.g. Sandbrook 1986). It is therefore no wonder that 'obedience has to be extracted by the threat of force or the inducement of personal advantage', instead of being 'unproblematically extended' because those who obey feel morally inclined to do so (Mars 1986: 17). It is thus revealing that 'only thrice in post-colonial African history has a change of incumbents come about through the electoral processes'. Moreover, 'since 1966, 40 to 50 per cent of the regimes in the continent have been military in origin and in states not under military rule, intervention by the security forces remains a tangible threat' (Young 1986: 37, 41). In Africa, the military coup has become an institutionalized 'vehicle for ruler displacement', a feature which came to dominate the African political scene when it became clear that 'political monopolies guaranteeing incumbents indefinite prolongation of their mandates were becoming the rule' (ibid. 37).

There are of course many complex factors accounting for the volatile political situation of most African countries, and it is increasingly being acknowledged that they can be properly understood only if they are put in the right historical perspective. Three important points will be briefly mentioned here. First, many African states have inherited from the colonial period arbitrary and absurd boundaries which tend to make the objective of national unity comparatively difficult to achieve. What Hart has said about West Africa could easily be extended to other areas as well: 'The further balkanization of West Africa as the price of independence has only increased the problem of borders by multiplying them' (Hart 1982: 103). This is especially distressing in view of the long tradition of continuous flows of goods and people across large parts of Africa.

Second, historical studies have shown that the ethnic problem—which is an important destabilizing factor in post-independence Africa—has been largely 'fabricated' by the colonial powers in order to increase their administrative, political, and even religious control over the people subjected to their rule. Thus, Noronha considers that 'ethnic consciousness, if not born through colonialism, was reaffirmed and strengthened' (Noronha 1985: 65), while, for Coquery-Vidrovitch, the impact of colonialism has been to cause a shift from 'ethnic' to 'tribalist' identity feeling among African people (Coquery-Vidrovitch 1985: 127–35; see also Bayart 1989: 65–86).[41] Unfortunately, the

[41] By 'tribalisme', Coquery-Vidrovitch apparently means 'the manipulation of ethnic feeling' in order to further particularistic interests on the basis of race criteria. Such manipulation could be driven very far indeed. In Zambia, in order to avoid the costs of large-scale unemployment in the copper mines during cyclical downturns, the colonial government instituted an administrative procedure of purely artificial 'tribalization'. To retain rural land rights, urban dwellers (like factory workers) had to be 'tribalized', that is they had to affiliate with the political officials of a rural community and establish membership in a kin group belonging to that community. In times of crisis, laid-off workers could thus reincorporate themselves into the rural economy 'quickly and peacefully', with no cost for the colonial Treasury (Bates 1984: 249).

policy of granting concessions and privileges on the basis of tribal affiliations has not been discontinued by independent African states. On the contrary, ethnic identity has become an important criterion for rationing access to scarce government or administrative posts as well as to the monopoly rents allocated by the state bureaucracy (Platteau 1984: 78–83). As aptly noted by Young, 'The politically ambitious had discovered that crystallizing ethnic consciousness was the swiftest and surest way to attract a political clientele' (Young 1986: 36).

Nevertheless, it would be wrong to infer from the above that ethnic affiliations are always an essential dimension of the African state. In fact, the common denominator of African political systems is that they are all structured by rival networks of political factions articulated around individuals, families, religious, socio-cultural, and economic groups, subgroups, sects, castes, etc. These factions are often engaged in merciless struggles for access to power and to the wealth and material privileges which automatically reward the power-holders (Bayart 1989: 261–80). And it is precisely because these struggles are so fierce (since the stakes are so big) that the state in Africa 'is being imposed in the most elementary sense of the term' (ibid. 300).

Third, the political project of many African states at the time of independence was to follow a 'socialist/populist strategy', that is a strategy directed towards instituting 'a rational and non-conflictual development process' by giving a central role to the state 'in relation to both overall regulation and direct intervention in the production process itself' (Brett 1986: 24). It was grounded on a domestic class alliance made of disparate elements which were supposed to transcend their own particularistic interests in the name of nationalist emancipation and progress. Such a project was bound to fail and to weaken the state structure not only because the responsibilities entrusted to the state clearly exceeded its capabilities, but also because it eschewed the crucial question of how and among whom to allocate the scarce resources available. In a rather paradoxical way, African countries have often attempted to escape or postpone the inevitable setting of priorities and to alleviate the accompanying class, regional, or ethnic tensions by increasing their dependence on foreign capital (both public and private), thus thwarting their initial plan of national emancipation.

*Paternalistic and instrumentalist biases in the institutional approach to rural development*  Political instability tends to discourage investments and risk-taking in agriculture, and to jeopardize long-term efforts to reduce population pressure on limited land resources. Similar adverse effects result from the 'control orientation' (Leonard) or the 'top-down bias' of the institutional approach to rural development followed by many African governments. The latter have usually ignored the important lesson that self-sustaining growth of the rural economy cannot occur 'without a policy designed to make positive use of indigenous community institutions and organizational principles as a basis for modern rural development institutions' (Hayami and Kikuchi 1981: 225). Instead of building up on indigenous village-community organizations and mechanisms of decentralized decision-making—that is, instead of starting with what already exists and encouraging local associations or voluntary agencies to promote organizational development from below and to diversify institutional responsibilities (what Hyden has called the 'greenhouse' approach—1986: 71–6)—they have almost systematically preferred to establish highly centralized and bureaucratized institutions, often entrusted with monopoly or monopsonistic powers.

Thus, for example, Africa is well known for her long tradition of informal savings clubs—known as 'tontines' in West Africa—which in many cases are run by women on the basis of extremely sound principles of savings management. As has been pointed out, these clubs could well have been developed into small credit unions with a view to providing 'the base for small, cost-effective credit operations through links with more formal banking institutions' (Leonard 1986: 194). Instead, most African governments opted for setting up from the top complex multifunctional co-operatives one function of which is to provide credit to their members according to rather rigid administrative procedures. Tragically enough, women are normally deprived of access to membership on the ground that households are adequately represented by their male head. To take another example, instead of supporting traditional rural artisans by helping them to acquire better tools, learn new techniques, and adapt to new market opportunities (intensive agriculture requires better agricultural implements), many African governments have preferred to follow a largely inefficient and expensive top-down approach. As described by Michael Lipton, this approach involves 'the training of largely unskilled and inexperienced would-be entrepreneurs, mollycoddled in subsidised and capital-intensive "industrial estates" for a few years of market-unrelated "training", and then either sent out to sink (or, rarely, swim) alone, or permitted to pressurise their way to endlessly prolonged "estate" cocooning' (Lipton 1985: 80; see also Please and Amoako 1984: 57).

More generally, in a world dominated by pervasive production externalities and by high information and transaction costs, local associations—that is, typically, non-market institutions grounded upon tight social interactions —must develop to undertake collective actions and to create public goods, particularly around resources that are becoming increasingly scarce (Hayami and Kikuchi 1981: 11–23). If large-scale organizations cannot be dispensed with in some specific circumstances (e.g. in the cases where construction of dams or large canals is required to ensure adequate distribution of water), they ought to be avoided whenever and wherever possible, because they tend to encourage free-riding and to give rise to all sorts of incentive problems.

Two central considerations seem to have led African leaders to believe that agricultural institutions subsumed under central government control are more appropriate and more reliable than private voluntary organizations, possibly based on lineage and extended family connections. For one thing, rural masses were regarded as too amorphous and too exposed to merchants' exploitation to be capable of raising their standard of living without the constant protection and support of the state (*the paternalistic bias*). For another thing, public institutions were considered as the best way to make small-scale rural produ-cers efficient instruments of government policies and programs, particularly those geared towards increasing agricultural exports and public revenues (*the instrumentalist bias*). At a more general level, the notion largely prevailed that 'economies can be developed like armies under a single command' (Hyden 1986: 65).

In many countries, the main rural institutions set up by the administration and the political system have taken the form of co-operative structures. As a rule, two chief tasks were assigned to them, both of which are revealing of the instrumental role reserved for the peasantry in most African strategies of national development. First, on the political plane, rural co-operatives were supposed to organize the villagers with a view to facilitating the transmission, towards the rural masses, of political orientations and instructions decided at the top. Second, at the economic level, their planned function was to serve as a relay between state societies, parastatals, and government departments on the one hand, and the mass of petty rural producers on the other hand. In more concrete terms, they were conceived as a kind of channel through which the state would distribute modern agricultural inputs and credit, convey market information, and collect the agricultural produce (mainly export products). It is no exaggeration to say that rural co-operatives, far from being partners or pressure groups with which the government has to negotiate, are in fact 'the lower element of state apparatuses' (Gentil 1986: 75).

In so far as co-operatives are considered and organized as a simple extension of the administration and the government, it is not surprising that the latter feel perfectly entitled continuously to intervene in the affairs of the former, by deciding and formalizing their rules of functioning (including the conditions of membership, the size of the co-operative, etc.), by appointing the chairman, by imposing certain activities (such as the cultivation of some crops or the building up of certain social infrastructures), by exercising permanent finan-cial control, and so forth. In some extreme cases, like that of rural state organizations in Mali (the 'Groupements ruraux de production et de secours mutuel'), the government had even dispensed with the co-operative façade to organize the peasantry in a more direct and ruthless fashion (1960–8). Adhesion was made compulsory to all villagers and the administration (then under the strong influence of the dominant political party, the US/RDA) was authorized to 'influence' the election of village chiefs and peasant delegates (Gentil 1986: 61–73). In the particular case of the Office du Niger, government irrigation schemes were run like military work camps and extension officers were acting both as technical advisers and as police guards (Coulibaly 1985: 218–22). The 'villagization' programme of Nyerere in Tanzania also suffered from continuous and demoralizing interferences from the state bureaucracy, thus preventing the emergence of self-determining and democratic collective groups (Kitching 1982: 104–24; Putterman 1985: 181–6; Swantz 1987). Unfortunately, examples of this kind could be multiplied *ad infinitum*.

*Social costs of the 'control model'*    Given the above set-up, the attitude of African smallholders who regard the co-operatives as 'belonging to the government, and not to the peasants' (Gentil 1986: 202; see also Jacquemot 1981; Geschiere 1984; Marty 1985) is perfectly understandable. Many such reactions have been actually observed. Thus, Tanzanian peasants perceived the 'collective fields' instituted under the 'villagization' programme as 'farms of the government' (Putterman 1985: 184), while on government irrigation schemes it is not rare that tenants 'feel and behave as if they were government labourers' (FAO 1986: Annex IV, ch. 5, para. 5.28). In Senegal, for example, smallholders regard the irrigated fields of the SAED as the 'gardens of the state' and, accordingly, they consider that maintenance of the infrastructure is the exclusive responsibility of the state, which does not fail to engender serious tensions with the extension and supervision personnel (Matthieu 1983a, 291). Evidently, the latter participate in the process of peasant alienation since they tend to behave as state employees (which they often actually are) and not as agents of the agricultural communities which they are supposed to serve. Moreover, they frequently embitter the relations between the peasants and the agricultural state services because of their 'lack of interest in peasant cooperation, except insofar as it serves personal and government aims'; and because of their 'habits of authoritarianism and attitudes of disdain for peasants' by which they convince themselves that they have finally succeeded in rising over their own peasant roots (Putterman 1985: 185).[42]

As could also be expected, rural small-scale producers use all sorts of defensive strategies or evasive reactions to thwart—or to minimize the effects of—the government's attempts at enrolling them against their will. African peasantries excel in the 'art of runaway' and are prone to seize all 'exit options' open to them (Bayart 1989: 308–15). Some of their strategies have been depicted by Dominique Gentil: putting in a minimum amount of effort when the compulsion is too strong (in collective fields); simulating submission while abstaining from undertaking any concrete action; sending a few village leaders or dummies to meetings which they will attend passively without making any commitment on behalf of the village community; taking maximum advantage of what the state offers, for instance, borrowing as much as possible and repaying as little as possible; selling a few bags of agricultural produce to the marketing co-operative while disposing of the largest possible portion of the

---

[42] It is revealing that in an official document the government of Mali has criticized rural agents of the central administration for the 'omnipotent power they have vested themselves with' and for the way they have 'traumatized' the population during 18 years of national independence (Government of Mali 1984: 9).

harvest through illegal channels (Gentil 1986: 147–8). The main defect of the top-down control model is now evident: it lies in the serious incentive problems that it inevitably creates at the level of rural producers. In the absence of participatory decision-making, the latter tend to consider themselves not as genuine members of the institutions which are supposed to be run for their benefit, but as simple customers or hired labourers with all the attendant consequences in terms of risks of labour-shirking, asset mismanagement, output underreporting, and other 'moral hazard' problems. The fact that such problems involve large social costs is too well known to deserve further elaboration.

What needs to be borne in mind, however, is that advantages distributed by co-operative societies or other rural organizations are far from being equally shared among the members or other potential beneficiaries. As in the case of access to land rights (see above, pp. 364–6), the old (rural) élite and the new (urban/rural) élite have managed to secure a preferential access to state favours. In most cases, this has been done by using traditional networks of clientelist relations to get 'elected' to key positions in the above organizations; or by establishing privileged relations with influential bureaucrats, party leaders, and government representatives who are often keen to distribute patronage in return for personal advantages or party support. As a consequence, far from being eroded by the emergence of so-called 'democratic', 'co-operative', or 'people's' organizations in the countryside, the structure of vertical leadership within African villages has actually been strengthened by the convenient alliance of rural élites and the new bureaucratic class.

Inequitable mechanisms for distributing state-channelled resources (credit, subsidies, modern agricultural inputs or tools, irrigation equipment, etc.) are particularly important and self-reinforcing with respect to the development of intensive agriculture. Indeed, access to the best lands belonging to the public domain is normally pre-conditioned on access to modern inputs on the ground that land belongs to he who can till it properly. In a rather cynical way, a customary principle of land allocation is thus invoked to justify growing socio-economic differentiation in African agriculture. This is what happens, for example, in the Senegal river valley, where good irrigated lands are often allocated to rich urban dwellers and to traditional village leaders because only they possess the equipment required to exploit them according to the rules of the SAED (Mathieu 1985a: 658–62, 1987).[43]

*Autocratic legacy of the colonial system*   To some extent, the problems which have been highlighted above are typical of most Third World countries. Where

---

[43] The positive experience of Ronkh village (on the Senegal river), where a group of rural youth could get access to a portion of SAED-allocated irrigated lands, actually confirms this analysis. Indeed, it is mainly because this group was led by an educated person who decided to put an end to his teaching career but could still act as a 'broker' for the villagers *vis-à-vis* the urban authorities, and because the group was strongly motivated, courageous, but also full of political tact, that it could eventually succeed in obtaining support from the SAED (Gentil 1986: 206–16).

Africa distinguishes herself, however, is in the comparatively high degree of authoritarianism commonly displayed in her top-down approaches to rural development, and in the strong resistance that such authoritarian modes of conduct oppose to change. To understand these two characteristics, one does not have to go very far back into African history since it was mainly during the colonial period that the control orientation of many present African political systems was shaped. Young has thus pointedly remarked (1) that contemporary African states remain 'deeply marked by the hegemonial pretensions and authoritarian legacy of the colonial state' since 'in innumerable ways, the peremptory, prefectoral command style of the colonial state remains embedded in its successor'; and (2) that the colonial state was much more authoritarian in Africa than in Asia and Latin America, with the result that subjugation and exclusion of civil society was particularly thorough in the former continent (Young 1986: 33–4, 46). The second feature is ascribed to two facts. On the one hand, 'the African colonial state was implanted in a highly competitive environment where consolidation of its rule was an immediate requirement'. On the other hand, the colonial class in Africa 'had a more profound conviction of its cultural, biological, and technological superiority, and a more systematically negative view of its subject population than was the case elsewhere' (ibid. 34).

With particular respect to rural/local organizations, a fascinating study on co-operative movements in West Africa (Gentil 1986) has revealed that the co-operative societies at present existing in the countries concerned are an almost exact replica of the colonial SIP, SP, SMPR, and SMDR (sociétés indigènes de prévoyance; sociétés de prévoyance; sociétés mutuelles de production rurale; sociétés mutuelles de développement rural). It is particularly worth noting that the latter societies were all considered to be part of the French colonial administrative system—Gentil calls them 'structures of a para-administrative type' (ibid. 43). This implied (1) that the colonial bureaucracy always took the initiative of creating them; (2) that it could use them towards achieving official objectives (in particular, the development of export cash crops and the collection of government revenues under the guise of membership fees); and (3) that it was entitled to intervene at every stage of their functioning. This intervention could go very far indeed since (French) province governors were automatically appointed chairmen of the 'co-operative' societies situated in their administrative territory, and since membership was often made compulsory for all the villagers (women and young people excepted) living in the area (ibid. 27–57). Even the ill-famed Office du Niger was in fact created in 1932 by the French to succeed the STIN (Service temporaire d'irrigation du Niger) which was a para-military organization run by military officers and relying upon a system of forced labour (Coulibaly 1985: 220).

Interestingly, village chiefs and their clients—provided that they professed allegiance to the new ruling power—were incorporated into the governing bodies of the colonial 'co-operative' societies. They were thus given a preferential treatment in the access to the resources, goods, and services provided through them. In fact, the political strategy of colonial powers consisted of incorporating submissive chieftains into the entire administrative machinery and not only into rural 'co-operative' organizations (Noronha 1985: 61–5; Coquery-Vidrovitch 1985: 112–27). In this way, even though they were not very high in the colonial hierarchy,[44] village chiefs came to be vested with enormous power at the local level: the power to allocate tribal lands; to collect revenue on behalf of the colonial state; to raise compulsory labour and to fix the criteria for selection of individuals; to punish defaulters when cropping programmes were imposed by the administration; and so forth. The whole political fabric of pre-colonial African societies was therefore perverted, since in these societies the village political sphere was traditionally 'plural' and the chief was not allowed to concentrate powers (Bates 1984: 245–8; Coquery-Vidrovitch 1985: 113, 126; Bayart 1989: 99–103). The result has been a hybrid and 'monstrous' creature vividly depicted by Coquery-Vidrovitch:

The 'chief' of today—whether the so-called 'traditional' chief or the modern bureau-crat—appears, strictly speaking, as a 'monster', that is as the combination, still badly effected and poorly understood, of two power systems which had initially nothing in common. Being so, he represents, at the least, an attempt at fusion between the old dominant groups and the new élites born from the colonization and decolonization processes. (Coquery-Vidrovitch 1985: 126–7—my translation)

In today's Africa, this 'monstrous' creature remains incorporated in a global political system of vertical relationships of personal subordination but, what makes matters still worse as compared with the colonial period, this system is now characterized by an almost complete 'patrimonialization of the state' (Young) as well as by chronic instability following the demise of colonial tutelage. The logic of this macropolitical system has been adequately captured by Young:

Abstract bureaucratic jurisprudence no longer sufficed after independence. Hostile cliques and conspiracies had to be pre-empted by ensuring placement of personnel at critical points in the state apparatus whose fidelity to the ruler was not simply formal, but immediate and personal. Thus rulers constructed an inner layer of control—key political operatives, top elements in the security forces, top technocrats in the financial institutions—whose fidelity was guaranteed by personal fealty as well as by hierarchical subordination. The surest basis for such fidelity is affinity of community or kinship . . . Beyond and often in addition to affinity, personal interest is the most reliable collateral for loyalty. Accordingly, rulers must reward generously and impose severe sanctions for any weakening of zeal. Thus public resources become a pool of benefits and prebends, while dismissal from office, confiscation of goods, and prosecution face those who show slackness in their personal fidelity. Holders of high office individually tend to become clients of the ruler and collectively a service class. (Young 1986: 38)

[44] In French colonies, the village chief was a simple assistant to the Commandant and derived no authority independent of the administration (Noronha 1985: 63; Coquery-Vidrovitch 1985: 121).

As is evident from the foregoing analysis, the preference for state control and direction and the authoritarian modes of conduct of most African rulers are a structural feature of contemporary societies in Africa. They answer the need of social control in a fluid political set-up dominated by ethnic and interdistrict competition, factional struggles, religious ties, and complicated relations of affection and patronage that cannot be encompassed by class analysis (Hyden 1986: 66; Bienen 1987: 298–300; Bayart 1989: 261–93). That the political economy of Africa described above is uncongenial to rural development hardly needs emphasis. It is sufficient to stress that villagers have many ways of expressing their resentment against a village chief who is not 'customary' but a creation of the colonial order. If they usually comply with his orders so long as he acts as a representative of the government (especially if these orders are backed up by administrative sanctions of superior links in the hierarchy), they are often found to hinder and to oppose him in his performance as a (pseudo-) traditional leader in the village (Geschiere 1984: 16–17). The ensuing cost in terms of lost opportunities of rural progress may be tremendous, since many African villages thus lack the minimum social cohesion and the leadership dynamics that are so badly needed to carry out communal projects of rural development, whether in the productive or in the social sphere.

## 6.5. Conclusion

African agriculture is confronted today with a dramatic challenge arising from both demand and supply factors. On the demand side, the picture is twofold: on the one hand, food consumption increases quickly, mainly as a result of very high rates of population growth, and, on the other hand, consumption patterns undergo drastic changes for a variety of reasons among which rapid rates of urbanization stand foremost. On the supply side, disappointing performances —although difficult to measure precisely due to the paucity and low reliability of the data available (see Berry 1984: 61–4)—can obviously not be attributed to a single factor or even to a small number of causes. While both supply and demand factors are responsible for the growing dependence of Africa on food imports and for the ensuing tightening of the continent's foreign exchange constraints, the poor performances of the agricultural sector and the gradual shift of consumption patterns towards import-intensive foods have combined to reduce the incomes of the majority of rural people.

In much of the specialized economic literature, attention has been essentially drawn to policy 'mistakes' currently made by African governments, either out of sheer ignorance of sound economic logic and unawareness of macroeconomic constraints, or because of considerations related to the 'political economy' of Africa understood in a narrow neoclassical sense (policies are the outcome of competition and interaction of organized groups made of rational individuals). The dominant image emerging from many such analyses is that of misguided, incompetent, exploitative, and corrupt states that are actually killing the peasantry from which they draw their living. Overvaluation of national currencies, urban food subsidies, and excessive reliance on foreign food aid programmes (all these policies having the effect of cheapening foreign foods artificially), high rates of effective taxation of agricultural production, inefficient distribution of agricultural inputs and food output, are considered to be the main factors acting as a brake on the expansion of domestic food supply. The main policy conclusion that seems to follow from such a diagnosis is that by just reversing the present policies and by redressing the existing economic distortions agricultural growth could be considerably stimulated. Admittedly, such reversals of economic policies will not be easily achieved since they require new political coalitions ready to call the 'old order' into question. Yet such a view has apparently been confirmed by policy changes in favour of agricultural producers during the last 10–15 years, usually imposed upon many African states by the world economic crisis and the 'instructions' issued by powerful international organizations (especially the IMF and the World Bank).

It would be absurd to pretend that the above school of thought is completely off the mark, since it has brought into focus a number of important problems that bear upon the agricultural situation in Africa. Moreover, bumper food harvests and grain surpluses recently recorded in several African countries (most notably in Mali and Sudan) seem to have partly resulted from policy reforms suggested by the price-focused doctrine, even though it is impossible to separate the influence of these reforms from the effect of exceptionally good climatic conditions. This said, the dominant view must be criticized, not only on its own ground because of internal weaknesses (both empirical and theoretical), but also and mainly because it has the effect of diverting attention from the most crucial issues confronting African agriculture today. Indeed, Africa will not be able to raise the incomes of the mass of rural smallholders on a sustainable basis, nor to reduce her food dependence with a view to sparing scarce foreign exchange for her industrialization, if rapid technical advances do not take place in the agricultural sector. More precisely, Africa has no choice but to generate and diffuse technological progress at a rate sufficiently rapid to cause regular increases in land productivity (so as to expand food supply despite the exhaustion of the 'land frontier'), and in labour productivity (so as to increase the real incomes of the farmers), probably at the cost of increased labour efforts. In the present context of Africa, the afore-mentioned challenge amounts to finding how African countries (particularly those below the Sahara desert) could make a significant shift from extensive to intensive farming and stock-raising practices.

When the question is posed in these terms, growth-inhibiting factors of a more structural type than those underlined in the 'price-focused' approach come to the foreground of analysis. More concretely, Africa appears to suffer from several serious handicaps which can be traced back to her colonial and pre-colonial history, or which result from specific characteristics of her physical environment. In many instances, she turns out to be at a disadvantage *vis-à-vis* other continents, Asia and Latin America in particular. This is not to say that such structural deficiencies and handicaps cannot or will not be overcome. But attempts at overcoming them will take considerable time, much energy, and large amounts of resources, while time runs against Africa and some badly needed resources (such as agricultural research personnel) are awfully scarce.

Six 'constraint areas' have been investigated in this paper. The underlying theses can be schematically formulated as follows:

1. In Africa, human settlements remain small and very scattered, with the result that the development of markets is slowed down and the per capita cost of providing numerous services to the rural population is quite high.

2. On the natural resources front, Africa is handicapped by the extraordinary diversity of her agroclimatic conditions; by the low quality and high fragility of her soils; by difficult and costly access to water; and by the inaccessibility of some of her best lands.

3. So far, African staple foods have not benefited from any technological breakthrough in high-yield varieties, a situation which must be ascribed to a variety of factors among which are: the structure of traditional consumption patterns; the small size of many African states; a large dispersion and a biased allocation of agricultural research efforts under the joint influence of 'export' and 'technological dependence' biases.

4. The transition from extensive to intensive agriculture and stock-raising is made more difficult because Africa has inherited an 'extensive culture' from her long history of long-fallow agriculture and pastoral nomadism.

5. Because land laws in Africa are at present in a state of transition and a dual system of land titles often prevails in the countryside, access to land is not properly guaranteed. As a consequence, land investment is discouraged and valuable resources are wasted in costly strategies of acquisition and protection of land rights.

6. Many African states are characterized by a high degree of political instability and by the 'control orientation' of their institutional approach to rural development. The 'paternalistic' and the 'instrumentalist' biases implied in this approach create many incentive problems for the rural sector, which turn out to be very expensive in terms of transaction costs and lost opportunities of agricultural growth.

From the above list of factors, it is evident that the problems which Africa will have to solve in order to trigger off new growth and development impulses in her agricultural sector do not lie wholly in the technological sphere. Changes in institutions and in the cultural and political systems will also be required. Moreover, it is worth stressing that the levels of income and the food security of the smallholder majority in Africa will not be improved unless serious attention is paid to equity issues and distributive effects of agricultural growth-promoting strategies. This is one of the main lessons from the discussion of the last two afore-mentioned constraints. As a matter of fact, in Africa as in Asia and Latin America—and contrary to a popular picture of Africa as a relatively egalitarian society—there is a high risk that the growth of sustainable productive income-earning opportunities in the countryside will bypass the poorer and politically weaker segments of rural populations, while encouraging the emergence of a small group of progressive rich farmers with a privileged access to valuable resources.

It is equally important to note that in many African countries—particularly in the arid and semi-arid areas—removing or reducing the various constraints that hamper agricultural growth will not be sufficient to grant new purchasing power to small family-operated farms. Strategies promoting diversification of rural production and creation of new off-farm employment opportunities will be needed—mainly during the dry season in areas where the rainy season is very short—to supplement the farm incomes of African smallholders. Priority should of course be given to activities having potential linkages with agricultural production or producing simple consumption and capital goods demanded by—or of potential use to—rural dwellers.

It would however be a mistake to think that, in the near future, development of non-agricultural activities could make technical change in agriculture superfluous or even wasteful. Indeed, given that in many instances investments in non-agricultural activities are likely to be much more import-intensive than investments in agricultural intensification in which labour investments play a considerable role, a relative neglect of agriculture would have two adverse effects upon the balance of payments. First, there is the effect resulting from the rising food import bill and, second, increasing imports of intermediate and capital goods will be required to create and sustain employment opportunities outside the agricultural sector. The problem is further complicated by the fact that the prospects of non-agricultural exports are rather bleak for Africa today. Furthermore, if non-agricultural activities are developed in the countryside to the detriment of agricultural production, the cost of transporting food will be high given the low population densities in most African countries. If, on the contrary, these activities are spatially concentrated, the acceleration of already fast-rising urbanization rates will entail considerable social costs besides causing rapid population depletion in entire regions of the continent.

There is not doubt that the challenge facing African agriculture today is tremendous. For one thing, given that populations grow very rapidly, all the changes required in technology, institutions, and cultural systems to solve problems of declining labour productivity and environmental degradation must occur simultaneously and within a short span of time. There is thus a serious risk that these changes will 'fail to emerge at a sufficiently rapid pace to prevent decline in human welfare' (Pingali and Binswanger 1986: 27). For another thing, difficulties are compounded by the fact that Africa's food crisis has deep historical roots which can be traced back to pre-colonial times (e.g. the lack of tradition of productive links between African cities and the rural hinterland) and to the colonial era (e.g. the export bias in agricultural research and the role of the colonial legacy in shaping contemporary African states). When placed in its right historical perspective, this crisis therefore appears to be far more difficult to overcome than many current prescriptions for simple policy reforms tend to suggest.

This is perhaps a disappointing conclusion for those who expect scientists to prescribe clear recipes for helping Africa out of her awkward agricultural predicament. Yet, the role of any structural analysis is precisely to shake off naïve beliefs in the illusory power of short-term policy measures to solve long-term development problems. Besides—and in a more positive way— it points to the necessity of carrying out in-depth country case-studies before venturing to suggest measures or strategies for agricultural development that must inevitably, to a large extent, be country specific. In effect, the main purpose of this paper was to identify sensible 'problem areas' which should be carefully investigated in the case of each African country or region contemplating the redress of present imbalances. In the very process of this identification, some schematization was unavoidable and idiosyncrasies were left out of the picture so that the issues highlighted could be made relevant for a large number of countries belonging to the African continent.

# References

ABOYADE, O. (1987), 'Growth Strategy and the Agricultural Sector', in Mellor *et al.* (1987).

AGARWAL, N. (1983), *The Development of a Dual Economy: A Theoretical Analysis* (Calcutta: K. P. Bagchi & Cy).

ANDRAE, G., and BECKMAN, B. (1986), *The Wheat Trap: Bread and Underdevelopment in Nigeria* (London: Zed).

ANSON-MEYER, M. (1985), 'Les illusions de l'autosuffisance alimentaire: Exemple du Bénin, du Ghana, du Nigéria et du Togo', in Gagey, F. (ed.), *Comprendre l'économie africaine* (Paris: Éditions L'Harmattan); repr. from *Mondes en développement*, 41–2 (1983).

ASKARI, H., and J. T. CUMMINGS (1977), 'Estimating the Agricultural Supply Response with the Nerlove Model: A Survey', *International Economic Review*, 18/2, June.

BACHELET, M. (1986), 'Réformes agro-foncières et développement', in Verdier, R., and Rochegude, A. (eds.), *Systèmes fonciers à la ville et au village* (Paris: L'Harmattan).

BATES, R. H. (1981), *Markets and States in Tropical Africa: The Political Basis of Agricultural Policies* (Berkeley, Calif.: University of California Press).

——(1984), 'Some Conventional Orthodoxies in the Study of Agrarian Change', *World Politics*, 26/2.

——and LOFCHIE, M. F. (eds.) (1980), *Agricultural Development in Africa: Issues of Public Policy* (New York: Praeger).

BAYART, J. F. (1989), *L'État en Afrique: La politique du ventre* (Paris: Fayard).

BERG, E., *et al.* (1986), 'La réforme de la politique céréalière dans le Sahel' (Paris: OCDE and CILSS (No. 38132)).

BERG, R. J., and WHITAKER, J. S. (eds.) (1986), *Strategies for African Development* (Berkeley, Calif.: University of California Press).

BERRY, S. (1980), 'Rural Class Formation in West Africa', in Bates and Lofchie (1980).

——(1984), 'The Food Crisis and Agrarian Change in Africa: A Review Essay', *African Studies Review*, 27/2, June.

BÉZY, F., PEEMANS, J.-P., and WAUTELET, J.-M. (1981), *Accumulation et sous-développement au Zaïre 1960–1980* (Louvain-la-Neuve: Presses universitaires de Louvain).

BIENEFELD, M. (1986), 'Analysing the Politics of African State Policy: Some Thoughts on Robert Bates' Work', *IDS Bulletin*, 17/1, Jan.

BIENEN, H. (1987), 'Domestic Political Considerations for Food Policy', in Mellor *et al.* (1987).

BINSWANGER, H. P., *et al.* (1985), 'Estimates of Agricultural Supply Response from Time Series of Cross-Country Data', EPOLS Division Working Paper (Washington, DC: World Bank).

——and ROSENZWEIG, M. R. (1986), 'Behavioural and Material Determinants of Production Relations in Agriculture', *Journal of Development Studies*, 22/3, Apr.

BOND, M. A. (1983), 'Agricultural Responses to Prices in Sub-Saharan African Countries', *IMF Staff Papers*, 30.

BONIN, J. P., and PUTTERMAN, L. (1987), *Economics of Cooperation and the Labor-Managed Economy* (London and New-York: Harwood Academic Publishers).

BOSERUP, E. (1965), *The Conditions of Agricultural Growth* (London: Allen & Unwin).
——(1981), *Population and Technology* (Oxford: Basil Blackwell).
BOUTILLIER, J. L. (1963), 'Les rapports du système foncier toucouleur et de
    l'organisation sociale et économique traditionnelle: Leur évolution actuelle',
    in Biebuyck, D. (ed.), *African Agrarian Systems* (London: Oxford University
    Press).
——(1980), 'Irrigated Farming in the Senegal River Valley' (Department of Agri-
    culture Economics, Purdue University).
BRAY, F. (1983), 'Patterns of Evolution in Rice-Growing Societies', *Journal of Peasant
    Studies*, 11/1, Oct.
——(1986), *The Rice Economies: Technology and Development in Asian Societies*
    (Oxford: Basil Blackwell).
BRETT, E. A. (1973), *Colonialism and Underdevelopment in East Africa* (London:
    Heinemann).
——(1986), 'State Power and Economic Inefficiency: Explaining Political Failure in
    Africa', *IDS Bulletin*, 17/1, Jan.
CHRISTODOULU, D. (1966), *Basic Agrarian Structural Issues in the Adjustment of African
    Customary Tenures to the Needs of Agricultural Development* (Rome: FAO).
CILSS (1979), *La politique céréalière dans les pays du Sahel: Actes du Colloque de
    Nouakchott* (Paris: Comité permanent inter-états de lutte contre la sécheresse dans le
    Sahel (CILSS)).
COHEN, J. (1980), 'Land Tenure and Rural Development in Africa', in Bates and
    Lofchie (1980).
COLCLOUGH, C. (1985), 'Competing Paradigms—and Lack of Evidence—in the
    Analysis of African Development', in Rose (1985).
COLLIER, P. (1983), 'Oil and Inequality in Nigeria', in Ghai and Radwan (eds.), 1983,
    191–248.
——and LAL D. (1981), 'Poverty and Growth in Kenya', World Bank Staff Working
    Paper No. 389 (Washington, DC: World Bank).
COLLINSON, M. (1987), 'Potential and Practice in Food Production Technology
    Development: Eastern and Southern Africa', in Mellor *et al.* (1987).
COMMINS, S. K., LOFCHIE, M. F., and PAYNE, R. (eds.) (1986), *Africa's Agrarian Crisis:
    The Roots of Famine* (London: Frances Pinter).
COQUERY-VIDROVITCH, C. (1982), 'Le régime foncier rural en Afrique noire', in Le
    Bris *et al.* (1982).
——(1985), *Afrique noire: Permanences et ruptures* (Paris: Payot).
COULIBALY, C. (1985), 'Intérêts de classes, politique alimentaire et sujétion des
    producteurs: Le Cas de l'Office du Niger au Mali', in Haubert *et al.* (1985).
COWEN, M. (1982), 'The British State and Agrarian Accumulation in Kenya', in
    Fransman, M. (ed.), *Industry and Accumulation in Africa* (London: Heinemann).
DELGADO, C., MELLOR, J., and BLACKIE, M. (1987), 'Strategic Issues in Food
    Production in Sub-Saharan Africa', in Mellor *et al.* (1987).
——and RANADE, C. (1987), 'Technological Change and Agricultural Labor Use', in
    Mellor *et al.* (1987).
DELOR-VANDUEREN, A. (1988), *Démographie, Agriculture et Environement—Le cas du
    Burundi*, Université Catholique de Louvain, mimeo.
DEMSETZ, H. (1967), 'Toward a Theory of Property Rights', *American Economic
    Review*, 57/2, May.

DIEMER, G., and VAN DER LAAN, E. (1987), *L'irrigation au Sahel—La crise des périmetres irrigués et la voie haalpulaar* (Paris and Wageningen: Karthala and CTA).

DORNER, P. (1972), *Land Reform and Economic Development* (Kingsport: Kingsport Press).

DUPRIEZ, H. (1980), *Paysans d'Afrique noire* (Nivelles: Terres et Vie).

EICHER, C. (1984), 'Facing Up to Africa's Food Crisis', in Eicher and Staatz (1984).

——(1985), 'Famine Prevention in Africa: The Long View', in *Food for the Future* (The Philadelphia Society).

——(1986a), 'Transforming African Agriculture', *Hunger Project Papers*, 4, Jan.

——(1986b), 'Western Science and African Hunger', Inaugural Lecture for the 1985/6 Foreign Francqui Lecture, the Catholic University of Leuven, (Belgium).

——(1986c), 'Strategic Issues in Combating Hunger and Poverty in Africa', in Berg and Whitaker (1986).

——and BAKER, D. C. (1982), 'Research on Agricultural Development in Sub-Saharan Africa: A Critical Survey', MSU International Development Paper No. 1 (East Lansing, Mich.: Michigan State University, Department of Agricultural Economics).

——and MANGWIRO, F. (1986), 'A Critical Assessment of the FAO Report on SADCC Agriculture and Agricultural Sector Studies', background paper prepared for a SADCC Meeting, Harare, July (Rome: FAO).

——and STAATZ, J. M. (eds.) (1984), *Agricultural Development in the Third World* (Baltimore, Md. and London: Johns Hopkins).

ENGELHARD, P. and T. BEN ABDALLAH (1986), *Enjeux de l'aprés-barrage-vollée du Sénégal* (Dakar: ENDA et République Française, Ministère de la Coopération).

EVENSON, R. E. (1978), 'The Organization of Research to Improve Crops and Animals in Low Income Countries', in Schultz, T. W. (ed.), *Distortions in Agricultural Incentives* (Bloomington, Ind., and London: Indiana University Press).

FACAGRO and ISA (1989), *Séminaire sur l'étude des systèmes d'exploitation agricole au Burundi* (Bujumbura: Faculté des Sciences Agronomiques and Institut des Sciences Agronomiques).

FALLERS, L. A. (1961), 'Are African Cultivators to be called "Peasants"?', *Current Anthropology*, 2/2.

FAO (1984), *Capacité potentielle de charge démographique des terres du monde en développement*, Technical Report FPA/INT/513 (Rome: FAO).

——(1985), *The State of Food and Agriculture 1984* (Rome: FAO).

——(1986), *African Agriculture: The Next 25 Years* (Rome: FAO (Main Report + 5 Appendices)).

——(various years), *Production Yearbook and Trade Yearbook* (Rome: FAO)

FAUCHER, J. J., and SCHNEIDER, H. (1985), 'Agricultural Crisis: Structural Constraints, Prices and Other Policy Issues', in Rose (1985).

GALLI, R. E. (1987), 'On Peasant Productivity: The Case of Guinea-Bissau', *Development and Change*, 18/1, Jan.

GENTIL, D. (1986), *Les mouvements coopératifs en Afrique de l'Ouest* (Paris: L'Harmattan).

GEPHART, M. (1986), 'African States and Agriculture: Issues for Research', *IDS Bulletin*, 17/1, Jan.

GESCHIERE, P. (1984), 'Segmentary Societies and the Authority of the State: Problems in Implementing Rural Development in the Maka Villages of Southeastern Cameroon', *Sociologia ruralis*, 24/1.

GHAI, D., and RADWAN, S. (eds.) (1983), *Agrarian Policies and Rural Poverty in Africa* (Geneva: ILO).

————(1983), 'Growth and Inequality: Rural Development in Malawi, 1964–78', in Ghai and Radwan (eds.), 1983.

GHATAK, S., and INGERSENT, K. (1984), *Agriculture and Economic Development* (Brighton: Harvester).

GIRI, J. (1983), *Le Sahel demain* (Paris: Karthala).

——(1986), *L'Afrique en panne* (Paris: Karthala).

Government of Mali (1984), *Recueil de documents sur les tons villageois* (Bamako: Ministère du développement rural).

GUEYMARD, Y. (1985), 'L'évolution de la politique de commercialisation des céréales au Mali', in Haubert *et al.* (1985).

HART, K. (1982), *The Political Economy of West African Agriculture* (Cambridge: Cambridge University Press).

HARVEY, C. (1983), 'The Case of Malawi', *IDS Bulletin*, 14/1, Jan.

HAUBERT, M., and FRELIN, C. (1985), 'Quelle autosuffisance?', in Haubert et al. (1985).

————and TRONG NAM TRAN, N. (eds.), *Politiques alimentaires et structures sociales en Afrique noire* (Paris: Presses universitaires de France).

HAYAMI, Y., and KIKUCHI, M. (1981), *Asian Village Economy at the Crossroads: An Economic Approach to Institutional Change* (Tokyo: University of Tokyo Press).

——and RUTTAN, V. (1985), *Agricultural Development: An International Perspective* (Baltimore, Md., and London: Johns Hopkins).

HELLEINER, G. (1975), 'Smallholder Decision Making: Tropical African Evidence', in Reynolds, L. (ed.), *Agriculture in Development Theory* (New Haven, Conn., and London: Yale University Press).

——(1979), 'Aid and Dependence in Africa: Issues for Recipients', in Shaw, T. M., and Heard, K. A. (eds.), *The Politics of Africa: Dependence and Development* (New York: Africana Pub. Co.).

HERDT, R. (1970), 'A Disaggregate Approach to Aggregate Supply', *American Journal of Agricultural Economics*, 52/4, Nov.

HESSELING, G., and MATHIEU, P. (1986), 'Stratégies de l'État et des populations par rapport à l'espace', in Crousse, B., Le Bris, E., and Le Roy, E. (eds.), *Espaces disputés en Afrique noire: Pratiques foncières locales* (Paris: Karthala).

HILL, P. (1963), *The Migrant Cocoa-Farmers of Southern Ghana* (Cambridge: Cambridge University Press).

HYDEN, G. (1986), 'African Social Structure and Economic Development', in Berg and Whitaker (1986).

IFPRI (1986), 'Food in the Third World: Past Trends and Projections to 2000', Research Report No. 52 (Washington, DC: IFPRI).

IFRI (1986), *RAMSES 86/87: Rapport annuel mondial sur le système économique et les stratégies* (Paris: éditions Atlas économica pour l'Institut français des relations internationales).

ISHIKAWA, S. (1981), *Essays on Technology, Employment and Institutions in Economic Development* (Tokyo: Kinokuniya Cy.).

Islands of Peace (1984, 1985, 1986), *Annual Reports on the Timbuktu Project* (Huy).

JACQUEMOT, P. (ed.) (1981), *Mali: Le paysan et l'État* (Paris: L'Harmattan).

JOHNSTON, B. F. (1986), 'Governmental Strategies for Agricultural Development', in Berg and Whitaker (1986).

——and KILBY, P. (1975), *Agriculture and Structural Transformation: Economic Strategies in Late-Developing Countries* (London: Oxford University Press).

JUDD, M. A., BOYCE, J. K., and EVENSON, R. E. (1986), 'Investing in Agricultural Supply: The Determinants of Agricultural Research and Extension Investment', *Economic Development and Cultural Change*, 35/1, Oct.

KÉBÉ, Y. (1981), 'L'agriculture malienne, le paysan, sa terre et l'État', in Jacquemot (1981).

KEMP, T. (1983), *Industrialization in the Non-Western World* (London and New York: Longman).

KITCHING, G. (1982), *Development and Underdevelopment in Historical Perspective* (London and New York: Methuen).

KODJO, E. (1985), *Et demain l'Afrique* (Paris: Stock).

KRISHNA, RAJ (1970), 'Models of the Family Farm', in Wharton, C. R. (ed.), *Subsistence Agriculture and Economic Development* (London: Frank Cass).

——(1984), 'Price and Technology Policies', in Eicher and Staatz (1984).

LE BRIS, E., LE ROY, E., and LEIMDORFER, F. (eds.) (1982), *Enjeux fonciers en Afrique noire* (Paris: Karthala).

LEE, E. (1979), 'Egalitarian Peasant Farming and Rural Development: The Case of South Korea', in Ghai, D., Khan, A. R., Lee, E., and Radwan, S. (eds.), *Agrarian Systems and Rural Development* (London: Macmillan).

LELE, U. (1975), *The Design of Rural Development: Lessons from Africa* (Baltimore, Md.: Johns Hopkins).

——(1976), 'Designing Rural Development Programs: Lessons from Past Experience in Africa', *Economic Development and Cultural Change*, 24/2, Jan.

——(1984), 'Rural Africa: Modernization, Equity, and Long-Term Development', in Eicher and Staatz (1984).

——(1985), 'Terms of Trade, Agricultural Growth, and Rural Poverty in Africa', in Mellor and Desai (1985).

LEONARD, D. K. (1986), 'Putting the Farmer in Control: Building Agricultural Institutions', in Berg and Whitaker (1986).

LIPTON, M. (1977), *Why the Poor Stay Poor* (London: Maurice Temple Smith).

——(1985), 'Indian Agricultural Development and African Food Strategies: A Role for EC?', in Callewaert, W. M., and Kumar, R. (eds.), *EEC—India: Towards a Common Perspective* (Leuven: Peeters).

——(1987), 'Agriculture and Central Physical Grid Infrastructure', in Mellor *et al.* (1987).

MAROT, E. (1987), *Autosuffisance alimentaire: Une stratégie pour le développement économique et la sécurité alimentaire?* (Namur: Faculté des sciences économiques et sociales).

MARS, T. (1986), 'State and Agriculture in Africa: A Case of Means and Ends', *IDS Bulletin*, 17/1, Jan.

MARTY, A. (1985), 'Crise rurale en milieu nord-sahélien et recherche coopérative', unpublished Ph.D. thesis, Université François Rabelais, Tours.

MASAKI, N. (1987), 'Élevage bovin chez les Suku de Feshi' (Zaïre), unpublished Ph.D. thesis, Fondation universitaire luxembourgeoise, Arlon.

MATHIEU, P. (1983a), 'Agriculture irriguée et cultures traditionnelles de décrue dans la zone du lac de Guiers', in *Le Lac de Guiers: Problématique de l'environnement et de développement* (Institut des sciences de l'environnement, Université de Dakar).

——(1983b), 'Présence ou absence des travailleurs et avenir du travail dans les aménagements hydro-agricoles', *Mondes en développement*, 11/43–4.

——(1985a), 'L'aménagement de la vallée du fleuve Sénégal: Transformations institutionnelles et objectifs coûteux de l'autosuffisance alimentaire', *Mondes en développement*, 13/52.

——(1985b), 'Évaluation du périmètre de Korioumé: Île de paix de Tombouctou' (Huy: ASBL 'Les Iles de paix').

——(1987), 'Agriculture irriguée, réforme foncière et stratégies paysannes dans la vallée du fleuve Sénégal, 1960–1985', unpublished Ph.D. thesis, Fondation universitaire luxembourgeoise, Arlon.

MATLON, P. (1987), 'Potential and Practice in Food Production Technology Development: The West African Semiarid Tropics', in Mellor *et al.* (1987).

MELLOR, J. (1968), 'The Functions of Agricultural Prices in Economic Development', *Indian Journal of Agricultural Economics*, 23/1.

——(1970), 'The Subsistence Farmer in Traditional Economies', in Wharton, C. (ed.), *Subsistence Agriculture and Economic Development* (London: Frank Cass).

——(1984), 'Agricultural Development and the Intersectoral Transfer of Resources', in Eicher and Staatz (1984).

——and DELGADO, C. (1987), 'Food Production in Sub-Saharan Africa', Food Policy Statement No. 7, Jan. (Washington, DC: IFPRI).

——— and BLACKIE, M. (eds.) (1987), *Accelerating Food Production in Sub-Saharan Africa* (Baltimore, Md., and London: Johns Hopkins).

——and DESAI, G. (eds.) (1985), *Agricultural Change and Rural Poverty: Variations on a Theme by Dharm Narain* (Baltimore, Md., and London: Johns Hopkins).

——and JOHNSTON, B. F. (1984), 'The World Food Equation: Interrelations among Development, Employment, and Food Consumption', *Journal of Economic Literature*, 22, June.

MILLAR, J. R. (1976), 'What is Wrong with the "Standard Story"?', *Problems of Communism*, July–Aug.

MINVIELLE, J. P. (1977), *La structure foncière du Waalo Fuutanké* (Office de la recherche scientifique et technique d'outre-mer (ORSTOM), Dakar Centre).

MONFERRER, D. (1985), 'L'introduction de l'agriculture capitaliste en Afrique et ses conséquences: Le Cas du Gabon', in Haubert *et al.* (1985).

MOORE, M. (1987), 'Interpreting Africa's Crisis: Political Science versus Political Economy', *IDS Bulletin*, 18/4, Oct.

MORRISON, S. (1986), 'Dilemmas of Sustaining Parastatal Success: The Botswana Meat Commission', *IDS Bulletin*, 17/1, Jan.

MORRISSON, C. (1985), 'Agricultural Production and Government Policy in Burkina Faso and Mali', in Rose (1985).

MYRDAL, G. (1963), *Economic Theory and Underdeveloped Regions* (London: Methuen & Co Ltd.).

NAKAJIMA, C. (1970), 'Subsistence and Commercial Family Farms: Some Theoretical Models of Subjective Equilibrium', in Wharton, C. R. (ed.), *Subsistence Agriculture and Economic Development* (London: Frank Cass).

NORONHA, R. (1985), 'A Review of the Literature on Land Tenure Systems in

Sub-Saharan Africa', Research Unit of The Agriculture and Rural Development Department, Report No. ARU 43 (Washington, DC: World Bank).

OYEJIDE, T. A. (1987), 'Food Policy and the Choice of Trade Regime', in Mellor *et al.* (1987).

PACEY, A., and PAYNE, P. (eds.) (1985), *Agricultural Development and Nutrition* (London: Hutchinson).

PAULINO, L. (1987), 'The Evolving Food Situation', in Mellor *et al.* (1987).

PAUSEWANG, S. (1987), 'Who is the Peasant? Experience with Rural Development in Zambia', Derap Working Papers, No. A 371, (Bergen: Chr. Michelsen Institute).

PENNISI, G. (1986), 'Le Sahel cherche de nouveaux équilibres', *Cooperazione*, 60 (French edn.).

PINGALI, P. L., BIGOT, Y., and BINSWANGER, H. P. (1987), *Agricultural Mechanization and the Evolution of Farming Systems in Sub-Saharan Africa* (Baltimore, Md., and London: Johns Hopkins).

——and BINSWANGER, H. P. (1986), 'Population Density, Market Access and Farmer-Generated Technical Change in Sub-Saharan Africa', Agriculture and Rural Development Department, Report No. ARU 58 (Washington, DC: World Bank).

PLATTEAU, J.-P. (1978), *Les économistes classiques et le sous-développement* (Paris: Presses universitaires de France).

——(1984), 'Das Paradoxon des Staates in wirtschaftlich rückständigen Ländern', *Osterreichische Zeitschrift für Soziologie*, 4/9.

——(1985), 'India as an Engine of Green Revolution in Africa?', in Callewaert, W. M., and Kumar, R. (eds.), *EEC—India: Towards a Common Perspective* (Leuven: Peeters).

——(1987), 'The Problems of Consistency and Relevance in Malthus's Analysis of Underdevelopment', Cahier de recherche de la faculté des sciences économiques et sociales (Namur).

PLATTEAU, J. P. (forthcoming), *Land Reform and Structural Adjustment in SubSaharan Africa: Controversies and Guidelines* (Rome: FAO).

PLEASE, S., and AMOAKO, K. Y. (1984), 'The World Bank's Report on Accelerated Development in Sub-Saharan Africa: A Critique of Some of the Criticism', *African Studies Review*, 27/4, Dec.

POTTIER, J. (1986), 'Village Responses to Food Marketing Alternatives in Northern Zambia: The Case of the Mambwe Economy', *IDS Bulletin*, 17/1, Jan.

PUTTERMAN, L. (1985), 'Extrinsic versus Intrinsic Problems of Agricultural Co-operation: Anti-incentivism in Tanzania and China', *Journal of Development Studies*, 21/2, Jan.

RAYNAUT, C. (1976), 'Transformation du système de production et inégalité économique: Le Cas d'un village haoussa (Niger)', *Revue canadienne des études africaines*, 10/2.

——(1983), 'La crise des systèmes de production agro-pastorale au Niger et en Mauritanie', in Raynaut, C. (ed.), *Milieu naturel, techniques, rapports sociaux* (Paris: Éditions du Centre national de la recherche scientifique).

ROBERTSON, A. F. (1987), *The Dynamics of Productive Relationships: African Share Contracts in Comparative Perspective* (Cambridge: Cambridge University Press).

ROSE, T. (1985), *Crisis and Recovery in Sub-Saharan Africa* (Paris: OECD).

SANDBROOK, R. (1986), 'The State and Economic Stagnation in Tropical Africa', *World Development*, 14/3.

SCANDIZZO, P. L., and C. BRUCE (1980), 'Methodology for Measuring Agricultural Price Incentive Effects', *World Bank Staff Working Papers*, No. 394, June.

SCHÄFER, H. B. (1987), 'Farm Prices and Agricultural Production in Developing Countries', *Intereconomics*, 22/3, May/June.

SEN, A. K. (1966), 'Peasants and Dualism, with or without Surplus Labour', *Journal of Political Economy*, 74/5, Oct.

——(1981), *Poverty and Famines: An Essay on Entitlement and Deprivation* (Oxford: Oxford University Press).

SINGLETON, M. (1983), 'Présence et absence de barrages en Afrique', paper given at the international conference 'Barrages en terre et développement des zones rurales en Afrique', École polytechnique de Thiès et AUPELF, Senegal.

SPENCER, D. S. C. (1986), 'Agricultural Research: Lessons of the Past, Strategies for the Future', in Berg and Whitaker (1986).

SWAINSON, N. (1986), 'Public Policy in the Development of Export Crops: Pineapples and Tea in Kenya', *IDS Bulletin*, 17/1, Jan.

SWANTZ, M.-L. (1987), 'Development: From Bottom to Top or Top to Bottom? Grassroots Dynamics and Directed Development—The Case of Tanzania', Paper 87/106 (Centre for Development Studies, Universiteit Antwerpen).

TER KUILE, C. (1987), 'Potential and Practice in Food Production Technology Development: The Humid and Subhumid Tropics', in Mellor *et al.* (1987).

TIMMER, C. P. (1986), *Getting Prices Right: The Scope and Limits of Agricultural Price Policy* (Ithaca, NY: Cornell University Press).

TOYE, J. (1987), *Dilemmas of Development* (Oxford: Basil Blackwell).

TYAGI, D. S. (1987), 'Domestic Terms of Trade and their Effect on Supply and Demand of Agricultural Sector', *Economic and Political Weekly*, 22/13, Mar. Review of Agriculture.

VON BRAUN, J., and WEBB, P. (1989), 'The Impact of New Crop Technology on the Agricultural Division of Labor in a West African Setting', *Economic Development and Cultural Change*, 37/3.

WEIGEL, J. Y. (1982a), 'Organisation foncière et opération de développement: Le Cas Soninke au Sénégal', in Le Bris *et al.* (1982).

——(1982b), *Migration et production domestique des Soninké du Sénégal* (Paris: Office de la recherche scientifique et technique d'outre-mer (ORSTOM)).

WILLIAMSON, O. (1985), *The Economic Institution of Capitalism* (New York: Free Press).

World Bank (1981), *Accelerated Development in Sub-Saharan Africa: An Agenda for Action* (Washington, DC: World Bank).

——(1984), *World Development Report: 1984* (Washington, DC: World Bank).

——(1986a), *Poverty and Hunger: Issues and Options for Food Security in Developing Countries* (Washington, DC: World Bank).

——(1986b), *World Development Report: 1986* (Washington, DC: World Bank).

YOTOPOULOS, P. (1985), 'Middle-Income Classes and Food Crises: The "New" Food–Feed Competition', *Economic Development and Cultural Change*, 33/3, Apr.

YOUNG, C. (1986), 'Africa's Colonial Legacy', in Berg and Whitaker (1986).

# NAME INDEX

# SUBJECT INDEX